Oliver Jamieson

Gorran P.S

2007.

Best wishes.

CHAMBERS

MINI
School
DICTIONARY

CHAMBERS

CHAMBERS
An imprint of Chambers Harrap Publishers Ltd
7 Hopetoun Crescent, Edinburgh, EH7 4AY

First published by Chambers Harrap Publishers Ltd 2005
© Chambers Harrap Publishers Ltd 2005

A CIP catalogue record for this book is available from the
British Library.

ISBN 0550 10147 0

Project Manager: Ian Brookes
Editor: Alice Grandison
Editorial Assistance: Susan Dunsmore, Megan Thomson
Publishing Manager: Patrick White
Prepress Manager: Sharon McTeir
Prepress Controller: Clair Simpson

Designed and typeset by Chambers Harrap Publishers Ltd, Edinburgh
Printed in China by Toppan

Contents

Preface

Chambers Mini School Dictionary is specially designed for use by students aged 9-14 (up to Key Stage 3 of the National Curriculum and level E of the Scottish curriculum). It is compact and portable, yet also manages to cover the basic vocabulary of current English and pays special attention to essential terms from the subjects that form the school curriculum.

The dictionary contains a number of features that make it especially suitable for school use. Inflected forms (such as plurals and past tenses) which could prove difficult to spell are shown in full, and special notes in shaded boxes help with confusable words, spelling and grammar. Pronunciation help is provided for tricky words.

Students using this book should first take some time to go through the *How to use the dictionary* section that follows. This section demonstrates the structure of a dictionary entry, showing how and where to find all the different types of information that the dictionary provides.

We have also included a supplement to the dictionary containing a **language workshop** including clear and detailed explanations of essential language concepts such as nouns, verbs and punctuation, and also a **dictionary quiz**.

Whether for looking up meanings and spellings, or simply browsing for pleasure, we hope students will enjoy using this handy reference book.

www

To help make best use of Chambers School titles, teachers can download photocopiable versions of the workshop material, along with games and exercises, from our website at **www.chambers.co.uk**

How to use the dictionary

Main entry words appear in large bold type.

misspell *verb* to spell wrongly ∎ **misspelling** *noun*

misspell ▶ misspells, misspelling, misspelled or misspelt

Sometimes examples are given to show how a word is used.

misspent *adjective* spent unwisely, wasted: *misspent youth*

mist *noun* a cloud of moisture in the air; thin fog or drizzle ∎ **misty** *adjective* ∎ **mist up** or **mist over** to cover or become covered with mist

mistake *verb* **1** to misunderstand, be wrong or make an error about **2** to take (one thing or person) for another ∎ *noun* a wrong action or statement; an error

If you do not simply add *s*, *ing* or *ed* to make the different tenses of a verb, then these forms are shown.

mistake *verb* ▶ mistakes, mistaking, mistaken, mistook

mistaken *adjective* making an error, unwise

mister *full form of* **Mr**

mistletoe *noun* a plant with white berries, used as a Christmas decoration

mistreat *verb* to treat badly; abuse

If you do not simply add *s* to make the plural form of a noun, then the plural is shown.

mistress *noun* (*plural* **mistresses**) **1** a female teacher **2** a female owner of a dog *etc* **3** a woman skilled in an art **4** a woman who is the lover though not the legal wife of a man **5** *full form of* **Mrs**

vi

mistrust *noun* a lack of trust or confidence in ▪ *verb* to have no trust or confidence in

> Parts of speech (or word classes), eg *noun*, *verb* and *adjective*, are spelled out in full.

misunderstand *verb* to take a wrong meaning from what is said or done

misunderstanding *noun* **1** a mistake about a meaning **2** a slight disagreement

misuse *noun* bad or wrong use ▪ *verb* **1** to use wrongly **2** to treat badly

mite *noun* something very small, *eg* a tiny child

mitigate *verb* to make (punishment, anger, *etc*) less great or severe: *reasonable efforts must be made to mitigate the risks to society* ▪ **mitigation** *noun*

> Words which come from the main entry word sometimes appear at the end of an entry.

✱ Do not confuse with: **militate**. It may be helpful to remember that the idea of fighting is contained in the word **MILITate** (in common with 'military' and 'militia') but not in **mitigate**

> If a word can be confused with another word, a note is given in a box.

mitosis *noun* the division of a cell nucleus to form two new nuclei

mitre *noun* **1** the pointed head-dress worn by archbishops and bishops **2** a slanting joint between two pieces of wood

mitt *or* **mitten** *noun* a glove without separate divisions for the

Pronunciation guide

This dictionary gives you help when the pronunciation of a word is difficult to work out. Pronunciations are given in brackets and signalled by the word *pronounced*, as in:

oesophagus (*pronounced* ee-**sof**-*ag*-us)

The system used is designed to allow you to work out how a word is pronounced immediately, without having to refer to a key. The syllables are separated by hyphens, and the stressed syllable (the syllable pronounced with most emphasis) is shown in thick black type. Any vowel or group of vowels which is pronounced as a neutral 'uh' sound is shown in italic type.

A few sounds are difficult to show in normal English letters. Here is a guide to the letter combinations that are used to show these sounds:

Consonants

'ng'	shows the sound as in ri**ng**
'ngg'	shows the sound as in fi**ng**er
'th'	shows the sound as in **th**in
'dh'	shows the sound as in **th**is
'sz'	shows the sound as in deci**s**ion, mea**s**ure
'kh'	shows the sound as in lo**ch**

Vowels

'uw'	shows the sound as in b**oo**k, p**u**t
'oo'	shows the sound as in m**oo**n, l**o**se
'ah'	shows the sound as in **ar**m, d**a**nce
'aw'	shows the sound as in s**aw**, ign**ore**
'er'	shows the sound as in f**er**n, b**ir**d, h**ear**d
'ei'	shows the sound as in d**ay**, s**a**me
'ai'	shows the sound as in m**y**, p**i**ne
'oi'	shows the sound as in b**oy**, s**oi**l
'oh'	shows the sound as in b**o**ne, n**o**, th**ough**
'ow'	shows the sound as in n**ow**, b**ough**

Sound combinations

'eer'	shows the sound as in n**ear**, b**eer**, t**ier**
'eir'	shows the sound as in h**air**, c**are**, th**ere**
'oor'	shows the sound as in p**oor**, s**ure**
'air'	shows the sound as in f**ire**, h**igher**

Labels used
in the dictionary

Some of the words and meanings in the dictionary have labels in italics to show you the subject area or the type of language in which the word or meaning is used. Some of these labels are explained in the list below. Any labels not on the list appear in full and should not require an explanation (for example *golf* and *music*).

Brit	used generally in British English, but not in American or other forms of English
derogatory	a word that is insulting about the person or thing referred to
euphemistic	used instead of a more direct term to refer to an unpleasant subject
feminine	the form of a word used when it refers to a female
formal	used mainly in formal English
informal	often used in spoken or informal English
Irish	used in Irish English
offensive	a word which could offend the person addressed
old	rarely used in English today
Scottish	used in Scottish English
slang	a very informal word which is less generally acceptable than *informal* words
trademark	a word which is registered as a trademark
US	used in American (and often Canadian) English, rather than in British English

A

a *or* **an** *adjective* **1** one: *a knock at the door* **2** any: *an ant* **3** in, to or for each: *four times a day*

✱ The form *a* is used before words beginning with a consonant, eg knock; *an* is used before words beginning with a vowel, eg ant

aardvark *noun* a nocturnal African mammal with a large snout

aback *adverb*: **taken aback** surprised or slightly shocked

abandon *verb* **1** to leave, without meaning to return to **2** to give up (an idea *etc*) ▪ *noun* lack of inhibition: *dancing with gay abandon* ▪ **abandoned** *adjective*

| **abandon** ▶ abandon*s*, abandon*ing*, abandon*ed*

abashed *adjective* embarrassed, confused

abate *verb* to make or grow less ▪ **abatement** *noun*

abattoir (*pronounced* ab-a-twahr) *noun* a place where animals are slaughtered

abbess *noun* (*plural* **abbesses**) the female head of an abbey or a convent

abbey *noun* (*plural* **abbeys**) **1** a monastery or convent ruled by an abbot or an abbess **2** the church now or formerly attached to such a monastery or convent

abbot *noun* the male head of an abbey

abbreviate *verb* to shorten (a word, phrase, *etc*)

abbreviation *noun* a shortened form of a word or group of words, eg *BBC* for *British Broadcasting Corporation*

abdicate *verb* to give up (a position or responsibility, especially that of king or queen) ▪ **abdication** *noun*

abdomen *noun* the part of the body between the chest and the hips ▪ **abdominal** *adjective*

abduct *verb* to take away by force ▪ **abduction** *noun* ▪ **abductor** *noun*

abhor *verb* to hate, or look upon with horror ▪ **abhorrent** *adjective*

| **abhor** ▶ abhor*s*, abhor*ring*, abhor*red*

abide *verb* to put up with, tolerate ▪ **abide by** to keep, act according to

abiding *adjective* lasting
ability *noun* (*plural* **abilities**) **1** power or means to do something **2** talent
ablaze *adjective* **1** burning fiercely **2** gleaming like fire
able *adjective* **1** having the power or means (to do something) **2** clever
able-bodied *adjective* **1** fit and healthy **2** not disabled
ably *adverb* in an efficient or competent way
abnormal *adjective* **1** not normal (in behaviour *etc*) **2** unusual
abnormality *noun* (*plural* **abnormalities**) **1** something which is abnormal **2** the condition of being abnormal
abnormally *adverb* unusually; unnaturally
aboard *adverb & preposition* on (to) or in(to) (a ship or aeroplane)
abode *noun, formal* a home
abolish *verb* to stop or put an end to (*eg* a custom, law, *etc*) ▪ **abolition** *noun*
abominable *adjective* **1** hateful **2** very bad, terrible ▪ **abominably** *adverb*
Abominable Snowman a large animal believed to exist in the Himalayas (*also called:* **Yeti**)
Aboriginal *or* **Aborigine** (*pronounced* a-bor-ij-i-nee) *noun* a member of the people who were the original inhabitants of Australia ▪ **Aboriginal** *adjective*

abort *verb* to end a pregnancy deliberately by having an abortion
abortion *noun* an operation to end an unwanted or dangerous pregnancy
abound *verb* to be very plentiful
about *preposition* **1** around: *look about you* **2** near (in time, size, *etc*): *about ten o'clock* **3** here and there in: *scattered about the room* ▪ *adverb* **1** around: *stood about waiting* **2** in motion or in action: *running about* **3** in the opposite direction: *turned about and walked away* ▪ **about to** on the point of (doing something)
above *preposition* **1** over, in a higher position than **2** greater than **3** too good for: *above criticism* ▪ *adverb* **1** at, in or to a higher position, rank, *etc* **2** earlier on (in a letter *etc*)
above board open and honest
abrasion *noun* a graze on the body
abrasive *adjective* **1** rough and scratchy **2** having a harsh and rude manner ▪ *noun* something used for rubbing or polishing ▪ **abrasively** *adverb*
abreast *adverb* side by side ▪ **abreast of** up to date with
abridge *verb* to shorten (a book, story, *etc*) ▪ **abridgement** *or* **abridgment** *noun*
abroad *adverb* in another country
abrupt *adjective* **1** sudden,

without warning **2** of speech or behaviour: bad-tempered or snappy ▪ **abruptly** adverb ▪ **abruptness** noun

abscess noun (plural **abscesses**) a boil or other swelling filled with pus

abscond verb to run away secretly: absconded with the money

abseil (pronounced ab-sayl) verb to let yourself down a rock face using a double rope

absence noun the state of being away

absent adjective away, not present

absentee noun someone who is absent

absenteeism noun continual absence from school or work

absently adverb in a dreamy way

absent-minded adjective forgetful ▪ **absent-mindedly** adverb

absolute adjective complete, not limited by anything

absolutely adverb completely, certainly

absolute zero the lowest possible temperature of matter, equal to $-273.15°C$

absolution noun forgiveness, pardon

absolve verb, formal to pardon: absolve me of my sins

absorb verb **1** to soak up (liquid) **2** to take up the whole attention of

absorbent adjective able to

soak up liquid ▪ **absorbency** noun

absorption noun **1** the act of absorbing **2** complete mental concentration

abstain verb **1** to refuse to cast a vote for or against **2 abstain from something** to hold yourself back from it

abstention noun **1** the act of choosing not to do something, especially not to take food or alcohol **2** a refusal to vote

abstract adjective **1** existing only as an idea, not as a real thing **2** of art: using shapes and patterns to represent things

abstraction noun absent-mindedness

absurd adjective clearly inappropriate, unsuitable or wrong; ridiculous ▪ **absurdity** noun (plural **absurdities**) ▪ **absurdly** adverb

abundance noun a plentiful supply

abundant adjective plentiful

abuse verb (pronounced a-byooz) **1** to use wrongly **2** to insult or speak unkindly to; treat badly ▪ noun (pronounced a-byooss) **1** wrongful use **2** insulting language or behaviour

abusive adjective insulting or rude ▪ **abusively** adverb

abysmal adjective very bad; terrible ▪ **abysmally** adverb

abyss (pronounced a-bis) noun (plural **abysses**) an apparently bottomless hole or pit

acacia (*pronounced a-kay-sha*) *noun* a family of thorny shrubs and trees

academic *adjective* 1 concerned with theoretical education or complicated ideas 2 not practical: *purely of academic interest* 3 of a university *etc* ▪ *noun* a university or college teacher ▪ **academically** *adverb*

academy *noun* (*plural* **academies**) 1 a college for special study or training 2 a society for encouraging science or art 3 in Scotland, a senior school

accelerate *verb* to increase in speed

acceleration *noun* an increasing of speed; the rate of increase of speed

accelerator *noun* a lever or pedal used to increase the speed of a car *etc*

accent *noun* 1 (a mark indicating) stress on a syllable or word 2 a mark used in written French to show the quality of a vowel 3 emphasis: *purely of academic interest be on hard work* 4 the way in which words are pronounced in a particular area *etc*

accentuate *verb* to make more obvious; emphasize

accept *verb* 1 to take something offered 2 to agree or submit to

🖊️ Do not confuse with: **except**

acceptable *adjective* satisfactory; pleasing ▪ **acceptably** *adverb*

acceptance *noun* the act of accepting

access *noun* right or means of approach or entry

🖊️ Do not confuse with: **excess**

accessible *adjective* easily approached or reached

accessory *noun* (*plural* **accessories**) 1 an item chosen to match or complement a piece of clothing or an outfit, *eg* a piece of jewellery, a handbag, *etc* 2 a helper, especially in crime

accident *noun* 1 an unexpected event causing injury 2 a mishap 3 chance: *by accident*

accidental *adjective* happening by chance ▪ **accidentally** *adverb*

acclaim *noun* enthusiastic praise

acclaimed *adjective* highly praised

acclimatize *or* **acclimatise** *verb* to accustom to another climate or situation

accommodate *verb* to make room for

accommodating *adjective* making an effort to be helpful

accommodation *noun* a place to live or to stay, lodgings

accompaniment *noun* 1 something that accompanies 2 the music played while a singer sings *etc*

accompanist *noun* someone who plays an accompaniment

accompany *verb* 1 to go or be with 2 to play an instrument (*eg* a piano) while a singer sings *etc*

accompany ► accompan*ies*, accompany*ing*, accompan*ied*

accomplice *noun* someone who helps another person, especially to commit a crime

accomplish *verb* 1 to complete 2 to manage to do

accomplished *adjective* 1 completed 2 skilled, talented

accomplishment *noun* 1 completion 2 a personal talent or skill

accord *verb* 1 to agree (with) 2 to give, grant ■ *noun* an official agreement ■ **of your own accord** of your own free will

accordance *noun* agreement: *in accordance with*

according *adverb*: **according to** 1 as told by 2 in relation to

accordingly *adverb* 1 in a way which suits what has just been said or what is happening 2 therefore

accordion *noun* a musical instrument with bellows, a keyboard and metal reeds

accordionist *noun* an accordion player

accost *verb* to approach and speak to in a forceful or threatening way

account *verb*: **1 account for** to give a reason for **2 account for** to make up: *tax accounts for most of the price of a gallon of petrol* ■ *noun* 1 a bill 2 a record of finances 3 a description of events *etc*; an explanation ■ **on account of** because of

accountable *adjective* answerable, responsible

accountant *noun* a keeper or inspector of financial accounts ■ **accountancy** *noun*

accrue *verb* to accumulate, collect

accumulate *verb* 1 to collect 2 to increase

accumulation *noun* 1 a collection 2 a mass or pile

accuracy *noun* exactness

accurate *adjective* correct, exact ■ **accurately** *adverb*

accursed *adjective* hateful

accusation *noun* 1 the act of accusing 2 a statement accusing someone of something

accuse *verb*: **accuse someone of something** to claim that someone has done something wrong ■ **the accused** the person charged with a crime *etc*

accuser *noun* a person who accuses or blames

accustom *verb* to make familiar with

accustomed *adjective* 1 used to 2 usual

ace *noun* 1 the one on playing-cards 2 an expert 3 *tennis* an unreturned first serve ■ *adjective*, *informal* excellent

acetylene *noun* a gas used for giving light and heat

ache *noun* a continuous pain
■ *verb* to be in continuous pain

achieve *verb* 1 to get (something) done, accomplish 2 to win

achievement *noun* 1 the gaining of something, usually after working hard for it 2 something that has been done or gained by effort

acid *noun* a substance that dissolves in water to produce hydrogen ions and which can dissolve certain metals to form salts (*contrasted with*: **alkali**) ■ *adjective* 1 of taste: sharp 2 sarcastic ■ **acidic** *adjective*

acidify *verb* to make or become acid

| acidify ► acidifies,
| acidifying, acidified

acidity *noun* the state of being acid

acid rain rain containing sulphur and nitrogen compounds and other pollutants

acknowledge *verb* 1 to admit the truth of something 2 to admit that you know or are aware of something 3 to (write to) say you have received something 4 to express gratitude or thanks
■ **acknowledgement** *or* **acknowledgment** *noun*

acne *noun* a common skin disease with pimples

acorn *noun* the fruit of the oak tree

acoustic *adjective* 1 of hearing or sound 2 played without an amplifier

acoustics *noun* 1 *singular* the study of sound 2 *plural* the characteristics of a room *etc* which affect the way sound is heard in it

acquaint *verb*: **acquaint someone with** to make someone familiar with

acquaintance *noun* 1 knowledge 2 someone whom you know slightly

acquiesce *verb* to agree
■ **acquiescence** *noun*
■ **acquiescent** *adjective*

acquire *verb* to obtain, get
■ **acquired** *adjective* gained; not something you were born with or have inherited

acquisition *noun* 1 the act of getting 2 something got

acquit *verb* to declare (someone) innocent of a crime
■ **acquit yourself well** to do well, be successful

| acquit ► acquits, acquitting,
| acquitted

acquittal *noun* a legal judgement of 'not guilty'

acre *noun* a land measure of 4840 square yards or about 4000 square metres

acreage *noun* the number of acres in a piece of land

acrid *adjective* harsh, bitter

acrimonious *adjective* bitter; accusing

acrimony *noun* bitterness of feeling or speech

acrobat *noun* someone who performs gymnastic tricks, tightrope-walking, *etc*

acrobatic *adjective* able to perform gymnastic tricks; agile

acronym *noun* a word formed from the initial letters of other words, *eg* radar for radio detecting and ranging

across *adverb & preposition* to or at the other side (of) ■ **across the board** involving everyone or everything; sweeping

acrylic *noun* 1 a synthetically produced fibre 2 paint containing acrylic material ■ *adjective* made with this fibre

act *verb* 1 to do something 2 to behave in a particular way: *act foolishly* 3 to play a dramatic role on stage, film, *etc* ■ *noun* 1 something done 2 a government law 3 a section of a play ■ **act up** *informal* to behave or act wrongly or badly

action *noun* 1 a deed, an act 2 a law case 3 dramatic events portrayed in a film, play, *etc*

activate *verb* to start (something) working

active *adjective* 1 busy; lively 2 able to perform physical tasks 3 *grammar* describing the form of a verb in which the subject performs the action of the verb,

eg 'the dog bit the postman' (*compare with*: **passive**) ■ **actively** *adverb* in a way which involves doing things: *actively involved in nature conservation*

activity *noun* (*plural* **activities**) 1 the state of being active 2 anything that you do, either for pleasure or as part of an organized programme

actor *noun* someone who acts a part in a play or film

actress *noun* (*plural* **actresses**) a female actor

actual *adjective* real, existing in fact

actuality *noun* fact; reality

actually *adverb* really, in fact, as a matter of fact

actuate *verb* to put into action

acumen *noun* quickness of understanding

acupuncture *noun* a method of treating illness by piercing the skin with needles

acute *adjective* 1 quick at understanding 2 sudden and severe (*compare with*: **chronic**) 3 of an angle: less than a right angle (*contrasted with*: **obtuse**)

■ **acutely** *adverb* extremely, painfully ■ **acuteness** *noun* the quality of being acute, used especially of mental perception

acute accent a forward-leaning stroke (´) placed over letters in some languages to show their pronunciation

AD *abbreviation* in the year of our

Lord (from Latin *anno Domini*). Used with a date, *eg* AD1900, to show that it refers to the time after, and not before, the birth of Christ

ad *noun, informal* an advertisement

adage *noun* an old saying, a proverb

adagio *noun* a slow-paced piece of music

adamant *adjective* not going to change your mind or opinion

Adam's apple the natural lump which sticks out from a man's throat

adapt *verb*: adapt to to make suitable for; alter so as to fit

adaptable *adjective* easily altered to suit new conditions

adaptation *noun* a change in the form of something to make it suitable for another situation or purpose

adaptor *noun* a device allowing an electrical plug to be used in a socket for which it was not designed, or several plugs to be used on the same socket

add *verb* 1 to make one thing join another to give a sum total or whole 2 to mix in 3 to say further ■ add up 1 to combine, grow to a large quantity 2 to make sense, seem logical

adder *noun* the common name of the viper, a poisonous snake

addict *noun* 1 someone who is dependent on a drug 2 *informal*

someone who is extremely fond of a hobby: *a chess addict*

addicted *adjective*: addicted to unable to do without

addiction *noun* an urgent desire to take a drug *etc*

addictive *adjective* more and more difficult to do without, the more often it is used

addition *noun* 1 the act of adding 2 something added

additional *adjective* extra; more than usual ■ additionally *adverb* as well as that

additive *noun* a chemical *etc* added to another substance

address *verb* 1 to speak to 2 to write the address on (a letter *etc*) ■ *noun* (*plural* addresses) 1 the name of the house, street, and town where someone lives *etc* 2 a name and location where you can be contacted by e-mail 3 a speech

adenoids *noun plural* tissue at the back of the nose which can swell and make it difficult to breathe

adept *adjective* very skilful

adequacy *noun* being adequate; sufficiency

adequate *adjective* sufficient, enough ■ adequately *adverb*

adhere *verb* 1 to stick (to) 2 to give support (to), be loyal (to)

adherent *adjective* sticking (to) ■ *noun* a follower or supporter of a cause *etc* ■ adherence *noun*

adhesion *noun* the act of sticking (to)

adhesive *adjective* sticky, gummed ▪ *noun* something which makes things stick to each other

ad hoc set up for a particular purpose only

Adi Granth the holy book of the Sikh religion

ad infinitum (*pronounced* ad in-fi-**nai**-tum) for ever

adjacent *adjective*: **adjacent to** lying next to

adjective *noun* a word which tells something about a noun, *eg* 'the *black* cat', 'times are *hard*'

adjoin *verb* to be joined to ▪ **adjoining** *adjective*

adjourn *verb* 1 to stop (a meeting *etc*) with the intention of continuing it at another time or place 2 **adjourn to somewhere** to go to another place ▪ **adjournment** *noun*

adjudicate *verb* 1 to give a judgement on (a dispute *etc*) 2 to act as a judge at a competition ▪ **adjudication** *noun*

adjudicator *noun* someone who adjudicates

adjust *verb* to rearrange or alter to suit the circumstances ▪ **adjustable** *adjective* ▪ **adjustment** *noun*

ad-lib *verb* to speak without plan or preparation ▪ *adjective* without preparation

| **ad-lib** *verb* ▶ ad-libs, ad-libbing, ad-libbed |

administer *verb* 1 to manage or

govern 2 to carry out (the law *etc*) 3 to give (help, medicine, *etc*)

administrate *verb* to manage or govern

administration *noun* 1 management 2 (the body that carries on) the government of a country *etc*

administrative *adjective* having to do with management or government

administrator *noun* someone involved in the administration of a country *etc*

admirable *adjective* worthy of being admired ▪ **admirably** *adverb*

admiral *noun* the commander of a navy

admire *verb* 1 to think very highly of 2 to look at with pleasure ▪ **admiration** *noun* ▪ **admirer** *noun*

admissible *adjective* allowable

admission *noun* 1 (the price of) being let in 2 anything admitted

admit *verb* 1 to let in 2 to acknowledge the truth of, confess 3 **admit of something** to leave room for, allow

| **admit** ▶ admits, admitting, admitted |

admittance *noun* the right or permission to enter

admittedly *adverb* as I must admit

admonish *verb* 1 to warn 2 to rebuke, scold

admonition *noun* a warning

ad nauseam to a tiresome degree

ado *noun* trouble, fuss

adolescent *noun* someone between a child and an adult in age ■ *adjective* of this age ■ **adolescence** *noun*

adopt *verb* 1 to take as your own (especially a child of other parents) 2 to take (*eg* precautions), choose formally ■ **adoption** *noun*

adoptive *adjective* adopted, taken as your own: *her adoptive country*

adorable *adjective* very lovable

adoration *noun* 1 worship 2 great love

adore *verb* 1 to love very much 2 to worship

adorn *verb* to decorate (with ornaments *etc*)

adornment *noun* ornament

adrenal gland either of two glands, one above each kidney, producing important hormones

adrenalin *or* **adrenaline** *noun* a hormone produced in response to fear, anger, *etc*, preparing the body for quick action

adrift *adverb & adjective* drifting, floating

adroit *adjective* skilful

ADSL *abbreviation, computing* Asymmetric Digital Subscriber Line, a fast Internet connection over a phone line

adulation (*pronounced* ad-yoo-lei-shun) *noun* great flattery

adult *adjective* grown up ■ *noun* a grown-up person

adultery *noun* unfaithfulness to a husband or wife ■ **adulterer**, **adulteress** *noun*

adulthood *noun* the state of being an adult

advance *verb* 1 to go forward 2 to put forward (a plan *etc*) 3 to help the progress of 4 to pay before the usual or agreed time ■ *noun* 1 movement forward 2 improvement 3 a loan of money ■ **in advance** beforehand

advanced *adjective* well forward in progress

advancement *noun* progress

advantage *noun* 1 a better position, superiority 2 gain or benefit ■ *verb* to help, benefit ■ **take advantage of** to make use of (a situation, person, *etc*) in such a way as to benefit yourself

advantageous *adjective* profitable; helpful

advent *noun* 1 coming, arrival 2 **Advent** in the Christian Church, the four weeks before Christmas

adventure *noun* a bold or exciting undertaking or experience

adventurer *noun* someone who takes risks, especially in the hope of making a lot of money

adventurous *adjective* taking risks, liking adventure

adverb *noun* a word which gives a more definite meaning to a verb, adjective, or other adverb, *eg* 'eat slowly,' 'extremely hard,' 'very carefully' ▪ **adverbial** *adjective*

adversary *noun* (*plural* **adversaries**) an enemy; an opponent

adverse *adjective* unfavourable

adversity *noun* (*plural* **adversities**) misfortune

advert *noun, informal* an advertisement

advertise *verb* 1 to make known to the public 2 to stress the good points of (a product for sale)

advertisement *noun* a photograph, short film, *etc* intended to persuade the public to buy a particular product

advice *noun* something said as a help to someone trying to make a decision

* Do not confuse with: **advise**. To help you remember: 'ice' is a noun, 'ise' is not!

advisable *adjective* wise, sensible ▪ **advisability** *noun*

advise *verb* 1 to give advice to 2 to recommend (an action *etc*) ▪ **adviser** or **advisor** *noun*

* Do not confuse with: **advice**. To help you remember: 'ice' is a noun ... so 'ise' must be the verb!

advisory *adjective* advice-giving

advocate *noun* (*pronounced* ad-vo-kat) 1 someone who pleads for another 2 in Scotland, a court lawyer ▪ *verb* (*pronounced* ad-vo-keit) to argue for or recommend

aeon or **eon** (*pronounced* ee-on) *noun* a very long period of time, an age

aerate *verb* to put air or another gas into (a liquid)

aerial *adjective* 1 of, in or from the air 2 placed high up or overhead ▪ *noun* a wire or rod (or a set of these) by which radio or television signals are received or sent

aero- *prefix* of air or aircraft

aerobatics *noun plural* stunts performed by an aircraft

aerobic *adjective* needing or using oxygen to live

aerobics *noun singular* a system of physical exercise which aims to strengthen the heart and lungs by increasing the body's oxygen consumption

aerodrome *noun* a landing and maintenance station for aircraft

aerodynamic *adjective* designed to promote more efficient movement through air

aeronautics *noun singular* the science or art of navigation in the air

aeroplane or *US* **airplane** *noun* an engine-powered flying machine with fixed wings (*short form:* plane)

aerosol *noun* a container of liquid and gas under pressure, from which the liquid is squirted as a mist

aesthetic *adjective* **1** of beauty or its appreciation **2** artistic, pleasing to the eye ▪ **aesthetically** *adverb*

afar *adverb, formal* a long way away

affable *adjective* pleasant, easy to speak to ▪ **affability** *noun*

affair *noun* **1** events *etc* connected with one person or thing: *the Watergate affair* **2** affairs personal concerns, transactions, *etc* **3** business, concern: *not your affair* **4** a love affair

affect *verb* **1** to act upon **2** to have an effect on; move the feelings of **3** to pretend to feel *etc*

⟡ Do not confuse with: **effect**. **Affect** is usually a verb. **Effect** is usually a noun. 'To AFFECT' means 'to have an EFFECT on'

affectation *noun* pretence

affected *adjective* **1** moved in your feelings **2** not natural, sham

affecting *adjective* moving the feelings

affection *noun* a strong liking

affectionate *adjective* loving

affidavit (*pronounced* af-i-**dei**-vit) *noun, law* a written statement made on oath

affiliated *adjective*: **affiliated to** connected with or attached to ▪ **affiliation** *noun*

affinity *noun* (*plural* **affinities**) a close likeness or agreement

affirm *verb* to state firmly ▪ **affirmation** *noun*

affirmative *adjective* saying 'yes'

affix *verb* to attach to

afflict *verb* to give continued pain or suffering to

affliction *noun* great suffering, misery

affluence *noun* wealth

affluent *adjective* wealthy

afford *verb* to be able to pay for

afforest *verb* to cover land with forest ▪ **afforestation** *noun*

affront *verb* to insult openly ▪ *noun* an insult

afloat *adverb & adjective* floating

afoot *adverb* happening or about to happen

aforesaid *adjective* said or named before: *the aforesaid person*

afraid *adjective* **1** struck with fear **2** *informal* sorry to have to admit that

afresh *adverb* starting again

aft *adverb* near or towards the stern of a vessel

after *preposition* **1** later in time than **2** following: *one after another* **3** in memory or honour of: *named after his father* **4** in pursuit of **5** about: *asked after her health* **6** despite: *after all my efforts, it still didn't work* **7** in the style of: *after Rubens* ▪ *adverb* later in time or place
▪ *conjunction* later than the time

when ■ **after all 1** all things
considered **2** despite everything
said or done before

after- *prefix* later in time or
place: *aftertaste/afterthought*

afterbirth *noun* the placenta
and membranes expelled from
the uterus after giving birth

aftermath *noun* the bad results
of something

afternoon *noun* the time
between noon and evening
■ *adjective* taking place in the
afternoon

aftershave *noun* a lotion used
on the face after shaving

afterthought *noun* a later
thought

afterwards *adverb* later

again *adverb* **1** once more **2** in or
into the original state, place, *etc*:
there and back again **3** on the
other hand

against *preposition* **1** in
opposition to **2** in the opposite
direction to **3** on a background of
4 close to, touching **5** as
protection from: *guard against
infection*

age *noun* **1** a long period of time **2**
the time someone or something
has lived or existed ■ *verb* to grow
or make visibly older ■ **of age**
legally an adult

| **age** *verb* ► ages, age*ing* or
| ag*ing*, ag*ed*

aged *adjective* **1** (*pronounced* eij-
id) old **2** (*pronounced* eijd) of the
age of

ageism *noun* discrimination on
grounds of age ■ **ageist** *adjective*

agency *noun* (*plural* **agencies**) **1**
the office or business of an agent
2 action, means by which
something is done

agenda *noun* a list of things to be
done, especially at a meeting

agent *noun* **1** someone who acts
for another **2** someone or
something that causes an effect **3**
a spy **4** a substance that can
cause a chemical reaction
(*compare with*: **reagent**)

aggravate *verb* **1** to make worse
2 *informal* to annoy ■ **aggravating**
adjective ■ **aggravation** *noun*

aggregate *noun* a total

aggressive *adjective* **1** ready to
attack first **2** quarrelsome
■ **aggression** *noun* ■ **aggressively**
adverb ■ **aggressor** *noun*

aggrieved *adjective* hurt, upset

aghast *adjective* struck with
horror

agile *adjective* active, nimble
■ **agility** *noun*

agitate *verb* **1** to stir up **2** to
excite, disturb ■ **agitated**
adjective ■ **agitation** *noun*

agitator *noun* someone who
stirs up others

agnostic *noun* someone who
believes it is impossible to know
whether God exists or not
■ **agnosticism** *noun*

ago *adverb* in the past

agog *adjective* eager, excited

agonize *or* **agonise** *verb* (to

cause) to worry intensely or suffer great anxiety about something

agonized *adjective* showing great pain or suffering

agonizing *adjective* causing great pain or suffering

agony *noun* (*plural* **agonies**) great pain

agoraphobia (*pronounced* ag-ra-**foh**-bi-*a*) *noun* great fear of open spaces

agrarian *adjective* of farmland or farming

agree *verb* **1** to be alike in opinions, decisions, *etc* **2** to say that you will do something **3** **agree with 4** **agree with** to cause no problems in digestion **5** to be the same or consistent, fit together

agreeable *adjective* **1** pleasant **2** ready to agree ▪ **agreeably** *adverb*

agreement *noun* **1** likeness (especially of opinions) **2** a written statement making a bargain

agri- *prefix* of fields, land use, or farming

agriculture *noun* the cultivation of the land; farming ▪ **agricultural** *adjective*

agro- *prefix* of fields, land use, or farming: *agrobiology* (= the study of plant nutrition)/*agrochemical* (= a chemical used in farming the land)

aground *adjective & adverb* stuck on the bottom of the sea or a river

ahead *adverb* in front; in advance

-aholic *or* **-oholic** *suffix* having an addiction to: *workaholic*/*chocoholic*

aid *verb* to help, assist ▪ *noun* help

AIDS *or* **Aids** *abbreviation* Acquired Immune Deficiency Syndrome

ailing *adjective* **1** troubled, in a bad state: *the ailing steel industry* **2** ill

ailment *noun* an illness

aim *verb* **1** to point at (especially with a gun) **2** to intend to do **3** to have as your purpose ▪ *noun* **1** the act of, or skill in, aiming **2** the point aimed at, goal, intention

aimless *adjective* without aim or purpose ▪ **aimlessly** *adverb*

air *noun* **1** the mixture of gases (mainly oxygen and nitrogen) which we breathe; the atmosphere **2** a light breeze **3** fresh air **4** space overhead **5** a tune **6** the look or manner (of a person) ▪ *verb* **1** to expose to the air **2** to make known (an opinion *etc*)

airbag *noun* a bag which automatically inflates inside a car on impact to protect the driver from injury

airbed *noun* a mattress which can be inflated

airborne *adjective* in the air, flying

air-conditioned *adjective*

equipped with a system for filtering and controlling the temperature of the air ∎ **air-conditioner** noun ∎ **air-conditioning** noun

aircraft noun (plural **aircraft**) a flying machine

aircraft carrier a warship on which aircraft can take off and land

air force the branch of the armed forces using aircraft

airgun noun a gun worked by means of compressed air

airing noun 1 the act of exposing to the air: give the room an airing 2 the act of talking about something openly: give your views an airing

airless adjective stuffy, with no circulation of fresh air

airline noun a company which provides travel by aeroplane

airlock noun 1 a bubble in a pipe obstructing the flow of a liquid 2 a compartment with two doors for entering and leaving an airtight spaceship etc

airplane US for **aeroplane**

airport noun a place where aircraft land and take off, with buildings for customs, waiting-rooms, etc

air raid an attack by aeroplanes

airship noun a large balloon which can be steered and driven

airstream noun a flow of air

airtight adjective made so that air cannot pass in or out

airy adjective 1 of or like the air 2 well supplied with fresh air

aisle (pronounced ail) noun 1 the side part of a church 2 a passage between seats in a theatre etc

ajar adverb & adjective partly open

aka abbreviation also known as

akimbo adverb with hand on hip and elbow bent outward

akin adjective similar

à la carte adjective & adverb 1 according to the menu 2 each dish chosen and priced separately

alacrity noun briskness, cheerful readiness

alarm noun 1 sudden fear 2 something which rouses to action or gives warning of danger ∎ verb to frighten ∎ **alarming** adjective

alarmist noun someone who frightens others needlessly

alas exclamation a cry showing grief

albatross noun (plural **albatrosses**) a type of large seabird

albino noun (plural **albinos**) a person or animal with no natural colour in their skin, hair and eye irises

album noun 1 a book with blank pages for holding photographs, stamps, etc 2 a record, CD, etc with multiple tracks

albumen noun the white of eggs

alchemy noun an early form of chemistry aimed at changing other metals into gold

alcohol *noun* **1** a type of chemical compound used in dyes, perfumes, *etc* **2** the compound ethanol, found in alcoholic drinks **3** drink containing ethanol

alcoholic *adjective* of or containing alcohol ▪ *noun* someone addicted to alcohol

alcoholism *noun* addiction to alcohol

alcove *noun* a recess in a room's wall

alder *noun* a type of tree which grows beside ponds and rivers

ale *noun* a drink made from malt, hops, *etc*; beer

alert *noun* signal to be ready for action ▪ *verb* to make alert, warn ▪ *adjective* **1** watchful **2** quick-thinking

algae (*pronounced* al-gi *or* al-ji) *noun plural* a group of simple plants which includes seaweed

algebra *noun* a part of mathematics in which letters and signs are used to represent numbers

alias *adverb* also known as ▪ *noun* (*plural* **aliases**) a false name

alibi *noun* **1** the plea that someone charged with a crime was elsewhere when it was done **2** the state or fact of being elsewhere when a crime was committed

alien *adjective* foreign ▪ *noun* a foreigner

alienate *verb* to make someone unfriendly, probably by causing them to feel unwanted or rejected

alight *verb* **1** to climb *etc* down: *alight from the train* **2** to settle, land ▪ *adjective & adverb* on fire, burning

| **alight** *verb* ▶ **alights**, **alight**ing, **alight**ed

align *verb* **1** to set in line **2** to take sides in an argument *etc*: *align yourself with environmentalists*

alignment *noun* arrangement in a line

alike *adjective* like one another, similar ▪ *adverb* in the same way, similarly

alimony *noun* an allowance paid by a husband to his wife, or a wife to her husband, when they are legally separated

alive *adjective* **1** living **2** full of activity ▪ **alive to** aware of

alkali *noun* a substance such as soda or potash that dissolves in water to produce a certain type of ions containing hydrogen and oxygen (*compare with*: **acid**) ▪ **alkaline** *adjective* ▪ **alkalinity** *noun*

alkaline-earth metal a metallic element, such as magnesium or calcium, that is only found in nature in compounds

alkane *noun* a hydrocarbon whose carbon atoms form chains linked by single bonds

alkene *noun* a hydrocarbon

whose carbon atoms form chains linked by one or more double bonds

all *adjective & pronoun* **1** every one (of) **2** the whole (of) ▪ *adverb* wholly, completely ▪ **all in 1** with everything included: *came to five pounds all in* **2** *informal* exhausted ▪ **all ready** totally ready

✸ Do not use this as an alternative spelling for 'already'

▪ **all right** in a normal state; not hurt, unhappy, or feeling strange

✸ It is best to avoid the spelling 'alright', since some people say it is incorrect

▪ **all together** together as a group

✸ Do not use this as an alternative spelling for 'altogether'

▪ **all ways** in every way possible

✸ Do not use this as an alternative spelling for 'always'

Allah *noun* in Islam, God
allege *verb* to say without proof ▪ **allegation** *noun*
alleged *adjective* claimed to be: *the alleged criminal* ▪ **allegedly** *adverb*
allegiance *noun* loyalty
allele *noun* any of the forms of a gene for a specific trait
alleluia see hallelujah
allergy *noun* (*plural* **allergies**)

abnormal sensitiveness of the body to something ▪ **allergic** *adjective*
alleviate *verb* to make lighter, lessen ▪ **alleviation** *noun*
alley *noun* (*plural* **alleys**) **1** a narrow passage or lane **2** an enclosure for bowls or skittles
alliance *noun* a joining together of two people, nations, *etc*, for a common cause
allied *adjective* joined by an alliance
alligator *noun* a large reptile like a crocodile
alliteration *noun* the repetition of the same sound at the beginning of two or more words close together, *eg* 'round and round the rugged rock' or 'sing a song of sixpence' ▪ **alliterative** *adjective*
allocate *verb* to allot, share out, reserve for a particular purpose ▪ **allocation** *noun*
allot *verb* to give each person a share of

| **allot ►** allots, allot*ting*, allot*ted*

allotment *noun* **1** the act of allotting **2** a small plot of ground for growing vegetables *etc*
allow *verb* **1** to let (someone do something) **2 allow for** to take into consideration (in sums, plans, *etc*) **3** to admit, confess ▪ **allowable** *adjective*
allowance *noun* a fixed sum or amount given regularly ▪ **make**

allowances for to treat differently because of taking into consideration special circumstances *etc*

alloy *noun* a mixture of two or more metals

allude *verb*: **allude to** to refer to indirectly or in passing

⚠ Do not confuse with: **elude**

allure *verb* to tempt, draw on by promises *etc* ▪ **alluring** *adjective*

allusion *noun* an indirect reference

⚠ Do not confuse with: **delusion** and **illusion**. An **allusion** is a comment which **alludes to** something

allusive *adjective* referring indirectly, hinting

⚠ Do not confuse with: **elusive** and **illusive**. **Allusive** is related to the verb **allude** and the noun **allusion**

alluvium *noun* (*plural* **alluvia**) earth, sand, *etc* brought down and left by rivers in flood ▪ **alluvial** *adjective*

ally *verb* to join yourself to by treaty *etc* ▪ *noun* (*plural* **allies**) someone in alliance with another; a friend

| **ally** *verb* ► **allies**, ally*ing*, alli*ed*

almanac *noun* a calendar for any year, with information about the phases of the moon *etc*

almighty *adjective* having much power ▪ **the Almighty** God

almond *noun* the kernel of the fruit of the almond-tree

almost *adverb* very nearly but not quite

alms *noun plural* gifts to the poor

aloft *adverb* 1 on high 2 upward

alone *adjective* not accompanied by others, solitary ▪ *adverb* 1 only, without anything else 2 not accompanied by others ▪ **leave alone** to let be, leave undisturbed

along *preposition* 1 by the side of or near 2 over the length of: *walk along the road* ▪ *adverb* onward: *come along!* ▪ **along with** together with

alongside *preposition* beside ▪ *adverb* near a ship's side

aloof *adjective & adverb* 1 at a distance, apart 2 showing no interest in others

aloud *adverb* so as to be heard

alpha *noun* the first letter of the Greek alphabet

alphabet *noun* letters of a language given in a fixed order

alphabetical *or* **alphabetic** *adjective* in the order of the letters of the alphabet

alpine *adjective* of the Alps or other high mountains

alps *noun plural* high mountains

already *adverb* 1 before this or that time 2 now, before the expected time

✸ If you write 'all ready' as two words, it has the very different meaning of 'totally ready': *Are you all ready for the big day?*

✸ **alright** It is best to spell this as two words: 'all right'. Some people consider the spelling 'alright' to be incorrect

alsatian *noun* a breed of large wolf-like dog

also *adverb* in addition, besides, too

also-ran *noun* someone or something that competed (as in a race) but was not among the winners

altar *noun* **1** a raised place for offerings to a god **2** in Christian churches, the communion table

altercation *noun* an argument or quarrel

alter *verb* to change ■ **alteration** *noun*

alter ego a second self

alternate *verb* (pronounced ol-te-neit) of two things: to do or happen in turn ■ *adjective* (pronounced ol-**tern**-at) happening *etc* in turns: *on alternate days* (= every other day)

✸ Do not confuse: **alternate** and **alternative**. 'To ALTERNATE' is to move between two possibilities. **Alternate** is the adjective from this verb

alternating current an electric current that reverses its direction at regular intervals (short form: **AC**)

alternative *adjective* offering a second possibility ■ *noun* a second possibility, a different course of action

alternator *noun* a generator producing alternating current

although *conjunction* though, in spite of the fact that

altitude *noun* height above sea level

alto *noun* (plural **altos**) *music* **1** the male voice of the highest pitch **2** the female voice of lowest pitch (also called: **contralto**)

altogether *adverb* **1** considering everything, in all **2** completely: *not altogether satisfied*

✸ If you write 'all together' as two words, it has the very different meaning of 'together in a group': *It's great to be all together for Christmas*

aluminium *or US* **aluminum** *noun* an element, a very light metal

always *adverb* **1** for ever **2** every time

✸ If you write 'all ways' as two words, it has the very different meaning of 'in every way possible': *I've tried all ways to tell her, but she just won't listen*

Alzheimer's disease an illness affecting the brain in middle-aged and elderly people and causing reduced mental ability

am *abbreviation* before noon (from Latin *ante meridiem*)

am *see* be

amalgam *noun* a mixture (especially of metals)

amalgamate *verb* 1 to join together, combine 2 to mix ■ amalgamation *noun*

amass *verb* to collect in large quantity

amateur *noun* someone who takes part in a thing for the love of it, not for money (*contrasted with:* **professional**) ■ *adjective* doing something for the love of it

amateurish *adjective* not done properly; not skilful

amaze *verb* to surprise greatly ■ amazed *adjective* ■ amazement *noun* ■ amazing *adjective* ■ amazingly *adverb*

ambassador *noun* 1 an official sent to another country to look after the interests of their country and government 2 a representative

amber *noun* a hard yellowish fossil resin used in making jewellery ■ *adjective* 1 made of amber 2 of the colour of amber

ambidextrous *adjective* able to use both hands with equal skill

ambience *noun* environment, atmosphere ■ ambient *adjective*

ambiguity *noun* (*plural*

ambiguities) uncertainty in meaning

ambiguous *adjective* 1 having two possible meanings 2 not clear

♦ Do not confuse with: ambivalent

ambition *noun* the desire for success, power, fame, *etc* ■ ambitious *adjective* ■ ambitiously *adverb*

ambivalent *adjective* having two contrasting feelings or attitudes towards something ■ ambivalence *noun*

♦ Do not confuse with: ambiguous

amble *verb* to walk in an unhurried relaxed way ■ *noun* an unhurried walk

ambulance *noun* a vehicle for carrying the sick or injured

ambush *noun* (*plural* ambushes) the act of lying hidden in order to make a surprise attack ■ *verb* to attack suddenly from a position of hiding

amenable *adjective* open to advice or suggestion ■ amenability *noun* ■ amenably *adverb*

amend *verb* 1 to correct, improve (a text or statement) by making small additions 2 to alter (a text or statement) slightly by making small additions ■ **make amends** to make up for having done wrong

✎ Do not confuse with: **emend**. **Amending** involves making changes or improvements. **Emending** consists simply of getting rid of errors

amendment noun a change, often in something written

amenity noun (plural **amenities**) a pleasant or convenient feature of a place etc

amethyst noun a precious stone of a bluish-violet colour

amiable adjective likeable; friendly ■ **amiability** noun ■ **amiably** adverb

amicable adjective friendly ■ **amicably** adverb

amid or **amidst** preposition in the middle of, surrounded by

✎ Use 'amid' or 'amidst' when the thing or things doing the surrounding cannot be counted: amidst the confusion/sitting amidst the wild poppies. Use 'among' or 'amongst' when the thing or things can be counted: celebrate your birthday among friends

amino acid a compound which contains carbon, oxygen, hydrogen and nitrogen, and joins with others to form proteins

amiss adjective wrong ■ adverb wrongly; badly

ammeter noun a device for measuring electrical current

ammonia noun a strong-smelling gas made of hydrogen and nitrogen

ammunition noun gunpowder, shot, bullets, bombs, etc

amnesia noun loss of memory

amnesiac noun & adjective (someone) suffering from amnesia

amnesty noun (plural **amnesties**) a general pardon of wrongdoers

amoeba (pronounced a-mee-ba) noun (plural **amoebas** or **amoebae** –pronounced a-mee-bi or a-mee-bai) a very simple form of animal life found in ponds etc

amok or **amuck** adverb: **run amok** to go mad and do a lot of damage, run riot

among or **amongst** preposition **1** surrounded by or in the middle of **2** giving each a part **3** in the group of: among all her novels, this is the best

✎ Use 'among' or 'amongst' when the thing or things doing the surrounding can be counted. Use 'amid' or 'amidst' when the thing or things cannot be counted

amoral adjective incapable of distinguishing between right and wrong ■ **amorality** noun

✎ Do not confuse with: **immoral**. An **amoral** person behaves badly because they do not understand the difference between right and wrong. An **immoral** person behaves badly in the full knowledge that what they are doing is wrong

amorous *adjective* loving; ready or inclined to love

amount *noun* **1** total, sum **2** a quantity ▪ **amount to** to add up to

amp *noun* **1** an ampère **2** *informal* an amplifier

ampère *noun* the standard unit of electric current

ampersand *noun* the character (&) representing *and*

amphibian *noun* **1** an animal that lives on land and in water **2** a vehicle for use on land and in water ▪ *adjective* living on land and water

amphibious *adjective* living or operating on land and water

amphitheatre *noun* a theatre with seats surrounding a central arena

ample *adjective* **1** plenty of **2** large enough ▪ **amply** *adverb*

amplification *noun* the process or product of making something louder, larger, or more detailed

amplifier *noun* an electrical device for increasing loudness

amplify *verb* to make louder

amplify ► amplifies,
amplifying, amplified

amputate *verb* to cut off (especially a human limb) ▪ **amputation** *noun*

amputee *noun* someone who has had a limb amputated

amrit *noun* **1** a Sikh ceremonial drink **2** the ceremony in which amrit is drunk

amuck *another spelling of* amok

amuse *verb* **1** to make laugh **2** to give pleasure to ▪ **amusement** *noun*

amusing *adjective* funny

an *see* a

anabolic steroids steroids used to increase the build-up of body tissue, especially muscle

anaconda *noun* a large South American water snake

anaemia *or US* **anemia** *noun* a shortage of red cells in the blood

anaemic *adjective* **1** suffering from anaemia **2** pale or ill-looking

anaerobic *adjective* not requiring oxygen to live

anaesthetic *or US* **anesthetic** *noun* a substance which produces lack of feeling for a time in a part of the body, or which makes someone unconscious

anaesthetist *noun* a doctor trained to administer anaesthetics ▪ **anaesthetize** *or* **anaesthetise** *verb*

anagram *noun* a word or sentence formed by reordering the letters of another word or sentence, *eg veil* is an anagram of *evil*

anal *adjective* of the anus

analgesic *adjective* causing pain to be reduced

analogue *adjective* **1** of a device: changing continuously rather than in a series of steps **2** of a clock: with 12 numbered divisions and pointers (hands) on a dial showing the time

analogy *noun* (*plural* **analogies**) a likeness, resemblance in certain ways

analyse *or US* **analyze** *verb* **1** to break down, separate into parts **2** to examine in detail

analysis *noun* (*plural* **analyses**) **1** a breaking up of a thing into its parts **2** a detailed examination (of something)

analyst *noun* **1** someone who analyses **2** a psychiatrist or psychologist

analyze *US spelling of* **analyse**

anarchic *or* **anarchical** *adjective* **1** refusing to obey any rules **2** in a state of disorder or confusion

anarchist *noun* someone who believes in anarchy

anarchy *noun* **1** lack or absence of government **2** disorder or confusion

anatomist *noun* a person who specializes in the study of the human body

anatomy *noun* **1** the study of the parts of the body **2** the body

ancestor *noun* a person from whom someone is descended by birth; a forefather ▪ **ancestral** *adjective*

ancestry *noun* line of ancestors

anchor *noun* a heavy piece of iron, with hooked ends, for holding a ship fast to the bed of the sea *etc* ▪ *verb* **1** to fix by anchor **2** to let down the anchor

anchorage *noun* a place where a ship can anchor

anchorman, anchorwoman *noun* the main presenter of a television news programme *etc*

anchovy *noun* (*plural* **anchovies**) a type of small fish of the herring family

ancient *adjective* **1** very old **2** of times long past

ancillary *adjective* serving or supporting something more important

and *conjunction* **1** joining two statements, pieces of information, *etc*: *black and white* **2** in addition to: *2 and 2 makes 4*

android *noun* a robot in human form

anecdote *noun* a short, interesting or amusing story, usually true ▪ **anecdotal** *adjective*

anemometer *noun* an instrument for measuring the speed of the wind

anemone (*pronounced a-nem-o-ni*) *noun* a type of woodland or garden flower

aneurism *noun* a dangerous swelling of an artery

angel *noun* **1** a messenger or attendant of God **2** a very good or beautiful person ▪ **angelic**

adjective as perfectly sweet and good as an angel

anger *noun* a bitter feeling against someone, annoyance, rage ▪ *verb* to make angry

angina *noun* a form of heart disease causing acute chest pains

angle *noun* **1** the V-shape made by two lines meeting at a point **2** a corner **3** a point of view ▪ *verb* to try to get by hints *etc*: *angling for a job*

angler *noun* someone who fishes with a rod and line

Anglican *adjective* of the Church of England ▪ *noun* a member of the Church of England

anglicize *or* **anglicise** *verb* **1** to put into the English language **2** to make English in character ▪ **anglicization** *noun*

angling *noun* the sport of fishing with a rod and line

Anglo-Saxon *adjective & noun* **1** (of) the people of England before the Norman Conquest **2** (of) their language

angry *adjective* feeling or showing anger ▪ **angrily** *adverb*

|angry ► angrier, angriest

anguish *noun* very great pain or distress

anguished *adjective* in misery and suffering

angular *adjective* **1** having angles **2** thin, bony ▪ **angularity** *noun*

animal *noun* **1** a living being

which can feel and move of its own accord **2** an animal other than a human ▪ *adjective* of or like an animal

animate *verb* (pronounced an-im-eit) **1** to give life to **2** to make lively ▪ *adjective* (pronounced an-im-*at*) living

animated *adjective* **1** lively **2** made to move as if alive ▪ **animatedly** *adverb*

animation *noun* **1** liveliness **2** a film made from a series of drawings that give the illusion of movement when shown in sequence

animator *noun* an artist who works in animation

animosity *noun* a strong feeling of dislike

anion *noun* an ion with negative charge

aniseed *noun* a seed with a flavour like that of liquorice

ankle *noun* the joint connecting the foot and leg

annals *noun plural* yearly historical accounts of events

annex *verb* **1** to take possession of **2** to add, attach ▪ *noun* (*also spelled* **annexe**) a building added to another ▪ **annexation** *noun*

annihilate *verb* to destroy completely ▪ **annihilation** *noun*

anniversary *noun* (*plural* **anniversaries**) the day of each year when a particular event is remembered

annotate *verb* **1** to make notes

upon **2** to add notes or explanation to ■ **annotation** noun

announce verb to make publicly known ■ **announcement** noun

announcer noun someone who announces programmes on TV etc, or reads the news

annoy verb to make rather angry; irritate ■ **annoyance** noun

annual adjective yearly ■ noun **1** a plant that lives only one year **2** a book published yearly

annually adverb every year

annul verb **1** to put an end to **2** to declare no longer valid ■ **annulment** noun

| annul ► annuls, annulling, annulled

anode noun the positive electrode in a battery (contrasted with: **cathode**)

anoint verb to smear with ointment or oil

anomaly noun (plural anomalies) something unusual ■ **anomalous** adjective

anon abbreviation anonymous

anonymous adjective without the name of the author, giver, etc being known or given ■ **anonymously** adverb

anorak noun a hooded waterproof jacket

anorexia noun an emotional illness causing the sufferer to refuse food and become sometimes dangerously thin (also called: **anorexia nervosa**)

anorexic adjective of or suffering from anorexia ■ noun someone suffering from anorexia

another adjective **1** a different (thing or person) **2** one more of the same kind ■ pronoun an additional thing of the same kind

answer verb **1** to speak, write, etc in return or reply **2** to find the result or solution (of a sum, problem, etc) ■ noun **1** something said, written, etc in return or reply **2** a solution ■ **answer back** to give a cheeky or aggressive answer to someone in authority ■ **answer for 1** to be responsible for **2** to suffer for, be punished for

answerable adjective responsible: answerable for her actions

ant noun a very small insect which lives in organized colonies

antagonism noun hostility, opposition

antagonist noun **1** an enemy **2** an opponent

antagonistic adjective opposed (to), unfriendly, hostile

antagonize or **antagonise** verb to make an enemy of, cause dislike

Antarctic adjective of the South Pole or regions round it

ante- prefix before

anteater noun an American animal with a long snout which feeds on ants and termites

antecedent noun someone who lived at an earlier time; an ancestor

antelope *noun* a graceful, swift-running animal like a deer

antenatal *adjective* **1** before birth **2** relating to pregnancy: *antenatal clinic*

antenna *noun* **1** (*plural* **antennae** – *pronounced* an-ten-ee) an insect's feeler **2** (*plural* **antennas**) an aerial

anthem *noun* **1** a piece of music for a church choir **2** any song of praise

ant-hill *noun* an earth mound built by ants as a nest

anthology *noun* (*plural* **anthologies**) a collection of specially chosen poems, stories, *etc*

anthracite *noun* coal that burns with a hot, smokeless flame

anthrax *noun* an infectious disease of cattle, sheep, *etc*, sometimes transferred to humans

anthropoid *adjective* of apes: resembling humans

anthropology *noun* the study of mankind ▪ **anthropological** *adjective* ▪ **anthropologist** *noun*

anti- *prefix* against, opposite: *anti-terrorist*

antibiotic *noun* a medicine taken to kill disease-causing bacteria

antibody *noun* (*plural* **antibodies**) a substance produced in the human body to fight bacteria *etc*

anticipate *verb* **1** to look forward to, expect **2** to see or know in advance **3** to act before (someone or something) ▪ **anticipation** *noun* ▪ **anticipatory** *adjective*

anticlimax *noun* a dull or disappointing ending

anticlockwise *adjective* & *adverb* in the opposite direction to the hands of a clock

antics *noun plural* tricks, odd or amusing actions

anticyclone *noun* a circling movement of air round an area of high air pressure, causing calm weather

antidote *noun* something given to act against the effect of poison

antifreeze *noun* a chemical with a low freezing point, added to a car radiator to prevent freezing

antigen *noun* a substance that stimulates the production of antibodies

antihistamine *noun* a medicine used to treat an allergy

antipathy *noun* extreme dislike

antiperspirant *noun* a substance applied to the body to reduce sweating

antipodes (*pronounced* an-tip-od-eez) *noun plural* places on the earth's surface exactly opposite each other, especially Australia and New Zealand in relation to Europe ▪ **antipodean** *adjective*

antiquarian *noun* a dealer in antiques

antiquated *adjective* grown old, or out of fashion

antique *noun* an old, interesting or valuable object from earlier times ■ *adjective* **1** old, from earlier times **2** old-fashioned

antiquity *noun* (*plural* **antiquities**) **1** ancient times, especially those of the Greeks and Romans **2** great age **3**

antiquities objects from earlier times

antiseptic *adjective* germ-destroying ■ *noun* a chemical *etc* which destroys germs

antisocial *adjective* **1** not fitting in with, harmful to other people **2** disliking the company of other people

antithesis *noun* (*plural* **antitheses**) the exact opposite

antler *noun* the horn of a deer

antonym *noun* a word which means the opposite of another, *eg* 'big' and 'small', or 'brave' and 'cowardly'

anus *noun* the lower opening of the bowels through which faeces pass

anvil *noun* a metal block on which blacksmiths hammer metal into shape

anxiety *noun* (*plural* **anxieties**) worry about what may happen

anxious *adjective* **1** worried **2** full of worry or uncertainty **3** eager, keen ■ **anxiously** *adverb*

any *adjective* **1** some: *is there any milk?* **2** every, no matter which: *any day will suit* ■ *pronoun* some: *there aren't any left* ■ *adverb* at all: *I can't work any faster* ■ **at any rate** in any case, whatever happens

anybody *pronoun* any person

anyhow *adverb* **1** in any case **2** carelessly: *scattered anyhow over the floor*

anyone *pronoun* any person

anything *pronoun* something of any kind

anyway *adverb* at any rate

anywhere *adverb* in any place

apart *adverb* **1** aside **2** in or into pieces: *came apart in my hands* **3** in opposite directions ■ **apart from 1** separate, or separately, from **2** except for

apartheid *noun* the political policy of keeping people of different races apart

apartment *noun* **1** a room in a house **2** *US* a flat

apathy *noun* lack of feeling or interest ■ **apathetic** *adjective*

ape *noun* a member of a group of animals related to monkeys, but larger, tailless and walking upright ■ *verb* to imitate

aperitif (*pronounced* a-pe-ri-teef) *noun* a drink taken before a meal

aperture *noun* an opening, a hole

apex *noun* (*plural* **apexes** or **apices**) the highest point of anything

aphid (*pronounced* ei-fid) *noun* a

small insect which feeds on plants

apiarist *noun* someone who keeps or studies bees

apiary *noun* (*plural* **apiaries**) a place where bees are kept

apiece *adverb* to or for each one: *three chocolates apiece*

aplomb *noun* self-confidence

apocalypse *noun* the destruction of the world ▪ **apocalyptic** *adjective*

apocryphal (*pronounced* a-**pok**-rif-al) *adjective* unlikely to be true

apogee *noun* the point of an orbit furthest from the earth

apologetic *adjective* expressing regret ▪ **apologetically** *adverb*

apologize *or* **apologise** *verb* to express regret, say you are sorry

apology *noun* (*plural* **apologies**) an expression of regret for having done wrong

apoplexy *noun* sudden loss of ability to feel, move, *etc*, a stroke ▪ **apoplectic** *adjective*

apostle *noun* a religious preacher, especially one of the disciples of Christ

apostrophe *noun* **1** a mark (') indicating possession: *the minister's cat* **2** a similar mark indicating that a letter *etc* has been missed out, *eg isn't* for *is not*

appal *verb* to horrify, shock

| **appal** ▶ appal**s**, appal**ling**, |
| appal**led** |

appalling *adjective* shocking

apparatus *noun* **1** an instrument or machine **2** instruments, tools or material required for a piece of work

apparel *noun* a formal or literary word for clothing

apparent *adjective* easily seen, evident ▪ **apparently** *adverb*

apparition *noun* **1** something remarkable which appears suddenly **2** a ghost

appeal *verb* **1** to ask earnestly (for help *etc*) **2** *law* to take a case that has been lost to a higher court **3** **appeal to someone** to be pleasing to someone ▪ *noun* **1** a request for help **2** *law* the taking of a case to a higher court

appealing *adjective* arousing liking or sympathy

appear *verb* **1** to come into view **2** to arrive **3** to seem ▪ **appearance** *noun*

appease *verb* to soothe or satisfy, especially by giving what was asked for

appendicitis *noun*, *medicine* inflammation of the appendix

appendix *noun* (*plural* **appendices** *or* **appendixes**) **1** a part added at the end of a book **2** a small worm-shaped part of the bowels

appetite *noun* **1** desire for food **2** taste or enthusiasm (for)

appetizer *or* **appetiser** *noun* a snack taken before a main meal

appetizing *adjective* tempting to the appetite

applaud *verb* **1** to show approval of by clapping the hands **2** to express strong approval of and admiration for: *I applaud her decision*

applause *noun* a show of approval by clapping

apple *noun* a round firm fruit, usually red or green

appliance *noun* a tool, instrument, machine, *etc*

applicable *adjective* **1** able to be applied **2** suitable, relevant

applicant *noun* someone who applies or asks

application *noun* **1** the act of applying **2** something applied, *eg* an ointment **3** a formal request, usually on paper **4** hard work, close attention **5** *computing* (full form **application program**) a computer program which performs a special function, such as word processing, Web browsing, spreadsheet, image editing, *etc* (*compare with*: **operating system**)

applicator *noun* a tool or device for applying something

applied *adjective* used practically and not just in theory

apply *verb* **1** to put on (an ointment *etc*) **2** to use: *apply these rules* **3** to ask formally (for) **4** to be suitable or relevant **5** apply to to affect ■ **apply yourself** to work hard

apply ► applies, applying, applied

appoint *verb* **1** to fix (a date *etc*) **2** to place in a job ■ **appointed** *adjective* (meaning 1): *at the appointed time*

appointment *noun* **1** the act of appointing **2** a job, a post **3** an arrangement to meet someone

apportion *verb* to divide in fair shares

apposite *adjective* suitable, appropriate

appraise *verb* to estimate the value or quality of ■ **appraisal** *noun*

appreciable *adjective* noticeable, considerable

appreciate *verb* **1** to see or understand the good points, beauties, *etc* of **2** to understand **3** to rise in value ■ **appreciation** *noun*

apprehend *verb* to arrest

apprehension *noun* **1** arrest **2** fear or nervousness

apprehensive *adjective* afraid

apprentice *noun* someone who is learning a trade ■ **apprenticeship** *noun*

approach *verb* **1** to come near **2** to be nearly equal to **3** to speak to in order to ask for something ■ *noun* (*plural* **approaches**) **1** a coming near to **2** a way leading to a place

approachable *adjective* **1** able to be reached **2** easy to speak to, friendly

appropriate *adjective* suitable, fitting ■ **appropriately** *adverb*

approval noun **1** permission **2** satisfaction, favourable judgement ■ **on approval** on trial, for return to a shop if not bought

approve verb **1** to agree to, permit **2** to think well (of)

approximate adjective (pronounced ap-**rok**-sim-at) more or less accurate ■ verb (pronounced ap-**rok**-sim-eit): **approximate to** to be or come near to ■ **approximately** adverb

approximation noun a rough estimate

apricot noun an orange-coloured fruit like a small peach

April noun the fourth month of the year

apron noun **1** a garment worn to protect the front of the clothes **2** a hard surface for aircraft to stand on

apropos adverb: **apropos of** in connection with, concerning

apt adjective **1** likely (to) **2** suitable, fitting ■ **aptly** adverb

aptitude noun talent, ability

aptness noun suitability

aqua- prefix of or relating to water

aqualung noun a breathing apparatus worn by divers

aquamarine noun **1** a type of bluish-green precious stone **2** a bluish-green colour ■ adjective bluish-green

aquarium noun (plural **aquaria** or **aquariums**) a tank or tanks for keeping fish or water animals

aquatic adjective living, growing or taking place in water

aqueduct noun a bridge for taking a canal etc across a valley

aqueous adjective **1** relating to water **2** dissolved in water

arable adjective of land: used for growing crops

arbiter noun **1** a judge, an umpire, someone chosen by opposing parties to decide between them **2** someone who sets a standard or has influence

arbitrary adjective **1** fixed according to opinion, not objective rules **2** occurring haphazardly ■ **arbitrarily** adverb

arbitrate verb to act as a judge between people or their claims etc ■ **arbitration** noun ■ **arbitrator** noun

arc noun part of the circumference of a circle; a curve

arcade noun a covered walk, especially one with shops on both sides

arch noun (plural **arches**) the curved part above people's heads in a gateway or the curved support for a bridge, roof, etc ■ adjective mischievous, roguish ■ verb to raise or curve in the shape of an arch

arch- prefix chief, main: arch-enemy

archaeology noun the study of the people of earlier times from the remains of their buildings etc

- archaeological *adjective*
- archaeologist *noun*

archaic *adjective* no longer used, old-fashioned

archangel *noun* a chief angel

archbishop *noun* a chief bishop

archdeacon *noun* a clergyman next in rank below a bishop

archduke *noun, history* the title of the ruling princes of Austria

archer *noun* someone who shoots arrows from a bow

archery *noun* the sport of shooting with a bow and arrows

archetype *noun* the original pattern or model from which copies are made ■ **archetypal** *adjective*

archipelago *noun* (*plural* **archipelagoes** *or* **archipelagos**) a group of small islands

architect *noun* someone who plans and designs buildings

architecture *noun* 1 the study of building 2 the style of a building ■ **architectural** *adjective*

archive *noun* a place on a computer for storing files that are rarely used

archives *noun plural* 1 historical papers, written records, *etc* 2 a building *etc* in which these are kept

archway *noun* a passage or road beneath an arch

arc lamp *or* **arc light** a bright lamp lit by a special kind of electric current

Arctic *or* **arctic** *adjective* 1 (*usually* **Arctic**) of the district round the North Pole 2 (*usually* **arctic**) very cold

ardent *adjective* eager, passionate ■ **ardently** *adverb*
■ **ardour** *noun*

arduous *adjective* difficult

are *see* be

area *noun* 1 the extent of a surface measured in square metres *etc* 2 a region, a piece of land or ground

arena *noun* 1 any place for a public contest, show, *etc* 2 *history* the centre of an amphitheatre *etc* where gladiators fought

argon *noun* an inert gas present in the air, used in light bulbs

arguable *adjective* that can be argued as being true

arguably *adverb* in certain people's opinion (although this opinion could be disagreed with)

argue *verb* 1 to quarrel in words 2 to try to prove by giving reasons (that) 3 **argue for** *or* **against something** to give reasons for or against something as a way of persuading people 4 **argue someone into** *or* **out of something** to persuade someone, by arguing with them, to do or not to do something

| **argue** ► argues, argu*ing*, argu*ed*

argument *noun* 1 a heated discussion, quarrel 2 reasoning (for or against something)

argumentative *adjective* fond of arguing

aria *noun* a song for solo voice in an opera

arid *adjective* **1** dry **2** of climate: hot and dry ■ **aridity** or **aridness** *noun*

arise *verb* **1** to rise up **2** to come into being

| **arise** ► arise*s*, aris*ing*, arose, arise*n*

aristocracy *noun* those of the nobility and upper class

aristocrat *noun* a member of the aristocracy

aristocratic *adjective* of the aristocracy

arithmetic *noun* a way of counting and calculating by using numbers

ark *noun* the covered boat used by Noah in the Biblical story of the Flood

arm *noun* **1** the part of the body between the shoulder and the hand **2** anything jutting out like this **3** arms weapons ■ *verb* to equip with weapons ■ **twist someone's arm** to persuade someone forcefully

armada *noun* a fleet of armed ships

armadillo *noun* (*plural* **armadillos**) a small American animal whose body is protected by bony plates

armaments *noun plural* equipment for war, especially the guns of a ship, tank, *etc*

armchair *noun* a chair with arms at each side

armed *adjective* carrying a weapon, now especially a gun

armistice *noun* a halt in fighting during war, a truce

armour *noun*, *history* a protective suit of metal worn by knights

armoured *adjective* of a vehicle: protected by metal plates

armoury *noun* (*plural* **armouries**) a store for military arms

armpit *noun* the hollow under the arm at the shoulder

army *noun* (*plural* **armies**) **1** a large number of soldiers armed for war **2** a great number of anything

aroma *noun* a sweet smell

aromatherapy *noun* a healing therapy involving massage with plant oils

arose *past form* of **arise**

around *preposition* **1** in a circle about **2** on all sides of, surrounding **3** all over, at several places in: *scattered around the room* **4** somewhere near in time, place, amount: *I left him around here* /*around three o'clock* ■ *adverb* all about, in various places: *people stood around* ■ **get around 1** of a story: to become known to everyone **2** to be active

arousal *noun* **1** the state of being stimulated or excited **2** awakening (of feelings)

arouse *verb* **1** to awaken **2** to stir, move (a feeling or person)

arpeggio *noun, music* a chord with the notes played in rapid succession, not at the same time

arrange *verb* **1** to put in some order **2** to plan, settle

arrangement *noun* **1** a pattern or particular order **2** an agreed plan

array *noun* **1** order, arrangement **2** clothing **3** *maths* a set of counters, numbers, *etc* ordered in rows and columns ▪ *verb* **1** to put in order **2** to dress, adorn

arrears *noun plural*: **in arrears** not up to date; behind with payments

arrest *verb* **1** to seize, capture, especially by power of the law **2** to stop **3** to catch (the attention *etc*) ▪ *noun* **1** capture by the police **2** stopping ▪ **arresting** *adjective* striking, capturing the attention

arrival *noun* **1** the act of arriving **2** someone or something that arrives

arrive *verb* to reach a place ▪ **arrive at** to reach, come to (a decision *etc*)

arrogant *adjective* proud, haughty, self-important ▪ **arrogance** *noun* ▪ **arrogantly** *adverb*

arrow *noun* **1** a straight, pointed weapon shot from a bow **2** an arrow shape, *eg* on a road sign, showing direction

arsenal *noun* a factory or store for weapons, ammunition, *etc*

arsenic *noun* an element that, combined with oxygen, makes a strong poison

arson *noun* the crime of setting fire to a house *etc* on purpose ▪ **arsonist** *noun*

art *noun* **1** drawing, painting, sculpture, *etc* **2** **arts** non-scientific school or university subjects

artefact *or* **artifact** *noun* a human-made object

arterial *adjective* of or like arteries

arterial road a main road carrying traffic

artery *noun* (*plural* **arteries**) a tube which carries blood from the heart to pass through the body

artesian well a well in which water rises to the surface by natural pressure

artful *adjective* wily, cunning ▪ **artfully** *adverb*

arthritis *noun* a condition causing swollen and painful joints ▪ **arthritic** *adjective*

artichoke *noun* a thistle-like plant with edible flowers

article *noun* **1** a thing, object **2** a composition in a newspaper, journal, *etc* **3** a section of a document **4** *grammar* the name of the words *the, a, an*

articulate *adjective* (*pronounced* ah-tik-yu-lat) **1** speaking clearly **2** expressing thoughts clearly ■ *verb* (*pronounced* ah-**tik**-y-u-leit) to express clearly ■ **articulation** *noun*

articulated lorry a lorry with a cab which can turn at an angle to the main part of the lorry, making cornering easier

artifact *another spelling of* artefact

artificial *adjective* not natural; man-made ■ **artificially** *adverb*

artificial intelligence the ability of computers to perform actions thought to require human intelligence, *eg* problem solving

artillery *noun* **1** big guns **2** an army division that uses these

artisan *noun* someone who does skilled work with their hands

artist *noun* **1** someone who paints pictures **2** someone skilled in anything **3** an artiste

artiste *noun* a performer in a theatre, circus, *etc*

artistic *adjective* **1** of artists **2** having a talent for art

artistry *noun* skill as an artist

artless *adjective* simple, frank

as *adverb & conjunction* in phrases expressing comparison or similarity: *as good as his brother* ■ *conjunction* **1** while, when **2** because, since **3** in the same way that ■ *adverb* for instance ■ **as if** *or* **as though** as it would be if ■ **as well (as)** too, in addition (to)

asbestos *noun* a thread-like mineral which can be woven and will not burn

ascend *verb* **1** to climb, go up **2** to rise or slope upwards ■ **ascend the throne** to be crowned king or queen

ascendancy *or* **ascendency** *noun* control (over)

ascendant *or* **ascendent** *adjective* rising

ascent *noun* **1** an upward move or climb **2** a slope upwards; a rise

ascertain *verb* **1** to find out **2** to make certain

ascetic *noun* someone who keeps away from all kinds of pleasure

ascribe *verb* to consider (something) as belonging (to)

asexual reproduction reproduction that does not involve the union of male and female reproductive cells

ash *noun* (*plural* **ashes**) **1** a type of hard-wood tree with silvery bark **2 ashes** what is left after anything is burnt

ashamed *adjective* feeling shame

ashen *adjective* very pale

ashore *adverb* on or on to the shore

ashtray *noun* a small dish for the ash from cigarettes

Ash Wednesday in the Christian Church, the first day of Lent

aside *adverb* on or to one side; apart ■ *noun* words spoken which those nearby are not supposed to hear

asinine *adjective* stupid

ask *verb* **1** to request information about **2** to invite ▪ **ask after someone** to make enquiries about someone's health and wellbeing

askance *adverb* off the straight ▪ **look askance at** to look at with suspicion or disapproval

askew *adverb* off the straight, to one side

asleep *adjective* **1** sleeping **2** of limbs: numbed

asp *noun* a small poisonous snake

asparagus *noun* a plant whose young shoots are eaten as a vegetable

aspect *noun* **1** look, appearance **2** view, point of view **3** a side of a building *etc* or the direction it faces

aspen *noun* a kind of poplar tree

asphalt *noun* a tarry mixture used to make pavements, paths, *etc*

asphyxia *noun* suffocation by smoke or other fumes

asphyxiate *verb* to suffocate ▪ **asphyxiation** *noun*

aspidistra *noun* a kind of pot plant with large leaves

aspiration *noun* a goal which you hope to achieve

aspire *verb*: **aspire to** to try to achieve or reach (something difficult, ambitious, *etc*)

aspirin *noun* a pain-killing drug

aspiring *adjective* trying or wishing to be

ass *noun* (*plural* **asses**) **1** a donkey **2** a stupid person

assail *verb* to attack

assailant *noun* an attacker

assassin *noun* someone who assassinates, a murderer

assassinate *verb* to murder (especially a politically important person) ▪ **assassination** *noun*

assault *noun* an attack, especially a sudden one ▪ *verb* to attack

assault course a series of physical obstacles to be jumped, climbed, *etc*

assemblage *noun* a collection, a gathering

assemble *verb* **1** to bring (people) together **2** to put together (a machine *etc*) **3** to meet together

assembly *noun* (*plural* **assemblies**) **1** a putting together **2** a gathering of people, especially for a special purpose

assembly line a series of machines and workers that an article passes along in the stages of its manufacture

assent *verb* to agree ▪ *noun* agreement

assert *verb* **1** to state firmly **2** to insist on (a right *etc*) ▪ **assertion** *noun* ▪ **assert yourself** to make yourself noticed, heard, *etc*

assertive *adjective* forceful, inclined to assert yourself

assess *verb* **1** to estimate the value, power, *etc* of **2** to fix an amount (to be paid in tax *etc*) ▪ **assessment** *noun*

assessor *noun* someone who assesses

asset *noun* **1** an advantage, a help **2 assets** the property of a person, company, *etc*

assiduous *adjective* persevering; hard-working

assign *verb* **1** to give to someone as a share or task **2** to fix (a time or place): *assign a date for the meeting*

assignation *noun* an appointment to meet

assignment *noun* **1** an act of assigning **2** a task given

assimilate *verb* to take in: *assimilate all the information* ▪ **assimilation** *noun*

assist *verb* to help ▪ **assistance** *noun*

assistant *noun* **1** a helper, *eg* to a senior worker **2** someone who serves in a shop *etc*

assizes *noun plural* formerly the name of certain law courts in England and Wales

associate *verb* **1 associate with** to keep company with **2 associate yourself with** to join with in partnership or friendship **3** to connect in thought: *associates gardening with hard work* ▪ *adjective* joined or connected

(with) ▪ *noun* a friend, partner, companion

association *noun* **1** a club, society, union, *etc* **2** a partnership, friendship **3** a connection made in the mind

assorted *adjective* various, mixed

assortment *noun* a variety, a mixture

assuage *verb* to soothe, ease (pain, hunger, *etc*)

assume *verb* **1** to take upon yourself: *assume responsibility* **2** to take as true without further proof, take for granted **3** to put on (a disguise *etc*)

assumed *adjective* false or pretended

assumption *noun* **1** the act of assuming **2** something taken for granted

assurance *noun* **1** a feeling of certainty; confidence **2** a promise **3** insurance

assure *verb* **1** to make (someone) sure: *I assured him of my intention to return home* **2** to state positively (that)

assured *adjective* certain; confident

asterisk *noun* a star (*) used in printing for various purposes, especially to point out a footnote or insertion

astern *adverb* at or towards the back of a ship

asteroid *noun* one of thousands of small, rocky objects that orbit the sun

asthma *noun* an illness causing coughing, difficulty in breathing, *etc*

asthmatic *adjective* suffering from asthma ■ *noun* someone with asthma

astonish *verb* to surprise greatly ■ **astonished** *adjective* ■ **astonishing** *adjective*

astonishment *noun* amazement, wonder

astound *verb* to surprise greatly, amaze ■ **astounding** *adjective*

astral *adjective* of the stars

astray *adverb* out of the right way, straying

astride *adverb* with legs apart ■ *preposition* with legs on each side of

astringent *noun* a lotion *etc* used for closing up the skin's pores ■ *adjective* 1 used for closing the pores 2 of manner: sharp, sarcastic

astro- or **astr-** *prefix* of or relating to stars or outer space

astrology *noun* the study of the stars and planets and their supposed influence over people's lives ■ **astrologer** *noun*

astronaut *noun* someone who travels in space

astronomer *noun* someone who studies astronomy

astronomical *adjective* 1 of astronomy 2 of a number: very large

astronomy *noun* the study of the stars and their movements

astute *adjective* cunning, clever ■ **astutely** *adverb*

asunder *adverb* a literary word meaning 'apart' or 'into pieces'

asylum *noun* 1 a place of refuge or safety 2 *old* a home for the mentally ill

asymmetrical *adjective* displaying asymmetry; lopsided in appearance ■ **asymmetrically** *adverb*

asymmetry *noun* the inequality in size, shape or position of two halves on either side of a dividing line (*contrasted with*: **symmetry**)

at *preposition* 1 showing position, time, *etc*: *I'll be at home/at 7 o'clock* 2 towards: *working at getting fit* 3 with or by: *annoyed at her* 4 occupied with; in a state of: *at play/at liberty* ■ **at all** in any way

ate *past form* of eat

atheism *noun* belief that there is no God

atheist *noun* someone who does not believe in a God ■ **atheistic** *adjective*

athlete *noun* someone good at sport, especially running, gymnastics, *etc*

athlete's foot a fungus which affects the feet

athletic *adjective* 1 of athletics 2 good at sports; strong, powerful

athletics *noun singular* running, jumping, *etc* or competitions in these

-athon or **-thon** *suffix* forms

nouns describing events, usually for charity, which are long in terms of time or endurance: *telethon* (= a very long television programme)/*talkathon* (= a long talking-session)

atlas *noun* (*plural* **atlases**) a book of maps

atmosphere *noun* **1** the air round the earth **2** any surrounding feeling: *friendly atmosphere*

atmospheric *adjective* **1** of the atmosphere **2** of a place, piece of art, *etc*: conveying a mood or impression

atmospheric pressure the pressure exerted by the atmosphere at the earth's surface, due to the weight of the air

atmospherics *noun plural* air disturbances causing crackling noises on the radio *etc*

atoll *noun* a coral island or reef

atom *noun* **1** the smallest part of an element, consisting of protons and neutrons **2** anything very small

atom bomb *or* **atomic bomb** a bomb in which the explosion is caused by nuclear energy

atomic *adjective* **1** relating to an atom or atoms **2** using nuclear energy

atomic number the number of protons in the nucleus of an atom

atomizer *or* **atomiser** *noun* an instrument for discharging liquids in a fine spray

atone *verb* to make up for wrongdoing ▪ **atonement** *noun*

atrocious *adjective* **1** cruel or wicked **2** *informal* very bad

atrocity *noun* (*plural* **atrocities**) **1** a terrible crime **2** *informal* something very ugly

attach *verb* **1** to fasten or join (to) **2** to think of (something) as having: *don't attach any importance to it*

attaché (*pronounced* a-tash-ei) *noun* a junior member of an embassy staff

attaché case a small case for papers *etc*

attached *adjective* **1** fastened **2** attached to fond of

attachment *noun* **1** something attached **2** a joining by love or friendship **3** an electronic file sent with an e-mail message

attack *verb* **1** to fall upon suddenly or violently **2** to speak or write against ▪ *noun* **1** an act of attacking **2** a fit (of an illness *etc*)

attain *verb* to reach; gain

attainable *adjective* able to be attained

attainment *noun* **1** an act of attaining **2** a thing attained, an achievement or accomplishment

attempt *verb* to try ▪ *noun* a try or effort

attend *verb* **1** to be present at **2** attend to something to pay attention to something **3** to wait on, look after **4** to accompany

attendance *noun* **1** the fact of

being present **2** the number of people present

attendant *noun* someone employed to look after a public place, shop, *etc* ▪ *adjective* accompanying, related

attention *noun* **1** careful notice **2** concentration **3** care **4** *military* a stiffly straight standing position: *stand to attention*

attentive *adjective* **1** giving or showing attention **2** polite ▪ **attentively** *adverb*

attic *noun* a room just under the roof of a house

attire *verb* to dress ▪ *noun* clothing

attitude *noun* a way of thinking or feeling

attorney *noun* (*plural* **attorneys**) **1** someone with legal power to act for another **2** *US* a lawyer

attract *verb* **1** to draw to or towards **2** to arouse liking or interest

attraction *noun* **1** the power of attracting **2** something which attracts visitors *etc*

attractive *adjective* **1** good-looking, likeable **2** pleasing: *attractive prices*

attribute *verb* (*pronounced* a-**trib**-yoot) **1** to state or consider as the source or cause of **2** to state as the author or creator of: *attributed to Rembrandt* ▪ *noun* (*pronounced* **a**-trib-yoot) a characteristic or feature

aubergine (*pronounced* oh-be-szeen) *noun* an oval dark purple fruit, eaten as a vegetable

auburn *adjective* of hair: reddish-brown in colour

auction *noun* a public sale in which articles are sold to the highest bidder ▪ *verb* to sell by auction

auctioneer *noun* someone who sells by auction

audacious *adjective* daring, bold ▪ **audacity** *noun*

audible *adjective* able to be heard

audience *noun* **1** a number of people gathered to watch or hear a performance *etc* **2** a formal interview with someone important

audio *noun* the reproduction of recorded or radio sound ▪ *adjective* relating to such sound

audio- *prefix* of or relating to sounds which can be heard

audio-typist *noun* a typist able to type from a recording on a tape recorder

audio-visual *adjective* concerned with hearing and seeing at the same time

audit *verb* to examine accounts officially ▪ *noun* an official examination of a company's accounts

audition *noun* a hearing to test an actor, singer, *etc*

auditor *noun* someone who audits accounts

auditorium *noun* (*plural*

auditoria or **auditoriums**) the part of a theatre *etc* where the audience sits

auditory *adjective* of hearing

augment *verb* to increase in size, number or amount ▪ **augmentation** *noun*

augur *verb*: **augur well** (or **ill**) to be a good (or bad) sign for the future

August *noun* the eighth month of the year

august *adjective* full of dignity, stately

aunt *noun* a father's or a mother's sister, or an uncle's wife

au pair a foreign person, usually a girl, who does domestic duties in return for board, lodging and pocket money

aural *adjective* relating to the ear

●* Do not confuse with: **oral**. Oral means 'relating to the mouth'. It may help to think of the 'O' as looking like an open mouth, and to remember that many words related to listening start with 'AU', like 'audition' and 'auditorium'

aurora borealis a display of lights that sometimes appears in the sky in northern regions

auspices *noun plural*: **under the auspices of** under the control or supervision of

auspicious *adjective* favourable; promising luck

austere *adjective* **1** severe

2 without luxury; simple, sparse ▪ **austerity** *noun*

authentic *adjective* true, real, genuine ▪ **authentically** *adverb* ▪ **authenticity** *noun*

authenticate *verb* to show to be true or real ▪ **authentication** *noun*

author *noun* the writer of a book, poem, play, *etc*

authoritative *adjective* stated by an expert or someone in authority

authority *noun* (*plural* **authorities**) **1** power or right **2** someone whose opinion is reliable, an expert **3** someone or a body of people having control (over something) **4 authorities** people in power

authorize or **authorise** *verb* **1** to give (a person) the power or the right to do something **2** to give permission (for something to be done) ▪ **authorization** *noun*

autism *noun* a disability affecting a person's ability to relate to and communicate with other people ▪ **autistic** *adjective*

auto- or **aut-** *prefix* **1** self: *autobiography* **2** self-caused or automatic **3** of or relating to cars

autobiographer *noun* the writer of an autobiography

autobiography *noun* (*plural* **autobiographies**) the story of someone's life, written or told by themselves ▪ **autobiographical** *adjective*

autograph *noun* **1** someone's own signature **2** someone's own handwriting ■ *verb* to write your own name on

automate *verb* to make automatic by introducing machines *etc*

automatic *adjective* **1** of a machine *etc*: self-working **2** of an action: unconscious, without thinking ■ *noun* **1** something automatic (*eg* an automatic washing-machine) **2** a kind of self-loading gun ■ **automatically** *adverb*

automatic pilot 1 a device which can be set to control an aircraft on a course **2** doing something unthinkingly

automation *noun* the use of machines for controlling other machines in factories *etc*

automaton *noun* (*plural* **automata**) **1** a mechanical toy or machine made to look and move like a human **2** someone who acts mindlessly, like a machine

automobile *noun*, *US* a car

autonomy *noun* the power or right of a country to govern itself ■ **autonomous** *adjective*

autopsy *noun* (*plural* **autopsies**) an examination of a body after death

autumn *noun* the season of the year following summer, when leaves change colour and fruits are ripe

autumnal *adjective* **1** relating to autumn **2** like that or those of autumn

auxiliary *adjective* supplementary, additional ■ *noun* (*plural* **auxiliaries**) a helper, an assistant

auxiliary verb a short verb, *eg* 'be', 'do', 'have' or 'can', used with other verbs to show the tense *etc*, *eg* 'must' in 'I must go'

avail *verb*: **avail yourself of** to make use of ■ *noun*: **to no avail** without any effect, of no use

available *adjective* able or ready to be made use of ■ **availability** *noun*

avalanche *noun* **1** a mass of snow and ice sliding down from a mountain **2** a great amount

avant-garde *adjective* ahead of fashion, very modern

avarice *noun* greed, especially for riches ■ **avaricious** *adjective*

avenge *verb* to take revenge for (a wrong)

| **avenge** ► avenge*s*, avengi*ng*, avenge*d*

avenue *noun* **1** a tree-lined street or approach to a house **2** a means, a way: *avenue of escape*

average *noun* the result obtained by adding several amounts and dividing the total by the number of amounts, *eg* the average of 3, 7, 9, 13 is 8 (32÷4) ■ *adjective* **1** ordinary, usual; of medium size *etc* **2** obtained by working out an average: *the* *average cost* ■ *verb* **1** to form an average **2** to find the average of

averse *adjective* not fond of, opposed (to)

aversion *noun* **1** extreme dislike or distaste **2** something that is hated

avert *verb, formal* **1** to turn away or aside **2** to prevent from happening

aviary *noun* (*plural* **aviaries**) a place for keeping birds

aviation *noun* the practice of flying or piloting aircraft

aviator *noun* an aircraft pilot

avid *adjective* eager, greedy: *an avid reader* ■ **avidity** *noun*

avocado *noun* (*plural* **avocados**) **1** a pear-shaped fruit with a rough peel and rich, creamy flesh **2** a light, yellowish-green colour

avoid *verb* to escape, keep clear of ■ **avoidable** *adjective* ■ **avoidance** *noun*

avoirdupois (*pronounced* av-wah-dyoo-pwah*) *noun* the system of measuring weights in pounds and ounces (*compare with*: **metric system**)

avow *verb, formal* to declare openly ■ **avowal** *noun* ■ **avowed** *adjective*

await *verb* to wait for

awake *verb* **1** to rouse from sleep **2** to stop sleeping ■ *adjective* not asleep

awaken *verb* **1** to awake **2** to arouse (interest *etc*)

awakening *noun* the act or process of waking up or coming into existence: *the awakening of unfamiliar feelings*

award *verb* **1** to give, grant (a prize *etc*) **2** to grant legally ■ *noun* something that is awarded, a prize

aware *adjective* **1** having knowledge (of), conscious (of) **2** alert ■ **awareness** *noun*

away *adverb* **1** to or at a distance from the speaker or person spoken to **2** in the proper place: *put the toys away* **3** in the opposite direction: *he turned away* **4** into nothing: *the sound died away* ■ **do away with** to abolish, get rid of ■ **get away with** to do (something) without being punished ■ **right** *or* **straight away** immediately

awe *noun* wonder or admiration mixed with fear ■ *verb* to affect with awe

awesome *adjective* **1** causing fear **2** *informal* remarkable, admirable

awestruck *adjective* full of awe

awful *adjective* **1** *informal* bad: *an awful headache* **2** *informal* very great: *an awful lot* **3** terrible: *I feel awful*

awfully *adverb, informal* very, extremely

awkward *adjective* **1** clumsy, not graceful **2** difficult to deal with ■ **awkwardly** *adverb* ■ **awkwardness** *noun*

awl *noun* a pointed tool for boring small holes

awning *noun* a covering of canvas *etc* providing shelter

awry *adjective & adverb* **1** not according to plan, wrong **2** crooked

axe *noun* (*plural* **axes**) a tool for chopping ▪ *verb* **1** to cancel (a plan *etc*) **2** to reduce greatly (costs, services, *etc*)

axiom *noun* an accepted truth

axis *noun* (*plural* **axes**) **1** the line, real or imaginary, on which a thing turns **2** the axis of the earth, from North to South Pole, around which the earth turns

axle *noun* the rod on which a wheel turns

ayatollah *noun* a religious leader of the Shiah sect of Islam

aye *adverb* yes ▪ *noun* a vote in favour of something

azure *adjective* sky-coloured, clear blue

B

babble *verb* to talk indistinctly or foolishly ▪ *noun* indistinct or foolish talk

babe *noun* **1** a baby **2** *informal* a girl or young woman

baboon *noun* a large monkey with a dog-like snout

baby *noun* (*plural* **babies**) a very young child, an infant ▪ *verb* to treat like a baby

> **baby** *verb* ▶ **babies**, baby**ing**, babi**ed**

babysit *verb* to look after a child while its parents are out

> **babysit** ▶ babysit**s**, babysit**ting**, babysat

babysitter *noun* someone who looks after a child while its parents are out

bachelor *noun* **1** an unmarried man **2** someone who has been awarded a degree at a university: *Bachelor of Arts*

bacillus (*pronounced* ba-**sil**-us) *noun* (*plural* **bacilli** – *pronounced* ba-**sil**-ai) a rod-shaped germ

back *noun* **1** the part of the human body from the neck to the base of the spine **2** the upper part of an animal's body **3** the part of anything situated behind **4** *football etc* a player positioned behind the forwards ▪ *adjective* of or at the back ▪ *adverb* **1** to or in the place from which someone or something came **2** to or in a former time or condition: *thinking back to their youth* ▪ *verb* **1** to move backwards **2** to bet on (a horse *etc*) **3** (*often* **back up**) to help or support ▪ **back down** to change your opinion *etc* ▪ **back out 1** to move out backwards **2** to excuse yourself from keeping to an agreement ▪ **put someone's back up** to irritate someone

backbone *noun* **1** the spine **2** the main support of something **3** firmness, resolve

backfire *verb* **1** of a vehicle: to make an explosive noise in the exhaust pipe **2** of a plan: to go wrong

backgammon *noun* a game similar to draughts, played with dice

background *noun* **1** the space behind the principal figures of a picture **2** details that explain something **3** someone's family and upbringing

backhand *noun, tennis* a stroke played with the back of the hand facing the ball

backing *noun* **1** support **2** a musical accompaniment on a recording

backlash *noun* a violent reaction against something

backstroke *noun* a stroke used in swimming on the back

backward *adjective* **1** to or towards the back **2** slow in learning or development

backwards *adverb* **1** towards the back **2** in a reverse direction; back to front **3** towards the past

backwater *noun* a place not affected by what is happening in the outside world

bacon *noun* pig's flesh salted and dried, used as food

bacteria *noun plural* (*singular* **bacterium**) germs found in air, water, living and dead bodies, and especially decaying matter ▪ **bacterial** *adjective*

bad *adjective* **1** not good; wicked **2** not of a good standard: *bad workmanship* **3** (often **bad for**) harmful or unpleasant **4** of food: rotten, decaying **5** severe, serious: *bad dose of flu* **6** unwell ▪ **badly** *adverb* **1** not well **2** seriously **3** very much

badge *noun* a mark or sign or brooch-like ornament giving some information about the wearer

badger *noun* a burrowing animal of the weasel family which comes out at night ▪ *verb* to pester or annoy

badminton *noun* a game resembling tennis, played with shuttlecocks

baffle *verb* to be too difficult for; puzzle, confound ▪ **baffling** *adjective*

bag *noun* a holder or container, often of a soft material ▪ *verb* **1** to secure possession of, claim: *bag a seat* **2** to kill (game) in a hunt

| **bag** *verb* ► bags, bagg*ing*, bagg*ed*

baggage *noun* luggage

baggy *adjective* of clothes: large and loose

bagpipes *noun plural* a wind instrument made up of a bag and several pipes

baguette *noun* a long narrow loaf of bread

bail[1] *noun* money given to bail out a prisoner ▪ **bail out** to obtain temporary release of (an untried prisoner) by giving money which will be forfeited if they do not return for trial

⚹ Do not confuse with: **bale**

bail[2] *verb*: **bail out** to bale out

bail[3] *noun, cricket* one of the crosspieces on the top of the wickets

⚹ Do not confuse with: **bale**

bailiff *noun* **1** an officer who

works for a sheriff **2** a landowner's agent

bait *noun* **1** food put on a hook to make fish bite, or in a trap to attract animals **2** something tempting or alluring ■ *verb* **1** to put bait on a hook *etc* **2** to worry, annoy

baize *noun* a coarse woollen cloth

bake *verb* **1** to cook in an oven **2** to dry or harden in the sun or in an oven

baker *noun* someone who bakes or sells bread *etc* ■ **bakery** *noun* a place used for baking in

baking soda bicarbonate of soda

balaclava or **balaklava** *noun* a knitted covering for the head and neck

balance *noun* **1** steadiness: *lost my balance and fell over* **2** the money needed to make the two sides of an account equal ■ *verb* **1** to be the same in weight **2** to make both sides of an account the same **3** to make or keep steady: *balanced it on her head*

balcony *noun* (*plural* **balconies**) **1** a platform built out from the wall of a building **2** an upper floor or gallery in a theatre *etc*

bald *adjective* **1** without hair **2** plain, frank: *a bald statement*

balding *adjective* going bald

bale [1] *noun* a large tight bundle of cotton, hay, *etc*

●* Do not confuse with: **bail**

bale [2] *verb*: **bale out 1** to escape by parachute from an aircraft in an emergency **2** to scoop water out of a boat (also **bail out**)

balk *verb*: **balk at something** to refuse to do it

ball [1] *noun* **1** anything round: *ball of wool* **2** the round or roundish object used in playing many games ■ **on the ball** *informal* in touch with a situation, alert

ball [2] *noun* a formal party at which dancing takes place

ballad *noun* **1** a narrative poem with a simple rhyme scheme, usually in verses of four lines **2** a simple song

ballast *noun* sand, gravel, *etc* put into a ship to steady it

ball-bearings *noun plural* small steel balls that sit loosely in grooves and ease the movement of one machinery part over another

ballerina *noun* a female ballet dancer

ballet *noun* a form of stylized dancing which tells a story by mime

ballistic missile a self-guided missile which falls on to its target

balloon *noun* a bag filled with gas to make it float in the air, especially one made of thin rubber used as a toy *etc* ■ *verb* to puff or swell out

ballot *noun* a way of voting in

secret by marking a paper and putting it into a special box ▪ *verb* to collect votes from by ballot

ballpoint *noun* a pen with a tiny ball as the writing point

ballroom *noun* a large room used for public dances *etc*

balm *noun* a sweet-smelling healing ointment

balmy *adjective* 1 mild, gentle; soothing: *balmy air* 2 sweet-smelling

balsa *or* **balsawood** *noun* a lightweight wood from a tropical American tree

bamboo *noun* the woody, jointed stem of a type of very tall grass

bamboozle *verb* to trick, puzzle

ban *noun* an order forbidding something ▪ *verb* to forbid officially (the publication of a book *etc*)

| **ban** *verb* ► bans, ban*ning*, ban*ned*

banal *adjective* lacking originality or wit, commonplace ▪ **banality** *noun*

banana *noun* the long yellow fruit of a type of tropical tree

band *noun* 1 a group of people 2 a group of musicians playing together 3 a strip of some material to put round something 4 a stripe (of colour *etc*) 5 a group of wavelengths for radio broadcasts ▪ *verb* to join together

bandage *noun* a strip of cloth *etc* or special dressing for a wound

bandit *noun* an outlaw, robber, especially a member of a gang of robbers

bandwagon *noun*: **jump** *or* **climb on the bandwagon** to join something because it is successful or popular

bandwidth *noun* 1 the width of a band of radio or television frequencies 2 the amount of information that can be conveyed in a link between computers

bandy *adjective* of legs: bent outward at the knee

bane *noun* a cause of ruin or trouble: *the bane of my life*

bang *noun* 1 a sudden, loud noise 2 a heavy blow ▪ *verb* 1 to close with a bang, slam 2 to hit, strike

banger *noun* a type of firework that bangs

bangle *noun* a large ring worn on an arm or leg

banish *verb* 1 to order to leave a country) 2 to drive away (doubts, fear, *etc*)

banister *noun* the posts and handrail of a staircase

banjo *noun* (*plural* **banjoes** *or* **banjos**) a stringed musical instrument like a guitar, with a long neck and a round body

bank *noun* 1 a mound or ridge of earth *etc* 2 the edge of a river 3 a place where money is lent, put for safety, *etc* 4 a place where blood *etc* is stored till needed 5 a public bin for collecting items for recycling: *bottle bank* ■ **bank on** to depend on, count on

banker *noun* someone who manages a bank

bank holiday a day on which all banks and many shops *etc* are closed

banking *noun* the business conducted by banks

banknote *noun* a piece of paper money issued by a bank

bankrupt *noun* someone who has no money to pay their debts ■ *adjective* unable to pay debts ■ **bankruptcy** *noun* (*plural* **bankruptcies**)

banner *noun* **1** a large flag carried in processions *etc*, often hung between two poles **2** any flag

banns *noun plural* a public announcement of a forthcoming marriage

banquet *noun* a ceremonial dinner

bantam *noun* a small kind of hen

banter *verb* to tease in fun ■ *noun* light teasing

baptize or **baptise** *verb* **1** to dip in, or sprinkle with, water as a sign of admission into the Christian Church **2** to christen, give a name to ■ **baptism** *noun*

bar *noun* **1** a rod of solid material **2** a broad line or band **3** a piece, a cake: *bar of soap* **4** a hindrance, a block **5** a bank of sand *etc* at the mouth of a river **6** a room, or

counter, where drinks are served in a public house, hotel, *etc* **7** a public house **8** the rail at which prisoners stand for trial **9** the lawyers who plead in a court **10** a time division in music ■ *preposition* except ■ *verb* **1** to fasten with a bar **2** to exclude, shut out

bar *verb* ► **bars**, **barr***ing*, **barr***ed*

barb *noun* the backward-pointing spike on an arrow, fish-hook, *etc*

barbarian *noun* an uncivilized person ■ *adjective* uncivilized

barbaric *adjective* **1** uncivilized **2** extremely cruel ■ **barbarity** *noun*

barbecue *noun* **1** a frame on which to grill food over an open fire **2** an outdoor party providing food from a barbecue ■ *verb* to cook (food) on a barbecue

barbed wire wire with regular clusters of sharp points, used for fencing *etc*

barber *noun* a men's hairdresser

bar chart a chart or graph which uses horizontal or vertical blocks or bars to show amounts

bare *adjective* **1** uncovered, naked **2** plain, simple **3** empty ■ *verb* to uncover, expose ■ **barely** *adverb* hardly, scarcely

barefaced *adjective* impudent, unashamed: *barefaced lie*

bargain *noun* **1** an agreement, especially about buying or selling

2 something bought cheaply ▪ *verb* to argue about a price *etc* ▪ **bargain for** to expect: *more than he bargained for* ▪ **into the bargain** in addition, besides

barge *noun* a flat-bottomed boat used on rivers and canals ▪ *verb* **1** to rush clumsily **2** to push or bump (into) **3** to push your way (into) rudely

baritone *noun* **1** a male singing voice between tenor and bass **2** a singer with this voice

bark[1] *noun* the noise made by a dog *etc* ▪ *verb* **1** to give a bark **2** to speak sharply or angrily

bark[2] *noun* the rough outer covering of a tree's trunk and branches

barley *noun* a grain used for food and for making malt liquors and spirits

barley sugar sugar candied by melting and cooling to make a sweet

barman *noun* a man serving drinks at a bar

bar mitzvah a Jewish ceremony to mark a boy's coming of age

barn *noun* a building in which grain, hay, *etc* is stored

barnacle *noun* a type of shellfish which sticks to rocks, ships' hulls, *etc*

barometer *noun* an instrument which measures the weight or pressure of the air and shows changes in the weather

baron *noun* **1** a nobleman, the lowest in the British peerage **2** a powerful person, especially in a business: *drug baron*

baroness *noun* (*plural* **baronesses**) a baron's wife or a female baron

baronet *noun* the lowest title that can be passed on to an heir

barracks *noun plural* a place for housing soldiers

barracuda *noun* a large tropical sea fish which feeds on other fish

barrage *noun* **1** heavy gunfire against an enemy **2** an overwhelming number

barrel *noun* **1** a wooden cask with curved sides **2** the metal tube of a gun through which the shot is fired

barren *adjective* not able to reproduce, infertile

barricade *noun* a barrier put up to block a street *etc* ▪ *verb* **1** to block or strengthen against attack **2** to shut behind a barrier

barrier *noun* **1** a strong fence *etc* used for enclosing or keeping out **2** an obstacle

barrister *noun* a lawyer who pleads cases in English or in Irish courts

barrow *noun* a small hand-cart

barter *verb* to give one thing in exchange for another ▪ *noun* trading by exchanging goods without using money

basalt *noun* a hard, dark-coloured rock thrown up as lava from volcanoes

base noun **1** something on which a thing stands or rests **2** the lowest part **3** a place from where an expedition, military action, etc is carried out **4** chemistry a compound that can neutralize acids ■ verb to use as a foundation: based on the facts

baseball noun a North American ball game in which players make a circuit of four bases on a field

baseless adjective without foundation; untrue

basement noun a storey below ground level in a building

bash verb to hit hard ■ noun a heavy blow ■ **have a bash** informal to have an attempt

basic adjective **1** of or forming a base **2** necessary, fundamental ■ **basically** adverb fundamentally, essentially

basil noun a sweet-smelling herb used in cooking

basin noun **1** a wide, open dish **2** a bowl for washing the hands etc in a bathroom **3** the land drained by a river and its tributaries

basis noun (plural **bases**) **1** something on which a thing rests, a foundation: the basis of their friendship **2** the main ingredient

bask verb **1** to lie in warmth **2** to enjoy, feel great pleasure (in)

basket noun a container made of strips of wood, rushes, etc woven together

basketball noun a team game in which goals are scored by

throwing a ball into a raised net

bass[1] (pronounced beis) noun (plural **basses**) **1** the low part in music **2** a deep male singing voice **3** a singer with this voice

bass[2] (pronounced bas) noun (plural **bass** or **basses**) a kind of fish of the perch family

bass clef a musical sign (𝄢), placed on a stave to fix the pitch of the notes

bassoon noun a musical wind instrument with low notes

baste verb to spoon fat over (meat) while roasting to keep (it) from drying out

bat[1] noun a shaped piece of wood etc for striking a ball in some games ■ verb to use the bat in cricket etc

| **bat** verb ▶ bats, batting, batted

bat[2] noun a mouse-like flying animal

bat[3] verb to flutter (eyelids etc)

| **bat** ▶ bats, batting, batted

batch noun (plural **batches**) a quantity of things made etc at one time

bated adjective: **with bated breath** anxiously

bath noun **1** a vessel which holds water in which to wash the body **2** the water in which to wash **3** a washing of the body in water **4** **baths** a public building with an artificial pool for swimming ■ verb to wash (oneself or another person) in a bath

bathe *verb* **1** to swim in water **2** to wash gently **3** to take a bath

bathroom *noun* a room containing facilities for washing yourself and usually a lavatory

bat mitzvah a Jewish ceremony to mark a girl's coming of age

baton *noun* **1** a small wooden stick **2** a light stick used by a conductor of music

batsman, batswoman a someone who bats in cricket *etc*

battalion *noun* a part of a regiment of foot soldiers

batter *verb* to hit repeatedly ▪ *noun* a beaten mixture of flour, milk and eggs, for cooking ▪ **battered** *adjective* **1** beaten, ill-treated **2** worn out by use **3** dipped in batter and fried

battering-ram *noun, history* a heavy beam used as a weapon for breaking through walls *etc*

battery *noun* (*plural* **batteries**) **1** a device for storing and transmitting electricity **2** a series of cages *etc* in which hens are kept for egg-laying

battle *noun* a fight, especially between armies ▪ *verb* to fight

battlement *noun* a wall on the top of a building, with openings or notches for firing through

battleship *noun* a heavily armed and armoured warship

bauble *noun* a brightly-coloured ornament of little value

bawl *verb* to shout or cry out loudly

bay *noun* **1** a wide inlet of the sea in a coastline **2** a space in a room *etc* set back, a recess **3** a compartment in an aircraft ▪ *verb* of dogs: to bark ▪ **hold at bay** to fight off

bayonet *noun* a steel stabbing blade that can be fixed to the muzzle of a rifle

bazaar *noun* **1** a sale of goods for charity *etc* **2** an Eastern market-place

BC *abbreviation* before Christ: *55BC*

be *verb* **1** to live, exist: *there may be some milk left* **2** to have a position, quality, *etc*: *she wants to be a dentist*

> **be ▸** *present forms* am, are, is; *past forms* was, were; *past participle* been

beach *noun* (*plural* **beaches**) the shore of the sea *etc*, especially when sandy or pebbly ▪ *verb* to drive or haul a boat up on the beach

beacon *noun* a flashing light or other warning signal

bead *noun* **1** a small pierced ball of glass, plastic, *etc*, used in needlework or jewellery-making **2** a drop of liquid: *beads of sweat*

beagle *noun* a small hound used in hunting hares

beak *noun* the hard, horny part of a bird's mouth with which it gathers food

beaker *noun* a tall cup or glass, usually without a handle

beam noun 1 a long straight piece of wood or metal 2 a shaft of light 3 a radio signal ■ verb 1 to shine 2 to smile broadly

bean noun 1 a pod-bearing plant 2 the seed of this used as food

bear[1] noun a heavy animal with shaggy fur and hooked claws

bear[2] verb 1 formal to carry 2 to endure, put up with 3 to produce (fruit, children, etc) ■ **bear in mind** to remember, take into account ■ **bear out** to confirm ■ **bear with** to be patient with
| **bear** verb ▶ bears, bearing, bore, borne or born

●* **born** is used as the past participle for meaning 3 only; otherwise the form is **borne**: I couldn't have borne it any longer

bearable adjective able to be borne or endured

beard noun the hair that grows on a man's chin and cheeks

bearer noun a carrier or messenger

bearing noun 1 behaviour 2 direction 3 connection: it has no bearing on the issue 4 part of a machine supporting a moving part

beast noun 1 a four-footed animal 2 a brutal person ■ **beastly** adjective 1 behaving like an animal 2 horrible 3 unpleasant

beat verb 1 to hit repeatedly 2 to overcome, defeat 3 of a pulse: to move or throb in the normal way 4 to mark (time) in music 5 to stir (a mixture etc) with quick movements ■ noun 1 a stroke 2 the regular round of a police officer etc ■ **beaten** adjective 1 of metal: shaped 2 of earth: worn smooth by treading 3 defeated ■ **beat up** to injure by repeated hitting, kicking, etc
| **beat** verb ▶ beats, beating, beat, beaten

beautiful adjective very attractive or pleasing in appearance, sound, etc ■ **beautifully** adverb

beautify verb to make beautiful
| **beautify** ▶ beautifies, beautifying, beautified

beauty noun (plural **beauties**) 1 very attractive or pleasing appearance, sound, etc 2 a very attractive person, especially a woman

beaver noun 1 an animal that can gnaw through wood and dam streams 2 **Beaver** a member of the most junior branch of the Scout Association

because conjunction for the reason that ■ adverb: **because of** on account of

beck noun: **at someone's beck and call** obeying all their orders or requests

beckon verb to make a sign (with the hand) to summon someone

become verb 1 to come to be: she

became angry **2** to suit: *that tie becomes you* ▪ **becoming** *adjective* **1** suiting well **2** of behaviour: appropriate, suitable

bed *noun* **1** a place on which to rest or sleep **2** a plot for flowers *etc* in a garden **3** the bottom of a river *etc*

bedclothes *noun plural* bedcovers

bedding *noun* mattress, bedcovers, *etc*

bedlam *noun* a place full of uproar and confusion

bedraggled *adjective* wet and untidy

bedridden *adjective* kept in bed by weakness, illness, *etc*

bedroom *noun* a room for sleeping

bedspread *noun* a top cover for a bed

bedstead *noun* a frame supporting a bed

bee *noun* a winged insect that makes honey in wax cells

beech *noun* (*plural* **beeches**) a forest tree with grey smooth bark

beef *noun* the flesh of an ox or cow, used as food

beefburger *noun* a flattened cake of minced beef

beefy *adjective* stout, muscular

beehive *noun* a dome or box in which bees are kept

beeline *noun*: **make a beeline for** to go directly towards

been *see* be

beer *noun* an alcoholic drink flavoured with hops

beet *noun* a plant with a carrot-like root, one type (**sugar beet**) used as a source of sugar, the other (**beetroot**) used as a vegetable

beetle *noun* an insect with four wings, the front pair forming hard covers for the back pair

befall *verb, formal* to happen to, strike

| **befall** ▶ befalls, befalling, befell, befallen

before *preposition* **1** in front of **2** earlier than **3** rather than, in preference to: *I'd die before telling him* ▪ *adverb* **1** in front **2** earlier ▪ *conjunction* earlier than the time that

beforehand *adverb* previously, before the time when something else is done

befriend *verb* to act as a friend to, help

beg *verb* **1** to ask for money *etc* from others **2** to ask earnestly

| **beg** ▶ begs, begging, begged

began *past form of* begin

beggar *noun* **1** someone who begs for money **2** a very poor person

begin *verb* to make a start on ▪ **beginner** *noun* ▪ **beginning** *noun*

| **begin** ▶ begins, beginning, began, begun

begrudge *verb* to grudge, envy

beguile *verb* to captivate

begun *past participle* of **begin**

behalf *noun*: **on behalf of 1** as the representative of **2** in aid of: *collecting on behalf of the homeless*

behave *verb* **1** to act (in a certain way): *he always behaves badly at parties* **2** to conduct yourself well ▪ **behaviour** *noun*

behead *verb* to cut off the head of

behind *preposition* **1** at or towards the back of **2** after **3** in support of, encouraging ▪ *adverb* **1** at the back **2** not up to date

behold *verb*, *formal* to look (at), see

beige *noun* a light brown colour

being *noun* **1** existence **2** a living person or thing

belated *adjective* arriving late ▪ **belatedly** *adverb*

belch *verb* **1** to bring up wind from the stomach through the mouth **2** of a fire *etc*: to send up (smoke *etc*) violently

belfry *noun* (*plural* **belfries**) the part of a steeple or tower in which the bells are hung

belief *noun* **1** what someone thinks to be true **2** faith

believable *adjective* able to be believed; possible

believe *verb* **1** to think of as true or as existing **2** to trust (in) **3** to think or suppose ▪ **make believe** to pretend

Belisha beacon *Brit* a pole with an orange globe on top, marking a pedestrian crossing

belittle *verb* to make to seem small or unimportant

bell *noun* a hollow metal object which gives a ringing sound when struck by the tongue or clapper inside

belligerent *adjective* quarrelsome, aggressive ▪ **belligerence** *noun*

bellow *verb* to roar like a bull ▪ *noun* a deep roar

bellows *noun plural* an instrument for making a blast of air, *eg* to increase a fire

belly *noun* (*plural* **bellies**) the abdomen

belly button *informal* the navel

belly dance a sensuous dance performed by women with circling movements of the stomach and hips

belly flop an inexpert dive landing face down on the water

belong *verb* **1** to be someone's property **2** to be a member of (a club *etc*) **3** to be born in or live in **4** of an object: to have its place in ▪ **belongings** *noun plural* what someone possesses

beloved *adjective* much loved, very dear ▪ *noun* someone much loved

below *preposition* lower in position, amount, *etc* than ▪ *adverb* **1** in a lower position **2** further on in a book *etc*

belt *noun* **1** a strip of leather,

cloth, *etc* worn around the waist **2** a continuous band on a machine for conveying objects in a factory *etc* ■ *verb* **1** to put a belt round **2** to beat with a belt

bemoan *verb* to weep about, mourn

bench *noun* (*plural* **benches**) **1** a long seat **2** a table where work is carried out **3 the bench** the judges of a court

bend *verb* **1** to curve **2** to stoop ■ *noun* **1** a curve **2** a turn in a road
| **bend** *verb* ► bends, bending, bent

beneath *preposition* **1** under, in a lower position than **2** covered by: *wearing a black dress beneath her coat* **3** considered too low a task *etc* for: *sweeping floors was beneath him* ■ *adverb* below

benefactor *noun* someone who does good to others

beneficial *adjective* bringing gain or advantage (to)

beneficiary *noun* (*plural* **beneficiaries**) someone who receives a gift, an advantage, *etc*

benefit *noun* **1** something good to receive or have done to you **2** money received from social security or insurance schemes ■ *verb* **1** to do good to **2** to gain advantage: *benefited from the cut in interest rates*
| **benefit** *verb* ► benefits, benefiting, benefited

benevolence *noun* tendency to

do good; kindliness ■ **benevolent** *adjective* kindly

benign (*pronounced* bi-**nain**) *adjective* **1** gentle, kindly **2** of disease: not causing death (*contrasted with*: **malignant**)

bent *noun* a natural liking or aptitude (for something) ■ *adjective* curved, crooked ■ *verb*, *past form of* **bend** ■ **be bent on** to be determined to

bequeath *verb* to leave by will

bequest *noun* money, property, *etc* left in a will

bereaved *adjective* suffering from the recent death of a relative or friend ■ **bereavement** *noun*

bereft *adjective* lacking, deprived (of)

beret (*pronounced* be-rei) *noun* a flat, round hat

berry *noun* (*plural* **berries**) a small juicy fruit enclosing seeds

berserk *adverb* in a frenzy, mad

berth *noun* **1** a room for sleeping in a ship *etc* **2** the place where a ship is tied up in a dock ■ *verb* to moor (a ship)

beseech *verb* to ask earnestly

beside *preposition* **1** by the side of, near **2** compared with: *beside her sister, she seems quite shy* ■ **be beside yourself** to lose self-control ■ **beside the point** irrelevant

besides *preposition* **1** in addition to: *he has other friends, besides me* **2** other than, except: *nothing in the fridge besides some cheese*

■ *adverb* **1** also, moreover **2** in addition: *plenty more besides*

besiege *verb* **1** to surround (a town *etc*) with an army **2** to crowd round; overwhelm

| **besiege** ► besieges, besieging, besieged

besotted *adjective*: **besotted with** foolishly fond of

best *adjective* good in the most excellent way ■ *adverb* in the most excellent way ■ **make the best of** to do as well as possible with

bestial *adjective* like a beast, beastly

best man someone who attends a man who is being married

bestow *verb* to give

best part the largest or greatest part

bestseller *noun* a book *etc* which sells exceedingly well

bet *noun* money put down to be lost or kept depending on the outcome of a race *etc* ■ *verb* to place a bet

| **bet** *verb* ► bets, betting, bet or betted

betray *verb* **1** to give up (secrets, friends, *etc*) to an enemy **2** to show signs of ■ **betrayal** *noun*

betroth *verb, formal*: **betrothed to** engaged to be married to

better *adjective* **1** good to a greater degree, of a more excellent kind **2** healthier **3** completely recovered from illness ■ *adverb* in a more

excellent way ■ *verb* to improve ■ **better off** in a better position, wealthier ■ **get the better of** to defeat, overcome

between *preposition* **1** in or through the space dividing two people or things **2** in parts, in shares to: *divide the chocolates between you* **3** from one thing to another: *the road between Edinburgh and Glasgow* **4** comparing one to the other: *the difference between them*

bevel *noun* a slanting edge ■ *verb* to give a slanting edge to ■ **bevelled** *adjective*

| **bevel** *verb* ► bevels, bevelling, bevelled

beverage *noun* a drink

bevy *noun* (*plural* **bevies**) a group of women or girls

bewail *verb* to mourn loudly over

beware *verb* to watch out for (something dangerous)

bewilder *verb* to puzzle, confuse ■ **bewildering** *adjective* ■ **bewilderment** *noun* confusion

bewitch *verb* to put under a spell; charm ■ **bewitching** *adjective* charming; very beautiful

beyond *preposition* **1** on the far side of **2** later than **3** more than: *beyond the call of duty* **4** too far gone for: *beyond repair* **5** too difficult or confusing for: *it's beyond me!* ■ *adverb* on or to the far side, further away

bi- *prefix* **1** having two: *biped/*

bipolar (= having two poles or extremities)/bicycle **2** occurring twice in a certain period, or once in every two periods: *bi-monthly*

biannual *adjective* happening twice a year

💧* Do not confuse with: biennial

bias *noun* the favouring of one person or point of view over any others ▪ *verb* to give a bias to

| **bias** *verb* ▸ bias*es*, bias*ing* or bias*sing*, bias*ed* or bias*sed*

bib *noun* **1** a piece of cloth put under a child's chin to protect their clothes from food stains *etc* **2** a part of an apron, overalls, *etc* above the waist, covering the chest

Bible *noun* the holy book of the Christian Church ▪ **Biblical** *adjective*

bibliography *noun* (*plural* **bibliographies**) a list of books (about a subject)

bicarbonate of soda a white crystalline compound used to make dough rise when baked (*also called*: **baking soda**)

biceps *noun singular* the muscle in front of the upper part of the arm

bicker *verb* to quarrel over small matters

bicycle *noun* a vehicle with two wheels, driven by foot-pedals

bid *verb* **1** to offer a price (for) **2** to tell, say: *bidding her farewell*

▪ *noun* **1** an offer of a price **2** a bold attempt

| **bid** *verb* ▸ bids, bidd*ing*, bade or bid, bidd*en* or bid

bidet (*pronounced* **beed**-ei) *noun* a low wash-basin for washing the lower body and feet

biennial *adjective* happening once every two years

💧* Do not confuse with: biannual

big *adjective* **1** large in size, amount, extent, *etc* **2** important

| **big** ▸ big*ger*, big*gest*

bigamy *noun* the crime or fact of having two wives or two husbands at once ▪ **bigamist** *noun* ▪ **bigamous** *adjective*

bigot *noun* someone with narrow-minded, prejudiced beliefs ▪ **bigoted** *adjective* prejudiced ▪ **bigotry** *noun*

bike *noun*, *informal* a bicycle

bikini *noun* (*plural* **bikinis**) a woman's brief two-piece bathing suit

bilateral *adjective* **1** having two sides **2** affecting two sides, parties, *etc*

bilberry *noun* a type of plant with an edible dark-blue berry

bile *noun* a fluid coming from the liver

bilge *noun* **1** the broadest part of a ship's bottom **2** (*also called*: **bilgewater**) water which lies in a ship's bottom **3** *informal* nonsense

bilingual *adjective* using or fluent in two languages

bilious *adjective* ill with too much bile; nauseated

bill *noun* **1** a bird's beak **2** an account for money **3** an early version of a law before it has been passed by parliament

billet *noun* a lodging, especially for soldiers ∎ *verb* to lodge (soldiers) in private houses

billiards *noun singular* a game played with a cue and balls on a table

billion *noun* **1** (originally *US*) a thousand millions (1,000,000,000) **2** *old* a million millions (1,000,000,000,000)

billow *noun* **1** a great wave **2** a mass of something such as smoke rising on or being swept along by the wind ∎ *verb* to be filled and swelled with, or moved along by, the wind ∎ **billowy** *adjective* giving the impression of billowing

billy goat a male goat

bin *noun* a container for storing goods or rubbish ∎ *verb* **1** to put in a bin **2** to throw away

| **bin** *verb* ▶ bins, binning, binned

binary *adjective* made up of two

binary digit 1 either of the two digits 0 and 1 **2** the smallest unit of information (usually in short form **bit**)

binary number a number represented by a combination of the digits 0 and 1

bind *verb* **1** to tie with a band **2** to fasten together **3** to make to promise

| **bind** ▶ binds, binding, bound

bindi *or* **bhindi** *noun* a circular mark worn as a decoration on the face

binding *noun* **1** anything that binds **2** the cover, stitching, *etc* which holds a book together

binge *verb* to eat and drink too much ∎ *noun* a spell of eating or drinking too much

bingo *noun* a popular gambling game using numbers

binoculars *noun plural* a small double telescope

bio- *prefix* of or relating to life or living organisms

biochemistry *noun* the study of the chemical composition and processes of living matter

biodegradable *adjective* able to be broken down into parts by bacteria

biographer *noun* someone who writes a biography

biography *noun* (*plural* **biographies**) a written account of someone's life ∎ **biographical** *adjective*

biological *adjective* **1** relating to the way that living organisms grow and behave **2** relating to biology

biology *noun* the study of living things ∎ **biologist** *noun*

bionics *noun singular* the use of

natural systems as models for artificial systems ■ **bionic** *adjective*

biopsy *noun* the removal of a sample of body tissue for medical examination

biosphere *noun* the parts of the land, sea and atmosphere in which organisms live

biotechnology *noun* the use of living organisms or biological substances to perform an industrial task or manufacture a product

biped *noun* an animal with two feet, *eg* a bird

birch *noun* (*plural* **birches**) **1** a type of tree with silvery bark **2** a bundle of birch twigs, used for beating

bird *noun* a feathered, egg-laying creature

bird of prey a bird (*eg* a hawk) which kills and eats small animals or birds

bird's-eye view a wide view, as would be seen from above

birdwatching *noun* the study of birds in their natural surroundings

Biro *noun, trademark* a type of ballpoint pen

birth *noun* the very beginning of someone's life

birthday *noun* **1** the day on which someone is born **2** the date of this day each year

birthmark *noun* a mark on the body from birth

birthright *noun* the right which someone may claim because of their parentage

biscuit *noun* dough baked hard in a small cake

bisect *verb* to cut in two equal parts

bishop *noun* a high-ranking member of the clergy (next below an archbishop) in the Roman Catholic Church and the Church of England

bison *noun* (*plural* **bison**) a large wild ox with shaggy hair and a fat hump

bistro *noun* (*plural* **bistros**) a small bar or restaurant

bit[1] *noun* **1** a small piece **2** a small tool for boring **3** the part of the bridle which the horse holds in its mouth **4** *computing* a binary digit, the smallest unit of information

bit[2] *past form of* **bite**

bitch *noun* (*plural* **bitches**) a female dog, wolf, *etc*

bitchy *adjective* spiteful, malicious

bite *verb* to grip, cut or tear with the teeth ■ *noun* **1** a grip with the teeth **2** the part bitten off **3** a nibble at a fishing bait **4** a wound caused by an animal's or insect's bite

| **bite** *verb* ► bites, bit*ing*, bit, bitt*en*

bitmap *noun, computing* a method of screen display where each small element (**pixel**) is

assigned to one or more bits of memory ∎ *verb* to display something using this method
∎ **bitmapped** *adjective*
∎ **bitmapping** *noun*

| **bitmap** *verb* ▶ bitmaps, bitmapping, bitmapped

bitten *past participle* of **bite**

bitter *adjective* **1** unpleasant to the taste; sour **2** harsh: *bitter cold* **3** resentful, angry through disappointment

bittern *noun* a bird resembling a heron

bitterness *noun* the quality of being bitter

bitty *adjective* piecemeal, scrappy

bivouac *noun* an overnight camp outdoors without a tent
∎ *verb* to sleep outdoors without a tent

| **bivouac** *verb* ▶ bivouacs, bivouacking, bivouacked

bi-weekly *adjective* happening twice a week or once every two weeks

bizarre *adjective* odd, strange

blab *verb* to let out a secret

| **blab** ▶ blabs, blabbing, blabbed

black *adjective* dark and colourless ∎ *noun* black colour
∎ **black out** to become unconscious

black-and-blue *adjective* badly bruised

black belt an award for skill in judo, karate, and other martial arts

blackberry *noun* (*plural* **blackberries**) a blackish-purple soft fruit growing on a prickly stem

blackbird *noun* a type of black, thrush-like bird

blackboard *noun* a dark-coloured board for writing on in chalk

blacken *verb* **1** to make black or dark **2** to spoil the reputation of

black eye a bruised area round the eye as the result of a blow

blackguard *noun*, *old* a wicked person

black hole a region in space whose gravity is so strong that not even light can escape from it

black ice a thin transparent layer of ice on a road *etc*

blackleg *noun* someone who works when other workers are on strike

blacklist *noun* a list of people to be refused credit, jobs, *etc* ∎ *verb* to put on a blacklist

black magic magic performed for an evil purpose; witchcraft

blackmail *noun* the crime of threatening to reveal secrets unless money is paid ∎ *verb* to threaten by blackmail
∎ **blackmailer** *noun*

black market illegal or dishonest buying and selling

blackout *noun* **1** total darkness caused by putting out or covering all lights **2** a temporary loss of consciousness

black pudding sausage made with blood

black sheep someone who is considered a failure or outsider in a group

blacksmith *noun* someone who makes or repairs iron goods, especially horseshoes

black tie formal evening dress

black widow a very poisonous American spider, the female of which often eats her mate

bladder *noun* **1** the organ in which urine collects in the body **2** a bag with thin, membrane-like walls

blade *noun* **1** the cutting part of a knife, sword, *etc* **2** a leaf of grass or wheat

blame *verb* to find fault with; consider responsible for ■ *noun* fault; responsibility for something bad ■ **blameless** *adjective*

blancmange (*pronounced* bla-monsz) *noun* a jelly-like pudding made with milk

bland *adjective* **1** mild, not strong or irritating **2** dull, insipid

blank *adjective* **1** clear, unmarked **2** expressionless ■ *noun* **1** an empty space **2** a cartridge without a bullet

blanket *noun* **1** a bedcovering of wool *etc* **2** a widespread, soft covering: *blanket of snow* ■ *adjective* covering a group of things: *blanket agreement*

blare *verb* to sound loudly ■ *noun* a loud sound, *eg* on a trumpet

blasé (*pronounced* blah-**zei**) *adjective* indifferent, unconcerned, especially because of being already familiar with something

blaspheme *verb* **1** to speak irreverently of a god **2** to swear, curse ■ **blasphemer** *noun* ■ **blasphemous** *adjective* ■ **blasphemy** *noun* (*plural* **blasphemies**) **1** the act of speaking irreverently of a god **2** a swear-word

blast *noun* **1** a blowing or gust of wind **2** a loud note, *eg* on a trumpet **3** an explosion ■ *verb* **1** to break (stones, a bridge, *etc*) by explosion **2** to produce a loud noise ■ *exclamation* damn! ■ **at full blast** as quickly, strongly, *etc* as possible

blast-off *noun* the moment of the launching of a rocket

blatant *adjective* very obvious; shameless ■ **blatantly** *adverb*

blaze *noun* a rush of light or flame ■ *verb* **1** to burn with a strong flame **2** to throw out a strong light

blazer *noun* a light jacket often worn as part of a uniform

bleach *verb* to whiten, remove the colour from ■ *noun* (*plural* **bleaches**) a substance which bleaches, used for cleaning, whitening clothes, *etc*

bleak *adjective* dull and cheerless; cold, unsheltered
■ **bleakly** *adverb* sadly, wistfully
■ **bleakness** *noun*

bleary *adjective* of eyes: tired and inflamed ■ **blearily** *adverb*

bleat *verb* **1** to cry like a sheep **2** to complain in an irritating or whining way ■ *noun* **1** a sheep's cry **2** an irritating whine

bleed *verb* to lose blood

| **bleed** ► **bleeds**, **bleeding**, **bled**

bleeding *noun* a flow of blood

bleep *noun* a high-pitched intermittent sound ■ *verb* to give out such a sound

bleeper *noun* an electronic device using a bleep as a signal

blemish *noun* (*plural* **blemishes**) a stain; a fault or flaw ■ *verb* to stain, spoil

blend *verb* to mix together
■ *noun* a mixture

blender *noun* an electric machine which mixes thoroughly and liquidizes food

bless *verb* **1** to wish happiness to **2** to make happy **3** to make holy
■ **blessed** *or* (in poetry *etc*) **blest** *adjective* **1** happy; fortunate **2** made holy, consecrated

blessing *noun* **1** a wish or prayer for happiness **2** a source of happiness or relief

blight *noun* **1** a disease which makes plants wither **2** a cause of destruction ■ *verb* to destroy

blind *adjective* unable to see

■ *noun* a window screen ■ *verb* **1** to make blind **2** to dazzle
■ **blindness** *noun*

blind alley 1 a street open only at one end **2** anything which leads nowhere

blindfold *noun* a bandage or cover which is put over a person's eyes to prevent them from seeing ■ *adjective* with the eyes bandaged or covered, so as not to see ■ *verb* to apply a blindfold to

blindly *adverb* without knowledge or direction

blindman's buff a game in which a blindfold person tries to catch others

blink *verb* **1** to close the eyes for a moment **2** to shine unsteadily

blinkers *noun plural* pieces of leather over a horse's eyes to prevent it seeing in any direction except in front

bliss *noun* very great happiness
■ **blissful** *adjective* bringing feelings of great happiness; lovely

blister *noun* a thin bubble on the skin full of watery matter ■ *verb* to rise up in a blister

blithe *adjective* happy, merry
■ **blithely** *adverb*

blitz *noun* (*plural* **blitzes**) **1** an air attack **2** a sudden violent attack

blizzard *noun* a fierce storm of wind and snow

bloated *adjective* swollen, puffed out

blob *noun* **1** a drop of liquid **2** a round spot

block noun 1 a lump of wood, stone, etc 2 a connected group of buildings 3 an obstruction ▪ verb to hinder, prevent from progress

blockade verb to surround a fort or country so that food etc cannot reach it ▪ noun the surrounding of a place in this way

blockage noun 1 an obstruction 2 something that causes an obstruction

blond adjective fair-haired

blonde adjective having fair skin and light-coloured hair ▪ noun a woman with this colouring

blood noun 1 the red liquid which flows in the bodies of human beings and animals 2 someone's descent or parentage

bloodcurdling adjective causing chilling fear

blood group any one of the types into which human blood is classified

bloodhound noun a breed of large dog with a good sense of smell

bloodless adjective without bloodshed

blood pressure the pressure of the blood in the vessels as it circulates through the body

bloodshed noun violent loss of life, slaughter

bloodshot adjective of eyes: inflamed with blood

bloodstream noun the flow of blood around the body

bloodthirsty adjective cruel, eager to kill

blood vessel a tube in the body through which blood circulates, eg a vein or artery

bloody adjective 1 covered with blood 2 extremely violent, gory

bloom verb 1 of a plant: to flower 2 to be in good health ▪ noun a flower

bloomers noun plural loose underpants with legs gathered above the knee

blossom noun 1 a flower 2 the flowers on a fruit tree ▪ verb 1 to produce flowers 2 to open out, develop, flourish

blot noun 1 a spot of ink 2 a stain ▪ verb to spot, stain ▪ **blot out** to remove from sight or memory

| **blot** verb ▸ blots, blotting, blotted

blotch noun (plural blotches) a spot or patch of colour etc ▪ verb to mark with blotches ▪ **blotched** adjective ▪ **blotchy** adjective with skin or another surface which is temporarily an uneven colour

blouse noun a loose piece of clothing for the upper body

blow noun 1 a hard stroke or knock, eg with the fist 2 informal a sudden piece of bad luck ▪ verb 1 of wind: to move around 2 to drive air upon or into ▪ **blow over** to pass and be forgotten ▪ **blow up** to destroy by explosion

| **blow** verb ▸ blows, blowing, blew, blown

blowtorch or **blowlamp** noun a tool for aiming a very hot flame at a particular spot

blowy adjective windy

blubber noun the fat of whales and other sea animals

bludgeon noun a short stick with a heavy end ■ verb to hit (someone) with a heavy object

blue noun the colour of a clear sky ■ adjective 1 of this colour 2 informal unhappy, depressed
■ **out of the blue** unexpectedly ■ **the blues** 1 a type of slow, sad music 2 low spirits, depression

bluebell noun the wild hyacinth

blue blood royal or aristocratic blood

bluebottle noun a large fly with a blue abdomen

blue-chip adjective of a business company: reliable for investment; prestigious

blueprint noun a plan of work to be done

bluff adjective 1 rough and cheerful in manner 2 frank, outspoken ■ verb to try to deceive by pretending self-confidence ■ noun deception, trickery

blunder verb to make a bad mistake ■ noun a bad mistake

blunderbuss noun (plural blunderbusses) a short hand-gun with a wide mouth

blunt adjective 1 having an edge or point that is not sharp 2 rough in manner ■ verb to make less

sharp or less painful ■ **bluntly** adverb frankly, straightforwardly

blur noun an indistinct area of something; a smudge, a smear ■ verb to make indistinct, smudge ■ **blurred** adjective

| **blur** verb ▶ blurs, blurring, blurred

blurt verb: **blurt out** to speak suddenly and without thinking

blush noun (plural blushes) a red glow on the face caused by embarrassment etc ■ verb to go red in the face

bluster verb 1 to blow strongly 2 to boast loudly ■ noun 1 a blasting wind 2 empty boasting ■ **blustery** adjective very windy

boa noun a long scarf of fur or feathers

boa constrictor a large snake which kills its prey by winding itself round it and crushing it

boar noun 1 a male pig 2 a wild pig

board noun 1 a sheet of wood 2 a group of people who run a business 3 food: bed and board ■ verb to enter (a ship, aeroplane, etc) ■ **boarder** noun someone who receives food and lodging

boarding house a house where paying guests receive meals at a fixed price

boarding school a school in which food and lodging is given

boast verb 1 to talk proudly about yourself 2 to have (something worth being proud of): *the hotel boasts magnificent views* ■ noun an act of boasting

boastful *adjective* with a tendency to boast

boat *noun* a vessel for sailing or rowing; a ship ■ *verb* to sail about in a boat

boatswain or **bosun** (*both pronounced* boh-sun) *noun* an officer who looks after a ship's boats, rigging, *etc*

bob *verb* **1** to move up and down rapidly **2** to cut (hair) to about neck level ■ *noun* a bobbed haircut

| **bob** *verb* ► bobs, bobb*ing*, bobb*ed*

bobbin *noun* a reel or spool on which thread is wound

bobble *noun* **1** a woolly ball for decorating hats *etc* **2** a little ball on the surface of fabric

bobsleigh *noun* a long sledge or two short sledges joined together with one long seat

bode *verb*: **bode well** (or **ill**) to be a good (or bad) sign

bodice *noun* the close-fitting part of a woman's or a child's dress above the waist

bodily *adjective* of the body

bodkin *noun*, *old* a large blunt needle

body *noun* (*plural* **bodies**) **1** the whole or main part of a human being or animal **2** a corpse **3** the main part of anything **4** a mass of people

bodyguard *noun* someone or a group of people whose job is to protect another person from harm or attack

bog *noun* a marsh ■ **boggy** *adjective* marshy ■ **bog down** to prevent from making progress

boggle *verb* to be astonished at

bogus *adjective* false

bohemian *noun* someone who lives outside social conventions, especially an artist or writer ■ *adjective* of the lifestyle of a bohemian

boil *verb* **1** of a liquid: to reach the temperature at which it turns to vapour **2** to bubble up owing to heat **3** *informal* to be hot ■ *noun* a kind of inflamed swelling

boiler *noun* a container in which water is heated or steam is produced

boiling point the temperature at which a liquid turns to vapour (*eg* for water, 100°C)

boisterous *adjective* wild, noisy

bold *adjective* **1** daring, full of courage **2** cheeky **3** striking, well-marked **4** of printing type: thick and clear ■ **boldly** *adverb*

bollard *noun* a short post on a street used for traffic control

Bolshevik *noun*, *history* a member of the Extreme Socialist Party in revolutionary Russia

bolster *noun* a long cylindrical pillow ■ **bolster up** to support

bolt *noun* a small metal sliding bar used to fasten a door *etc*

- *verb* **1** to fasten with a bolt **2** to swallow (food) hurriedly **3** to rush away, escape ▪ **bolt upright** sitting with a very straight back

bomb *noun* **1** a case containing explosive or other harmful material thrown, dropped, timed to go off automatically, *etc* **2 the bomb** the nuclear bomb ▪ *verb* to drop bombs on

bombard *verb* **1** to attack with artillery **2** to overwhelm (with): *bombarded with letters* ▪ **bombardment** *noun*

bomber *noun* **1** an aeroplane built for bombing **2** someone who throws or plants bombs

bombshell *noun* a startling piece of news

bond *noun* **1** something which binds, *eg* a rope **2** something which brings people together: *music was a bond between them*

bone *noun* **1** a hard material forming the skeleton of animals **2** one of the connected pieces of a skeleton ▪ *verb* to take the bones out of (meat *etc*)

bonfire *noun* a large fire in the open air

bonnet *noun* **1** a decorative woman's hat, fastened under the chin **2** the covering over a car engine

bonny *adjective* good-looking; pretty

bonus *noun* (*plural* **bonuses**) **1** an extra payment in addition to wages **2** something extra

bony *adjective* **1** full of bones **2** not fleshy, thin

boo *verb* to make a sound of disapproval ▪ *noun* a sound of disapproval

booby prize a prize for the person who is last in a competition

booby trap a device hidden or disguised as something harmless, intended to injure the first person to come near it

book *noun* **1** a number of pages bound together **2** a written work which has appeared, or is intended to appear, in the form of a book ▪ *verb* to order (places *etc*) beforehand

book-keeping *noun* the keeping of accounts ▪ **book-keeper** *noun*

booklet *noun* a small paperback book

bookmaker *noun* someone who takes bets and pays winnings

bookmark *noun* **1** something inserted in the pages of a book to mark a place **2** a record of the location of a favourite Internet site, web page, *etc* ▪ *verb* to make an electronic record of (a favourite Internet site *etc*)

boom *verb* **1** to make a hollow sound or roar **2** to increase in prosperity, success, *etc* ▪ *noun* **1** a loud, hollow sound **2** a rush or increase of trade, prosperity, *etc*

boomerang *noun* a curved piece of wood which when

thrown returns to the thrower, a traditional hunting weapon of Australian Aboriginals

boost *verb* to push up, raise, increase ▪ *noun* an increase, a rise

booster *noun* **1** a device for increasing the power of a machine *etc* **2** the first of several stages of a rocket

boot *noun* **1** a heavy shoe covering the foot and lower part of the leg **2** *Brit* a place for stowing luggage in a car **3** the start of a computer from its start-up programs **4** a kick ▪ *verb* to kick ▪ **boot up** to start (a computer) by running its start-up programs

booth *noun* **1** a covered stall, *eg* at a market **2** a small compartment for telephoning, voting, *etc*

booty *noun* plunder, gains taken in war *etc*

border *noun* **1** the edge or side of anything **2** the boundary of a country **3** a flowerbed in a garden ▪ *verb*: **border on** to be near to

borderline *noun* **1** the line dividing two countries *etc* **2** the line dividing two things ▪ *adjective* on the borderline between one thing and another: *a borderline pass*

bore[1] *verb* **1** to make a hole by piercing **2** to weary, be tiresome to ▪ *noun* **1** a pierced hole **2** a tiresome person or thing ▪ **bored** *adjective*

bore[2] *past form of* **bear**[2]

boredom *noun* lack of interest; weariness

boring *adjective* not at all interesting

born *adjective* by birth, natural: *a born actor* ▪ **be born** of a baby: to come out of the mother's womb

○✱ Do not confuse: **born** and **borne**. Born is used for the past participle of **bear** when referring to the birth of a child; otherwise the form is **borne**: *I couldn't have borne it any longer*

borne *past participle of* **bear**[2]

○✱ Do not confuse: **borne** and **born**

borough *noun* **1** *history* a town with special privileges granted by royal charter **2** a town that elects Members of Parliament

borrow *verb* to get on loan ▪ **borrower** *noun*

bosom *noun* **1** the breast **2** the midst, centre: *bosom of her family* ▪ *adjective* of a friend: close, intimate

boss *noun* (*plural* **bosses**) a manager, a chief ▪ *verb* to order about in a high-handed way

bossy *adjective* tending to boss others, domineering

bosun *see* **boatswain**

botanist *noun* someone who studies botany

botany *noun* the study of plants ▪ **botanic** *or* **botanical** *adjective*

botch *verb* **1** to mend clumsily **2** to do badly ▪ *noun* a badly done piece of work

both *adjective & pronoun* the two, the one and the other ▪ *adverb* equally, together: *both willing and able*

bother *verb* **1** to be a nuisance to **2** to take time or trouble over something ▪ *noun* trouble, inconvenience

bottle *noun* a hollow narrow-necked vessel for holding liquids ▪ *verb* to put in a bottle ▪ **bottle up** to keep in, hold back (feelings)

bottle bank a skip collecting empty glass containers for recycling

bottleneck *noun* **1** a narrow part of a road likely to become crowded with traffic **2** a stage in a process where progress is held up

bottom *noun* **1** the lowest part or underside of anything **2** the buttocks

bottomless *adjective* extremely deep

bough *noun* a branch of a tree

bought *past form* of **buy**

boulder *noun* a large stone

bounce *verb* **1** to jump up after striking the ground *etc* **2** to make (a ball *etc*) do this ▪ *noun* a jumping back up ▪ **bouncy** *adjective* ▪ **bounce back** to recover after a setback or trouble

bouncer *noun* someone employed to force troublemakers to leave a place

bound[1] *noun* **1** a leap, a jump **2** **bounds** borders, limits ▪ *verb* to jump, leap ▪ **bound for** ready to go to, on the way to ▪ **bound to** certain to ▪ **out of bounds** beyond the permitted limits

bound[2] *past form* of **bind**

boundary *noun* (*plural* **boundaries**) an edge, a limit

boundless *adjective* having no limit, vast

bountiful *or* **bounteous** *adjective* generous; plentiful

bounty *noun* (*plural* **bounties**) **1** a gift; generosity **2** a reward

bouquet *noun* a bunch of flowers

bout *noun* **1** a round in a contest **2** a spell, a fit

boutique *noun* a small shop selling fashionable clothes *etc*

bow[1] (*pronounced* bow) *verb* **1** to bend **2** to nod the head or bend the body in greeting ▪ *noun* **1** a bending of the head or body **2** the front part of a ship

bow[2] (*pronounced* boh) *noun* **1** anything in the shape of a curve or arch **2** a weapon for shooting arrows, made of a stick of springy wood bent by a string **3** a looped knot, usually decorative **4** an instrument used to produce the sounds from the strings of a violin *etc*

bowels *noun plural* the intestines

bowl *noun* **1** a basin for holding

liquids **2** a heavy wooden ball, used in skittles *etc* **3** bowls a game played on a green with specially weighted bowls ■ *verb* **1** to play at bowls **2** *cricket* to send the ball at the wicket **3** *cricket* to put out by knocking the wicket with the ball ■ **bowler** *noun* **1** someone who plays bowls **2** someone who bowls in cricket **3** a hat with a rounded top ■ **bowl over** to surprise greatly

bowling *noun* **1** the game of bowls **2** the game of tenpin bowling

bow tie a neck tie with two loops and a knot

box *noun* (*plural* **boxes**) **1** a case for holding anything **2** an evergreen shrub or tree **3** an enclosure of private seats in a theatre ■ *verb* **1** to put in a box **2** to confine in a small space **3** to engage in the sport of boxing

boxer *noun* **1** someone who boxes as a sport **2** a breed of large smooth-haired dog with a head like a bulldog's

boxer shorts loose-fitting men's underpants

boxing *noun* the sport of fighting with the fists wearing padded gloves

Boxing Day the first weekday after Christmas Day

box office an office where theatre tickets *etc* may be bought

boy *noun* a male child

boycott *verb* to refuse to do business or trade with ■ *noun* a refusal to trade or do business

boyfriend *noun* a male friend, especially in a romantic relationship

boyhood *noun* the time of being a boy

boyish *adjective* **1** of a girl: having an appearance or behaviour which gives an impression of masculinity **2** of a man: having an appearance or behaviour which gives an impression of youthfulness

bra *noun* an article of women's underwear for supporting the breasts

brace *noun* **1** an instrument which draws things together and holds them firmly **2** a piece of wire fitted over teeth to straighten them **3** a pair of pheasant, grouse, *etc* when shot **4** a carpenter's tool for boring **5** **braces** shoulder-straps for holding up trousers ■ *verb* to strengthen, give firmness to

bracelet *noun* a circular ornament placed around the wrist

bracken *noun* a coarse kind of fern

bracket *noun* **1** a support for something fastened to a wall **2** each of a pair of written or printed marks, *eg* (), [ ], used to group together several words **3** a grouping, category ■ *verb* **1** to enclose in brackets **2** to group together

brag *verb* to boast ▪ *noun* a boast
brag *verb* ▶ brags, bragging, bragged

Brahman *or* **Brahmin** *noun* (*plural* **Brahmans** *or* **Brahmins**) one of the highest-ranking groups of Hindus

braid *verb* to plait (the hair) ▪ *noun* 1 a plait of hair 2 decorative ribbon used as trimming

braille *noun* a system of raised marks on paper which blind people can read by feeling

brain *noun* the part of the body inside the skull, the centre of feeling and thinking

brainwash *verb* to force (someone) to believe something by using constant pressure ▪ **brainwashing** *noun*

brainwave *noun* a good idea

brainy *adjective, informal* clever

braise *verb* to stew (meat) in a small amount of liquid

brake *noun* a part of a vehicle used for stopping or slowing down ▪ *verb* to slow down by using the brake(s)

bramble *noun* 1 the blackberry bush 2 its fruit

bran *noun* the inner husks of wheat *etc*, separated from flour after grinding

branch *noun* (*plural* **branches**) 1 an arm-like limb of a tree 2 a shop, bank, *etc* that is part of a large group ▪ *verb* to spread out like branches

brand *noun* 1 a make of goods with a special trademark 2 a permanent mark made by a red-hot iron ▪ *verb* 1 to mark with a brand 2 to mark permanently; impress deeply 3 to mark with disgrace: *branded as a thief*

brandish *verb* to wave (a weapon *etc*) about

brand-new *adjective* absolutely new

brandy *noun* (*plural* **brandies**) an alcoholic spirit made from wine

brass *noun* (*plural* **brasses**) 1 metal made by mixing copper and zinc 2 *music* brass wind instruments ▪ *adjective* 1 made of brass 2 playing brass musical instruments: *brass section*

brat *noun* a disapproving name for a child

bravado *noun* a show of bravery, bold pretence

brave *adjective* ready to meet danger, pain, *etc* without showing fear; courageous, noble ▪ *verb* to face or meet boldly and without fear ▪ *noun* a Native American warrior

bravery *noun* the quality of being brave and acting with courage

bravo *exclamation* well done!

brawl *noun* a noisy quarrel; a fight ▪ *verb* to quarrel or fight noisily

brawn *noun* muscle power ▪ **brawny** *adjective* big and strong

bray noun a cry like that of an ass ■ verb to cry like an ass

brazen adjective impudent, shameless ■ **brazenly** adverb

brazier noun an iron basket for holding burning coals

breach noun (plural **breaches**) 1 a break, a gap 2 a breaking of a law, a promise, etc ■ verb to make a gap or opening in

bread noun food made of flour or meal and baked

breadth noun 1 distance from side to side, width 2 extent: breadth of knowledge

breadwinner noun someone who earns a living for a family

break verb 1 to (cause to) fall to pieces or apart 2 to act against (a law, promise, etc) 3 to interrupt (a silence) 4 to tell (news) 5 to check, soften the effect of (a fall) 6 to cure (a habit) 7 of a boy's voice: to drop to a deep male tone ■ noun 1 an opening 2 a pause 3 informal a lucky chance ■ **break down 1** to divide into parts 2 of an engine: to fail 3 to be overcome with weeping or nervous exhaustion ■ **break in** to tame, train (a wild horse etc) ■ **break into** to enter by force ■ **break out 1** to appear suddenly 2 to escape 3 **break out in something** to become covered (with a rash etc) ■ **break up 1** to (cause to) fall to pieces or apart 2 to separate, leave one another

break verb ▶ breaks,

breaking, broke, broken

breakage noun 1 the act of breaking 2 something broken

breakdown noun 1 a division into parts 2 a collapse from nervous exhaustion etc

breaker noun a large wave

breakfast noun the first meal of the day ■ verb to eat this meal

break-in noun illegal forced entry of a house etc with intent to steal

breakthrough noun a sudden success after some effort

breast noun 1 either of the milk-producing glands on a woman's body 2 the front part of a human or animal body between neck and belly 3 a part of a jacket or coat which covers the breast

breaststroke noun a stroke used in swimming where the arms and legs are pushed forwards then sideways

breath noun 1 the air drawn into and then sent out from the lungs 2 an instance of breathing 3 a very slight breeze

♦* Do not confuse: **breath** and **breathe**

Breathalyser noun, trademark a device into which someone breathes to indicate the amount of alcohol in their blood

breathe verb to draw in and send out air from the lungs

breathe ▶ breathes, breathing, breathed

♦* Do not confuse: **breathe** and **breath**

breather noun a rest or pause

breathless adjective 1 breathing very fast, panting 2 excited

breathtaking adjective very surprising or impressive

bred past form of breed

breeches (pronounced brich-iz) noun plural trousers reaching to just below the knee

breed verb 1 to produce (children or a family) 2 to mate and rear (animals) 3 to cause: dirt breeds disease ■ noun 1 a group of animals etc descended from the same ancestor 2 type, sort: a new breed of salesmen ■ breeder noun someone who breeds certain animals

| breed verb ▶ breeds, breeding, bred

breeding noun 1 the act of producing or rearing 2 good manners; education and training

breeze noun a gentle wind

breezy adjective 1 windy, gusty 2 bright, lively ■ breezily adverb

breve noun a long musical note (⊩◁⊪) which is 8 beats in length

brevity noun shortness, conciseness

brew verb 1 to make beer 2 to make (tea etc) 3 to be gathering or forming: there's trouble brewing ■ brewer noun someone who brews beer etc

brewery noun (plural breweries) a place where beer is made

briar or **brier** noun 1 the wild rose 2 a heather plant whose wood is used for making tobacco pipes

bribe noun a gift of money etc given to persuade someone to do something ■ verb to give a bribe to

| bribe verb ▶ bribes, bribing, bribed

bribery noun the act of bribing someone to do something

brick noun 1 a block of baked clay for building 2 a toy building-block of wood etc

bricklayer noun someone whose job it is to build with bricks

bridal adjective of a bride or a wedding

bride noun a woman about to be married, or newly married

bridegroom noun a man about to be married, or newly married

bridesmaid noun a woman who attends the bride at a wedding

bridge[1] noun 1 a structure built to carry a track or road across a river etc 2 the captain's platform on a ship 3 the bony part of the nose 4 a thin piece of wood holding up the strings of a violin etc ■ verb 1 to be a bridge over; span 2 to build a bridge over 3 to get over (a difficulty)

| bridge verb ▶ bridges, bridging, bridged

bridge[2] noun a card game for two pairs of players

bridle noun the harness on a horse's head to which the reins are attached ■ verb 1 to put on a bridle 2 to toss the head indignantly

brief adjective short; taking a short time ■ noun a set of notes giving information or instructions, especially to a lawyer about a law case ■ verb to instruct or inform ■ **briefly** adverb

briefcase noun a flat case for carrying papers

briefs noun plural close-fitting underpants

brier another spelling of briar

brigade noun a body of soldiers, usually two battalions

brigadier noun a senior army officer

brigand noun, old a robber, a bandit

bright adjective 1 shining; full of light 2 clever 3 cheerful

brighten verb to make or grow bright

brilliant adjective 1 very clever 2 sparkling 3 informal very good, excellent ■ **brilliance** noun ■ **brilliantly** adverb

brim noun 1 the edge of a cup etc 2 the protruding lower edge of a hat or cap

brine noun salt water ■ **briny** adjective

bring verb 1 to fetch, lead or carry (to a place) 2 to cause to come: the medicine brings him relief ■ **bring about** to cause

■ **bring home to** to make (someone) realize (something) ■ **bring off** to do (something) successfully ■ **bring to** to revive ■ **bring up 1** to rear, feed and educate 2 to mention 3 informal to vomit

| **bring** ► brings, bringing, brought

brink noun the edge of a cliff etc ■ **on the brink of** almost at the point of, on the verge of

brisk adjective 1 moving quickly: a brisk walk 2 lively and efficient: a brisk manner ■ **briskly** adverb

bristle noun a short, stiff hair on an animal, a brush, etc ■ verb 1 of hair etc: to stand on end 2 to show anger and indignation ■ **bristly** adjective having bristles; rough

brittle adjective hard but easily broken

broach verb to begin to talk about: broached the subject

broad adjective 1 wide, extensive 2 of an accent etc: strong, obvious ■ **broadly** adverb 1 widely 2 generally: broadly speaking, we're all afraid of the same things

broadband adjective 1 of telecommunications: operating across a wide range of frequencies 2 computing accommodating data from a wide range of sources, eg telephone, television, etc

broadcast verb to transmit (a programme etc) on radio or television ■ *noun* a programme transmitted on radio or television ■ **broadcaster** *noun*

broaden *verb* to make or grow broader

broad-minded *adjective* tolerant and liberal

broadsheet *noun* a large-format quality newspaper (*compare with:* **tabloid**)

brocade *noun* a silk cloth on which fine patterns are sewn

broccoli *noun* a hardy variety of cauliflower with small green or purple flower-heads

brochure (*pronounced* broh-**shoor** *or* broh-**shur**) *noun* a booklet, a pamphlet

brogue[1] (*pronounced* brohg) *noun* a strong shoe

brogue[2] (*pronounced* brohg) *noun* a broad accent in speaking

broil *verb* to make or be very hot

broke *past form of* **break**
■ *adjective, informal* having no money

broken *past participle of* **break**

broker *noun* someone who buys and sells stocks and shares for others ■ *verb* **1** to act as a broker **2** to negotiate on behalf of others: *broker a deal*

bromide *noun* a chemical used as a sedative

bronchitis (*pronounced* brong-**kait**-*is*) *noun* an illness affecting the windpipe, causing difficulty in breathing

bronco *noun* (*plural* **broncos**) *US* a half-tamed horse

brontosaurus *noun* a large dinosaur

bronze *noun* a golden-brown mixture of copper and tin
■ *adjective* of this colour
■ **bronzed** *adjective* suntanned

bronze medal a medal given to a competitor who comes third

brooch (*pronounced* brohch) *noun* (*plural* **brooches**) an ornament pinned to the clothing

brood *verb* **1** of a hen *etc*: to sit on eggs **2** to think anxiously for some time ■ *noun* **1** a number of young birds hatched at one time **2** young animals or children of the same family

broody *adjective* **1** moody, thoughtful **2** *informal* of a woman: wanting to have babies

brook *noun* a small stream

broom *noun* **1** a type of shrub with yellow flowers **2** a brush for sweeping

broomstick *noun* the handle of a broom

broth *noun* soup, especially one made with vegetables

brother *noun* **1** a male born of the same parents as yourself **2** a companion, a fellow-worker

brotherhood *noun* **1** comradeship between men **2** a men's association

brother-in-law *noun* **1** the brother of your husband or wife

2 the husband of your sister or sister-in-law

brotherly *adjective* like a brother; affectionate

brought *past form* of bring

brow *noun* **1** a forehead **2** an eyebrow **3** the edge of a hill

browbeat *verb* to bully

brown *noun* a dark colour, the colour of dark soil or wood ▪ *adjective* **1** of this colour **2** *informal* suntanned

brownie *noun* **1** a helpful fairy or goblin **2** a Brownie Guide

Brownie Guide a member of the junior branch of the Guides

browse *verb* **1** to glance through a range of books, shop merchandise, *etc* **2** to feed on the shoots or leaves of plants

browser *noun* a computer program used for searching and managing data from the World Wide Web

bruise *noun* a discoloured area on the skin, the surface of fruit, *etc*, where it has been struck ▪ *verb* to cause bruises (to)

brunette *noun* a woman with dark brown hair

brunt *noun*: **bear** *or* **take the brunt** to take the chief strain

brush *noun* (*plural* **brushes**) **1** an instrument with tufts of bristles, hair, *etc* for smoothing the hair, cleaning, painting, *etc* **2** a disagreement, a brief quarrel **3** the tail of a fox **4** undergrowth ▪ *verb* **1** to pass a brush over **2** to remove by sweeping **3** to touch lightly in passing

Brussels sprout a type of vegetable with sprouts like small cabbages on the stem

brutal *adjective* cruel or violent ▪ **brutality** *noun*

brute *noun* **1** an animal **2** a cruel person

brutish *adjective* like a brute, savage, coarse

bubble *noun* **1** a thin ball of liquid blown out with air **2** a small ball of air in anything ▪ *verb* to rise in bubbles

bubbly *adjective* **1** full of bubbles **2** lively, vivacious ▪ *noun*, *informal* champagne; sparkling wine

buccaneer *noun*, *old* a pirate ▪ **buccaneering** *adjective* like a pirate

buck *noun* **1** the male of the deer, goat, hare and rabbit **2** *US informal* a dollar ▪ *verb* of a horse *etc*: to attempt to throw a rider by rapid jumps into the air

bucket *noun* a container for water *etc*

buckle *noun* a clip for fastening straps or belts ▪ *verb* to fasten with a buckle

bud *noun* the first shoot of a tree or plant ▪ *verb* to produce buds

| **bud** *verb* ▸ buds, budd*ing*, budd*ed*

Buddhism *noun* a religion that follows the teachings of Buddha ▪ **Buddhist** *noun & adjective*

budding *adjective* showing signs of becoming: *budding author*

budge *verb* to move slightly, stir

| **budge** ► budges, budging, budged

budgerigar *noun* a kind of small parrot often kept as a pet

budget *noun* 1 a government plan for the year's spending 2 any plan of future spending ▪ *verb* to allow for in a budget

budgie *noun*, *informal* a budgerigar

buff *noun* 1 a light yellowish brown colour 2 an enthusiast, a fan ▪ *verb* to polish

buffalo *noun* (*plural* **buffaloes**) 1 a large Asian ox, used to draw loads 2 the North American bison

buffer *noun* something which lessens the force of a blow or collision

buffet[1] (*pronounced* buf-it) *verb* to strike, knock about ▪ *noun* a slap or a blow

buffet[2] (*pronounced* buwf-ei) *noun* a range of dishes set out at a party *etc* for people to serve themselves

buffoon *noun* a clown, fool ▪ **buffoonery** *noun* silly behaviour, clowning around

bug *noun* 1 a small, especially irritating, insect 2 a disease germ 3 a tiny hidden microphone for recording conversations 4 a problem in a computer program causing errors in its execution

▪ *verb* 1 to conceal a microphone in (a room *etc*) 2 *informal* to annoy, harass

| **bug** *verb* ► bugs, bugging, bugged

bugbear *noun* something that frightens or annoys

buggy *noun* (*plural* **buggies**) a child's pushchair

bugle *noun* a small military trumpet ▪ **bugler** *noun* someone who plays the bugle

build *verb* to put together the parts of anything ▪ *noun* physique, physical character ▪ **builder** *noun*

| **build** *verb* ► builds, building, built

building *noun* 1 the act or trade of building (houses *etc*) 2 a house or other built dwelling *etc*

building society an institution like a bank which accepts investments and whose main business is to lend people money to buy a house

built *past form* of build

built-up *adjective* of an area: containing houses and other buildings

bulb *noun* 1 the rounded part of the stem of an onion, tulip, *etc*, in which they store their food 2 a glass globe surrounding the element of an electric light ▪ **bulbous** *adjective* bulb-shaped

bulge *noun* a swelling ▪ *verb* to swell out

bulge *verb* ► bulges, bulging, bulged

bulimia *noun* an eating disorder in which bingeing is followed by self-induced vomiting or purging ■ **bulimic** *adjective* suffering from bulimia

bulk *noun* 1 large size 2 the greater part: *the bulk of the population*

bulky *adjective* taking up a lot of room ■ **bulkily** *adverb*

bull *noun* the male of animals of the ox family, also of the whale, elephant, *etc*

bulldog *noun* a breed of strong, fierce-looking dog

bulldoze *verb* 1 to use a bulldozer on 2 to force

bulldozer *noun* a machine for levelling land and clearing away obstacles

bullet *noun* 1 the piece of metal fired from a gun 2 a small shape, such as a circle or square, highlighting each of the various points on a piece of writing

bulletin *noun* a report of current news, someone's health, *etc*

bullet-proof *adjective* not able to be pierced by bullets

bullfight *noun* a public entertainment in Spain *etc*, in which a bull is baited and usually killed ■ **bullfighter** *noun*

bullfinch *noun* a small pink-breasted bird

bullion *noun* gold or silver in the form of bars *etc*

bullock *noun* a young bull

bull's-eye *noun* the mark in the middle of a target

bully *noun* (*plural* **bullies**) someone who unfairly uses their size and strength to hurt or frighten others ■ *verb* to act like a bully ■ **bullying** *noun*

bully *verb* ► bullies, bullying, bullied

bulrush *noun* (*plural* **bulrushes**) a large strong reed which grows on, in or near water

bulwark (*pronounced* buwl-wak) *noun* 1 a strong defensive wall 2 a prop, a defence

bum[1] *noun, Brit slang* the buttocks

bum[2] *noun, US slang* a tramp ■ *adjective* useless, dud

bumbag *noun* a carrying pouch strapped round the waist

bumblebee *noun* a type of large bee

bump *verb* 1 to strike heavily 2 to knock by accident ■ *noun* 1 the sound of a heavy blow 2 an accidental knock 3 a raised lump ■ **bumpy** *adjective*

bumper *noun* a bar round the front and back of a car's body to protect it from damage ■ *adjective* large

bumpkin *noun* a clumsy, awkward, country person

bumptious *adjective* self-important

bun *noun* 1 a sweet roll made of egg dough 2 hair wound into a rounded mass

bunch noun (plural **bunches**) a number of things tied together or growing together ▪ verb to crowd together

bundle noun a number of things loosely bound together ▪ verb 1 to tie in a bundle 2 to push roughly

bung noun the stopper of the hole in a barrel, bottle, etc ▪ verb to stop up with a bung

bungalow noun a one-storey detached house

bungee jumping the sport of jumping from a height with strong rubber ropes attached to the ankles so that the jumper bounces up before reaching the ground

bungle verb 1 to do badly or clumsily 2 to deal with or manage badly ▪ noun a clumsy or mishandled action

bunion noun a lump or swelling on the joint of the big toe

bunk noun a narrow bed, eg in a ship's cabin

bunk bed one of a pair of narrow beds one above the other

bunker noun 1 a sand-filled pit on a golf course 2 an underground shelter 3 a large box for keeping coal

bunny noun (plural **bunnies**) a child's name for a rabbit

Bunsen burner a gas-burner used in laboratories

bunting[1] noun 1 a thin cloth used for making flags 2 flags

bunting[2] noun a bird of the finch family

buoy noun 1 a floating mark acting as a guide or warning for ships 2 a float, eg a lifebuoy

buoyant adjective 1 able to float 2 cheerful, bouncy ▪ **buoyancy** noun

bur another spelling of **burr**

burden noun 1 a load 2 something difficult to bear, eg poverty or sorrow ▪ **burdensome** adjective

bureau noun (plural **bureaux** or **bureaus**) 1 a writing table 2 an office

bureaucracy (pronounced byoo-**rok**-ra-si) noun government by officials ▪ **bureaucrat** noun an administrative official ▪ **bureaucratic** adjective 1 involving bureaucracy 2 full of complicated and irritating official procedures

burglar noun someone who breaks into a house to steal

burglary noun (plural **burglaries**) a break-in into a house by a person who wants to steal things

burgle verb to commit burglary

burial noun the placing of a body under the ground after death

burly adjective broad and strong

burn verb 1 to set fire to 2 to be on fire, or scorching 3 to injure by burning 4 to record data onto (a compact disc) ▪ noun an injury or mark caused by fire

| **burn** verb ▶ burns, burning, burnt or burned

burner noun 1 the part of a lamp or gas jet from which the flame rises 2 a CD burner

burnt past form of **burn**

burp verb, informal to bring up wind through the mouth from the stomach

burr or **bur** noun the prickly seedcase or head of certain plants

burrow noun a hole or passage in the ground dug by certain animals for shelter ■ verb to make a passage beneath the ground

burst verb 1 to break suddenly (after increased pressure) 2 to move, speak, etc suddenly or violently ■ noun 1 an instance of something breaking suddenly 2 a sudden activity: burst of gunfire

| **burst** verb ► bursts, bursting, burst

bury verb 1 to place (a dead body etc) under the ground 2 to cover, hide

| **bury** ► buries, burying, buried

bus noun (plural **buses**) a large road vehicle, often used for public transport

busby noun (plural **busbies**) a tall fur hat worn by soldiers in certain regiments

bush noun (plural **bushes**) 1 a growing thing between a plant and a tree in size 2 wild, unfarmed country in Africa etc

bushy adjective growing thickly ■ **bushiness** noun

business noun (plural **businesses**) 1 someone's work or job 2 trade, commerce 3 a matter of personal interest or concern

businesslike adjective practical, methodical, alert and prompt

businessman, **businesswoman** noun someone who works in commerce

busk verb to play or sing in the street for money ■ **busker** noun

bus stop an official stopping place for buses

bust noun 1 a woman's breasts 2 a sculpture of someone's head and shoulders

bustle verb to busy oneself noisily ■ noun noisy activity, fuss

busy adjective having a lot to do ■ **busily** adverb ■ **busy yourself with** to occupy yourself with

| **busy** ► busier, busiest

busybody noun (plural **busybodies**) someone nosey about others

but conjunction 1 showing a contrast between two ideas etc: my brother can swim but I can't 2 except that, without that: it never rains but it pours ■ preposition except, with the exception of ■ adverb only

butcher noun someone whose work is to carve up meat and sell it ■ verb 1 to kill and carve up (an animal) for food 2 to kill cruelly

butchery *noun* great or cruel slaughter

butler *noun* the chief male servant in a household

butt *noun* **1** a large cask, a barrel **2** someone of whom others make fun **3** the thick heavy end of a rifle *etc* **4** the end of a finished cigarette or cigar **5** a push with the head **6** *US slang* the buttocks ■ *verb* to strike with the head ■ **butt in** to interrupt, interfere

butter *noun* a fatty food made by churning cream ■ *verb* to spread over with butter

buttercup *noun* a plant with a cup-like yellow flower

butterfly *noun* (*plural* **butterflies**) **1** a kind of insect with large, often patterned wings **2** a swimming stroke where the arms are swung forwards in a circling motion

buttermilk *noun* the milk that is left after butter has been made

butterscotch *noun* a hard toffee made with butter

buttocks *noun plural* the two fleshy parts of the body on which you sit

button *noun* **1** a knob or disc of metal, plastic, *etc* used to fasten clothing **2** a knob pressed to work an electrical device ■ *verb* to fasten by means of buttons

buttonhole *noun* a hole through which a button is passed ■ *verb* to catch the attention of

(someone) and force them to listen

buttress *noun* (*plural* **buttresses**) a support on the outside of a wall

buxom *adjective* plump and pretty

buy *verb* to get in exchange for money ■ *noun* a purchase ■ **buyer** *noun*

| **buy** *verb* ► buys, buy*ing*, bought

buzz *verb* **1** to make a humming noise like bees **2** *informal* to call, telephone ■ *noun* (*plural* **buzzes**) **1** a humming sound **2** *informal* a phone call

buzzard *noun* a large bird of prey

buzzer *noun* a signalling device which makes a buzzing noise

buzzword *noun* a word well-established in a particular jargon, its use suggesting up-to-date specialized knowledge

by *adverb* **1** near: *a crowd stood by, watching* **2** past: *people strolled by* **3** aside: *money put by for an emergency* ■ *preposition* **1** next to, near **2** past **3** through, along, across **4** indicating the person who does something: *written by Robert Burns* **5** of time: not after **6** by means of: *by train* **7** to the extent of: *taller by a head* **8** used to express measurements, compass directions, *etc*: *6 metres by 4 metres/north by northwest* **9**

in the quantity of: *sold by the pound*

bye[1] *or* **bye-bye** *exclamation, informal* goodbye

bye[2] *noun, cricket* **1** a ball bowled past the wicket **2** a run made from this

by-election *noun* an election for parliament during a parliamentary session

bygone *adjective* past

■ **bygones** *noun plural* old grievances or events that have been, or should be, forgotten

by-law *or* **bye-law** *noun* a local (not a national) law

bypass *noun* a road built round a town *etc* so that traffic need not pass through it ■ *verb* to go around or avoid

by-product *noun* something useful obtained during the manufacture of something else

bystander *noun* someone who stands watching an event or accident

byte *noun, computing* a unit used to measure data or memory

byword *noun* someone or something well-known for a particular quality

C

cab *noun* **1** a taxi **2** in the past, a hired carriage

cabaret (*pronounced* **kab**-*a*-rei) *noun* an entertainment consisting of a variety of songs, comedy, dancing, *etc*

cabbage *noun* a type of vegetable with edible leaves

cabin *noun* **1** a wooden hut **2** a small room used for living quarters in a ship **3** the part of a commercial aircraft containing passenger seating

cabin crew the flight attendants on a commercial airline

cabinet *noun* **1** a cupboard which has shelves and doors **2** a similar container for storage *etc* **3** a wooden case with drawers **4** a selected number of government ministers who decide on policy

cabinet-maker *noun* a maker of fine furniture

cable *noun* **1** a strong rope or thick metal line **2** a line of covered telegraph wires laid under the sea or underground **3** a telegram sent by such a line **4** an underground wire **5** *informal* cable television

cable car a small carriage suspended from a moving cable

cable television a service transmitting television programmes to individual subscribers by underground cable

cacao *noun* a tree from whose seeds cocoa and chocolate are made

cache *noun* **1** a store or hiding place for ammunition, treasure, *etc* **2** things hidden

cackle *noun* **1** the sound made by a hen or goose **2** a laugh which sounds like this

cactus *noun* (*plural* **cactuses** *or* **cacti**) a type of prickly plant

caddie *noun* an assistant who carries a golfer's clubs

caddy *noun* (*plural* **caddies**) a box for keeping tea fresh

cadet (*pronounced* ka-**det**) *noun* **1** an officer trainee in the armed forces or police service **2** a school pupil who takes military training

cadge *verb* to beg ■ **cadger** *noun*

| **cadge** ▶ cadges, cadging, cadged

Caesarean (*pronounced* se-*zeir*-ri-*an*) *adjective* of a birth: performed by cutting through the walls of the mother's abdomen ■ *noun* (*also called:* **Caesarean section**) a Caesarean birth or operation

café *noun* a small restaurant serving coffee, tea, snacks, *etc*

cafeteria *noun* a self-service restaurant

caffeine *noun* a stimulating drug found in coffee and tea

caftan *or* **kaftan** *noun* a long-sleeved, ankle-length Middle-Eastern garment

cage *noun* a barred enclosure for birds or animals ■ *verb* to close up in a cage

| **cage** *verb* ► cages, caging, caged

cagey *or* **cagy** *adjective* unwilling to speak freely; wary
■ **caginess** *noun*

cagoule *noun* a lightweight anorak

cahoots *noun plural*: **in cahoots with** in collusion with

cairn *noun* **1** a heap of stones marking a grave, or on top of a mountain **2** a breed of small terrier

cajole *verb* to coax by flattery
■ **cajolery** *noun*

cake *noun* **1** a baked piece of dough made from flour, eggs, sugar, *etc* **2** something pressed into a lump: *cake of soap* ■ *verb* to become dry and hard

calamine *noun* a pink powder containing a zinc salt, used to make a skin-soothing lotion

calamitous *adjective* extremely unfortunate, disastrous

calamity *noun* (*plural* **calamities**) a great disaster, a misfortune

calcium *noun* a silvery-white metallic element which forms the chief part of lime and is a basic component of teeth, bones and leaves

calculate *verb* **1** to count, work out by mathematics **2** to think out in an exact way

calculating *adjective* thinking selfishly

calculation *noun* a mathematical reckoning, a sum

calculator *noun* a machine which makes mathematical calculations

calculus *noun* a mathematical system of calculation

calendar *noun* a table or list showing the year divided into months, weeks and days

calf [1] *noun* (*plural* **calves**) **1** the young of a cow or ox **2** the young of certain other mammals, *eg* an elephant or whale

calf [2] *noun* (*plural* **calves**) the back of the lower part of the leg

calibre *or US* **caliber** *noun* **1** the measurement across the opening of a tube or gun **2** of a person: quality of character, ability

♦* This is one of a large number of words which are spelled with an **-re** ending in British English, but with an **-er** in American English, *eg* centre/center, metre/meter, lustre/luster

calico *noun* a patterned kind of cotton cloth

call *verb* 1 to cry aloud 2 to name 3 to summon 4 to make a short visit 5 to telephone ■ *noun* 1 a loud cry 2 a short visit 3 a telephone conversation ■ **call off** to cancel

call centre a building where workers provide a company's telephone services

calling *noun* a vocation, a job

callipers *or* **calipers** *noun plural* 1 an instrument like compasses, used to measure thickness 2 **calliper** a splint to support the leg, made of two metal rods

callous *adjective* cruel, hardhearted ■ **callously** *adverb* ■ **callousness** *noun*

♦* Do not confuse with: **callus**

callus *noun* (*plural* **calluses**) an area of thickened or hardened skin

♦* Do not confuse with: **callous**

calm *adjective* 1 still or quiet 2 not anxious or flustered ■ *noun* 1 absence of wind 2 quietness,

peacefulness ■ *verb* to make peaceful ■ **calmly** *adverb*

calorie *noun* 1 a measure of heat 2 a measure of the energy-giving value of food

calve *verb* to give birth to a calf

calypso *noun* (*plural* **calypsos**) a West Indian improvised song

calyx (*pronounced* kal-iks) *noun* (*plural* **calyces** – *pronounced* kal-i-seez – *or* **calyxes**) the outer covering or cup of a flower

camaraderie *noun* comradeship, fellowship

camber *noun* a slight curve on a road *etc* making the middle higher than the sides

camcorder *noun* a hand-held device combining a video camera and video recorder

came *past form of* **come**

camel *noun* an animal native to Asia and Africa, with a humped back, used for transport

cameo *noun* (*plural* **cameos**) a gem or stone with a figure carved in relief

camera *noun* an instrument for taking photographs

camisole *noun* a woman's undervest with thin shoulder straps

camomile *noun* a plant with pale yellow flowers, used as a medicinal herb

camouflage (*pronounced* kam-ouf-lahsz) *noun* 1 the disguising of the appearance of something to blend in with its background

2 natural protective colouring in animals ▪ *verb* to disguise by camouflage

camp *noun* **1** a group of tents, caravans, *etc* forming a temporary settlement **2** fixed military quarters ▪ *verb* **1** to pitch tents **2** to set up a temporary home ▪ **camper** *noun*

campaign *noun* **1** organized action in support of a cause or movement **2** a planned series of battles or movements during a war ▪ *verb* **1** to organize support **2** to serve in a military campaign ▪ **campaigner** *noun*

camp bed a small portable folding bed

camphor *noun* a pungent solid oil obtained from a cinnamon tree, or a synthetic substitute for it, used to repel insects *etc*

campsite *noun* an area set aside for pitching tents

campus *noun* (*plural* **campuses**) the grounds and buildings of a university or college

can[1] *verb* **1** to be able to (do something) **2** to have permission to (do something)

| **can**[1] ► *present form* **can**, *past form* **could**

can[2] *noun* a sealed tin container for preserving food or liquids ▪ *verb* to put into a sealed tin to preserve

| **can**[2] *verb* ► **cans**, **can**n*ing*, **can**n*ed*

canal *noun* an artificial waterway for boats

canary *noun* (*plural* **canaries**) a songbird with yellow plumage, kept as a pet

cancan *noun* a high-kicking dance performed by women

cancel *verb* **1** to put off permanently, call off **2** to mark for deletion by crossing with lines ▪ **cancellation** *noun* ▪ **cancel out** to make ineffective by balancing each other

| **cancel** ► **cancels**, **cancel**l*ing*, **cancel**l*ed*

cancer *noun* a serious disease in which cells in the body grow rapidly into lumps which can spread and may cause death ▪ **cancerous** *adjective*

candid *adjective* frank, open, honest ▪ **candidly** *adverb*

candidacy *or* **candidature** *noun* the state of being a candidate for something

candidate *noun* **1** an entrant for an examination, or competitor for a job, prize, *etc* **2** an entrant in a political election

candied *adjective* cooked or coated in sugar

candle *noun* a stick of wax containing a wick, used for giving light

candlestick *noun* a holder for a candle

candour *or US* **candor** *noun* frankness, honesty

candy *noun* **1** sugar crystallized

by boiling **2** *US* (*plural* **candies**) sweets, chocolate

candy floss a fluffy mass of spun sugar served on a stick

cane *noun* **1** the woody stem of bamboo, sugar cane, *etc* **2** a walking stick ▪ *verb* to beat with a cane

cane sugar sugar extracted from sugar cane

canine *adjective* of dogs

canine tooth a sharp-pointed tooth found on each side of the upper and lower jaw

canister *noun* a tin or other container for tea *etc*

canker *noun* **1** a spreading sore **2** a disease in trees, plants, *etc*

cannabis *noun* a narcotic drug obtained from the hemp plant

canned music pre-recorded bland music

cannibal *noun* someone who eats human flesh ▪ **cannibalism** *noun* ▪ **cannibalistic** *adjective*

cannon *noun* a large gun mounted on a wheel-carriage

✒* Do not confuse with: **canon**

cannonball *noun* a solid metal ball shot from a cannon

cannot *verb* **1** used with another verb to express inability to do something: *I cannot understand this* **2** used to refuse permission: *he cannot see me today*

canny *adjective* wise, shrewd, cautious ▪ **cannily** *adverb*

canoe *noun* a light narrow boat driven by paddles

canon *noun* **1** a member of the Anglican clergy connected with a cathedral **2** a list of saints

✒* Do not confuse with: **cannon**

canonization or **canonisation** *noun* the process of making someone a saint

canonize or **canonise** *verb* to put on the list of saints

canopy *noun* (*plural* **canopies**) a canvas or cloth covering suspended over a bed *etc*

cant[1] *noun* **1** insincere talk **2** the slang or vocabulary used by a particular group of people

cant[2] *noun* a slope, an incline ▪ *verb* to tilt from a level position

can't *short for* cannot

cantankerous *adjective* crotchety, bad-tempered, quarrelsome

cantata *noun* a short piece of music for a choir

canteen *noun* **1** a place serving food and drink **2** a case for storing cutlery

canter *verb* to move at an easy gallop ▪ *noun* an easy gallop

cantilever *noun* a large projecting bracket used to support a balcony or staircase

cantilever bridge a bridge consisting of upright piers with cantilevers extending to meet one another

canton noun a federal state in Switzerland

canvas noun (plural **canvases**) 1 coarse, strong cloth used for sails, tents, etc 2 a piece of this stretched and used for painting on

canvass verb to go round asking for votes, money, etc ■ **canvasser** noun

canyon noun a deep, steep-sided river valley

cap noun 1 a peaked soft hat 2 a lid, a top ■ verb 1 to put a cap on 2 to set a limit to (a budget etc) 3 to do better than, improve on 4 to select for a national sports team

| **cap** verb ► **caps**, **cap**ping, **cap**ped

capability noun (plural **capabilities**) the ability, potential or skill to do something

capable adjective able to cope with difficulties without help

capably adverb in an efficient and confident way

capacious adjective roomy, wide

capacitor noun a device for collecting and storing electricity

capacity noun (plural **capacities**) 1 power of understanding 2 ability to do something: capacity for growth 3 the amount that something can hold 4 post, position: in my capacity as leader

cape¹ noun a thick shawl or covering for the shoulders

cape² noun a point of land running into the sea

caper¹ verb to leap, dance about ■ noun 1 a leap 2 informal a prank, an adventure

caper² noun the flower-bud of a shrub, pickled or salted for eating

capillary noun (plural **capillaries**) a tiny blood vessel ■ adjective very fine, like a hair

capital adjective 1 chief, most important 2 bringing a possible punishment of death: capital offence 3 informal excellent 4 of a letter: written or printed in upper case, eg A, B or C ■ noun 1 the chief city of a country 2 an upper-case letter 3 money for running a business 4 money invested, accumulated wealth

capitalism noun a system in which a country's wealth is owned by individuals, not by the State

capitalist noun someone who supports or practises capitalism ■ **capitalistic** adjective

capitalize or **capitalise** verb 1 to write in capital letters 2 to turn to your advantage

capital punishment punishment by death

capitulate verb to give in to an enemy

capitulation noun the act of giving in to an enemy

cappuccino (pronounced kap-e-chee-no) noun (plural **cappuccinos**) coffee made with frothy milk

caprice *noun* a sudden, impulsive change of mind or mood

capricious *adjective* full of caprice; impulsive, fickle

capsize *verb* to upset, overturn

capstan *noun* a device used for winding in heavy ropes on a ship or quay

capsule *noun* 1 a small gelatine case containing a dose of medicine *etc* 2 a dry seed-pod on a plant 3 a self-contained, detachable part of a spacecraft

captain *noun* 1 the commander of a company of soldiers, a ship or an aircraft 2 the leader of a sports team, club, *etc* ▪ *verb* to lead

captaincy *noun* (*plural* **captaincies**) the rank of captain

caption *noun* the words that accompany a newspaper article, photograph, *etc*

captivate *verb* to charm, fascinate

captive *noun* a prisoner ▪ *adjective* 1 taken or kept prisoner 2 not able to get away: *captive audience*

captivity *noun* 1 the state of being a prisoner 2 the enclosure of an animal in a zoo *etc*, not in the wild

captor *noun* someone who takes a prisoner

capture *verb* 1 to take by force 2 to get hold of; seize: *capture the imagination* ▪ *noun* the act of capturing

car *noun* a small enclosed motor vehicle

carafe *noun* a bottle for serving wine, water, *etc*

caramel *noun* 1 sugar melted and browned 2 a sweet made with sugar and butter

carat *noun* 1 a measure of purity for gold 2 a measure of weight for gemstones

💧* Do not confuse with: carrot

caravan *noun* 1 a covered vehicle with living accommodation drawn behind a car 2 a number of travellers *etc* crossing the desert together

caraway *noun* a plant with spicy seeds used in cooking

carbohydrate *noun* a compound of carbon, hydrogen and oxygen, *eg* sugar or starch

carbon *noun* an element of which charcoal is one form

carbonate *noun* a compound which contains the chemical group CO_3 ▪ *verb* to add carbon dioxide to something, *eg* a fizzy drink ▪ **carbonated** *adjective*

carbon copy 1 a copy of a document made by using carbon paper 2 an exact copy

carbon dioxide a gas present in the air and breathed out by humans and animals

carbon monoxide a poisonous gas with no smell

carbon paper paper coated

with black ink, interleaved between ordinary paper when typing to produce exact copies

carbuncle *noun* an inflamed swelling under the skin

carburettor or **carburetter** or *US* **carburetor** *noun* the part of a car engine which changes the petrol into vapour

carcass or **carcase** *noun* the dead body (of an animal)

carcinogen *noun* a substance that encourages the growth of cancer

carcinogenic *adjective* causing cancer

carcinoma *noun* (*plural* **carcinomas** or **carcinomata**) a cancerous growth

card *noun* **1** very thick paper **2** an illustrated, folded square of paper sent in greeting *etc* **3 cards** any of the many types of games played with a pack of special cards

cardboard *noun* very thick, stiff paper

cardiac *adjective* of the heart

cardigan *noun* a knitted woollen jacket

cardinal *adjective* principal, important ■ *noun* the highest rank of priest in the Roman Catholic Church

cardinal number a number which expresses quantity, *eg* 1, 2, 3 (*contrasted with*: **ordinal number**)

care *noun* **1** close attention **2** worry, anxiety **3** protection,

keeping ■ *verb* to be concerned or worried ■ **care for 1** to look after **2** to feel affection or liking for ■ **take care** to be careful; watch out

career *noun* life work; trade, profession ■ *verb* to run rapidly and wildly

carefree *adjective* having no worries

careful *adjective* attentive, taking care ■ **carefully** *adverb*

careless *adjective* paying little attention; not taking care ■ **carelessly** *adverb*

carer *noun* someone who looks after someone who cannot look after themselves

caress *verb* to touch gently and lovingly ■ *noun* (*plural* **caresses**) a gentle touch

caretaker *noun* someone who looks after a building

careworn *adjective* worn out by anxiety

cargo *noun* (*plural* **cargoes**) a ship's load

caribou *noun* the North American reindeer

caricature *noun* a picture of someone which exaggerates certain of their features ■ *verb* to draw a caricature of ■ **caricaturist** *noun*

carnage *noun* slaughter, killing

carnation *noun* a type of garden flower, often pink, red or white

carnival *noun* a celebration with merriment, feasting, *etc*

carnivore *noun* a flesh-eating animal

carnivorous *adjective* eating meat or flesh

carol *noun* a hymn or song sung at Christmas

caroller *noun* a person who sings carols

carolling *noun* the singing of carols

carousel *noun* 1 *US* a merry-go-round 2 a rotating conveyor belt for luggage at an airport *etc*

carp[1] *noun* a freshwater fish found in ponds

carp[2] *verb* to find fault with small errors; complain about nothing

car park a place where cars *etc* may be left for a time

carpel *noun* the female part of a flower

carpenter *noun* a worker in wood, *eg* for building

carpentry *noun* the trade of a carpenter

carpet *noun* the woven covering of floors, stairs, *etc* ▪ *verb* to cover with a carpet

carriage *noun* 1 a vehicle for carrying people 2 the act or cost of carrying 3 a way of walking; bearing

carrier *noun* 1 someone who carries goods 2 a machine or container for carrying 3 someone who passes on a disease

carrier pigeon a pigeon used to carry messages

carrion *noun* rotting animal flesh

carrot *noun* a vegetable with an edible orange-coloured root

🖊️✳ Do not confuse with: **carat**

carry *verb* 1 to pick up and take to another place 2 to contain and take to a destination: *cables carrying electricity* 3 of a voice: to be able to be heard at a distance ▪ **carried away** overcome by emotion; overexcited ▪ **carry on** to continue (doing) ▪ **carry out** to accomplish; succeed in doing

| **carry** ▶ carries, carry*ing*, carr*ied*

carry-on *noun* a fuss, a to-do

cart *noun* 1 a horse-drawn vehicle used for carrying loads 2 a small wheeled vehicle pushed by hand ▪ *verb* to drag, haul

cart-horse *noun* a large, heavy work-horse

cartilage *noun* a strong elastic material in the bodies of humans and animals; gristle

carton *noun* a small container made of cardboard, plastic, *etc*

cartoon *noun* 1 a comic drawing, or strip of drawings, often with a caption 2 an animated film 3 a drawing used as the basis for a large painting *etc*

cartoonist *noun* someone who draws cartoons

cartridge *noun* 1 a case holding the powder and bullet fired by a gun 2 a spool of film or tape enclosed in a case

cartwheel *noun* 1 the wheel of a

cart **2** a sideways somersault with hands touching the ground

carve verb **1** to make or shape by cutting **2** to cut up (meat) into slices

cascade noun **1** a waterfall **2** an abundant hanging display: *cascade of curls* ■ verb to fall like or in a waterfall

case noun **1** a container or outer covering **2** that which happens, an occurrence **3** a statement of facts, an argument **4** state of affairs, what is true: *if that is the case* **5** a trial in a law-court

casement noun **1** a window-frame **2** a window that swings on hinges

cash noun money in the form of coins and notes ■ verb to turn into, or change for, money ■ **cash in on** to profit from

cash card a card issued by a bank etc that allows the holder to use a cash dispenser

cashew noun a kidney-shaped nut produced by a tropical tree

cashier noun someone who looks after the receiving and paying of money

cashmere noun fine soft goat's wool

cash register a machine for holding money that records the amount put in

casino (pronounced ka-**see**-noh) noun (plural **casinos**) a building in which gambling takes place

cask noun a barrel containing wine etc

casket noun **1** a small box for holding jewels etc **2** US a coffin

cassava noun a tropical plant with roots from which tapioca is obtained

casserole noun **1** a covered ovenproof dish for cooking and serving food **2** food cooked in a casserole

cassette noun **1** a small case for film, magnetic recording tape, etc **2** the magnetic tape itself

cassock noun a long robe worn by priests

cast verb **1** to throw, fling **2** to throw off; drop, shed **3** to shape in a mould **4** to choose (actors) for a play or film **5** to give a part to (an actor etc) ■ noun **1** something shaped in a mould **2** plaster encasing a broken limb **3** the actors in a play ■ **cast off** used by someone else, second-hand

| **cast** verb ► casts, cast**ing**, cast

castanets noun plural hollow shells of ivory or hard wood, clicked together to accompany a dance

castaway noun a deserted or shipwrecked person

caste noun a class or rank of people, especially in India

caster another spelling of **castor**

castigate verb to scold, punish ■ **castigation** noun

castle noun a fortified house or fortress

castor or **caster** noun a small wheel, eg on the legs of furniture

castor oil or **caster oil** a kind of palm oil used medicinally

castor sugar or **caster sugar** very fine granulated sugar

castrate verb to remove the testicles of

casual adjective **1** happening by chance: casual encounter **2** not regular, temporary: casual labour **3** informal: casual clothes **4** not careful, unconcerned: casual attitude ▪ **casually** adverb

casualty noun (plural **casualties**) **1** someone who is killed or wounded **2** a casualty department

casualty department a hospital department for treating accidental injuries etc

cat noun **1** a sharp-clawed furry animal kept as a pet **2** an animal of the family which includes lions, tigers, etc

catalogue noun an ordered list of names, books, objects for sale, etc ▪ verb **1** to list in order **2** to compile details of (a book) for a library catalogue

catalyst noun **1** a substance which helps a chemical reaction without itself changing **2** something that brings about a change

catalytic converter a device containing catalysts, attached to car engines to reduce the polluting gases produced

catamaran noun a boat with two parallel hulls

catapult noun a small forked stick with a piece of elastic attached, used for firing small stones

cataract noun **1** a waterfall **2** a disease of the outer eye

catarrh noun inflammation of the lining of the nose and throat causing a discharge

catastrophe noun a sudden disaster

catastrophic adjective disastrous, absolutely terrible

cat burglar a burglar who breaks into houses by climbing walls etc

catch verb **1** to take hold of, capture **2** to take (a disease) **3** to be in time for: catch the last train **4** to surprise (in an act): caught him stealing ▪ noun **1** a haul of fish etc **2** something you are lucky to have got or won **3** a hidden flaw or disadvantage **4** a fastening ▪ **catchy** adjective of a tune: easily remembered ▪ **catch on** to become popular ▪ **catch up on 1** to draw level with, overtake **2** to get up-to-date with (work etc)

| **catch** verb ► catch*es*, catch*ing*, caught

catching adjective infectious

catchment area 1 an area from which a river or reservoir draws its water supply **2** an area from which the pupils in a school are drawn

catchphrase *noun* a phrase which is popular for a while

catchword *noun* a word which is popular for a while

categorical *adjective* allowing no doubt or argument

categorically *adverb* in such a sure way that there can be no discussion or argument

categorize or **categorise** *verb* to divide into categories

category *noun* (*plural* **categories**) a class or group of similar people or things

cater *verb* **1** to provide food **2** to supply what is required: *cater for all tastes*

caterer *noun* someone whose job is to provide ready-prepared food and drinks for people

caterpillar *noun* the larva of an insect that feeds on plant leaves

caterwaul *verb* to howl or yell like a cat

cat flap a small door set in a larger door to allow a cat entry and exit

catgut *noun* cord made from sheep's stomachs, used to make strings for violins, harps, *etc*

cathedral *noun* **1** the church of a bishop **2** the chief church in a bishop's district

catherine-wheel *noun* a firework which rotates as it burns

cathode *noun* the negative electrode in a battery (*contrasted with:* **anode**)

cathode ray tube a device in a television set *etc*, which causes a narrow beam of electrons to strike against a screen

Catholic *adjective* of the Roman Catholic Church

catholic *adjective* wide, comprehensive: *a catholic taste in literature*

catkin *noun* a tuft of small flowers on certain trees, *eg* the willow and hazel

cat-o'-nine-tails *noun* a whip with nine lashes

cat's cradle a children's game of creating patterns by winding string around the fingers

Cat's-eye *noun*, *trademark* a small mirror fixed in a road surface to reflect light at night

cattle *noun plural* oxen, bulls and cows, and other grass-eating animals of this family

caught *past form of* **catch**

cauldron *noun* a large pan

cauliflower *noun* a kind of cabbage with an edible white flower-head

cause *noun* **1** that which makes something happen **2** a reason for action: *cause for complaint* **3** an aim for which a group or person works ■ *verb* to make happen

causeway *noun* a raised road over wet ground or shallow water

caustic *adjective* **1** burning, corroding **2** bitter, severe: *caustic wit*

caution *noun* carefulness

because of potential danger **2** a warning ■ *verb* to warn

cautionary *adjective* giving a warning

cautious *adjective* careful, showing caution

cavalcade *noun* a procession on horseback, in cars, *etc*

cavalier *noun*, *history* a supporter of the king in the English Civil War of the 17th century

cavalry *noun* soldiers mounted on horses

cave *noun* a hollow place in the earth or in rock ■ **cave in** to fall or collapse inwards

caveman, **cavewoman** *noun* a prehistoric cave-dweller

cavern *noun* a deep hollow place in the earth

cavernous *adjective* huge and hollow

caviare or **caviar** *noun* the pickled eggs of the sturgeon

cavity *noun* (*plural* **cavities**) **1** a hollow place, a hole **2** a decayed hollow in a tooth

cavort *verb* to dance or leap around

caw *verb* to call like a crow ■ *noun* a crow's call

CD *abbreviation* compact disc

CD burner or **CD recorder** a device used to record data onto compact discs

CD-ROM *abbreviation* compact disc read-only memory

cease *verb* to come or bring to an end

ceasefire *noun* **1** an order to stop firing weapons **2** an agreed, although maybe temporary, end to active hostilities

ceaseless *adjective* without stopping

cedar *noun* a large evergreen tree with a hard sweet-smelling wood

cede *verb* to yield, give up

ceilidh or *Irish* **ceili** (*pronounced* kei-li) *noun* an event involving traditional Scottish or Irish dancing, sometimes combined with musical performances

ceiling *noun* **1** the inner roof of a room **2** an upper limit

celandine *noun* a small yellow wild-flower

celebrate *verb* to commemorate an event (*eg* a birthday or marriage) by going out, having a party, *etc* ■ **celebrated** *adjective* famous ■ **celebration** *noun*

celebrity *noun* (*plural* **celebrities**) **1** a famous person, a star **2** fame

celery *noun* a type of vegetable with edible fibrous stalks

celestial *adjective* **1** of the sky **2** heavenly

cell *noun* **1** a small room in a prison, monastery, *etc* **2** the smallest, fundamental part of living things **3** the part of an electric battery containing electrodes

cellar *noun* an underground room used for storing coal, wine, *etc*

cellist (*pronounced* chel-ist) *noun* someone who plays the cello

cello (*pronounced* chel-oh) *noun* (*short for* **violoncello**) a stringed musical instrument, similar in shape to a violin but much larger

cellophane *noun, trademark* a thin transparent wrapping material

cellphone *noun* a pocket telephone for use in a cellular radio system based on a network of transmitters

cellular *adjective* made of or having cells

celluloid *noun* a very hard elastic substance used for making photographic film *etc*

cellulose *noun* a substance found in plants and wood used to make paper, textiles, *etc*

Celsius *adjective* **1** of a temperature scale: consisting of a hundred degrees, on which water freezes at 0° and boils at 100° **2** of a degree: measured on this scale: *10° Celsius*

Celtic *adjective & noun* **1** (of) a group of ancient peoples of Europe, or their descendants in Wales, Scotland and Ireland **2** (of) their languages

cement *noun* **1** the mixture of clay and lime used to secure bricks in a wall **2** something used to make two things stick together ▪ *verb* **1** to put together with cement **2** to join firmly, fix: *cemented their friendship*

cemetery *noun* (*plural* cemeteries) a place where the dead are buried

cenotaph *noun* a monument to someone or a group buried elsewhere

censer *noun* a container for burning incense in a church

♦* Do not confuse: **censer**, **censor** and **censure**

censor *noun* someone whose job is to examine books, films, *etc* with power to delete any of the contents ▪ *verb* to examine (books *etc*) in this way

♦* Do not confuse: **censor**, **censer** and **censure**

censure *noun* blame, expression of disapproval ▪ *verb* to blame, criticize

♦* Do not confuse: **censure**, **censer** and **censor**

census *noun* (*plural* **censuses**) a periodical official count of the people who live in a country

♦* Do not confuse with: **consensus**

cent *noun* a coin which is the hundredth part of a larger coin, *eg* of a euro or a US dollar

centenary *noun* (*plural* **centenaries**) a hundredth anniversary; the hundredth year since an event took place

centigrade *adjective* **1** of a temperature scale: consisting of a hundred degrees **2** measured on this scale: *5° centigrade* **3** Celsius

centigram or **centigramme**
noun (abbrev **cg**) a hundredth part
of a gram

centilitre noun (abbrev **cl**) a
hundredth part of a litre

centimetre noun (abbrev **cm**) a
hundredth part of a metre

centipede noun a small
crawling insect with many legs

central adjective **1** belonging to
the centre **2** chief, main: *central
point of the argument*

central heating heating of a
building by water, steam or air
from a central point

centralize or **centralise** verb to
group in a single place

central locking a system
whereby all the doors of a vehicle
are locked by the locking of the
driver's door

central nervous system the
brain and spinal cord

centre or US **center** noun **1** the
middle point or part **2** a building
used for some special activity:
sports centre ■ verb to put in the
centre

| centre verb ▶ centres,
| centring, centred

♣* This is one of a large
number of words which are
spelled with an **-re** ending in
British English, but with an **-er**
in American English eg
metre/meter, calibre/caliber,
lustre/luster

centrifugal adjective moving
away from the centre

centripetal adjective moving
towards the centre

centurion noun, history a
commander of 100 Roman
soldiers

century noun (plural **centuries**)
1 a hundred years **2** cricket a
hundred runs

ceramic adjective **1** made of
pottery **2** of pottery-making
■ noun **1** something made of
pottery **2** ceramics the art of
pottery

cereal noun **1** grain used as food
2 a breakfast food prepared from
grain

cerebral adjective of the brain

cerebral palsy a disorder
caused by brain injury at birth,
causing poor muscle control

ceremonial adjective with or of
ceremony ■ **ceremonially** adverb

ceremony noun (plural
ceremonies) the formal acts that
accompany an important event:
marriage ceremony

certain adjective **1** sure; not to be
doubted **2** fixed, settled **3**
particular but unnamed: *certain
places*

certainly adverb **1** definitely,
without any doubt **2** of course

certainty noun (plural
certainties) **1** a sure thing **2** the
quality of being certain

certificate noun a written or
printed statement giving details

of a birth, passed examination, *etc*

certify *verb* to put down in writing as an official promise or statement *etc*

| **certify** ► certif**ies**, certify**ing**, certif**ied**

chador (*pronounced* **chud**-er) *noun* a thick veil worn by Muslim women

chafe *verb* 1 to make hot or sore by rubbing 2 to wear away by rubbing 3 to become annoyed

chaff *noun* 1 husks of corn left after threshing 2 something of little value 3 good-natured teasing ■ *verb* to tease jokingly

chaffinch *noun* (*plural* **chaffinches**) a small songbird of the finch family

chagrin (*pronounced* **sha**-grin) *noun* annoyance, irritation

chain *noun* 1 a number of metal links or rings passing through one another 2 chains these used to tie a prisoner's limbs; fetters 3 a number of connected things: *mountain chain* 4 a group of shops owned by one person or company 5 a number of atoms of an element joined together ■ *verb* to fasten or imprison with a chain

chain letter a letter containing promises or threats, requesting the recipient to send a similar letter to several other people

chain mail armour made of iron links

chain reaction a chemical process in which each reaction in turn causes a similar reaction

chain saw a power-driven saw with teeth on a rotating chain

chain store one of several shops under the same ownership

chair *noun* 1 a seat for one person with a back to it 2 a chairman or chairwoman

chairlift *noun* a row of chairs on a rotating cable for carrying people up mountains *etc*

chairman, **chairperson**, **chairwoman** *noun* someone who presides at or is in charge of a meeting

chalet (*pronounced* **shal**-ei) *noun* 1 a small wooden house used by holidaymakers 2 a summer hut used by Swiss herdsmen in the Alps

chalice *noun* a cup for wine, used *eg* in church services

chalk *noun* 1 a type of limestone 2 a compressed stick of coloured powder used for writing or drawing ■ *verb* to mark with chalk

chalky *adjective* 1 of chalk 2 white, pale

challenge *verb* 1 to question another's right to do something 2 to ask (someone) to take part in a contest, *eg* to settle a quarrel ■ *noun* 1 a questioning of another's right 2 a call to a contest

challenger *noun* someone who challenges a person such as a champion to a competition for their status

challenging *adjective* interesting but difficult

chamber *noun* **1** a room **2** a place where a parliament meets **3** a room where legal cases are heard by a judge **4** an enclosed space or cavity **5** the part of a gun that holds the cartridges

chamber music music for a small group of players, suitable for performance in a room rather than a large hall

chameleon (*pronounced ka-meel-*yon) *noun* a small lizard able to change its colour to match its surroundings

chamois *noun* **1** (*pronounced* **sham-**wah) a goat-like deer living in mountainous country **2** (*pronounced* **sham-**i) (*also spelt* **shammy**) a soft leather made from its skin

champagne *noun* a type of white sparkling wine

champion *noun* **1** someone who has beaten all others in a competition **2** a strong supporter of a cause ■ *verb* to support the cause of

championship *noun* a contest to find a champion

chance *noun* **1** a risk, a possibility **2** something unexpected or unplanned **3** an opportunity ■ *verb* **1** to risk **2** to happen by accident ■ *adjective* happening by accident ■ **chance upon** to meet or find unexpectedly

chancellor *noun* a high-ranking government minister
■ **Chancellor of the Exchequer** the minister in the British cabinet in charge of government spending

chancy *adjective* risky

chandelier *noun* a fixture hanging from the ceiling with branches for holding lights

change *verb* **1** to make or become different **2** to give up or leave (a job, house, *etc*) for another **3** to put on different clothes **4** to give (money of one kind) in exchange for (money of another kind) ■ *noun* **1** the act of making or becoming different **2** another set of clothing **3** money in the form of coins **4** money returned when a buyer gives more than the price of an article

| **change** *verb* ► changes, changing, changed

changeable *adjective* likely to change; often changing

channel *noun* **1** the bed of a stream **2** a passage for ships **3** a narrow sea **4** a groove; a gutter **5** a band of frequencies for radio or television signals ■ *verb* to direct into a particular course

| **channel** *verb* ► channels, channelling, channelled

chant *verb* to recite in a singing manner ■ *noun* a singing recitation

Chanukkah *see* **Hanukkah**

chaos *noun* disorder, confusion

chaotic *adjective* disordered, confused

chap *noun, informal* a man

chapati *or* **chapatti** *noun* a round of unleavened Indian bread

chapel *noun* **1** a small church **2** a small part of a larger church

chaperon *or* **chaperone** *noun* a woman who attends a younger one when she goes out in public ■ *verb* to act as a chaperon to

chaplain *noun* a member of the clergy accompanying an army, navy, *etc*

chapped *adjective* of skin: cracked by cold or wet weather

chapter *noun* a division of a book

char *verb* to burn until black

| **char** ▶ chars, charr*ing*, charr*ed*

character *noun* **1** the nature and qualities of someone **2** self-control, firmness **3** someone noted for eccentric behaviour **4** someone in a play, story or film

characteristic *noun* a typical and noticeable feature of someone or something ■ *adjective* typical

characteristically *adverb* typically, as always

characterize *or* **characterise** *verb* to be typical of

charade *noun* **1** a ridiculous pretence **2 charades** a game in which players have to guess a word from gestures representing its sound or meaning

charcoal *noun* wood burnt black, used for fuel or sketching

charge *verb* **1** to accuse **2** to ask (a price) **3** to ask to do; give responsibility for **4** to attack in a rush ■ *noun* **1** accusation for a crime **2** a price, a fee **3** an attack **4** care, responsibility ■ **in charge** in command or control

| **charge** *verb* ▶ charges, charg*ing*, charg*ed*

chariot *noun, history* a wheeled carriage used in battle

charisma *noun* a personal quality that impresses others

charismatic *adjective* full of charisma or charm

charitable *adjective* giving to the poor; kindly

charity *noun* (*plural* **charities**) **1** donation of money to the poor *etc* **2** an organization which collects money and gives it to those in need **3** kindness, humanity

charlatan (*pronounced* shah-lat-an) *noun* someone who claims greater powers or abilities than they really have

charm *noun* **1** something thought to have magical powers **2** a magical spell **3** personal power to attract ■ *verb* **1** to please greatly, delight **2** to put under a spell

charming *adjective* lovely, delightful

chart *noun* **1** a table or diagram giving particular information **2** a geographical map of the sea **3** a rough map ■ *verb* to make into a chart; plot

charter *noun* a written paper showing the official granting of rights, lands, *etc* ■ *verb* to hire (a boat, aeroplane, *etc*)

chartered *adjective* **1** qualified under the regulations of a professional body: *chartered surveyor* **2** hired for a purpose

charwoman *noun* a woman hired to do domestic cleaning *etc*

chase *verb* to run after, pursue ■ *noun* a pursuit, a hunt

chasm (*pronounced* ka-zm) *noun* **1** a steep drop between high rocks *etc* **2** a wide difference; a gulf

chassis (*pronounced* shas-i) *noun* (*plural* **chassis** – *pronounced* shas-iz) **1** the frame, wheels and machinery of a car **2** an aeroplane's landing carriage

chaste *adjective* pure, virtuous

chastity *noun* sexual purity and virtue

chat *verb* to talk in an easy, friendly way ■ *noun* a friendly conversation

| **chat** *verb* ► chats, chatt*ing*, chatt*ed*

chat room a place on the Internet where people can exchange messages

chat show a radio or TV programme in which personalities talk informally with their host

chatter *verb* **1** to talk idly or rapidly; gossip **2** of teeth: to rattle together because of cold

chatterbox *noun* someone who talks a great deal

chatty *adjective* willing to talk, talkative

chauffeur (*pronounced* shoh-fer) *noun* someone employed to drive a car

chauvinism *noun* **1** extreme nationalism or patriotism **2** sexism towards women
■ **chauvinist** *noun* ■ **chauvinistic** *adjective*

cheap *adjective* **1** low in price, inexpensive **2** of little value, worthless

cheapen *verb* to make cheap

cheaply *adverb* for a low price

cheat *verb* **1** to deceive **2** to act dishonestly to gain an advantage ■ *noun* **1** someone who cheats **2** a dishonest trick

check *verb* **1** to bring to a stop **2** to hold back, restrain **3** to see if (a total *etc*) is correct or accurate **4** to see if (a machine *etc*) is in good condition or working properly ■ *noun* **1** a sudden stop **2** a restraint **3** a test of correctness or accuracy **4** a pattern of squares ■ **check in** *or* **check out** to record your arrival at or departure from (a hotel *etc*)

> ✱ Do not confuse with: **cheque**

checked *adjective* patterned with squares

checkered *another spelling of* **chequered**

checkers *another spelling of* **chequers**

checkmate *noun, chess* a position from which the king cannot escape

checkout *noun* a place where payment is made in a supermarket

cheek *noun* **1** the side of the face below the eye **2** insolence, disrespectful behaviour

cheeky *adjective* impudent, insolent ▪ **cheekily** *adverb*

cheep *verb* to make a faint sound like a small bird ▪ *noun* the sound of a small bird

cheer *noun* a shout of approval or welcome ▪ *verb* **1** to shout approval **2** to encourage, urge on ▪ **cheer up** to make or become less gloomy

cheerful *adjective* happy, in good spirits ▪ **cheerfully** *adverb*

cheerio *exclamation* goodbye!

cheerless *adjective* sad, gloomy

cheers *exclamation* **1** good health! **2** regards, best wishes

cheery *adjective* lively and merry ▪ **cheerily** *adverb*

cheese *noun* a solid food made from milk

cheesecake *noun* a cake with a biscuit base topped with sweet cream cheese

cheesy *adjective* **1** tasting of cheese **2** of a smile: broad **3** *informal* inferior, cheap

cheetah *noun* a member of the cat family with a spotted coat, the fastest land mammal

chef *noun* a head cook in a restaurant

chemical *adjective* relating to the reactions between elements *etc* ▪ *noun* a substance formed by or used in a chemical process

chemist *noun* someone who makes up and sells medicines; a pharmacist

chemistry *noun* the study of the elements and the ways they combine or react with each other

chemotherapy (*pronounced* keem-oh-**the**-rap-i) *noun* treatment of infectious diseases or cancer using chemical compounds

cheque *or US* **check** *noun* a written order to a banker to pay money from a bank account to another person

⚠️ Do not confuse with: check

chequered *or* **checkered** *adjective* marked like a chessboard

chequers *or* **checkers** *noun singular* the game of draughts

cherish *verb* to protect and treat with fondness or kindness

cherry *noun* (*plural* **cherries**) **1** a small bright-red fruit with a stone **2** the tree that produces this fruit

cherub *noun* (*plural* **cherubs** *or* **cherubim**) **1** an angel with a plump, childish face and body **2** a beautiful child

chess *noun* a game for two players in which pieces are moved in turn on a board marked in alternate black and white squares

chessman or **chesspiece** *noun* one of the figures which you move on a chessboard when playing chess

chest *noun* **1** a large strong box **2** the part of the body between the neck and the stomach

chestnut *noun* **1** a reddish-brown edible nut (**sweet chestnut**), or the tree that produces it **2** a reddish-brown inedible nut (**horse chestnut**), or the tree that produces it **3** a reddish-brown horse

chest of drawers a piece of furniture fitted with a set of drawers

chevron *noun* a V-shape, eg on a badge or road sign

chew *verb* to break up (food) with the teeth before swallowing

chic *adjective* smart and fashionable

chick *noun* a chicken

chicken *noun* the young of birds, especially of domestic poultry ▪ *adjective, informal* cowardly

chickenfeed *noun* **1** food for poultry **2** something paltry or worthless

chickenpox *noun* an infectious disease which causes red, itchy spots

chickpea *noun* a plant of the pea family with a brown edible seed

chicory *noun* a plant with sharp-tasting leaves eaten in salads

chide *verb* to scold with words

chief *adjective* main, most important ▪ *noun* a leader or ruler

chiefly *adverb* mainly, for the most part

chieftain *noun* the head of a clan or tribe

chiffon *noun* a thin flimsy material made of silk or nylon

chihuahua (*pronounced* chi-wah-wah) *noun* a breed of very small dog, originally from Mexico

chilblain *noun* a painful swelling on hands and feet, caused by constricted blood vessels in cold weather

child *noun* (*plural* **children**) **1** a young human being **2** a son or daughter

childhood *noun* the time of being a child

childish *adjective* **1** of or like a child **2** silly, immature ▪ **childishly** *adverb*

childlike *adjective* innocent

childminder *noun* a person who is paid to look after other people's children in his or her home

children *plural* of **child**

chili *another spelling of* **chilli**

chill *noun* **1** coldness **2** an illness that causes fever and shivering **3** lack of warmth or enthusiasm ▪ *verb* **1** to make cold **2** to refrigerate

chilli or **chili** noun 1 the hot-tasting pod of a kind of pepper, sometimes dried for cooking 2 a dish or sauce made with this

chilly adjective cold

|chilly ► chillier, chilliest

chime noun 1 the sound of bells ringing 2 chimes a set of bells, eg in a clock ■ verb 1 to ring 2 of a clock: to strike

chimney noun (plural chimneys) a passage allowing smoke or heated air to escape from a fire

chimpanzee noun a type of African ape

chin noun the part of the face below the mouth

china noun 1 a fine kind of earthenware; porcelain 2 articles made of this

chink noun 1 a narrow opening 2 the sound of coins etc striking together

chintz noun (plural chintzes) a cotton cloth with brightly coloured patterning

chip verb to break or cut small pieces (from or off) ■ noun 1 a small piece chipped off 2 a part damaged by chipping 3 a long thin piece of fried potato 4 see integrated circuit

|chip verb ► chips, chipping, chipped

chipmunk noun a kind of small N American squirrel

chiropodist noun someone who treats minor disorders and diseases of the feet

chiropody noun the profession of caring for people's feet and treating minor foot problems such as verrucas and corns

chirp or **chirrup** verb of a bird: to make a sharp, shrill sound

chirpy adjective merry, cheerful

chisel noun a metal tool to cut or hollow out wood, stone, etc ■ verb to cut with a chisel

|chisel verb ► chisels, chiselling, chiselled

chivalrous adjective gallant, showing traditional good manners especially to women

chivalry noun kindness, especially towards women or the weak

chive noun an onion-like herb used in cooking

chloride noun a compound which contains chlorine and another element

chlorinate verb to add chlorine to

chlorine noun a yellowish-green gas with a sharp smell, used as a bleach and disinfectant

chloroform noun a liquid whose vapour causes unconsciousness if inhaled

chlorophyll noun a green pigment in some plants and algae that traps light energy to use in photosynthesis

chock-a-block adjective completely full or congested

chocolate noun 1 a sweet made from the seeds of the cacao tree

2 (*also called*: **cocoa**) a drink made from these seeds

choice *noun* **1** the act or power of choosing **2** something chosen ▪ *adjective* of a high quality

choir *noun* a group or society of singers

choke *verb* **1** to stop or partly stop the breathing of **2** to block or clog (a pipe *etc*) **3** to have your breathing stopped or interrupted, *eg* by smoke ▪ *noun* a valve in a petrol engine which controls the inward flow of air

cholera (*pronounced* kol-*e-ra*) *noun* an infectious intestinal disease, causing severe vomiting and diarrhoea

cholesterol *noun* a substance found in body cells which carries fats through the bloodstream

choose *verb* **1** to select and take from two or several things **2** to decide, prefer to

| choose ► chooses,
| choosing, chose, chosen

choosy *adjective* difficult to please

chop *verb* to cut into small pieces ▪ *noun* **1** a chopping blow **2** a slice of meat containing a bone

| chop *verb* ► chops,
| chopping, chopped

chopper *noun* **1** a knife or axe for chopping **2** *informal* a helicopter

choppy *adjective* of the sea: not calm, having small waves

chopsticks *noun plural* a pair of small sticks of wood, ivory,

etc used for eating Chinese food

choral *adjective* sung by or written for a choir

chord *noun* **1** a musical sound made by playing several notes together **2** a straight line joining any two points on a curve

🔹* Do not confuse with: **cord**

chore *noun* a dull, boring job

choreographer *noun* a person who designs dances and dance steps

choreography *noun* the arrangement of dancing and dance steps

chortle *verb* to laugh, chuckle

chorus *noun* (*plural* **choruses**) **1** a band of singers and dancers **2** a part of a song repeated after each verse

chose *past form* of **choose**

chosen *past participle* of **choose**

christen *verb* to baptize and give a name to

christening *noun* the ceremony of baptism

Christian *noun* a believer in Christianity ▪ *adjective* of Christianity

Christianity *noun* the religion which follows the teachings of Christ

Christian name a first or personal name

Christmas *noun* an annual Christian holiday or festival, in memory of the birth of Christ, held on 25 December

Christmas Eve 24 December

Christmassy *adjective* typical of, or suitable for, Christmas

Christmas tree an evergreen tree hung with lights, decorations and gifts at Christmas

chromatography *noun*, *chemistry* a technique for separating the substances in a mixture

chromium *noun* a hard metallic element which does not rust and is used to plate other metals

chromosome *noun* a rod-like part of a body cell that determines the characteristics of an individual

chronic *adjective* **1** of a disease: long-term and progressing slowly (*compare with*: **acute**) **2** *informal* very bad ▪ **chronically** *adverb*

chronicle *noun* a record of events in order of time ▪ *verb* to write down events in order ▪ **chronicler** *noun*

chronological *adjective* arranged in the order of the time of happening ▪ **chronologically** *adverb*

chronology *noun* the arrangement of events in the order they occurred

chrysalis *noun* an insect (especially a butterfly or moth) in its early stage of life, with no wings and encased in a soft cocoon

chrysanthemum *noun* a type of colourful garden flower with a large bushy head

chubby *adjective* plump

| **chubby** ► chubb*ier*, chubb*iest*

chuck *verb* to throw, toss ▪ **chuck out** *informal* **1** to throw away, get rid of **2** to expel

chuckle *noun* a quiet laugh ▪ *verb* to laugh quietly

chug *verb* of a vehicle: to move along making a thudding noise

| **chug** ► chug*s*, chugg*ing*, chugg*ed*

chum *noun*, *informal* a close friend

chummy *adjective* very friendly

chump *noun* **1** *informal* an idiot **2** a piece of lamb or mutton cut from the loin

chunk *noun* a thick piece

chunky *adjective* heavy, thick

| **chunky** ► chunk*ier*, chunk*iest*

church *noun* (*plural* **churches**) **1** a building for public, especially Christian, worship **2** any group of people who meet together for worship

churchyard *noun* a burial ground next to a church

churlish *adjective* bad-mannered, rude

churn *noun* a machine for making butter from milk ▪ *verb* **1** to make (butter) in a churn **2** to shake or stir about violently

chute *noun* **1** a sloping trough for sending water, parcels, *etc* to a lower level **2** a sloping structure for children to slide down, with steps for climbing back up

chutney noun (plural **chutneys**) a sauce made with vegetables or fruits and vinegar

cider noun an alcoholic drink made from fermented apple juice

cigar noun a roll of tobacco leaves for smoking

cigarette noun a tube of fine tobacco enclosed in thin paper

cinder noun a burnt-out piece of coal

cine camera a hand-held camera for making films

cinema noun 1 a place where films are shown 2 films as an art form or industry

cinnamon noun a yellowish-brown spice obtained from the bark of an Asian tree

cipher noun a secret writing, a code

circle noun 1 a figure formed from an endless curved line 2 something in the form of a circle; a ring 3 a society or group of people 4 a tier of seats in a theatre etc ■ verb 1 to enclose in a circle 2 to move round in a circle

circuit noun 1 a movement in a circle 2 a connected group of places, events, etc: the American tennis circuit 3 the path of an electric current

circuitous adjective not direct, roundabout

circular adjective round, like a circle ■ noun a letter sent round to a number of people

circulate verb 1 to move round 2 to send round

circulation noun 1 the act of circulating 2 the movement of the blood 3 the total sales of a newspaper or magazine

circumference noun 1 the outside line of a circle 2 the length of this line

circumspect adjective wary, cautious

circumstance noun 1 a condition of time, place, etc which affects someone, an action or an event 2 **circumstances** the state of someone's financial affairs

circumstantial adjective of evidence: pointing to a conclusion without giving absolute proof

circus noun (plural **circuses**) a travelling company of acrobats, clowns, etc

cirrhosis noun a disease of the liver

cirrus noun a fleecy kind of cloud

cistern noun a tank for storing water

citadel noun a fortress within a city

citation noun 1 something quoted 2 a summons to appear in court 3 official recognition of an achievement or action

cite verb 1 to quote as an example or as proof 2 to summon to appear in court

⚠* Do not confuse with: **sight** and **site**

citizen *noun* someone who lives in a city or state

citizenship *noun* the rights or state of being a citizen

citrus fruit one of a group of fruits including the orange, lemon and lime

city *noun* (*plural* **cities**) 1 a large town 2 a town with a cathedral

civic *adjective* relating to a city or citizens

civil *adjective* 1 relating to a community 2 non-military, civilian 3 polite

civil engineer an engineer who plans bridges, roads, *etc*

civilian *noun* someone who is not in the armed forces ■ *adjective* non-military

civility *noun* politeness, good manners

civilization *or* **civilisation** *noun* 1 making or becoming civilized 2 life under a civilized system 3 a particular culture: *a prehistoric civilization*

civilize *or* **civilise** *verb* to bring (a people) under a regular system of laws, education, *etc*

civilized *or* **civilised** *adjective* living under a system of laws, education, *etc*; not savage

civil rights the rights of a citizen

civil servant someone who works in the civil service

civil service the paid administrative officials of the country, excluding the armed forces

civil war war between citizens of the same country

claim *verb* 1 to demand as a right 2 to state as a truth; assert (that) ■ *noun* an act of claiming

claimant *noun* someone who makes a claim

clairvoyant *adjective* able to see into the future, or to contact the spirit world ■ *noun* someone with clairvoyant powers ■ **clairvoyance** *noun*

clam *noun* a large shellfish with two shells hinged together

clamber *verb* to climb awkwardly or with difficulty

clammy *adjective* moist and sticky

clamour *noun* a loud, continuous noise or outcry ■ *verb* 1 to cry aloud 2 to make a loud demand (for)

clamp *noun* a piece of metal, wood, *etc* used to fasten things together ■ *verb* to bind with a clamp ■ **clamp down on** to suppress firmly

clan *noun* 1 a number of families with the same surname, traditionally under a single chieftain 2 a sect, a clique

clandestine *adjective* hidden, secret, underhand

clang *verb* to make a loud, deep ringing sound ■ *noun* a loud, deep ring

clank noun a sound like that made by metal hitting metal ■ verb to make this sound

clansman, clanswoman noun a member of a clan

clap noun 1 the noise made by striking together two things, especially the hands 2 a burst of sound, especially thunder ■ verb 1 to strike noisily together 2 to strike the hands together to show approval

| **clap** verb ► claps, clapping, clapped

clapper noun the tongue of a bell

claptrap noun meaningless words, nonsense

claret noun a type of red wine

clarify verb 1 to make clear and understandable 2 to make (a liquid) clear and pure

| **clarify** ► clarifies, clarifying, clarified

clarinet noun a musical wind instrument, usually made of wood

clarinettist noun someone who plays the clarinet

clarity noun clearness

clash noun (plural clashes) 1 a loud noise made by striking swords etc 2 a disagreement, a fight ■ verb 1 to bang noisily together 2 to disagree 3 of events: to take place at the same time 4 of two colours etc: not to look well together

clasp noun 1 a hook or pin for fastening 2 an embrace ■ verb 1 to hold closely; grasp 2 to fasten

class noun (plural classes) 1 a rank or order of people or things 2 a group of school pupils or students taught together 3 a group of plants or animals with something in common ■ verb 1 to place in a class 2 to arrange in some order

classic noun 1 a great book or other work of art 2 something typical and influential of its kind 3 classics the study of ancient Greek and Latin literature ■ adjective 1 excellent 2 standard, typical of its kind: *a classic example* 3 simple and elegant in style

classical adjective 1 of a classic or the classics 2 of music: serious, not light

classification noun 1 the activity of arranging things into classes or categories 2 the label or name that you give something in order to indicate its class or category

classify verb 1 to arrange in classes 2 to put into a class or category 3 to declare (information) to be secret ■ classified adjective

| **classify** ► classifies, classifying, classified

classmate noun a fellow pupil or student in your class

classroom noun a room in a school or college where lessons take place

classy *adjective* elegant, stylish

clatter *noun* a noise of plates *etc* banged together

clause *noun* **1** a part of a sentence containing a verb **2** a part of a will, act of parliament, *etc*

claustrophobia *noun* an abnormal fear of enclosed spaces

claustrophobic *adjective* suffering from or affected by claustrophobia

claw *noun* **1** an animal's or bird's foot with hooked nails **2** a hooked nail on one of these feet ■ *verb* to scratch or tear

clay *noun* soft, sticky earth, often used to make pottery, bricks, *etc*

clean *adjective* **1** free from dirt; pure **2** neat, complete: *a clean break* ■ *verb* to make clean; free from dirt ■ **cleanly** *adverb*

cleaner *noun* someone employed to clean a building *etc*

cleanliness (*pronounced* klen-li-nes) *noun* the quality of being free from dirt

cleanse (*pronounced* klenz) *verb* to make clean

cleanser *noun* a substance that cleanses, especially the skin

clear *adjective* **1** bright, undimmed **2** free from mist or cloud: *clear sky* **3** transparent **4** free from difficulty or obstructions **5** easy to see, hear or understand ■ *verb* **1** to make clear **2** to empty **3** to free from blame **4** to leap over without touching **5** of the sky: to become bright ■ **clearness** *noun* ■ **clear out** *or* **clear off** to go away

clearance *noun* **1** the activity of getting rid of all the things which are in a certain place so that a new start can be made: *a clearance sale* (= a cut-price sale in a shop to get rid of all the old stock) **2** permission to do something

clear-cut *adjective* distinct, obvious

clearing *noun* land free of trees

clearly *adverb* **1** obviously **2** in a clear way

cleavage *noun* **1** splitting **2** the way in which two things are split or divided **3** the hollow between a woman's breasts

cleaver *noun* a heavy knife for splitting meat carcases *etc*

clef *noun* a musical sign, 𝄞 (**treble clef**) or 𝄢 (**bass clef**), placed on a stave to fix the pitch of the notes

cleft *noun* an opening made by splitting; a crack

cleft palate a deformity in the roof of the mouth, present in some people at birth

clench *verb* to press firmly together

clergy *noun plural* the ministers of the Christian Church

clergyman, **clergywoman** *noun* a Christian minister

cleric *noun* a member of the clergy

clerical *adjective* **1** relating to office work **2** of the clergy

clerk *noun* an office worker who writes letters, keeps accounts, *etc*

clever *adjective* quick in learning and understanding ▪ **cleverly** *adverb*

cliché (*pronounced* klee-shei) *noun* an idea, phrase, *etc* that has been used too much and has little meaning

click *noun* a short sharp sound like a clock's tick ▪ *verb* to make this sound

client *noun* **1** a customer of a shop *etc* **2** someone who goes to a lawyer *etc* for advice

clientele (*pronounced* klee-en-tel *or* klai-en-tel) *noun* the customers of a lawyer, shopkeeper, *etc*

cliff *noun* a very steep, rocky slope, especially by the sea

cliffhanger *noun* a story that keeps you in suspense until the end

climate *noun* **1** the weather conditions of a particular area **2** general condition or situation: *the present political climate*

climax *noun* (*plural* **climaxes**) the point of greatest interest or importance in a situation

climb *verb* **1** to go to the top of **2** to go up using hands and feet **3** to slope upward ▪ *noun* an act of climbing

climber *noun* **1** someone who

climbs **2** a plant which climbs up walls *etc*

clinch *verb* to settle (an argument, bargain, *etc*) ▪ *noun* (*plural* **clinches**) **1** *boxing* a position in which the boxers hold each other with their arms **2** a passionate embrace

clincher *noun* the thing which settles (an argument, bargain, *etc*)

cling *verb* to stick or hang on (to) ▪ **clingy** *adjective*

| **cling** ► **clings**, **cling***ing*, **clung**

clingfilm *noun* thin transparent plastic material used to wrap food

clinic *noun* a place or part of a hospital where a particular kind of treatment is given

clinical *adjective* **1** of a clinic **2** of medicine: involving direct contact with patients **3** objective, cool and unemotional

clinically *adverb* according to medical diagnosis: *clinically depressed*

clink *noun* a ringing sound of knocked glasses *etc*

clip *verb* **1** to cut (off) **2** to fasten with a clip ▪ *noun* **1** something clipped off **2** a small fastener

| **clip** *verb* ► **clips**, **clip***ping*, **clip***ped*

clique *noun* a small group of people who help each other but keep others at a distance

cloak *noun* **1** a loose outer

garment **2** something which hides: *cloak of darkness* ■ *verb* **1** to cover as with a cloak **2** to hide

cloakroom *noun* a place where coats, hats, *etc* may be left for a time

clock *noun* a machine for measuring time ■ **clock in** *or* **clock out** to record your time of arrival at, or departure from, work

clockwise *adjective* turning or moving in the same direction as the hands of a clock

clockwork *adjective* worked by machinery such as that of a clock

clod *noun* **1** a thick lump of turf **2** a stupid man

clodhopper *noun* a stupid clumsy person

clog *noun* a shoe with a wooden sole ■ *verb* to block (pipes *etc*)

| **clog** *verb* ► clogs, clogging, clogged

cloister *noun* a covered-in walk in a monastery or convent ■ **cloistered** *adjective* **1** shut up in a monastery *etc* **2** sheltered

clone *noun* **1** a cell or organism from a single ancestor **2** a genetically-engineered copy of a sequence of DNA *etc* ■ *verb* **1** to grow a new cell or organism from a single cell **2** to make copies of a DNA sequence

close[1] *adjective* **1** near in time, place, *etc* **2** without fresh air, stuffy **3** beloved, very dear **4** decided by a small amount:

a close contest ■ *noun* a narrow passage off a street

close[2] *verb* **1** to shut **2** to finish ■ *noun* the end

closed *adjective*, *maths* **1** of a curve: having no end points, as in a circle **2** of a set: having as members the results of an operation (*eg* addition) on other members of the set

closed-circuit television a system of television cameras and receivers for use in shops *etc*

closely *adverb* **1** carefully: *listen closely* **2** strongly, intimately **3** in a way that brings things close together: *packed closely together*

closet *noun*, *US* a cupboard

close-up *noun* a film or photograph taken very near the subject

closure *noun* the act of closing

clot *noun* **1** a lump that forms in blood, cream, *etc* **2** *informal* an idiot ■ *verb* to form into clots

| **clot** *verb* ► clots, clotting, clotted

cloth *noun* **1** woven material of cotton, wool, silk, *etc* **2** a piece of this

clothe *verb* **1** to put clothes on **2** to provide with clothes

clothes *noun plural* things worn to cover the body and limbs, *eg* shirt, trousers, skirt

clothing *noun* clothes

cloud *noun* a mass of tiny drops of water or ice floating in the sky ■ *verb* to become dim or blurred

■ **clouded** *adjective* ■ **cloudless** *adjective*

cloudburst *noun* a sudden heavy fall of rain

cloudy *adjective* 1 darkened with clouds 2 not clear or transparent

clout *noun, informal* 1 a blow 2 influence, power ■ *verb, informal* to hit

clove *noun* 1 a flower bud of the clove tree, used as a spice 2 a small section of a bulb of garlic

cloven-hoofed *adjective* having a divided hoof like an ox, sheep, *etc*

clover *noun* a field plant with leaves usually in three parts

clown *noun* 1 a comedian with a painted face and comical clothes in a circus 2 a fool

cloying *adjective* over-sweet, sickly

club *noun* 1 a heavy stick 2 a stick used to hit the ball in golf 3 a group of people who meet for social events *etc* 4 the place where these people meet 5 **clubs** one of the four suits in playing-cards ■ *verb* to beat with a club

■ **club together** to put money into a joint fund for some purpose

┃ **club** *verb* ► **club**s, **club**b*ing*, **club**b*ed*

cluck *noun* a sound like that made by a hen ■ *verb* to make this sound

clue *noun* a sign or piece of evidence that helps to solve a mystery

clump *noun* a cluster of trees or shrubs ■ *verb* to walk heavily

clumsy *adjective* 1 awkward in movement or actions 2 tactless, thoughtless ■ **clumsily** *adverb*

┃ **clumsy** ► **clumsi**er, **clumsi**est

clung *past form of* **cling**

cluster *noun* 1 a bunch of fruit *etc* 2 a crowd ■ *verb* to group together in clusters

clutch *verb* 1 to hold firmly 2 to seize, grasp ■ *noun (plural* **clutches)** 1 a grasp 2 part of a car engine used for changing gears

clutter *noun* 1 a muddled or disordered collection of things 2 disorder, confusion, untidiness ■ *verb* to fill or cover in an untidy, disordered way

co- *prefix* joint, working with, together with: *co-author/co-driver*

coach *noun (plural* **coaches)** 1 a bus for long-distance travel 2 a closed, four-wheeled horse carriage 3 a railway carriage 4 a trainer or instructor ■ *verb* to train or help to prepare for an examination, sports contest, *etc*

coagulate *verb* to thicken; clot

coal *noun* a black substance dug out of the earth and used for burning, making gas, *etc*

coal gas the mixture of gases obtained from coal, used for lighting and heating

coalition *noun* a joining together of different parts or groups

coal mine a mine from which coal is dug

coarse *adjective* **1** not fine in texture; rough, harsh **2** vulgar

coarsen *verb* to make coarse

coast *noun* the border of land next to the sea ■ *verb* **1** to sail along or near a coast **2** to move without the use of power on a bike, in a car, *etc*

coastal *adjective* of or on the coast

coastguard *noun* someone who acts as a guard along the coast to help those in danger in boats *etc*

coat *noun* **1** an outer garment with sleeves **2** an animal's covering of hair or wool **3** a layer of paint ■ *verb* to cover with a coat or layer

coating *noun* a covering

coat of arms the badge or crest of a family

coax *verb* to persuade to do what is wanted without using force

cob *noun* **1** a head of corn, wheat, *etc* **2** a male swan

cobalt *noun* a silvery metal

cobble *noun* (*also called:* **cobblestone**) a rounded stone used in paving roads ■ *verb* **1** to mend (shoes) **2** to repair roughly or hurriedly

cobbled *adjective* of streets: paved with cobbles

cobbler *noun* someone who mends shoes

cobra *noun* a poisonous snake found in India and Africa

cobweb *noun* a spider's web

cocaine *noun* a narcotic drug

cock *noun* **1** the male of most kinds of bird, especially of the farmyard hen **2** a hammer-like part of a gun which fires the shot ■ *verb* **1** to draw back the cock of a gun **2** to set (the ears) upright to listen

cockatoo *noun* a kind of parrot

cockerel *noun* a young cock

cocker spaniel a breed of small spaniel

cockle *noun* a type of shellfish

cockney *noun* (*plural* **cockneys**) **1** someone born in the East End of London **2** the speech characteristic of this area

cockpit *noun* the space for the pilot or driver in an aeroplane or small boat

cockroach *noun* (*plural* **cockroaches**) a type of crawling insect

cocksure *adjective* very confident, often without cause

cocktail *noun* a mixed alcoholic drink

cocky *adj* ~~ve~~ conceited, self-confident

cocoa *noun* ~~made from~~ the ground see ~~~~e cacao tree

coconut *noun* the large, hard-shelled nut of a type of palm tree

cocoon *noun* a protective covering of silk spun by the larva of a butterfly, moth, *etc*

cod *noun* (*plural* **cod**) a fish much

used as food, found in the northern seas

code *noun* **1** a way of signalling or sending secret messages, using letters *etc* agreed beforehand **2** a book or collection of laws, rules, *etc*

codger *noun* an old, eccentric man

codify *verb* to arrange in an orderly way, classify

| **codify** ► codifies, codifying, codified

coeducation *noun* the education of boys and girls together ■ **coeducational** *adjective*

coefficient *noun*, *maths* a number appearing before a variable *eg* 5 in $5x$

coerce *verb* to make to do; force, compel ■ **coercion** *noun*

coexist *verb* to exist at the same time ■ **coexistence** *noun*

coffee *noun* a drink made from the roasted, ground beans of the coffee shrub

coffer *noun* a chest for holding money, gold, *etc*

coffin *noun* a box in which a dead body is buried or cremated

cog *noun* a tooth on a wheel

cognac *noun* a kind of French brandy

cogwheel *noun* a toothed wheel

cohere *verb* to stick together

coherence *noun* connection between thoughts, ideas, *etc*

coherent *adjective* **1** sticking

together **2** clear and logical in thought or speech

cohesion *noun* the act of sticking together

cohesive *adjective* of a group: consisting of members who are closely linked together or associated with each other

cohort *noun* **1** *history* a tenth part of a Roman legion **2** a follower or companion

coil *verb* to wind in rings; twist ■ *noun* a wound arrangement of hair, rope, *etc*

coin *noun* a piece of stamped metal used as money ■ *verb* **1** to make metal into money **2** to make up (a new word *etc*)

coinage *noun* **1** the system of coins used in a country **2** a newly-made word

coincide *verb* **1** (often **coincide with**) to be the same as: *his story coincides with mine* **2** (often **coincide with**) to happen at the same time as

coincidence *noun* the occurrence of two things simultaneously without planning

coincidental *adjective* happening by chance, the result of a coincidence ■ **coincidentally** *adverb*

coke *noun* **1** a type of fuel made by heating coal till the gas is driven out **2** *informal* cocaine

cola *noun* a soft drink made from the nuts of a tropical tree

colander *noun* a bowl with small

holes in it for straining vegetables *etc*

cold *adjective* **1** low in temperature **2** lower in temperature than is comfortable **3** unfriendly ■ *noun* **1** the state of being cold **2** an infectious disease causing shivering, running nose, *etc* ■ **coldly** *adverb* ■ **coldness** *noun*

cold-blooded *adjective* **1** of fishes *etc*: having cold blood **2** cruel; lacking in feelings

cold sore a blister on or near the mouth, caused by a contagious virus similar to that which causes genital herpes

cold war a power struggle between nations without open warfare

coleslaw *noun* a salad made from raw cabbage

colic *noun* a severe stomach pain

collaborate *verb* **1** to work together (with) **2** to work with (an enemy) to betray your country
■ **collaboration** *noun*
■ **collaborator** *noun*

● Do not confuse with: **corroborate**

collage (*pronounced* ko-**lahzs**) *noun* a design made of scraps of paper pasted on wood, card, *etc*

collapse *verb* **1** to fall or break down **2** to cave or fall in **3** to become unable to continue ■ *noun* a falling down or caving in

collapsible *adjective* of a chair *etc*: able to be folded up

collar *noun* **1** a band, strip, *etc* worn round the neck **2** part of a garment that fits round the neck

collarbone *noun* either of two bones joining the breast bone and shoulder blade

collate *verb* **1** to examine and compare **2** to gather together and arrange in order

collateral *noun* something that is offered as a guarantee that a debt will be repaid

colleague *noun* someone who works in the same company *etc* as yourself

collect *verb* **1** to bring together **2** to gather together

collected *adjective* **1** gathered together **2** calm, composed

collection *noun* **1** the act of collecting **2** a number of objects or people **3** money gathered at a meeting, *eg* a church service

collective *adjective* of several things or people, not of one: *collective decision*

collector *noun* someone who collects a particular group of things

college *noun* **1** a building housing students, forming part of a university **2** a higher-education institute

collide *verb* to come together with great force; clash

collie *noun* a breed of long-haired dog with a pointed nose

colliery noun (plural **collieries**) a coal mine

collision noun 1 a crash between two moving vehicles etc 2 a disagreement, a clash of interests etc

colloquial adjective used in everyday speech but not in formal writing or speaking

collude verb to plot secretly with someone

collusion noun a secret or clandestine agreement

cologne noun light perfume made with plant oils and alcohol

colon[1] noun a punctuation mark (:) used eg to introduce a list of examples

colon[2] noun a part of the bowels

colonel (pronounced ker-nel) noun a senior army officer, in charge of a regiment

colonial adjective of colonies abroad

colonist noun a settler

colonize or **colonise** verb 1 to set up a colony in 2 to settle people in (a colony)

colony noun (plural **colonies**) 1 a group of settlers or the settlement they make in another country 2 a group of people, animals, etc of the same type living together

colossal adjective huge, enormous

colour or US **color** noun 1 a quality that an object shows in the light, eg redness, blueness, etc 2 a shade or tint ■ verb 1 to put

colour on 2 to influence: coloured my attitude to life ■ **off colour** unwell

colour-blind adjective unable to distinguish certain colours, eg red and green

colourful adjective 1 brightly coloured 2 vivid, interesting

colouring noun 1 shade or combination of colours 2 complexion

colourless adjective 1 without colour 2 dull, bland

colt noun a young horse

column noun 1 an upright stone or wooden pillar 2 something of a long or tall, narrow shape 3 a vertical line of print, figures, etc on a page 4 a regular feature in a newspaper

columnist noun someone who writes a regular newspaper column

coma noun unconsciousness lasting a long time

comb noun 1 a toothed instrument for separating or smoothing hair, wool, etc 2 the crest of certain birds 3 a collection of cells for honey ■ verb 1 to arrange or smooth with a comb 2 to search through thoroughly

combat verb to fight or struggle against ■ noun a fight or struggle

combatant noun someone who is fighting ■ adjective fighting

combative adjective taking delight in fights and quarrels

combination noun 1 a joining together of things or people 2 a set of things or people combined 3 a series of letters or figures dialled to open a safe

combine verb to join together

combine harvester a machine that both cuts and threshes crops

combustible adjective liable to catch fire and burn ■ noun anything that will catch fire

combustion noun burning

come verb 1 to move towards this place (contrasted with: **go**) 2 to draw near: Christmas is coming 3 to arrive: we'll have tea when you come 4 to happen, occur: the index comes at the end ■ **come about** to happen ■ **come across** or **come upon** to meet or find accidentally ■ **come by** to obtain ■ **come into** to inherit ■ **come round** or **come to** to recover from a faint etc ■ **come upon** to come across

| come ► comes, coming, came

comedian noun a performer who tells jokes, acts in comedy, etc

comedy noun (plural **comedies**) a light-hearted or amusing play (contrasted with: **tragedy**)

comet noun a kind of star which has a tail of light

comfort verb to help, soothe (someone in pain or distress) ■ noun 1 ease; quiet enjoyment 2 something that brings ease and happiness

comfortable adjective 1 at ease; free from trouble, pain, etc 2 giving comfort 3 having enough money for a pleasant lifestyle

comfortably adverb 1 easily, happily, or without any problems 2 in a way which involves no pain or physical irritation

comfy adjective, informal comfortable

| comfy ► comfier, comfiest

comic adjective 1 of comedy 2 amusing, funny ■ noun 1 a professional comedian 2 a children's magazine with illustrated stories etc

comical adjective funny, amusing ■ **comically** adverb

comic strip a strip of small pictures outlining a story

comma noun a punctuation mark (,) indicating a pause in a sentence

command verb 1 to give an order 2 to be in charge of ■ noun 1 an order 2 control: in command of the situation

commandant noun an officer in command of a place or of troops

commander noun 1 someone who commands 2 a naval officer next in rank below captain

commandment noun an order or command

commando noun (plural **commandoes**) a soldier in an army unit trained for special tasks

commemorate verb 1 to bring to memory by some solemn act

2 to serve as a memorial of
■ **commemoration** noun

commence verb to begin

commencement noun the start
or beginning

commend verb to praise

commendable adjective
praiseworthy

commendation noun praise

comment noun **1** a remark **2** a
criticism ■ verb to remark on;
criticize

commentary noun (plural
commentaries) a description of
an event etc by someone who is
watching it

commentator noun someone
who gives or writes a
commentary

commerce noun the buying and
selling of goods between people
or nations; trade, dealings

commercial adjective **1** of
commerce **2** paid for by
advertisements: commercial
radio ■ noun an advertisement on
radio, TV, etc ■ **commercially**
adverb

commiserate verb to
sympathize (with)

commiserations noun plural an
expression of sympathy when
someone has failed to do or
achieve something

commission noun **1** the act of
committing **2** a document giving
authority to an officer in the
armed forces **3** an order for a work
of art **4** a fee for doing business on

another's behalf **5** a group of
people appointed to investigate
something ■ verb to give a
commission or power to

commissionaire noun a
uniformed doorkeeper

commissioner noun **1** someone
with high authority in a district **2** a
member of a commission

commit verb **1** to give or hand
over; entrust **2** to make a promise
to do **3** to do, bring about: commit
a crime

| **commit** ► commits,
| committing, committed

commitment noun **1** a promise
2 a task that must be done

committed adjective strong in
belief or support

committee noun a number of
people chosen from a larger body
to attend to special business

commodity noun (plural
commodities) **1** an article to be
bought or sold **2** commodities
goods, produce

commodore noun an officer
next above a captain in the navy

common adjective **1** shared by
all or many **2** seen or happening
often **3** ordinary, normal ■ noun
land belonging to the people of a
town, parish, etc

commoner noun someone who
is not a member of the ruling
classes

commonplace adjective
ordinary

common room a sitting room

for the use of a group in a school
etc

Commons or **House of Commons** *noun* the lower House of Parliament

common sense practical good sense

commonwealth *noun* an association of self-governing states

commotion *noun* a disturbance among several people

communal *adjective* common, shared

commune *noun* a group of people living together, sharing work *etc*

communicable *adjective* able to be passed on to others: *communicable disease*

communicate *verb* 1 to make known, tell 2 to pass on 3 to get in touch (with) 4 to have a connecting door

communication *noun* 1 a means of conveying information 2 a message 3 a way of passing from place to place

communicative *adjective* willing to give information, talkative

communion *noun* 1 the act of sharing thoughts, feelings, *etc*; fellowship 2 **Communion** in the Christian Church, the celebration of the Lord's supper

communism *noun* a form of socialism where industry is controlled by the state

communist *adjective* of communism ■ *noun* someone who believes in communism

community *noun* (*plural* **communities**) 1 a group of people living in one place 2 the public in general

commute *verb* to travel regularly between two places, *eg* between home and work

commuter *noun* someone who regularly travels some distance from their home to work

compact *adjective* fitted or packed closely together ■ *noun* a bargain or agreement

compact disc a small disc on which digitally recorded sound is registered as a series of pits to be read by a laser beam

companion *noun* someone or something that accompanies; a friend

companionship *noun* friendship; the act of accompanying

company *noun* (*plural* **companies**) 1 a gathering of people 2 a business firm 3 a part of a regiment 4 companionship

comparable *adjective* roughly similar or equal in some way

comparative *adjective* 1 judged by comparing with something else; relative: *comparative improvement* 2 near to being: *a comparative stranger* ■ *noun*, *grammar* the degree of an adjective or adverb between

positive and superlative, *eg* blacker, better, more courageous
- **comparatively** *adverb* in comparison to others: *comparatively easy*

compare *verb* 1 to set things together to see how similar or different they are 2 to liken

comparison *noun* the act of comparing

compartment *noun* a separate part or division, *eg* of a railway carriage

compass *noun* (*plural* **compasses**) 1 an instrument with a magnetized needle for showing direction 2 **compasses** an instrument with one fixed and one movable leg for drawing circles

compassion *noun* pity for another's suffering; mercy
compassionate *adjective* pitying, merciful

compatibility *noun* the natural tendency for two or more people or groups to get on well together

compatible *adjective* 1 able to live with, agree with, *etc* 2 of pieces of electronic equipment: able to be connected and used together

compatriot *noun* a fellow-countryman or -countrywoman

compel *verb* to force to do something

> compel ▶ compel*s*, compel*ling*, compel*led*

compelling *adjective* 1 convincing 2 fascinating

compensate *verb* to make up for wrong or damage done, especially by giving money
- **compensation** *noun*

compère *noun* someone who introduces acts as part of an entertainment ▪ *verb* to act as compère

compete *verb* to try to beat others in a race *etc*

competent *adjective* 1 capable, efficient 2 skilled; properly trained or qualified
- **competence** *noun*
- **competently** *adverb*

competition *noun* 1 a contest between rivals 2 rivalry

competitive *adjective* 1 of sport: based on competitions 2 fond of competing with others

competitor *noun* someone who competes; a rival

compilation *noun* 1 a collection of several short, related pieces of writing, music or information 2 the activity of compiling something

compile *verb* to make (a book *etc*) from information that has been collected

compiler *noun* a person whose job consists of compiling

complacency or
complacence *noun* a lazy attitude resulting from an exaggerated belief in your own security

complacent *adjective* self-satisfied and with a tendency to be lazy ■ **complacently** adverb

complain verb 1 to express dissatisfaction about something 2 to grumble

complaint noun 1 a statement of dissatisfaction 2 an illness

complement noun 1 something which completes or fills up 2 the full number or quantity needed to fill something

🖊 Do not confuse with: **compliment**. Remember COMPLEment and COMPLEte are related in meaning, and the first six letters of both words are the same

complementary adjective together making up a whole

🖊 Do not confuse with: **complimentary**. Complementary is related to the noun **complement**

complete adjective 1 having nothing missing; whole 2 finished ■ verb 1 to finish 2 to make whole ■ **completion** noun

completely adverb totally, absolutely

complex adjective 1 made up of many parts 2 complicated, difficult ■ noun (plural complexes) 1 an exaggerated reaction, an obsession: has a complex about her height 2 a group of related buildings: sports complex

complexion noun the colour or look of the skin of the face

complexity noun (plural complexities) the quality of being complicated or difficult

compliance noun the act of complying; agreement with another's wishes

compliant adjective yielding, giving agreement

complicate verb to make difficult

complicated adjective difficult to understand; detailed

complication noun 1 a difficulty 2 a development in an illness which makes things worse

compliment noun 1 an expression of praise or flattery 2 **compliments** good wishes ■ verb to praise, congratulate

🖊 Do not confuse with: **complement**. Remember, if you make a compliment, you are being polite, and an 'I' comes after the 'L' in both words

complimentary adjective 1 flattering, praising 2 given free: complimentary ticket

🖊 Do not confuse with: **complementary**. Complimentary is related to the noun **compliment**

comply verb to agree to do something that someone else orders or wishes

| **comply** ► complies, complying, complied

component *noun* one of several parts, *eg* of a machine

compose *verb* **1** to put together or in order; arrange **2** to create (a piece of music, a poem, *etc*)

composed *adjective* quiet, calm

composer *noun* someone who writes music

composite *adjective* made up of parts

composition *noun* **1** the act of composing **2** a created piece of writing or music

compost *noun* a mixture of natural manures for spreading on soil

composure *noun* calmness, self-possession

compound *adjective* **1** made up of a number of different parts **2** not simple ■ *noun* **1** *chemistry* a substance formed from two or more elements **2** an enclosure round a building **3** a word made up of two or more words, *eg* tablecloth

comprehend *verb* to understand ■ **comprehension** *noun*

comprehensible *adjective* able to be understood

comprehensive *adjective* taking in or including much or all

comprehensive school a state-funded school providing all types of secondary education

compress *verb* (*pronounced* kom-**pres**) **1** to press together **2** to force into a narrower or smaller

space ■ *noun* (*pronounced* **kom**-pres) a pad used to create pressure on a part of the body or to reduce inflammation ■ **compression** *noun*

comprise *verb* **1** to include, contain **2** to consist of

◆※ Do not confuse with: **consist**. Remember, you do not need the word 'of' after **comprise**. You say *the exam comprises three parts*, but *the exam consists of three parts*

compromise *noun* an agreement reached by both sides giving up something ■ *verb* to make a compromise

compulsion *noun* a force driving someone to do something

compulsive *adjective* unable to stop yourself, obsessive: *compulsive liar*

◆※ Do not confuse: **compulsive** and **compulsory**

compulsory *adjective* **1** requiring to be done **2** forced upon someone

◆※ Do not confuse: **compulsory** and **compulsive**

compute *verb* to count, calculate

computer *noun* an electronic machine that stores and sorts information of various kinds

computerize *or* **computerise** *verb* **1** to transfer (a system or procedure) to computer control **2**

to install computers in (a place)
■ **computerization** *noun*

comrade *noun* a companion, a friend ■ **comradeship** *noun*

con *verb* to trick, play a confidence trick on ■ *noun* a trick, a deceit

| **con** *verb* ▶ cons, conn*ing*, conn*ed*

concave *adjective* hollow or curved inwards (*contrasted with*: **convex**)

conceal *verb* to hide, keep secret ■ **concealment** *noun*

concede *verb* **1** to give up, yield **2** to admit the truth of something

conceit *noun* a too high opinion of yourself; vanity

conceited *adjective* full of conceit; vain

conceivable *adjective* able to be imagined ■ **conceivably** *adverb*

conceive *verb* **1** to form in the mind, imagine **2** to become pregnant

concentrate *verb* **1** to direct all your attention or effort towards something **2** to bring together to one place ■ **concentration** *noun*

concentrated *adjective* made stronger or less dilute

concentration camp a prison camp for civilians, especially in Nazi Germany

concentric *adjective* of circles: placed one inside the other with the same centre point (*contrasted with*: **eccentric**)

concept *noun* a general idea about something

conception *noun* **1** the act of conceiving **2** an idea

concern *verb* **1** to have to do with **2** to make uneasy **3** to interest, affect ■ *noun* **1** anxiety **2** a cause of anxiety, a worry **3** a business ■ **concern yourself with** to be worried about

concerning *preposition* about: *concerning your application*

concert *noun* a musical performance

concertina *noun* a type of musical wind instrument, with bellows and keys

concerto *noun* (*plural* **concertos**) a long piece of music for a solo instrument with orchestral accompaniment

concession *noun* **1** a granting or allowing of something **2** something granted or allowed **3** a reduction in the price of something for children, the unemployed, senior citizens, *etc*

conciliate *verb* to win over (someone previously unfriendly or angry)

conciliation *noun* the act or process of making peace with a person or group

concise *adjective* brief, using few words

◆* Do not confuse with: **precise**

conclude verb 1 to end 2 to reach a decision or judgement; settle

concluding adjective last, final

conclusion noun 1 end 2 decision, judgement

conclusive adjective settling, deciding: conclusive proof

conclusively adverb in a way which leaves no doubt

concoct verb 1 to mix together (a dish or drink) 2 to make up, invent: concoct a story ■ concoction noun

concord noun agreement

concourse noun a large open space in a building etc

concrete adjective 1 solid, real 2 made of concrete ■ noun a mixture of gravel, cement, etc used in building

concur verb to agree

| concur ► concurs, concurring, concurred

concussion noun temporary harm done to the brain from a knock on the head

condemn verb 1 to blame 2 to sentence to (a certain punishment) 3 to declare (a building) unfit for use ■ condemnation noun

condensation noun 1 the act of condensing 2 drops of liquid formed from vapour

condense verb 1 to make to go into a smaller space 2 of steam: to turn to liquid

condescend verb to act towards someone as if you are better than them ■ condescending adjective ■ condescension noun

condiment noun a seasoning for food, especially salt or pepper

condition noun 1 the state in which anything is: in poor condition 2 something that must happen before some other thing happens 3 a point in a bargain, treaty, etc

conditional adjective depending on certain things happening ■ conditionally adverb

condolence noun 1 sharing in another's sorrow; sympathy 2 condolences an expression of sympathy

condone verb to allow (an offence) to pass unchecked

conducive adjective helping, favourable (to): conducive to peace

conduct verb (pronounced kon-dukt) 1 to lead, guide 2 to control, be in charge of 3 to direct (an orchestra) 4 to transmit (electricity etc) 5 to behave: conducted himself correctly ■ noun (pronounced kon-dukt) behaviour

conduction noun transmission of heat, electricity, etc

conductor noun 1 someone who directs an orchestra 2 someone who collects fares on a bus etc 3 something that transmits heat, electricity, etc

cone noun 1 a shape that is round at the bottom and comes to a point 2 the fruit of a pine or fir tree *etc* **3** an ice-cream cornet ■ **conic** *adjective*

confectionery *noun* sweets, cakes, *etc*

confederacy *noun* (*plural* **confederacies**) **1** a league, an alliance **2 Confederacy** *US history* the union of Southern states in the American Civil War

confederate *adjective* **1** joined together by treaty **2** *US history* supporting the Confederacy ■ *noun* someone acting in an alliance with others

confer *verb* to talk together

| confer ► confers, conferring, conferred

conference *noun* a meeting for discussion

confess *verb* to own up, admit to (wrong)

confessed *adjective* admitted, not secret

confession *noun* an admission of wrongdoing

confetti *noun plural* small pieces of coloured paper thrown at weddings or other celebrations

confidant *or feminine*

confidante *noun* someone trusted with a secret

  🔥 Do not confuse with: **confident**

confide *verb*: **confide in** to tell secrets to

confidence *noun* **1** trust, belief **2** self-assurance, boldness **3** something told privately

confidence trick a trick to get money *etc* from someone by first gaining their trust

confident *adjective* **1** very self-assured **2** certain of an outcome ■ **confidently** *adverb*

  🔥 Do not confuse with: **confidant** and **confidante**

confidential *adjective* to be kept as a secret: *confidential information* ■ **confidentially** *adverb*

confiding *adjective* trusting

confine *verb* **1** to shut up, imprison **2** to keep within limits

confinement *noun* **1** the state of being confined **2** imprisonment **3** the time of a woman's labour and childbirth

confines (*pronounced* kon-fainz) *noun plural* limits

confirm *verb* **1** to make sure **2** to show to be true **3** to admit into full membership of a church

confirmation *noun* **1** a making sure **2** proof **3** the ceremony by which someone is made a full member of a church

confirmed *adjective* settled in a habit *etc*: *a confirmed bachelor*

confiscate *verb* to take away, as a punishment ■ **confiscation** *noun*

conflict *noun* **1** a struggle, a contest **2** a battle **3** disagreement ■ *verb* of statements *etc*: to contradict each other

■ **conflicting** *adjective*

conform verb to follow the example of most people in behaviour, dress, etc

confound verb to puzzle, confuse

confront verb 1 to face, meet 2 to bring face to face (with)

confrontation noun a situation in which two people or groups are challenging each other openly

confuse verb 1 to mix up, disorder 2 to puzzle, bewilder ■ **confusion** noun

confusing adjective puzzling, bewildering

congeal verb to become solid, especially by cooling

conger (pronounced **kong**-ger) noun a kind of large sea-eel

congested adjective 1 overcrowded, especially with traffic 2 clogged ■ **congestion** noun

congratulate verb to express joy to (someone) at their success

congratulations noun plural an expression of joy at someone's success

congregate verb to come together in a crowd

congregation noun a gathering, especially of people in a church

congress noun (plural **congresses**) 1 a large meeting of people from different countries etc for discussion 2 **Congress** the parliament of the United States, consisting of the Senate and the House of Representatives

conical adjective cone-shaped

conifer noun a cone-bearing tree ■ **coniferous** adjective

conjecture noun a guess ■ verb to guess

conjunction noun, grammar a word that joins sentences or phrases, eg and, but

conjure verb to perform tricks that seem magical

conjuror or **conjurer** noun someone who performs conjuring tricks

conker noun 1 a horse chestnut 2 **conkers** a game in which conkers are tied on strings and players try to hit and break each other's

con man someone who regularly plays confidence tricks on people in order to cheat them out of money

connect verb to join or fasten together

connection noun 1 something that connects 2 a state of being connected 3 a train, aeroplane, etc which takes you to the next part of a journey 4 an acquaintance, a friend

connive verb: **connive at** to disregard (a misdeed)

connoisseur (pronounced kon-o-ser) noun someone with an expert knowledge of a subject: wine connoisseur

conquer verb 1 to gain by force 2 to overcome: conquered his fear of heights ■ **conqueror** noun

conquest *noun* something won by force

conscience *noun* an inner sense of what is right and wrong

conscientious *adjective* careful and diligent in work *etc*
■ **conscientiously** *adverb*

conscious *adjective* **1** aware of yourself and your surroundings; awake **2** aware, knowing **3** deliberate, intentional: *a conscious decision* ■ **consciously** *adverb* ■ **consciousness** *noun*

conscript *noun* (pronounced **kon**-skript) someone obliged by law to serve in the armed forces
■ *verb* (pronounced kon-**skript**) to compel to serve in the armed forces ■ **conscription** *noun*

consecutive *adjective* coming in order, one after the other

consensus *noun* an agreement of opinion

* Do not confuse with: **census**

consent *verb* to agree (to)
■ *noun* **1** agreement **2** permission

consequence *noun* something that follows as a result

conservation *noun* the maintaining of old buildings, the countryside, *etc* in an undamaged state

conservationist *noun* someone who encourages and practises conservation

conservative *adjective* **1** resistant to change **2** moderate,

not extreme ■ *noun* **1** someone of conservative views **2**

Conservative a supporter of the Conservative Party

Conservative Party a right-wing political party in the UK

conservatory *noun* (plural **conservatories**) a room with glass walls for growing plants, or a similar room used as a lounge, attached to and entered from the house

conserve *verb* to keep from being wasted or lost; preserve

consider *verb* **1** to think about carefully **2** to think of as, regard as **3** to pay attention to the wishes of (someone)

considerable *adjective* fairly large, substantial

considerably *adverb* substantially, quite a lot

considerate *adjective* taking others' wishes into account; thoughtful

consideration *noun* **1** serious thought **2** thoughtfulness for others

considering *preposition* taking into account: *considering your age*

consign *verb* to give into the care of

consignment *noun* a load, *eg* of goods

consist *verb* to be made up (of)

* Do not confuse with: **comprise**. You need the word

'of' after **consist**, but not after **comprise**. You say *the exam consists of three parts*, but *the exam comprises three parts*

consistency *noun* (*plural* **consistencies**) 1 thickness, firmness 2 the quality of always being the same

consistent *adjective* 1 not changing, regular 2 of statements *etc*: not contradicting each other ▪ **consistently** *adverb*

consolation *noun* something that makes trouble *etc* more easy to bear

consolation prize a prize sometimes given to someone coming second in a competition

console *verb* to comfort, cheer up

consolidate *verb* to make or become strong ▪ **consolidation** *noun*

consonant *noun* a letter of the alphabet that is not a vowel, *eg* b, c, d

conspicuous *adjective* clearly seen, noticeable ▪ **conspicuously** *adverb*

conspiracy *noun* (*plural* **conspiracies**) a plot by a group of people

conspirator *noun* someone who takes part in a conspiracy

conspire *verb* to plan or plot together

constable *noun* a junior police officer

constant *adjective* 1 never

stopping 2 never changing ▪ *noun, maths* a number that does not vary ▪ **constancy** *noun*

constantly *adverb* always

constellation *noun* a group of stars

constipated *adjective* suffering from constipation

constipation *noun* sluggish working of the bowels

constituency *noun* (*plural* **constituencies**) 1 a district which has a member of parliament 2 the voters in such a district

constituent *adjective* making or forming ▪ *noun* 1 a necessary part 2 a voter in a constituency

constitute *verb* 1 to establish 2 to form, make up 3 to be the equivalent of: *this action constitutes a crime*

constitution *noun* 1 the way in which something is made up 2 the natural condition of a body in terms of health *etc*: *a weak constitution* 3 a set of laws or rules governing a country or organization

constitutional *adjective* of a constitution ▪ *noun* a short walk for the sake of your health

constraint *noun* 1 compulsion, force 2 restraint, repression

constrict *verb* 1 to press together tightly 2 to surround and squeeze

construct *verb* to build, make

construction *noun* 1 the act of constructing 2 something built

3 the arrangement of words in a sentence

constructive *adjective* **1** of construction **2** helping to improve: *constructive criticism* ▪ **constructively** *adverb*

consul *noun* someone who looks after their country's affairs in a foreign country ▪ **consulate** *noun* the official residence of a consul

consult *verb* to seek advice or information from

consultant *noun* **1** someone who gives professional or expert advice **2** the senior grade of hospital doctor

consultation *noun* **1** the activity of looking in *eg* reference books for information **2** a meeting with someone to exchange ideas and opinions **3** discussion

consulting room a room where a doctor sees patients

consume *verb* **1** to eat up **2** to use (up) **3** to destroy

consumer *noun* someone who buys, eats or uses goods, energy, resources, *etc*

consumption *noun* **1** the act of consuming **2** an amount consumed

contact *noun* **1** touch **2** meeting, communication **3** an acquaintance; someone who can be of help ▪ *verb* to get into contact with

contact lens a plastic lens worn in contact with the eyeball

contagious *adjective* of disease: spreading from person to person, especially by touch

contain *verb* **1** to hold or have inside **2** to hold back: *couldn't contain her anger*

container *noun* a box, tin, jar, *etc* for holding anything

contaminate *verb* to make impure or dirty ▪ **contaminated** *adjective* ▪ **contamination** *noun*

contemplate *verb* **1** to look at or think about attentively **2** to intend ▪ **contemplation** *noun*

contemporary *adjective* belonging to the same time ▪ *noun* someone of roughly the same age as yourself

contempt *noun* complete lack of respect; scorn

contemptible *adjective* deserving scorn, worthless

⚫※ Do not confuse: **contemptible** and **contemptuous**. **Contemptible** is formed from **contempt** + **-ible** ► able to be scorned, worthy of scorn. It is used in phrases like *a contemptible little tell-tale*

contemptuous *adjective* scornful

contend *verb* to struggle against ▪ **contender** *noun* someone taking part in a contest

content *adjective* happy, satisfied ▪ *noun* **1** happiness, satisfaction **2 contents** that which is contained in anything ▪ *verb* to make happy, satisfy

contented *adjective* happy, content

contentment *noun* happiness, content

contest *verb* (pronounced kon-**test**) to fight for, argue against ▪ *noun* (pronounced **kon**-test) a fight, a competition

contestant *noun* someone who takes part in a contest

context *noun* **1** the place in a book *etc* to which a certain part belongs **2** the background of an event, remark, *etc*

continent *noun* one of the seven large divisions of the earth's land surface (Europe, Asia, Africa, Antarctica, Australia, North America, South America)

continental *adjective* **1** of a continent **2** *Brit* European **3** of climate: warm in summer and cool in winter, because of being inland

continental drift the gradual movement of the earth's continents

continental shelf the edge of a continent where it is submerged in shallow sea

contingency *noun* (*plural* **contingencies**) a chance happening

continual *adjective* happening again and again at close intervals

❖ Do not confuse with: **continuous**. Something which is **continual** happens often, but there are short breaks when it is not happening. Something which is **continuous** happens all the time without stopping. So you could talk about, for example, *continual* interruptions, but the *continuous* lapping of *waves on a beach*

continually *adverb* all the time, repeatedly

continuation *noun* **1** the act of continuing **2** a part that continues, an extension

continue *verb* to keep on, go on (doing something)

continuity *noun* the state of having no gaps or breaks

continuous *adjective* coming one after the other or in a steady stream without any gap or break ▪ **continuously** *adverb*

❖ Do not confuse with: **continual**

contort *verb* to twist or turn violently ▪ **contorted** *adjective* ▪ **contortion** *noun*

contortionist *noun* someone who can twist their body into strange shapes

contour *noun* (often **contours**) outline, shape

contour line a line drawn on a map through points all at the same height above sea level

contract *verb* (pronounced kon-trakt) **1** to become or make smaller **2** to bargain for **3** to promise in writing ■ *noun* (pronounced **kon**-trakt) a written agreement

contraction *noun* **1** a shortening **2** a shortened form of a word **3** a muscle spasm, *eg* during childbirth

contractor *noun* someone who promises to do work, or supply goods, at an arranged price

contradict *verb* to say the opposite of; deny ■ **contradiction** *noun*

contradictory *adjective* **1** contradicting something **2** of two pieces of information: contradicting each other

contralto *noun* (plural **contraltos**) the lowest singing voice in women (also called: **alto**)

contraption *noun* a machine, a device

contrary[1] (pronounced **kon**-tra-ri) *adjective* opposite ■ *noun* the opposite

contrary[2] (pronounced kon-**treir**-ri) *adjective* always doing or saying the opposite, perverse

contrast *verb* (pronounced kon-**trast**) **1** to compare so as to show differences **2** to show a marked difference from ■ *noun* (pronounced **kon**-trast) a difference between (two) things

contravene *verb* to break (a law *etc*) ■ **contravention** *noun*

contribute *verb* **1** to give (money, help, *etc*) along with others **2** to supply (articles *etc*) for a publication **3** to help to cause

contribution *noun* something given or supplied

contributor *noun* a person or thing that contributes

contributory *adjective* contributing to, or playing a part in, some result

con-trick *noun* a confidence trick

contrive *verb* **1** to plan **2** to bring about, manage

contrived *adjective* unconvincingly artificial

control *noun* **1** authority to rule, manage, restrain, *etc* **2** (often **controls**) means by which a driver keeps a machine powered or guided ■ *verb* **1** to exercise control over **2** to have power over ■ **controlled** *adjective* ■ **controller** *noun*

control tower an airport building from which landing and take-off instructions are given

controversial *adjective* likely to cause argument

controversy *noun* (plural **controversies**) an argument, a disagreement

conundrum *noun* a riddle, a question

conurbation *noun* a group of towns forming a single built-up area

convalesce *verb* to recover

health gradually after being ill
- **convalescence** *noun*

convalescent *noun* someone convalescing from illness

convection *noun* the spreading of heat by movement of heated air or water

convector *noun* a heater which works by convection

convene *verb* to call or come together

convener *noun* 1 someone who calls a meeting 2 the chairman or chairwoman of a committee

convenience *noun* 1 suitableness, handiness 2 a means of giving ease or comfort 3 *informal* a public lavatory

convenient *adjective* easy to reach or use, handy
- **conveniently** *adverb*

convent *noun* a building accommodating an order of nuns

convention *noun* 1 a way of behaving that has become usual, a custom 2 a large meeting, an assembly

conventional *adjective* 1 done by habit or custom 2 having traditional attitudes and behaviour ■ **conventionally** *adverb*

converge *verb* to come together, meet at a point ■ **convergence** *noun* ■ **convergent** *adjective*

conversation *noun* talk, exchange of ideas, news, *etc*

conversational *adjective* 1 of conversation 2 talkative

converse[1] (*pronounced* kon-vers) *verb* to talk

converse[2] (*pronounced* kon-vers) *noun* the opposite
- *adjective* opposite

convert *verb* (*pronounced* kon-vert) 1 to change (from one thing into another) 2 to turn from one religion to another ■ *noun* (*pronounced* kon-vert) someone who has been converted
- **conversion** *noun*

convertible *adjective* able to be changed from one thing to another ■ *noun* a car with a folding roof

convex *adjective* curved outwards (*contrasted with*: concave)

convey *verb* 1 to carry, transport 2 to send

conveyance *noun* the act of conveying

conveyor *or* **conveyor belt** *noun* an endless moving mechanism for conveying articles, especially in a factory

convict *verb* (*pronounced* kon-vikt) to declare or prove that someone is guilty ■ *noun* (*pronounced* kon-vikt) someone found guilty of a crime and sent to prison

conviction *noun* 1 the passing of a guilty sentence on someone in court 2 a strong belief

convince *verb* 1 to make (someone) believe that something is true 2 to persuade

(someone) by showing
■ **convinced** *adjective*

convoy *noun* 1 merchant ships protected by warships 2 a line of army lorries with armed guard

convulse *verb* to cause to shake violently

convulsion *noun* 1 a sudden stiffening or jerking of the muscles 2 a violent disturbance ■ **convulsive** *adjective*

coo *noun* a sound like that of a dove ■ *verb* to make this sound

cook *verb* to prepare (food) by heating ■ *noun* someone who cooks and prepares food

cooker *noun* a stove for cooking

cookery *noun* the art of cooking

cookie *noun* a biscuit

cool *adjective* 1 slightly cold 2 calm, not excited 3 *informal* good, fashionable ■ *verb* to make or grow cool; calm ■ **coolness** *noun*

coolly *adverb* 1 in a calm way 2 in a slightly unfriendly way

coop *noun* a box or cage for hens *etc* ■ *verb* to shut (up) as in a coop

co-op *see* co-operative society

co-operate *verb* to work or act together ■ **co-operation** *noun*

co-operative *adjective* helpful; willing to work together ■ *noun* a business or farm *etc* owned by the workers

co-operative society *or* **co-op** a trading organization in which the profits are shared among members

co-opt *verb* to choose (someone) to join a committee or other body

co-ordinate *verb* to make things fit in or work smoothly together ■ *noun* one of a set of numbers used to indicate the position of a point

co-ordination *noun* 1 the activity or skill of co-ordinating things 2 the ability to move and use the different parts of your body smoothly together

coot *noun* a water bird with a white spot on the forehead

cop *noun, slang* a police officer ■ *verb* to catch, seize ■ **cop it** to land in trouble ■ **cop out** to avoid responsibility

| **cop** *verb* ► cops, copp*ing*, copp*ed*

cope *verb* to struggle or deal successfully (with), manage

copious *adjective* plentiful ■ **copiously** *adverb*

copper *noun* 1 a hard reddish-brown metal 2 a reddish-brown colour 3 a coin made from copper

copse *or* **coppice** *noun* a wood of low-growing trees

copy *noun* (*plural* copies) 1 an imitation 2 a print or reproduction of a picture *etc* 3 an individual example of a certain book *etc* ■ *verb* 1 to make a copy of 2 to imitate

| **copy** *verb* ► copies, copy*ing*, copi*ed*

copyright *noun* the right of one

person or body to publish a book, perform a play, print music, *etc*
■ *adjective* of or protected by the law of copyright

coral *noun* a hard substance made from the skeletons of tiny animals

coral reef a rock-like mass of coral built up gradually from the seabed

cord *noun* 1 thin rope or strong string 2 a thick strand of anything

🖝* Do not confuse with: **chord**

cordial *noun* a refreshing drink

cordon *noun* a line of guards, police, *etc* to keep people back

corduroy *noun* a ribbed cotton cloth resembling velvet

core *noun* the inner part of anything, especially fruit ■ *verb* to take out the core of (fruit)

corgi *noun* a breed of short-legged dog

cork *noun* 1 the outer bark of a type of oak found in southern Europe *etc* 2 a stopper for a bottle *etc* made of cork ■ *adjective* made of cork ■ *verb* to plug or stop up with a cork

corkscrew *noun* a tool with a screw-like spike for taking out corks ■ *adjective* shaped like a corkscrew

cormorant *noun* a type of big seabird

corn *noun* 1 wheat, oats or maize

2 a small lump of hard skin, especially on a toe

cornea *noun* the transparent covering of the eyeball

corned beef salted tinned beef

corner *noun* 1 the point where two walls, roads, *etc* meet 2 a small secluded place 3 *informal* a difficult situation ■ *verb* to force into a position from which there is no escape

cornerstone *noun* 1 the stone at the corner of a building's foundations 2 something upon which much depends

cornet *noun* 1 a musical instrument like a small trumpet 2 an ice-cream in a cone-shaped wafer

cornflour *noun* finely ground maize flour

cornflower *noun* a type of plant, with a blue flower

cornice *noun* an ornamental border round a ceiling

corny *adjective* of a joke: old and stale

corona *noun* a halo of luminous gases around the sun

coronation *noun* the crowning of a king or queen

coroner *noun* a government officer who holds inquiries into the causes of sudden or accidental deaths

coronet *noun* 1 a small crown 2 a crown-like head-dress

corporal[1] *noun* the rank next below sergeant in the British army

corporal[2] *adjective* of the body

corporal punishment physical punishment by beating

corporation *noun* a body of people acting as one for administrative or business purposes

corps (*pronounced* kawr) *noun* (*plural* **corps** – *pronounced* kawz) **1** a division of an army **2** an organized group

🔸 Do not confuse: **corps** and **corpse**

corpse *noun* a dead body

corpuscle *noun* **1** a very small particle **2** a blood cell, red or white

correct *verb* **1** to remove errors from **2** to set right ▪ *adjective* **1** having no errors **2** true **3** suitable and acceptable

correction *noun* the putting right of a mistake

correspond *verb* **1** to write letters to **2** to be similar (to), match

correspondence *noun* **1** letters **2** likeness, similarity

correspondent *noun* **1** someone who writes letters **2** someone who contributes reports to a newspaper *etc*

corridor *noun* a passageway

corroborate *verb* to give evidence which strengthens evidence already given
▪ **corroboration** *noun*

🔸 Do not confuse with: **collaborate**

corrode *verb* **1** to rust **2** to eat away at, erode ▪ **corrosion** *noun*

corrosive *adjective* **1** able to destroy or wear away materials such as metal by reacting chemically with them **2** having the effect of gradually wearing down or destroying something

corrugated *adjective* folded or shaped into ridges

corrupt *verb* **1** to make evil or rotten **2** to make dishonest, bribe ▪ *adjective* **1** dishonest, taking bribes **2** bad, rotten

corruptible *adjective* able to be corrupted, usually because of being innocent or naive

corruption *noun* **1** dishonesty, often involving the taking of bribes **2** the process of taking away someone's innocence or goodness

corset *noun* a tight-fitting undergarment to support the body

cosh *noun* (*plural* **coshes**) a short heavy stick ▪ *verb* to hit with a cosh

cosmetic *noun* something designed to improve the appearance, especially of the face ▪ *adjective* applied as a cosmetic

cosmic *adjective* of the universe or outer space

cosmology *noun* astronomy

that deals with the evolution of the universe

cosmopolitan *adjective* **1** including people from many countries **2** familiar with, or comfortable in, many different countries

cosmos *noun* the universe

cosset *verb* to treat with too much kindness, pamper

cost *verb* **1** to be priced at **2** to cause the loss of: *the war cost many lives* ■ *noun* what must be spent or suffered in order to get something

| **cost** *verb* ► costs, cost*ing*, cost

costly *adjective* high-priced, valuable ■ **costliness** *noun*

costume *noun* **1** a set of clothes **2** clothes to wear in a play **3** fancy dress

costume jewellery inexpensive, imitation jewellery

cosy *adjective* warm and comfortable ■ *noun* (*plural* **cosies**) a covering to keep a teapot *etc* warm

| **cosy** *adjective* ► cosier, cosiest

cot *noun* a small high-sided bed for children

cot death the sudden unexplained death in sleep of an apparently healthy baby

cottage *noun* a small house, especially in the countryside or a village

cottage cheese a soft, white cheese made from skimmed milk

cotton *noun* **1** a soft fluffy substance obtained from the seeds of the cotton plant **2** cloth made of cotton ■ *adjective* made of cotton

cotton wool cotton in a fluffy state, used for wiping or absorbing

couch *noun* (*plural* **couches**) a sofa

cougar *noun, US* the puma

cough *noun* a noisy effort of the lungs to throw out air and harmful matter from the throat ■ *verb* to make this effort

could *verb* **1** the form of the verb **can**[1] used to express a condition: *he could afford it if he tried* **2** *past form* of the verb **can**[1]

council *noun* a group of people elected to discuss or give advice about policy, government, *etc*

✱ Do not confuse with: **counsel**

councillor *noun* a member of a council

counsel *noun* **1** advice **2** *US* someone who gives legal advice; a lawyer ■ *verb* to give advice to

| **counsel** ► counsels, counsel*ling*, counsel*led*

✱ Do not confuse with: **council**

counsellor *noun* someone who gives advice, or who is involved in counselling

count[1] *verb* **1** to find the total number of, add up **2** to say numbers in order (1, 2, 3, *etc*) **3** to think, consider: *count yourself lucky!* ■ *noun* **1** the act of counting **2** the number counted, *eg* of votes at an election **3** a charge, an accusation **4** a point being considered ■ **count on** to rely on, depend on

count[2] *noun* a nobleman in certain countries

countdown *noun* a count backwards to zero, the point where the action takes place

countenance *noun* **1** the face **2** the expression on someone's face ■ *verb* to tolerate, encourage

counter[1] *verb* to answer or oppose (a move, act, *etc*) by another ■ *adjective* opposed; opposite

counter[2] *noun* **1** a token used in counting **2** a small plastic disc used in ludo *etc* **3** a table across which payments are made in a shop

counter- *prefix* **1** against, opposing: *counter-argument* **2** opposite

counteract *verb* to block or defeat (an action) by doing the opposite

counterattack *noun* an attack made by the defenders upon an attacking enemy ■ *verb* to launch a counterattack

counterfeit *adjective* **1** not genuine, not real **2** made in imitation for criminal purposes ■ *verb* to make a copy of

counterfoil *noun* a part of a cheque, postal order, *etc* kept by the payer or sender

counterpart *noun* someone or something which is just like or which corresponds to another person or thing

counterpoint *noun* the combining of two or more melodies to make a piece of music

counter-tenor *noun* the highest alto male voice

countess *noun* **1** a woman of the same rank as a count or earl **2** the wife or widow of a count or earl

countless *adjective* too many to be counted, very many

country *noun* (*plural* **countries**) **1** a nation **2** a land under one government **3** the land in which someone lives **4** a district which is not in a town or city **5** an area or stretch of land ■ *adjective* belonging to the country

**countryman,
countrywoman** *noun* **1** someone who lives in a rural area **2** someone who belongs to the same country as you

countryside *noun* the parts of a country other than towns and cities

county *noun* (*plural* **counties**) a division of a country

coup (*pronounced* koo) *noun* **1** a

sudden outstandingly successful move or act **2** a coup d'état

coup d'état (*pronounced* koo dei-**tah**) a sudden and violent change in government

couple *noun* **1** a pair, two of a kind together **2** a husband and wife ■ *verb* to join together

couplet *noun* two lines of rhyming verse

coupling *noun* a link for joining railway carriages *etc*

coupon *noun* a piece of paper which may be exchanged for goods or money

courage *noun* bravery, lack of fear

courageous *adjective* brave, fearless

courgette *noun* a type of small marrow

courier *noun* **1** someone who acts as a guide for tourists **2** a messenger

course *noun* **1** a path in which anything moves **2** movement from point to point **3** a track along which athletes *etc* run **4** a direction to be followed **5** line of action **6** a part of a meal **7** a number of things following each other: *a course of twelve lectures* ■ *verb* to move quickly

court *noun* **1** an open space surrounded by houses **2** an area marked out for playing tennis *etc* **3** the people who attend a monarch *etc* **4** a royal residence **5** a room or building where legal cases are heard or tried ■ *verb* **1** to woo as a potential lover **2** to try to gain: *courting her affections*

courteous *adjective* polite; obliging ■ **courteously** *adverb*

courtesy *noun* politeness

courtier *noun* a member of a royal court

court-martial *noun* (*plural* **courts-martial** *or* **court-martials**) an internal court held to try those who break navy or army laws ■ *verb* to try in a court-martial

court-martial *verb* ▶ court-martials, court-martial*ing*, court-martial*led*

courtship *noun* the act or time of courting or wooing

courtyard *noun* a court or enclosed space beside a house

cousin *noun* the son or daughter of an uncle or aunt

covalent bond a chemical bond formed when electrons are shared by two atoms

cove *noun* a small inlet on the sea coast; a bay

cover *verb* **1** to put or spread something on or over **2** to hide **3** to stretch over: *the hills were covered with heather* **4** to include, deal with: *covering the news story* **5** to be enough for: *five pounds should cover the cost* ■ *noun* something that covers, hides or protects ■ **cover up 1** to cover completely **2** to conceal deliberately

coverage *noun* **1** an area covered **2** the extent of news covered by a newspaper *etc*

covert *adjective* secret, not done openly

cover-up *noun* a deliberate attempt to hide the truth, especially by people in authority

covet *verb* to desire eagerly, especially something belonging to another person

covetous *adjective* having a tendency to desire things, especially things which belong to other people

cow *noun* **1** the female of various types of ox, bred by humans for giving milk **2** the female of an elephant, whale, *etc* ▪ *verb* to frighten, subdue

coward *noun* someone who has no courage and shows fear easily ▪ **cowardly** *adjective*

cowardice *noun* lack of courage

cowboy *noun* a man who works with cattle on a ranch

cowed *adjective* frightened, subdued

cower *verb* to crouch down or shrink back through fear

cowgirl *noun* a woman who works with cattle on a ranch

cowherd *noun* someone who looks after cows

cowl *noun* **1** a hood, especially that of a monk **2** a cover for a chimney

cowslip *noun* a yellow wild flower

cox *noun* (*plural* **coxes**) short for **coxswain** ▪ *verb* to act as a coxswain

coxswain *noun* **1** someone who steers a boat **2** an officer in charge of a boat and crew

coy *adjective* too modest or shy

coyote (*pronounced* kai-oh-ti) *noun* (*plural* **coyote** or **coyotes**) a type of small North American wolf

crab *noun* a sea creature with a shell and five pairs of legs, the first pair of which have large claws

crab apple a type of small, bitter apple

crack *verb* **1** to (cause to) make a sharp, sudden sound **2** to break partly without falling to pieces **3** to break into (a boat or safe) **4** to decipher (a code) **5** to break open (a nut) **6** to make (a joke) ▪ *noun* **1** a sharp sound **2** a split, a break **3** a narrow opening **4** *informal* a sharp, witty remark ▪ *adjective* excellent: *a crack tennis player*

▪ **crack up** to go to pieces, collapse

cracked *adjective* **1** split, damaged **2** *informal* mad, crazy

cracker *noun* **1** a hollow paper tube containing a small gift, which breaks with a bang when the ends are pulled **2** a thin, crisp biscuit **3** *informal* something excellent

crackle *verb* to make a continuous cracking noise

crackling *noun* **1** a continuous

cracking sound **2** the rind or outer skin of roast pork

cradle *noun* a baby's bed, especially one which can be rocked

craft *noun* **1** a trade, a skill **2** a boat, a small ship

craftsman, **craftswoman** *noun* someone who works at a trade, especially with their hands

craftworker *noun* a craftsman or craftswoman

crafty *adjective* cunning, sly ▪ **craftily** *adverb*

crag *noun* a rough steep rock

craggy *adjective* **1** rocky **2** of a face: well-marked, lined

cram *verb* **1** to fill full, stuff **2** to learn up facts for an examination in a short time

| **cram** ▶ crams, cramm*ing*, cramm*ed*

cramp *noun* **1** a painful stiffening of the muscles **2** cramps an acute stomach pain ▪ *verb* **1** to confine in too small a space **2** to hinder, restrict

cramped *adjective* **1** without enough room **2** of handwriting: small and closely-written

cranberry *noun* (*plural* **cranberries**) a type of red, sour berry

crane *noun* **1** a large wading bird with long legs, neck and bill **2** a machine for lifting heavy weights ▪ *verb* to stretch out (the neck) to see round or over something

cranefly *noun* (*plural* **craneflies**) a long-legged, two-winged insect

cranium *noun* (*plural* **crania** or **craniums**) the skull

crank *noun* **1** a handle for turning an axle **2** a lever which converts a horizontal movement into a rotating one **3** an eccentric ▪ *verb* to start (an engine) with a crank

cranky *adjective* **1** odd, eccentric **2** cross, irritable

cranny *noun* (*plural* **crannies**) a small opening or crack

crape *another spelling* of **crêpe**

crash *noun* (*plural* **crashes**) **1** a noise of heavy things breaking or banging together **2** a collision causing damage, *eg* between vehicles **3** the failure of a business ▪ *adjective* short but intensive: *crash course in French* ▪ *verb* **1** to be involved in a crash **2** of a business: to fail **3** of a computer program: to break down, fail

crash-helmet *noun* a protective covering for the head worn by motorcyclists *etc*

crash-land *verb* to land (an aircraft) in an emergency, causing some structural damage ▪ **crash-landing** *noun*

crass *adjective* stupid ▪ **crassly** *adverb*

crate *noun* a container for carrying goods, often made of wooden slats

crater *noun* **1** the bowl-shaped mouth of a volcano **2** a hole made by an explosion

cravat noun a scarf worn in place of a tie

crave verb to long for (something) ■ **craving** noun

crawl verb 1 to move on hands and knees 2 to move slowly 3 to be covered (with): crawling with wasps 4 to be obsequious, fawn ■ noun 1 the act of crawling 2 a swimming stroke performed by kicking the feet and moving one arm at a time

crawler noun, informal an obsequious, fawning person

crayon noun a coloured pencil or stick for drawing

craze noun a temporary fashion or enthusiasm

crazy adjective mad, unreasonable ■ **crazily** adverb ■ **craziness** noun

creak verb to make a sharp, grating sound like a hinge in need of oiling ■ **creaky** adjective

cream noun 1 the fatty substance which forms on milk 2 something like this in texture: shaving cream 3 the best part: cream of society ■ verb 1 to take the cream from 2 to take away (the best part)

creamy adjective full of or like cream

crease noun 1 a mark made by folding 2 cricket a line showing the position of a batsman and bowler ■ verb 1 to make creases in 2 to become creased

create verb 1 to bring into being; make 2 informal to make a fuss

creation noun 1 the act of creating 2 something created

creative adjective having the ability to create, artistic ■ **creativity** noun

creator noun the person who has created something

creature noun an animal or person

crèche noun a nursery for children

credible adjective able to be believed ■ **credibility** noun

♦※ Do not confuse with: **credulous**

credit noun 1 recognition of good qualities, achievements, etc 2 good qualities 3 a source of honour: a credit to the family 4 trustworthiness in ability to pay for goods 5 the sale of goods to be paid for later 6 the side of an account on which payments received are entered 7 a sum of money in a bank account 8 **credits** the naming of people who have helped in a film etc ■ verb 1 to believe 2 to enter on the credit side of an account 3 **credit someone with** to believe them to have: I credited him with more sense

credit card a card allowing the holder to pay for purchased articles at a later date

creditor noun someone to whom money is owed

credulity noun willingness to

believe things which may be untrue

credulous *adjective* believing too easily

◆* Do not confuse with: **credible**

creed *noun* a belief, especially a religious one

creek *noun* **1** a small inlet or bay on the sea coast **2** a short river

creep *verb* **1** to move slowly and silently **2** to move with the body close to the ground **3** to shiver with fear or disgust: *makes your flesh creep* **4** of a plant: to grow along the ground or up a wall ■ *noun* **1** the act of creeping **2** *informal* an unpleasant person ■ **creep up on** to approach silently from behind

| **creep** *verb* ▶ creeps, creeping, crept

creeper *noun* a plant growing along the ground or up a wall

creepy *adjective* unsettlingly sinister

cremate *verb* to burn (a dead body) ■ **cremation** *noun*

crematorium *noun* (*plural* **crematoria** *or* **crematoriums**) a place where dead bodies are burnt

creosote *noun* an oily liquid made from wood tar, used to keep wood from rotting

crêpe *noun* **1** a type of fine, crinkly material **2** a thin pancake

crêpe paper paper with a crinkled appearance

crept *past form* of **creep**

crescendo *noun* a musical passage of increasing loudness

crescent *adjective* shaped like the new or old moon; curved ■ *noun* **1** something in a curved shape **2** a curved road or street

cress *noun* a plant with small, slightly bitter-tasting leaves, used in salads

crest *noun* **1** a tuft on the head of a cock or other bird **2** the top of a hill, wave, *etc* **3** feathers on top of a helmet **4** a badge

crestfallen *adjective* downhearted, discouraged

crevasse *noun* a deep split in snow or ice

◆* Do not confuse: **crevasse** and **crevice**

crevice *noun* a crack, a narrow opening

crew[1] *noun* **1** the people who man a ship, aircraft, *etc* **2** a gang, a mob ■ *verb* to act as a member of a crew

crew[2] *past form* of **crow**

crib *noun* **1** a manger **2** a child's bed **3** a ready-made translation of a school text *etc* ■ *verb* to copy someone else's work

| **crib** *verb* ▶ cribs, cribbing, cribbed

cribbage *noun* a type of card game in which the score is kept with a pegged board

crick noun a sharp pain, especially in the neck ▪ verb to produce a crick in

cricket noun 1 a game played with bats, ball and wickets, between two sides of 11 each 2 an insect similar to a grasshopper

cricketer noun someone who plays cricket

cried past form of **cry**

crime noun an act or deed which is against the law

criminal adjective 1 forbidden by law 2 very wrong ▪ noun someone guilty of a crime

crimp verb to press into small ridges

crimson noun a deep red colour ▪ adjective of this colour

cringe verb 1 to crouch or shrink back in fear 2 to behave in too humble a way

crinkle verb 1 to wrinkle, crease 2 to make a crackling sound

crinkly adjective wrinkled

cripple noun a disabled person ▪ verb to make lame ▪ **crippled** adjective

crisis noun (plural **crises**) 1 a deciding moment, a turning point 2 a time of great danger or suspense

crisp adjective 1 stiff and dry; brittle 2 cool and fresh: crisp air 3 firm and fresh: crisp lettuce ▪ noun a thin crisp piece of fried potato eaten cold ▪ **crispness** noun ▪ **crispy** adjective

criss-cross adjective having a pattern of crossing lines ▪ verb to move across and back

criterion noun (plural **criteria**) a means or rule by which something can be judged; a standard

critic noun 1 someone who judges the merits or faults of a book, film, etc 2 someone who finds faults in a thing or person

critical adjective 1 fault-finding 2 of criticism: critical commentary 3 of or at a crisis 4 very ill 5 serious, very important

criticism noun 1 a judgement or opinion on (something), especially one showing up faults 2 the act of criticizing

criticize or **criticise** verb 1 to find fault with 2 to give an opinion or judgement on

croak verb to make a low, hoarse sound ▪ noun a low, hoarse sound ▪ **croaky** adjective

crochet (pronounced kroh-shei) noun a form of knitting done with one hooked needle ▪ verb to work in crochet

crock noun 1 an earthenware pot or jar 2 an old and decrepit person or thing

crockery noun china or earthenware dishes

crocodile noun 1 a large reptile found in rivers in Asia, Africa, etc 2 a procession of children walking two by two

crocus noun (plural **crocuses**) a yellow, purple or white flower which grows from a bulb

croissant *noun* a curved roll of rich bread dough

crone *noun* an ugly old woman

crony *noun* (*plural* **cronies**) *informal* a close friend

crook *noun* **1** a shepherd's or bishop's stick bent at the end **2** a criminal ▪ *verb* to bend or form into a hook

crooked (*pronounced* **kruuk**-id) *adjective* **1** bent, hooked **2** dishonest, criminal

croon *verb* to sing or hum in a low voice ▪ **crooning** *noun*

crop *noun* **1** natural produce gathered for food from fields, trees or bushes **2** a part of a bird's stomach **3** a riding whip **4** a short haircut ▪ *verb* to cut short ▪ **crop up** to happen unexpectedly

| **crop** *verb* ► **crops**, **crop**ping, **crop**ped

cropper *noun*: **come a cropper 1** to fail badly **2** to have a bad fall

croquet (*pronounced* **kroh**-kei) *noun* a game in which players use long-handled mallets to drive wooden balls through hoops in the ground

cross *noun* (*plural* **crosses**) **1** a shape (×) or (+) formed of two lines intersecting in the middle **2** a crucifix **3** a street monument marking the site of a market *etc* **4** the result of breeding an animal or plant with one of another kind ▪ *verb* **1** to mark with a cross **2** to go to the other side of (a room, road, *etc*) **3** to lie or pass across **4**

to meet and pass **5** to go against the wishes of **6** to draw two lines across (a cheque) so that it can only be paid through a bank **7** to breed (one kind) with (another) ▪ *adjective* bad-tempered, angry ▪ **cross out** to delete (something) by drawing a line through it

crossbar *noun* **1** a horizontal bar between posts, especially goalposts **2** the horizontal bar on a man's bicycle

crossbow *noun* a bow fixed across a wooden stand with a device for pulling back the bowstring

cross-country *adjective* of a race: across fields *etc*, not on roads

cross-examine *verb* to question closely in court to test the accuracy of a statement *etc* ▪ **cross-examination** *noun*

cross-eyed *adjective* having a squint

crossfire *noun* gunfire coming from different directions

crossing *noun* **1** a place where a street, river, *etc* may be crossed **2** a journey over the sea

crossly *adverb* angrily

crossness *noun* bad temper, sulkiness

cross-purposes *noun plural* confusion in a conversation through misunderstanding

crossroads *noun singular* a place where roads cross each other

cross-section noun **1** a section made by cutting across something **2** a sample taken as representative of the whole

crossword noun a puzzle in which letters are written across into blank squares to form words

crotch noun the area between the tops of the legs

crotchet noun a musical note (♩) equivalent to a quarter of a whole note or semibreve

crotchety adjective bad-tempered

crouch verb **1** to stand with the knees well bent **2** of an animal: to lie close to the ground

crow noun **1** a large bird, generally black **2** the cry of a cock **3** the happy sounds made by a baby ▪ verb **1** to cry like a cock **2** to boast **3** of a baby: to make happy noises

| crow verb ▶ crows, crowing, crew or crowed

🔸* **crew** is used as the past form for meaning 1 only: *the cock crew*; otherwise the form is **crowed**: *crowed about his exam results*

crowbar noun a large iron bar used as a lever

crowd noun a number of people or things together ▪ verb **1** to gather into a crowd **2** to fill too full **3** to keep too close to; impede

crown noun **1** a jewelled headdress worn by monarchs on ceremonial occasions **2** the top of the head **3** the highest part of something ▪ verb **1** to put a crown on **2** to make a monarch

crow's-nest noun a sheltered and enclosed platform near the top of a ship's mast from which a lookout is kept

crucial adjective extremely important, critical ▪ **crucially** adverb

crucible noun a small container for melting metals *etc*

crucifix noun (plural **crucifixes**) a figure or picture of Christ fixed to the cross

crucifixion noun **1** the act of crucifying **2** death on the cross, especially that of Christ

crucify verb to put to death by fixing the hands and feet to a cross

| crucify ▶ crucifies, crucifying, crucified

crude adjective **1** not purified or refined: *crude oil* **2** roughly made or done **3** rude, blunt, tactless ▪ **crudely** adverb ▪ **crudity** noun

cruel adjective **1** causing pain or distress **2** having no pity for others' sufferings ▪ **cruelly** adverb ▪ **cruelty** noun (plural **cruelties**)

cruet noun **1** a small jar for salt, pepper, mustard, *etc* **2** two or more such jars on a stand

cruise verb to travel by car, ship, *etc* at a steady speed ▪ noun a journey by ship made for pleasure

cruiser *noun* a middle-sized warship

crumb *noun* a small bit of anything, especially bread

crumble *verb* 1 to break into crumbs or small pieces 2 to fall to pieces ■ *noun* a dish of stewed fruit *etc* topped with crumbs

crumbly *adjective* having a tendency to fall to pieces

crumpet *noun* a soft cake, toasted and eaten with butter

crumple *verb* 1 to crush into creases or wrinkles 2 to become creased 3 to collapse

crunch *verb* 1 to chew hard so as to make a noise 2 to crush ■ *noun* 1 a noise of crunching 2 *informal* a testing moment, a turning-point ■ **crunchy** *adjective*

crusade *noun* 1 a movement undertaken for some good cause 2 *history* a Christian expedition to regain the Holy Land from the Turks

crusader *noun* someone who goes on a crusade

crush *verb* 1 to squeeze together 2 to beat down, overcome 3 to crease, crumple ■ *noun* 1 a violent squeezing 2 a pressing crowd of people 3 a drink made by squeezing fruit

crushed *adjective* 1 squeezed, squashed 2 completely defeated or miserable

crust *noun* a hard outside coating, *eg* on bread, a pie, a planet

crustacean *noun* one of a large group of animals with a hard shell, including crabs, lobsters, shrimps, *etc*

crusty *adjective* 1 having a crust 2 cross, irritable

crutch *noun* (*plural* **crutches**) 1 a stick held under the armpit or elbow, used for support in walking 2 a support, a prop

crux *noun* the most important or difficult part of a problem

cry *verb* 1 to make a loud sound in pain or sorrow 2 to weep 3 to call loudly ■ *noun* (*plural* **cries**) a loud call ■ **cry off** to cancel

| **cry** *verb* ► cries, crying, cried

crying *adjective* 1 weeping 2 calling loudly

crypt *noun* an underground cell or chapel, especially one used for burial

cryptic *adjective* mysterious, difficult to understand
■ **cryptically** *adverb*

crystal *noun* 1 very clear glass, often used for making drinking glasses *etc* 2 the regular shape taken by each small part of certain substances, *eg* salt or sugar

crystalline *adjective* made up of crystals

crystallize or **crystallise** *verb* to form into the shape of a crystal

cub *noun* 1 the young of certain animals, *eg* foxes 2 a Cub Scout

cube *noun* 1 a solid body having six equal square sides 2 the answer to a sum in which a number is multiplied by itself twice: *8 is the cube of 2*

cube root the number which, multiplied by itself and then by itself again, gives a certain other number (*eg* 2 is the cube root of 8)

cubic *adjective* **1** of cubes **2** in the shape of a cube **3** in volume: *cubic metre*

cubicle *noun* a small room closed off in some way from a larger one

cuboid *noun* a solid body having six rectangular faces, the opposite faces of which are equal

Cub Scout a junior Scout

cuckoo *noun* a bird which visits Britain in summer and lays its eggs in the nests of other birds

cucumber *noun* a creeping plant with a long green fruit used in salads

cud *noun* food regurgitated by certain animals, *eg* sheep and cows

cuddle *verb* to put your arms round, hug ▪ *noun* a hug, an embrace ▪ **cuddly** *adjective* pleasant to cuddle

cudgel *noun* a heavy stick, a club ▪ *verb* to beat with a cudgel

> **cudgel** *verb* ▶ cudgels, cudgelling, cudgelled

cue[1] *noun* **1** a sign to tell an actor when to speak *etc* **2** a hint, an indication

cue[2] *noun* the stick used to hit a ball in billiards and snooker

cuff *noun* **1** the end of a sleeve near the wrist **2** a blow with the open hand ▪ *verb* to hit with the open hand ▪ **off the cuff** without planning or rehearsal

cufflinks *noun plural* a pair of ornamental buttons *etc* used to fasten a shirt cuff

cuisine (*pronounced* kwi-zeen) *noun* **1** the art of cookery **2** a style of cooking: *Mexican cuisine*

cul-de-sac *noun* a street closed at one end

cull *verb* **1** to gather **2** to choose from a group **3** to pick out (seals, deer, *etc*) from a herd and kill for the good of the herd ▪ *noun* such a killing

culminate *verb* **1** to reach the highest point **2** to reach the most important or greatest point, end (in) ▪ **culmination** *noun*

culpable *adjective* guilty, deserving blame

culprit *noun* **1** someone who is to blame for something **2** *English* and *US law* a prisoner accused but not yet tried

cult *noun* **1** a religious sect **2** a general strong enthusiasm for something: *the cult of physical fitness*

cultivate *verb* **1** to grow (vegetables *etc*) **2** to plough, sow **3** to try to develop and improve: *cultivated my friendship* ▪ **cultivation** *noun*

cultivated *adjective* **1** farmed, ploughed **2** educated, informed

cultural *adjective* **1** to do with a culture: *cultural differences* **2** to do with the arts: *a cultural visit to the gallery*

culture *noun* **1** a type of civilization with its associated customs: *ancient Greek culture* **2** development of the mind by education **3** educated tastes in art, music, *etc* **4** cultivation of plants

culvert *noun* an arched drain for carrying water under a road or railway

cumbersome *adjective* awkward to handle

cumulative *adjective* increasing with additions: *cumulative effect*

cumulus *noun* a kind of cloud made up of rounded heaps

cunning *adjective* **1** sly, clever in a deceitful way **2** skilful, clever ■ *noun* **1** slyness **2** skill, knowledge

cup *noun* **1** a hollow container holding liquid for drinking **2** an ornamental vessel given as a prize in sports events ■ *verb* to make (hands *etc*) into the shape of a cup

| **cup** *verb* ▶ cups, cupp*ing*, cupp*ed*

cupboard *noun* a shelved recess, or a box with drawers, used for storage

cupful *noun* (*plural* **cupfuls**) as much as fills a cup

cup-tie *noun* a game in a sports

competition for which the prize is a cup

curable *adjective* able to be treated and cured

curate *noun* a member of the Church of England clergy assisting a rector or vicar

curator *noun* someone who has charge of a museum, art gallery, *etc*

curb *verb* to hold back, restrain ■ *noun* a restraint

🔌 Do not confuse with: **kerb**

curd *noun* a thick substance that forms in milk as it turns to cheese

curdle *verb* to turn into curd

cure *noun* **1** freeing from disease, healing **2** something which frees from disease ■ *verb* **1** to heal **2** to get rid of (a bad habit *etc*) **3** to preserve by drying, salting, *etc*

curfew *noun* an order forbidding people to be out of their houses after a certain hour

curiosity *noun* (*plural* **curiosities**) **1** strong desire to find something out **2** something unusual, an oddity

curious *adjective* **1** anxious to find out **2** unusual, odd ■ **curiously** *adverb*

curl *verb* **1** to twist (hair) into small coils **2** of hair: to grow naturally in small coils **3** of smoke: to move in a spiral **4** to twist, form a curved shape **5** to play at the game of curling ■ *noun* a small coil or roll, *eg* of hair

curler *noun* **1** something used to make curls **2** someone who plays the game of curling

curlew *noun* a wading bird with very long slender bill and legs

curling *noun* a game played by throwing round, flat stones along a sheet of ice

curly *adjective* having curls

currant *noun* **1** a small black raisin **2** a berry of various kinds of soft fruit: *redcurrant*

⚫* Do not confuse: **currant** and **current**

currency *noun* (*plural* **currencies**) **1** the money used in a particular country **2** the state of being generally known: *the story gained currency*

current *adjective* belonging to the present time: *the current year* ■ *noun* a stream of water, air or electrical power moving in one direction

⚫* Do not confuse: **current** and **currant**

current account a bank account from which money may be withdrawn by cheque

curriculum *noun* the course of study at a university, school, *etc*

curriculum vitae a brief account of the main events of a person's life

curry *noun* (*plural* **curries**) a dish containing a mixture of spices with a strong, hot flavour ■ *verb* to make into a curry by adding spices

curry *verb* ► curries, currying, curried

curry powder a selection of ground spices used in making curry

curse *verb* **1** to use swearwords **2** to wish evil towards ■ *noun* **1** a wish for evil or a magic spell **2** an evil or a great misfortune or the cause of this

cursed *adjective* under a curse; hateful

cursor *noun* a flashing symbol that appears on a VDU screen to show the position for entering data

cursory *adjective* hurried

curt *adjective* of someone's way of speaking: clipped and unfriendly ■ **curtly** *adverb*

curtail *verb* to make less, reduce ■ **curtailment** *noun*

curtain *noun* a piece of material hung to cover a window, stage, *etc*

curtsy or **curtsey** *noun* (*plural* **curtsies**) a bow made by bending the knees

curvature *noun* **1** a curving or bending **2** a curved piece **3** an abnormal curving of the spine

curve *noun* **1** a rounded line, like part of the edge of a circle **2** a bend: *a curve in the road*

cushion *noun* **1** a fabric casing stuffed with feathers, foam, *etc*, for resting on **2** a soft pad

cushy *adjective*, *informal* easy and comfortable: *a cushy job*

custard noun a sweet sauce made from eggs, milk and sugar

custodian noun 1 a keeper 2 a caretaker, eg of a museum

custody noun 1 care, guardianship 2 imprisonment

custom noun 1 something done by habit 2 the regular or frequent doing of something; habit 3 the buying of goods at a shop 4 **customs** taxes on goods coming into a country 5 **customs** the government department that collects these

customary adjective usual

custom-built adjective built to suit a particular purpose

customer noun 1 someone who buys from a shop 2 informal a person: a slippery customer

customize or **customise** verb to make changes to (something) to suit particular needs or tastes

cut verb 1 to make a slit in, or divide, with a blade 2 to wound 3 to trim with a blade etc 4 to reduce in amount 5 to shorten (a play, book, etc) by removing parts 6 to refuse to acknowledge (someone you know) 7 to divide (a pack of cards) in two 8 to stop filming 9 informal to play truant from (school) ■ noun 1 a slit made by cutting 2 a wound made with something sharp 3 a stroke, a blow 4 a thrust with a sword 5 the way something is cut 6 the shape and style of clothes 7 a piece of

meat ■ **cut down 1** to take down by cutting 2 to reduce ■ **cut down on** to reduce the intake of ■ **cut in** to interrupt ■ **cut off 1** to separate, isolate 2 to stop: cut off supplies ■ **cut out 1** to shape (a dress etc) by cutting 2 informal to stop 3 of an engine: to fail

| **cut** verb ► cuts, cutting, cut

cut-and-dried adjective arranged carefully and exactly

cute adjective 1 smart, clever 2 pretty and pleasing

cuticle noun the skin at the bottom and edges of finger and toe nails

cutlass noun (plural **cutlasses**) a short broad sword

cutlery noun knives, forks, spoons, etc

cutlet noun a slice of meat with the bone attached

cut-price adjective sold at a price lower than usual

cut-throat adjective fiercely competitive ■ noun a ruffian

cutting noun 1 a piece cut from a newspaper 2 a trench cut in the earth or rock for a road etc 3 a shoot of a tree or plant ■ adjective wounding, hurtful

cuttlefish noun a type of sea creature like a squid

cyanide noun a kind of poison

cyber- prefix relating to computers or electronic media: cyberspace/cyber-selling

cybercafé noun a place which serves snacks and also has

several personal computers linked to the Internet for use by customers

cycle *noun* **1** a bicycle **2** a round of events following on from one another repeatedly **3** a series of poems, stories, *etc* written about a single person or event ■ *verb* to ride a bicycle

cycle lane a section of road marked off for cyclists to use

cyclist *noun* someone who rides a bicycle

cyclone *noun* **1** a violent storm with extremely strong winds **2** a system of winds blowing in a spiral

cygnet *noun* a young swan

💧* Do not confuse with: signet

cylinder *noun* **1** a solid or hollow tube-shaped object **2** in machines, car engines, *etc*, the hollow tube in which a piston works

cylindrical *adjective* shaped like a cylinder

cymbals *noun plural* brass, plate-like musical instruments, beaten together in pairs

cynic *noun* someone who believes the worst about people ■ **cynicism** *noun*

cynical *adjective* sneering; believing the worst of people ■ **cynically** *adverb*

cypress *noun* a type of evergreen tree

cyst *noun* a liquid-filled blister within the body or just under the skin

czar *another spelling of* **tsar**

czarina *another spelling of* **tsarina**

Dd

dab *verb* to touch gently with a pad *etc* to soak up moisture ■ *noun* **1** the act of dabbing **2** a gentle blow, a pat **3** a small kind of flounder

| **dab** *verb* ▶ dabs, dabbing, dabbed

dabble *verb* **1** to play in water with hands or feet **2** to do in a half-serious way or as a hobby: *dabble in computers*

dab hand *informal* an expert

dachshund (*pronounced* daks-huwnt *or* daks-huwnd) *noun* a breed of dog with short legs and a long body

dad *or* **daddy** *noun, informal* father

daffodil *noun* a type of yellow flower which grows from a bulb

daft *adjective* silly

dagger *noun* a short sword for stabbing

dahlia *noun* a type of garden plant with large flowers

daily *adjective & adverb* every day

dainty *adjective* small and neat ■ **daintily** *adverb*

dairy *noun* (*plural* **dairies**) **1** a building for storing milk and making butter and cheese **2** a shop which sells milk, butter, cheese, *etc*

dais *noun* (*plural* **daises**) a raised floor at the upper end of a hall

daisy *noun* (*plural* **daisies**) a small common flower with white petals

daisy chain a string of daisies threaded through each other's stems

dalai lama the spiritual leader of Tibetan Buddhism

dale *noun* low ground between hills

dally *verb* **1** to waste time idling or playing **2** to play (with) ■ **dalliance** *noun*

| **dally** ▶ dallies, dallying, dallied

Dalmatian *noun* a breed of large spotted dog

dam *noun* **1** a wall of earth, concrete, *etc* to keep back water **2** water kept in like this ■ *verb* **1** to keep back by a dam **2** to hold back, restrain (tears *etc*)

| **dam** *verb* ▶ dams, damming, dammed

damage noun 1 hurt, injury 2 **damages** money paid by one person to another to make up for injury, insults, etc ■ verb to spoil, make less effective or unusable

dame noun 1 a comic woman in a pantomime, played by a man in drag 2 **Dame** the title of a woman of the same rank as a knight

damn verb 1 to sentence to unending punishment in hell 2 to condemn as wrong, bad, etc ■ exclamation an expression of annoyance

damnably adverb, slang extremely

damnation noun unending punishment in hell

damning adjective leading to conviction or ruin

damp noun 1 moist air 2 wetness, moistness ■ verb 1 to wet slightly 2 to make less fierce or intense ■ adjective moist, slightly wet

dampen verb 1 to make or become damp; moisten 2 to lessen (enthusiasm etc)

damper noun, music a pad which touches the strings inside a piano, silencing each note after it has been played ■ **put a damper on something** to make it less cheerful

dampness noun the quality of being damp

damson noun a type of small dark-red plum

dance verb to move in time to music ■ noun 1 a sequence of steps in time to music 2 a social event with dancing ■ **dancer** noun ■ **dancing** noun & adjective

dandelion noun a type of common plant with a yellow flower

dandruff noun dead skin which collects under the hair and falls off in flakes

dandy noun, old (plural **dandies**) a man who pays great attention to his dress and looks

danger noun 1 something potentially harmful 2 potential harm: unaware of the danger

dangerous adjective 1 unsafe, likely to cause harm 2 full of risks ■ **dangerously** adverb

dangle verb to hang loosely

dank adjective moist, wet and cold

dapper adjective small and neat

dappled adjective marked with spots or splashes of colour

dare verb 1 to be brave or bold enough (to): I didn't dare tell him 2 to challenge: dared him to cross the railway line ■ **I dare say** I suppose

daredevil noun a rash person fond of taking risks ■ adjective rash, risky

daring adjective bold, fearless ■ noun boldness ■ **daringly** adverb

dark adjective 1 without light 2 black or near to black 3 gloomy 4 evil ■ noun absence of light, nightfall ■ **darkness** noun

darken verb to make or grow dark or darker

dark horse someone about whom little is known

darling noun 1 a word showing affection 2 someone dearly loved; a favourite

darn verb to mend (clothes) with crossing rows of stitches ■ noun a patch mended in this way

dart noun a pointed weapon for throwing or shooting ■ verb to move quickly and suddenly

dartboard noun the board used in playing the game of darts

darts noun singular a game in which small darts are aimed at a board marked off in circles and numbered sections

dash verb 1 to throw or knock violently, especially so as to break 2 to ruin (hopes) 3 to depress, sadden (spirits) 4 to rush with speed or violence ■ noun (plural **dashes**) 1 a rush 2 a short race 3 a small amount of a drink etc 4 a short line (–) to show a break in a sentence etc

dashboard noun a panel with dials, switches, etc in front of the driver's seat in a vehicle

dashing adjective 1 hasty 2 smart, elegant

data noun plural (singular **datum**) 1 available facts from which conclusions may be drawn 2 facts stored in a computer

database noun, computing a collection of systematically

stored files that are often connected with each other

date[1] noun 1 a statement of time in terms of the day, month and year, eg 23 December 1995 2 the time at which an event occurs 3 the period of time to which something belongs 4 an appointment ■ verb 1 to give a date to 2 to belong to a certain time: dates from the 12th century 3 to become old-fashioned

date[2] noun 1 a type of palm tree 2 its blackish, shiny fruit with a hard stone

datum singular of data

daub verb 1 to smear 2 to paint roughly

daughter noun a female child

daughter-in-law noun a son's wife

daunt verb 1 to frighten 2 to be discouraging

dawdle verb to move slowly ■ **dawdler** noun

dawn noun 1 the time when light first appears at the start of a day 2 a beginning: dawn of a new era ■ verb 1 to become day 2 to begin to appear ■ **dawn on** to become suddenly clear to (someone)

dawn chorus the singing of birds at dawn

day noun 1 the time of light, from sunrise to sunset 2 twenty-four hours, from one midnight to the next 3 the time or hours spent at work 4 (often **days**) a particular time or period: *in the days of steam*

daydream *noun* an imagining of pleasant events while awake ■ *verb* to imagine in this way

dayglo *noun*, *trademark* a luminously bright colour

daylight *noun* the light of day, sunlight

day-release *noun* time off from work for training or education

daze *verb* **1** to stun with a blow **2** to confuse, bewilder

dazzle *verb* **1** to shine on so as to prevent from seeing clearly **2** to shine brilliantly **3** to fascinate, impress deeply

deacon *noun* **1** the lowest rank of clergy in the Church of England **2** an official in some other churches

dead *adjective* **1** not living, without life **2** cold and cheerless **3** numb **4** not working; no longer in use **5** complete, utter **6** exact: *dead centre* ■ *adverb* **1** completely: *dead certain* **2** suddenly and completely: *stop dead* ■ *noun* **1** those who have died: *respect for the dead* **2** the time of greatest stillness *etc*: *the dead of night*

dead-beat *adjective* having no strength left

deaden *verb* to lessen (pain *etc*)

dead end a road *etc* closed at one end **2** a job *etc* not leading to promotion

dead heat a race in which two or more runners finish equal

deadline *noun* a date by which something must be done

deadlock *noun* a standstill resulting from a complete failure to agree

deadly *adjective* **1** likely to cause death, fatal **2** intense, very great: *deadly hush* ■ *adverb* intensely, extremely

deadpan *adjective* without expression on the face

deaf *adjective* **1** unable to hear **2** refusing to listen

deafen *verb* **1** to make deaf **2** to be unpleasantly loud

deafening *adjective* extremely loud

deal *noun* **1** an agreement, especially in business **2** an amount or quantity: *a good deal of paper* **3** the dividing out of playing-cards in a game ■ *verb* **1** to divide, give out **2** to trade (in) **3** to do business (with) ■ **deal with** to take action concerning, cope with

dealer *noun* **1** someone who deals out cards at a game **2** a trader

dean *noun* **1** the chief religious officer in a cathedral church **2** the head of a faculty in a university

dear *adjective* **1** high in price **2** highly valued; much loved ■ *noun* **1** someone who is loved **2** someone who is lovable or charming ■ *adverb* at a high price

dearly *adverb* **1** very much,

sincerely: *love someone dearly* **2** involving a great cost, either financially or in some other way

dearth (*pronounced* derth) *noun* a scarcity, shortage

death *noun* **1** the state of being dead, the end of life **2** the end of something: *the death of steam railways*

deathblow *noun* **1** a blow that causes death **2** an event that causes something to end

death knell 1 a bell announcing a death **2** something indicating the end of a scheme, hope, *etc*

deathly *adjective* **1** very pale or ill-looking **2** deadly

death wish a conscious or unconscious desire to die

debar *verb* to keep from, prevent
| **debar ►** debars, debar**ring**, debar**red**

debase *verb* **1** to lessen in value **2** to make bad, wicked, *etc*
■ **debased** *adjective*

debatable *adjective* arguable, doubtful

debate *noun* **1** a discussion, especially a formal one before an audience **2** an argument ■ *verb* to engage in debate, discuss

debauched *adjective* inclined to debauchery

debauchery *noun* excessive indulgence in drunkenness, lewdness, *etc*

debilitate *verb* to make weak

debit *noun* an amount owed, spent or deducted from a bank account ■ *verb* to mark down as a debit

debit card a plastic card which transfers money directly from a purchaser's account to a retailer's

debonair *adjective* of pleasant and cheerful appearance and behaviour

debris (*pronounced* deb-ree) *noun* **1** the remains of something broken, destroyed, *etc* **2** rubbish

debt *noun* what one person owes to another

debtor *noun* someone who owes a debt

debut *or* **début** (*pronounced* dei-byoo) *noun* the first public appearance, *eg* of an actor
■ *adjective* first before the public

deca- *or* **dec-** *prefix* ten, multiplied by ten: *decade/ decathlon*

decade *noun* **1** a period of ten years **2** a set or series of ten

decadence *noun* a falling from high to low standards in morals, the arts, *etc*

decadent *adjective* wicked, throwing away moral standards for the sake of pleasure

decaff *adjective*, *informal* decaffeinated

decaffeinated *adjective* with the caffeine removed

decagon *noun* a figure with ten sides

decamp *verb* to run away

decant *verb* to pour (wine *etc*) from a bottle into a decanter

decanter noun an ornamental bottle with a glass stopper for wine, whisky, etc

decapitate verb to cut the head from ■ **decapitation** noun

decathlon noun an athletics competition combining contests in ten separate disciplines

decay verb to become bad, worse or rotten, etc ■ noun the process of rotting or worsening ■ **decayed** adjective

decease noun, formal death

deceased adjective, formal dead ■ noun (**the deceased**) a dead person

deceit noun the act of deceiving

deceitful adjective inclined to deceive; lying ■ **deceitfully** adverb

deceive verb to tell lies to so as to mislead ■ **deceiver** noun

decelerate verb to slow down ■ **deceleration** noun

December noun the twelfth month of the year

decent adjective 1 respectable 2 good enough, adequate: decent salary 3 kind: decent of you to help ■ **decency** noun (meanings 1 and 3) ■ **decently** adverb

deception noun 1 the act of deceiving 2 something that deceives or is intended to deceive

deceptive adjective misleading: appearances may be deceptive ■ **deceptively** adverb

deci- prefix one-tenth: decimal/ decimate

decibel noun a unit of loudness of sound

decide verb 1 to make up your mind to do something: I've decided to take your advice 2 to settle (an argument etc)

decided adjective 1 clear: a decided difference 2 with your mind made up: he was decided on the issue

decidedly adverb definitely

deciduous adjective of a tree: having leaves that fall in autumn

decimal adjective 1 numbered by tens 2 of ten parts or the number 10 ■ noun a decimal fraction

decimal currency a system of money in which each coin or note is either a tenth of another or ten times another in value

decimal fraction a fraction expressed in tenths, hundredths, thousandths, etc, separated by a decimal point

decimalize or **decimalise** verb to convert (figures or currency) to decimal form ■ **decimalization** noun

decimal place a digit to the right of a decimal point, eg in 0.26, 2 is in the first decimal place

decimal point a dot used to separate units from decimal fractions, eg $0.1 = \frac{1}{10}$, $2.33 = \frac{233}{100}$

decimate verb to make much smaller in numbers

decipher verb 1 to translate (a code) into ordinary,

understandable language **2** to make out the meaning of **decision** noun **1** the act of deciding **2** clear judgement, firmness: *acting with decision*

decisive adjective **1** final, putting an end to a contest etc: *a decisive defeat* **2** showing decision and firmness ▪ **decisively** adverb

deck noun **1** a platform forming the floor of a ship, bus, etc **2** a pack of playing-cards ▪ verb to decorate, adorn

deckchair noun a collapsible chair of wood and canvas etc

declare verb **1** to make known (goods or income on which tax is payable) **2** to announce formally or publicly **3** to say firmly ▪ **declaration** noun

decline verb **1** to say 'no' to, refuse **2** to weaken, become worse ▪ noun a gradual worsening of health etc

decode verb to translate (a coded message) into ordinary, understandable language

decompose verb to rot, decay ▪ **decomposition** noun

décor noun the decoration of, and arrangement of objects in, a room etc

decorate verb **1** to add ornament to **2** to paint or paper the walls of (a room etc) ▪ **decoration** noun

decorative adjective **1** ornamental **2** pretty

decorator noun someone who decorates houses, rooms, etc

decoy verb to lead into a trap or into evil ▪ noun something or someone intended to lead another into a trap

decrease verb to make or become less in number ▪ noun a growing less

decree noun **1** an order, a law **2** a judge's decision ▪ verb to give an order

| **decree** verb ▶ decrees, decreeing, decreed

decrepit adjective **1** weak and infirm because of old age **2** in ruins or disrepair

dedicate verb **1** to devote yourself (to) **2** to inscribe or publish (a book etc) in tribute to someone or something ▪ **dedicated** adjective ▪ **dedication** noun

deduce verb to find out something by putting together all that is known

◆※ Do not confuse: **deduce** and **deduct**

deduct verb to subtract, take away (from)

deduction noun **1** a subtraction **2** finding something out using logic, or a thing which has been found out in this way

deed noun **1** something done, an act **2** law a signed statement or bargain

deem verb, formal to judge or consider: *deemed unsuitable for children*

deep *adjective* 1 being or going far down 2 hard to understand; cunning 3 involved to a great extent: *deep in debt* 4 intense, strong: *deep affection* 5 low in pitch ■ *noun* (**the deep**) the sea

deepen *verb* to make or become deep

deep-freeze *noun* a low-temperature refrigerator that can freeze and preserve food frozen for a long time

deer *noun* (*plural* **deer**) an animal with antlers in the male, such as the reindeer

deface *verb* to spoil the appearance of, disfigure

default *noun* a pre-set action taken by a computer system unless a user's instruction overrides it ■ **by default** because of a failure to do something

defeat *verb* to beat, win a victory over ■ *noun* an act of defeating or being defeated

defect *noun* a lack of something needed for completeness or perfection; a flaw

defective *adjective* faulty; incomplete

♦ Do not confuse with: **deficient**

defence or US **defense** *noun* 1 the act of defending against attack 2 a means or method of protection 3 *law* the argument defending the accused person in a case (*contrasted with*:

prosecution) 4 *law* the lawyer(s) putting forward this argument

defenceless *adjective* without defence

defend *verb* 1 to guard or protect against attack 2 *law* to conduct the defence of 3 to support against criticism

defendant *noun, law* the accused person in a law case

defensive *adjective* 1 used for defence 2 expecting criticism, ready to justify actions

defer *verb* 1 to put off to another time 2 to give way (to): *he deferred to my wishes*

| **defer** ▶ defers, defer**ring**, defer**red**

defiance *noun* open disobedience or opposition ■ **defiant** *adjective* ■ **defiantly** *adverb*

deficiency *noun* (*plural* **deficiencies**) 1 lack, want 2 an amount lacking

deficient *adjective* lacking in what is needed

♦ Do not confuse with: **defective**

deficit *noun* an amount by which a sum of money *etc* is too little

define *verb* 1 to fix the bounds or limits of 2 to state the exact meaning of

definite *adjective* 1 having clear limits, fixed 2 exact 3 certain, sure

definite article the name given to the adjective *the*

definitely *adverb* certainly, without doubt

definition *noun* **1** an explanation of the exact meaning of a word or phrase **2** sharpness or clearness of outline

definitive *adjective* **1** fixed, final **2** not able to be bettered: *definitive biography*

deflate *verb* to let the air out of (a tyre *etc*)

deflation *noun* **1** the letting out of air (from *eg* a tyre) **2** the feeling of disappointment which you get *eg* when your hopes have been dashed

deflect *verb* to turn aside (from a fixed course) ▪ **deflection** *noun*

deforestation *noun* the removal of all or most of the trees in a forested area

deform *verb* **1** to spoil the shape of **2** to make ugly

deformed *adjective* badly or abnormally formed

deformity *noun* (*plural* **deformities**) **1** something abnormal in shape **2** the fact of being badly shaped

defraud *verb* **1** to cheat **2** **defraud someone of something** to take or keep it from them by cheating or fraud

defrost *verb* to remove frost or ice (from); thaw

deft *adjective* clever with the hands, handy ▪ **deftly** *adverb*

defunct *adjective* no longer active or in use

defy *verb* **1** to dare to do something, challenge **2** to resist openly **3** to make impossible: *its beauty defies description*

| **defy** ► **defies**, **defy**ing, **defi**ed

degenerate *verb* to become or grow bad or worse

degrade *verb* to disgrace

degrading *adjective* humiliating and embarrassing

degree *noun* **1** a step or stage in a process **2** rank or grade **3** amount, extent **4** a unit of temperature **5** a unit by which angles are measured, one 360th part of the circumference of a circle **6** a certificate given by a university, gained by examination or given as an honour

dehydrate *verb* to lose excessive water from the body

dehydrated *adjective* weak and exhausted as a result of losing too much water from your body

dehydration *noun* a lack of sufficient water in the body

deign *verb* to act as if doing a favour: *she deigned to answer us*

deity (*pronounced* dei-it-i) *noun* (*plural* **deities**) a god or goddess

déjà vu (*pronounced* dei-zah voo) the feeling of having experienced something before

dejected *adjective* gloomy, dispirited ▪ **dejection** *noun*

delay verb 1 to put off, postpone 2 to keep back, hinder ■ noun 1 a postponement 2 a hindrance

delegate verb (pronounced del-ig-eit) to give (a task) to someone else to do ■ noun (pronounced del-ig-at) someone acting on behalf of another; a representative

delegation noun a group of delegates

delete verb to rub or strike out (eg a piece of writing) ■ **deletion** noun

deli noun, informal a delicatessen

deliberate adjective 1 intentional, not accidental 2 slow in deciding 3 not hurried ■ **deliberately** adverb

deliberation noun careful thought

delicacy noun (plural delicacies) 1 tact 2 something delicious to eat

delicate adjective 1 not strong, frail 2 easily damaged 3 fine, dainty 4 pleasant to taste 5 tactful 6 requiring skill or care: delicate operation

delicatessen noun a shop selling food cooked or prepared ready for eating

delicious adjective 1 very pleasant to taste 2 giving pleasure ■ **deliciously** adverb

delight verb 1 to please greatly 2 to take great pleasure (in) ■ noun great pleasure

delighted adjective very pleased

delightful adjective very pleasing ■ **delightfully** adverb

delinquent noun someone guilty of an offence

delirious adjective 1 raving, wandering in the mind 2 wildly excited ■ **deliriously** adverb

delirium noun 1 a delirious state, especially caused by fever 2 wild excitement

deliver verb 1 to hand over 2 to give out (eg a speech, a blow) 3 to set free, rescue 4 to assist at the birth of (a child)

delivery noun (plural deliveries) 1 a handing over, eg of letters 2 the birth of a child 3 a style of speaking

delta noun the triangular stretch of land at the mouth of a river

delude verb to deceive

deluge noun 1 a great flood of water 2 an overwhelming amount: deluge of work ■ verb to overwhelm

delusion noun a false belief, especially as a symptom of mental illness

♣ Do not confuse with: allusion and illusion. Delusion comes from the verb **delude**

delve verb to rummage, search through: delved in her bag for her keys

demand verb 1 to ask, or ask for, firmly 2 to insist: I demand that *you listen* **3** to require, call for: *demanding attention* ▪ noun **1** a forceful request **2** an urgent claim: *many demands on his time* **3** a need for certain goods *etc*

demeanour noun behaviour, conduct

demented adjective mad, insane

democracy noun government of the people by the people through their elected representatives

democrat noun **1** someone who believes in democracy **2** **Democrat** US a member of the American Democratic Party

democratic adjective **1** of or governed by democracy **2** **Democratic** US belonging to the American Democratic Party ▪ democratically adverb

demolish verb **1** to destroy completely **2** to pull down (a building *etc*) ▪ demolition noun

demon noun an evil spirit, a devil

demonstrate verb **1** to show clearly; prove **2** to show (a machine *etc*) in action **3** to express an opinion by marching, showing placards, *etc* in public

demonstration noun **1** a showing, a display **2** a public expression of opinion by a procession, mass meeting, *etc*

demonstrative adjective inclined to show feelings openly

demonstrator noun **1** a person who takes part in a public

demonstration to express their opinion about something **2** a person who explains how something works, or shows you how to do something

demoralize or **demoralise** verb to take away the confidence of ▪ demoralization noun

demote verb to reduce to a lower rank or grade ▪ demotion noun

demure adjective shy and modest ▪ demurely adverb

den noun the lair of a wild animal

denial noun the act of denying

denier (pronounced den-i-er) noun a unit of weight of nylon, silk, *etc*

denim noun a hard-wearing cotton cloth used for jeans, overalls, *etc*

denomination noun **1** name, title **2** a value of a coin, stamp, *etc* **3** a religious sect

denominator noun the lower number in a vulgar fraction by which the upper number is divided, *eg* the 3 in $\frac{2}{3}$ (*compare with*: **numerator**)

denote verb to mean, signify

denounce verb to accuse publicly of a crime

dense adjective **1** closely packed together; thick **2** very stupid ▪ densely adverb

density noun (plural densities) **1** thickness **2** weight (of water) in proportion to volume **3** *computing* the extent to which data can be held on a floppy disk

dent *noun* a hollow made by a blow or pressure ▪ *verb* to make a dent in

dental *adjective* of or for a tooth or teeth

dentist *noun* a doctor who examines teeth and treats dental problems

dentistry *noun* the work of a dentist

dentures *noun plural* a set of false teeth

denunciation *noun* a strongly expressed public criticism or condemnation

deny *verb* 1 to declare to be untrue 2 to refuse, forbid ▪ **deny yourself** to do without things you want or need

| deny ► denies, denying, denied

deodorant *noun* something that hides unpleasant smells

depart *verb* to go away

department *noun* a self-contained section within a shop, university, government, *etc*

departure *noun* 1 the act of leaving or going away 2 a break with something expected or traditional

depend *verb*: **depend on** 1 to rely on 2 to receive necessary financial support from 3 to be controlled or decided by

dependable *adjective* to be trusted

dependant *noun* someone who is kept or supported by another

⚫✴ Do not confuse: **dependant** and **dependent**

dependence *or* **dependency** *noun* the state of being dependent

dependent *adjective* relying or depending (on)

⚫✴ Do not confuse: **dependent** and **dependant**

depict *verb* to describe

deplete *verb* to make smaller in amount or number ▪ **depletion** *noun*

deplorable *adjective* regrettable; very bad

deploy *verb* to place in position ready for action

depopulate *verb* to reduce greatly in population ▪ **depopulated** *adjective* ▪ **depopulation** *noun*

deport *verb* to send (someone) out of a country ▪ **deportation** *noun*

depose *verb* to remove from a high position, especially a monarch from a throne

deposit *verb* 1 to put or set down 2 to put in for safe keeping, *eg* money in a bank ▪ *noun* 1 money paid in part payment of something 2 money put in a bank account 3 a solid that has settled at the bottom of a liquid

deposit account a bank account from which money must be withdrawn in person, not by cheque

depot (*pronounced* **dep-oh**) *noun* **1** a place where goods are stored **2** a building where railway engines, buses, *etc* are kept and repaired

depreciate *verb* **1** to lessen the value of **2** to fall in value
■ **depreciation** *noun*

depress *verb* to make gloomy or unhappy

depressed *adjective* gloomy, in low spirits

depressing *adjective* having the effect of making you gloomy or unhappy

depression *noun* **1** low spirits, gloominess **2** a hollow **3** a low period in a country's economy with unemployment, lack of trade, *etc* **4** a region of low atmospheric pressure

deprivation *noun* great hardship; lack of the basic necessities in life, *eg* food or human contact

deprive *verb*: **deprive of** to take away from

deprived *adjective* suffering from hardship; disadvantaged

depth *noun* **1** deepness **2** intensity, strength: *depth of colour*

deputize *or* **deputise** *verb* to take another's place, act as substitute

deputy *noun* (*plural* **deputies**) **1** a delegate, a representative **2** a second-in-command

deranged *adjective* mad, insane

derby *noun* (*plural* **derbies**) a sports event between two teams from the same area

derelict *adjective* broken-down, abandoned

dereliction *noun* neglect of what should be attended to: *dereliction of duty*

deride *verb* to laugh at, mock

derision *noun* mockery

derisive *adjective* mocking

derivative *adjective* not original
■ *noun* a word formed on the base of another word, *eg fabulous from fable*

derive *verb* **1** to be descended or formed (from) **2** to receive, obtain
■ **derivation** *noun*

dermatitis *noun* inflammation of the skin

derogatory *adjective* scornful, belittling, disparaging

derrick *noun* **1** a crane for lifting weights **2** a framework over an oil well that holds the drilling machinery

descant *noun, music* a tune played or sung above the main tune

descend *verb* **1** to go or climb down **2** to slope downwards **3** **descend from** to have as an ancestor: *descended from Napoleon*

descendant *noun* someone descended from another

descent *noun* **1** an act of descending **2** a downward slope

describe *verb* to give an account of in words

description *noun* 1 the act of describing 2 an account in words 3 sort, kind: *people of all descriptions*

desecrate *verb* to spoil (something sacred)

desert[1] *verb* 1 to run away from (the army) 2 to leave, abandon: *deserted his wife* ■ **deserter** *noun*

desert[2] *noun* a stretch of barren country with very little water

💧* Do not confuse with: **dessert**

desert island an uninhabited island in a tropical area

deserve *verb* to have earned as a right, be worthy of

deservedly *adverb* justly

deserving *adjective* 1 worthy of being rewarded or helped 2 **be deserving of something** to deserve it

desiccate *verb* to preserve by drying: *desiccated coconut*

💧* Do not confuse with: **desecrate**. Remember that **desecRate** and **sacRed** are related, and they both contain an **R**

design *verb* to make a plan of (eg a building) before it is made ■ *noun* 1 a plan, a sketch 2 a painted picture, pattern, *etc*

designate *verb* 1 to name or appoint 2 to point out

designing *adjective* crafty, cunning

desirable *adjective* pleasing; worth having

desire *verb* to wish for greatly ■ *noun* 1 a longing for 2 a wish

desk *noun* a table for writing, reading, *etc*

desolate *adjective* 1 deeply unhappy 2 empty of people, deserted

desolation *noun* deep sorrow

despair *verb* to give up hope ■ *noun* 1 lack of hope 2 a cause of despair: *she was the despair of her mother*

despatch *another spelling of* **dispatch**

desperate *adjective* 1 without hope, despairing 2 very bad, awful

desperately *adverb* very much, very intensely: *desperately in love*

desperation *noun* the feeling you have when your situation is so bad that you are prepared to do anything to get out of it

despicable *adjective* contemptible, hateful

despise *verb* to look on with contempt

despite *preposition* in spite of

despondent *adjective* downhearted, dejected ■ **despondency** *noun*

despot *noun* a ruler with unlimited power, a tyrant ■ **despotic** *adjective*

dessert *noun* fruits, sweets, *etc* served at the end of a meal

⚫※ Do not confuse with:
desert

destination *noun* the place to which someone or something is going

destine *verb* to set apart for a certain use

destiny *noun* (*plural* **destinies**) what is destined to happen; fate

destitute *adjective* lacking food, shelter, *etc*

destroy *verb* 1 to pull down, knock to pieces 2 to ruin 3 to kill

destroyer *noun* a type of fast warship

destruction *noun* 1 the act of destroying or being destroyed 2 ruin

destructive *adjective* doing great damage

detach *verb* to unfasten, remove (from)

detachable *adjective* able to be taken off: *detachable lining*

detached *adjective* 1 standing apart, by itself: *detached house* 2 not personally involved, showing no emotion

detachment *noun* the state of being detached

detail *noun* a small part, fact, item, *etc* ▪ *verb* to describe fully, give particulars of

detailed *adjective* with nothing left out

detain *verb* 1 to hold back 2 to keep late 3 to keep under guard

detect *verb* 1 to discover 2 to notice ▪ **detection** *noun*

detective *noun* someone who tries to find criminals or watches suspects

detention *noun* 1 imprisonment 2 a forced stay after school as punishment

deter *verb* to discourage or prevent through fear

| **deter** ► deters, deterring, deterred

detergent *noun* a soapless substance used with water for washing dishes *etc*

deteriorate *verb* to grow worse ▪ **deterioration** *noun*

determination *noun* 1 the fact of being determined 2 stubbornness, firmness of purpose

determine *verb* 1 to decide (on) 2 to fix, settle: *determined his course of action*

determined *adjective* 1 firmly decided; having a strong intention 2 fixed, settled

deterrent *noun* something, especially a threat of some kind, which deters or discourages people from a particular course of action

detest *verb* to hate greatly

detonate *verb* to (cause to) explode

detonator *noun* something which sets off an explosive

detour *noun* a circuitous route

detract *verb* to take away (from), lessen

detriment *noun* harm, damage, disadvantage

detrimental *adjective* disadvantageous (to), causing harm or damage

deuce (*pronounced* dyoos) *noun* 1 a playing-card with two pips 2 *tennis* a score of forty points each

devastate *verb* 1 to lay in ruins 2 to overwhelm with grief *etc*
■ **devastation** *noun*

develop *verb* 1 to (make to) grow bigger or more advanced 2 to acquire gradually: *developed a taste for opera* 3 to become active or visible 4 to unfold gradually 5 to use chemicals to make (a photograph) appear

Developing World a name for the underdeveloped countries in Africa, Asia and Latin America (*also called*: **Third World**)

development *noun* 1 growth in size or importance 2 work done on studying and improving on previous or basic models, designs or techniques 3 improvement of land so as to make it more fertile, useful or profitable 4 an occurrence that affects or influences a situation 5 the gradual unfolding of something *eg* a story 6 the process of using chemicals to make a photograph appear

deviate *verb* to turn aside, especially from a standard course

deviation *noun* something

which is different, or which departs from the normal course

device *noun* a tool, an instrument

🖋 Do not confuse with: **devise**. To help you remember: 'ice' is a noun, 'ise' is not!

devil *noun* 1 an evil spirit 2 Satan 3 a wicked person

devilish *adjective* very wicked

devious *adjective* 1 not direct, roundabout 2 not honest or straightforward

devise *verb* to make up, put together

🖋 Do not confuse with: **device**. To help you remember: 'ice' is a noun ... so 'ise' must be the verb!

devoid *adjective*: **devoid of** empty of, free from: *devoid of curiosity*

devolution *noun* the delegation of certain legislative powers to regional or national assemblies

devolutionist *noun* a supporter of devolution

devolve *verb* 1 to fall as a duty (on) 2 to delegate (power) to a regional or national assembly

devote *verb* to give up wholly (to)

devoted *adjective* 1 loving and loyal 2 given up (to): *devoted to her work*

devotee *noun* a keen follower

devotion *noun* great love

devour *verb* 1 to eat up greedily 2 to destroy

devout *adjective* **1** earnest, sincere **2** religious ▪ **devoutly** *adverb*

dew *noun* tiny drops of water which form from the air as it cools at night

dexterity *noun* skill, quickness ▪ **dexterous** *or* **dextrous** *adjective*

dhoti *noun* (*plural* **dhotis**) a piece of cloth worn around the hips by some Hindu men

di- *prefix* two, twice or double: *carbon dioxide* (= having molecules containing two oxygen atoms)

diabetes *noun* a disease in which there is too much sugar in the blood

diabetic *noun & adjective* (someone) suffering from diabetes

diabolical *adjective* devilish, very wicked

diagnose *verb* to identify (a cause of illness) after making an examination

diagnosis *noun* (*plural* **diagnoses**) the identification (of the cause of illness in a patient) by examination

diagonal *adjective* going from one corner to the opposite corner ▪ *noun* a line from one corner to the opposite corner ▪ **diagonally** *adverb*

diagram *noun* a drawing to explain something

dial *noun* **1** the face of a clock or watch **2** a rotating disc over the numbers on some telephones ▪ *verb* to call (a number) on a telephone using a dial or buttons

| **dial** *verb* ► dials, dialling, dialled

dialect *noun* a way of speaking found only in a certain area or among a certain group of people

dialogue *noun* a talk between two or more people

diameter *noun* a line which dissects a circle, passing through its centre

diamond *noun* **1** a very hard precious stone **2** an elongated, four-cornered shape (♦) **3 diamonds** one of the four suits in playing-cards

diaphragm *noun* a layer of muscle separating the lower part of the body from the chest

diarrhoea *noun* frequent emptying of the bowels, with too much liquid in the faeces

diary *noun* (*plural* **diaries**) **1** a record of daily happenings **2** a book detailing these

dice *or* **die** *noun* (*plural* **dice**) a small cube with numbered sides or faces, used in certain games ▪ *verb* (**dice**) to cut (food) into small cubes

dictate *verb* **1** to speak the text of (a letter *etc*) for someone else to write down **2** to give firm commands ▪ *noun* an order, a command

dictation *noun* the act of dictating

dictator *noun* an all-powerful ruler

dictatorial *adjective* like a dictator; domineering

dictionary *noun* (*plural* **dictionaries**) a book giving the words of a language in alphabetical order, together with their meanings

did *see* do

die¹ *verb* 1 to lose life 2 to wither ■ **die down** to become less intense

| **die** ▶ dies, dying, died

die² *noun* 1 a stamp or punch for making raised designs on money *etc* 2 *another word for* **dice**

diesel *noun* an internal combustion engine in which heavy oil is ignited by heat generated by compression

diet *noun* 1 food 2 a course of recommended foods, *eg* to lose weight ■ *verb* to eat certain kinds of food only, especially to lose weight

differ *verb* 1 **differ from** to be unlike 2 to disagree

| **differ** ▶ differs, differing, differed

difference *noun* 1 a point in which things differ 2 the amount by which one number is greater than another

different *adjective* 1 **different from** unlike 2 varying, not the same 3 unusual

differentiate *verb* to make a difference or distinction between

difficult *adjective* 1 not easy; hard to do, understand or deal with 2 hard to please

difficulty *noun* (*plural* **difficulties**) 1 lack of easiness; hardness 2 anything difficult 3 anything which makes something difficult; an obstacle, hindrance, *etc* 4 **difficulties** troubles

diffraction *noun* the spreading of a light wave when it encounters an obstacle

diffuse *verb* to spread in all directions

diffusion *noun* 1 the reflection of light in all directions 2 the way light passes through a transparent substance 3 *chemistry* the movement of ions or molecules from an area of higher concentration to a lower one

dig *verb* 1 to turn up (earth) with a spade *etc* 2 to make (a hole) by this means 3 to poke or push (something) into ■ *noun* 1 a poke, a thrust 2 an archaeological excavation

| **dig** ▶ digs, digging, dug

digest *verb* 1 to break down (food) in the stomach into a form that the body can make use of 2 to think over

digestion *noun* the act or power of digesting

digger *noun* a machine for digging

digit *noun* 1 a finger or toe 2 any of the numbers 0–9

digital *adjective* 1 using information supplied and stored as binary digits 2 of a clock: showing the time in the form of digits rather than with pointers on a dial

digital camera a camera which records photographic images in digital form to be viewed on a personal computer

digital recording the recording of sound by storing electrical pulses representing the audio signal on compact disc, *etc*

digital television or **digital TV** a method of TV broadcasting, using digital rather than traditional analogue signals

dignified *adjective* stately, serious

dignitary *noun* (*plural* **dignitaries**) someone of high rank or office

dignity *noun* manner showing a sense of your own worth or the seriousness of the occasion

digress *verb* to wander from the point in speaking or writing ▪ **digression** *noun*

dike or **dyke** *noun* 1 a wall; an embankment 2 a ditch

dilapidated *adjective* falling to pieces, needing repair

dilate *verb* to make or grow larger, swell out

dilemma *noun* a situation offering a difficult choice between two options

diligent *adjective* hard-working, industrious ▪ **diligence** *noun* ▪ **diligently** *adverb*

dilly-dally *verb* to loiter, waste time

| **dilly-dally** ▶ dilly-dall*ies*, dilly-dally*ing*, dilly-dall*ied*

dilute *verb* to lessen the strength of a liquid *etc*, especially by adding water ▪ *adjective* diluted ▪ **diluted** *adjective* ▪ **dilution** *noun*

dim *adjective* 1 not bright or clear 2 not understanding clearly, stupid ▪ *verb* to make or become dim

| **dim** *verb* ▶ dims, dimm*ing*, dimm*ed*

dime *noun* a tenth of a US or Canadian dollar, ten cents

dimension *noun* 1 a measurement of length, width or thickness 2 **dimensions** size, measurements

diminish *verb* to make or grow less

diminutive *adjective* very small

dimly *adverb* vaguely, not brightly or clearly

dimness *noun* haziness, half-light, lack of clarity

dimple *noun* a small hollow, especially on the cheek or chin

din *noun* a loud, lasting noise

dine *verb* to eat dinner

diner *noun* 1 someone who dines 2 a restaurant car on a train 3 *US* a small cheap restaurant

dinghy (*pronounced* ding-i) *noun* (*plural* **dinghies**) a small rowing boat

dingy (*pronounced* din-ji) *adjective* dull, faded or dirty-looking

dinner *noun* 1 a main evening meal 2 a midday meal, lunch

dinosaur *noun* any of various types of extinct giant reptile

dip *verb* 1 to plunge into a liquid quickly 2 to lower (*eg* a flag) and raise again 3 to slope down 4 to look briefly into (a book *etc*)
■ *noun* 1 a liquid in which anything is dipped 2 a creamy sauce into which biscuits *etc* are dipped 3 a downward slope 4 a hollow 5 a short bathe or swim

| **dip** *verb* ► dips, dipping, dipped

diploma *noun* a written statement conferring a degree, confirming a pass in an examination, *etc*

diplomacy *noun* 1 the business of making agreements, treaties, *etc* between countries 2 skill in making people agree, tact

diplomat *noun* someone engaged in diplomacy

diplomatic *adjective* 1 of diplomacy 2 tactful

dire *adjective* dreadful: *in dire need*

direct *adjective* 1 straight, not roundabout 2 frank, outspoken ■ *verb* 1 to point or aim at 2 to show the way 3 to order, instruct 4 to control, organize 5 to put a name and address on (a letter)

direct current an electric current flowing in one direction

direction *noun* 1 the act of directing 2 the place or point to which someone moves, looks, *etc* 3 an order 4 guidance 5

directions instructions on how to get somewhere

directly *adverb* 1 straight away, immediately 2 straight: *I looked directly at him* 3 just, exactly: *directly opposite*

directness *noun* frankness, with no effort to be tactful

director *noun* 1 a manager of a business *etc* 2 the person who controls the shooting of a film *etc*

directory *noun* (*plural* **directories**) 1 a book of names and addresses *etc* 2 a named group of files on a computer disk

dirge *noun* a lament; a funeral hymn

dirt *noun* any unclean substance, such as mud, dust, dung, *etc*

dirty *adjective* 1 not clean, soiled 2 obscene, lewd ■ *verb* to soil with dirt ■ **dirtily** *adverb*

| **dirty** *verb* ► dirties, dirtying, dirtied

disability *noun* (*plural* **disabilities**) something which disables

disable *verb* to take away power or strength from, cripple

disabled *adjective* having a severely restricted lifestyle as the result of an injury, or a physical or mental illness or handicap

disadvantage *noun* an unfavourable circumstance, a drawback

disadvantaged *adjective* suffering a disadvantage, especially poverty or homelessness

disadvantageous *adjective* not advantageous

disagree *verb* 1 (often disagree with) to hold different opinions (from) 2 to quarrel 3 disagree with of food: to make feel ill

disagreeable *adjective* unpleasant

disagreement *noun* a difference of opinion or quarrel

disallow *verb* not to allow

disappear *verb* to go out of sight, vanish ▪ **disappearance** *noun*

disappoint *verb* 1 to fail to come up to the hopes or expectations (of) 2 to fail to fulfil

disappointed *adjective* sad because your hopes or expectations have not been fulfilled

disappointment *noun* something which disappoints you, or the feeling of being disappointed

disapprove *verb* to have an unfavourable opinion (of) ▪ **disapproval** *noun*

disarm *verb* 1 to take (a weapon) away from 2 to get rid of war weapons

disarmament *noun* the removal or disabling of war weapons

disarray *noun* disorder

disaster *noun* an extremely unfortunate happening, often causing great damage or loss ▪ **disastrous** *adjective* ▪ **disastrously** *adverb*

disband *verb* to break up, separate

disbelief *noun* inability to believe something

disbelieve *verb* to not believe

disc *noun* 1 a flat, round shape 2 a pad of cartilage between vertebrae 3 a gramophone record

discard *verb* to throw away as useless

discern *verb* to see, realize

discernible *adjective* noticeable: discernible difference

discerning *adjective* quick at noticing; discriminating: a discerning eye

discharge *verb* 1 to unload (cargo) 2 to set free 3 to dismiss 4 to fire (a gun) 5 to perform (duties) 6 to let out (pus) ▪ *noun* 1 a discharging 2 dismissal 3 pus *etc* discharged from the body

disciple *noun* 1 someone who believes in another's teaching 2 one of the followers of Christ

discipline *noun* 1 training in an orderly way of life 2 order kept by means of control 3 punishment ▪ *verb* 1 to bring to order 2 to punish

disc jockey someone who

introduces and plays recorded music on the radio *etc*

disclose *verb* to uncover, reveal, make known

disclosure *noun* 1 the act of disclosing 2 something disclosed

disco *noun* (*plural* **discos**) an event or place where recorded music is played for dancing

discolour *or US* **discolor** *verb* to spoil the colour of; stain ▪ **discoloration** *noun*

discomfort *noun* lack of comfort, uneasiness

disconcert *verb* to upset, confuse

disconnect *verb* to separate, break the connection between

disconsolate *adjective* sad, disappointed

discontent *noun* dissatisfaction

discontented *adjective* dissatisfied, cross

discontinue *verb* to stop, cease to continue

discord *noun* 1 disagreement, quarrelling 2 *music* a jarring of notes

discount *noun* a small sum taken off the price of something: *10% discount* ▪ *verb* 1 to leave out, not consider: *completely discounted my ideas* 2 to allow for exaggeration in (*eg* a story)

discourage *verb* 1 to take away the confidence, hope, *etc* of 2 to try to prevent by showing dislike or disapproval ▪ **discouragement** *noun*

discouraging *adjective* giving little hope or encouragement

discover *verb* 1 to find out 2 to find by chance, especially for the first time

discovery *noun* (*plural* **discoveries**) 1 the act of finding or finding out 2 something discovered

discredit *verb* to disgrace ▪ *noun* disgrace

discreet *adjective* wisely cautious, tactful ▪ **discreetly** *adverb*

◆ Do not confuse with: **discrete**

discrepancy *noun* (*plural* **discrepancies**) a difference or disagreement between two things

discrete *adjective* separate, distinct

◆ Do not confuse with: **discreet**. It may help you to think of **Crete**, which is an island separate from the rest of Greece

discretion *noun* wise caution, tact

discriminate *verb* 1 to make differences (between), distinguish 2 to treat (people) differently because of their gender, race, *etc*

discrimination *noun* 1 ability to discriminate 2 unfair treatment on grounds of gender, race, *etc*

discus noun a heavy disc thrown in an athletic competition

discuss verb to talk about
- **discussion** noun

disdain noun scorn ■ **disdainful** adjective

disease noun illness

diseased adjective affected by disease

disembark verb to put or go ashore

disentangle verb to free from a tangled or complicated state

disfigure verb to spoil the beauty or appearance of
- **disfigurement** noun

disgrace noun the state of being out of favour; shame ■ verb to bring shame on

disgraceful adjective shameful; very bad ■ **disgracefully** adverb

disgruntled adjective discontented, sulky

disguise verb 1 to change the appearance of 2 to hide (feelings etc) ■ noun 1 a disguised state 2 a costume etc which disguises

disgust noun 1 strong dislike, loathing 2 indignation ■ verb 1 to cause loathing, revolt 2 to make indignant ■ **disgusted** adjective

disgusting adjective sickening; causing disgust

dish noun (plural **dishes**) 1 a plate or bowl for food 2 food prepared for eating 3 a saucer-shaped aerial for receiving information from a satellite ■ verb 1 to serve (food) 2 to deal (out), distribute

dishearten verb to take away courage or hope from
- **disheartened** adjective
- **disheartening** adjective

dishevelled adjective untidy, with hair etc disordered

dishonest adjective not honest, deceitful ■ **dishonesty** noun

dishonour noun disgrace, shame ■ verb to cause shame to
- **dishonourable** adjective

disillusion verb to take away a false belief from

disillusioned adjective unhappy and disappointed after your happy impressions of something have been destroyed

disinclined adjective unwilling

disinfect verb to destroy disease-causing germs in

disinfectant noun a substance that kills germs

disintegrate verb to fall into pieces; break down
- **disintegration** noun

disinterested adjective unbiased, not influenced by personal feelings

❗✱ Do not confuse with: **uninterested**. It is generally a positive thing to be **disinterested** (= fair), especially if you are trying to make an unbiased decision. It is generally a negative thing to be **uninterested** (= bored)

disjointed adjective of speech etc: not well connected together

disk noun 1 US spelling of **disc** 2 computing a flat round magnetic plate used for storing data

disk drive computing part of a computer that records data on to and retrieves data from disks

dislike verb not to like, disapprove of ▪ noun disapproval

dislocate verb to put (a bone) out of joint

dislodge verb 1 to drive from a place of rest, hiding or defence 2 to knock out of place, often accidentally

disloyal adjective not loyal, unfaithful ▪ **disloyalty** noun

dismal adjective gloomy; sorrowful; sad

dismantle verb 1 to remove fittings, furniture, etc from 2 to take to pieces

dismay verb to make to feel hopeless, upset ▪ noun hopelessness or discouragement

dismiss verb 1 to send or put away 2 to remove (someone) from a job, sack ▪ **dismissal** noun

dismount verb to come down off a horse, bicycle, etc

disobedient adjective refusing or failing to obey

disobey verb to fail or refuse to do what is commanded
▪ **disobedience** noun

disorder noun 1 lack of order, confusion 2 a disease

disorderly adjective 1 out of order 2 behaving in a lawless (noisy) manner

disown verb to refuse or cease to recognize as your own

disparage verb to speak of as being of little worth or importance, belittle
▪ **disparaging** adjective

dispatch or **despatch** verb to send off (a letter etc) ▪ noun (plural **dispatches** or **despatches**) the act of sending off

dispel verb to drive away, make disappear

| **dispel** ▶ dispels, dispelling, dispelled

dispensable adjective able to be done without

dispense verb 1 to give out 2 to prepare (medicines) for giving out ▪ **dispense with something** to do without it

dispenser noun 1 a machine that issues something to you 2 a holder or container from which you can get something one at a time or in measured quantities

disperse verb 1 to scatter; spread 2 to (cause to) vanish

dispirited adjective sad, discouraged

displace verb 1 to put out of place 2 to disorder
▪ **displacement** noun

display verb to set out for show ▪ noun a show, exhibition

displease verb to offend, annoy

displeasure noun annoyance, disapproval

disposable adjective intended to be thrown away

disposal noun the act or process of getting rid of something ■ **at your disposal** available for your use

dispose verb 1 to arrange, settle 2 to get rid (of): *they disposed of the body*

disposed adjective inclined, willing ■ **be well disposed towards someone** to favour them and be inclined to treat them well

disposition noun nature, personality

disproportionate adjective too big or too little in comparison to something else

disprove verb to prove to be false

dispute verb to argue about ■ noun an argument, quarrel

disqualification noun the act of disqualifying someone or the state of being disqualified

disqualify verb to put out of a competition for breaking rules

| disqualify ► disqualifies, disqualifying, disqualified

disquiet noun uneasiness, anxiety

disregard verb to pay no attention to, ignore ■ noun neglect

disrepair noun a state of bad repair

disreputable adjective having a bad reputation, not respectable

disrepute noun bad reputation

disrespect noun rudeness, lack of politeness ■ **disrespectful** adjective

disrupt verb to throw (a meeting etc) into disorder

disruption noun an obstacle or disturbance

disruptive adjective causing disorder

dissatisfaction noun displeasure, annoyance

dissatisfy verb to bring no satisfaction, displease ■ **dissatisfied** adjective

| dissatisfy ► dissatisfies, dissatisfying, dissatisfied

dissect verb to cut into parts for examination ■ **dissection** noun

dissent verb 1 to have a different opinion 2 to refuse to agree ■ noun disagreement

disservice noun harm, a bad turn

dissident noun someone who disagrees, especially with a political regime

dissimilar adjective not the same ■ **dissimilarity** noun (plural dissimilarities)

dissolute adjective living without discipline or morals

dissolve verb 1 to melt 2 to break up 3 to put an end to

dissuade verb to persuade not to do something ■ **dissuasion** noun

distance noun 1 the space between things 2 a far-off place or point: *in the distance* 3 coldness of manner

distant adjective 1 far off or far

apart in place or time: *distant land* **2** not close: *distant cousin* **3** cold in manner

distantly *adverb* **1** with a dreamy or cold manner **2** not closely: *distantly related*

distaste *noun* dislike

distasteful *adjective* disagreeable, unpleasant

distil *verb* **1** to purify (liquid) by heating to a vapour and cooling **2** to extract the spirit or essence from **3** to (cause to) fall in drops ▪ **distiller** *noun*

| **distil** ► distils, distil*ling*, distil*led*

distillery *noun* (*plural* **distilleries**) a place where whisky, brandy, *etc* is distilled

distinct *adjective* **1** clear; easily seen or noticed: *a distinct improvement* **2** different: *the two languages are quite distinct*

⚫※ Do not confuse: **distinct** and **distinctive**

distinction *noun* **1** a difference **2** outstanding worth or merit

distinctive *adjective* different, special, easily recognizable

⚫※ Do not confuse: **distinctive** and **distinct**

distinguish *verb* **1** to recognize a difference (between) **2** to mark off as different **3** to recognize

distinguished *adjective* **1** outstanding, famous **2** dignified

distort *verb* **1** to twist out of

shape **2** to turn or twist (a statement *etc*) from its true meaning **3** to make (a sound) unclear and harsh ▪ **distortion** *noun*

distract *verb* **1** to divert (the attention) **2** to trouble, confuse

distracted *adjective* mad with pain, grief, *etc*

distraction *noun* **1** something which diverts your attention **2** anxiety, confusion **3** amusement **4** madness

distraught *adjective* extremely agitated or anxious

distress *noun* **1** pain, trouble, sorrow **2** a cause of suffering ▪ *verb* to cause pain or sorrow to ▪ **distressed** *adjective* ▪ **distressing** *adjective*

distribute *verb* **1** to divide among several **2** to spread out widely ▪ **distribution** *noun*

district *noun* a region of a country or town

distrust *noun* lack of trust, suspicion ▪ *verb* to have no trust in ▪ **distrustful** *adjective*

disturb *verb* **1** to confuse, worry, upset **2** to interrupt

disturbance *noun* **1** an outbreak of violent behaviour, especially in public **2** an act of disturbing, agitating or disorganizing **3** psychological damage or illness

disturbed *adjective* **1** *psychology* mentally or emotionally ill or damaged **2** **disturbed about something** very anxious about it **3** full of trouble and anxiety

disuse *noun* the state of being no longer used

disused *adjective* no longer used

ditch *noun* (*plural* **ditches**) a long narrow hollow trench dug in the ground, especially to carry water

dither *verb* **1** to hesitate, be undecided **2** to act in a nervous, uncertain manner ▪ *noun* a state of indecision

ditto *noun* (often written as **do**) the same as already written or said

ditto marks a character (") written below a word in a text, meaning it is to be repeated

divan *noun* **1** a long, low couch without a back **2** a bed without a headboard

dive *verb* **1** to plunge headfirst into water **2** to swoop through the air **3** to go down steeply and quickly ▪ *noun* an act of diving

dive-bomb *verb* to bomb from an aircraft in a steep downward dive ▪ **dive-bomber** *noun*

diver *noun* someone who works under water using special breathing equipment

diverge *verb* to separate and go in different directions; differ

diverse *adjective* different, various

diversify *verb* to make or become different or varied

| diversify ▶ diversifies, diversifying, diversified

diversion *noun* **1** an alteration to a traffic route **2** an amusement

diversity *noun* difference; variety

divert *verb* **1** to turn aside, change the direction of **2** to entertain, amuse

diverting *adjective* entertaining, amusing

divide *verb* **1** to separate into parts **2** to share (among) **3** to (cause to) go into separate groups **4** *maths* to find out how many times one number contains another

dividend *noun* **1** an amount to be divided (*compare with*: **divisor**) **2** a share of profits from a business

dividers *noun plural* measuring compasses

divine *adjective* **1** of a god; holy **2** *informal* splendid, wonderful

division *noun* **1** the act of dividing **2** something that separates; a barrier **3** a section, especially of an army

divisor *noun* the number by which another number (the **dividend**) is divided

divorce *noun* **1** the legal ending of a marriage **2** a complete separation ▪ *verb* **1** to end a marriage with **2** to separate (from)

divulge *verb* to let out, make known (a secret *etc*)

Diwali or **Dewali** *noun* the Hindu and Sikh festival of lamps, celebrated in October or November

dizzy *adjective* **1** giddy, confused **2** causing giddiness: *from a dizzy height*

DJ *abbreviation* disc jockey

djinn (*pronounced* jeen *or* jin) *noun plural* (*singular* **djinni** – *pronounced* **jeen**-i *or* jin-**ee**) a group of spirits in Islamic folklore

DNA *abbreviation* deoxyribonucleic acid, a compound carrying genetic instructions for passing on hereditary characteristics

do *verb* **1** to carry out, perform (a job *etc*) **2** to perform an action on, *eg* clean (dishes), arrange (hair), *etc* **3** to act: *do as you please* **4** to get on: *I hear she's doing very well* **5** to be enough: *a pound will do* **6** used to avoid repeating a verb: *I seldom see him now, and when I do, he ignores me* **7** used with a more important verb (1) in questions: *do you see what I mean?* (2) in sentences with **not**: *I don't know*; or (3) for emphasis: *I do hope she'll be there* ■ **do away with** to put an end to, destroy ■ **do out of** to swindle out of ■ **do up 1** to fasten **2** to renovate

| **do** ▶ **does**, **doing**, **did**, **done**

docile *adjective* tame, easy to manage

dock *noun* **1** (often **docks**) a deepened part of a harbour where ships go for loading, repair, *etc* **2** the box in a law court where

the accused person stands **3** a weed with large leaves ■ *verb* **1** to put in or enter a dock **2** to clip or cut short **3** of a spacecraft: to join on to another craft in space

docker *noun* someone who works in the docks

docket *noun* a label listing the contents of something

dockyard *noun* a naval harbour with docks, stores, *etc*

doctor *noun* **1** someone trained in and licensed to practise medicine **2** someone with the highest university degree in any subject ■ *verb* to tamper with, alter

doctrine *noun* a belief that is taught

document *noun* a written statement giving proof, information, *etc*

documentary *noun* (*plural* **documentaries**) a film giving information about real people or events ■ *adjective* **1** of or in documents: *documentary evidence* **2** of a documentary

dodder *verb* to shake, tremble, especially as a result of old age

doddery *adjective* shaky or slow because of old age

doddle *noun*, *informal* an easy task

dodge *verb* to avoid by a sudden or clever movement ■ *noun* a trick

dodo *noun* (*plural* **dodoes** *or* **dodos**) a type of large extinct bird

doe noun the female of certain animals, eg a deer, rabbit or hare

dog noun 1 a four-footed animal often kept as a pet 2 one of the dog family which includes wolves, foxes, etc ■ verb 1 to follow and watch constantly 2 to hamper, plague: dogged by ill health

| dog verb ▶ dogs, dogging, dogged

dog collar 1 a collar for dogs 2 the stiff white collar of a vicar

dog-eared adjective of a page: turned down at the corner

dogfish noun a kind of small shark

dogged (pronounced dog-id) adjective determined, stubborn ■ doggedly adverb

doggy adjective of or for dogs ■ noun, informal a child's name for a dog

doggy-paddle noun a simple style of swimming

dogma noun an opinion, especially religious, accepted or fixed by an authority

dogmatic adjective stubbornly forcing your opinions on others ■ dogmatically adverb

do-gooder noun someone who tries to help others in a self-righteous way

dogsbody noun, informal someone who is given unpleasant or dreary tasks to do

dog's breakfast or **dog's dinner** noun a complete mess

dog's life a life of misery

dog-tired adjective completely worn out

doily or **doyley** noun (plural doilies or doyleys) a perforated paper napkin put underneath cakes etc

doings noun plural actions

dole verb to deal (out) in small amounts ■ noun, informal unemployment benefit

doleful adjective sad, unhappy ■ dolefully adverb

doll noun a toy in the shape of a small human being

dollar noun the main unit of currency in several countries, eg the USA, Canada, Australia and New Zealand

dolphin noun a type of sea animal like a porpoise

dolt noun a stupid person

domain noun 1 a kingdom 2 an area of interest or knowledge

domain name computing in e-mail and Web site addresses, the name and location of the server

dome noun 1 the shape of a half sphere or ball 2 the roof of a building etc in this shape ■ domed adjective

domestic adjective 1 of the home or house 2 of an animal: tame, domesticated 3 not foreign, of your own country

domesticated adjective 1 of an animal: tame, used for farming etc 2 fond of doing housework, cooking, etc

domesticity noun home life

dominant adjective ruling; most powerful or important
■ **dominance** noun

dominate verb 1 to have command or influence over 2 to be most strong, or most noticeable: the castle dominates the skyline 3 to tower above, overlook ■ **domination** noun

domineering adjective overbearing, like a tyrant

dominion noun 1 rule, authority 2 an area with one ruler or government

domino noun (plural **dominoes**) a piece used in the game of dominoes

dominoes noun singular a game played on a table with pieces marked with dots, each side of which must match a piece placed next to it

don noun a college or university lecturer ■ verb to put on (a coat etc)

| **don** verb ► dons, donning, donned

donate verb to present a gift

donation noun a gift of money or goods

done past participle of **do**
■ adjective finished

donkey noun (plural **donkeys**) a type of animal with long ears, related to the horse (also called: **ass**)

donor noun 1 a giver of a gift 2 someone who agrees to let their body organs be used for transplant operations

don't short for do not

doom noun 1 judgement; fate 2 ruin

doomed adjective 1 destined, condemned 2 bound to fail or be destroyed

door noun 1 a hinged barrier which closes the entrance to a room or building 2 the entrance itself

doorstep noun the step in front of the door of a house

doorway noun the space filled by a door, the entrance

dope noun, informal 1 the drug cannabis 2 an idiot ■ verb to drug

dormant adjective sleeping, inactive

dormitory noun (plural **dormitories**) a room with beds for several people

dormouse noun (plural **dormice**) a small animal which hibernates

dosage noun the proper size of dose

dose noun 1 a quantity of medicine to be taken at one time 2 a bout of something unpleasant ■ verb to give medicine to

dossier (pronounced dos-i-eh) noun a set of papers containing information about a certain person or subject

dot noun a small, round mark ■ verb 1 to mark with a dot 2 to scatter

dot verb ▶ dots, dott*ing*, dott*ed*

dotcom adjective of a company: trading on the Internet ■ noun a dotcom company

dote verb: **dote on** to be foolishly fond of

double verb **1** to multiply by two **2** to fold ■ noun **1** twice as much **2** someone so like another as to be mistaken for them ■ adjective **1** containing twice as much **2** made up of two of the same sort **3** folded over ■ **double back** to turn sharply and go back the way you have come ■ **double up** to writhe in pain

double agent a spy paid by two rival countries, but loyal to only one

double bass a type of large stringed musical instrument played by plucking the strings

double-breasted adjective of a coat: with one half of the front overlapping the other

double-click verb, computing to click the button of a mouse two times in rapid succession

double-cross verb to cheat

double-decker noun a bus with two floors

double-Dutch noun incomprehensible talk, gibberish

double glazing two sheets of glass in a window to keep in the heat or keep out noise

double-take noun a second look at something surprising or confusing

double-time noun payment for overtime work etc at twice the usual rate

doubly adverb **1** extra, especially **2** in two ways

doubt verb **1** to be unsure or undecided about **2** to think unlikely ■ noun a lack of certainty or trust; suspicion

doubtful adjective **1** doubtful about something unsure about it **2** unlikely, uncertain or unreliable **3** strange, raising suspicion

doubtless adverb probably

dough noun a mass of flour, moistened and kneaded

doughnut noun a ring-shaped cake fried in fat

dour (pronounced door or dow-er) adjective dull, humourless

dove noun a pigeon

dovecote noun a pigeon-house

dowdy adjective not smart, badly dressed

down[1] adverb **1** towards or in a lower position: fell down **2** to a smaller size: grind down **3** to a later generation: handed down from mother to daughter **4** on the spot, in cash: £10 down
■ preposition **1** towards or in the lower part of: rolled down the hill **2** along: strolling down the road
■ adjective going downwards: the down escalator ■ **go down with** or **be down with** to become or be ill with

down[2] noun light, soft feathers

downcast adjective sad

downfall *noun* ruin, defeat

downhearted *adjective* discouraged

downhill *adjective* going downwards ▪ *adverb* downwards

download *verb* to transfer (information from the Internet) from one computer to another ▪ *noun* 1 an act of downloading 2 something downloaded

downpour *noun* a heavy fall of rain

downright *adjective* utter: *downright idiocy* ▪ *adverb* utterly

downs *noun plural* low, grassy hills

downstairs *adjective* on a lower floor of a building ▪ *adverb* to a lower floor

downstream *adverb* further down a river, in the direction of its flow

downtrodden *adjective* kept in a lowly, inferior position

downward *adjective* moving down, descending ▪ **downwards** *adverb* from higher to lower; down

downy *adjective* soft, feathery

dowry *noun* (*plural* **dowries**) money and property brought by a woman to her husband on their marriage

doyley *another spelling of* **doily**

doze *verb* to sleep lightly ▪ *noun* a light, short sleep

dozen *noun* twelve

drab *adjective* dull, monotonous

draft *noun* 1 a rough outline, a sketch 2 a group of people selected for a special purpose 3 *US* forced enrolment into the armed forces ▪ *verb* 1 to make a rough plan 2 to select for a purpose 3 *US* to force to join the armed forces

▶ Do not confuse with: **draught**

drag *verb* 1 to pull roughly 2 to move slowly and heavily 3 to trail along the ground ▪ *noun*, *informal* 1 a dreary task 2 a tedious person 3 clothes for one sex worn by the other 4 *physics* a force that slows down movement through a liquid or gas

dragon *noun* 1 an imaginary fire-breathing, winged reptile 2 a fierce, intimidating person

dragonfly *noun* a winged insect with a long body and double wings

drain *verb* 1 to clear (land) of water by trenches or pipes 2 to drink the contents of (a glass *etc*) 3 to use up completely ▪ *noun* a channel or pipe used to carry off water *etc*

drainage *noun* the drawing-off of water by rivers, pipes, *etc*

drained *adjective* 1 emptied of liquid 2 sapped of strength

drake *noun* a male duck

drama *noun* 1 a play for acting in the theatre 2 exciting or tense action

dramatic *adjective* 1 relating to

plays **2** exciting, thrilling **3** unexpected, sudden ▪ **dramatically** *adverb*

dramatist *noun* a playwright

dramatize *or* **dramatise** *verb* **1** to turn into a play for the theatre **2** to make vivid or sensational ▪ **dramatization** *noun*

drank *past form of* drink

drape *verb* to arrange (cloth) to hang gracefully ▪ *noun* (**drapes**) *US* curtains

drastic *adjective* severe, extreme ▪ **drastically** *adverb*

draught *noun* **1** a current of air **2** **draughts** a game for two, played by moving pieces on a board marked with squares

💥 Do not confuse with: draft

draughtsman, **draughtswoman** *noun* **1** someone employed to draw plans **2** someone skilled in drawing

draughty *adjective* full of air currents, chilly

draw *verb* **1** to make a picture with pencil, crayons, *etc* **2** to pull after or along **3** to attract: *drew a large crowd* **4** to obtain money from a fund: *drawing a pension* **5** to approach, come: *night is drawing near* **6** to score equal points in a game ▪ *noun* **1** an equal score **2** a lottery ▪ **draw on** to use as a resource: *drawing on experience* ▪ **draw out 1** to lengthen **2** to persuade

(someone) to talk and be at ease ▪ **draw up 1** to come to a stop **2** to move closer **3** to plan, write out (a contract *etc*)

| **draw** *verb* ▶ draws, drawing, drew, drawn

drawback *noun* a disadvantage

drawbridge *noun* a bridge at the entrance to a castle which can be drawn up or let down

drawer *noun* **1** someone who draws **2** (*pronounced* drawr) a sliding box fitting into a chest, table, *etc*

drawing *noun* a picture made by pencil, crayon, *etc*

drawing pin a pin with a large flat head for fastening paper on a board *etc*

drawing room a sitting room

drawl *verb* to speak in a slow, lazy manner ▪ *noun* a drawling voice

drawn *past participle of* draw

dread *noun* great fear ▪ *verb* to be greatly afraid of ▪ **dreaded** *adjective*

dreadful *adjective* **1** terrible **2** *informal* very bad ▪ **dreadfully** *adverb*

dreadlocks *noun* thick, twisted strands of hair

dream *noun* **1** a series of images and sounds in the mind during sleep **2** something imagined, not real **3** something very beautiful **4** a hope, an ambition ▪ *verb* to have a dream ▪ **dream up** to invent

dream verb ► dream**s**, dream**ing**, dream**t** or dream**ed**

dreamy adjective **1** sleepy, half-awake **2** vague, dim **3** informal beautiful ▪ **dreamily** adverb

dreary adjective gloomy, cheerless ▪ **drearily** adverb

dredge verb **1** to drag a net or bucket along a river bed or seabed to bring up fish, mud, etc **2** to sprinkle with (sugar or flour) ▪ noun an instrument for dredging a river etc

dredger noun **1** a ship which digs a channel by lifting mud from the bottom **2** a perforated jar for sprinkling sugar or flour

dregs noun plural **1** sediment on the bottom of a liquid **2** last remnants **3** a worthless or useless part

drench verb to soak

dress verb **1** to put on clothes or a covering **2** to prepare (food etc) for use **3** to arrange (hair) **4** to treat and bandage (wounds) ▪ noun (plural **dresses**) **1** a one-piece woman's garment combining skirt and top **2** a style of clothing: formal dress ▪ adjective of clothes: for formal use: a dress shirt

dresser noun a kitchen sideboard for dishes

dressing noun **1** a covering **2** a seasoned sauce poured over salads etc **3** a bandage

dressing-gown noun a loose, light coat worn indoors over pyjamas etc

dressmaking noun making women's clothes ▪ **dressmaker** noun

dress rehearsal the final rehearsal of a play, in which the actors wear their costumes

dressy adjective stylish, smart

drew past form of **draw**

drey noun (plural **dreys**) a squirrel's nest

dribble verb **1** to (cause to) fall in small drops **2** to let saliva run down the chin **3** football to move the ball forward by short kicks

dried see **dry**

drift noun **1** snow, sand, etc driven by the wind **2** the direction in which something is driven **3** the general meaning of someone's words ▪ verb **1** to go with the tide or current **2** to be driven into heaps by the wind **3** to wander about **4** to live aimlessly

drifter noun someone who drifts

drill verb **1** to make a hole in **2** to make with a drill **3** to exercise (soldiers) ▪ noun **1** a tool for making holes in wood etc **2** military exercise

drily another spelling of **dryly**

drink verb **1** to swallow (a liquid) **2** to take alcoholic drink, especially excessively ▪ noun **1** liquid to be drunk **2** alcoholic liquids ▪ **drink in** to listen to eagerly ▪ **drink to** to drink a toast to ▪ **drink up** to finish a drink

drink verb ► drinks, drinking, drank, drunk

drip verb 1 to fall in drops 2 to let (water etc) fall in drops ■ noun 1 a drop 2 a continual dropping, eg of water 3 a device for adding liquid slowly to a vein etc

drip verb ► drips, dripping, dripped

drip-dry verb to dry (a garment) by hanging it up to dry without wringing it first

dripping noun fat from roasting meat

drive verb 1 to control or guide (a car etc) 2 to go in a vehicle: driving to work 3 to force or urge along 4 to hurry on 5 to hit hard (a ball, nail, etc) ■ noun 1 a journey in a car 2 a private road to a house 3 an avenue or road 4 energy, enthusiasm 5 a campaign: a drive to save the local school 6 a hard stroke with a club or bat

drive verb ► drives, driving, drove, driven

drive-in noun, US a cinema where the audience watches the screen while staying in their cars

drivel noun, informal nonsense

driven past participle of **drive**

driver noun someone who drives a car etc

drizzle noun light rain ■ verb to rain lightly ■ **drizzly** adjective

droll adjective funny, amusing

drone verb 1 to make a low humming sound 2 to speak in a dull boring voice ■ noun 1 a low humming sound 2 a dull boring voice 3 the low-sounding pipe of a set of bagpipes 4 a male bee 5 a lazy, idle person

drool verb 1 to produce saliva 2 to anticipate something in an obvious way

droop verb 1 to hang down 2 to grow weak or discouraged

drop noun 1 a small round or pear-shaped blob of liquid 2 a small quantity 3 a fall from a height ■ verb 1 to fall suddenly 2 to let fall 3 to fall in drops 4 to set down from a car etc 5 to give up, abandon (a friend, habit, etc) ■ **drop back** to fall behind others in a group ■ **drop in** to pay a brief visit ■ **drop off** to fall asleep ■ **drop out** to withdraw from a class, from society, etc

drop verb ► drops, dropping, dropped

drop-down menu see **pull-down menu**

droplet noun a tiny drop

droppings noun plural animal or bird dung

dross noun 1 scum produced by melting metal 2 waste material, impurities 3 coal dust 4 anything worthless

drought noun a period of time when no rain falls

drove noun 1 a number of moving cattle or other animals 2 **droves** a great number of people ■ verb, past form of **drive**

drover noun someone who drives cattle

drown verb 1 to die by suffocating in water 2 to kill (someone) in this way 3 to flood or soak completely 4 to block out (a sound) with a louder one

drowsy adjective sleepy ■ **drowsily** adverb

| **drowsy** ► drowsier, drowsiest

drubbing noun a thrashing

drudge verb to do very humble or boring work ■ noun someone who does such work

drudgery noun hard, uninteresting work

drug noun 1 a substance used in medicine to treat illness, kill pain, etc 2 a stimulant or narcotic substance taken habitually for its effects ■ verb 1 to administer drugs to 2 to make to lose consciousness by drugs

| **drug** verb ► drugs, drugging, drugged

drum noun 1 a musical instrument of skin etc stretched on a round frame and beaten with sticks 2 a cylindrical container: oil drum ■ verb 1 to beat a drum 2 to tap continuously with the fingers ■ **drummer** noun

| **drum** verb ► drums, drumming, drummed

drumstick noun 1 a stick for beating a drum 2 the lower part of the leg of a cooked chicken etc

drunk adjective showing the effects (giddiness, unsteadiness, etc) of drinking too much alcohol ■ noun someone who is drunk, or habitually drunk ■ verb, past participle of **drink**

drunkard noun a drunk

drunken adjective 1 habitually drunk 2 caused by too much alcohol: drunken stupor 3 involving much alcohol: drunken spree ■ **drunkenness** noun

dry adjective 1 not moist or wet 2 thirsty 3 uninteresting: makes very dry reading 4 reserved, matter-of-fact 5 of wine: not sweet 6 of a sense of humour: funny in a quiet, subtle way ■ verb to make or become dry

| **dry** verb ► dries, drying, dried

dry-clean verb to clean (clothes etc) with chemicals, not with water

dryly or **drily** adverb 1 in a reserved, matter-of-fact, emotionless way 2 with quiet, subtle humour

dryness noun the quality of being dry

dry rot a disease causing wood to become dry and crumbly

dual adjective double; made up of two

◆* Do not confuse with: **duel**

dual carriageway a road divided by a central barrier or boundary, with each side used by traffic moving in one direction

dub *verb* **1** to declare (a knight) by touching each shoulder with a sword **2** to name or nickname **3** to add sound effects to a film **4** to give (a film) a new soundtrack in a different language

| **dub** ▶ dubs, dubb*ing*, dubb*ed*

dubious *adjective* **1** doubtful, uncertain **2** probably dishonest

duchess *noun* (*plural* **duchesses**) **1** a woman of the same rank as a duke **2** the wife or widow of a duke

duck *noun* **1** a web-footed bird, with a broad flat beak **2** *cricket* a score of no runs ■ *verb* **1** to lower the head quickly as if to avoid a blow **2** to push (someone's head) under water ■ **duck out** (**of**) to avoid responsibility (for)

duck-billed platypus *see* platypus

duckling *noun* a baby duck

duct *noun* a pipe for carrying liquids, electric cables, *etc*

ductile *adjective* easily led, yielding

dud *adjective*, *informal* useless, broken

due *adjective* **1** owed, needing to be paid **2** expected to arrive *etc* **3** proper, appropriate: *due care* ■ *adverb* directly: *due south* ■ *noun* **1** something you have a right to: *give him his due* **2** dues the amount of money charged for belonging to a club *etc* ■ due

to brought about by, caused by

duel *noun*, *history* a formalized fight with pistols or swords between two people ■ *verb* to fight in a duel

🔹 Do not confuse with: **dual**

duet (*pronounced* dyoo-**et**) *noun* a piece of music for two singers or players

duffel bag a cylindrical canvas bag tied with a drawstring

duffel coat a heavy woollen coat, fastened with toggles

dug *past form* of dig

dugout *noun*, *sport* a bench beside the pitch for team managers, trainers, and extra players

duke *noun* a nobleman next in rank below a prince

dull *adjective* **1** not lively **2** slow to understand or learn **3** not exciting or interesting **4** of weather: cloudy, not bright or clear **5** not bright in colour **6** of sounds: not clear or ringing **7** blunt, not sharp **8** of pain: present in the background, but not acute ■ *verb* to make dull ■ **dullness** *noun* ■ **dully** *adverb*

duly *adverb* at the proper or expected time; as expected

dumb *adjective* **1** without the power of speech **2** silent **3** *informal* stupid

dumbfounded *adjective* astonished

dumbly *adverb* in silence

dummy noun (plural **dummies**)
1 a mock-up of something used
for display 2 a model used for
displaying clothes etc 3 an
artificial teat used to comfort a
baby

dummy run a try-out, a
practice

dump verb 1 to throw down
heavily 2 to unload and leave
(rubbish etc) ■ noun a place for
leaving rubbish ■ **in the dumps**
feeling low or depressed

dumpling noun a cooked ball of
dough

dumpy adjective short and thick
or fat

dunce noun a stupid or slow-
learning person

dune noun a low hill of sand

dung noun animal faeces,
manure

dungarees noun plural trousers
made of coarse, hard-wearing
material with a bib

dungeon noun a dark
underground prison

duo noun 1 a pair of musicians or
performers 2 people considered
a pair

dupe noun someone easily
cheated ■ verb to deceive, trick

duplicate adjective exactly the
same ■ noun an exact copy ■ verb
to make a copy or copies of
■ **duplication** noun

durable adjective lasting, able to
last; wearing well ■ **durability**
noun

duration noun the time a thing
lasts

during preposition 1 throughout
all or part of: we lived here during
the war 2 at a particular point
within: she died during the night

dusk noun twilight, partial
dark

dusky adjective dark-coloured

dust noun 1 fine grains or specks
of earth, sand, etc 2 fine powder
■ verb 1 to free from dust 2 to
sprinkle lightly with powder

dustbin noun a container for
household rubbish

duster noun a cloth for removing
dust

dust jacket a paper cover on a
book

dustman noun someone
employed to collect household
rubbish

dusty adjective covered with
dust

dutiful adjective obedient
■ **dutifully** adverb

duty noun (plural **duties**) 1
something a person ought to do 2
an action required to be done 3 a
tax 4 **duties** the various tasks
involved in a job

duty-free adjective not taxed

duvet noun a quilt stuffed with
feathers or synthetic material,
used instead of blankets

DVD abbreviation digital
versatile disk

dwarf noun (plural **dwarfs** or
dwarves) an undersized person,

animal or plant ▪ *verb* to make to appear small by comparison ▪ *adjective* not growing to full or usual height: *dwarf cherry-tree*

dwell *verb* **1** to live, inhabit, stay **2 dwell on** to think habitually about something

dwindle *verb* to grow less, waste away

dye *verb* to give a colour to (fabric *etc*) ▪ *noun* a powder or liquid for colouring

| **dye** *verb* ► dyes, dye*ing*, dy*ed*

dying *present participle of* **die**[1]

dyke *another spelling of* **dike**

dynamic *adjective* forceful, energetic ▪ **dynamically** *adverb*

dynamics *noun singular* the scientific study of movement and force

dynamite *noun* a type of powerful explosive

dynamo *noun* (*plural* **dynamos**) a machine for turning the energy produced by movement into electricity

dynasty *noun* (*plural* **dynasties**) a succession of monarchs, leaders, *etc* of the same family

dysentery *noun* an infectious disease of the intestines causing fever, pain and diarrhoea

dyslexia *noun* difficulty in learning to read and in spelling

dyslexic *noun & adjective* (someone) suffering from dyslexia

E

each *adjective* of two or more things: every one taken individually ■ *pronoun* every one individually ■ **each other** used when an action takes place between two or more people

eager *adjective* keen, anxious to do or get (something) ■ **eagerly** *adverb*

eagle *noun* a kind of large bird of prey

ear *noun* **1** the part of the body through which you hear sounds **2** a head (of corn *etc*)

eardrum *noun* the membrane in the middle of the ear

earl *noun* a member of the British aristocracy between a marquis and a viscount

earlobe *noun* the soft fleshy part at the bottom of the human ear

early *adjective* **1** in good time **2** at or near the beginning **3** sooner than expected ■ *adverb* at a time sooner than expected or necessary: *the bus left early*

| **early** ► earli*er*, earli*est*

earmark *verb* to mark or set aside for a special purpose

earn *verb* **1** to receive (money) for work **2** to deserve

earnest *adjective* serious, serious-minded ■ *noun* seriousness ■ **earnestly** *adverb* ■ **in earnest** meaning what you say or do

earnings *noun plural* pay for work done

earphones *noun plural* a pair of small speakers fitting in or against the ear for listening to a radio *etc*

ear-piercing *adjective* very loud or shrill

earplugs *noun plural* a pair of plugs placed in the ears to block off outside noise

earring *noun* a piece of jewellery worn on the ear

earshot *noun* the distance at which a sound can be heard

earth *noun* **1** the third planet from the sun; our world **2** its surface **3** soil **4** the hole of a fox, badger, *etc* **5** an electrical connection with the ground ■ *verb* to connect electrically with the ground

earthenware *noun* pottery, dishes made of clay

earthly *adjective* of the earth as opposed to heaven

earthquake *noun* a shaking of the earth's crust

earthshattering *adjective* of great importance

earthworm *noun* the common worm

earthy *adjective* 1 like soil 2 covered in soil 3 coarse and natural, not refined

earwig *noun* a type of insect with pincers at its tail

ease *noun* 1 freedom from difficulty 2 freedom from pain, worry or embarrassment 3 rest from work ■ *verb* 1 to make or become less painful or difficult 2 to move carefully and gradually

easel *noun* a stand for an artist's canvas while painting *etc*

easily *adverb* 1 without difficulty 2 without pain, worry or discomfort 3 obviously, clearly, beyond doubt or by a long way 4 more quickly or more readily than most people

easiness *noun* the quality of being or feeling easy

east *noun* one of the four chief directions, that in which the sun rises ■ *adjective* in or from the east

Easter *noun* 1 the Christian celebration of Christ's rising from the dead 2 the weekend when this is celebrated each year, sometime in spring

easterly *adjective* coming from or facing the east

eastern *adjective* of the east

eastward *or* **eastwards** *adjective & adverb* towards the east

easy *adjective* 1 not hard to do 2 free from pain, worry or discomfort

┃**easy** ► eas*ier*, eas*iest*

eat *verb* 1 to chew and swallow (food) 2 to destroy gradually, waste away

┃**eat** ► eats, eat*ing*, ate, eaten

eatable *adjective* fit to eat; edible

eaves *noun plural* the edge of a roof overhanging the walls

eavesdrop *verb* to listen secretly to a private conversation ■ **eavesdropper** *noun*

ebb *noun* 1 the flowing away of the tide after high tide 2 a lessening, a worsening ■ *verb* 1 to flow away 2 to grow less or worse

ebony *noun* a type of black, hard wood ■ *adjective* 1 made of ebony 2 black

eccentric *adjective* 1 odd, acting strangely 2 of circles: not having the same centre (*contrasted with*: **concentric**)

eccentricity *noun* (*plural* **eccentricities**) oddness of manner or conduct

echo *noun* (*plural* **echoes**) the repetition of a sound by its striking a surface and coming back ■ *verb* 1 to send back sound 2 to repeat (a thing said)

éclair *noun* an oblong sweet pastry filled with cream

eclipse *noun* 1 the covering of the whole or part of the sun (**solar eclipse**) or moon (**lunar eclipse**), *eg* when the moon comes between the sun and the earth 2 loss of position or prestige ■ *verb* 1 to throw into the shade 2 to blot out (someone's achievement) by doing better

eco- *prefix* relating to the environment: *ecofriendly/eco-summit*

ecological *adjective* 1 having to do with plants, animals, *etc* and their natural surroundings 2 concerned with protecting and preserving plants, animals and the natural environment ■ **ecologically** *adverb*

ecologist *noun* someone who studies, or is an expert in, ecology

ecology *noun* the study of plants, animals, *etc* in relation to their natural surroundings

e-commerce *noun, computing* buying and selling of goods on the Internet and World Wide Web

economic *adjective* 1 concerning economy 2 making a profit

economical *adjective* thrifty, not wasteful

economics *noun singular* the study of how money is created and spent

economist *noun* someone who studies, or is an expert in, economics

economize *or* **economise** *verb* to be careful in spending or using

economy *noun (plural economies)* 1 the management of a country's finances 2 the careful use of something, especially money

ecosystem *noun* a community of living things and their relationship with their environment

ecstasy *noun (plural ecstasies)* very great joy or pleasure ■ **ecstatic** *adjective* ■ **ecstatically** *adverb*

eczema *noun* a skin disease causing red swollen patches on the skin

eddy *noun (plural eddies)* a circling current of water or air running against the main stream

edge *noun* 1 the border of anything, farthest from the middle 2 a line joining two vertices in a figure 3 sharpness: *put an edge on my appetite* 4 advantage: *Brazil had the edge at half-time* ■ *verb* 1 to put a border on 2 to move little by little ■ **on edge** nervous, edgy

edgeways *adverb* sideways

edging *noun* a border, a fringe

edgy *adjective* unable to relax, irritable

edible *adjective* fit to be eaten

edit *verb* to prepare (a text, film, *etc*) for publication or broadcasting

edition *noun* 1 the form in which

a book *etc* is published after being edited **2** the copies of a book, newspaper, *etc* printed at one time **3** a special edition of a newspaper, *eg* for a local area

editor *noun* **1** someone who edits a book, film, *etc* **2** the chief journalist of a newspaper or section of a newspaper

educate *verb* to teach (people), especially in a school or college

educated *adjective* knowledgeable and cultured, as a result of receiving a good education

education *noun* **1** the process or system of teaching in schools and other establishments **2** the development of a person's knowledge

educational *adjective* **1** concerned with formal teaching **2** concerned with giving information, rather than simply entertaining or amusing **3** interesting from the point of view of teaching you something which you did not know before

eel *noun* a long, ribbon-shaped fish

eerie *adjective* causing fear of the unknown ▪ **eerily** *adverb*

effect *noun* **1** the result of an action **2** strength, power: *the pills had little effect* **3** an impression produced: *the effect of the sunset* **4** use, operation: *that law is not yet in effect* ▪ *verb* to bring about

◆* Do not confuse with: **affect**. **Effect** is usually a noun. **Affect** is usually a verb. 'To AFFECT' means 'to have an EFFECT on'

effective *adjective* **1** producing the desired effect **2** actual

effectual *adjective* able to do what is required

effeminate *adjective* unmanly, woman-like

effervesce *verb* **1** to froth up **2** to be very lively, excited, *etc*
▪ **effervescence** *noun*
▪ **effervescent** *adjective*

efficient *adjective* able to do things well; capable ▪ **efficiency** *noun* ▪ **efficiently** *adverb*

effigy *noun* (*plural* **effigies**) a likeness of a person carved in stone, wood, *etc*

effort *noun* **1** an attempt using a lot of strength or ability **2** hard work

effrontery *noun* impudence

eg *abbreviation* for example (from Latin *exempli gratia*)

egg *noun* **1** an oval shell containing the embryo of a bird, insect or reptile **2** (*also called:* **ovum**) a human reproductive cell **3** a hen's egg used for eating ▪ **egg on** to urge, encourage

ego *noun* **1** the conscious self **2** self-conceit, egoism

egoism *or* **egotism** *noun* the habit of considering only your own interests, selfishness

■ **egoist** or **egotist** noun ■ **egoistic** or **egotistic** adjective

Eid or **Eid-ul-Fitr** noun a Muslim festival celebrating the end of Ramadan

eiderdown noun **1** soft feathers from the eider, a type of northern sea-duck **2** a feather quilt

eight noun the number 8
■ adjective 8 in number

eighteen noun the number 18
■ adjective 18 in number

eighteenth adjective the last of a series of eighteen ■ noun one of eighteen equal parts

eighth adjective the last of a series of eight ■ noun one of eight equal parts

eightieth adjective the last of a series of eighty ■ noun one of eighty equal parts

eighty noun the number 80
■ adjective 80 in number

either adjective & pronoun **1** one or other of two: either bus will go there **2** each of two, both: there is a crossing on either side of the road
■ conjunction used with **or** to show alternatives: either he goes or I do ■ adverb any more than another: that won't work either

eject verb **1** to throw out **2** to force to leave a house, job, etc
■ **ejection** noun

eke verb: **eke out 1** to make go further or last longer by adding to: eked out the stew with more vegetables **2** to make a living with difficulty

elaborate verb (pronounced i-lab-o-reit) (often **elaborate on**) to explain fully ■ adjective (pronounced i-lab-o-rat) highly detailed or decorated

elapse verb of time: to pass

elastic adjective able to stretch and spring back again, springy ■ noun a piece of cotton etc interwoven with rubber to make it springy

elated adjective in high spirits, very pleased ■ **elation** noun

elbow noun the joint where the arm bends ■ verb to push with the elbow, jostle

elbow-room noun plenty of room to move

elder[1] adjective older ■ noun someone who is older

elder[2] noun a type of tree with purple-black berries

elderberry noun (plural **elderberries**) a berry from the elder tree

elderly adjective nearing old age

eldest adjective oldest

elect verb to choose by voting

election noun the choosing by vote of people to sit in parliament etc

electric or **electrical** adjective produced or worked by electricity

electrician noun someone skilled in working with electricity

electricity noun a form of energy used to give light, heat and power

electric shock a violent jerking

of the body caused by an electric current passing through it

electrify *verb* **1** to supply with electricity **2** to excite greatly

| **electrify** ► electrifies, electrifying, electrified

electrocute *verb* to kill by an electric current ■ **electrocution** *noun*

electrode *noun* a conductor through which an electric current enters or leaves a battery *etc*

electromagnet *noun* a piece of soft metal magnetized by an electric current
■ **electromagnetic** *adjective*

electron *noun* a very light particle with the smallest possible charge of electricity, which orbits the nucleus of an atom (*see also* **neutron, proton**)

electronic *adjective* of or using electrons or electronics

electronics *noun singular* a branch of physics dealing with electrons and their use in machines *etc*

elegant *adjective* **1** graceful, well-dressed, fashionable **2** of clothes *etc*: well-made and tasteful ■ **elegance** *noun*
■ **elegantly** *adverb*

elegy *noun* (*plural* elegies) a poem written on someone's death

element *noun* **1** a part of anything **2** a substance that cannot be split chemically into simpler substances, *eg* oxygen, iron, *etc* **3** circumstances which

suit someone best: *she is in her element when singing* **4** a heating wire carrying the current in an electric heater **5** elements basic facts or skills **6** elements the powers of nature, the weather

elementary *adjective* **1** at the first stage **2** simple

elephant *noun* a very large animal with a thick skin, a trunk and two ivory tusks

elevate *verb* to raise to a higher position

elevator *noun, US* a lift in a building

eleven *noun* **1** the number 11 **2** a team of eleven players, *eg* for cricket ■ *adjective* 11 in number

elevenses *noun plural* coffee, biscuits, *etc* taken around eleven o'clock in the morning

eleventh *adjective* the last of a series of eleven ■ *noun* one of eleven equal parts

elf *noun* (*plural* elves) a tiny, mischievous supernatural creature

eligible *adjective* fit or worthy to be chosen, especially for marriage ■ **eligibility** *noun*

eliminate *verb* **1** to get rid of **2** to exclude, omit ■ **elimination** *noun*

élite *or* **elite** (*pronounced* ei-leet) *noun* a part of a group selected as, or believed to be, the best

elk *noun* a very large deer found in N Europe and Asia, related to the moose

ellipse noun (plural **ellipses**) an oval shape

elm noun a tree with a rough bark and leaves with saw-like edges

elocution noun 1 the art of what is thought to be correct speech 2 style of speaking

elongate verb to stretch out lengthwise, make longer

elope verb to run away from home to get married

eloquent adjective 1 good at expressing thoughts in words 2 persuasive ■ **eloquence** noun

else adverb otherwise: come inside or else you will catch cold ■ adjective other than the person or thing mentioned: someone else

elsewhere adverb in or to another place

elucidate verb to make (something) easy to understand

elude verb 1 to escape by a trick 2 to be too difficult to remember or understand

⚫* Do not confuse with: **allude**

elusive adjective hard to catch

⚫* Do not confuse with: **allusive** and **illusive**. **Elusive** comes from the verb **elude**

e-mail or **email** noun electronic mail, messages exchanged across a network of computers

embalm verb to preserve (a dead body) from decay by treating it with spices or chemicals

embankment noun a bank of earth or stone to keep back water, or carry a railway over low-lying places

embargo noun (plural **embargoes**) an official order forbidding something, especially trade with another country

embark verb 1 to go on board ship 2 **embark on** to start (a new career etc)

embarrass verb to make to feel uncomfortable and self-conscious ■ **embarrassed** adjective ■ **embarrassing** adjective ■ **embarrassment** noun

embassy noun (plural **embassies**) the offices and staff of an ambassador in a foreign country

embellish verb 1 to decorate 2 to add details to (a story etc) ■ **embellishment** noun

ember noun a piece of wood or coal glowing in a fire

embezzle verb to use for yourself money entrusted to you ■ **embezzlement** noun

emblazon verb 1 to decorate, adorn 2 to show in bright colours or conspicuously

emblem noun 1 an image which represents something: the dove is the emblem of peace 2 a badge

embodiment noun a person or thing that perfectly symbolizes some idea or quality

embody verb to express, give form to: embodying the spirit of the age embody ► embodies, embodying, embodied

embrace verb **1** to throw your arms round in affection **2** to include **3** to accept, adopt eagerly ▪ noun an affectionate hug

embroider verb **1** to decorate with designs in needlework **2** to add false details to (a story)

embroidery noun **1** the art or practice of sewing designs on to cloth **2** the designs sewn on to cloth

embryo noun (plural **embryos**) the young of an animal or plant in its earliest stage

emend verb a rather formal word meaning 'to remove faults or errors from' ▪ **emendation** noun

⬥ Do not confuse with: **amend**. Emending consists simply of deleting errors. Amending involves making changes or improvements

emerald noun a bright green precious stone

emerge verb **1** to come out **2** to become known or clear

emergency noun (plural **emergencies**) an unexpected event requiring very quick action

emigrant noun someone who emigrates

emigrate verb to leave your country to settle in another ▪ **emigration** noun

⬥ Do not confuse with: **immigrate**. You are **E**migrating when you leave your home country (the E comes from the Latin meaning 'from'). You **IM**migrate to the country where you plan to start living (the IM comes from the Latin meaning 'into')

eminent adjective famous, notable

⬥ Do not confuse with: **imminent**

eminently adverb very, obviously

emit verb to send or give out (light, sound, etc) ▪ **emission** noun

emit ► emits, emitting, emitted

emotion noun a feeling that disturbs or excites the mind, eg fear, love, hatred

emotional adjective **1** moving the feelings **2** of a person: having feelings easily excited ▪ **emotionally** adverb

empathize or **empathise** verb to share another person's feelings etc

empathy noun the ability to share another person's feelings etc

emperor noun the ruler of an empire

emphasis noun **1** stress placed on a word or words in speaking

2 greater attention or importance: *the emphasis is on playing, not winning*

emphasize *or* **emphasise** *verb* to put emphasis on; call attention to

emphatic *adjective* spoken strongly: *an emphatic 'no'* ▪ **emphatically** *adverb*

empire *noun* a group of nations *etc* under the same ruling power

employ *verb* **1** to give work to **2** to use **3** to occupy the time of

employee *noun* someone who works for an employer

employer *noun* someone who gives work to employees

employment *noun* work, occupation

empower *verb* **1** to authorize **2** to give self-confidence to

empress *noun* the female ruler of an empire

empty *adjective* **1** containing nothing or no one **2** unlikely to result in anything: *empty threats* ▪ *verb* to make or become empty ▪ **emptiness** *noun*

| **empty** *verb* ► **empties**, **emptying**, **emptied**

empty-handed *adjective* bringing or gaining nothing

empty-headed *adjective* flighty, irresponsible

emu *noun* a type of Australian bird which cannot fly

emulate *verb* to try to do as well as, or better than

emulsion *noun* a milky liquid,

especially that made by mixing oil and water

enable *verb* to make it possible for, allow

enact *verb* **1** to act, perform **2** to make a law

enamel *noun* **1** a glassy coating fired on to metal **2** a paint with a glossy finish **3** the smooth white coating of the teeth ▪ *verb* to coat or paint with enamel ▪ **enamelling** *noun*

| **enamel** *verb* ► **enamels**, **enamelling**, **enamelled**

enamoured *adjective*: **enamoured of** fond of

encapsulate *verb* to capture the essence of; describe briefly and accurately

enchant *verb* **1** to delight, please greatly **2** to put a spell or charm on

enchanting *adjective* delightful, charming

enchantment *noun* **1** a feeling of delight and wonder **2** a spell or charm

encircle *verb* to form a circle around

enclose *verb* **1** to put inside an envelope with a letter *etc* **2** to put (*eg* a wall) around

enclosure *noun* **1** the act of enclosing **2** something enclosed *eg* a small field with a high fence or wall round it

encompass *verb* to surround; to include

encore *noun* **1** an extra

performance of a song *etc* in reply to audience applause **2** a call for an encore

encounter *verb* **1** to meet by chance **2** to come up against (a difficulty, enemy, *etc*) ∎ *noun* **1** a meeting **2** a fight

encourage *verb* **1** to give hope or confidence to **2** to urge (to do)
∎ **encouragement** *noun*
∎ **encouraging** *adjective*

encroach *verb* to go beyond your rights or land and interfere with someone else's ∎ **encroachment** *noun*

encyclopedia *or*
encyclopaedia *noun* a reference book containing information on many subjects, or on a particular subject

encyclopedic *or*
encyclopaedic *adjective* giving complete information

end *noun* **1** the last point or part **2** death **3** the farthest point of the length of something **4** a result aimed at **5** a small piece left over ∎ *verb* to bring or come to an end

endanger *verb* to put in danger or at risk

endear *verb* to make dear or more dear

endearing *adjective* appealing

endeavour *verb* to try hard (to) ∎ *noun* a determined attempt

ending *noun* the last part

endorse *verb* to give your support to something said or written ∎ **endorsement** *noun*

endow *verb* **1** to give money for the buying and upkeep of: *he endowed a bed in the hospital* **2** to give a talent, quality, *etc* to: *nature endowed her with a good brain*
∎ **endowment** *noun*

endurance *noun* the power of enduring

endure *verb* to bear without giving way; last

enemy *noun* (*plural* **enemies**) **1** someone hostile to another; a foe **2** someone armed to fight against another

energetic *adjective* active, lively
∎ **energetically** *adverb*

energy *noun* (*plural* **energies**) **1** strength to act, vigour **2** a form of power, *eg* electricity, heat, *etc*

enforce *verb* to cause (a law *etc*) to be carried out ∎ **enforcement** *noun*

engage *verb* **1** to begin to employ (workers *etc*) **2** to book in advance **3** to take or keep hold of (someone's attention *etc*) **4** to be busy with, be occupied (in)

engaged *adjective* **1** bound by a promise of marriage **2** busy with something **3** of a telephone: in use

engagement *noun* **1** a promise of marriage **2** an appointment to meet

engaging *adjective* pleasant, charming

engine *noun* **1** a machine which converts heat or other energy into motion **2** the part of a train which pulls the coaches

engineer noun **1** someone who works with, or designs, engines or machines **2** someone who designs or makes bridges, roads, etc ■ verb to bring about by clever planning

engineering noun the science of designing machines, roadmaking, etc

engrave verb **1** to draw with a special tool on glass, metal, etc **2** to make a deep impression on: engraved on his memory

engraving noun a print made from a cut-out drawing in metal or wood

engross verb to take up the whole interest or attention

engulf verb to swallow up wholly

enhance verb to improve, make greater or better

enigma noun something or someone difficult to understand, a mystery ■ **enigmatic** adjective

enjoy verb **1** to take pleasure in **2** to experience, have (something beneficial): enjoying good health ■ **enjoy yourself** to have a pleasant time

enjoyable adjective pleasant and satisfying

enjoyment noun **1** pleasure and satisfaction **2** the experiencing or having (of something beneficial)

enlarge verb to make larger

enlargement noun **1** an increase in size **2** a larger photograph made from a smaller one **3** maths a transformation that produces a larger figure with its dimensions in the same ratio (compare with: **reflection**, **rotation**, **translation**)

enlighten verb **1** to give more knowledge or information to **2** to correct the false beliefs of

enlightenment noun new understanding or awareness

enlist verb **1** to join an army etc **2** to obtain the support and help of

enliven verb to make more active or cheerful

enormity noun **1** hugeness **2** extreme badness

enormous adjective very large

enormously adverb **1** very greatly, a great deal **2** extremely

enough adjective & pronoun (in) the number or amount wanted or needed ■ adverb as much as is wanted or necessary

enquire see inquire

enquiring see inquiring

enquiry see inquiry

enrage verb to make angry

enrich verb to make something richer in quality or value
■ **enriched** adjective

enrol or **enroll** verb to enter (a name) in a register or list
■ **enrolment** noun

| enrol ▶ enrols, enrolling, enrolled

ensemble noun **1** the parts of a thing taken together **2** an outfit of clothes **3** a group of musicians

ensue verb **1** to follow, come after **2** to result (from)

ensure *verb* to make sure

> ♣* Do not confuse with:
> **insure**

entail *verb* to bring as a result, involve

entangle *verb* 1 to make tangled or complicated 2 to involve (in difficulties)

enter *verb* 1 to go or come in or into 2 to put (a name *etc*) on to a list 3 to take part (in) 4 to begin (on)

enterprise *noun* 1 an undertaking, especially if risky or difficult 2 boldness in trying new things 3 a business concern

enterprising *adjective* inventive, clever, original, go-ahead

entertain *verb* 1 to amuse 2 to receive as a guest 3 to give a party 4 to consider (*eg* a suggestion)

entertainer *noun* someone who entertains professionally

entertaining *adjective* amusing

entertainment *noun* 1 performances and activities that amuse and interest people 2 a performance or activity organized for the public

enthral *verb* to give great delight to

| enthral ▸ enthral*s*,
| enthral*ling*, enthral*led*

enthuse *verb* to be enthusiastic (about)

enthusiasm *noun* great interest and keenness

enthusiast *noun* someone who is very keen on a certain activity

enthusiastic *adjective* greatly interested, very keen
■ **enthusiastically** *adverb*

entice *verb* to attract with promises, rewards, *etc*

enticement *noun* a bribe, an attractive promise

enticing *adjective* very attractive and tempting

entire *adjective* whole, complete

entirely *adverb* utterly, wholly, fully, absolutely

entirety *noun* whole and complete state

entitle *verb* 1 to give a name to (a book *etc*) 2 to give (someone) a right to ■ **entitlement** *noun*

entity *noun* (*plural* **entities**) something which exists; a being

entrance[1] (*pronounced* **en**-trans) *noun* 1 a place for entering, *eg* a door 2 the act of coming in 3 the right to enter

entrance[2] (*pronounced* in-**trahns**) *verb* 1 to delight, charm 2 to bewitch ■ **entrancing** *adjective*

entrant *noun* someone who goes in for a race, competition, *etc*

entreat *verb* to ask earnestly

entreaty *noun* (*plural* **entreaties**) earnest request or plea

entrepreneur (*pronounced* on-tre-pre-**ner**) *noun* someone who undertakes an enterprise, often involving financial risk

entrust *verb* to place in someone else's care

entry noun (plural **entries**) **1** the act of entering **2** a place for entering, a doorway **3** a name or item in a record book

E-number noun an identification code for food additives

envelop (pronounced in-**vel**-op) verb **1** to cover by wrapping **2** to surround entirely: enveloped in mist

envelope noun a wrapping or cover, especially for a letter

enviable adjective worth envying, worth having

envious adjective feeling envy ■ **enviously** adverb

environment noun surroundings, circumstances in which someone or an animal lives ■ **environmental** adjective

environmentalist noun a person who works to protect the environment

envisage verb **1** to visualize, picture in the mind **2** to consider, contemplate

envoy (pronounced **en**-voi) noun a messenger, especially one sent to deal with a foreign government

envy noun (plural **envies**) greedy desire for someone else's property, qualities, etc ■ verb to feel envy for

| **envy** verb ► envies, envying, envied

enzyme noun a substance produced in a living body which affects the speed of chemical changes

eon another spelling of aeon

ephemeral adjective very short-lived, fleeting

epic noun a long poem, story, film, etc about heroic deeds ■ adjective **1** of an epic; heroic **2** large-scale, impressive

epicentre or US **epicenter** noun the centre of an earthquake

epidemic noun a widespread outbreak of a disease etc

epidermis noun the top covering of the skin

epilepsy noun an illness causing attacks of unconsciousness and convulsions

epileptic adjective **1** suffering from epilepsy **2** of epilepsy ■ noun someone suffering from epilepsy

episode noun **1** one of several parts of a story etc **2** an interesting event

epitaph noun words on a gravestone about a dead person

epitome (pronounced i-**pit**-om-i) noun a perfect example or representative of something: the epitome of good taste

epitomize or **epitomise** verb to be the perfect example of something

epoch noun an extended period of time, often marked by a series of important events

equal adjective **1** of the same size, value, quantity, etc **2** evenly balanced **3 equal to** able, fit for: *not equal to the job* ■ *noun* someone of the same rank, cleverness, *etc* as another ■ *verb* **1** to be or make equal to **2** to be the same as ■ **equally** *adverb*

| **equal** *verb* ► equal*s*, equal*ling*, equal*led*

equality *noun* equal treatment for all the people in a group or society

equalize *or* **equalise** *verb* to make equal

equalizer *or* **equaliser** *noun* a goal *etc* which makes the score in a game equal

equate *verb* **1** to regard or treat as the same **2** to state as being equal

equation *noun* a statement, especially in mathematics, that two things are equal

equator *noun* an imaginary line around the earth, halfway between the North and South Poles

equatorial *adjective* on or near the equator

equestrian *adjective* **1** of horse-riding **2** on horseback

equilateral *adjective* of a triangle or other polygon: with all sides equal (*compare with:* **isosceles**)

equilibrium *noun* **1** equal balance between weights, forces, *etc* **2** a balanced state of mind or feelings

equine *adjective* of or like a horse

equinox *noun* either of the times (about 21 March and 23 September) when the sun crosses the equator, making night and day equal in length ■ **equinoctial** *adjective*

equip *verb* to supply with everything needed for a task

| **equip** ► equip*s*, equip*ping*, equip*ped*

equipment *noun* a set of tools *etc* needed for a task; an outfit

equity *noun* **1** fairness, just dealing **2 Equity** the trade union for the British acting profession

equivalent *adjective* equal in value, power, meaning, *etc* ■ *noun* something that is the equal of another

era *noun* a period in history: *the Elizabethan era*

eradicate *verb* to get rid of completely ■ **eradication** *noun*

erase *verb* **1** to rub out **2** to remove

eraser *noun* something which erases, a rubber

erect *verb* **1** to build **2** to set upright ■ *adjective* standing straight up

erection *noun* **1** the act of erecting **2** something erected or erect

ermine *noun* **1** a stoat **2** its white fur

erode *verb* to wear away, destroy gradually

erosion *noun* **1** a gradual destruction: *the erosion of my* *confidence* **2** *geography* the gradual wearing away of the land by water, wind, *etc*

err *verb* **1** to make a mistake **2** to sin

errand *noun* a short journey to carry a message, buy something, *etc*

erratic *adjective* **1** irregular, not following a fixed course **2** not steady or reliable in behaviour ■ **erratically** *adverb*

erroneous *adjective* wrong, mistaken ■ **erroneously** *adverb*

error *noun* **1** a mistake **2** wrongdoing

erupt *verb* to break out or through

eruption *noun* **1** an outburst from a volcano **2** a rash or spot on the skin

escalate *verb* to increase in amount, intensity, *etc* ■ **escalation** *noun*

escalator *noun* a moving staircase

escapade *noun* an adventure

escape *verb* **1** to get away safe or free **2** of gas *etc*: to leak **3** to slip from memory: *his name escapes me* ■ *noun* the act of escaping

escapism *noun* the tendency to escape from reality by daydreaming *etc* ■ **escapist** *noun & adjective*

escarpment *noun* a steep side of a hill or rock

escort *noun* someone who accompanies others for protection, courtesy, *etc* ■ *verb* to act as escort to

Eskimo *noun* (*plural* **Eskimos**) an Inuit

especial *adjective* **1** special, extraordinary **2** particular

especially *adverb* particularly

> ❧ Do not confuse with: **specially**. Especially means 'particularly, above all': *I like making cakes, especially for birthdays*. Specially means 'for a special purpose': *I made this cake specially for your birthday*.

espionage *noun* spying, especially by one country to find out the secrets of another

esplanade *noun* a level roadway, especially along a seafront

espresso *noun* strong coffee made by extraction under high pressure

essay *noun* a written composition

essence *noun* **1** the most important part or quality of something **2** a concentrated extract from a plant *etc*

essential *adjective* absolutely necessary ■ *noun* an absolute requirement

essentially *adverb* **1** basically **2** necessarily

establish *verb* **1** to settle in position **2** to found, set up **3** to show to be true, prove (that)

established *adjective* 1 firmly set up 2 accepted, recognized

establishment *noun* a place of business, residence, *etc*

estate *noun* 1 a large piece of private land 2 someone's total possessions 3 land built on with houses, factories, *etc*: *industrial estate*

estate agent someone who sells and leases property for clients

estate car a car with an inside luggage compartment and a rear door

esteem *verb* to think highly of; value ▪ *noun* high value or opinion

esteemed *adjective* respected, valued

estimate *verb* (*pronounced* es-tim-eit*) to judge roughly the size, amount or value of something ▪ *noun* (*pronounced* es-tim-at*) a rough judgement of size *etc*

estimation *noun* opinion, judgement

estranged *adjective* no longer friendly; separated

estuary *noun* (*plural* **estuaries**) the wide lower part of a river, up which the tide travels

etc *or* **&c** *abbreviation* and other things of the same sort

etch *verb* to draw on metal or glass by eating out the lines with acid

eternal *adjective* 1 lasting for ever 2 seemingly endless

eternally *adverb* for ever

eternity *noun* 1 time without end 2 the time or state after death

ether *noun* a colourless liquid used as an anaesthetic, or to dissolve fats

ethical *adjective* having to do with right behaviour, justice, duty; right, just, honourable ▪ **ethically** *adverb*

ethics *noun singular* 1 the study of right and wrong 2 (belief in) standards leading to right, ethical behaviour

ethnic *adjective* 1 of race or culture 2 of the culture of a particular race or group ▪ **ethnically** *adverb*

etiquette *noun* rules governing correct social behaviour

EU *abbreviation* European Union

eucalyptus *noun* (*plural* **eucalyptuses** *or* **eucalypti**) a large Australian evergreen tree whose leaves produce a pungent oil

euphemism *noun* a vague word or phrase used to refer to an unpleasant subject, *eg* 'passed on' for 'died' ▪ **euphemistic** *adjective*

euphonium *noun* a brass musical instrument with a low tone

euphoria *noun* a feeling of great happiness, joy ▪ **euphoric** *adjective*

Euro- *prefix* of Europe or the European Union: *Euro-budget/Eurocrat*

euro *noun* the unit of currency of the European Union, made up of 100 cents

euthanasia *noun* the killing of someone painlessly, especially to end suffering

evacuate *verb* to (cause to) leave especially because of danger; make empty ■ **evacuation** *noun*

evacuee *noun* someone who has been evacuated (from danger)

evade *verb* to avoid or escape, especially by cleverness or trickery

evaluate *verb* to find or state the value of ■ **evaluation** *noun*

evangelical *adjective* 1 spreading Christian teaching 2 strongly supporting and speaking for some cause

evangelist *noun* a person who spreads Christian teaching or supports and speaks for some cause

evaporate *verb* to change into vapour ■ **evaporation** *noun*

evasion *noun* 1 the act of evading 2 an attempt to avoid the point of an argument or accusation

evasive *adjective* with the purpose of evading; not straightforward

eve *noun* 1 the evening or day before a festival: *New Year's Eve* 2 the time just before an event: *the eve of the revolution*

even *adjective* 1 level, smooth 2 equal 3 of a number: able to be divided by 2 without a remainder (*contrasted with*: **odd**) 4 calm ■ *adverb* 1 used to emphasize another word: *even harder* 2 exactly, just ■ *verb* to make even or smooth ■ **even out** to become equal

even-handed *adverb* fair, unbiased

evening *noun* the last part of the day and early part of the night

evenly *adverb* 1 levelly, smoothly 2 equally 3 calmly

evenness *noun* the quality of being even

evensong *noun* an evening service in the Anglican Church

event *noun* 1 an important happening 2 an item in a sports programme *etc*

eventful *adjective* exciting

eventual *adjective* 1 final 2 happening as a result

eventuality *noun* (*plural* **eventualities**) a possible happening

eventually *adverb* at last, finally

ever *adverb* 1 always, for ever 2 at any time, at all: *I won't ever see her again* 3 that has existed, on record: *the best ever*

evergreen *noun* a tree with green leaves all the year round

everlasting *adjective* lasting for ever, eternal

evermore *adverb*, *old* forever

every *adjective* each of several things without exception ■ **every**

other one out of every two, alternate

everybody or **everyone** pronoun each person without exception

everyday adjective 1 daily 2 common, usual

everything pronoun all things

everywhere adverb in every place

evict verb to force (someone) out of their house, especially by law ∎ **eviction** noun

evidence noun 1 a clear sign; proof 2 information given in a law case

evident adjective easily seen or understood

evidently adverb seemingly, obviously

evil adjective wicked, very bad; malicious ∎ noun wickedness

evocative adjective evoking memories or atmosphere

evoke verb to draw out, produce: evoking memories of their childhood

evolution noun 1 gradual development 2 the belief that the higher forms of life have gradually developed out of the lower ∎ **evolutionary** adjective

evolve verb to develop gradually

ewe noun a female sheep

ex- prefix 1 no longer, former: ex-husband/ex-president 2 outside, not in: ex-directory number

exact adjective 1 accurate, precise 2 careful ∎ verb to compel

to pay, give, etc: exacting revenge

exacting adjective 1 asking too much 2 wearying, tiring

exactly adverb 1 precisely 2 as a reply to something someone has said: 'that's right' or 'I agree'

exactness noun accuracy, correctness

exaggerate verb to make to seem larger or greater than reality ∎ **exaggeration** noun

exalt verb 1 to raise in rank 2 to praise 3 to make joyful

exam noun an examination

examination noun 1 a formal test of knowledge or skill 2 a close inspection or inquiry 3 formal questioning

examine verb 1 to put questions to (pupils etc) to test knowledge 2 to question (a witness) 3 to look at closely, inquire into 4 to look over (someone's body) for signs of illness ∎ **examiner** noun

example noun 1 something taken as a representative of its kind 2 a warning

exasperate verb to make very angry ∎ **exasperation** noun

excavate verb 1 to dig, scoop out 2 to uncover by digging

excavation noun 1 the act of digging out 2 a hollow made by digging

exceed verb to go beyond, be greater than

exceedingly adverb very

excel verb 1 to do very well 2 to be better than

excel ► excels, excelling, excelled

excellence *noun* the fact of being excellent, very high quality

excellent *adjective* unusually or extremely good

except *preposition* leaving out, not counting ■ *conjunction* with the exception (that) ■ *verb* to leave out, not to count ■ **except for** with the exception of

excepting *preposition* except

exception *noun* 1 something left out 2 something unlike the rest: *an exception to the rule* ■ **take exception to** to object to, be offended by

exceptional *adjective* standing out from the rest

exceptionally *adverb* very, extremely

excerpt *noun* a part chosen from a whole work

☛ Do not confuse with: **exert**

excess *noun* (*pronounced* ik-ses) 1 a going beyond what is usual or proper 2 the amount by which one thing is greater than another 3 **excesses** very bad behaviour ■ *adjective* (*pronounced* ek-ses) beyond the amount allowed

☛ Do not confuse with: **access**

excessive *adjective* too much, too great, *etc* ■ **excessively** *adverb*

exchange *verb* to give (one

thing) and get another in return ■ *noun* 1 the act of exchanging 2 exchanging money of one country for that of another 3 the difference between the value of money in different places: *rate of exchange* 4 a central office or building: *telephone exchange* 5 a place where business shares are bought and sold

exchequer *noun* a government office concerned with a country's finances ■ **Chancellor of the Exchequer** see **chancellor**

excitable *adjective* easily excited

excite *verb* 1 to rouse the feelings of 2 to move to action

excited *adjective* unable to be calm because of extreme feelings of happiness, impatience or arousal

excitement *noun* the state of being excited

exciting *adjective* creating feelings of excitement

exclaim *verb* to cry or shout out

exclamation *noun* a sudden shout

exclamation mark a punctuation mark (!) used for emphasis, or to indicate surprise *etc*

exclude *verb* 1 to shut out 2 to prevent from sharing 3 to leave out of consideration ■ **exclusion** *noun*

exclusive *adjective* 1 only open to certain people; select: *an*

exclusive club **2** not available elsewhere: *exclusive offer*
■ **exclusive of** not including

excommunicate *verb* to expel from membership of a Church
■ **excommunication** *noun*

excrement *noun* the waste matter cast out by humans or animals

excrete *verb* to discharge (waste matter) from the body ■ **excretion** *noun*

excruciating *adjective* **1** of pain *etc*: very severe **2** painfully bad: *an excruciating performance*

excursion *noun* an outing for pleasure, *eg* a picnic

excusable *adjective* pardonable

excuse *verb* (*pronounced* eks-**kyooz**) **1** to forgive, pardon **2** to set free from a duty or task ■ *noun* (*pronounced* eks-**kyoos**) an explanation for having done something wrong

execute *verb* **1** to perform **2** to carry out: *execute commands* **3** to put to death legally

execution *noun* **1** a doing or performing **2** killing by order of the law

executioner *noun* someone with the job of putting condemned prisoners to death

executive *adjective* having power to act or carry out laws
■ *noun* **1** the part of a government with such power **2** a business manager

executor *noun* someone who

sees that the requests stated in a will are carried out

exemplary *adjective* worth following as an example

exemplify *verb* **1** to be an example of **2** to demonstrate by example

| **exemplify** ► exemplif*ies*, exemplify*ing*, exemplif*ied*

exempt *verb* to grant freedom from an unwelcome task, payment, *etc* ■ *adjective* free (from), not liable for payment *etc*
■ **exemption** *noun*

exercise *noun* **1** a task for practice **2** a physical routine for training muscles *etc* ■ *verb* **1** to give exercise to **2** to use: *exercise great care*

◆＊ Do not confuse with: **exorcize**

exert *verb* to bring into action, use: *exerting great influence*
■ **exert yourself** to make a great effort

◆＊ Do not confuse with: **excerpt**

exertion *noun* effort, hard work

exhale *verb* to breathe out
■ **exhalation** *noun*

exhaust *verb* **1** to tire out **2** to use up completely **3** to say all that can be said about (a subject *etc*)
■ *noun* a device for expelling waste fumes from internal combustion engines

exhausted *adjective* **1** tired out

2 emptied; used up ■ **exhaustion** *noun*

exhaustive *adjective* extremely thorough

exhibit *verb* to show; put on public display ■ *noun* something on display in a gallery *etc*

exhibition *noun* a public show, an open display

exhibitionism *noun* a tendency to try to attract people's attention

exhibitionist *noun* someone who tries to get people's attention all the time, a show-off

exhibitor *noun* a person who has presented something belonging to them for display at an exhibition

exhilarate *verb* to make joyful or lively, refresh ■ **exhilarating** *adjective* ■ **exhilaration** *noun*

exile *noun* **1** someone who lives outside their own country, by choice or unwillingly **2** a period of living in a foreign country ■ *verb* to drive (someone) away from their own country; banish

exist *verb* **1** to be, have life; live **2** to live in poor circumstances

existence *noun* life, being

exit *noun* **1** a way out **2** the act of going out: *a hasty exit*

exodus *noun* a going away of many people (especially those leaving a country for ever)

exonerate *verb* to free from blame

exorbitant *adjective* going

beyond what is usual or reasonable: *exorbitant price*

exorcism *noun* the act of driving away evil spirits

exorcist *noun* a person who drives evil spirits away

exorcize *or* **exorcise** *verb* **1** to drive out (an evil spirit) **2** to free from possession by an evil spirit

  ✦ Do not confuse with: **exercise**

exotic *adjective* **1** coming from a foreign country **2** unusual, colourful

expand *verb* **1** to grow wider or bigger **2** to open out

expanse *noun* a wide stretch of land *etc*

expansion *noun* a growing, stretching or spreading

expansive *adjective* **1** spreading out **2** talkative, telling much ■ **expansively** *adverb*

expect *verb* **1** to think of as likely to happen or arrive soon **2** to think, assume

expectancy *noun* the feeling of excitement that you get when you know something good is about to happen

expectant *adjective* **1** hopeful, expecting **2** waiting to become: *expectant mother*

expectation *noun* a firm belief or hope that something will happen

expecting *adjective, informal* pregnant

expedient *adjective* done for speed or convenience rather than fairness or truth ▪ *noun* something done to get round a difficulty

expedition *noun* **1** a journey with a purpose, often for exploration **2** people making such a journey

expel *verb* **1** to drive or force out **2** to send away in disgrace, *eg* from a school

| **expel** ▶ expel*s*, expel*ling*, expel*led*

expend *verb* to spend, use up

expenditure *noun* an amount spent or used up, especially money

expense *noun* **1** cost **2** a cause of spending **3** expenses money spent in carrying out a job *etc*

expensive *adjective* costing a lot of money ▪ **expensively** *adverb*

experience *noun* **1** an event in which you are involved **2** knowledge gained from events, practice, *etc* ▪ *verb* to go through, undergo

experienced *adjective* skilled, knowledgeable

experiment *noun* a trial, a test (of an idea, machine, *etc*) ▪ *verb* to carry out experiments

experimental *adjective* of something new: being done for the first time to see how successful it will be

expert *adjective* highly skilful or knowledgeable (in a particular

subject) ▪ *noun* someone who is highly skilled or knowledgeable ▪ **expertly** *adverb*

expertise *noun* skill

expire *verb* **1** to die **2** to come to an end, become invalid: *your visa has expired*

expiry *noun* the end or finish

explain *verb* **1** to make clear **2** to give reasons for

explanation *noun* a statement which makes clear something difficult or puzzling; a reason (*eg* for your behaviour)

explanatory *adjective* intended to make clear

explicable *adjective* able to be explained

explicit *adjective* plainly stated or shown; outspoken, frank ▪ **explicitly** *adverb*

explode *verb* **1** to blow up like a bomb with a loud noise **2** to prove to be wrong or unfounded

exploit *noun* (pronounced **eks**-ploit) a daring deed; a feat ▪ *verb* (pronounced eks-**ploit**) **1** to make use of unfairly **2** to make good use of (resources *etc*) ▪ **exploitation** *noun*

exploration *noun* **1** travel for the sake of discovery **2** the act of searching or searching for something thoroughly

exploratory *adjective* having the purpose of discovering things

explore *verb* **1** to make a journey of discovery **2** to think about very carefully, research ▪ **explorer** *noun*

explosion *noun* a sudden violent burst or blow-up

explosive *adjective* **1** liable to explode **2** hot-tempered ■ *noun* something that will explode, eg gunpowder

export *verb* (*pronounced* eks-**pawt**) **1** to sell goods *etc* in a foreign country **2** to send data from one computer, program, *etc* to another ■ *noun* (*pronounced* eks-pawt) **1** an act of exporting **2** something exported

expose *verb* **1** to place in full view **2** to show up (a hidden crime *etc*) **3** to lay open to the sun or wind **4** to allow light to reach and act on (a film)

exposure *noun* **1** the state of being allowed to experience something or be affected by something **2** appearance or mention in public, eg on television or in newspapers **3** the extremely harmful effects of severe cold on a person's body **4** the fact of revealing something about someone, usually something unpleasant, that has been kept secret **5** a single photograph or frame on a film

expound *verb* to explain fully

express *verb* **1** to show by action **2** to put into words ■ *adjective* **1** clearly stated: *express instructions* **2** sent in haste: *express messenger* ■ *noun* a fast train, bus, *etc*

expression *noun* **1** the look on someone's face **2** showing meaning or emotion through language, art, *etc* **3** a show of emotion in an artistic performance *etc* **4** a word or phrase **5** *maths* a symbol or combination of symbols

expressive *adjective* expressing meaning or feeling clearly

expulsion *noun* **1** the act of driving or forcing a person or thing out **2** the sending away of someone in disgrace, eg from a school

exquisite (*pronounced* eks-kwiz-it *or* iks-**kwiz**-it) *adjective* **1** extremely beautiful **2** excellent **3** very great, utter: *exquisite pleasure*

extend *verb* **1** to stretch, make longer **2** to hold out: *extended a hand* **3** to last, carry over: *my holiday extends into next week*

extension *noun* **1** a part added to a building **2** an additional amount of time on a schedule, holiday, *etc* **3** a telephone connected with a main one

extensive *adjective* **1** wide; covering a large space **2** happening in many places **3** wide-ranging, sweeping: *extensive changes* ■ **extensively** *adverb*

extent *noun* **1** the space something covers **2** degree: *to a great extent*

exterior *adjective* on the outside; outer ■ *noun* the outside of a building *etc*

exterminate verb to kill off completely (a race, a type of animal, etc), wipe out ■ **extermination** noun
external adjective outside; on the outside
extinct adjective 1 of an old volcano: no longer erupting 2 no longer found alive
extinction noun making or becoming extinct
extinguish verb 1 to put out (fire etc) 2 to put an end to
extinguisher noun a spray containing chemicals for putting out fires
extol verb to praise greatly
| extol ► extols, extolling, extolled
extort verb to take by force or threats ■ **extortion** noun
extortionate adjective of a price: much too high
extra adjective more than is usual or necessary; additional ■ adverb unusually; more than is average: extra large ■ noun 1 something extra 2 someone employed to be one of a crowd in a film
extra- prefix outside, beyond
extract verb (pronounced eks-trakt) 1 to draw or pull out, especially by force: extract a tooth 2 to remove selected parts of a book etc 3 to draw out by pressure or chemical action ■ noun (pronounced eks-trakt) 1 an excerpt from a book etc 2 a

substance obtained by extraction: vanilla extract
extraction noun 1 the act of extracting 2 someone's descent or lineage: of Irish extraction
extraordinary adjective 1 not usual, exceptional 2 very surprising ■ **extraordinarily** adverb
extraterrestrial adjective from outside the earth ■ noun a being from another planet
extravagant adjective 1 spending too freely; wasteful 2 too great, overblown: extravagant praise ■ **extravagance** noun ■ **extravagantly** adverb
extravaganza noun an extravagant creation or production
extreme adjective 1 far from the centre 2 far from the ordinary or usual 3 very great: extreme sadness ■ noun an extreme point
extremely adverb very, exceptionally
extremist noun someone who carries ideas foolishly far ■ **extremism** noun
extremity noun (plural extremities) 1 a part or place furthest from the centre 2 great distress or pain 3 **extremities** the hands and feet
extricate verb to free from (difficulties etc)
extrovert noun an outgoing, sociable person (contrasted with: **introvert**)

exuberant *adjective* in very high spirits ■ **exuberance** *noun* ■ **exuberantly** *adverb*

exude *verb* to give off in large amounts

exult *verb* to be very glad, rejoice greatly: *exulting in their victory* ■ **exultant** *adjective* ■ **exultation** *noun*

eye *noun* **1** part of the body with which you see **2** the ability to notice: *an eye for detail* **3** sight **4** something the shape of an eye, *eg* the hole in a needle ■ *verb* to look at with interest

| **eye** *verb* ▶ eyes, eye*ing*, eye*d*

eyeball *noun* the round part of the eye; the eye itself (the part between the eyelids)

eyebrow *noun* the hairy ridge above the eye

eye-catching *adjective* drawing attention; striking

eyelash *noun* one of the hairs on the edge of the eyelid

eyelet *noun* a small hole for a shoelace *etc*

eyelid *noun* the skin covering of the eye

eye-opener *noun* that which shows up something unexpected

eyesight *noun* the ability to see

eyesore *noun* anything that is ugly (especially a building)

eye tooth a canine tooth

eyewash *noun* a lotion for the eye

eyewitness *noun* someone who sees a thing done (*eg* a crime committed)

eyrie (*pronounced* **ee**-*e*-ri) *noun* the nest of an eagle or other bird of prey

fable *noun* a story about animals *etc*, including a lesson or moral

fabric *noun* cloth

fabricate *verb* to make up (lies) ■ **fabrication** *noun*

fabulous *adjective* 1 *informal* very good, excellent 2 imaginary, mythological

fabulously *adverb* extremely, unbelievably

façade *noun* 1 the front of a building 2 a deceptive appearance or act; a mask

face *noun* 1 the front part of the head 2 the front of anything 3 appearance 4 one of the flat surfaces of a solid figure ■ *verb* 1 to turn or stand in the direction of 2 to stand opposite to ■ **face up to** to meet or accept boldly

facelift *noun* 1 a surgical operation to smooth and firm the tissues of the face 2 a renovating process, especially one applied to the outside of a building

face pack a cosmetic paste applied to the face and left to dry before being peeled or washed off

facet *noun* 1 a side of a many-sided object, *eg* a cut gem 2 an aspect; a characteristic

facetious (*pronounced* fa-see-shus) *adjective* not meant seriously; joking ■ **facetiously** *adverb*

facial *adjective* of the face

facilitate *verb* to make easy

facility *noun* 1 ease 2 skill, ability 3 **facilities** buildings, equipment, *etc* provided for a purpose: *sports facilities*

facsimile *noun* an exact copy

fact *noun* 1 something known or held to be true 2 reality ■ **in fact** actually, really

faction *noun* a group that is part of a larger group

factor *noun* 1 something affecting the course of events 2 someone who does business for another 3 a number which exactly divides into another (*eg* 3 is a factor of 6)

factorize *or* **factorise** *verb* to find the factors of a number or expression ■ **factorization** *noun*

factory *noun* (*plural* **factories**) a workshop producing goods in large quantities

factual *adjective* consisting of facts; real, not fictional

faculty *noun* (*plural* **faculties**)

1 power of the mind, *eg* reason **2** a natural power of the body, *eg* hearing **3** ability, aptitude **4** a department of study in a university

fad *noun* **1** an odd like or dislike **2** a temporary fashion ■ **faddy** *adjective*

fade *verb* **1** to (make to) lose colour or strength **2** to disappear gradually, *eg* from sight or hearing

faeces *or US* **feces** (*pronounced* **fees**-eez) *noun plural* solid excrement

fag *noun* **1** *informal* tiring work **2** *slang* a cigarette

Fahrenheit *noun* a temperature scale on which water freezes at 32° and boils at 212° ■ *adjective* measured on this scale: *70° Fahrenheit*

fail *verb* **1** to (declare to) be unsuccessful **2** to break down, stop **3** to lose strength **4** to be lacking or insufficient **5** to disappoint

failing *noun* a fault; a weakness

failure *noun* **1** the act of failing **2** someone or something which fails

faint *adjective* **1** lacking in strength, brightness, *etc* **2** about to lose consciousness: *feel faint* ■ *verb* **1** to become faint **2** to fall down unconscious ■ *noun* a loss of consciousness

faintly *adverb* dimly, not clearly

faintness *noun* **1** lack of strength, brightness, *etc* **2** a feeling of weakness, as if you were about to lose consciousness

fair [1] *adjective* **1** of a light colour: *fair hair* **2** of weather: clear and dry **3** unbiased, just **4** good enough but not excellent **5** beautiful

fair [2] *noun* **1** a large market held at fixed times **2** an exhibition of goods from different producers *etc*: *craft fair* **3** a travelling collection of merry-go-rounds, stalls, *etc*

◆※ Do not confuse with: **fare**

fairly *adverb* **1** in a just and reasonable way **2** rather, reasonably **3** only moderately, to a limited extent

fairness *noun* the quality of being reasonable or just in your treatment of people

fairway *noun* the mown part on a golf course, between the tee and the green

fair-weather friend someone who is a friend only when things are going well

fairy *noun* (*plural* **fairies**) a small imaginary creature, human in shape, with magical powers

fairy light a small coloured light for decorating Christmas trees *etc*

fairy story *or* **fairy tale 1** a traditional story of fairies, giants, *etc* **2** *informal* a lie

faith *noun* **1** trust **2** belief in a religion or creed

faithful *adjective* **1** loyal;

keeping your promises **2** true, accurate **3** believing in a particular religion or creed
■ **faithfully** *adverb*

fake *adjective* not genuine, forged ■ *noun* **1** someone who is not what they pretend to be **2** a forgery ■ *verb* to make an imitation or forgery of

falcon *noun* a kind of bird of prey

fall *verb* **1** to drop down **2** to become less **3** of a fortress *etc*: to be captured **4** to die in battle **5** to happen, occur: *Christmas falls on a Monday this year* ■ *noun* **1** a dropping down **2** something that falls: *a fall of snow* **4** *US* autumn **5** an accident involving falling **6** ruin, downfall, surrender **7** falls a waterfall ■ **fall in love** to begin to be in love ■ **fall out with** to quarrel with ■ **fall through** of a plan: to fail, come to nothing

| **fall** *verb* ▶ falls, falling, fell, fallen

fallout *noun* radioactive dust resulting from the explosion of an atomic bomb *etc*

fallow *adjective* of land: left unsown for a time after being ploughed

false *adjective* **1** untrue **2** not real, fake **3** not natural: *false teeth*
falseness *noun* quality of being false

falsetto *noun* a singing voice forced higher than its natural range

falsify *verb* to make false, alter for a dishonest purpose: *falsified his tax forms*

| **falsify** ▶ falsifies, falsifying, falsified

falter *verb* to stumble or hesitate

fame *noun* the quality of being well-known, renown

famed *adjective* famous

familiar *adjective* **1** well-known **2** seen, known, *etc* before **3** well-acquainted (with) **4** over-friendly, cheeky ■ **familiarity** *noun*

familiarize *or* **familiarise** *verb* to make quite accustomed or acquainted (with)

family *noun* (*plural* **families**) **1** a couple and their children **2** the children alone **3** a group of people related to one another

famine *noun* a great shortage of food

famished *adjective* very hungry

famous *adjective* well-known, having fame

famously *adverb*, *informal* very well: *get along famously*

fan[1] *noun* **1** a device or appliance for making a rush of air **2** a small hand-held device for cooling the face ■ *verb* to cause a rush of air with a fan ■ **fan out** to spread out in the shape of a fan

| **fan** *verb* ▶ fans, fanning, fanned

fan[2] *noun* an admirer, a devoted follower

fanatic *noun* someone who is over-enthusiastic about something

fanatical *adjective* wildly or excessively enthusiastic
■ **fanatically** *adverb*

fancier *noun* someone whose hobby is to keep prize animals, birds, *etc*: *a pigeon fancier*

fanciful *adjective* **1** inclined to have fancies **2** imaginary, not real

fancy *noun* (*plural* **fancies**) **1** a sudden liking or desire **2** imagination **3** something imagined ■ *adjective* not plain, elaborate ■ *verb* **1** to picture, imagine **2** to have a liking for a sudden wish for **3** to think without being sure

fancy *verb* ► fanci*es*, fanci*ing*, fanci*ed*

fancy dress an elaborate costume worn *eg* for a party, often representing a famous character

fanfare *noun* a loud flourish from a trumpet or bugle

fang *noun* **1** a long tooth of a wild animal **2** the poison-tooth of a snake

fanlight *noun* a window above a door, usually semi-circular

fantastic *adjective* **1** very unusual, strange **2** *informal* excellent

fantasy *noun* (*plural* **fantasies**) **1** an imaginary scene, story, *etc* **2** an idea not based on reality

far *adverb* **1** at or to a long way: *far off* **2** very much: *far better* ■ *adjective* **1** a long way off, distant: *a far country* **2** more distant: *the far side*

far *adjective* ► far*ther*, far*thest*

farce *noun* **1** a play with far-fetched characters and plot **2** a ridiculous situation

fare *verb* to get on (either well or badly): *they fared well in the competition* ■ *noun* **1** the price of a journey **2** a paying passenger in a taxi *etc* **3** food

◆* Do not confuse with: **fair**

farewell *exclamation & noun* goodbye

far-fetched *adjective* very unlikely: *a far-fetched story*

farm *noun* **1** an area of land for growing crops, breeding and feeding animals, *etc* **2** a place where certain animals, fish, *etc* are reared: *a salmon farm* ■ *verb* to work on a farm ■ **farm out** to give (work) to others to do for payment

farmer *noun* the owner or tenant of a farm

farmhouse *noun* the house attached to a farm

farmyard *noun* the yard surrounded by farm buildings

far-sighted *adjective* foreseeing what is likely to happen and preparing for it

farther and **farthest** *see* far

fascinate *verb* to charm, attract irresistibly

fascinating *adjective* extremely interesting

fascination *noun* an intense and deep interest

fashion *noun* **1** the style in which something is made, especially clothes **2** a way of behaving or dressing which is popular for a time **3** a manner, a way: *acting in a strange fashion* ■ *verb* to shape, form

fashionable *adjective* up-to-date, agreeing with the latest style

fast *adjective* **1** quick-moving of a clock: showing a time in advance of the correct time **2** of dyed colour: fixed, not likely to wash out ■ *adverb* **1** quickly **2** firmly: *stand fast* **3** soundly, completely: *fast asleep* ■ *verb* to go without food voluntarily, *eg* for religious reasons ■ *noun* a period of not eating

fasten *verb* to fix; make firm by tying, nailing, *etc* ■ **fastener** or **fastening** *noun*

fat *noun* an oily substance made by the bodies of animals and by plants ■ *adjective* **1** having a lot of fat; plump **2** thick, wide

fatal *adjective* causing death or disaster

fatality *noun* (*plural* **fatalities**) a death, especially caused by accident or disaster

fate *noun* **1** what the future holds; fortune, luck **2** end, death: *met his fate bravely*

fated *adjective* doomed

fateful *adjective* with important consequences; crucial, significant

father *noun* **1** a male parent **2** a priest ■ *verb* to be the father of

fatherhood *noun* the state of being a father

father-in-law *noun* the father of someone's husband or wife

fatherly *adjective* kind and protective

fathom *noun* a measure of depth of water (6 feet, 1.83 metres) ■ *verb* to understand, get to the bottom of

fatigue *noun* great tiredness ■ *verb* to tire out

fatten *verb* to make or become fat

fatty *adjective* containing a lot of fat

fatty acid one of a group of acids found in animal and vegetable fats

fault *noun* **1** a mistake **2** a flaw, something bad or wrong, *eg* with a machine **3** a long crack in the earth's surface where a section of the rock layer has slipped

faultless *adjective* perfect ■ **faultlessly** *adverb*

faulty *adjective* having a fault or faults

faun *noun* a mythological creature, half human and half animal

🖝 Do not confuse with: **fawn**

fauna *noun* the animals of a district or country as a whole

favour *noun* **1** a kind action

2 goodwill, approval **3** a gift, a token ▪ *verb* **1** to show preference for **2** to be an advantage to

favourable *adjective* **1** showing approval **2** advantageous, helpful (to)

favourably *adverb* in a positive or advantageous way

favourite *adjective* best liked ▪ *noun* **1** a best-loved person or thing **2** a competitor, horse, *etc* expected to win a race

favouritism *noun* showing favour towards one person *etc* more than another

fawn¹ *noun* **1** a young deer **2** a light yellowish-brown colour ▪ *adjective* of this colour

fawn² *verb* **1** to show affection as a dog does **2** **fawn on** to flatter in a grovelling fashion

> ❡ Do not confuse with: **faun**

fax *noun* **1** a machine that scans a document electronically and transfers the information by a telephone line to a receiving machine that produces a corresponding copy **2** a document copied and sent in this way ▪ *verb* **1** to send by fax **2** to send a fax message to

fear *noun* an unpleasant feeling caused by danger, evil, *etc* ▪ *verb* to be afraid of

fearful *adjective* **1** timid, afraid **2** terrible **3** *informal* very bad: *a fearful headache*

fearfully *adverb* **1** timidly,

showing fear **2** extremely, dreadfully

fearless *adjective* brave, daring ▪ **fearlessly** *adverb*

fearsome *adjective* inspiring fear; frightening

feasible *adjective* able to be done, likely ▪ **feasibility** *noun* ▪ **feasibly** *adverb*

feast *noun* **1** a rich and plentiful meal **2** a festival day commemorating some event ▪ *verb* to eat or hold a feast

feat *noun* a deed requiring some effort

feather *noun* one of the growths which form the outer covering of a bird

feathery *adjective* **1** covered in feathers **2** soft **3** light

feature *noun* **1** an identifying mark, a characteristic **2** a special article in a newspaper *etc* **3** the main film in a cinema programme **4** a special attraction **5 features** the various parts of someone's face, *eg* eyes, nose, *etc* ▪ *verb* **1** to have as a feature **2** to take part (in) **3** to be prominent in

February *noun* the second month of the year

fed *past form of* **feed**

federal *adjective* joined by treaty or agreement

federation *noun* a group of states *etc* joined together for a common purpose, a league

fee *noun* a price paid for work done, or for a special service

feeble *adjective* weak ▪ **feebly** *adverb*

feed *verb* **1** to give food to **2** to eat food ▪ *noun* food for animals ▪ **fed up** tired, bored and disgusted

⎰ **feed** *verb* ► feed*s*, feed*ing*, fed

feedback *noun* **1** responses and reactions (to something) **2** *computing* the process in which part of the output of a system is returned to the input, to regulate the following output

feel *verb* **1** to explore by touch **2** to experience, be aware of: *he felt no pain* **3** to believe, consider **4** to think (yourself) to be: *I feel ill* **5** to be sorry (for): *we felt for her in her grief* ▪ *noun* an act of touching

⎰ **feel** *verb* ► feel*s*, feel*ing*, felt

feeler *noun* one of two thread-like parts on an insect's head for sensing danger *etc*

feeling *noun* **1** sense of touch **2** emotion **3** affection **4** an impression, belief

feelings *noun plural* what someone feels inside; emotions

feet *plural* of foot

feline *adjective* **1** of or relating to cats **2** like a cat

fell [1] *verb* to cut down (a tree)

fell [2] *past form* of fall

fellow *noun* **1** a member of an academic society, college, *etc* **2** a man, a boy

fellowship *noun* **1** comradeship, friendship **2** an award to a university graduate

felt [1] *noun* a type of rough cloth made of rolled and pressed wool

felt [2] *past form* of feel

female *adjective* of the sex which produces children ▪ *noun* a human or animal of this sex

feminine *adjective* **1** of or relating to women **2** characteristic of women

femininity *noun* **1** the circumstance of being a woman **2** the quality of being feminine, or of having physical and mental characteristics traditionally thought suitable and essential for women

feminism *noun* a social and cultural movement aiming to win equal rights for women ▪ **feminist** *noun & adjective*

fen *noun* low marshy land, often covered with water

fence *noun* a railing, hedge, *etc* for closing in animals or land ▪ *verb* **1** to close in with a fence **2** to fight with swords

fencing *noun* **1** material for fences **2** the sport of fighting with swords, using blunted weapons

fend *verb*: **fend for yourself** look after and provide for yourself

ferment *verb* to change by fermentation

fermentation *noun* a reaction caused by bringing certain substances together, *eg* by adding yeast to dough in bread-making

fern noun a plant with no flowers and feather-like leaves

ferocious adjective fierce, savage ■ **ferociously** adverb

ferret noun a small weasel-like animal

ferry verb to carry over water by boat, or overland by aeroplane ■ noun (plural **ferries**) a boat which carries passengers and cars etc across a channel

| **ferry** verb ► ferries, ferrying, ferried

fertile adjective 1 able to produce children or young 2 full of ideas, creative, productive ■ **fertility** noun

fertilize or **fertilise** verb 1 to make (soil etc) fertile 2 to start the process of reproduction in an egg or plant by combining them with sperm or pollen ■ **fertilization** noun

fertilizer or **fertiliser** noun manure or chemicals used to make soil more fertile

fervour or US **fervor** noun enthusiasm, zeal

fester verb of a wound: to produce pus because of infection

festival noun 1 a celebration; a feast 2 a season of musical, theatrical or other performances

festive adjective 1 of a feast 2 in a happy, celebrating mood

festivity noun (plural **festivities**) a celebration, a feast

fetch verb to go and get

fete or **fête** noun a public event with stalls, competitions, etc to raise money

fetters noun plural, formal chains for imprisonment

feud (pronounced fyood) noun a private, drawn-out war between families, clans, etc

fever noun an above-normal body temperature and quickened pulse

feverish adjective 1 having a slight fever 2 excited 3 too eager, frantic

few adjective not many: only a few tickets left ■ **quite a few** several, a considerable number

| **few** ► fewer, fewest

fiancé noun the man a woman is engaged to marry

fiancée noun the woman a man is engaged to marry

fiasco noun (plural **fiascos**) a complete failure

fib verb to lie about something unimportant ■ noun an unimportant lie ■ **fibber** noun

| **fib** verb ► fibs, fibbing, fibbed

fibre noun 1 a thread or string 2 the essence or material of something: the fibre of her being 3 roughage in foods

fibreglass noun a lightweight material made of very fine threads of glass, used for building boats etc

fickle adjective changeable; not stable or loyal

fiction noun stories about

imaginary characters and events

fictional *adjective* imagined, created for a story

◆* Do not confuse: **fictional** and **fictitious**

fictitious *adjective* **1** not real, imaginary **2** untrue

fiddle *noun*, *informal* **1** a violin **2** a tricky or delicate operation **3** a cheat, a swindle ■ *verb* **1** to play the violin **2** to play aimlessly (with) **3** to interfere, tamper (with) **4** *informal* to falsify (accounts *etc*) with the intention of cheating

fiddly *adjective* needing delicate or careful handling

fidget *verb* to move about restlessly

field *noun* **1** a piece of enclosed ground for pasture, crops, sports, *etc* **2** an area of land containing a natural resource: *coalfield* **3** a branch of interest or knowledge ■ *verb*, *cricket*, *rounders*, *etc* to catch the ball and return it

field day a day of unusual activity or success

fielder *noun* someone whose role is to catch and return the ball in cricket, rounders, *etc*

field marshal the highest ranking army officer

fieldwork *noun* practical work done outside the classroom or home

fiend *noun* **1** an evil spirit **2** a wicked person **3** an extreme enthusiast: *a crossword fiend*

fiendish *adjective* **1** evil or wicked **2** extremely bad **3** very complicated or clever

fierce *adjective* **1** very angry-looking, hostile, likely to attack **2** intense, strong: *fierce competition* ■ **fiercely** *adverb*

fiery *adjective* **1** like fire **2** quick-tempered, volatile

fiesta *noun* a religious festival or carnival

fifteen *noun* the number 15 ■ *adjective* 15 in number

fifteenth *adjective* the last of a series of fifteen ■ *noun* one of fifteen equal parts

fifth *adjective* the last of a series of five ■ *noun* one of five equal parts

fiftieth *adjective* the last of a series of fifty ■ *noun* one of fifty equal parts

fifty *noun* the number 50 ■ *adjective* 50 in number

fig *noun* **1** a soft roundish fruit with thin, dark skin and red pulp containing many seeds **2** the tree which bears it

fight *verb* **1** to struggle with fists, weapons, *etc* **2** to quarrel **3** to go to war with ■ *noun* a struggle; a battle

| **fight** *verb* ▶ fights, fight*ing*, fought

fighter *noun* **1** someone who fights **2** a fast military aircraft armed with guns

figure *noun* **1** outward form or shape **2** a number **3** a geometrical shape **4** an unidentified person: *a shadowy figure approached* **5** a diagram or drawing on a page ▪ *verb* to appear, take part: *he figures in the story* ▪ **figure out** to work out, understand

file *noun* **1** a loose-leaf book *etc* to hold papers **2** an amount of computer data held under a single name **3** a line of soldiers *etc* walking one behind another **4** a steel tool with a roughened surface for smoothing wood, metal, *etc* ▪ *verb* **1** to put (papers *etc*) in a file **2** to rub with a file **3** to walk in a file

file extension *computing* the 2- or 3-letter suffix, *eg* doc, bmp, xls, *etc*, at the end of a computer file name, separated from the rest of the name by a full stop and showing the file format

fill *verb* **1** to put (something) into until there is no room for more **2** to become full: *her eyes filled with tears* **3** to satisfy, fulfil (a requirement *etc*) **4** to put something in a hole to stop it up ▪ **fill in 1** to fill (a hole) **2** to complete (a form *etc*) **3** to do another person's job while they are absent ▪ **fill up** to fill completely

fillet *noun* a piece of meat or fish with bones removed ▪ *verb* to remove the bones from

| **fillet** *verb* ▶ fillets, filleting, filleted

filling *noun* something used to fill a hole or gap ▪ *adjective* of food: satisfying

filling-station *noun* a garage which sells petrol

filly *noun* (*plural* fillies) a young female horse

film *noun* **1** a thin skin or coating **2** a chemically-coated strip of celluloid on which photographs are taken **3** a narrative photographed on celluloid and shown in a cinema, on television, *etc* ▪ *verb* **1** to photograph on celluloid **2** to develop a thin coating: *his eyes filmed over*

filter *noun* **1** a strainer for removing solid material from liquids or gases **2** a green arrow on a traffic light signalling one lane of traffic to move while the main stream is held up ▪ *verb* **1** to strain through a filter **2** to move or arrive gradually: *the news filtered through*

| **filter** *verb* ▶ filters, filtering, filtered

filth *noun* **1** dirt **2** obscene words or pictures

filthy *adjective* **1** very dirty **2** obscene, lewd

fin *noun* a flexible projecting part of a fish's body used for balance and swimming

final *adjective* **1** last **2** allowing of no argument ▪ *noun* the last contest in a competition

finale (*pronounced* fi-**nah**-lei)

noun the last part of anything (eg a concert)

finalize or **finalise** verb to put (eg plans) in a final or finished form

finally adverb in the end, at last, eventually, lastly

finance noun **1** money affairs **2** the study or management of these **3 finances** the money someone has to spend ▪ verb to supply with sums of money ▪ **financial** adjective ▪ **financially** adverb

finch noun (plural **finches**) a small bird

find verb **1** to come upon accidentally or after searching **2** to discover **3** to judge to be: finds it hard to live on her pension ▪ **find out** to discover, detect

| **find** verb ► finds, finding, found

fine[1] adjective **1** made up of very small pieces, drops, etc **2** not coarse: fine linen **3** thin, delicate **4** slight: a fine distinction **5** beautiful, handsome **6** of good quality; pure **7** bright, not rainy **8** well, healthy

fine[2] noun money to be paid as a punishment ▪ verb to compel to pay (money) as punishment

finesse noun cleverness and subtlety in handling situations etc

finger noun one of the five branching parts of the hand ▪ verb to touch with the fingers

fingerprint noun the mark made by the tip of a finger, used by the police as a means of identification

fingertip noun the very end of a finger

finish verb **1** to end or complete the making of **2** to stop: when do you finish work today? ▪ noun **1** the end (eg of a race) **2** the last coating of paint, polish, etc

finished adjective **1** ended, complete **2** of a person: ruined, not likely to achieve further success etc

fir noun a kind of cone-bearing tree

fire noun **1** the heat and light given off by something burning **2** a mass of burning material, objects, etc **3** a heating device: electric fire ▪ verb **1** to make (a gun) explode, shoot **2** informal to dismiss from a job

| **fire** verb ► fires, firing, fired

fire alarm a device to sound a bell etc as a warning of fire

firearm noun a gun eg a pistol

fire brigade a company of firefighters

fire engine a vehicle carrying firefighters and their equipment

fire escape a means of escape from a building in case of fire

firefighter noun someone whose job it is to put out fires

firefly noun a type of insect which glows in the dark

fireguard noun a framework of

iron placed in front of a fireplace for safety

fireman, **firewoman** a firefighter

fireplace *noun* a recess in a room below a chimney for a fire

firewall *noun* a piece of software that stops unauthorized access to a computer network

firework *noun* **1** a device that produces colourful patterns when set on fire, used for entertainments at night **2 fireworks** *informal* angry behaviour

firm *adjective* **1** not easily moved or shaken **2** with mind made up ▪ *noun* a business company

first *adjective & adverb* before all others in place, time or rank ▪ *adverb* before doing anything else

first-aid *noun* treatment of a wounded or sick person before the doctor's arrival

first-class *adjective* of the highest standard, best kind, *etc*

first-hand *adjective* direct

first minister the leader of the parliament in Scotland, Northern Ireland or Wales

first-rate *adjective* first-class

fish *noun* (*plural* **fish** or **fishes**) a kind of animal that lives in water and breathes through gills ▪ *verb* **1** to try to catch fish with a rod, nets, *etc* **2** to search (for) **3** to try to obtain: *fish for compliments*

fisherman *noun* a man who fishes, especially for a living

fishmonger *noun* someone who sells fish for eating

fishy *adjective* **1** like a fish **2** doubtful, arousing suspicion

fission *noun* splitting

fissure *noun* a crack

fist *noun* a tightly-shut hand

fit *adjective* **1** suited to a purpose; proper **2** in good training or health ▪ *noun* a sudden attack or spasm of laughter, illness, *etc* ▪ *verb* **1** to be of the right size or shape **2** to be suitable

| **fit** *verb* ▶ fits, fit*ting*, fit*ted*

fitness *noun* good physical health and strength

fitting *adjective* suitable ▪ *noun* something fixed or fitted in a room, house, *etc*

five *noun* the number 5 ▪ *adjective* 5 in number

fix *verb* **1** to make firm; fasten **2** to mend, repair

fixed *adjective* settled; set in position

fixture *noun* **1** a piece of furniture *etc* fixed in position **2** an arranged sports match or race

fizz *verb* to make a hissing sound ▪ *noun* a hissing sound

fizzle or **fizzle out** *verb* to fail, coming to nothing

fizzy *adjective* of a drink: forming bubbles on the surface

flabbergasted *adjective* very surprised

flabby *adjective* not firm, soft, limp; weak, feeble

flag *noun* 1 a piece of cloth with a distinctive design, representing a country, party, *etc* 2 (*also called*: **flagstone**) a flat paving-stone ▪ *verb* to become tired or weak

| **flag** *verb* ▶ flags, flagg*ing*, flagged

flagrant *adjective* openly wicked

flagstone *see* flag

flair *noun* talent, skill

flake *noun* 1 a thin slice or chip of anything 2 a very small piece of snow *etc* ▪ *verb* to form into flakes ▪ **flake off** to break off in flakes

flaky *adjective* forming flakes, crumbly

flamboyant *adjective* 1 splendidly coloured 2 too showy, gaudy

flame *noun* the bright leaping light of a fire ▪ *verb* 1 to burn brightly 2 *computing slang* to send abusive electronic mail (to)

flaming *adjective* burning

flamingo *noun* (*plural* **flamingos** *or* **flamingoes**) a type of long-legged bird with pink or white plumage

flammable *adjective* easily set on fire

> ●⋆ **Flammable** and **inflammable** mean the same thing

flan *noun* a flat, open tart

flank *noun* the side of an animal's body, of an army, *etc* ▪ *verb* 1 to go by the side of 2 to be situated at the side of

flannel *noun* 1 loosely woven woollen fabric 2 a small towel or face cloth

flap *noun* 1 anything broad and loose-hanging 2 the sound of a wing *etc* moving through air 3 a panic ▪ *verb* 1 to hang down loosely 2 to move with a flapping noise 3 to get into a panic

| **flap** *verb* ▶ flaps, flapp*ing*, flapped

flapjack *noun* a biscuit made with rolled oats, butter and sugar

flare *verb* 1 to blaze up 2 to widen towards the edge ▪ *noun* a bright light, especially one used at night as a signal, to show the position of a boat in distress, *etc* ▪ **flared** *adjective*

| **flare** *verb* ▶ flares, flar*ing*, flared

flash *noun* (*plural* **flashes**) 1 a quick burst of light 2 a moment, an instant ▪ *verb* 1 to shine out suddenly 2 to pass quickly

flashy *adjective* showy, gaudy

flask *noun* 1 a narrow-necked bottle 2 a small flat bottle 3 an insulated bottle or vacuum flask

flat *adjective* 1 level: *a flat surface* 2 of a drink: no longer fizzy 3 leaving no doubt, downright: *a flat denial* 4 below the right musical pitch 5 of a tyre: punctured 6 dull, uninteresting ▪ *adverb* stretched out: *lying flat* on her back ■ *noun* **1** an apartment on one storey of a building **2** *music* a sign (♭) which lowers a note by a semitone **3** a punctured tyre ■ **flat out** as fast as possible; with as much effort as possible

flatfish *noun* a flat-bodied fish with its eyes on the upper surface, *eg* a sole

flatly *adverb* in a definite or emphatic way

flatness *noun* the quality of being flat

flat race a race over level ground

flat rate a rate which is the same in all cases

flatten *verb* to make or become flat

flatter *verb* to praise insincerely ■ **flattery** *noun*

flaunt *verb* to display in an obvious way: *flaunted his wealth*

◆* Do not confuse with: **flout**. Remember that the use of **flaunt** is perfectly illustrated in the well-known phrase 'if you've got it, **flaunt** it'. On the other hand, when you **flout** something, you treat it with contempt instead of showing it off, *eg* you might **flout** the rules or **flout** tradition

flavour *noun* **1** taste: *lemon flavour* **2** quality or atmosphere: *an exotic flavour* ■ *verb* to give a taste to

flavouring *noun* an ingredient used to give a particular taste: *chocolate flavouring*

flaw *noun* a fault, an imperfection

flawless *adjective* with no faults or blemishes

flax *noun* a plant whose fibres are woven into linen cloth

flea *noun* a small, wingless, blood-sucking insect with great jumping power

fleck *noun* a spot, a speck

flecked *adjective* marked with spots or patches

fled *past form* of **flee**

fledgling *noun* a young bird with fully-grown feathers

flee *verb* to run away from danger *etc*

│ **flee** ► flees, flee*ing*, fled

fleece *noun* **1** a sheep's coat of wool **2** a garment made of fluffy, warm fabric

fleecy *adjective* soft and fluffy like wool

fleet *noun* a number of ships

fleeting *adjective* passing quickly ■ **fleetingly** *adverb*

flesh *noun* **1** the soft tissue which covers the bones of humans and animals **2** meat **3** the body **4** the soft eatable part of fruit ■ **fleshy** *adjective*

flew *past form* of **fly**

flex *verb* to bend ■ *noun* a length of covered wire attached to electrical devices

flexible *adjective* **1** easily bent

2 willing to adapt to new or different conditions ▪ **flexibility** noun

flexitime noun a system in which an agreed number of hours' work is done at times chosen by the worker

flick verb **1** to strike lightly with a quick movement **2** to remove (dust etc) with a movement of this kind ▪ noun a quick, sharp movement

flicker verb **1** to flutter **2** to burn unsteadily ▪ noun a brief trace: a flicker of hope

flight noun **1** the act of flying **2** a journey by plane **3** a number (of steps)

flighty adjective changeable, impulsive

flimsy adjective **1** thin; easily torn or broken etc **2** weak: a flimsy excuse

flinch verb to move or shrink back in fear, pain, etc

fling verb to throw ▪ noun **1** a throw **2** a brief romantic affair

| **fling** verb ► flings, flinging, flung

flint noun a kind of hard stone ▪ adjective made of flint

flip verb to toss lightly ▪ noun a light toss or stroke

| **flip** verb ► flips, flipping, flipped

flippant adjective joking, not serious ▪ **flippancy** noun ▪ **flippantly** adverb

flipper noun **1** a limb of a seal, walrus, etc **2** a webbed rubber shoe worn by divers

flirt verb to play at courtship without any serious intentions ▪ noun someone who flirts ▪ **flirtation** noun

flirtatious adjective fond of flirting

flit verb to move quickly and lightly from place to place

| **flit** ► flits, flitting, flitted

float verb to keep on the surface of a liquid without sinking ▪ noun **1** a cork etc on a fishing line **2** a van delivering milk etc **3** a platform on wheels, used in processions

flock[1] noun **1** a number of animals or birds together **2** the congregation of a church ▪ verb **1** **flock to** to go to in large numbers or in a large crowd **2** **flock together** to gather in a crowd

flock[2] noun a shred or tuft of wool

flog verb **1** to beat, lash **2** slang to sell ▪ **flogging** noun

| **flog** ► flogs, flogging, flogged

flood noun **1** a great flow, especially of water **2** a great quantity: a flood of letters ▪ verb **1** to (cause to) overflow **2** to cover or fill with water

floodlight verb to illuminate with floodlighting ▪ noun a light used to floodlight

| **floodlight** verb ►

floodlights, floodlight*ing*, floodlit

floodlighting *noun* strong artificial lighting to illuminate an exterior or stage

floor *noun* **1** the base level of a room on which people walk **2** a storey of a building: *a third-floor flat* ▪ *verb* **1** to make a floor **2** *informal* to fall or sit down suddenly and heavily **3** *informal* to puzzle: *floored by the question*

flop *verb* **1** to sway or swing about loosely **2** to fall or sit down suddenly and heavily **3** to fail badly ▪ *noun* **1** an act of flopping **2** a complete failure

flop *verb* ► flops, flopp*ing*, flopp*ed*

floppy *adjective* flopping, soft and flexible

floppy disk a flexible computer disk, often in a harder case, used to store data

flora *noun* the plants of a district or country as a whole

floral *adjective* (made) of flowers

florist *noun* a seller or grower of flowers

floss *noun* thin, often waxed thread for passing between the teeth to clean them ▪ *verb* to clean (teeth) with dental floss

flotilla *noun* a fleet of small ships

flotsam *noun* floating objects washed from a ship or wreck

flounce[1] *verb* to walk away suddenly and impatiently, *eg* in anger

flounce[2] *noun* a gathered

decorative strip sewn on to the hem of a dress

flounder[1] *verb* **1** to struggle to move your legs and arms in water, mud, *etc* **2** to have difficulty speaking or thinking clearly, or in acting efficiently

♦* Do not confuse with: **founder**

flounder[2] *noun* a small flatfish

flour *noun* finely-ground wheat

flourish *verb* **1** to be successful, especially financially **2** to grow well, thrive **3** to wave or brandish as a show or threat ▪ *noun* (*plural* **flourishes**) **1** a fancy stroke in writing **2** a sweeping movement with the hand, sword, *etc* **3** showy splendour

floury *adjective* **1** covered with flour **2** powdery

♦* Do not confuse with: **flowery**

flout *verb* to treat with contempt, defy openly: *flouted the speed limit*

♦* Do not confuse with: **flaunt**

flow *verb* **1** to run, as water **2** to move or come out in an unbroken run ▪ *noun* a smooth or unbroken run: *flow of ideas* ▪ **flowing** *adjective*

flow chart a diagram showing a sequence of operations

flower *noun* the part of a plant or tree from which fruit or seeds

grow ■ *verb* of plants *etc*: to produce a flower

flowery *adjective* 1 full of or decorated with flowers 2 using fine-sounding, fancy language

❧* Do not confuse with: **floury**

flown *see* **fly**

flu *noun, informal* influenza

fluctuate *verb* 1 to vary in number, price, *etc* 2 to be always changing ■ **fluctuation** *noun*

fluent *adjective* finding words easily in speaking or writing, without any awkward pauses ■ **fluency** *noun*

fluff *noun* soft, downy material ■ *verb* 1 to spoil something by doing it badly or making a mistake 2 **fluff up** *or* **out** to shake or arrange into a soft mass ■ **fluffy** *adjective*

fluid *noun* a substance whose particles can move about freely, a liquid or gas ■ *adjective* flowing

fluke *noun* an accidental or unplanned success

flume *noun* a water chute

flung *past form of* **fling**

fluorescent *adjective* giving off light when exposed to ultraviolet light or X-rays ■ **fluorescence** *noun*

fluoride *noun* a chemical added to water or toothpaste to prevent tooth decay

fluoridize, fluoridise *or* **fluoridate** *verb* to add fluoride to

flurry *noun* (*plural* **flurries**) a sudden rush of wind *etc*

flush *noun* (*plural* **flushes**) 1 a reddening of the face 2 freshness, glow ■ *verb* 1 to become red in the face 2 to clean by a rush of water ■ *adjective* **flush with** having the surface level with the surface around

fluster *noun* excitement caused by hurry ■ *verb* to harass, confuse

flute *noun* a high-pitched musical wind instrument

flutter *verb* to move (eyelids, wings, *etc*) back and forth quickly ■ *noun* 1 a quick beating of the pulse *etc* 2 nervous excitement: *in a flutter*

flux *noun* an ever-changing flow: *in a state of flux*

fly *noun* (*plural* **flies**) 1 a small winged insect 2 a fish-hook made to look like a fly to catch fish 3 a flap of material with buttons or a zip, especially at the front of trousers ■ *verb* 1 to move through the air on wings or in an aeroplane 2 to run away

| **fly** *verb* ▶ flies, fly*ing*, flew, flown

flyer *noun* a small poster or advertising sheet

flying saucer a disc-shaped object believed to be an alien spacecraft

flyover *noun* a road built on pillars to cross over another

foal *noun* a young horse

foam *noun* a mass of small

bubbles on liquids ■ *verb* to produce foam ■ **foamy** *adjective*

foam rubber a sponge-like form of rubber for stuffing chairs, mattresses, *etc*

fob[1] *noun* **1** a small watch pocket **2** an ornamental chain hanging from such a pocket

fob[2] *verb* to force to accept (something worthless): *I won't be fobbed off with a silly excuse*

focal *adjective* central, pivotal: *focal point*

focus *noun* (*plural* **focuses** or **foci**) **1** the meeting point for rays of light **2** the point to which light, a look, or someone's attention is directed ■ *verb* **1** to get the right length of ray of light for a clear picture **2** to direct (one's attention *etc*) to one point

| **focus** *verb* ► **focus**es, **focus**ing, **focus**ed

fodder *noun* dried food, *eg* hay or oats, for farm animals

foe *noun*, *formal* an enemy

foetus *or US* **fetus** *noun* a young human being or animal in the womb or egg

fog *noun* thick mist ■ **foggy** *adjective*

fogy *or* **fogey** *noun* someone with old-fashioned views

foil *verb* to defeat, disappoint ■ *noun* metal in the form of paper-thin sheets

foist *verb* to palm off (something undesirable) on someone

fold *noun* **1** a laying of one part

on top of another **2** an enclosure for sheep *etc* ■ *verb* to lay one part on top of another

folder *noun* a cover to hold papers

foliage *noun* leaves

folk *noun* **1** people **2** a nation, race **3 folks** family or relations

folklore *noun* the study of the customs, beliefs, stories, *etc* of a group of people

folk music traditional music of a particular culture

folksong *noun* a traditional song passed on orally

follow *verb* **1** to go or come after **2** to happen as a result **3** to act according to: *follow your instincts* **4** to understand: *I don't follow you* **5** to work at (a trade)

follower *noun* **1** someone who follows **2** a supporter, disciple

following *noun* supporters: *the team has a large following* ■ *adjective* next in time ■ *preposition* after, as a result of

folly *noun* (*plural* **follies**) foolishness

fond *adjective* loving; tender ■ **fond of** having a liking for

fondle *verb* to caress

fondly *adverb* with fondness

fondness *noun* **1** affection, love, tenderness **2** liking

font[1] *noun* **1** a basin holding water for baptism **2** a main source: *a font of knowledge*

font[2] *or* **fount** *noun* a particular style of letters and characters

food noun that which living beings eat

food chain the sequence in which food is transferred from one living thing to another in an ecosystem, *eg* plants which are eaten by herbivores which may then be eaten by carnivores

food processor an electrical appliance for chopping, blending, *etc* food

fool noun 1 a silly person 2 a dessert made of fruit, sugar and whipped cream ▪ verb 1 to deceive 2 to play the fool ▪ **fool about** to behave in a playful or silly manner

foolhardy adjective rash, taking foolish risks

foolish adjective unwise, ill-considered ▪ **foolishly** adverb

foolproof adjective unable to go wrong

foolscap noun paper for writing or printing, 17 × 13 inches (43 × 34 centimetres)

foot noun (plural **feet**) 1 the part of the leg below the ankle 2 the lower part of anything 3 twelve inches, 30 centimetres ▪ verb to pay (a bill)

football noun 1 a game played by two teams of 11 on a field with a round ball 2 *US* a game played with an oval ball which can be handled or kicked 3 a ball used in football

foothill noun a smaller hill at the foot of a mountain

foothold noun 1 a place to put the foot in climbing 2 a firm position from which to begin something

footing noun 1 balance 2 degree of friendship, seniority, *etc*

footlight noun a light at the front of a stage, which shines on the actors

footnote noun a note at the bottom of a page

footpath noun 1 a path or track for walkers 2 a pavement

footprint noun a mark of a foot

footstep noun the sound of someone's foot when walking

footwear noun shoes *etc*

for preposition 1 sent to or to be given to: *a letter for you* 2 towards: *headed for home* 3 during (an amount of time): *waited for three hours* 4 on behalf of: *for me* 5 because of: *for no good reason* 6 as the price of: *£5 for a ticket* 7 in order to obtain: *only doing it for the money*

forage verb to search for food, fuel, *etc*

foray noun 1 a raid 2 a brief journey

forbade past form of **forbid**

forbid verb to order not to

| **forbid** ► forbids, forbidd*ing*, forbade, forbidd*en*

forbidden adjective not allowed

forbidding adjective rather frightening

force noun 1 strength, violence 2 the police 3 a group of workers, soldiers, *etc* **4 forces** those in the army, navy and air force ▪ *verb* **1** to make, compel **2** to get by violence: *force an entry* **3** to break open

forced *adjective* done unwillingly or with effort: *a forced laugh*

forceful *adjective* **1** acting with power **2** persuasive, convincing, powerful ▪ **forcefully** *adverb* ▪ **forcefulness** *noun*

forceps *noun* surgical pincers for holding or lifting

ford *noun* a shallow crossing-place in a river

forearm *noun* the part of the arm between elbow and wrist

foreboding *noun* a feeling of coming evil

forecast *verb* to tell about beforehand, predict ▪ *noun* a prediction

forefather *noun*, *formal* an ancestor

forefinger *noun* the finger next to the thumb (*also called*: **index finger**)

forefront *noun* the very front

foregoing *adjective* preceding, going before

foregone *adjective*: **a foregone conclusion** a result that can be guessed rightly in advance

foreground *noun* the part of a view or picture nearest to the person looking at it

forehead *noun* the part of the face above the eyebrows

foreign *adjective* **1** belonging to another country **2** not belonging naturally in a place *etc*: *a foreign body in an eye* **3** not familiar

foreigner *noun* someone from another country

foreleg *noun* an animal's front leg

foreman *noun* (*plural* **foremen**) **1** an overseer of a group of workers **2** the leader of a jury

foremost *adjective* the most famous or important

forerunner *noun* an earlier example or sign of what is to follow

foresee *verb* to see or know beforehand

| **foresee** ► **foresees**, **foreseeing**, **foresaw**, **foreseen**

foresight *noun* ability to see what will happen later

forest *noun* a large piece of land covered with trees

forestall *verb* to upset someone's plan by acting earlier than they expect

forestry *noun* the science of forest-growing

foretell *verb* to tell in advance, prophesy

| **foretell** ► **foretells**, **foretelling**, **foretold**

foretold *past form of* foretell

forever *or* **for ever** *adverb* **1** for all time **2** continually: *forever complaining* ▪ *noun* **1** an endless period of time **2** *informal* a very long time

foreword (*pronounced* faw-werd) *noun* a piece of writing at the beginning of a book

 ☀ Do not confuse with: **forward**. It is helpful to remember that the foreWORD in a book is made up of WORDs

forfeit *verb* to lose (a right) as a result of doing something ▪ *noun* something given in compensation or punishment for an action, *eg* a fine

forge *noun* 1 a blacksmith's workshop 2 a furnace in which metal is heated ▪ *verb* 1 to hammer (metal) into shape 2 to imitate for criminal purposes 3 to move steadily on: *forged ahead with the plan* ▪ **forger** *noun*

| **forge** *verb* ► forges, forging, forged

forgery *noun* (*plural* **forgeries**) 1 something imitated for criminal purposes 2 the act of criminal forging

forget *verb* to lose or put away from the memory

| **forget** ► forgets, forgetting, forgot, forgotten

forgetful *adjective* likely to forget, having a tendency to forget things ▪ **forgetfully** *adverb*

forgive *verb* 1 to be no longer angry with 2 to overlook (a fault, debt, *etc*)

| **forgive** ► forgives, forgiving, ▪ forgave, forgiven

forgiveness *noun* pardon

forgiving *adjective* merciful, willing to forgive other people for their faults

forgot and **forgotten** *see* forget

fork *noun* 1 a pronged tool for piercing and lifting things 2 the point where a road, tree, *etc* divides into two branches ▪ *verb* to divide into two branches *etc*

fork-lift truck a power-driven truck with steel prongs that can lift and carry heavy packages

forlorn *adjective* pitiful, unhappy

form *noun* 1 shape or appearance 2 kind, type 3 a paper with printed questions and space for answers 4 a long seat 5 a school class ▪ *verb* 1 to give shape to 2 to make

formal *adjective* 1 of manner: cold, business-like 2 done according to custom or convention ▪ **formally** *adverb*

formality *noun* (*plural* **formalities**) something which must be done but has little meaning: *the nomination was only a formality*

format *noun* 1 the size, shape, *etc* of a printed book 2 the design or arrangement of an event, *eg* a television programme 3 *computing* the description of the way data is arranged on a disk ▪ *verb* 1 to arrange into a specific format 2 *computing* to arrange data for use on a disk **3** *computing* to prepare (a disk) for use by dividing it into sectors

| **format** *verb* ▶ formats, formatting, formatted

formation *noun* **1** the act of forming **2** arrangement, *eg* of aeroplanes in flight

former *adjective* **1** of an earlier time **2** of the first-mentioned of two (contrasted with: **latter**)

formerly *adverb* in earlier times; previously

formidable *adjective* **1** fearsome, frightening **2** difficult to overcome

formula *noun* (*plural* **formulae** *or* **formulas**) **1** a set of rules to be followed **2** an arrangement of signs or letters used in chemistry, arithmetic, *etc* to express an idea briefly, *eg* H_2O = water

formulate *verb* **1** to set down clearly **2** to make into a formula

forsake *verb* to desert

| **forsake** ▶ forsakes, forsaking, forsook, forsaken

fort *noun* a place of defence against an enemy

forth *adverb* forward, onward

forthcoming *adjective* **1** happening soon **2** willing to share knowledge; friendly and open

forthright *adjective* outspoken, straightforward

fortieth *adjective* the last of a series of forty ▪ *noun* one of forty equal parts

fortifications *noun plural* walls

etc built to strengthen a position

fortify *verb* to strengthen against attack

| **fortify** ▶ fortifies, fortifying, fortified

fortnight *noun* two weeks

fortnightly *adjective & adverb* once a fortnight

fortress *noun* (*plural* **fortresses**) a fortified place

fortunate *adjective* lucky ▪ **fortunately** *adverb*

fortune *noun* **1** luck (good or bad) **2** a large sum of money

forty *noun* the number 40 ▪ *adjective* 40 in number

forward *adjective* **1** advancing **2** near or at the front **3** too quick to speak or act, pert ▪ *verb* to send on (letters) ▪ *adverb* forwards

> ● Do not confuse with: **foreword**. It is helpful to remember that for**WARD** is an indication of direction, similar to back**WARDS** and home**WARDS**

forwards *adverb* onward, towards the front .

fossil *noun* the hardened remains of the shape of a plant or animal found in rock

fossil fuel a fuel derived from the remains of ancient plants and animals, *eg* coal and natural gas

fossilize *or* **fossilise** *verb* to change into a fossil

foster *verb* **1** to bring up or nurse

(a child not your own) **2** to help on, encourage

foster-child *noun* a child fostered by a family

foster-parent *noun* someone who brings up a fostered child

fought *past form of* fight

foul *adjective* **1** very dirty **2** smelling or tasting bad **3** stormy: *foul weather* ▪ *verb* **1** to dirty **2** to play unfairly ▪ *noun* a breaking of the rules of a game

foul play a criminal act

found[1] *verb* to establish, set up

found[2] *past form of* find

foundation *noun* **1** that on which anything rests **2**

foundations the underground structure supporting a building

founder[1] *verb* of a ship: to sink

◆* Do not confuse with: flounder

founder[2] *noun* someone who founds

foundry *noun* (*plural* **foundries**) a workshop where metal is melted and cast

fount *see* font[2]

fountain *noun* **1** a rising jet of water **2** the pipe or structure from which it comes

fountain pen a pen with a metal nib and a cartridge of ink

four *noun* the number 4 ▪ *adjective* 4 in number

fourteen *noun* the number 14 ▪ *adjective* 14 in number

fourteenth *adjective* the last of a series of fourteen ▪ *noun* one of fourteen equal parts

fourth *adjective* the last of a series of four ▪ *noun* **1** one of four equal parts **2** *music* an interval of four notes

fowl *noun* a bird, especially a domestic cock or hen

fox *noun* (*plural* **foxes**) a wild animal related to the dog, with reddish-brown fur and a long bushy tail

foxglove *noun* a tall wild flower

foxhound *noun* a breed of dog trained to chase foxes

foxtrot *noun* a ballroom dance made up of walking steps and turns

foyer (*pronounced* **foi**-ei) *noun* an entrance hall to a theatre, hotel, *etc*

fraction *noun* **1** a part, not a whole number, *eg* $\frac{1}{3}$ **2** a small part

fracture *noun* a break in something hard, especially in a bone of the body

fragile *adjective* easily broken ▪ **fragility** *noun*

fragment *noun* a part broken off; something not complete

fragrance *noun* sweet scent

fragrant *adjective* sweet-smelling

frail *adjective* **1** weak **2** easily tempted to do wrong

frailty *noun* (*plural* **frailties**) weakness

frame *verb* **1** to put a frame round **2** to put together, construct

■ *noun* **1** a case or border round anything **2** build of human body **3** state (of mind)

frame *verb* ▶ frames, framing, framed

framework *noun* the outline or skeleton of something

franc *noun* the former standard unit of French and Belgian money, still used in some countries

franchise *noun* a right to sell the goods of a particular company

frank *adjective* open, speaking your mind

frankincense *noun* a sweet-smelling resin used as incense

frankly *adverb* openly

frankness *noun* the quality of being frank

frantic *adjective* wildly excited or anxious ■ **frantically** *adverb*

fraternal *adjective* brotherly; of a brother ■ **fraternally** *adverb*

fraud *noun* **1** deceit, dishonesty **2** an impostor; a fake

fray *verb* to wear away

freak *noun* **1** an unusual event **2** an odd or eccentric person **3** *informal* a keen fan: *film freak*

freckle *noun* a small brown spot on the skin

free *adjective* **1** not bound or shut in **2** generous **3** frank, open **4** costing nothing ■ *verb* **1** to make or set free **2** free someone from or of something to get rid of it for them

-free *adjective* (added to another word) not containing or involving: *additive-free*

freedom *noun* liberty

freelance *or* **freelancer** *noun* someone working independently (such as a writer who is not employed by any one newspaper)

free-range *adjective* **1** of poultry: allowed to move about freely and feed out of doors **2** of eggs: laid by poultry of this kind

freestyle *adjective* of swimming, skating, *etc*: in which any style may be used

freeware *noun*, *computing* software programs offered to the public at no cost

freewheel *verb* to travel on a bicycle or car, especially downhill, without using mechanical power

freeze *verb* **1** to turn into ice **2** to make (food) very cold in order to preserve **3** to go stiff with cold, fear, *etc* **4** to fix (prices or wages) at a certain level

freeze *verb* ▶ freezes, freezing, froze, frozen

freezer *noun* a type of cabinet in which food is made, or kept, frozen

freezing point the point at which liquid becomes a solid (of water, 0°C)

freight *noun* **1** load, cargo **2** a charge for carrying a load ■ *verb* to load with goods

freighter *noun* a ship or aircraft that carries cargo

French fries US fried potatoes

French toast bread dipped in egg and fried

French window a long window also used as a door

frenetic adjective frantic

frenzied adjective mad
- **frenziedly** adverb

frenzy noun 1 a fit of madness 2 wild excitement

frequency noun (plural **frequencies**) 1 the rate at which something happens 2 the number per second of vibrations, waves, etc

frequent adjective (pronounced **free**k-went) happening often
- **verb** (pronounced frik-**went**) to visit often

fresh adjective 1 new, unused 2 newly made or picked; not preserved: fresh fruit 3 cool, refreshing: fresh breeze 4 not tired 5 cheeky, impertinent • adverb newly: fresh-laid eggs

freshen verb 1 to make fresh 2 of a wind: to grow stronger

freshly adverb newly, recently

freshwater adjective of inland rivers, lakes, etc, not of the sea

fret[1] verb to worry or show discontent

| **fret** ► **frets**, fret**ting**, fret**ted**

fret[2] noun one of the ridges on the neck of a guitar

fretful adjective showing feelings of worry or discontent

friar noun a member of one of the Roman Catholic brotherhoods, especially someone who has vowed to live in poverty

friction noun 1 the rubbing of two things together 2 the wear caused by rubbing 3 quarrelling, bad feeling

Friday noun the sixth day of the week

fridge noun, informal a refrigerator

fried see fry[1]

friend noun someone who likes and knows well another person

friendly adjective 1 kind 2 friendly with on good terms with
- noun (plural **friendlies**) a sports match that is not part of a competition • **friendliness** noun

-friendly adjective (added to another word) 1 not harmful towards: dolphin-friendly 2 compatible with or easy to use for: child-friendly

friendship noun the state of being friends; mutual affection

frieze noun 1 a part of a wall below the ceiling, often ornamented with designs 2 a picture on a long strip of paper etc, often displayed on a wall

frigate noun a small warship

fright noun sudden fear: gave me a fright

frighten verb to make afraid
- **frightening** adjective

frightful adjective 1 causing terror 2 informal very bad

frightfully adverb **1** very badly **2** extremely

frill noun **1** an ornamental edging **2** an unnecessary ornament ■ **frilly** adjective

fringe noun **1** a border of loose threads **2** hair cut to hang over the forehead ■ verb to edge round

Frisbee noun, trademark a plastic plate-like object skimmed through the air as a game

frisk verb **1** to skip about playfully **2** informal to search someone closely for concealed weapons etc

frisky adjective lively, playful and keen to have fun ■ **friskily** adverb

fritter[1] noun a piece of fried batter containing fruit etc

fritter[2] verb to waste, squander

frivolity noun (plural **frivolities**) lack of seriousness; playfulness

frivolous adjective playful, not serious ■ **frivolously** adverb

frizzy adjective of hair: massed in small curls

fro adverb: **to and fro** forwards and backwards

frock noun a woman's or girl's dress

frock-coat noun a man's double-breasted coat that reaches down to the knees

frog noun a small greenish jumping animal living on land and in water

frogman noun, informal an underwater diver with flippers and breathing apparatus

frolic noun a merry, light-hearted playing ■ verb to play light-heartedly

frolic verb ► frolics, frolicking, frolicked

from preposition **1** used before the place, person, etc that is the starting point of an action etc: sailing from England to France **2** used to show separation: keep away from there

front noun **1** the part of anything nearest the person who sees it **2** the part which faces the direction in which something moves **3** the fighting line in a war **4** the dividing zone between warm and cold air ■ adjective at or in the front

frontier noun a boundary between countries

frost noun **1** frozen dew **2** the coldness of weather needed to form ice ■ verb to cover with frost

frosted adjective having an appearance as if covered in frost, eg glass with a specially roughened surface

frosty adjective **1** of weather: cold enough for frost to form **2** cold, unwelcoming: a frosty look

froth noun foam on liquids ■ verb to throw up foam ■ **frothy** adjective

frown verb to wrinkle the brows in deep thought, disapproval, etc ■ noun **1** a wrinkling of the brows

2 a disapproving look ■ **frown on** to look upon with disapproval

froze and **frozen** see freeze

frugal adjective **1** careful in spending, thrifty **2** costing little, small: a frugal meal

fruit noun the part of a plant containing the seed

fruitful adjective **1** producing plenty of fruit **2** producing good results: a fruitful meeting

fruitless adjective useless, done in vain

fruit machine a gambling machine into which coins are put

frustrate verb to make to feel powerless

frustration noun **1** a feeling of irritation and annoyance as a result of being powerless or unable to do something **2** the bringing to nothing or spoiling of something

fry[1] verb to cook in hot fat ■ noun food cooked in hot fat

| fry verb ▶ fries, frying, fried

fry[2] noun a young fish ■ **small fry** unimportant people or things

fuchsia noun a plant with long hanging flowers

fuddle verb to confuse, muddle

fudge noun a soft, sugary sweet

fuel noun a substance such as coal, gas or petrol, used to keep a fire or an engine going

fugitive noun someone who is running away from the police etc

fulfil verb to carry out (a task, promise, etc)

fulfil ▶ fulfils, fulfilling, fulfilled

fulfilment noun **1** successful completion, accomplishment **2** satisfaction with things achieved

full adjective **1** holding as much as can be held **2** plump: full face **3**

full of having a great deal or plenty of ■ adverb (used with adjectives) fully: full-grown

fullback noun a defensive player in football etc, the nearest to their team's goal-line

full moon the moon when it appears at its largest

full stop a punctuation mark (.) placed at the end of a sentence

full-time adjective for the whole of the working week: a full-time job (compare with: part-time)

fully adverb entirely, completely

fumble verb **1** to use the hands awkwardly **2** to drop (a thrown ball etc)

fume verb **1** to give off smoke or vapour **2** to be in a silent rage

fume verb ▶ fumes, fuming, fumed

fumes noun plural smoke, vapour

fun noun enjoyment, a good time ■ **make fun of** to tease, make others laugh at

function noun **1** a special job, use or duty of a machine, person, part of the body, etc **2** an arranged public gathering **3** maths the relation of every element in a set (the **domain**) to a single element

of another set (the **codomain**)
■ *verb* **1** to work, operate: *the engine isn't functioning properly* **2** to carry out usual duties: *I can't function at this time in the morning*

functional *adjective* **1** designed to be efficient rather than decorative; plain **2** in working order

fund *noun* **1** a sum of money for a special purpose: *charity fund* **2** a store or supply

fundamental *adjective* **1** of great or far-reaching importance **2** basic, essential ■ *noun* **1** a necessary part **2 fundamentals** the groundwork, the first stages

funeral *noun* the ceremony of burial or cremation

funfair *noun* an amusement park

fungus *noun* (*plural* **fungi** – *pronounced* **fungg**-i) **1** a soft, spongy plant growth, *eg* a mushroom **2** disease-growth on animals and plants

funky *adjective, informal* **1** of jazz and pop music: unsophisticated, earthy and soulful, like early blues **2** fashionable, trendy

funnel *noun* **1** a cone ending in a tube, for pouring liquids into bottles **2** a tube or passage for escape of smoke, air, *etc* ■ *verb* to pass through a funnel; channel

| **funnel** *verb* ► **funnels**, **funnelling**, **funnelled**

funny *adjective* **1** amusing **2** odd
■ **funnily** *adverb*

funny bone part of the elbow which gives a prickly feeling when knocked

fur *noun* **1** the short fine hair of certain animals **2** their skins covered with fur **3** a coating on the tongue, on the inside of kettles, *etc* ■ *verb* to line or cover with fur

| **fur** *verb* ► **furs**, **furring**, **furred**

furious *adjective* **1** extremely angry **2** stormy **3** fast, energetic and rather disorganized
■ **furiously** *adverb*

furlong *noun* one-eighth of a mile (220 yards, 201.17 metres)

furnace *noun* a very hot oven for melting iron ore, making steam for heating, *etc*

furnish *verb* **1** to fit up (a room or house) completely **2** to supply: *furnished with enough food for a week*

furnishings *noun plural* fittings, furniture

furniture *noun* movable articles in a house, *eg* tables, chairs

furore (*pronounced* fyoo-**raw**-rei) *noun* uproar; excitement

furrow *noun* **1** a groove made by a plough **2** a deep groove **3** a deep wrinkle ■ *verb* **1** to cut deep grooves in **2** to wrinkle: *furrowed brow*

furry *adjective* covered with fur

further *adverb & adjective* to a

greater distance or degree; in addition ▪ *verb* to help on or forward

furthermore *adverb* in addition to what has been said

furthest *adverb & adjective* to the greatest distance or degree

furtive *adjective* stealthy, sly ▪ **furtively** *adverb*

fury *noun* violent anger

fuse *verb* 1 to melt 2 to join together 3 to put a fuse in (a plug *etc*) 4 of a circuit *etc*: to stop working because of the melting of a fuse ▪ *noun* 1 easily-melted wire put in an electric circuit for safety 2 any device for causing an explosion to take place automatically

| **fuse** *verb* ► fuses, fusing, fused

fuselage *noun* the body of an aeroplane

fusion *noun* 1 melting 2 a merging: *a fusion of musical traditions*

fuss *noun* 1 unnecessary activity, excitement or attention, often about something unimportant 2 strong complaint ▪ *verb* 1 to be unnecessarily concerned about details 2 to worry too much

fussy *adjective* 1 over-elaborate 2 difficult to please; choosy 3 partial, in favour of one thing over another: *either will do; I'm not fussy* ▪ **fussily** *adverb* ▪ **fussiness** *noun*

futile *adjective* useless; having no effect

futility *noun* uselessness

futon (*pronounced* foo-ton) *noun* a sofa bed with a low frame and detachable mattress

future *adjective* happening later in time ▪ *noun* 1 the time to come: *foretell the future* 2 the part of your life still to come: *planning for their future* 3 *grammar* the tense used to describe future actions or states, *eg* 'our friends *will arrive*'

fuzz *noun* fine, light hair or feathers

fuzzy *adjective* 1 covered with fuzz, fluffy 2 tightly curled

gabble *verb* to talk fast, chatter ■ *noun* fast talk

gable *noun* the triangular area of wall at the end of a building with a ridged roof

gadget *noun* a small simple machine or tool

Gaelic *noun* **1** the language of the Scottish Highlands **2** the Irish language ■ *adjective* written or spoken in Gaelic

gag *verb* to silence by stopping the mouth ■ *noun* **1** a piece of cloth *etc* put in or over someone's mouth to silence them **2** *informal* a joke

| **gag** *verb* ► gag**s**, gag**ging**, gag**ged**

gaggle *noun* a flock of geese

gaiety and **gaily** *see* gay

gain *verb* **1** to win; earn **2** to reach **3** to get closer, especially in a race: *gaining on the leader* **4** of a clock: to go ahead of correct time **5** to take on (*eg* weight) ■ *noun* **1** something gained **2** profit

gait *noun* way or manner of walking

🔸 Do not confuse with: **gate**

gala *noun* **1** a public festival

2 a sports meeting: *swimming gala*

galaxy *noun* (*plural* **galaxies**) a system of stars ■ **the Galaxy** the Milky Way

gale *noun* a strong wind

gall *noun* bitterness of feeling ■ *verb* to annoy

gallant *adjective* **1** brave; noble **2** polite or attentive towards women

gallantry *noun* gallant behaviour

galleon *noun*, *history* a large Spanish sailing ship

gallery *noun* (*plural* **galleries**) **1** a long passage **2** the top floor of seats in a theatre **3** a room or building for showing artworks

galley *noun* (*plural* **galleys**) **1** *history* a long, low-built ship driven by oars **2** a ship's kitchen

galling *adjective* annoying, frustrating

gallivant *verb* to travel or go out for pleasure

gallon *noun* a measure for liquids (8 pints, 4.546 litres)

gallop *verb* **1** to move by leaps **2** to (cause to) move very fast ■ *noun* a fast pace

gallows *noun singular* a wooden framework on which criminals were hanged

galore *adverb* in plenty: *whisky galore*

galoshes *noun plural* waterproof shoes worn over other shoes

galvanize or **galvanise** *verb* **1** to stimulate by electricity **2** to coat (iron *etc*) with zinc

gamble *verb* **1** to play games for money **2** to risk money on the result of a game, race, *etc* **3** to take a wild chance ■ *noun* a risk; a bet on a result

gambol *verb* to leap playfully

| **gambol** ▸ gambol*s*, gambol*ling*, gambol*led*

game *noun* **1** a contest played according to rules **2 games** an athletics competition **3** wild animals and birds hunted for sport ■ *adjective* plucky

gamekeeper *noun* someone who looks after game birds, animals, fish, *etc*

gamete *noun* a germ cell

gaming *noun & adjective* gambling

gamma ray an electromagnetic ray that is stronger than an X-ray

gammon *noun* leg of a pig, salted and smoked

gander *noun* a male goose

gang *noun* **1** a group of people who meet regularly **2** a team of criminals

gangrene *noun* the rotting of some part of the body

gangster *noun* a member of a gang of criminals

gangway *noun* **1** a passage between rows of seats **2** a movable bridge leading from a quay to a ship

gannet *noun* a large white sea bird

gantry *noun* (*plural* **gantries**) a platform or structure for supporting a travelling crane *etc*

gap *noun* an opening or space between things

gape *verb* **1** to open the mouth wide (as in surprise) **2** to be wide open

garage *noun* **1** a building for storing a car (or cars) **2** a shop which carries out car repairs and sells petrol, oil, *etc*

garbage *noun* rubbish

garble *verb* to mix up, muddle

garden *noun* a piece of ground on which flowers or vegetables are grown ■ *verb* to work in a garden

gardener *noun* someone who tends a garden

gargle *verb* to rinse the throat with a liquid, without swallowing

gargoyle *noun* a grotesque carving of a human or animal head, jutting out from a roof

garish *adjective* tastelessly over-bright

garland *noun* flowers or leaves tied or woven into a circle

garlic *noun* an onion-like plant

with a strong smell and taste, used in cooking

garment noun an article of clothing

garnet noun a semi-precious stone, usually red in colour

garnish verb to decorate (a dish of food) ■ noun (plural **garnishes**) a decoration on food

garret noun an attic room

garrison noun a body of troops for guarding a fortress

garrulous adjective fond of talking

garter noun a broad elastic band to keep a stocking up

gas noun (plural **gases**) **1** a substance like air (though you can smell some gases) **2** a natural or manufactured form of this which will burn and is used as a fuel ■ verb to poison with gas

> **gas** verb ▶ gases, gassing, gassed

gaseous adjective in gas form

gash noun (plural **gashes**) a deep, open cut ■ verb to cut deeply into

gasket noun a layer of padding used to make airtight or gas-tight joints

gas mask a covering for the face to prevent breathing in poisonous gas

gasp noun the sound made by a sudden intake of breath ■ verb **1** to breathe with difficulty **2** to say breathlessly **3** informal to want badly: gasping for a cup of tea

gastric adjective relating to the stomach

gasworks noun a place where gas is made

gate noun **1** a door across an opening in a wall, fence, etc **2** the number of people at a football match **3** the total entrance money paid by those at a football match

■✴ Do not confuse with: **gait**

gateau (pronounced gat-oh) noun (plural **gateaus** or **gateaux**) a rich cake, usually layered and filled with cream

gatecrash verb to go to a party uninvited ■ **gatecrasher** noun

gateway noun **1** an opening containing a gate **2** an entrance **3** computing a connection between networks

gather verb **1** to bring together, or meet, in one place **2** to pick (flowers etc) **3** to learn, come to the conclusion (that)

gathering noun a crowd

gaudy adjective showy; vulgarly bright in colour ■ **gaudily** adverb

gauge (pronounced geij) verb **1** to measure **2** to make a guess ■ noun a measuring device

gaunt adjective thin, haggard

gauntlet noun a long glove (often of leather) with a guard for the wrist, used by motorcyclists etc ■ **throw down the gauntlet** to offer a challenge

gauze noun thin cloth that can be seen through

gawky adjective awkward

gay *adjective* **1** homosexual **2** lively; merry; full of fun **3** brightly coloured ▪ *noun* a homosexual ▪ **gaiety** *noun* ▪ **gaily** *adverb*

gaze *verb* to look steadily ▪ *noun* a fixed look

gazelle *noun* a small deer

gazette *noun* a newspaper, especially one having lists of government notices

gear *noun* **1** clothing and equipment needed for a particular job, sport, *etc* **2** a connection by means of a set of toothed wheels between a car engine and the wheels ▪ *verb*: **gear to** to adapt to, design for what is needed

geese *plural* of **goose**

gel *noun* a jelly-like substance

gelatine *noun* a jelly-like substance made from hooves, animal bones, *etc*, and used in food

gem *noun* **1** a precious stone, especially when cut **2** something greatly valued

gender *noun* (in grammar, especially in languages other than English) any of three types of noun, masculine, feminine or neuter

gene *noun* the basic unit of heredity responsible for passing on specific characteristics from parents to offspring

general *adjective* **1** not detailed, broad: *a general idea of the person's interests* **2** involving

everyone: *general election* **3** to do with several different things: *general knowledge* **4** of most people: *the general opinion* ▪ *noun* a high-ranking army officer

generalize *verb* to make a broad general statement, meant to cover all individual cases ▪ **generalization** *noun*

generally *adverb* **1** usually, in most cases **2** by most people: *generally known*

general practitioner a doctor who treats most ordinary illnesses

generate *verb* to produce, bring into being

generation *noun* **1** creation, making **2** a step in family descent **3** people born at about the same time: *the 90s generation*

generator *noun* a machine for making electricity *etc*

generous *adjective* giving plentifully; kind ▪ **generosity** *noun* ▪ **generously** *adverb*

genesis *noun* beginning, origin

genetic *adjective* **1** relating to genes **2** inherited through genes ▪ **genetically** *adverb*

genetic engineering the science of changing the genes of an organism to change its characteristics

genetics *noun singular* the study of the way characteristics are passed from one generation to the next

genial *adjective* good-natured

genie *noun* a guardian spirit

genitals *noun plural* the organs of sexual reproduction

genius *noun (plural geniuses)* **1** unusual cleverness **2** someone who is unusually clever

genocide *noun* the deliberate extermination of a race of people

gent *noun, informal* a man

genteel *adjective* good-mannered, especially excessively

gentile *noun* a non-Jew

gentility *noun* **1** aristocracy **2** good manners, refinement, often in excess

gentle *adjective* **1** mild-mannered, not brutal **2** mild, not extreme: *gentle breeze* **3** having a pleasant light or soft quality, not harsh or forceful ▪ **gentleness** *noun* ▪ **gently** *adverb*

gentleman *noun (plural gentlemen)* **1** a man, especially one of noble birth **2** a well-mannered man

gentlemanly *adjective* behaving in a polite manner

gentry *noun* a wealthy, land-owning class of people

gents *noun singular* a men's public toilet

genuine *adjective* **1** real, not fake or pretended **2** honest and straightforward ▪ **genuinely** *adverb* ▪ **genuineness** *noun*

genus *noun (plural genera)* a group of living things made up of a number of kinds

geographer *noun* someone who studies geography

geography *noun* the study of the surface of the earth and its inhabitants ▪ **geographic** *or* **geographical** *adjective*

geologist *noun* someone who studies geology

geology *noun* the study of the earth's history as shown in its rocks and soils ▪ **geological** *adjective*

geometric *or* **geometrical** *adjective* **1** relating to geometry **2** of a shape or pattern: made up of angles and straight lines

geometry *noun* the branch of mathematics which deals with the study of lines, angles, and figures

geranium *noun* a plant with thick leaves and bright red or pink flowers

gerbil *noun* a small, rat-like desert animal, often kept as a pet

geriatric *adjective* dealing with old people

geriatrics *noun singular* the health and care of the elderly

germ *noun* a small living organism which can cause disease

German measles an infectious disease, similar to, but milder than, measles

German shepherd a breed of large wolf-like dog (*also called*: **alsatian**)

germ cell the reproductive cell

of a plant or animal (*also called*: **gamete**)

germinate *verb* to begin to grow; sprout ▪ **germination** *noun*

gesticulate *verb* to wave hands and arms about in excitement *etc* ▪ **gesticulation** *noun*

gesture *noun* **1** a meaningful action with the hands, head, *etc* **2** an action expressing your feelings or intent

get *verb* **1** to go and find, take hold of, obtain **2** to go or move **3** to cause to be done: *get your hair cut* **4** to receive **5** to cause to be in some condition: *get the car started* **6** to arrive: *what time did you get home?* **7** to catch or have (a disease) **8** to become: *get rich* ▪ **get at 1** to reach **2** to hint at **3** to criticize continually ▪ **get away with** to escape punishment for ▪ **get on with** to be on friendly terms with ▪ **get over** to recover from ▪ **get up 1** to stand up **2** to get out of bed

get ► gets, gett*ing*, got; *US* gets, gett*ing*, got, gott*en*

◆* **Get** is one of the most overused words in the English language. Make sure **you** don't use it too much!

geyser (*pronounced* **geez**-er) *noun* a natural hot spring

ghastly *adjective* **1** very ill: *feeling ghastly* **2** horrible, ugly **3** very pale, death-like **4** very bad ▪ **ghastliness** *noun*

gherkin *noun* a small pickled cucumber

ghetto *noun* (*plural* **ghettos** *or* **ghettoes**) a poor residential part of a city in which a certain group (especially of immigrants) lives

ghost *noun* the spirit of a dead person

ghostly *adjective* like a ghost

ghoul *noun* **1** an evil spirit which robs dead bodies **2** someone unnaturally interested in death and disaster ▪ **ghoulish** *adjective*

giant *noun* **1** an imaginary being, like a human but enormous **2** a very tall or large person ▪ *adjective* huge

gibber *verb* **1** to speak nonsense **2** to make meaningless noises; babble

gibberish *noun* words without meaning; rubbish

gibbon *noun* a large, tailless ape

gibe *another spelling of* **jibe**

giblets *noun plural* eatable organs from the inside of a chicken *etc*

giddy *adjective* **1** unsteady, dizzy **2** causing dizziness: *from a giddy height* ▪ **giddiness** *noun*

gift *noun* **1** something freely given, *eg* a present **2** a natural talent

gifted *adjective* having special natural power or ability

gigabyte *noun* a measure of computer data or memory, equal to 1024 megabytes

gigantic *adjective* huge, of giant size

giggle *verb* to laugh in a nervous or silly manner ▪ *noun* a nervous or silly laugh

gild *verb* to cover with beaten gold

◆※ Do not confuse with: **guild**

gill *noun* one of the openings on the side of a fish's head through which it breathes

gilt *noun* beaten gold used for gilding ▪ *adjective* **1** covered with thin gold **2** gold in colour

◆※ Do not confuse with: **guilt**. Gilt is a past participle of the verb 'gild'

gimmick *noun* something meant to attract attention

gin *noun* an alcoholic drink made from grain, flavoured with juniper berries

ginger *noun* a hot-tasting root, used as a seasoning in food ▪ *adjective* **1** flavoured with ginger **2** reddish-brown in colour: *ginger hair*

gingerbread *noun* cake flavoured with ginger

gingerly *adverb* very carefully and gently

Gipsy *another spelling of* **Gypsy**

giraffe *noun* an African animal with very long legs and neck

girder *noun* a beam of iron, steel or wood used in building

girdle *noun* **1** a belt for the waist

2 a tight-fitting piece of underwear to slim the waist

girl *noun* a female child or young woman

girlfriend *noun* a female friend, especially in a romantic relationship

girlish *adjective* of a woman's appearance or behaviour: attractively youthful, like that of a girl

girth *noun* measurement round the middle

gist *noun* the main points or ideas of a story, argument, *etc*

give *verb* **1** to hand over freely or in exchange **2** to utter (a shout or cry) **3** to break, crack: *the bridge gave under the weight of the train* **4** to produce: *this lamp gives a good light* ▪ **giver** *noun* ▪ **give away 1** to hand over (something) to someone without payment **2** to betray ▪ **give in** to yield ▪ **give rise to** to cause ▪ **give up 1** to hand over **2** to yield **3** to stop, abandon (a habit *etc*) ▪ **give way 1** to yield **2** to collapse **3** to let traffic crossing your path go before you

| give ▶ gives, giving, gave, given

giveaway *noun* (*plural* **giveaways**) something that you say or do which reveals a secret to other people

given *adjective* stated or specified: *on a given day*

glacial *adjective* of ice or glaciers

glacier *noun* a slowly-moving

river of ice in valleys between high mountains

glad *adjective* **1** pleased **2** giving pleasure: *glad tidings* ▪ **gladly** *adverb* ▪ **gladness** *noun*

gladden *verb* to make glad

glade *noun* an open space in a wood

gladiator *noun*, *history* in ancient Rome, a man trained to fight with other men or with animals for the amusement of spectators

glamorous *adjective* **1** dressing and behaving in a way which people find fascinating and attractive **2** fashionable and extravagant

glamour *noun* fascination, charm, beauty, especially artificial

glance *noun* a quick look ▪ *verb* to take a quick look at ▪ **glance off** to hit and fly off sideways

gland *noun* a part of the body which takes substances from the blood and stores them for later use or elimination by the body

glandular *adjective* of, or affecting, the glands

glare *noun* **1** an unpleasantly bright light **2** an angry or fierce look ▪ *verb* **1** to shine with an unpleasantly bright light **2** to look angrily

glaring *adjective* **1** dazzling **2** very clear, obvious: *glaring mistake* ▪ **glaringly** *adverb*

glass *noun* (*plural* **glasses**) **1** a

hard transparent substance made from metal and other oxides **2** **glasses** spectacles **3** a drinking vessel made of glass ▪ *adjective* made of glass

glassy *adjective* **1** of eyes: without expression **2** of surfaces, especially water: smooth and shiny with no ripples

glaze *verb* **1** to cover with a thin coating of glass or other shiny stuff **2** to ice (a cake *etc*) **3** to put panes of glass in a window **4** of eyes: to become glassy ▪ *noun* **1** a shiny surface **2** sugar icing

glazier *noun* someone who sets glass in window frames

gleam *verb* **1** to glow **2** to flash ▪ *noun* **1** a beam of light **2** brightness

glean *verb* to collect, gather

glee *noun* joy

gleeful *adjective* merry, usually in a mischievous way ▪ **gleefully** *adverb*

glen *noun* in Scotland, a long narrow valley

glib *adjective* **1** speaking smoothly and fluently (often insincerely and superficially) **2** quick and ready, but showing little thought: *glib reply* ▪ **glibly** *adverb*

glide *verb* **1** to move smoothly and easily **2** to travel by glider ▪ *noun* the act of gliding

glider *noun* an aeroplane without an engine

glimmer *noun* **1** a faint light **2** a

faint indication: *a glimmer of hope*
■ *verb* to burn or shine faintly

glimpse *noun* a brief view ■ *verb* to get a brief look at

glint *verb* to sparkle, gleam
■ *noun* a sparkle, a gleam

glisten *verb* to sparkle

glitter *verb* to sparkle ■ *noun* **1** sparkling **2** shiny granules used for decorating paper *etc*

glittery *adjective* shiny, sparkling

gloat *verb* to look at or think about with malicious joy

global *adjective* **1** of or affecting the whole world **2** applying generally: *global increase in earnings*

globalization or **globalisation** *noun* expansion of a company or an industry all over the world

global warming an increase in the temperature of the earth's atmosphere, great enough to cause changes in the earth's climate

globe *noun* **1** the earth **2** a ball with a map of the world drawn on it **3** a ball, a sphere

globule *noun* **1** a droplet **2** a small ball-shaped piece

gloom *noun* dullness, darkness; sadness

gloomy *adjective* **1** sad, depressed **2** miserable, depressing **3** dimly lit ■ **gloomily** *adverb* ■ **gloominess** *noun*

glorify *verb* **1** to make glorious **2** to praise highly

glorify ► glorif*ies*, glorify*ing*, glorif*ied*

glorious *adjective* **1** splendid **2** deserving great praise **3** delightful ■ **gloriously** *adverb*

glory *noun* (*plural* **glories**) **1** fame, honour **2** great show, splendour ■ *verb* to rejoice, take great pleasure (in)

gloss *noun* brightness on the surface ■ *verb* **1** to make bright **2** **gloss over** to try to hide (a fault *etc*) by treating it quickly or superficially

glossary *noun* (*plural* **glossaries**) a list of words with their meanings

glossy *adjective* shiny, highly polished

glove *noun* a covering for the hand with a separate covering for each finger

glow *verb* **1** to burn without flames **2** to give out a steady light **3** to be flushed from heat, cold, *etc* **4** to be radiant with emotion: *glow with pride* ■ *noun* **1** a glowing state **2** great heat **3** bright light

glower *verb* to stare (at) with a frown

glowing *adjective* **1** giving out a steady light **2** flushed **3** radiant **4** full of praise

glucose *noun* a sugar found in fruits *etc*

glue *noun* a substance for sticking things together ■ *verb* to join with glue

glum *adjective* sad, gloomy
- **glumly** *adverb*

glut *noun* an over-supply

gluten *noun* a sticky protein found in wheat and certain other cereals

glutton *noun* **1** someone who eats too much **2** someone who is eager for anything: *a glutton for punishment*

gluttony *noun* greediness in eating

glycerine *noun* a colourless, sticky, sweet-tasting liquid

gnarled *adjective* twisted through age and use

gnash *verb* to grind (the teeth)

gnat *noun* a small blood-sucking fly, a midge

gnaw *verb* to bite at with a scraping action

gnome *noun* a small, imaginary, human-like creature who lives underground, often guarding treasure

gnu (*pronounced* noo *or* nyoo) *noun* a type of African antelope

go *verb* **1** to move **2** to leave **3** to lead: *that road goes north* **4** to become: *go mad* **5** to work: *the car is going at last* **6** to intend (to do) **7** to be removed or taken **8** to be given, awarded, *etc*: *the first prize goes to Mona* ▪ *noun* **1** the act or process of going **2** energy, spirit **3** *informal* an attempt, a try ▪ **go about** to try, set about ▪ **go ahead** to proceed (with), begin on ▪ **go along with** to agree with ▪ **go**

back on to fail to keep (a promise *etc*) ▪ **go for 1** to aim to get **2** to attack ▪ **go off 1** to explode **2** to become rotten **3** to come to dislike ▪ **go on 1** to continue **2** to talk too much ▪ **go round** to be enough for everyone ▪ **go under** to be ruined

| **go** *verb* ▶ goes, going, went, gone

goad *verb* to urge on by annoying

go-ahead *adjective* eager to succeed ▪ *noun* permission to act

goal *noun* **1** the upright posts between which the ball is to be driven in football and other games **2** a score in football and other games **3** anything aimed at or wished for

goat *noun* an animal of the sheep family with horns and a long-haired coat

gob *noun*, *slang* the mouth

gobble *verb* **1** to eat quickly **2** to make a noise like a turkey

go-between *noun* someone who helps two people to communicate with each other

goblet *noun* **1** a large cup without handles **2** a drinking glass with a stem

goblin *noun* a mischievous, ugly spirit in folklore

gobstopper *noun* a hard round sweet for sucking

god *noun* a male supernatural being who is worshipped ▪ **God** *noun* the creator and ruler of the world in the Christian, Jewish, *etc* religions

god-daughter *noun* a girl for whom a godmother or godfather is responsible

goddess *noun* a female supernatural being who is worshipped

godfather *noun* a man who agrees to see that a child is brought up according to the beliefs of the Christian Church

godly *adjective* holy, living well

godmother *noun* a woman who agrees to see that a child is brought up according to the beliefs of the Christian Church

godsend *noun* a very welcome piece of unexpected good fortune

godson *noun* a boy for whom a godmother or godfather is responsible

goggles *noun plural* spectacles for protecting the eyes from dust, sparks, *etc*

go-kart *noun* a small low-powered racing car

gold *noun* a precious yellow metal ▪ *adjective* 1 made of gold 2 golden in colour

golden *adjective* 1 of or like gold 2 very fine

golden wedding the 50th anniversary of a wedding

goldfinch *noun* a small colourful bird

goldfish *noun* a golden-yellow Chinese carp, often kept as a pet

gold medal a medal given to a competitor who comes first

goldsmith *noun* a maker of gold articles

golf *noun* a game in which a ball is struck with a club and aimed at a series of holes on a large open course

golf club 1 a club used in golf 2 a society of golf players 3 the place where they meet

golfer *noun* someone who plays golf

gondola *noun* a canal boat used in Venice

gondolier *noun* a person who rows a gondola

gone *past participle* of go

gong *noun* a metal plate which makes a booming sound when struck, used to summon people to meals *etc*

good *adjective* 1 having desired or positive qualities 2 having a positive effect: *fruit is good for you* 3 virtuous 4 kind 5 pleasant, enjoyable 6 substantial, sufficiently large: *a good income*

goodbye *noun* (*plural* **goodbyes**) what you say when leaving people

good-for-nothing *adjective* useless, lazy

goodly *adjective* 1 large 2 ample, plentiful

good-natured *adjective* kind, cheerful

goodness *noun* the quality of

being good ■ *exclamation* an exclamation of surprise

goods *noun plural* **1** personal belongings **2** things to be bought and sold

goodwill *noun* **1** kind wishes **2** a good reputation in business

goose *noun* (*plural* **geese**) a web-footed bird larger than a duck

gooseberry *noun* a sour-tasting, pale green berry

goosebumps or **goosepimples** *noun plural* small bumps on the skin caused by cold or fear

gopher *noun* **1** a small, burrowing rodent **2** *computing* a piece of software used to search for or index services on the Internet

gore[1] *noun* a mass of blood ■ *verb* to run through with horns, tusks, *etc*

gore[2] *noun* a triangular-shaped piece of cloth in a garment *etc*

gorge *noun* **1** the throat **2** a narrow valley between hills ■ *verb* to eat greedily till full: *gorging himself on chocolate biscuits*

| **gorge** *verb* ► **gorges**, **gorging**, **gorged**

gorgeous *adjective* **1** beautiful, very attractive **2** showy, splendid **3** *informal* excellent, very enjoyable

gorilla *noun* the largest kind of ape

♦* Do not confuse with: **guerrilla**

gormless *adjective*, *Brit* stupid, senseless

gorse *noun* a prickly bush with yellow flowers

gory *adjective* full of gore; bloody

gosling *noun* a young goose

go-slow *noun* a slowing of speed at work as a form of protest

gospel *noun* **1** the teaching of Christ **2** *informal* the absolute truth

gossamer *noun* **1** fine spider-threads floating in the air or lying on bushes **2** a very thin material

gossip *noun* **1** talk, not necessarily true, about other people's personal affairs *etc* **2** someone who listens to and passes on gossip ■ *verb* **1** to engage in gossip **2** to chatter

| **gossip** *verb* ► **gossips**, **gossiping**, **gossiped**

got *past form of* **get**

gouge *noun* a chisel with a hollow blade for cutting grooves ■ *verb* to scoop (out)

| **gouge** *verb* ► **gouges**, **gouging**, **gouged**

goulash *noun* (*plural* **goulashes**) a stew of meat and vegetables, flavoured with paprika

gourd *noun* **1** a large fleshy fruit **2** the skin of a gourd used to carry water *etc*

gourmet (*pronounced* **goor-**

mei) *noun* someone who loves good wines or food

gout *noun* a painful swelling of the smaller joints, especially of the big toe

govern *verb* 1 to rule, control 2 to put into action the laws *etc* of a country

governess *noun* a woman who teaches young children at their home

government *noun* 1 rule; control 2 those who rule and administer the laws of a country

governor *noun* someone who rules a state or country *etc*

gown *noun* 1 a woman's formal dress 2 a loose robe worn by members of the clergy, lawyers, teachers, *etc*

grab *verb* 1 to seize or grasp suddenly 2 to secure possession of quickly 3 to get in a hurry ■ *noun* a sudden grasp or catch

| **grab** *verb* ▶ grab*s*, grab*bing*, grab*bed*

grace *noun* 1 beauty of form or movement 2 a short prayer at a meal 3 the title of a duke or archbishop: *Your Grace* 4 favour, mercy: *by God's grace*

graceful *adjective* 1 beautiful in appearance or movement 2 done in a neat way 3 polite ■ **gracefully** *adverb*

gracious *adjective* kind, polite ■ **graciously** *adverb*

grade *noun* a step or placing according to quality or rank; class

■ *verb* to arrange in order, *eg* from easy to difficult

gradient *noun* 1 a slope on a road, railway, *etc* 2 the amount of a slope, worked out by dividing the vertical distance by the horizontal distance

gradual *adjective* step by step; going slowly but steadily ■ **gradually** *adverb*

graduate *verb* (*pronounced* grad-yoo-eit) to pass university examinations and receive a degree ■ *noun* (*pronounced* grad-yoo-at) someone who has done so

graduation *noun* the act of getting a degree from a university, or the ceremony to celebrate this

graffiti *noun plural* words or drawings scratched or painted on a wall *etc*

graft *verb* 1 to fix (skin) from one part of the body on to another part 2 to transfer (a part of the body) from one person to another ■ *noun* living tissue (*eg* skin) which is grafted

grain *noun* 1 a seed *eg* of wheat, oats 2 corn in general 3 the run of the lines of fibre in wood, leather, *etc*

gram *or* **gramme** *noun* the basic unit of weight in the metric system

grammar *noun* 1 the correct use of words in speaking or writing 2 the rules applying to a particular language

grammar school a kind of secondary school

grammatical *adjective* correct according to rules of grammar
■ **grammatically** *adverb*

gramme *another spelling of* gram

gramophone *noun, old* a record-player

gran *noun, informal* a grandmother

granary *noun* (*plural* **granaries**) a place where grain is stored

grand *adjective* great; noble; fine

grandchild *noun* a son's or daughter's child

grand-daughter *noun* a son's or daughter's daughter

grandeur *noun* greatness

grandfather *noun* a father's or mother's father

grandiose *adjective* planned on a large scale

grandmother *noun* a father's or mother's mother

grandparent *noun* a grandmother or grandfather

grand piano a piano with a large flat top

grandson *noun* a son's or daughter's son

grandstand *noun* rows of raised seats at a sports ground giving a good view

granite *noun* a hard rock of greyish or reddish colour

granny *noun* (*plural* **grannies**) *informal* a grandmother

grant *verb* **1** to give, allow (something asked for) **2** to admit as true ■ *noun* money awarded for a special purpose

granted *or* **granting** *conjunction* (often with **that**) even if, assuming ■ **take for granted 1** to assume that something will happen without checking **2** to treat (someone) casually, without respect or kindness

granule *noun* a tiny grain or part

grape *noun* the green or black smooth-skinned berry from which wine is made

grapefruit *noun* a sharp-tasting fruit like a large yellow orange

grapevine *noun* a climbing plant that produces grapes ■ **the grapevine** the spreading of information through casual conversation

graph *noun* lines drawn on squared paper to show changes in quantity, *eg* in temperature, money spent ■ **graphical** *adjective*

graphic *adjective* relating to writing, drawing or painting ■ *noun* a painting, print, illustration or diagram
■ **graphically** *adverb*

graphics *noun singular* the art of drawing according to mathematical principles ■ *noun plural* **1** the pictures in a magazine **2** the use of computers to display data in a pictorial form **3** pictures produced by computer

graphite *noun* a form of carbon used in making pencils

grapple verb: **grapple with 1** to struggle with **2** to try to deal with (a problem etc)

grasp verb **1** to clasp and grip with the fingers or arms **2** to understand ■ noun **1** a grip with the hand or arms **2** someone's power of understanding

grasping adjective greedy, mean

grass noun (plural **grasses**) **1** the plant covering fields of pasture **2** a kind of plant with long narrow leaves, eg wheat, reeds, bamboo

grasshopper noun a type of jumping insect

grass snake a type of harmless snake

grassy adjective covered with grass

grate noun a framework of iron bars for holding a fire ■ verb **1** to rub down into small pieces **2** to make a harsh, grinding sound **3** to irritate

grateful adjective **1** feeling thankful **2** showing or giving thanks ■ **gratefully** adverb

grater noun an instrument with a rough surface for rubbing cheese etc into small pieces

gratification noun pleasure; satisfaction

gratify verb to please; satisfy
| **gratify** ▶ **gratifies**, **gratifying**, **gratified**

grating noun a frame of iron bars

gratitude noun thankfulness; desire to repay kindness

gratuitous adjective uncalled-for, done without good reason: gratuitous violence ■ **gratuitously** adverb

grave noun a pit in which a dead person is buried ■ adjective **1** serious, important **2** not cheerful, solemn ■ **gravely** adverb ■ **gravity** noun

grave accent (pronounced grahv) a backward-leaning stroke (`) placed over letters in some languages to show their pronunciation

gravel noun small stones or pebbles

gravestone noun a stone placed to mark a grave

graveyard noun a place where the dead are buried, a cemetery

gravity noun **1** seriousness, importance: gravity of the situation **2** the force which attracts things towards earth and causes them to fall to the ground

gravy noun (plural **gravies**) a sauce made from juices of meat that is cooking

graze verb **1** to feed on (growing grass) **2** to scrape the skin of **3** to touch lightly in passing ■ noun **1** a scraping of the skin **2** a light touch

grease noun **1** thick animal fat **2** an oily substance ■ verb to smear with grease, apply grease to

grease paint theatrical make-up

greasy adjective **1** full of, or covered in, grease **2** of skin:

having a slightly moist appearance because the body releases a lot of natural oils into it **3** wet and slippery

great *adjective* **1** very large **2** powerful **3** very important, distinguished **4** very talented **5** of high rank, noble **6** *informal* excellent, very good ▪ **greatness** *noun*

great-grandchild *noun* the son or daughter of a grandson or grand-daughter

great-grandfather *noun* the father of a grandfather or grandmother

great-grandmother *noun* the mother of a grandfather or grandmother

greatly *adverb* very much

greed *noun* great and selfish desire for food, money, *etc*

greedy *adjective* full of greed ▪ **greedily** *adverb*

green *adjective* **1** of the colour of growing grass *etc* **2** inexperienced, naive **3** concerned with care of the environment ▪ *noun* **1** the colour of growing grass **2** a piece of ground covered with grass **3** **Green** a member of the Green Party, an environmentalist **4** **greens** green vegetables for food

green belt open land surrounding a city

greenery *noun* green plants

green fingers *informal* skill at gardening

greenfly *noun* (*plural* **greenfly**) a bright green, small insect which attacks plants

greengage *noun* a kind of plum, green but sweet

greengrocer *noun* someone who sells fresh vegetables

greenhouse *noun* a building with large glass panes in which plants are grown

greenhouse effect the warming-up of the earth's surface due to excess carbon dioxide and other gases (**greenhouse gases**) in the atmosphere

Green Party a political party concerned with conserving natural resources and decentralizing political and economic power

greet *verb* **1** to meet someone with kind words **2** to say hello *etc* to **3** to react to, respond to: *greeted the news with relief*

greeting *noun* **1** words of welcome or kindness **2** reaction, response

gregarious *adjective* sociable, liking the company of others

grenade *noun* a small bomb thrown by hand

grew *past form* of **grow**

grey *or US* **gray** *adjective* of a colour between black and white ▪ *noun* **1** grey colour **2** a grey horse

greyhound *noun* a breed of fast-running dog

grid *noun* **1** a grating of bars **2** a network of lines, *eg* for helping to find a place on a map **3** a network of wires carrying electricity over a wide area

grid reference a set of numbers or letters used to indicate a place on a grid

grief *noun* deep sorrow, especially after bereavement

grievance *noun* a cause for complaining

grieve *verb* to feel or cause to feel grief or sorrow

grievous *adjective* **1** painful; serious **2** causing grief

grill *verb* **1** to cook directly under heat (provided by an electric or gas cooker) **2** to question closely ▪ *noun* the part of a cooker used for grilling

grille *noun* a metal grating over a door, window, *etc*

grim *adjective* **1** stern, fierce-looking **2** terrible; very unpleasant **3** unyielding, stubborn ▪ **grimly** *adverb*

grimace *noun* a twisting of the face in fun or pain ▪ *verb* to make a grimace

grime *noun* dirt

grimy *adjective* covered with a layer of ground-in dirt

grin *verb* to smile broadly ▪ *noun* a broad smile

| **grin** *verb* ► grins, grin*ning*, grin*ned*

grind *verb* **1** to crush to powder **2** to sharpen by rubbing **3** to rub together ▪ *noun* hard or unpleasant work

| **grind** *verb* ► grinds, grind*ing*, ground

grindstone *noun* a revolving stone for grinding or sharpening tools ▪ **keep your nose to the grindstone** to work hard without stopping

grip *noun* **1** a firm hold, a grasp **2** a way of holding or grasping; control ▪ *verb* to take a firm hold of

| **grip** *verb* ► grips, grip*ping*, grip*ped*

gripping *adjective* commanding attention, compelling

grisly *adjective* frightful, hideous

♣* Do not confuse with: **grizzly**

gristle *noun* a tough elastic substance in meat ▪ **gristly** *adjective*

grit *noun* **1** a mixture of rough sand and gravel, spread on icy surfaces **2** courage ▪ *verb* **1** to apply grit to (an icy surface) **2** to clench: *grit your teeth*

| **grit** *verb* ► grits, grit*ting*, grit*ted*

gritty *adjective* **1** covered in grit or having a texture like grit **2** courageous **3** honest in the portrayal of harsh realities ▪ **grittiness** *noun*

grizzled *adjective* grey; mixed with grey

grizzly *adjective* grey in colour ▪ *noun* (*plural* **grizzlies**) *informal* a grizzly bear

🔆 Do not confuse with: **grisly**

grizzly bear a type of large bear of North America

groan *verb* to moan in pain, disapproval, *etc* ▪ *noun* a moaning sound

grocer *noun* a dealer in certain kinds of food and household supplies

groceries *noun plural* food *etc* sold by grocers

groggy *adjective* weak and light-headed after illness or blows

groin *noun* the part of the body where the inner thigh joins the torso

groom *noun* **1** a bridegroom **2** someone in charge of horses ▪ *verb* **1** to look after (a horse) **2** to make smart and tidy

groove *noun* a furrow, a long hollow ▪ *verb* to cut a groove (in)

grope *verb* to search (for) by feeling as if blind

gross *adjective* **1** coarse **2** very fat **3** of money: total, before any deductions for tax *etc*: *gross profit* **4** *US informal* disgusting, revolting ▪ *noun* twelve dozen

grossly *adverb* extremely

grossness *noun* coarseness

grotesque *adjective* very odd or unnatural-looking

grotto *noun* (*plural* **grottoes** or **grottos**) a cave

grotty *adjective* dirty or shabby

grotty *adjective* ▸ grotti**er**, grotti**est**

ground¹ *noun* **1** the surface of the earth **2** (also **grounds**) a good reason: *ground for complaint* **3** **grounds** lands surrounding a large house *etc* **4** **grounds** dregs: *coffee grounds* ▪ *verb* **1** to prevent (aeroplanes) from flying **2** to prevent (someone in your charge) from going out

ground² *past form* of **grind**

ground floor the storey of a building at street level

grounding *noun* the first steps in learning something

groundless *adjective* without reason

groundwork *noun* the first stages of a task

group *noun* a number of people or things together ▪ *verb* **1** to form or gather into a group **2** to classify

grouse¹ *noun* (*plural* **grouse**) a game bird hunted on moors and hills

grouse² *noun* (*plural* **grouses**) a grumble, a complaint ▪ *verb* to grumble, complain

grove *noun* a small group of trees

grovel *verb* to be overly humble

grovel ▸ grovel**s**, grovel**ling**, grovel**led**

grow *verb* **1** to become bigger or stronger **2** to become: *grow old* **3** to rear, cause to grow (plants, trees, *etc*)

grow ▸ grow**s**, grow**ing**, grew, grown

growl *verb* to utter a deep sound like a dog ▪ *noun* an angry dog's deep sound

grown *past form of* grow

growth *noun* 1 growing 2 increase 3 something that grows 4 something abnormal that grows on the body

grub *noun* 1 the form of an insect after being hatched from the egg, *eg* a caterpillar 2 *informal* food

grubby *adjective* dirty ▪ **grubbily** *adverb* ▪ **grubbiness** *noun*

grudge *verb* 1 to be unwilling to grant, accept or allow 2 to give unwillingly or reluctantly ▪ *noun* a feeling of resentment

gruel *noun* a thin mixture of oatmeal boiled in water

gruelling *adjective* straining, exhausting

gruesome *adjective* horrible

gruff *adjective* 1 rough in manner 2 of a voice: deep and harsh

grumble *verb* to complain in a bad-tempered, discontented way ▪ *noun* a complaint

grumpy *adjective* cross, bad-tempered ▪ **grumpily** *adverb*

grunge *noun, informal* grime, dirt ▪ **grungy** *adjective*

grunt *verb* to make a sound like that of a pig ▪ *noun* a pig-like snort

guarantee *noun* 1 a promise to do something 2 a statement by the maker that something will work well ▪ *verb* to give a guarantee

guard *verb* to keep safe from danger or attack ▪ *noun* 1 someone or a group whose duty it is to protect 2 a screen *etc* which protects from danger 3 someone in charge of a railway train or coach

guarded *adjective* careful, not revealing much

guardian *noun* 1 someone with the legal right to take care of an orphan 2 someone who protects or guards ▪ **guardianship** *noun*

guerrilla *noun* one of a small band which makes sudden attacks on a larger army but does not fight openly ▪ *adjective* of fighting: in which many small bands acting independently make sudden raids on an enemy

♦ Do not confuse with: gorilla

guess *verb* 1 to say without sure knowledge 2 *US* to suppose ▪ *noun* (*plural* **guesses**) an estimate

guesswork *noun* guessing

guest *noun* a visitor received and entertained in another's house or in a hotel *etc*

guffaw *verb* to laugh loudly ▪ *noun* a loud laugh

guidance *noun* help or advice towards doing something

guide *verb* 1 to show the way to, lead, direct 2 to influence ▪ *noun*

1 someone who shows tourists around **2** someone who leads travellers on a route unfamiliar to them **3** a guidebook **4 Guide** a girl belonging to the Guides organization

guidebook *noun* a book with information for tourists about a place

guide dog a dog trained to guide a blind person safely

guild *noun* **1** an association for those working in a particular trade or profession **2** a society, a social club

♦* Do not confuse with: **gild**

guile *noun* cunning, deceit

guillotine *noun, history* an instrument with a falling blade used for executing by beheading ▪ *verb* to behead with the guillotine

guilt *noun* **1** a sense of shame **2** blame for wrongdoing, *eg* breaking the law

♦* Do not confuse with: **gilt**

guilty *adjective* **1** ashamed about something bad you have done **2** having done something wrong **3** officially judged to have committed a crime

guinea *noun* **1** an old British gold coin **2** a sum of money equal to £1.05

guinea pig 1 a rodent about the size of a rabbit **2** someone used as the subject of an experiment

guise *noun* appearance, dress, especially in disguise

guitar *noun* a stringed musical instrument with frets and a waisted body

gulf *noun* a large inlet of the sea

gull *noun* a seagull

gullet *noun* a passage by which food goes down into the stomach

gullible *adjective* easily tricked

gully *noun* (*plural* **gullies**) a channel worn by water

gulp *verb* to swallow quickly and in large mouthfuls ▪ *noun* a sudden fast swallowing

gum *noun* **1** the firm flesh in which the teeth grow **2** sticky juice got from some trees and plants **3** a sticky substance used as glue **4** a flavoured gummy sweet, chewing gum ▪ *verb* to stick with gum

| **gum** *verb* ▶ gums, gum*ming*, gum*med*

gummy *adjective* sticky

gumption *noun* good sense

gum tree a tree that gives gum or gum resin, especially the eucalyptus

gun *noun* any weapon firing bullets or shells

gunfire *noun* the firing of guns

gunpowder *noun* an explosive in powder form

gurgle *verb* **1** of water: to make a bubbling sound **2** to make such a sound, *eg* in pleasure

guru *noun* **1** a Hindu spiritual

teacher **2** a revered instructor, a mentor

gush *verb* **1** to flow out in a strong stream **2** to talk at length with exaggerated emotions ▪ *noun* (*plural* **gushes**) a strong or sudden flow

gusset *noun* a piece of material sewn into a seam join to strengthen or widen part of a garment

gust *noun* a sudden blast of wind

gusto *noun* enthusiasm

gusty *adjective* windy

gut *noun* **1** a narrow passage in the lower part of the body in which food is broken down **2** animal intestines used as strings for musical instruments **3 guts** spirit, courage ▪ *verb* **1** to take out the inner parts of: *gut a fish* **2** to destroy completely, especially by fire: *gutted the building*

| **gut** *verb* ▸ guts, gut*ting*, gut*ted*

gutter *noun* a water channel on a roof, at the edge of a roadside, *etc*

guttural *adjective* harsh in sound, as if formed in the throat

guy[1] *noun* **1** *Brit* an effigy of Guy Fawkes, traditionally burned on 5 November **2** *informal* a man

guy[2] *noun* a steadying rope for a tent *etc*

guzzle *verb* to eat or drink greedily

gym *noun, informal* **1** a gymnasium **2** gymnastics

gymkhana *noun* a meeting for competitions, especially in horse-riding

gymnasium *noun* (*plural* **gymnasiums** *or* **gymnasia**) a building or room equipped for physical exercises

gymnast *noun* someone who does gymnastics

gymnastic *adjective* relating to gymnastics

gymnastics *noun plural* exercises to strengthen the body

Gypsy *or* **Gipsy** *noun* (*plural* **Gypsies** *or* **Gipsies**) a member of a wandering people; a Romany

gyrate *verb* to whirl round

H h

habit *noun* **1** something you are used to doing **2** someone's usual behaviour **3** the dress of a monk or nun

habitable *adjective* fit to live in

habitat *noun* the natural home of an animal or plant

habitual *adjective* usual, formed by habit

habitually *adverb* usually, as a matter of habit

hack *verb* **1** to cut or chop up roughly **2** to use a computer to get unauthorized access to other systems ◼ *noun* a writer who does hard work for low pay

hacker *noun* **1** a skilled computer operator **2** someone who breaks into government or commercial computer systems

hackles *noun plural* **1** the feathers on the neck of a farmyard cock **2** the hair on a dog's neck ◼ **make someone's hackles rise** to make them angry

hackneyed *adjective* overused, not fresh or original: *hackneyed phrase*

hacksaw *noun* a saw for cutting metal

had *past form* of **have**

haddock *noun* (*plural* **haddock** *or* **haddocks**) a small edible N Atlantic fish

Hadith *noun* the collection of traditions about Mohammed

haemoglobin *or US*
hemoglobin (*both pronounced* heem-o-glohb-in) *noun* the oxygen-carrying substance in red blood cells

haemophilia *or US*
hemophilia (*both pronounced* heem-o-fil-i-*a*) *noun* a hereditary disease causing extreme bleeding when the sufferer is cut

haemophiliac *or US*
hemophiliac (*both pronounced* heem-o-fil-i-ak) *noun* someone suffering from haemophilia

haemorrhage *or US*
hemorrhage *noun* a large amount of bleeding

hag *noun* **1** an ugly old woman **2** a witch

haggard *adjective* gaunt and hollow-eyed, from tiredness

haggis *noun* (*plural* **haggises**) a Scottish dish made from chopped sheep's offal and oatmeal

haggle *verb* to argue determinedly over a price

haiku noun a Japanese form of poem written in three lines of 5, 7 and 5 syllables

hail[1] verb 1 to greet, welcome 2 to call to, attract the attention of
■ noun a call from a distance
■ **hail from** to come from, belong to

hail[2] noun frozen raindrops
■ verb to shower with hail

hailstone noun a piece of hail

hair noun a thread-like growth on the skin of an animal; the whole mass of these (as on the head)

hair-breadth or **hair's-breadth** noun a very small distance

haircut noun 1 an act of cutting the hair 2 a hairstyle

hairdresser noun someone who cuts, washes and sets hair

hairdryer noun an electrical device which blows hot air to dry hair

hair-raising adjective terrifying

hairspray noun a fine spray to fix a hairstyle

hairstyle noun a way of cutting or wearing the hair

hairy adjective covered with hair
■ hairiness noun

hajj or **hadj** noun the Muslim pilgrimage to Mecca

hajji or **hadji** noun (plural **hajjis** or **hadjis**) a Muslim who has made the pilgrimage to Mecca

hake noun an edible seafish similar to a cod

halal noun meat from animals that have been slaughtered according to Islamic law
■ adjective from animals slaughtered in this way

half noun (plural **halves**) one of two equal parts ■ adjective 1 being one of two equal parts 2 not full or complete: a half smile
■ adverb partly, to some extent

half-baked adjective not properly thought out, incomplete

half-board noun a hotel charge for bed, breakfast and another meal

half-brother noun a brother sharing only one parent

half day a day in which someone attends school or work only in the morning or afternoon

half-hearted adjective not eager

half-life noun the time in which the radioactivity of a substance falls to half its original value

half-mast adverb of a flag: hoisted halfway up the mast to show that someone important has died

half moon the moon when half is visible

half-sister noun a sister sharing only one parent

half-term noun a short holiday halfway through a school or college term

half-time noun an interval halfway through a sports game

halfway adverb & adjective at or

to a point equally far from the
beginning and the end

halibut *noun* a large edible
flatfish

hall *noun* **1** (*also called:* hallway)
a passage at the entrance to a
house **2** a large public room

hallelujah *or* **halleluia**
exclamation expressing praise to
God (*also:* **alleluia**)

hallmark *noun* **1** a mark put on
gold and silver articles to show
quality **2** a characteristic sign: *the
hallmarks of a good essay*

hallo *another spelling of* **hello**

hallowed *adjective, old* holy,
sacred

Hallowe'en *noun* the evening of
31 October, traditionally a time
when spirits are believed to be
around

hallucinate *verb* to see
something that is not actually
there ■ **hallucination** *noun*

hallway *see* **hall**

halo *noun* (*plural* **haloes** *or* **halos**)
1 a circle of light surrounding *eg*
the sun or moon **2** a circle of light
depicted around the head of a
saint *etc* as a sign of holiness

halogen *noun* one of a group of
elements that includes chlorine
and iodine

halt *verb* to come or bring to a
stop ■ *noun* a stop, a standstill:
call a halt

halter *noun* a head-rope for
holding and leading a horse

halve *verb* to divide in two

ham[1] *noun* a pig's thigh salted
and dried

ham[2] *noun, informal* **1** an actor
who overacts **2** an amateur radio
operator

hamburger *noun* a round cake
of minced beef, cooked by frying
or grilling

ham-fisted *adjective* clumsy

hamlet *noun* a small village

hammer *noun* **1** a tool with a
heavy metal head for beating
metal, driving nails, *etc* **2** a
striking piece in a clock, piano,
pistol, *etc* ■ *verb* **1** to drive or
shape with a hammer **2** to defeat
overwhelmingly

hammock *noun* a length of
netting, canvas, *etc* hung up
by the corners, and used as a
bed

hamper[1] *verb* to hinder, impede

hamper[2] *noun* a large basket
with a lid

hamster *noun* a small rodent
with large cheek pouches, often
kept as a pet

hamstring *noun* a tendon at the
back of the knee

hand *noun* **1** the part of the
human body at the end of the arm
2 a pointer, *eg* on a clock **3** help,
aid **4** a measure (four inches, 10.16
centimetres) for the height of
horses **5** a worker, a labourer **6**
side, direction: *left-hand side* **7** a
group of playing-cards dealt to
someone **8** clapping, applause: *a
big hand* ■ *verb* **1** to pass

(something) with the hand **2 hand over** to give

handbag noun a small bag for personal belongings

handbook noun a small book giving information or directions

handcuffs noun plural steel bands joined by a short chain, put round the wrists of prisoners

handful noun (plural **handfuls**) **1** as much as can be held in one hand **2** a small amount **3** a difficult and demanding child, pet, etc

handicap noun **1** something that makes an action more difficult **2** a disadvantage, such as having to run a greater distance, given to the best competitors in a race **3** a physical or mental disability ▪ verb **1** to give a handicap to **2** to burden, impede

| handicap ► handicaps, handicapping, handicapped

handicapped adjective **1** having or given a handicap **2** physically or mentally disabled

handicraft noun skilled work done by hand, not machine

hand-in-hand adjective holding hands

handiwork noun **1** thing(s) made by hand **2** something done by a particular person etc

handkerchief noun a small cloth for wiping the nose etc

handle verb **1** to touch, hold or use with the hand **2** to manage, cope with ▪ noun the part of

anything meant to be held in the hand

handlebars noun plural a steering bar at the front of a bicycle with a handle at each end

handler noun someone who trains and works with an animal, eg a police dog

hand-me-down noun a second-hand piece of clothing, especially one that used to belong to another member of the family

handout noun a sheet or bundle of information given out at a lecture etc

hand-picked adjective chosen carefully

handrail noun a narrow rail running alongside a staircase

handshake noun a greeting made by taking hold of another person's hand

handsome adjective **1** good-looking **2** generous: a handsome gift

hands-on adjective involving practical experience

handstand noun an act of balancing on the hands with the legs in the air

handwriting noun writing with pen or pencil ▪ **handwritten** adjective

handy adjective **1** useful or convenient to use **2** easily reached, near **3** clever with the hands

handyman noun a man who does odd jobs

hang *verb* **1** to fix or be fixed to a point off the ground **2** to be suspended in the air **3 hang down** to droop or fall downwards **4** to attach (wallpaper) to a wall **5** (*past form* **hanged**) to put a prisoner to death by putting a rope round their neck and letting them fall ▪ **hang about** *or* **hang around** to remain near, loiter ▪ **hang back** to hesitate ▪ **hang on 1** to depend on **2** to wait, linger

| **hang** ▶ hangs, hang*ing*, hung *or* hang*ed*

hangar *noun* a shed for aeroplanes

🖐 Do not confuse: **hangar** and **hanger**

hanger *noun* a piece of wood, wire or plastic on which a coat *etc* is hung

hanger-on *noun* (*plural* **hangers-on**) someone who stays near someone in the hope of gaining some advantage

hang-gliding *noun* a form of gliding by hanging in a harness under a large kite

hanging *noun* an execution in which the prisoner is hanged

hangman *noun* an executioner who hangs people

hangover *noun* uncomfortable after-effects of being drunk

hanker *verb* to long for: *hankering after a chocolate biscuit*

hankie *or* **hanky** *noun* (*plural* **hankies**) *informal* a handkerchief

Hanukkah (*pronounced* hah-nuk-a) *or* **Chanukkah** *noun* the Jewish festival of lights held in mid-December

haphazard *adjective* depending on chance, without planning or system ▪ **haphazardly** *adverb*

hapless *adjective* unlucky

haploid *adjective* of a cell: having a single set of chromosomes

happen *verb* **1** to take place **2** to occur by chance **3** to chance to do

happening *noun* an event

happy *adjective* **1** joyful **2** contented **3** fortunate, lucky: *a happy coincidence* **4** willing: *happy to help* ▪ **happily** *adverb* ▪ **happiness** *noun*

| **happy** ▶ happi*er*, happi*est*

happy-go-lucky *adjective* easy-going, taking things as they come

harangue *noun* a loud aggressive speech ▪ *verb* to deliver a harangue

harass *verb* to annoy persistently, pester ▪ **harassment** *noun*

harbour *noun* a place of shelter for ships ▪ *verb* **1** to give shelter or refuge **2** to store in the mind: *harbouring ill will*

hard *adjective* **1** solid, firm **2** not easily broken or put out of shape **3** not easy to do, understand, *etc* **4** not easy to bear **5** having no kind or gentle feelings ▪ *adverb* strongly, violently ∎ **hard of hearing** rather deaf

hardback *noun* a book bound in a hard cover (*compare with:* **paperback**)

hardboard *noun* light strong board made from compressed wood pulp

hard disk *computing* a hard-cased disk able to store large amounts of data, fixed into a base unit

hard drive a disk drive that reads data stored on hard disk

harden *verb* to make hard

hard-hearted *adjective* having no kind feelings

hardline *adjective* refusing to change or compromise: *a hardline socialist*

hard lines or **hard luck** bad luck

hardly *adverb* scarcely; only just; with difficulty

hardness *noun* the state of being hard

hardship *noun* something difficult to bear

hard shoulder the surfaced strip on the outer edges of a motorway, used when stopping in an emergency

hard up short of money

hardware *noun* **1** goods made from metal or wood **2** the casing, processor, disk drives, *etc* of a computer, not the programs which it runs (*contrasted with:* **software**)

hardy *adjective* strong, robust, tough ∎ **hardiness** *noun*

hare *noun* a fast-running animal, like a large rabbit

hare-brained *adjective* mad, foolish

hare-lip *noun* a split in the upper lip at birth

harem (*pronounced* hei-rem *or* hah-**reem**) *noun* the women's rooms in an Islamic house

hark *exclamation* listen! ∎ **hark back to** to recall or refer to (a previous time, remark, *etc*)

harlequin *noun* a comic pantomime character wearing a multicoloured costume

harm *noun* hurt, damage ∎ *verb* **1** to wound, damage **2** to do wrong to

harmful *adjective* having a bad or damaging effect on people or things

harmless *adjective* **1** safe, *eg* to eat, use or touch **2** causing no annoyance or disturbance to anyone

harmonic *adjective* relating to harmony

harmonica *noun* a mouth organ

harmonious *adjective* **1** pleasant-sounding **2** peaceful, without disagreement

harmonize or **harmonise** *verb* **1** to agree, go well (with) **2** *music* to add the different parts to a melody

harmony *noun* (*plural* **harmonies**) **1** agreement of one part, colour or sound with another **2** agreement between people **3** *music* a part intended to agree in sound with the melody

harness *noun* the leather and other fittings used for guiding a horse ▪ *verb* to put a harness on a horse

harp *noun* a triangular, stringed musical instrument played upright by plucking with the fingers ▪ **harp on about** to talk too much about

harpoon *noun* a spear tied to rope, used for killing whales ▪ *verb* to strike with a harpoon

harpsichord *noun* an early musical instrument with keys, played like a piano

harrow *noun* a frame with iron spikes for breaking up lumps of earth

harrowing *adjective* very distressing

harry *verb* to harass, worry

| harry ► harries, harrying, harried

harsh *adjective* rough, bitter; cruel ▪ **harshly** *adverb*

hart *noun* the stag or male deer, especially from the age of six years

harvest *noun* **1** the time of the year when ripened crops are gathered in **2** the crops gathered at this time ▪ *verb* to gather in (a crop)

has *see* have

has-been *noun* someone no longer important or popular

hash *noun* a dish of chopped meat *etc* ▪ **make a hash of** to spoil completely

hassle *verb* to cause problems for ▪ *noun* difficulty, trouble

haste *noun* speed, hurry

hasten *verb* to hurry (on)

hasty *adjective* hurried; done without thinking ▪ **hastily** *adverb*

hat *noun* a covering for the head

hatch *noun* (*plural* **hatches**) a door or cover over an opening in a floor, wall, *etc* ▪ *verb* **1** to produce young from eggs **2** to form and set working: *hatch a plan*

hatchback *noun* a car with a sloping rear door which opens upwards

hatchet *noun* a small axe

hate *verb* to dislike very much ▪ *noun* great dislike

hateful *adjective* horrible, causing hatred

hatred *noun* extreme dislike

hat-trick *noun* **1** *cricket* the putting out of three batsmen by three balls in a row **2** *football* three goals scored by the same player **3** any action performed three times in a row

haughty *adjective* proud, looking on others with scorn ▪ **haughtily** *adverb*

haul *verb* to drag, pull with force ▪ *noun* **1** a strong pull **2** a rich find, booty

haulage *noun* the carrying of goods

haunch *noun* (*plural* **haunches**)

1 the fleshy part of the hip **2** a leg and loin of meat, especially venison

haunt *verb* **1** to visit often **2** of a ghost: to inhabit, linger in (a place) ▪ *noun* a place often visited

haunted *adjective* inhabited by ghosts

have *verb* **1** used with another verb to show that an action is in the past and completed: *we have decided to move house* **2** to own, possess **3** to hold, contain **4** to give birth to **5** to suffer from: *have a cold* **6** to cause to be done: *have your hair cut*

| have ► has, having, had

haven *noun* a place of safety

haversack *noun* a bag made of canvas *etc* with shoulder-straps, for carrying on the back

havoc *noun* great destruction

hawk *noun* a bird of prey like a falcon ▪ *verb* to carry goods about for sale

hawthorn *noun* a prickly tree with white flowers and small red berries

hay *noun* cut and dried grass, used as cattle food

hay fever an allergic reaction with effects like a bad cold, caused by pollen *etc*

haystack *or* **hayrick** *noun* hay built up into a mound

haywire *adjective* tangled, in a state of disorder

hazard *noun* **1** chance **2** risk of

harm or danger ▪ *verb* **1** to risk **2** to put forward (a guess) at the risk of being wrong

hazardous *adjective* dangerous, risky

haze *noun* a thin mist

hazel *noun* a nut-producing tree of the birch family ▪ *adjective* light greenish-brown in colour

hazelnut *noun* a light brown nut produced by the hazel tree

hazy *adjective* **1** misty **2** not clear, vague ▪ **hazily** *adverb* ▪ **haziness** *noun*

he *pronoun* a male person or animal already spoken about (used only as the subject of a verb): *he ate a banana*

head *noun* **1** the uppermost part of the body, containing the brain, skull, *etc* **2** someone's mind **3** a person in charge, a chief **4 heads** the side of a coin showing the head of a monarch or leader ▪ *verb* **1** to lead **2** to go in front of **3** to go in the direction of: *heading for home* **4** to hit (a ball) with the head **5 head off** to turn aside, deflect: *head off an attack*

headache *noun* a pain in the head

headband *noun* a band worn round the head

headboard *noun* a board across the top end of a bed

headdress *noun* a covering for the head

header *noun*, *football* a striking of the ball with the head

headfirst *adverb* **1** with the head first **2** rashly, without thinking

heading *noun* the title of a book or chapter

headland *noun* a point of land running out into the sea, a cape

headlight *noun* a strong light on the front of a car *etc*

headline *noun* a line in large letters at the top of a newspaper article

headlong *adverb* headfirst

headmaster *noun* a man who is the principal teacher of a school

headmistress *noun* a woman who is the principal teacher of a school

head-on *adjective & adverb* with the head or front first

headphones *noun plural* a listening device that fits over the ears

headquarters *noun singular & noun plural* place from which the chief officers of an army *etc* control their operations; the chief office (of a business *etc*)

headrest *noun* a support for the head in a vehicle *etc*

head start a boost or advantage at the beginning of something

headstrong *adjective* determined, stubborn

headteacher *noun* the principal teacher of a school

headway *noun* forward movement

heal *verb* to make or become healthy or sound; cure ■ **healer** *noun*

health *noun* **1** someone's physical condition **2** good or natural physical condition ■ **healthily** *adverb*

health centre a building where nurses and doctors hold clinics

health food food considered to be beneficial to health

health visitor a trained nurse who visits people in their homes

healthy *adjective* **1** in good health or condition **2** encouraging good health

heap *noun* **1** a pile of things thrown one on top of another **2** a great many (of) ■ *verb* to throw in a pile

hear *verb* **1** to receive (sounds) by the ear **2** to listen to **3** to be told, understand: *I hear you want to speak to me*

| **hear** ▶ hears, hearing, heard

hearing *noun* **1** the act or power of listening **2** an investigation and listening to evidence

hearing aid a small electronic device worn on or in the ear to help hearing

hearsay *noun* gossip, rumour

hearse *noun* a car for carrying a dead body to the grave *etc*

heart *noun* **1** the part of the body which acts as a blood pump **2** the inner or chief part of anything: *the heart of the problem* **3** courage: *take heart* **4** will, enthusiasm: *his heart isn't in it* **5** love, affection:

with all my heart **6** a sign (♥) representing a heart, or often love **7 hearts** one of the four suits in playing-cards

heartache *noun* sorrow, grief

heart attack a sudden and painful interruption in the functioning of the heart

heartbeat *noun* **1** the pulsing of the heart **2** a single pulsing action of the heart

heartbreak *noun* great sorrow or grief ▪ **heartbreaking** *adjective*

heartbroken *adjective* very upset, very sad

heartburn *noun* a burning feeling in the chest after eating; indigestion

hearten *verb* to cheer on, encourage

heart failure the sudden stopping of the heart's beating

heartfelt *adjective* felt deeply, sincere

hearth *noun* a fireplace

heartily *adverb* **1** cheerfully and with great enthusiasm **2** thoroughly, absolutely: *heartily sick of his moaning*

heartless *adjective* cruel

heart-rending *adjective* very moving, very upsetting

heartstrings *noun plural* inmost feelings of love

heart-throb *noun* a very attractive person, with whom others fall in love

heart-to-heart *noun* a frank, intimate discussion

hearty *adjective* **1** of a meal: large, satisfying **2** eager, over-cheerful

heat *noun* **1** high temperature **2** a round in a competition, race, *etc* ▪ *verb* to make or become hot

heath *noun* barren, open country

heathen *noun* someone who does not believe in an established religion, especially someone who worships idols ▪ *adjective* of heathens, pagan

heather *noun* a plant with small purple or white flowers growing on moorland

heat wave a period of hot weather

heave *verb* **1** to lift by force **2** to throw **3** to rise and fall **4** to produce, let out (a sigh)

heaven *noun* **1** the sky (often **the heavens**) **2** the dwelling place of God; paradise **3** any place of great happiness

heavenly *adjective* **1** living in heaven **2** *informal* delightful

heavenly bodies the sun, moon and stars

heavily *adverb* **1** with great force, in great amount **2** to a serious or great extent, intensely **3** loudly and deeply: *sighing heavily* **4** in a thick, solid-looking way: *heavily built*

heavy *adjective* **1** of great weight **2** great in amount, force, *etc* **3** not easy to bear **4** loud and deep: *heavy breathing* **5** having a thick, solid appearance: *a heavy oak table*

heavy-duty *adjective* designed to withstand very hard wear

heavy-handed *adjective* clumsy, awkward

heavy industry industries such as coal-mining, steel-making, shipbuilding, *etc*, using heavy equipment

heavyweight *noun* **1** a boxer in the highest weight category **2** someone very important or powerful

Hebrew *noun* an ancient language spoken in its modern form by Jews in Israel

heckle *verb* to shout insults at, or ask awkward questions of, a public speaker ▪ **heckler** *noun*

hectare *noun* 10 000 square metres

hectic *adjective* rushed

hedge *noun* a fence of bushes, shrubs, *etc* ▪ *verb* **1** to shut in with a hedge **2** to avoid giving a straight answer

hedgehog *noun* a small animal with prickly spines on its back

hedgerow *noun* a row of bushes forming a hedge

heed *verb* to give attention to, listen to

heedless *adjective* careless

heel *noun* the back part of the foot ▪ *verb* **1** to put a heel on (a shoe) **2** of a ship: to lean over

hefty *adjective* **1** powerful, muscular **2** heavy

Hegira *noun* the Islamic era, dating from AD622

heifer (*pronounced* hef-er) *noun* a young cow

height *noun* **1** the state of being high **2** distance from bottom to top **3** the highest point

heighten *verb* to make more intense

heinous (*pronounced* heen-us) *adjective* extremely bad, atrocious: *heinous crime*

heir *noun* a person who legally inherits a title or property on the death of the owner

heiress *noun* a woman or girl who is expected to inherit a large amount of property or money

heirloom *noun* something that has been handed down in a family from generation to generation

held *past form of* **hold**

helicopter *noun* a flying machine kept in the air by propellers rotating on a vertical axis

helium *noun* a very light gas

helix *noun* a screw-shaped coil

hell *noun* **1** a place of punishment of the wicked after death **2** the dwelling place of the Devil **3** any place of great misery or pain

hello *or* **hallo** *or* **hullo** *noun* (*plural* **hellos** *or* **helloes** *etc*) a greeting used between people

helm *noun* the wheel or handle by which a ship is steered

helmet *noun* an armoured or

protective covering for the head

helmsman *noun* the person who steers a ship

help *verb* 1 to aid, do something useful for 2 to give the means for doing something to 3 to stop yourself from (doing): *I can't help liking him* ▪ *noun* aid, assistance ▪ **helper** *noun*

helpful *adjective* useful, giving help ▪ **helpfully** *adverb*

helping *noun* a share, especially of food

helpless *adjective* useless; powerless ▪ **helplessly** *adverb*

helter-skelter *adverb* in a great hurry, in confusion ▪ *noun* a spiral slide in a fair *etc*

hem *noun* the border of a garment doubled down and stitched ▪ *verb* to put or form a hem on ▪ **hem in** to surround

| **hem** *verb* ▶ hems, hemm*ing*, hemm*ed*

hemisphere *noun* half of the earth: *western hemisphere*

hemline *noun* the height of a hem on a dress or skirt

hemlock *noun* a poisonous plant with spotted leaves

hemp *noun* a plant used for making ropes, bags, sails, *etc*

hen *noun* 1 a female bird 2 a female domestic fowl

hence *adverb* 1 from this place or time: *ten years hence* 2 for this reason: *hence, I am unable to go*

henceforth *adverb* from now on

henchman *noun* a follower; a servant

henna *noun* a reddish plant dye used for colouring the hair *etc*

henpecked *adjective* of a husband: dominated by his wife

hepatitis *noun* inflammation of the liver caused by one of several viruses

heptagon *noun* a seven-sided figure ▪ **heptagonal** *adjective*

her *pronoun* a female person already spoken about (used only as the object in a sentence): *have you seen her?* ▪ *adjective* belonging to such a person: *her house*

herald *noun* 1 something that is a sign of future things 2 *history* someone who carried and read important notices ▪ *verb* 1 to announce loudly 2 to be a sign of

heraldry *noun* the study of coats of arms, crests, *etc*

herb *noun* a plant used in the making of medicines or in cooking

herbal *adjective* of or using herbs

herbalism *noun* the study and use of plants in medicine

herbivore *noun* an animal which feeds on plants ▪ **herbivorous** *adjective*

herd *noun* a group of animals of one kind ▪ *verb* to group together like a herd of animals

here *adverb* at, in or to this place

hereabouts *adverb* approximately in this place

hereafter *adverb* after this ▪ the hereafter life after death

hereby *adverb* by this means

hereditary *adjective* passed on from parents to children

heredity *noun* the passing on of physical qualities from parents to children

heresy (*pronounced* he-re-si) *noun* (*plural* **heresies**) an opinion which goes against the official (especially religious) view ▪ **heretic** (*pronounced* he-re-tik) *noun*

heritage *noun* something passed on by or inherited from an earlier generation

hermaphrodite (*pronounced* her-maf-ro-dait) *noun* an animal which has the qualities of both male and female sexes

hermit *noun* someone who lives alone, often for religious reasons

hermitage *noun* the dwelling of a hermit

hernia *noun* the bursting out of part of an internal organ through a weak spot in surrounding body tissue

hero *noun* (*plural* **heroes**) **1** someone much admired for their bravery **2** the chief male character in a story, film, *etc*

heroic *adjective* **1** brave as a hero **2** of heroes ▪ **heroically** *adverb*

heroin *noun* a very addictive drug derived from morphine

heroine *noun* **1** a woman much admired for her bravery **2** the chief female character in a story, film, *etc*

heroism *noun* bravery

heron *noun* a large water bird, with long legs and neck

herring *noun* (*plural* **herring** or **herrings**) an edible sea fish with silvery colouring, which moves in large shoals

hers *pronoun* something belonging to a female person already spoken about: *the idea was hers*

herself *pronoun* **1** used reflexively: *she washed herself* **2** used for emphasis: *she herself won't be there*

hertz *noun* a unit of frequency for radio waves *etc*

hesitant *adjective* undecided about whether to do something or not, because of anxiety or worry about the possible results ▪ **hesitancy** *noun*

hesitate *verb* **1** to pause because of uncertainty **2** to be unwilling (to do something): *I hesitate to ask* ▪ **hesitation** *noun*

heterosexual *noun* someone who is sexually attracted to the opposite sex ▪ *adjective* attracted to the opposite sex (*contrasted with:* **homosexual**) ▪ **heterosexuality** *noun*

hew *verb* to cut or shape with an axe *etc*

| **hew** ▸ hews, hew*ing*, hew*ed*,

hewn or hewed

hexagon noun a six-sided figure ▪ **hexagonal** adjective

hey exclamation expressing surprise or dismay or to attract someone's attention

heyday noun the time of greatest strength, the prime

hi exclamation, informal **1** hello **2** hey

hibernate verb of an animal: to pass the winter in a sleep-like state ▪ **hibernation** noun

hiccup noun **1** a sharp gasp, caused by laughing, eating, drinking, etc **2 hiccups** a fit of such gasping **3** a minor setback or difficulty ▪ verb to make a hiccuping sound

hidden adjective **1** concealed, out of sight **2** unknown: hidden meaning

hide[1] verb to put or keep out of sight

hide ► hides, hiding, hid, hidden

hide[2] noun the skin of an animal

hideous adjective **1** horrible, ghastly **2** very ugly

hideout noun a place where someone goes to hide or to get away from others

hiding noun a beating

hierarchy noun a number of people or things arranged in order of rank

hieroglyphics noun plural ancient Egyptian writing, in which pictures are used as letters

hi-fi adjective short for **high-fidelity** ▪ noun, informal high-quality equipment for reproducing recorded sound

higgledy-piggledy adverb & adjective in a complete muddle

high adjective **1** raised far above **2** extending far upwards, tall **3** well up on any scale of measurement, rank, etc **4** great, large: high prices **5** of sound: shrill, acute in pitch ▪ adverb **1** far above in the air **2** well up on any scale **3** to a high degree

high chair a tall chair with a small detachable table, for young children

high-fidelity adjective reproducing sound very clearly

high jinks lively games or play

high jump an athletics contest in which competitors jump over a high bar which is raised after every jump

Highlander noun someone who comes from the Highlands

Highlands noun: the Highlands a mountainous region, especially the north of Scotland

highlight noun **1** a bright spot or area in a picture **2** a lighter patch in hair etc made obvious by bright light **3** the most memorable part or experience ▪ verb to emphasize, make the focus of attention

highlighter noun a coloured felt-tip pen used to mark but not obscure lines of text

highly adverb 1 very 2 in an approving way: *I've always thought highly of him*

highly-strung adjective nervous, easily excited

Highness noun a title of a monarch

high-rise adjective of a building: having many storeys ▪ noun a building with many storeys

high school a secondary school

high-spirited adjective bold, lively

high tech or **hi tech** noun, short for **high-technology**, referring to the use of advanced, especially electronic, equipment and devices ▪ adjective (**high-tech**) modern and sophisticated

high tide or **high water** the time when the tide is farthest up the shore

highway noun the public road

Highway Code a set of official rules for road users in Britain

highwayman noun a robber who attacked people on the public road

hijack verb to steal (a car, aeroplane, *etc*) while it is moving, forcing the driver or pilot to take a new route ▪ noun the action of hijacking a vehicle *etc* ▪ **hijacker** noun

hike verb to travel on foot through countryside ▪ noun a country walk ▪ **hiker** noun

hilarious adjective extremely funny

hilarity noun great amusement and laughter

hill noun a mound of high land, less high than a mountain

hillock noun a small hill

hilly adjective covered with hills

hilt noun the handle of a sword

him pronoun a male person already spoken about (used only as the object in a sentence): *I saw him yesterday*

himself pronoun 1 used reflexively: *he cut himself shaving* 2 used for emphasis: *he wrote it himself*

hind noun a female deer ▪ adjective placed behind

hinder verb to keep back, delay, prevent

hindmost adjective farthest behind

hindrance noun something that hinders

hindsight noun realizing what should have been done after an event

Hinduism noun a religion whose followers believe people who die are born again in different bodies ▪ **Hindu** noun & adjective

hinge noun a joint on which a door, lid, *etc* turns ▪ verb 1 to move on a hinge 2 to depend (on): *everything hinges on the weather*

hint noun 1 a remark which suggests a meaning without stating it clearly 2 a slight impression, a suggestion ▪ verb to suggest without stating clearly

hinterland *noun* an area lying inland from the coast

hip[1] *noun* the part of the side of the body just below the waist

hip[2] *noun* the fruit of the wild rose

hip[3] *adjective* very fashionable, trendy

hip flask a small pocket flask for alcohol

hip-hop *noun* a popular culture movement which started in the US in the early 1980s and is associated with rap music, breakdancing, graffiti and baggy sports clothes

hippie *noun* a member of a youth movement rebelling against conventional society, dress codes, *etc*

hippo *short for* hippopotamus

hippopotamus *noun* (*plural* **hippopotami** *or* **hippopotamuses**) a large African animal living in and near rivers (often shortened to **hippo**)

hire *noun* money paid for work done, or for the use of something belonging to another person ▪ *verb* to give or get the use of by paying money

hire-purchase *noun* a way of buying an article by paying for it in instalments

hirsute *adjective* hairy, shaggy

his *adjective* belonging to him: *his book* ▪ *pronoun* the one belonging to him: *her parents are older than his*

hiss *verb* to make a sound like a snake ▪ *noun* (*plural* **hisses**) such a sound, made to show anger or displeasure

historian *noun* someone who studies or writes history

historic *adjective* important, likely to be remembered

historical *adjective* **1** of history **2** true of something in the past

history *noun* (*plural* **histories**) **1** the study of the past **2** a description of past events, society, *etc*

histrionics *noun plural* an exaggerated show of strong feeling

hit *verb* **1** to strike with a blow **2** to occur suddenly to: *it finally hit me* ▪ *noun* **1** a blow, a stroke **2** a shot which hits a target **3** a success **4** a successful song, recording, *etc* **5** an instance of a computer file, especially a Web site, being contacted ▪ **hit upon** to come upon, discover

| **hit** *verb* ► hits, hitt*ing*, hit

hit-and-miss *adjective* haphazard, sometimes working and sometimes not

hit-and-run *adjective* of a driver: driving away after causing injury without reporting the accident

hitch *verb* **1** to fasten with a hook *etc* **2** to lift with a jerk **3** to hitch-hike ▪ *noun* (*plural* **hitches**) **1** a jerk **2** an unexpected stop or delay

hitch-hike *verb* to travel by getting lifts in other people's vehicles ▪ **hitch-hiker** *noun*

hi tech *another spelling of* **high tech**

hither *adverb* to this place

hitherto *adverb* until now

hitman *noun, slang* someone employed to kill or attack others

HIV *abbreviation* human immuno-deficiency virus

hive *noun* **1** place where bees live **2** a busy place: *hive of industry*

hoard *noun* a hidden store of treasure, food, *etc* ▪ *verb* to store up secretly

❖ Do not confuse with: **horde**

hoarding *noun* a fence of boards

hoarse *adjective* having a harsh voice, *eg* from a cold or cough

hoax *noun* (*plural* **hoaxes**) a trick played to deceive ▪ *verb* to play a hoax on

hob *noun* the top of a cooker, with rings for heating *etc*

hobble *verb* to walk with short unsteady steps

hobby *noun* (*plural* **hobbies**) a favourite way of passing your spare time

hobby-horse *noun* a toy wooden horse

hobgoblin *noun* a mischievous fairy

hobnob *verb* to attend social events in company (with)

hobnob ► hobnobs, hobnobbing, hobnobbed

hockey *noun* an eleven-a-side ball-game played with clubs curved at one end

hoe *noun* a tool used for weeding, loosening earth, *etc* ▪ *verb* to use a hoe

hog *noun* a pig ▪ *verb, informal* to take or use selfishly

hog *verb* ► hogs, hogging, hogged

Hogmanay *noun* the name in Scotland for 31 December and the celebrations held that night

hoist *verb* to lift, raise ▪ *noun* a lift, an elevator for goods

hold *verb* **1** to keep in your possession or power; have **2** to contain **3** to occupy (a position *etc*) **4** to put on, organize ▪ *noun* **1** grip, grasp **2** influence: *a hold over the others* **3** a large space for carrying a ship's cargo ▪ **hold forth** to speak at length ▪ **hold off** to delay or refrain from doing something ▪ **hold on** to wait ▪ **hold out** to refuse to give in ▪ **hold over** to keep till later ▪ **hold up 1** to support **2** to hinder **3** to attack and demand money from

hold *verb* ► holds, holding, held

holdall *noun* a large carrying bag with a zip

holder *noun* **1** a container **2** someone who holds (a position *etc*)

hold-up noun **1** an armed attempt at robbery **2** a delay, or something that causes it

hole noun **1** an opening in something solid **2** a pit, a burrow **3** a miserable place

holiday noun **1** a day when businesses etc are closed **2** a period away from work for rest

holiness noun **1** the quality of being holy or sacred **2** Your Holiness the official form of address used for the leader of a religion eg the Pope

hollow adjective **1** having empty space inside, not solid **2** false, unreal: hollow smile ▪ noun **1** a sunken place **2** a dip in the land ▪ verb to scoop (out)

holly noun (plural **hollies**) an evergreen shrub with scarlet berries and prickly leaves

holocaust noun a great destruction (by fire) ▪ **the Holocaust** the mass killing of Jews by the German Nazis in World War II

hologram noun a 3-D image created by laser beams

holster noun a case for a pistol

holy adjective **1** of or like God **2** religious, righteous **3** for religious use; sacred

| holy ► holier, holiest

homage noun a show of respect; an acknowledgement of superiority

home noun **1** the place where someone lives **2** the house of someone's family **3** a centre or place of origin: the home of country music **4** a place where children, the elderly, etc live and are looked after ▪ adjective **1** of someone's house or family: home comforts **2** domestic, not foreign: home affairs ▪ adverb towards home

home economics the study of how to run a home

homely adjective plain but pleasant

home-made adjective made at home

homeopathic or **homoeopathic** adjective of or using homeopathy

homeopathy or **homoeopathy** noun the treatment of illness by small quantities of substances that produce symptoms similar to those of the illness

home page computing the first page that appears on a computer screen after a connection is made to the Internet, or the access page of a Web site

homesick adjective longing for home

home truth a frank statement of something true but unpleasant

homewards adverb towards home

homework noun work for school etc done at home

homing adjective of a pigeon:

having the habit of making for home

homosexual *noun* someone who is sexually attracted to the same sex ▪ *adjective* sexually attracted to the same sex (*contrasted with*: **heterosexual**) ▪ **homosexuality** *noun*

hone *verb* to sharpen (a knife *etc*)

honest *adjective* truthful; not inclined to steal, cheat, *etc*

honestly *adverb* 1 truthfully 2 without cheating or stealing *etc* 3 when you are trying to convince someone of something: really

honesty *noun* the quality of being honest, truthful or trustworthy

honey *noun* 1 a sweet, thick fluid made by bees from the nectar of flowers 2 *informal* sweetheart, dear

honeycomb *noun* a network of wax cells in which bees store honey

honeymoon *noun* a holiday spent immediately after marriage ▪ *verb* to spend a honeymoon

honeysuckle *noun* a climbing shrub with sweet-smelling flowers

honk *noun* a noise like the cry of the wild goose or the sound of a motor horn ▪ *verb* to make this sound

honorary *adjective* 1 done to give honour 2 without payment

honour *or US* **honor** *noun* 1 respect for truth, honesty, *etc*

2 fame, glory 3 reputation, good name 4 a title of respect, especially to a judge: *Your Honour* 5 a privilege 6 **honours** recognition given for exceptional achievements ▪ *verb* 1 to give respect to 2 to give high rank to

honourable *adjective* worthy of honour

hood *noun* 1 a covering for the head 2 a protective cover for anything

hoodwink *verb* to deceive

hoof *noun* (*plural* **hoofs** or **hooves**) the horny part on the feet of certain animals (*eg* horses)

hook *noun* 1 a bent piece of metal *etc* for hanging things on 2 a piece of metal on the end of a line for catching fish

hookah *or* **hooka** *noun* a tobacco pipe in which the smoke is drawn through water

hooked *adjective* 1 curved, bent 2 caught by a hook 3 *slang* addicted to, fascinated by

hooligan *noun* a wild, unruly person

hooliganism *noun* unruly behaviour

hoop *noun* a thin ring of wood or metal

hooray *another spelling of* **hurrah**

hoot *verb* 1 to sound (a siren, car horn, *etc*) 2 of an owl: to call, cry 3 to laugh loudly ▪ *noun* 1 the sound made by a car horn, siren or owl 2 a shout of scorn or disgust **3** *informal* someone or something extremely funny

hooter *noun* a siren or horn which makes a hooting sound

Hoover *noun, trademark* a vacuum cleaner

hoover *verb* to vacuum (a floor *etc*)

hop[1] *verb* to leap on one leg ■ *noun* a short jump on one leg
> hop *verb* ► hops, hopp*ing*, hopp*ed*

hop[2] *noun* a climbing plant with bitter-tasting fruits used in brewing beer

hope *noun* **1** the state of expecting or wishing something good to happen **2** something desired ■ *verb* to expect or wish good to happen

hopeful *adjective* **1** confident or optimistic about something **2** promising, encouraging

hopefully *adverb* **1** with hope **2** used when expressing hopes: 'I hope that...'

hopeless *adjective* **1** without hope **2** very bad ■ **hopelessly** *adverb*

hopscotch *noun* a hopping game over lines drawn on the ground

horde *noun* a large crowd or group

♦* Do not confuse with: hoard

horizon *noun* **1** the imaginary line formed where the earth

meets the sky **2** the limit of someone's experience or understanding

horizontal *adjective* lying level or flat ■ **horizontally** *adverb*

hormone *noun* a substance produced by certain glands of the body, which acts on a particular organ ■ **hormonal** *adjective*

horn *noun* **1** a hard growth on the heads of certain animals, *eg* deer, sheep **2** part of a car which gives a warning sound **3** a brass wind instrument (originally made of horn)

horned *adjective* having horns

hornet *noun* a kind of large wasp

hornpipe *noun* a lively sailor's dance

horny *adjective* hard like horn

horoscope *noun* a prediction of someone's future based on the position of the stars at their birth

horrendous *adjective, informal* awful, terrible

horrible *adjective* **1** very unpleasant **2** very bad, awful ■ **horribly** *adverb*

horrid *adjective* hateful; very unpleasant

horrific *adjective* **1** terrifying **2** awful, very bad ■ **horrifically** *adverb*

horrify *verb* to frighten greatly, shock ■ **horrifying** *adjective*
> horrify ► horrif*ies*, horrify*ing*, horrif*ied*

horror *noun* **1** great fear, terror **2** something which causes fear

3 an unruly or demanding child

horse *noun* **1** a four-footed animal with hooves and a mane **2** a wooden frame for drying clothes on **3** a piece of gymnastic equipment for vaulting ∎ **on horseback** riding on a horse

horse chestnut a tree which produces a shiny, inedible nut (a conker)

horseplay *noun* rough play, fooling around

horsepower *noun* a unit of mechanical power for car engines (*short form:* **hp**)

horseradish *noun* a plant with a sharp-tasting root which is used in sauces

horseshoe *noun* **1** a shoe for horses, made of a curved piece of iron **2** a horseshoe-shaped thing

horticulture *noun* the study and art of gardening
∎ **horticultural** *adjective*

hose *noun* a rubber tube for carrying water

hosiery *noun* stockings, tights, *etc*

hospice *noun* a home providing special nursing care for incurable invalids

hospitable *adjective* showing kindness to guests or strangers

hospital *noun* a building for the treatment of the sick and injured

hospitality *noun* the quality of being hospitable, or of being friendly and welcoming to guests and strangers, entertaining them

with food or drink, or providing them with accommodation

host[1] *noun* **1** someone who welcomes and entertains guests **2** an innkeeper or hotel-keeper **3** the person on a television or radio show who introduces guests and performers to the audience, or interviews them

host[2] *noun* a very large number

hostage *noun* someone held prisoner by an enemy to make sure that an agreement will be kept to

hostel *noun* a building providing rooms for students *etc*

hostelry *noun* (*plural* **hostelries**), *old* an inn

hostess *noun* **1** a woman who welcomes and entertains guests **2** an air hostess

hostile *adjective* **1** of an enemy **2** not friendly **3** showing dislike or opposition (to)

hostility *noun* **1** unfriendliness, dislike **2** (*plural* **hostilities**) acts of warfare

hot *adjective* **1** very warm **2** spicy **3** passionate
│ hot ▶ hot*ter*, hot*test*

hot air meaningless talk

hotbed *noun* a centre or breeding ground for anything: *a hotbed of rebellion*

hot-blooded *adjective* passionate, easily angered

hot dog a hot sausage in a long roll

hotel *noun* a building with

several rooms which people can pay to stay in for a number of nights

hotfoot *adverb* in great haste

hotheaded *adjective* inclined to act rashly without thinking

hothouse *noun* a heated greenhouse for plants

hotline *noun* a direct telephone line to an important person

hound *noun* a dog used in hunting ■ *verb* to hunt, pursue

hour *noun* sixty minutes, the 24th part of a day

hourglass *noun* an instrument which measures the hours by the running of sand from one glass into another

hourly *adjective* happening or done every hour ■ *adverb* every hour

house *noun* 1 a building in which people live 2 a household ■ *verb* to provide a house for; accommodate

houseboat *noun* a river barge with a cabin for living in

housebreaker *noun* someone who breaks into a house to steal ■ **housebreaking** *noun*

household *noun* the people who live together in a house

householder *noun* someone who owns or pays the rent of a house

housekeeper *noun* someone employed to look after the running of a house

house-proud *adjective* proud of keeping your house clean and tidy

house-trained *adjective* of a pet: trained to go outdoors to pass urine and faeces

housewarming *noun* a party held when someone moves into a new house

housewife *noun* a woman who looks after a house and her family

housework *noun* the work involved in keeping a house clean and tidy

housing *noun* accommodation, *eg* houses, flats, *etc*

hovel *noun* a small squalid dwelling

hover *verb* 1 to stay in the air in the same spot 2 to stay near, linger (about)

hovercraft *noun* a craft able to travel over land or sea supported on a cushion of air

how *adverb* 1 in what manner: *how are they getting there?* 2 to what extent: *how old are you?* 3 to a great extent: *how well you play* 4 by what means: *how do you switch this on?* 5 in what condition: *how is she?*

however *adverb* 1 no matter how 2 in spite of that

howl *verb* 1 to make a long, loud sound like that of a dog or wolf 2 to yell in pain, anger, *etc* 3 to laugh loudly ■ *noun* a howling sound

howler *noun*, *informal* a ridiculous mistake

HQ *abbreviation* headquarters

hub *noun* **1** the centre part of a wheel through which the axle passes **2** a thriving centre of anything: *the hub of the entertainment industry*

hubbub *noun* a confused sound of many voices

huddle *verb* to crowd together ■ *noun* a close group

hue *noun* colour, shade

hue and cry a commotion, a fuss

huff *noun* a fit of bad temper and sulking

huffy *adjective* inclined to sulk; peevish

hug *verb* **1** to hold tightly with the arms **2** to keep close to: *hugging the kerb* ■ *noun* a tight embrace

| **hug** *verb* ► hugs, hugg*ing*, hugg*ed*

huge *adjective* extremely big

hula hoop a light hoop for spinning round the waist

hulk *noun* an old ship unfit for use

hulking *adjective* big and clumsy

hull *noun* the body or framework of a ship

hullabaloo *noun* a noisy disturbance

hullo *another spelling* of **hello**

hum *verb* **1** to make a buzzing sound like that of bees **2** to sing with the lips shut **3** of a place: to be noisily busy ■ *noun* **1** the noise of bees **2** any buzzing, droning sound

| **hum** *verb* ► hums, humm*ing*, humm*ed*

human *adjective* **1** relating to people as opposed to animals or gods **2** having natural qualities, feelings, *etc* ■ *noun* a man, woman or child

humane *adjective* kind, showing mercy, gentle ■ **humanely** *adverb*

humanitarian *adjective* kind to fellow human beings

humanity *noun* **1** people in general **2** kindness, gentleness

humble *adjective* **1** modest, meek **2** not of high rank, unimportant ■ *verb* to make to feel low and unimportant

humbug *noun* **1** nonsense, rubbish **2** a kind of hard mint-flavoured sweet

humdrum *adjective* dull, not exciting

humid *adjective* of air *etc*: moist, damp

humidity *noun* dampness

humiliate *verb* to make to feel humble or ashamed; hurt someone's pride ■ **humiliating** *adjective* ■ **humiliation** *noun*

humility *noun* a humble state of mind; meekness

hummingbird *noun* a small brightly-coloured bird which beats its wings rapidly making a humming noise

humorist *noun* a comedian, a comic writer

humorous *adjective* funny, amusing

humour *or US* **humor** *noun* **1** the ability to see things as amusing or ridiculous **2** funniness; the amusing side of anything: *the humour of the situation* **3** state of mind; temper, mood ▪ *verb* to do as someone else wishes in order to please them

hump *noun* **1** a lump, a mound **2** a lump on the back

humpback *noun* **1** a back with a hump **2** someone with a hump on their back ▪ *adjective* of a bridge: rising and falling so as to form a hump shape

hunch *noun* (*plural* **hunches**) a suspicion that something is untrue or is going to happen *etc* ▪ *verb* to draw (your shoulders) up towards your ears and forward towards your chest, giving your body a rounded, stooping appearance

hunchback *noun* humpback

hunchbacked *adjective* humpbacked

hundred *noun* the number 100 ▪ *adjective* 100 in number

hundredth *adjective* the last of a hundred (things *etc*) ▪ *noun* one of a hundred equal parts

hundredweight *noun* 112 pounds, 50.8 kilograms (often written **cwt**)

hung *past form of* **hang**

hunger *noun* **1** a desire for food **2** a strong desire for anything ▪ *verb* **1** to go without food **2** to long (for)

hungover *adjective* suffering from a hangover

hungry *adjective* wanting or needing food ▪ **hungrily** *adverb*

hunt *verb* **1** to chase animals or birds for food or sport **2** to search (for) ▪ *noun* **1** a chase of wild animals **2** a search

huntsman, huntswoman *noun* someone who hunts

hurdle *noun* **1** a light frame to be jumped over in a race **2** a difficulty which must be overcome

hurl *verb* to throw with force

hurlyburly *noun* a great stir, uproar

hurrah *or* **hurray** *exclamation* a shout of joy, approval, *etc*

hurricane *noun* a violent storm of wind blowing at a speed of over 75 miles (120 kilometres) per hour

hurried *adjective* done in a hurry ▪ **hurriedly** *adverb*

hurry *verb* **1** to act or move quickly **2** to make (someone) act quickly ▪ *noun* eagerness to act quickly, haste

| **hurry** *verb* ► **hurries**, **hurrying**, **hurried**

hurt *verb* **1** to cause pain or distress to **2** to injure physically, wound **3** to damage, spoil ▪ *noun* **1** pain, distress **2** damage

| **hurt** *verb* ► **hurts**, **hurting**, **hurt**

hurtful *adjective* causing pain, distress or damage

hurtle *verb* to rush at great speed

husband noun a married man (the partner of a **wife**)

hush exclamation be quiet! ■ noun, informal silence, quiet ■ verb to make quiet ■ **hush up** to stop (a scandal etc) becoming public

hush-hush adjective, informal top secret

husk noun the dry thin covering of certain fruits and seeds

husky[1] adjective of a voice: deep and rough ■ **huskily** adverb

husky[2] noun (plural **huskies**) a Canadian sledge-dog

hustle verb **1** to push rudely **2** to hurry

hut noun a small wooden building

hutch noun (plural **hutches**) a box in which pet rabbits are housed

hyacinth noun a sweet-smelling flower which grows from a bulb

hyaena another spelling of **hyena**

hybrid noun an animal or plant bred from two different kinds, eg a mule, which is a hybrid from a horse and an ass

hydrant noun a connection to which a hose can be attached to draw water off the main water supply

hydraulic adjective **1** carrying water **2** worked by water or other fluid

hydrocarbon noun a compound containing only carbon and hydrogen

hydroelectricity noun electricity obtained from water-power ■ **hydroelectric** adjective

hydrofoil noun a boat with a device which raises it out of the water as it speeds up

hydrogen noun the lightest gas, which with oxygen makes up water

hydrogen bomb an extremely powerful bomb using hydrogen

hyena or **hyaena** noun a dog-like wild animal with a howl sounding like laughter

hygiene noun the maintaining of cleanliness as a means to health ■ **hygienic** adjective

hymn noun a religious song of praise

hype noun, informal extravagant advertisement or publicity ■ verb to promote extravagantly

hyper- prefix to a greater extent than usual, excessive: hypersensitive

hyperactive adjective of a child: abnormally active

hyperlink noun, computing a piece of text a user can click on to take them to another file (also called: **link**)

hypertext noun electronic text containing cross-references which can be accessed by keystrokes etc

hyphen noun a short stroke (-) used to link or separate parts of a word or phrase: touch-and-go

hyphenate verb to join (two or

more words) with a hyphen
- **hyphenated** *adjective*
- **hyphenation** *noun*

hypnosis *noun* **1** a sleep-like state in which suggestions are obeyed **2** hypnotism

hypnotic *adjective* **1** of hypnosis or hypnotism **2** causing a sleep-like state

hypnotism *noun* the putting of someone into hypnosis
- **hypnotist** *noun*

hypnotize *or* **hypnotise** *verb* to put someone into hypnosis

hypochondria *noun* over-anxiety about your own health

hypochondriac *noun* someone who is over-anxious about their health, and who is inclined to think they are ill when they are perfectly healthy

hypocrite *noun* someone who pretends to be something they are not, or to believe something they do not ∎ **hypocrisy** *noun*
∎ **hypocritical** *adjective*

hypodermic *adjective* used for injecting drugs just below the skin

hypotenuse (*pronounced* hai-pot-*e*-nyooz) *noun* the longest side of a right-angled triangle

hypothermia *noun* an abnormally low body temperature caused by exposure to cold

hypothesis (*pronounced* hai-poth-*e*-sis) *noun* (*plural* **hypotheses**) something taken as true for the sake of argument

hypothetical *adjective* supposed, based on an idea or a possibility rather than on facts

hysterectomy *noun* (*plural* **hysterectomies**) surgical removal of the womb

hysteria *noun* **1** nervous excitement causing uncontrollable laughter, crying, *etc* **2** a nervous illness

hysterical *adjective* **1** suffering from a severe emotional disturbance, often as a result of shock **2** wild with panic, excitement or anger **3** very funny
∎ **hysterically** *adverb*

hysterics *noun plural* a fit of hysteria

I

I *pronoun* the word used by a speaker or writer in mentioning themselves (as the subject of a verb): *you and I*

ice *noun* **1** frozen water **2** ice-cream ▪ *verb* **1** to cover with icing **2** to freeze

ice age an age when the earth was mostly covered with ice

iceberg *noun* a huge mass of floating ice

icecap *noun* a permanent covering of ice, as at the North and South Poles

ice-cream *noun* a sweet creamy mixture, flavoured and frozen

ice hockey hockey played with a rubber disc (called a **puck**) on an ice rink

ice lolly a portion of frozen, flavoured water or ice-cream on a stick

ice-skate *noun* a skate for moving on ice

ice-skating *noun* the sport of moving about on ice wearing ice-skates

icicle *noun* a hanging, pointed piece of ice formed by the freezing of dropping water

icing *noun* powdered sugar, mixed with water or egg-white, spread on cakes or biscuits

icon *noun* **1** a painted or mosaic image of Christ or a saint (*also*: **ikon**) **2** *computing* a small graphic image which is clicked to access a particular program

icy *adjective* **1** covered with ice **2** very cold **3** unfriendly ▪ **icily** *adverb*

ID *abbreviation* identification ▪ *noun* a means of identification, *eg* a driving licence

I'd *short for* I would, I should *or* I had

idea *noun* **1** a thought, a notion **2** a plan

ideal *adjective* **1** perfect **2** existing in imagination only (*contrasted with*: **real**) ▪ *noun* the highest and best; a standard of perfection

idealism *noun* the belief that perfection can be reached

idealist *noun* someone who thinks that perfection can be reached ▪ **idealistic** *adjective*

idealize *or* **idealise** *verb* to think of as perfect ▪ **idealization** *noun*

ideally *adverb* in ideal circumstances

identical *adjective* the same in all details ▪ **identically** *adverb*

identification *noun* **1** an official document, such as a passport or driving licence, that proves who you are **2** the process of finding out who someone is or what something is

identify *verb* to claim to recognize, prove to be the same: *identified the man as his attacker* ▪ **identify with** to feel close to or involved with

| **identify ▸** identifies, identifying, identified

identity *noun* (*plural* **identities**) **1** who or what someone or something is **2** the state of being the same **3** *maths* an equation that works with all possible variables

ideology *noun* (*plural* **ideologies**) a set of ideas, often political or philosophical

idiocy *noun* feeble-mindedness, foolishness

idiom *noun* a common expression whose meaning cannot be guessed from the individual words, *eg* 'I'm feeling *under the weather*'

idiosyncrasy *noun* (*plural* **idiosyncrasies**) a personal oddness of behaviour ▪ **idiosyncratic** *adjective*

idiot *noun* a feeble-minded person; a fool

idiotic *adjective* extremely foolish, ridiculous ▪ **idiotically** *adverb*

idle *adjective* **1** not working **2** lazy **3** meaningless, without a useful purpose ▪ **idly** *adverb*

idler *noun* a person who wastes time or is reluctant to work

idol *noun* **1** an image worshipped as a god **2** someone much loved or honoured

idolize *or* **idolise** *verb* to adore, worship

idyllic *adjective* very happy and content, blissful

ie *abbreviation* that is, that means (from Latin *id est*)

if *conjunction* **1** on condition that, supposing that **2** whether: *do you know if she'll be there?*

igloo *noun* an Inuit snow hut

ignite *verb* **1** to set on fire **2** to catch fire

ignition *noun* **1** the act of setting on fire or catching fire **2** the sparking part of a motor engine

ignoble *adjective* dishonourable

ignominious *adjective* bringing disgrace or dishonour

ignoramus (*pronounced* ig-no-rei-mus) *noun* an ignorant person

ignorant *adjective* knowing little ▪ **ignorance** *noun*

ignore *verb* to take no notice of

iguana (*pronounced* ig-wah-na) *noun* a type of large lizard

ikon *another spelling* of **icon**

I'll *short for* I shall, I will

ill *adjective* unwell, sick ■ *adverb* badly ■ *noun* evil

ill-at-ease *adjective* uncomfortable

illegal *adjective* against the law ■ **illegality** *noun* (*plural* **illegalities**)

illegible *adjective* impossible to read ■ **illegibility** *noun*

illegitimate *adjective* born of parents not married to each other

ill-feeling *noun* dislike, resentment

illicit *adjective* unlawful, forbidden

illiterate *adjective* not able to read or write ■ **illiteracy** *noun*

illness *noun* disease, sickness

illogical *adjective* not logical, not showing sound reasoning ■ **illogicality** *noun* ■ **illogically** *adverb*

ill-treat *verb* to treat badly

illuminate *verb* to light up

illuminations *noun plural* a decorative display of lights

illusion *noun* 1 something which deceives the mind or eye 2 a mistaken belief

🖋 Do not confuse with: allusion and delusion

illusive *adjective* misleading, deceptive

🖋 Do not confuse with: allusive and elusive. Illusive is related to the noun illusion.

illusory *adjective* mistaken or untrue, despite seeming believable

illustrate *verb* to draw pictures for (a book *etc*)

illustration *noun* a picture in a book *etc*

illustrator *noun* someone who illustrates books *etc*

illustrious *adjective* famous, distinguished

ill-will *noun* dislike, resentment

I'm *short for* I am

image *noun* 1 a likeness made of someone or something 2 a striking likeness 3 a picture in the mind 4 public reputation

imagery *noun* words that suggest images, used to make a piece of writing more vivid

imaginary *adjective* existing only in the imagination, not real

🖋 Do not confuse with: imaginative

imagination *noun* the power of forming pictures in the mind of things not present or experienced

imaginative *adjective* 1 having a lively imagination 2 done with imagination

🖋 Do not confuse with: imaginary

imagine *verb* 1 to form a picture in the mind, especially of something that does not exist 2 to think, suppose

imam *noun* 1 the priest who leads the prayers in a mosque 2 **Imam** an Islamic leader

imbecile *noun* a feeble-minded person; a fool

imbibe *verb* to drink (in)

imbue *verb* to fill or affect (with): *imbued her staff with enthusiasm*

imitate *verb* to try to be the same as, copy

imitation *noun* a copy
■ *adjective* made to look like: *imitation leather*

imitator *noun* someone who copies, or tries to do the same things as, someone else

immaculate *adjective* spotless; very clean and neat
■ **immaculately** *adverb*

immaterial *adjective* of little importance

immature *adjective* not mature
■ **immaturity** *noun*

immediate *adjective* 1 happening straight away 2 close: *immediate family* 3 direct: *my immediate successor*

immediately *adverb* without delay

immemorial *adjective* going further back in time than can be remembered

immense *adjective* very large
■ **immensity** *noun*

immensely *adverb* greatly

immerse *verb* to plunge something into liquid so that it is completely covered ■ **immerse yourself in** to give your whole attention to

immersion *noun* 1 the plunging of something into liquid so that it

is completely covered 2 deep involvement in a certain subject or situation

immersion heater an electric water-heater inside a hot-water tank

immigrant *noun* someone who immigrates

immigrate *verb* to come into a country and settle there
■ **immigration** *noun*

🔹 Do not confuse with: **emigrate**. You **IMm**igrate to a new country where you plan to start living (the IM comes from the Latin meaning 'into'). You are **Emigrating** when you leave your original or home country (the E comes from the Latin meaning 'from')

imminent *adjective* about to happen: *imminent danger*

🔹 Do not confuse with: **eminent**

immobile *adjective* without moving ■ **immobility** *noun*

immobilize or **immobilise** *verb* to put out of action

immoral *adjective* 1 wrong, unscrupulous 2 sexually improper ■ **immorality** *noun*
■ **immorally** *adverb*

🔹 Do not confuse with: **amoral**. An **immoral** person behaves badly in the full knowledge that what they are doing is wrong. An **amoral** person behaves badly because they do not understand the difference between right and wrong

immortal *adjective* 1 living forever 2 famous forever

immortality *noun* unending life or fame

immortalize *or* **immortalise** *verb* to make immortal or famous forever

immovable *adjective* not able to be moved or changed ▪ **immovably** *adverb*

immune *adjective* 1 not likely to catch a particular disease 2 not able to be affected by: *immune to his charm* ▪ **immunity** *noun*

immunize *or* **immunise** *verb* to make someone immune to (a disease), especially by inoculation ▪ **immunization** *noun*

imp *noun* 1 a small malignant spirit 2 a mischievous child ▪ **impish** *adjective*

impact *noun* 1 the blow of one thing striking another; a collision 2 strong effect: *made an impact on the audience* ▪ *verb* to press firmly together ▪ **impact on** to affect strongly

impair *verb* to damage, weaken ▪ **impairment** *noun*

impala *noun* a large African antelope

impale *verb* to pierce through with a spear *etc*

impart *verb* to tell (information, news, *etc*) to others

impartial *adjective* not favouring one side over another; unbiased ▪ **impartiality** *noun* ▪ **impartially** *adverb*

impassable *adjective* of a road: not able to be driven along

impasse (*pronounced* **am**-pas) *noun* a situation from which there seems to be no way out

impassioned *adjective* moved by strong feeling

impassive *adjective* not easily moved by strong feeling ▪ **impassively** *adverb*

impatient *adjective* 1 restlessly eager 2 irritable, short-tempered ▪ **impatience** *noun* ▪ **impatiently** *adverb*

impeach *verb* to accuse publicly of, or charge with, misconduct ▪ **impeachment** *noun*

impeccable *adjective* faultless, perfect ▪ **impeccably** *adverb*

impede *verb* to hinder, keep back

impediment *noun* 1 a hindrance 2 a speech defect, *eg* a stutter or stammer

impel *verb* 1 to urge 2 to drive on

| **impel** ▶ impel*s*, impel*ling*, impel*led*

impending *adjective* about to happen

impenetrable *adjective* 1 not allowing light *etc* through 2 incomprehensible, inscrutable

imperative *adjective* 1 necessary, urgent 2 *grammar*

expressing command, eg look! or read this

imperceptible *adjective* so small as not to be noticed

imperfect *adjective* having a fault or flaw, not perfect ▪ *noun*, *grammar* the tense used to describe continuing or incomplete actions or states in the past, eg 'the birds *were singing*'

imperfection *noun* a fault or a flaw

imperfectly *adverb* not perfectly or thoroughly

imperial *adjective* 1 of an emperor or empire 2 commanding, superior

imperial system the system of weights and measures using inches and feet, ounces and pounds, *etc*

imperious *adjective* having an air of authority, haughty

impersonal *adjective* 1 not influenced by personal feelings 2 not connected with any person ▪ **impersonally** *adverb*

impersonate *verb* to dress up as, or act the part of, someone ▪ **impersonation** *noun*

impersonator *noun* someone who impersonates others

impertinent *adjective* cheeky, impudent ▪ **impertinence** *noun* ▪ **impertinently** *adverb*

impetuous *adjective* rushing into action, rash ▪ **impetuosity** *noun*

impetus *noun* moving force, motivation

impinge *verb*: **impinge on** or **impinge upon 1** to come in contact with **2** to trespass on, interfere with

implacable *adjective* not able to be soothed or calmed ▪ **implacably** *adverb*

implant *verb* (*pronounced* im-**plant**) to fix in, plant firmly ▪ *noun* (*pronounced* **im**-plant) an artificial organ, graft, *etc* inserted into the body

implement *noun* a tool ▪ *verb* to carry out, fulfil (eg a promise) ▪ **implementation** *noun*

implicate *verb* to bring in, involve

implication *noun* something meant though not actually said

implicit *adjective* **1** understood, meant though not actually said **2** unquestioning: *implicit obedience*

implode *verb* to collapse inwards suddenly ▪ **implosion** *noun*

implore *verb* to beg, entreat

imply *verb* to suggest: *her silence implies disapproval*

♦ Do not confuse with: **infer. Implying** is an action of expression – you **imply** something by dropping subtle hints about it. **Inferring** is an action of understanding – you **infer** something by drawing conclusions from what you have seen or heard

impolite *adjective* not polite, rude

imponderable *adjective* not able to be judged or evaluated

import *verb* (*pronounced* im-pawt) **1** to bring in (goods) from abroad for sale **2** to load a file, data, *etc* into a program ■ *noun* (*pronounced* **im**-pawt) **1** the act of importing **2** goods imported

important *adjective* worthy of attention; special ■ **importance** *noun* ■ **importantly** *adverb*

impose *verb* **1** to place (a tax *etc*) on **2 impose on** to take advantage of, inconvenience

imposing *adjective* impressive, commanding attention

imposition *noun* a burden, an inconvenience

impossible *adjective* **1** not able to be done or to happen **2** extremely difficult to deal with, intolerable ■ **impossibility** *noun* ■ **impossibly** *adverb*

impostor or **imposter** *noun* someone who pretends to be someone else in order to deceive

impoverish *verb* to make poor

impractical *adjective* lacking common sense

imprecise *adjective* not precise, vague

impregnable *adjective* too strong to be taken by attack

impresario *noun* (*plural* **impresarios**) the organizer of an entertainment

impress *verb* **1** to arouse the interest or admiration of **2** to mark by pressing upon **3** to fix deeply in the mind

impression *noun* **1** someone's thoughts or feelings about something **2** a deep or strong effect **3** a mark made by impressing **4** an act of imitating another person, especially for entertainment

impressionable *adjective* easily influenced or affected

impressionist *noun* an entertainer who impersonates people

impressive *adjective* having a strong effect on the mind

imprint *verb* to stamp, press

imprison *verb* to shut up as in a prison ■ **imprisonment** *noun*

improbable *adjective* not likely to happen ■ **improbability** *noun*

impromptu *adjective & adverb* without preparation or rehearsal

improper *adjective* **1** not suitable; wrong **2** indecent

improper fraction a fraction greater than 1 (as $\frac{5}{4}$, $\frac{11}{8}$)

impropriety *noun* (*plural* **improprieties**) something improper

improve *verb* to make or become better ■ **improvement** *noun*

improvise *verb* **1** to put together from available materials **2** to create (a tune, script, *etc*) spontaneously ■ **improvisation** *noun*

impudent *adjective* cheeky, insolent ▪ **impudence** *noun* ▪ **impudently** *adverb*

impulse *noun* a sudden urge resulting in sudden action

impulsive *adjective* acting on impulse, without taking time to consider ▪ **impulsively** *adverb*

impunity *noun* freedom from punishment, injury or loss

impure *adjective* mixed with other substances; not clean

impurity *noun* (*plural* **impurities**) **1** a small amount of something which is present in, and spoils the quality of, another substance **2** the state of being impure

in *preposition* **1** showing position in space or time: *in the garden* **2** showing state, manner, *etc*: *in cold blood* ▪ *adverb* **1** towards the inside, not out **2** in power **3** *informal* in fashion ▪ *adjective* **1** that is in, inside or coming in **2** *informal* fashionable ▪ **be in for 1** to be trying to get (a prize *etc*) **2** to be about to receive (trouble, punishment)

inability *noun* (*plural* **inabilities**) lack of power, means, *etc* (to do something)

inaccessible *adjective* not able to be easily reached or obtained

inaccurate *adjective* **1** not correct **2** not exact ▪ **inaccuracy** *noun* (*plural* **inaccuracies**)

inaction *noun* lack of action

inactive *adjective* **1** not active **2** not working, doing nothing

inactivity *noun* idleness; rest

inadequate *adjective* **1** not enough **2** unable to cope with a situation ▪ **inadequacy** *noun*

inadvertent *adjective* unintentional

inane *adjective* silly, foolish, mindless

inanimate *adjective* without life

inappropriate *adjective* not suitable

inarticulate *adjective* **1** unable to express yourself clearly **2** said indistinctly

inasmuch as because, since

inattentive *adjective* not paying attention ▪ **inattention** *noun*

inaugurate *verb* to mark the beginning of (*eg* a presidency) with a ceremony ▪ **inauguration** *noun*

inauspicious *adjective* unlucky, unlikely to end in success

inborn *adjective* existing from birth; natural: *inborn talent*

incapable *adjective* **1** unable (to do what is expected) **2** helpless (through drink *etc*)

incapacitate *verb* **1** to take away power, strength or rights **2** to disable

incapacity *noun* **1** inability **2** disability

incarcerate *verb* to imprison ▪ **incarceration** *noun*

incarnate *adjective* having human form

incense *verb* (pronounced in-sens) to make angry ■ *noun* (*pronounced* in-sens) a mixture of resins, gums, *etc* burned to give off fumes, especially in religious ceremonies

incentive *noun* something which encourages someone to do something

inception *noun* beginning

incessant *adjective* going on without pause

inch *noun* (*plural* **inches**) one twelfth of a foot (about 2.5 centimetres) ■ *verb* to move very gradually

incidence *noun* the frequency of something occurring

incident *noun* a happening

incidental *adjective* **1** happening in something in connection with something: *an incidental expense* **2** casual

incidentally *adverb* by the way

incinerate *verb* to burn to ashes ■ **incineration** *noun*

incinerator *noun* an apparatus for burning rubbish *etc*

incipient *adjective* beginning to exist: *an incipient dislike*

incision *noun* **1** cutting into something **2** a cut, a gash

incisor *noun* a front tooth

incite *verb* to move to action; urge on ■ **incitement** *noun*

inclement *adjective* of weather: stormy ■ **inclemency** *noun*

inclination *noun* liking, tendency

incline *verb* (*pronounced* in-klain) **1** to lean, slope (towards) **2** to have a liking for ■ *noun* (*pronounced* in-klain) a slope

inclined *adjective*: inclined to having a tendency, or a hesitant desire to

include *verb* to count in, along with others

inclusion *noun* the act of including something, or the fact that it is included

inclusive *adjective* including everything mentioned: *from Tuesday to Thursday inclusive is 3 days*

incognito (*pronounced* in-cog-neet-oh) *adjective & adverb* in disguise, with identity concealed

incoherent *adjective* **1** unconnected, disjointed **2** speaking in an unconnected, rambling way ■ **incoherence** *noun*

income *noun* personal earnings

incomparable *adjective* without equal

incompatible *adjective* **1** of statements: contradicting each other **2** of people: not suited, bound to disagree ■ **incompatibility** *noun*

incompetent *adjective* not good enough at doing a job ■ **incompetence** *noun*

incomplete *adjective* not finished

incomprehensible *adjective*

not able to be understood, puzzling

incongruous *adjective* **1** not matching well **2** out of place, unsuitable

inconsequential *adjective* unimportant ▪ **inconsequence** *noun*

inconsiderable *adjective* slight, unimportant

inconsiderate *adjective* not thinking of others

inconsistent *adjective* not consistent, contradicting ▪ **inconsistency** *noun*

inconsolable *adjective* not able to be comforted

inconspicuous *adjective* not noticeable

inconvenience *noun* minor trouble or difficulty

inconvenient *adjective* causing awkwardness or difficulty

incorporate *verb* **1** to contain as parts of a whole **2** to include, take account of

incorrect *adjective* wrong

incorrigible *adjective* too bad to be put right or reformed

increase *verb* (*pronounced* in-**krees**) to grow, make greater or more numerous ▪ *noun* (*pronounced* **in**-krees) **1** growth **2** the amount added by growth

increasingly *adverb* more and more

incredible *adjective* impossible to believe

🔹* Do not confuse:
incredible and **incredulous**. Incred**IBLE** means unbeliev**ABLE**. Incred**ULOUS** means unbeliev**ING**. You might, for example, be **incredulous** at (= unable to believe) another person's **incredible** (= unbelievable) stupidity

incredibly *adverb* extremely, unbelievably

incriminate *verb* to show that (someone) has taken part in a crime

incubate *verb* to brood, hatch

incubation period the time that it takes for a disease to develop from infection to the first symptoms

incubator *noun* **1** a large heated box for hatching eggs **2** a hospital crib for rearing premature babies

incur *verb* to bring (blame, debt, *etc*) upon yourself

| **incur** ▶ incurs, incurr*ing*, incurr*ed*

incurable *adjective* unable to be cured

incursion *noun* an invasion, a raid

indebted *adjective* having cause to be grateful: *we are indebted to you for your kindness*

indecent *adjective* offending against normal or usual standards of (especially sexual) behaviour ▪ **indecency** *noun*

indecision *noun* slowness in making up your mind, hesitation

indecisive *adjective* 1 not coming to a definite result 2 unable to make up your mind

indeed *adverb* 1 in fact: *she is indeed a splendid cook* 2 (used for emphasis) really: *did he indeed?* ▪ *exclamation* expressing surprise

indefinite *adjective* 1 not fixed, uncertain 2 without definite limits

indefinite article the name given to the adjectives *a* and *an*

indefinitely *adverb* for an indefinite period of time

indelible *adjective* unable to be rubbed out or removed ▪ **indelibly** *adverb*

indent *verb* to begin a new paragraph by going in from the margin

indentation *noun* 1 a hollow, a dent 2 an inward curve in an outline, coastline, *etc*

independent *adjective* 1 free to think or act for yourself 2 not relying on someone else for support, guidance, *etc* 3 of a country: self-governing ▪ **independence** *noun*

indestructible *adjective* not able to be destroyed

indeterminate *adjective* not fixed, indefinite

index *noun* (*plural* **indexes**) 1 an alphabetical list giving the page number of subjects mentioned in a book 2 (*plural* **indices**) *maths* an upper number which shows how many times a number is multiplied by itself (*eg* 4^3 means 4 × 4 × 4) (*also called*: **exponent**) 3 a numerical scale showing changes in the cost of living, wages, *etc*

index finger the forefinger

Indian summer a period of summer warmth in autumn

indicate *verb* to point out, show

indication *noun* a sign

indicative *adjective* pointing out, being a sign of: *indicative of his attitude*

indicator *noun* 1 something which indicates; a pointer 2 a flashing light on either side of a vehicle for signalling to other drivers

indices *plural* of **index** (meaning 2)

indifferent *adjective* 1 neither very good nor very bad 2 **indifferent to** showing no interest in ▪ **indifference** *noun*

indigenous *adjective* native to a country or area

indigestion *noun* discomfort or pain experienced in digesting food

indignant *adjective* angry, especially because of wrong done to yourself or others ▪ **indignation** *noun*

indigo *noun* a purplish-blue colour ▪ *adjective* purplish-blue

indirect *adjective* 1 not straight

or direct **2** not affecting or affected directly

indiscreet *adjective* **1** rash, not cautious **2** giving away too much information

indiscriminate *adjective* making no distinction between one person (or thing) and another: *indiscriminate killing*

indispensable *adjective* not able to be done without, necessary

indisposed *adjective* unwell

indisputable *adjective* not able to be denied

indistinct *adjective* not clear

indistinguishable *adjective* **1** difficult to make out **2** too alike to tell apart

individual *adjective* **1** relating to a single person or thing **2** distinctive, unusual ■ *noun* a single person or thing

individuality *noun* **1** separate existence **2** the quality of standing out from others

indivisible *adjective* not able to be divided

indoctrinate *verb* to fill with a certain teaching or set of ideas ■ **indoctrination** *noun*

indolent *adjective* lazy ■ **indolence** *noun*

indomitable *adjective* unconquerable, unyielding

indoor *adjective* done *etc* inside a building

indoors *adverb* in or into a building *etc*

indubitable *adjective* not to be doubted

induce *verb* **1** to persuade **2** to bring on, cause

indulge *verb* **1** to be inclined to give in to the wishes of; spoil **2** to give way to, not restrain

indulgence *noun* the act of indulging

indulgent *adjective* not strict, kind

industrial *adjective* **1** related to or used in trade or manufacture **2** of a country: having highly developed industry

industrialist *noun* someone involved in organizing an industry

industrialize *or* **industrialise** *verb* to introduce industry to (a place) ■ **industrialization** *noun*

industrious *adjective* hard-working

industry *noun* (*plural* **industries**) **1** a branch of trade or manufacture: *the clothing industry* **2** steady attention to work

inedible *adjective* not eatable

ineffective *adjective* useless, having no effect

ineffectual *adjective* achieving nothing

inefficient *adjective* **1** not efficient, not capable **2** wasting time, energy, *etc* ■ **inefficiency** *noun* (*plural* **inefficiencies**)

inelegant *adjective* not graceful ■ **inelegance** *noun*

ineligible *adjective* not qualified, not suitable to be chosen

inept *adjective* clumsy, badly done ▪ **ineptitude** *noun*

inequality *noun* (*plural* **inequalities**) lack of equality, unfairness

inert *adjective* **1** not moving or able to move **2** disinclined to move or act **3** not lively **4** chemically inactive

inert gas *see* **noble gas**

inertia *noun* **1** lack of energy or the will to move or act **2** *physics* the resistance of an object to a change in its state of motion *eg* when you try to stop a moving object, or to set a stationary object in motion

inescapable *adjective* unable to be avoided

inessential *adjective* not essential, unnecessary

inevitable *adjective* not able to be avoided ▪ **inevitability** *noun*

inexact *adjective* not exact, approximate

inexorable *adjective* not able to be persuaded; relentless

inexpensive *adjective* cheap in price

inexperience *noun* lack of (skilled) knowledge or experience ▪ **inexperienced** *adjective*

inexpert *adjective* unskilled, amateurish

inexplicable *adjective* not able to be explained

infallible *adjective* never making an error ▪ **infallibility** *noun*

infamous *adjective* having a very bad reputation; notorious, disgraceful

infamy *noun* public disgrace, notoriety

infancy *noun* very early childhood

infant *noun* a baby

infantile *adjective* **1** of babies **2** childish

infantry *noun* foot-soldiers

infatuated *adjective* filled with foolish love ▪ **infatuation** *noun*

infect *verb* **1** to fill with disease-causing germs **2** to pass on disease to **3** to pass on, spread (*eg* enthusiasm)

infection *noun* **1** a disease which can be spread to others **2** something that spreads widely and affects many people

infectious *adjective* likely to spread from person to person

infer *verb* to reach a conclusion from facts or reasoning: *I infer from what you say that you wish to resign*

| **infer** ▸ infers, infer*ring*, infer*red*

🞶 **Infer** is sometimes used to mean 'imply' or 'suggest': *'Are you inferring that I'm a liar?'*, but this use is considered incorrect by some people

inference *noun* a conclusion that you reach, based on information which you have been given

inferior *adjective* **1** lower in any way **2** not of best quality ▪ *noun* someone lower in rank *etc* ▪ **inferiority** *noun*

inferiority complex a constant feeling that you are less good in some way than other people

infernal *adjective*, *informal* annoying, blasted

inferno *noun* (*plural* **infernos**) a raging fire

infertile *adjective* **1** of soil: not producing much **2** not able to bear children or young ▪ **infertility** *noun*

infest *verb* to swarm over: *infested with lice*

infidel *noun* someone who does not believe in a particular religion (especially Christianity)

infidelity *noun* unfaithfulness, disloyalty

infighting *noun* rivalry or quarrelling between members of the same group

infiltrate *verb* to enter (an organization *etc*) secretly to spy or cause damage ▪ **infiltration** *noun*

infinite *adjective* without end or limit

infinitely *adverb* very much

infinitive *noun*, *grammar* the part of a verb which expresses the action but has no subject, *eg* I hate *to lose*

infinity *noun* space or time without end

infirm *adjective* feeble, weak

infirmary *noun* (*plural* **infirmaries**) a hospital

infirmity *noun* (*plural* **infirmities**) **1** a physical weakness **2** a character flaw

inflame *verb* **1** to make hot or red **2** to arouse passion in ▪ **inflamed** *adjective*

inflammable *adjective* easily set on fire

inflammation *noun* heat in a part of the body, with pain, redness and swelling

inflammatory *adjective* arousing passion (especially anger)

inflate *verb* **1** to blow up (a balloon, tyre, *etc*) **2** to puff up (with pride), exaggerate

inflation *noun* **1** the act of inflating **2** an economic situation in which prices and wages keep forcing each other to increase

inflection *noun* **1** change in the tone of your voice **2** a change in the basic form of a word to show tense, number, *etc* **3** the new form of a word which has been changed in this way: *the inflections of the verb 'find' are: 'finds', 'finding' and 'found'.*

inflexible *adjective* not yielding, unbending

inflict *verb* to bring down (blows, punishment, *etc*) on

influence *noun* the power to affect other persons or things ■ *verb* to have power over ■ **influential** *adjective*

influenza *noun* an infectious illness with fever, headache, muscle pains, *etc*

influx *noun* the arrival of large numbers of people

info *noun, informal* information

inform *verb* **1** to give knowledge to **2 inform on** to tell on, betray

informal *adjective* not formal; relaxed, friendly ■ **informality** *noun*

informant *noun* someone who informs

information *noun* knowledge, news

information technology the development and use of computer systems and applications

informative *adjective* giving information

informer *noun* someone who gives information to the police or authorities

infra-red *adjective* of rays of heat: with wavelengths longer than visible light

infrequent *adjective* rare, happening seldom

infringe *verb* to break (a rule or law) ■ **infringement** *noun*

infuriate *verb* to drive into a rage

infuriating *adjective* extremely annoying

infuse *verb* to fill the mind (with a desire *etc*)

ingenious *adjective* **1** skilful in inventing **2** cleverly thought out

ingenuity *noun* cleverness; quickness of ideas

ingot *noun* a block of metal (especially gold or silver) cast in a mould

ingrained *adjective* deeply fixed: *ingrained laziness*

ingratiate *verb* to work your way into someone's favour by flattery *etc* ■ **ingratiating** *adjective*

ingratitude *noun* lack of gratitude or thankfulness

ingredient *noun* one of the things of which a mixture is made

ingrown *adjective* of a nail: growing into the flesh

inhabit *verb* to live in

inhabitant *noun* someone who lives permanently in a place

inhalation *noun* the act of inhaling

inhale *verb* to breathe in

inhaler *noun* a device for breathing in medicine, steam, *etc*

inherent *adjective* inborn, belonging naturally

inherit *verb* **1** to receive property *etc* as an heir **2** to get (a characteristic) from your parents *etc*

inheritance *noun* something received by will when someone dies

inhibit *verb* to hold back, prevent

inhibited *adjective* unable to express your feelings

inhibition *noun* a holding back of natural impulses *etc*, restraint

inhospitable *adjective* unwelcoming, unfriendly

inhuman *adjective* not human; brutal ▪ **inhumanity** *noun*

inhumane *adjective* cruel

inimitable *adjective* impossible to imitate

initial *adjective* of or at the beginning: *initial difficulties* ▪ *noun* the letter beginning a word, especially someone's name ▪ *verb* to sign with the initials of your name

| **initial** *verb* ▶ initials, initial*ling*, initial*led*

initially *adverb* at first

initiate *verb* **1** to begin, start: *initiate the reforms* **2** to formally make someone a member of a society *etc* ▪ **initiation** *noun*

initiative *noun* **1** the right to take the first step **2** readiness to take a lead

inject *verb* **1** to force (a fluid *etc*) into the veins or muscles with a syringe **2** to put (*eg* enthusiasm) into ▪ **injection** *noun*

in-joke *noun* a joke only understood by a particular group

injure *verb* to harm, damage, wrong

injured *adjective* hurt; offended

injury *noun* (*plural* **injuries**) **1** hurt, damage, harm **2** a wrong

injustice *noun* **1** unfairness **2** a wrong

ink *noun* a coloured liquid used in writing, printing, *etc*

inkling *noun* a hint or slight sign

inland *adjective* **1** not beside the sea **2** happening inside a country ▪ *adverb* towards the inner part of a country

inland revenue taxes *etc* collected within a country

in-laws *noun plural, informal* relatives by marriage

inlet *noun* a small bay

inmate *noun* a resident, an occupant (especially of an institution)

inmost *adjective* the most inward, the farthest in

inn *noun* a small country hotel

innards *noun plural* inside parts

innate *adjective* inborn, natural

inner *adjective* **1** farther in **2** of feelings *etc*: hidden

innermost *adjective* farthest in; most secret

innings *noun singular* **1** a team's turn for batting in cricket **2** a turn, a go at something

innkeeper *noun* someone who keeps an inn

innocent *adjective* **1** not guilty, blameless **2** having no experience of how unpleasant people, and life in general, can be, and therefore tending to trust everyone **3** harmless **4** innocent

of lacking, without ■ **innocence** noun

innocuous adjective not harmful

innovation noun something new ■ **innovative** adjective

innuendo noun (plural **innuendoes**) an indirect reference, a hint

inoculate verb to inject (someone) with a mild form of a disease to prevent them later catching it ■ **inoculation** noun

inoffensive adjective harmless, giving no offence

inordinate adjective going beyond the limit, unreasonably great

inorganic adjective 1 not of animal or vegetable origin 2 of a chemical compound: not containing carbon

in-patient noun a patient who stays in a hospital during their treatment (contrasted with: **out-patient**)

input noun 1 an amount (of energy, labour, etc) put into something 2 data fed into a computer (contrasted with: **output**)

inquest noun a legal inquiry into a case of sudden death

inquire or **enquire** verb to ask

inquiring or **enquiring** adjective questioning, curious: inquiring mind

inquiry or **enquiry** noun (plural **inquiries** or **enquiries**) 1 a

question; a search for information 2 an official investigation

inquisitive adjective 1 very curious 2 fond of prying, nosey

inroad noun a raid, an advance ■ **make inroads into** to use up large amounts of

insane adjective mad, not sane ■ **insanity** noun

insatiable adjective not able to be satisfied: insatiable appetite

inscribe verb to write or engrave (eg a name) on a book, monument, etc

inscribed adjective, maths of a figure: enclosed by another figure

inscription noun the writing on a book, monument, etc

inscrutable adjective not able to be understood, mysterious

insect noun a small six-legged creature with wings and a body divided into sections

insecticide noun powder or liquid for killing insects

insecure adjective 1 not safe; not firm 2 lacking confidence, not feeling settled ■ **insecurity** noun

insensitive adjective 1 **insensitive to** not feeling: insensitive to cold 2 unsympathetic (to): insensitive to her grief 3 unappreciative, crass ■ **insensitivity** noun

inseparable adjective not able to be separated or kept apart ■ **inseparably** adverb

insert verb to put in or among ■ **insertion** noun

in-service *adjective* happening as part of someone's work

inset *noun* a small picture, map, *etc* in a corner of a larger one

inside *noun* **1** the side, space or part within **2** indoors ▪ *adjective* **1** being on or in the inside **2** indoor **3** coming from or done by someone within an organization ▪ *adverb* to, in or on the inside ▪ *preposition* to or on the inside of; within

insidious *adjective* likely to trap those who are not careful; treacherous

insight *noun* ability to consider a matter and understand it clearly

insignificant *adjective* of little importance ▪ **insignificance** *noun*

insincere *adjective* not sincere ▪ **insincerity** *noun*

insinuate *verb* **1** to hint (at a fault) **2** to put in gradually and secretly **3** to work yourself into (someone's favour *etc*)

insinuation *noun* a sly hint

insipid *adjective* **1** dull, without liveliness **2** tasteless, bland

insist *verb* **1** to urge something strongly **2** to refuse to give way, hold firmly to your intentions **3** to go on saying (that)

insistent *adjective* **1** insisting on having or doing something **2** forcing you to pay attention ▪ **insistence** *noun* ▪ **insistently** *adverb*

insolent *adjective* rude, impertinent, insulting ▪ **insolence** *noun*

insoluble *adjective* **1** not able to be dissolved **2** of a problem: not able to be solved ▪ **insolubility** *noun*

insomnia *noun* sleeplessness

inspect *verb* **1** to look carefully into, examine **2** to look over (troops *etc*) ceremonially

inspection *noun* careful examination

inspector *noun* **1** an official who inspects **2** a police officer below a superintendent and above a sergeant in rank

inspiration *noun* **1** something or someone that influences or encourages others **2** a brilliant idea

inspirational *adjective* inspiring, brilliant

inspire *verb* **1** to encourage, rouse **2** to be the source of creative ideas

inspired *adjective* **1** seeming to be aided by higher powers **2** brilliantly good

instability *noun* lack of steadiness or stability (especially in the personality)

install *or* **instal** *verb* **1** to place in position, ready for use **2** to introduce formally to a new job *etc* ▪ **installation** *noun*

install ▶ **installs** *or* **instals**, **installing**, **installed**

instalment *noun* **1** a part of a sum of money paid at fixed times until the whole amount is paid **2** one part of a serial story

instance noun an example, a particular case ■ **for instance** for example

instant adjective **1** immediate, urgent **2** able to be prepared almost immediately: instant coffee ■ noun **1** a very short time, a moment **2** point or moment of time

instantaneous adjective done or happening very quickly

instantly adverb immediately

instead adverb in place of someone or something ■ **instead of** in place of

instep noun the arching, upper part of the foot

instigate verb to stir up, encourage

instigation noun encouragement to take an action: decided to study the piano at his teacher's instigation

instil or **instill** verb to put in little by little (especially ideas into the mind)

| instil ► instils or instills, instilling, instilled

instinct noun a natural feeling or knowledge which someone has without thinking and without being taught

instinctive adjective due to instinct

institute noun a society, organization, etc or the building it uses

institution noun **1** an organization, building, etc established for a particular purpose (especially care or education) **2** an established custom ■ **institutional** adjective

instruct verb **1** to teach **2** to direct, command ■ **instructor** noun

instruction noun **1** teaching **2** a command **3 instructions** rules showing how something is to be used

instructive adjective containing or giving information or knowledge

instrument noun **1** something used for a particular purpose, a tool **2** a device for producing musical sounds, eg a piano, a harp

instrumental adjective **1** helpful in bringing (something) about **2** written for or played by musical instruments, without voice accompaniment

instrumentalist noun someone who plays on a musical instrument

insufferable adjective not able to be endured

insufficient adjective not enough ■ **insufficiency** noun

insular adjective narrow-minded, prejudiced

insulate verb to cover with a material that will not let through electrical currents, heat, frost, etc ■ **insulation** noun

insulin *noun* a substance used in the treatment of diabetes

insult *verb* to treat with scorn or rudeness ■ *noun* a rude or scornful remark

insulting *adjective* scornful, rude

insure *verb* to arrange for payment of a sum of money on (something) if it should be lost, damaged, stolen, *etc* ■ **insurance** *noun*

♦* Do not confuse with: **ensure**

intact *adjective* whole, unbroken

intake *noun* an amount of people or things taken in

intangible *adjective* 1 not able to be felt by touch 2 difficult to define or describe, not clear

integer *noun* a whole number, not a fraction

integral *adjective* of or essential to a whole

integrate *verb* 1 to fit parts together to form a whole 2 to enable (racial groups) to mix freely and live on equal terms ■ **integration** *noun*

integrated circuit interconnected electronic components etched on to a tiny piece of a semiconductor such as silicon (*also called:* **chip**)

integrity *noun* honesty

intellect *noun* the thinking power of the mind

intellectual *adjective* showing or requiring intellect ■ *noun* someone of natural ability or with academic interests

intelligence *noun* 1 mental ability 2 information sent, news

intelligent *adjective* clever, quick at understanding

intend *verb* to mean or plan to (do something)

intense *adjective* 1 very great 2 tending to feel strongly, deeply emotional ■ **intensely** *adverb*

intensify *verb* to increase, make more concentrated

| intensify ► intensifies, intensifying, intensified

intensity *noun* (*plural* **intensities**) strength, *eg* of feeling, colour, *etc*

intensive *adjective* very thorough, concentrated

intent *noun* purpose ■ *adjective* 1 with all your concentration (on), attentive 2 determined (to)

intention *noun* what someone means to do, an aim

intentional *adjective* done on purpose ■ **intentionally** *adverb*

inter (*pronounced* in-ter) *verb* to bury

| inter ► inters, interring, interred

inter- *prefix* between, among, together: *intermingle/ interplanetary*

interact *verb* to act on one another

interactive *adjective* allowing

two-way communication, *eg* between a computer and its user

intercede *verb* to act as peacemaker between two people, nations, *etc*
- **intercession** *noun*

intercept *verb* 1 to stop or seize on the way 2 to cut off, interrupt (a view, the light, *etc*) 3 *maths* to cut a line or surface with another line

interchange *noun* a junction of two or more major roads on separate levels

interchangeable *adjective* able to be used one for the other

intercom *noun* a telephone system in a building, aeroplane, *etc*

interest *noun* 1 special attention, curiosity 2 someone's personal concern or field of study 3 advantage, benefit 4 a sum paid for the loan of money ▪ *verb* to catch or hold the attention of

interested *adjective* having or taking an interest

interesting *adjective* holding the attention

interest rate a charge made for borrowing money, usually shown as a percentage of the amount borrowed

interface *noun*, *computing* a connection between two parts of the same system

interfere *verb* 1 interfere in to take part in what is not your business, meddle in 2 interfere

with to get in the way of, hinder, have a harmful effect on

interference *noun* 1 the act of interfering 2 the spoiling of radio or television reception by another station or disturbance from traffic *etc*

interim *noun* time between; the meantime ▪ *adjective* temporary

interior *adjective* 1 inner 2 inside a building ▪ *noun* the inside of anything

interjection *noun* a word or phrase of exclamation, *eg Ah!* and *Oh dear!*

interlock *verb* 1 to lock or clasp together 2 to fit into each other

interloper *noun* someone who enters without permission, an intruder

interlude *noun* 1 an interval 2 a short piece of music played between the parts of a play, film, *etc*

intermediary *noun* (*plural* **intermediaries**) someone who acts between two people, for example in trying to settle a quarrel

intermediate *adjective* in the middle; coming between

interminable *adjective* never-ending, boringly long

intermission *noun* an interval, a pause

intermittent *adjective* stopping every now and then and starting again

internal *adjective* 1 of the inner

part, especially of the body **2** inside, within a country, organization, etc

international adjective **1** happening between nations **2** concerning more than one nation **3** worldwide ■ noun a sports match between teams of two countries

Internet noun an international computer network linking users through telephone lines

interpret verb **1** to explain the meaning of something **2** to translate **3** to bring out the meaning of (music, a part in a play, etc) in performance **4** to take the meaning of something to be ■ **interpretation** noun

interpreter noun someone who translates (on the spot) the words of a speaker into another language

interrogate verb to examine by asking questions ■ **interrogation** noun ■ **interrogator** noun

interrupt verb **1** to stop (someone) while they are saying or doing something **2** to stop doing (something) **3** to get in the way of, cut off (a view etc) ■ **interruption** noun

intersect verb of lines: to meet and cross

intersection noun **1** the point where two lines cross **2** a crossroads

intersperse verb to scatter here and there

intertwine verb to twine or twist together

interval noun **1** a time or space between two things **2** a short pause in a programme etc

intervene verb **1** to come or be between, or in the way **2** to join in (in order to stop) a fight or quarrel between other persons or nations ■ **intervention** noun

interview noun a formal meeting of one person with others to apply for a job, give information to the media, etc ■ verb **1** to ask questions etc of in an interview **2** to conduct an interview

intestines noun plural the inside parts of the body, especially the bowels and passages leading to them ■ **intestinal** adjective

intimacy noun (plural intimacies) **1** close friendship **2** familiarity

intimate adjective **1** knowing a lot about, familiar (with) **2** of friends: very close **3** private, personal: intimate details ■ noun a close friend ■ **intimately** adverb

intimation noun a hint

intimidate verb to frighten or threaten into submission ■ **intimidating** adjective ■ **intimidation** noun

into preposition **1** to the inside **2** to a different state: a tadpole changes into a frog **3** maths expressing the idea of division: 2 into 4 goes twice

intolerable *adjective* not able to be endured

intolerant *adjective* not willing to put up with (people of different ideas, religion, *etc*) ■ **intolerance** *noun*

intonation *noun* the rise and fall of the voice

intone *verb* to speak in a singing manner, chant

intoxicate *verb* 1 to make drunk 2 to enthuse, excite

intoxication *noun* drunkenness

intranet *noun* a restricted network of computers, *eg* in a company

in-tray *noun* an office tray for letters and work still to be dealt with (*contrasted with*: **out-tray**)

intrepid *adjective* without fear, brave

intricate *adjective* complicated, having many twists and turns ■ **intricacy** *noun* (*plural* **intricacies**)

intrigue *noun* a secret plot ■ *verb* 1 to plot, scheme 2 to rouse the curiosity of, fascinate ■ **intriguing** *adjective*

intrinsic *adjective* belonging to something as part of its nature

introduce *verb* 1 to bring in or put in 2 to make (someone) known to another person

introduction *noun* 1 the introducing of someone or something 2 an essay at the beginning of a book *etc* briefly explaining its contents

introductory *adjective* coming at the beginning

introvert *noun* a person who tends to be uncommunicative and unsociable (*contrasted with*: **extrovert**)

intrude *verb* to thrust yourself into somewhere uninvited ■ **intrusion** *noun* ■ **intrusive** *adjective*

intruder *noun* someone who breaks in or intrudes

intuition *noun* 1 ability to understand something without thinking it out 2 an instinctive feeling or belief

Inuit *noun* 1 a native person living in or near the Arctic region, especially in Greenland, Canada and N Alaska 2 their language

inundate *verb* 1 to flood 2 to overwhelm: *inundated with work*

invade *verb* 1 to enter (a country *etc*) as an enemy to take possession 2 to interfere with (someone's rights, privacy, *etc*) ■ **invader** *noun* ■ **invasion** *noun*

invalid[1] (*pronounced* in-**val**-id) *adjective* not valid, not legally effective

invalid[2] (*pronounced* **in**-val-id) *noun* someone who is ill or disabled ■ *adjective* 1 ill or disabled 2 suitable for people who are ill or disabled

invalidate *verb* to prove to be wrong, or make legally ineffective

invaluable *adjective* priceless, essential

invariably *adverb* always

invasion *see* invade

invent *verb* 1 to make or think up for the first time 2 to make up (a story, an excuse) ▪ **inventor** *noun*

invention *noun* something invented

inventive *adjective* good at inventing, resourceful

inventory *noun* (*plural* **inventories**) a detailed list of contents

inverse *adjective* opposite, reverse ▪ *noun* 1 the opposite 2 *maths* one of two numbers that cancel each other out in a mathematical operation, *eg* the inverse of 3 in addition is -3, because $3 + -3 = 0$ ▪ **inversely** *adverb*

invert *verb* 1 to turn upside down 2 to reverse the order of

invertebrate *adjective* of an animal: not having a backbone ▪ *noun* an animal with no backbone, *eg* a worm or insect

inverted commas a pair of punctuation marks looking like one or two upside-down commas (' ' or " ") showing where direct speech begins and ends

invest *verb* to put money in a firm, property, *etc* to make a profit

investigate *verb* to search into with care ▪ **investigator** *noun*

investigation *noun* a careful search

investment *noun* 1 money

invested 2 something in which money is invested

investor *noun* someone who invests

invigilate *verb* to supervise (an examination *etc*) ▪ **invigilator** *noun*

invigorate *verb* to strengthen, refresh ▪ **invigorating** *adjective*

invincible *adjective* not able to be defeated or overcome ▪ **invincibility** *noun*

invisible *adjective* not able to be seen ▪ **invisibility** *noun*

invitation *noun* a request to do something

invite *verb* 1 to ask (someone) to do something, especially to come for a meal *etc* 2 to seem to ask for: *inviting punishment*

inviting *adjective* tempting, attractive

invoice *noun* a letter sent with goods with details of price and quantity ▪ *verb* to make such a list

invoke *verb* 1 to call upon in prayer 2 to ask for (*eg* help) ▪ **invocation** *noun*

involuntary *adjective* not done willingly or intentionally ▪ **involuntarily** *adverb*

involve *verb* 1 to have as a consequence, require 2 to take part (in), be concerned (in): *involved in publishing/involved in the scandal* ▪ **involvement** *noun*

involved *adjective* complicated

inward *adjective* 1 placed within 2 situated in the mind or soul

- *adverb* (also **inwards**) towards the inside

inwardly *adverb* **1** within **2** in your heart, privately

iodine *noun* a liquid chemical used to kill germs

ion *noun* an electrically-charged atom or group of atoms ▪ **ionic** *adjective*

ionic bond a chemical bond formed between ions with opposite charges

ionizer *or* **ioniser** *noun* a device which sends out negative ions to improve the quality of the air

IOU *noun, short for* I owe you, a note given as a receipt for money borrowed

IQ *abbreviation* intelligence quotient

irascible *adjective* easily made angry ▪ **irascibility** *noun*

irate *adjective* angry

ire *noun, formal* anger

iridescent *adjective* **1** coloured like a rainbow **2** shimmering with changing colours ▪ **iridescence** *noun*

iris *noun* (*plural* **irises**) **1** the coloured part of the eye around the pupil **2** a lily-like flower which grows from a bulb

irk *verb* to weary, annoy

iron (*pronounced* **ai**-on *or Scottish* **ai**-ron) *noun* **1** a common metal, widely used to make tools *etc* **2** a golf club (originally with an iron head) **3** an appliance for pressing clothes ▪ *adjective*

1 made of iron **2** stern, resolute: *iron will* **3** of a rule: not to be broken ▪ *verb* **1** to press (clothes) with an iron **2 iron out** to smooth out (difficulties)

ironic *or* **ironical** *adjective* **1** containing or expressing irony **2** of a person: frequently using irony ▪ **ironically** *adverb*

ironmonger *noun* a shopkeeper selling household tools, gardening equipment, *etc*

irony *noun* (*plural* **ironies**) **1** a form of humour in which someone says the opposite of what is obviously true **2** an absurd contradiction or paradox

irrational *adjective* **1** against logic or common sense **2** *maths* of a number: unable to be expressed as an integer or common fraction ▪ **irrationality** *noun*

irregular *adjective* **1** uneven, variable **2** against the rules ▪ **irregularity** *noun* (*plural* **irregularities**)

irrelevant *adjective* not having to do with what is being spoken about ▪ **irrelevance** *or* **irrelevancy** *noun* (*plural* **irrelevancies**)

irreplaceable *adjective* too good or rare to be replaced

irresistible *adjective* too strong or too charming to be resisted

irrespective *adjective* taking no account of: *irrespective of the weather*

irresponsible *adjective* having

no sense of responsibility, thoughtless

irreverent *adjective* having no respect, *eg* for holy things ■ **irreverence** *noun*

irrigate *verb* to supply (land) with water by canals *etc* ■ **irrigation** *noun*

irritable *adjective* cross, easily annoyed

irritant *noun* someone or something that causes annoyance or discomfort

irritate *verb* **1** to annoy **2** to cause discomfort to (the skin, eyes, *etc*) ■ **irritation** *noun*

-ish *suffix* **1** like: *girlish* **2** a little: *quietish*

Islam *noun* **1** the Muslim religion, founded by the prophet Mohammed **2** the Muslim world ■ **Islamic** *adjective*

island *noun* an area of land surrounded by water

islander *noun* an inhabitant of an island

isle *noun, formal* an island

-ism *suffix* **1** indicating a system, set of beliefs, *etc*: *socialism/ Buddhism* **2** indicating prejudice against a particular group: *racism/sexism*

isobar *noun* a line on a weather map connecting places where atmospheric pressure is the same

isolate *verb* **1** to place or keep separate from other people or things **2** to consider (something) by itself ■ **isolation** *noun*

isomer *noun* a chemical substance with the same molecular weight as another, but with its atoms in a different arrangement ■ **isomeric** *adjective*

isometric *adjective* of equal size

isosceles *adjective* of a triangle: with two sides equal (*compare with*: **equilateral**)

isotope *noun* an atom with the same atomic number as, but different mass number from, another

issue *verb* **1** to go or come out **2** to give out (orders *etc*) **3** to publish ■ *noun* **1** a flowing out **2** something published **3** one number in a series of magazines *etc* **4** result, consequence **5** a matter being discussed

IT *abbreviation* information technology

it *pronoun* **1** the thing spoken of: *I meant to bring the book, but I left it at home* **2** used in sentences with no definite subject: *it snowed today*

italics *noun plural* a kind of writing which *slopes to the right like this*

itch *noun* **1** an irritating feeling in the skin, made better by scratching **2** a strong desire ■ *verb* **1** to have an itch **2** to be impatient (to do), long (to) ■ **itchy** *adjective*

item *noun* a separate article in a list

itemize *or* **itemise** *verb* to list in items

itinerant *adjective* travelling from place to place, especially on business

itinerary *noun* (*plural* **itineraries**) a route or plan of a journey

-itis *suffix, medicine* used to describe diseases which involve inflammation: *tonsillitis* (= inflammation of the tonsils)

its *adjective* belonging to it: *keep the hat in its box*

◆※ Do not confuse: **its** and **it's**. **Its**, meaning 'belonging to it', is spelt with no apostrophe ('). **It's** means 'it is' or 'it has'

it's short for it is *or* it has

itself *pronoun* **1** used reflexively: *the cat licked itself* **2** used for emphasis or contrast: *after I've read the introduction, I'll begin the book itself*

ivory *noun* (*plural* **ivories**) the hard white substance which forms the tusks of the elephant, walrus, *etc*

ivy *noun* (*plural* **ivies**) a creeping evergreen plant

jab *verb* **1** to prod (someone) **2** to strike with a quick punch ■ *noun* **1** a prod **2** *informal* an injection

jabber *verb* to talk rapidly and indistinctly

jack *noun* **1** a device with a lever for raising heavy weights **2** (*also called*: **knave**) the playing-card between ten and queen ■ **jack up** to raise with a jack

jackal *noun* a dog-like wild animal

jackass *noun* a male ass

jackdaw *noun* a type of small crow

jacket *noun* **1** a short coat **2** a loose paper cover for a book

jacket potato a baked potato

jack-in-the-box *noun* a doll fixed to a spring inside a box that leaps out when the lid is opened

jack-knife *verb* of a vehicle and its trailer: to swing together to form a sharp angle

jackpot *noun* a fund of prize money which increases until someone wins it

Jacobean *adjective, history* relating to the period of James VI of Scotland, I of England (1603–1625)

Jacobite *noun, history* a supporter of James VII of Scotland, II of England and his descendants

Jacuzzi *noun, trademark* a bath fitted with a device that agitates the water

jade *noun* a hard green mineral substance used for ornaments

jaded *adjective* tired

jagged *adjective* rough-edged, uneven

jaguar *noun* a S American animal like a leopard

jail *noun* a prison

jailer *noun* someone in charge of a jail or prisoners

Jain *noun* a member of an Indian religion similar to Buddhism ■ **Jainist** *noun & adjective*

jam *noun* **1** fruit boiled with sugar till it is set **2** a crush **3** a blockage caused by crowding **4** *informal* a difficult situation ■ *verb* **1** to press or squeeze tight **2** to crowd full **3** to stick and so be unable to move

jam *verb* ▶ jams, jamm*ing*, jamm*ed*

jamb *noun* the side post of a door

jamboree *noun* **1** a large, lively

gathering **2** a rally of Scouts
jammy *adjective* covered or filled with jam

| **jammy** ► **jammi**er, **jammi**est

jam-packed *adjective* packed tightly, congested
jangle *verb* to make a harsh ringing noise
janitor *noun* a caretaker
January *noun* the first month of the year
jape *noun, informal* a trick, a practical joke
jar *noun* a glass or earthenware bottle with a wide mouth ■ *verb* **1** to have a harsh, startling effect **2** to be in disagreement

| **jar** *verb* ► **jar**s, **jar**ring, **jar**red

jargon *noun* special words used within a particular trade, profession, *etc*
jarring *adjective* harsh, startling
jasmine *noun* a shrub with white or yellow sweet-smelling flowers
jaundice *noun* a disease which causes the skin and eyes to turn yellow
jaundiced *adjective* having jaundice
jaunt *noun* a short journey for pleasure
jaunty *adjective* cheerful
javelin *noun* a long spear for throwing
jaw *noun* the lower part of the face, including the mouth and chin
jay *noun* a brightly-coloured bird like a crow

jaywalker *noun* someone who walks carelessly among traffic
jazz *noun* a style of music with a strong rhythm, based on African-American folk music ■ **jazz something up** to make it more lively or colourful
jazzy *adjective* **1** resembling or containing certain elements of jazz **2** colourful, flamboyant
JCB *noun* a type of mobile digger used in the construction industry
jealous *adjective* **1** wanting to have what someone else has; envious **2** guarding closely (possessions *etc*) ■ **jealousy** *noun*
jeans *noun plural* denim trousers
Jeep *noun, trademark* a small army motor vehicle
jeer *verb* to make fun of, scoff ■ *noun* a scoff
Jehovah *noun* the Hebrew God of the Old Testament
jelly *noun* (*plural* **jellies**) **1** fruit juice boiled with sugar till it becomes firm **2** a transparent wobbly food, often fruit-flavoured
jellyfish *noun* a sea animal with a jelly-like body
jemmy *noun* (*plural* **jemmies**) a burglar's iron tool
jeopardize or **jeopardise** *verb* to put in danger or at risk
jeopardy *noun* danger
jerk *verb* to give a sudden sharp movement ■ *noun* a sudden sharp movement
jerkin *noun* a type of short coat
jerky *adjective* moving or

coming in jerks ∎ **jerkily** *adverb*

jersey *noun* (*plural* **jerseys**) a sweater, pullover

jest *noun* a joke ∎ *verb* to joke

jester *noun, history* a fool employed to amuse a royal court *etc*

jet *noun* **1** a hard black mineral, used for ornaments and jewellery **2** a spout of flame, air or liquid **3** a jet plane

jet-black *adjective* very black

jet lag tiredness caused by the body's inability to cope with being in a new time zone

jet plane an aeroplane driven by jet propulsion

jetsam *noun* goods thrown overboard and washed ashore

jettison *verb* to throw overboard

jetty *noun* (*plural* **jetties**) a small pier

Jew *noun* someone who is of the race or religion of the Israelites

jewel *noun* a precious stone

jeweller *or US* **jeweler** *noun* someone who makes or sells articles made of precious jewels and metals

jewellery *or US* **jewelry** *noun* articles made or sold by a jeweller

Jewish *adjective* of the Jews

jib *noun* **1** a three-cornered sail at the front of a ship **2** the jutting-out arm of a crane

jibe *or* **gibe** *verb* to jeer, scoff ∎ *noun* a jeer

jiffy *noun, informal* a moment

jig *noun* a lively dance or tune

jigsaw *or* **jigsaw puzzle** *noun* a puzzle consisting of many different-shaped pieces that fit together to form a picture

jihad (*pronounced* jee-**had**) *noun* an Islamic holy war

jilt *verb* to cast aside (a lover) after previously encouraging them

jingle *noun* **1** a clinking sound like that of coins **2** a simple rhyme

jinx *noun* someone or something thought to bring bad luck

jitters *noun plural*: **have the jitters** to be very nervous

jittery *adjective* very nervous, shaking with nerves

jive *noun* a type of fast dancing

job *noun* **1** someone's daily work **2** any piece of work

job centre a government office where information about available jobs is shown

jockey *noun* (*plural* **jockeys**) someone who rides a horse in a race

jocular *adjective* joking, merry ∎ **jocularity** *noun* ∎ **jocularly** *adverb*

jodhpurs *noun plural* riding breeches, fitting tightly from knee to ankle

jog *verb* **1** to nudge, push slightly **2** to run at a gentle pace ∎ *noun* a gentle run ∎ **jogging** *noun*

| **jog** *verb* ▶ jogs, jog*ging*, jog*ged*

jogger *noun* someone who runs gently to keep fit

joggle *verb* to shake slightly

join *verb* 1 to put or come together 2 to connect, fasten 3 to become a member of 4 to come and meet ■ *noun* the place where two or more things join

joiner *noun* someone who makes wooden fittings, furniture, *etc*

joint *noun* 1 the place where two or more things join 2 the place where two bones are joined, *eg* an elbow or knee 3 meat containing a bone ■ *adjective* 1 united 2 shared among more than one

jointly *adverb* together

joist *noun* the beam to which the boards of a floor or the laths of a ceiling are nailed

joke *noun* something said or done to cause laughter ■ *verb* to make a joke, tease

joker *noun* 1 someone who jokes 2 an extra playing-card in a pack

jolliness *noun* merriment

jolly *adjective* merry

jolt *verb* 1 to shake suddenly 2 to go forward with sudden jerks ■ *noun* a sudden jerk

jostle *verb* to push or knock against

jot *noun* a very small amount ■ *verb* to write down hurriedly or briefly

| **jot** *verb* ▶ jots, jot**ting**, jot**ted**

jotter *noun* a book for taking notes

joule *noun* a unit of energy

journal *noun* 1 a personal account of each day's events; a diary 2 a newspaper, a magazine

journalism *noun* the business of recording daily events for the media ■ **journalist** *noun*
■ **journalistic** *adjective*

journey *noun* (*plural* **journeys**) a distance travelled ■ *verb* to travel

journeyman *noun* someone whose apprenticeship is finished

joust *noun*, *history* the armed contest between two knights on horseback at a tournament ■ *verb* to fight on horseback at a tournament

jovial *adjective* cheerful, good-humoured ■ **joviality** *noun*

joy *noun* gladness

joyful or **joyous** *adjective* full of joy

joyless *adjective* dismal

joyride *noun* a reckless trip for amusement in a stolen car
■ **joyrider** *noun*

joystick *noun* a control-lever for something *eg* an aeroplane, an invalid car or a video game

jubilant *adjective* full of rejoicing, triumphant ■ **jubilation** *noun*

jubilee *noun* celebrations arranged for the anniversary of a coronation *etc*

Judaism *noun* the Jewish religion or way of life ■ **Judaic** *adjective*

judder *noun* a strong vibration or jerky movement

judge *verb* 1 to make a decision

on (a law case) after hearing all the evidence **2** to form an opinion **3** to decide the winners in a competition *etc* ▪ *noun* **1** an official who hears cases in the law-courts and decides on them according to the country's or state's laws **2** someone skilled in evaluating anything: *a good judge of character*

judgement *or* **judgment** *noun* **1** a decision in a law case **2** an opinion **3** good sense in forming opinions

judicial *adjective* of a judge or court of justice

judiciary *noun* the judges of a country or state

judicious *adjective* wise

judo *noun* a Japanese form of wrestling for self-defence

jug *noun* a dish for liquids, with a handle and a shaped lip for pouring

juggernaut *noun* a large articulated lorry

juggle *verb* to toss a number of things (balls, clubs, *etc*) into the air and catch them in order ▪ **juggler** *noun*

jugular vein the large vein at the side of the neck

juice *noun* the liquid in vegetables, fruits, *etc*

juicy *adjective* full of juice

jukebox *noun* a coin-operated machine which plays selected records automatically

July *noun* the seventh month of the year

jumble *verb* to throw together without order, muddle ▪ *noun* a confused mixture

jumble sale a sale of odds and ends, cast-off clothing, *etc*

jumbo *noun* (plural **jumbos**) **1** a child's name for an elephant **2** a jumbo jet ▪ *adjective* very large

jumbo jet a large jet aircraft

jump *verb* **1** to leap **2** to make a sudden startled movement **3** to pass over without spending time on: *jumped forward a few chapters* ▪ *noun* **1** a leap **2** a sudden start

jumper *noun* a sweater, a jersey

jumpy *adjective* easily startled

junction *noun* a place or point of joining, especially of roads or railway lines

juncture *noun* point: *it's too early to decide at this juncture*

June *noun* the sixth month of the year

jungle *noun* a dense growth of trees and plants in tropical areas

junior *adjective* **1** younger **2** in a lower class or rank ▪ *noun* someone younger: *he is my junior*

juniper *noun* an evergreen shrub with berries and prickly leaves

junk *noun* worthless articles; rubbish

junk food food that is easy to prepare but provides little nourishment

junkie or **junky** noun (plural junkies) slang a drug addict

junk mail unwanted mail, especially advertising material

jurisdiction noun a legal authority or power

juror noun someone who serves on a jury

jury noun (plural juries) a group of people selected to reach a decision on whether an accused prisoner is guilty or not

just adjective fair in judgement; unbiased ■ adverb 1 exactly: just right 2 not long since: only just arrived 3 merely, only ■ **justly** adverb

justice noun 1 fairness in making judgements 2 what is right or rightly deserved

Justice of the Peace a citizen who acts as a judge for certain matters

justifiable adjective able to be justified or defended ■ **justifiably** adverb

justification noun good reason

justify verb 1 to prove or show to be right or desirable 2 printing to make (text) form an even margin down the page

| justify ► justifies, justifying, justified

jut verb to stand or stick out

| jut ► juts, jutting, jutted

jute noun fibre from certain plants for making sacking, canvas, etc

juvenile adjective 1 young; of young people 2 childish ■ noun a young person

K k

kaftan *another spelling* of **caftan**

kaleidoscope *noun* a tube held to the eye and turned, so that loose, coloured shapes reflected in two mirrors change patterns

kamikaze *noun, history* a Japanese pilot trained to make a suicidal attack ■ *adjective* suicidal, self-destructive

kangaroo *noun* a large Australian animal with long hindlegs and great jumping power, the female carrying its young in a pouch on the front of her body

kaput *adjective, slang* broken, not working

karaoke *noun* an entertainment of singing well-known songs against pre-recorded backing music

karate *noun* a Japanese form of unarmed fighting using blows and kicks

karma *noun* in Buddhist belief, someone's destiny as determined by their actions in a previous life

kayak *noun* 1 an Inuit sealskin canoe 2 a lightweight canoe for one person, manoeuvred with a single paddle

kebab *noun* small pieces of meat or vegetables cooked on a skewer

kedgeree *noun* a dish made with rice, fish and hard-boiled eggs

keel *noun* the piece of a ship's frame that lies lengthways along the bottom ■ **keel over** to overturn, fall over

keen¹ *adjective* 1 eager, enthusiastic 2 very sharp; bitingly cold ■ **keenness** *noun*

keen² *verb* to wail in grief; lament

keenly *adverb* intensely, passionately, alertly

keep *verb* 1 to hold on to, not give or throw away 2 to look after; feed and clothe 3 to have or use 4 to fulfil (a promise) 5 to remain in a position or state 6 (also **keep on**) to continue (doing something) 7 of food: to stay in good condition ■ *noun* food, board ■ **keep out** 1 to exclude 2 to stay outside ■ **keep up** to go on with, continue ■ **keep up with** to go as fast *etc* as

| **keep** *verb* ▶ keeps, keeping, kept

keeper *noun* someone who looks after something: *zookeeper*

keeping *noun* care, charge ▪ **in keeping with** suitable for or fitting in with

keepsake *noun* a gift in memory of an occasion *etc*

keg *noun* a small cask or barrel

kelvin *noun* a measure of temperature

kennel *noun* **1** a hut for a dog **2 kennels** a place where dogs can be looked after

kept *past form* of keep

kerb *noun* the edge of something, especially a pavement

🖎 Do not confuse with: **curb**

kernel *noun* a soft edible substance in the shell of a nut, or inside the stone of a fruit

kerosene *noun* paraffin oil

kestrel *noun* a type of small falcon which hovers

ketchup *noun* a flavouring sauce made from tomatoes *etc*

kettle *noun* a pot with a spout for heating liquids

kettledrum *noun* a drum made of a metal bowl covered with stretched skin *etc*

key *noun* **1** a device which is turned in a corresponding hole to lock or unlock, tighten, tune, *etc* **2** a lever pressed on a piano *etc* to produce a note **3** a button on a typewriter or computer keyboard which is pressed to type letters **4** the chief note of a piece of music **5** something which explains a mystery or deciphers a code ▪ *verb* to type on a typewriter or computer ▪ *adjective* important, essential

keyboard *noun* **1** the keys in a piano or organ arranged along a flat board **2** the keys of a typewriter or computer **3** an electronic musical instrument with keys arranged as on a piano *etc*

keyhole *noun* the hole in which a key of a door is placed

keynote *noun* **1** the chief note of a piece of music **2** the chief point about anything

keypad *noun* a device with buttons that can be pushed to operate a television, telephone, *etc*

kg *abbreviation* kilogram(s); kilogramme(s)

khaki *adjective* greenish-brown in colour ▪ *noun* **1** greenish-brown **2** cloth of this colour used for military uniforms

kibbutz *noun* (*plural* **kibbutzim**) a farming settlement in Israel in which all share the work

kick *verb* to hit or strike out with the foot ▪ *noun* a blow with the foot

kick-off *noun* the start (of a football game)

kid *noun* **1** *informal* a child **2** a young goat **3** the skin of a young goat ▪ *adjective* made of kid leather ■ *verb, informal* **1** to fool or deceive **2** to pretend

kid *verb* ► kids, kidding, kidded

kidnap *verb* to carry (someone) off by force, often demanding money in exchange for their release ■ **kidnapper** *noun* ■ **kidnapping** *noun*

kidnap ► kidnaps, kidnapping, kidnapped

kidney *noun* (*plural* kidneys) either of a pair of organs in the lower back which filter waste from the blood and produce urine

kidney bean a bean with a curved shape like a kidney

kill *verb* to put to death ■ *noun* the act of killing ■ **killer** *noun*

killing *noun*: **make a killing** to make a lot of money quickly

kiln *noun* a large oven or furnace for baking pottery, bricks, *etc* or for drying grain, hops, *etc*

kilo- *prefix* a thousand: *kilogram/kilometre*

🔷* In computing terminology **kilo-** does not mean exactly 1000, but 1024 ($= 2^{10}$)

kilobyte *noun* a measure of computer data or memory, equal to 1024 bytes

🔷* See note at entry for prefix 'kilo-'

kilogram *or* **kilogramme** *noun* a measure of weight equal to 1000 grams

kilometre *noun* a measure of length equal to 1000 metres

kilowatt *noun* a measure of electrical power equal to 1000 watts

kilt *noun* a pleated tartan skirt reaching to the knee, part of traditional Scottish dress

kilter *noun*: **out of kilter** out of sequence, off balance

kimono *noun* (*plural* kimonos) a loose Japanese robe, fastened with a sash

kin *noun* members of the same family, relations ■ **next of kin** your nearest relative

kind[1] *noun* a sort, type

kind[2] *adjective* having good feelings towards others; generous, gentle ■ **kindness** *noun*

kindergarten *noun* a nursery school

kind-hearted *adjective* kind

kindle *verb* **1** to light a fire **2** to catch fire

kindling *noun* material for starting a fire

kindly *adverb* in a kind way ■ *adjective* kind, warm-hearted ■ **kindliness** *noun*

kindly *adjective* ► kindlier, kindliest

kindred *adjective* of the same sort; related: *a kindred spirit*

kinetic *adjective* of or expressing motion: *kinetic energy*

king *noun* **1** the inherited male

ruler of a nation **2** a playing-card with a picture of a king **3** the most important chess piece

kingdom *noun* **1** the area ruled by a king **2** any of the three major divisions of the natural world, *ie* animal, vegetable or mineral

kingfisher *noun* a type of fish-eating bird with brightly-coloured feathers

kingpin *noun* the most important person in an organization

king-size *adjective* of a larger than usual size

kink *noun* a bend or curl in a rope, hair, *etc*

kinky *adjective* twisted, contorted

| **kinky** ► kink*ier*, kink*iest*

kinsfolk *noun plural* relations, relatives

kinsman, kinswoman *noun* a close relation

kiosk *noun* **1** a small stall for the sale of papers, sweets, *etc* **2** a telephone box

kipper *noun* a smoked and dried herring

kiss *verb* **1** to touch lovingly with the lips **2** to touch gently ■ *noun* (*plural* **kisses**) an affectionate touch with the lips ■ **the kiss of life** a method of restoring breathing by blowing into the person's mouth

kit *noun* an outfit of clothes, tools, *etc* necessary for a particular job

kitchen *noun* a room where food is cooked

kite *noun* **1** a light frame, covered with paper or other material, for flying in the air **2** a four-sided figure, with two pairs of equal sides that are not parallel

kitten *noun* a young cat

kitty[1] *noun* (*plural* **kitties**) a sum of money set aside for a purpose

kitty[2] *noun* (*plural* **kitties**) *informal* a cat or kitten

kiwi *noun* a fast-running almost wingless bird of New Zealand

kiwi fruit an edible fruit with a thin hairy skin and bright green flesh

kleptomania *noun* an uncontrollable desire to steal
■ **kleptomaniac** *noun & adjective*

km *abbreviation* kilometre(s)

knack *noun* a special talent

knapsack *noun* a bag for food, clothes, *etc* slung on the back

knave *noun* **1** a cheating rogue **2** in playing-cards, the jack

knead *verb* to work (dough *etc*) by pressing with the fingers

knee *noun* the joint at the bend of the leg

kneecap *noun* the flat round bone on the front of the knee joint

kneel *verb* to go down on one or both knees

| **kneel** ► kneel*s*, kneel*ing*, knelt

knew *past form* of **know**

knickerbockers *noun plural*

loose breeches tucked in at the knee

knickers *noun plural* women's or girls' underpants

knick-knack *noun* a small, ornamental article

knife *noun* (*plural* **knives**) a tool for cutting

knight *noun* **1** *history* an aristocrat trained to use arms **2** a rank, with the title *Sir*, which is not inherited by a son **3** a piece used in chess ■ *verb* to raise to the rank of knight

knighthood *noun* the rank of a knight

knit *verb* **1** to form a garment from yarn or thread by making a series of knots using knitting needles **2** to join closely

| **knit** ► knits, knitt*ing*, knitt*ed*

knitting *noun* work done by knitting

knob *noun* **1** a small rounded projection **2** a round door-handle

knock *verb* **1** to strike, hit **2** to drive or be driven against **3** to tap on a door to have it opened ■ *noun* **1** a sudden stroke **2** a tap (on a door) ■ **knock back** *informal* to eat or drink greedily ■ **knock down 1** to demolish **2** *informal* to reduce in price ■ **knock off** *informal* to stop work for the day ■ **knock out** to hit (someone) hard enough to make them unconscious ■ **knock up 1** to put together hastily **2** to knock on someone's door to wake them up

knocker *noun* a hinged weight on a door for knocking with

knock-kneed *adjective* having knees that touch in walking

knoll *noun* a small rounded hill

knot *noun* **1** a hard lump, *eg* one made by tying string, or found in wood at the join between trunk and branch **2** a tangle **3** a measure of speed for ships (about 1.85 kilometre per hour) ■ *verb* to tie in a knot

| **knot** *verb* ► knots, knott*ing*, knott*ed*

knotted *adjective* full of knots

knotty (*pronounced* not-i) *adjective* **1** having knots **2** difficult, complicated: *a knotty problem*

| **knotty** ► knottier, knottiest

know *verb* **1** to be aware or sure of **2** to recognize

| **know** ► knows, know*ing*, knew, known

knowing *adjective* clever; cunning

knowingly *adverb* **1** intentionally **2** in a way that shows you understand something which is secret or which has not been directly expressed

knowledge *noun* **1** that which is known **2** information **3** ability, skill

knowledgeable *adjective*

showing or having knowledge

known *past participle* of **know**

knuckle *noun* a joint of the fingers ∎ **knuckle under** to give in, yield

knuckle-duster *noun* a metal covering worn on the knuckles as a weapon

koala *noun* an Australian tree-climbing animal resembling a small bear

kookaburra *another word* for **laughing jackass**

Koran *noun* the sacred book of Islam

kosher *adjective* pure and clean according to Jewish law

kowtow *verb* to act with excessive respect

krypton *noun* an inert gas present in the air, used in fluorescent lighting

kudos (*pronounced* **kyood**-os) *noun* fame, glory

kung-fu *noun* a Chinese form of self-defence

L

lab *noun, informal* a laboratory

label *noun* a small written note fixed onto something listing its contents, price, *etc* ■ *verb* **1** to fix a label to **2** to call something by a certain name

label *verb* ▶ labels, label*ling*, label*led*

laboratory *noun* (*plural* **laboratories**) a place where scientific experiments are performed

laborious *adjective* requiring hard work; wearisome

labour *or US* **labor** *noun* **1** hard work **2** workers on a job **3** the process of childbirth ■ *verb* to work hard to move slowly or with difficulty

laboured *adjective* showing signs of effort

labourer *noun* someone who does heavy unskilled work

Labour Party one of the chief political parties of Great Britain, which has the aim of representing the working people and achieving greater social equality

labrador *noun* a large black or fawn-coloured dog, often used for retrieving game after it has been shot

laburnum *noun* a tree with large clusters of yellow flowers and poisonous seeds

labyrinth *noun* a maze

lace *noun* **1** a cord for fastening shoes *etc* **2** decorative fabric made with fine thread ■ *verb* to fasten with a lace

lack *verb* **1** to be in want **2** to be without ■ *noun* want, need

lackadaisical *adjective* bored, half-hearted

lackey *noun* (*plural* **lackeys**) **1** a male personal servant **2** someone who acts like a slave

lacklustre *or US* **lackluster** *adjective* dull, insipid

lacquer *noun* a varnish ■ *verb* to varnish

lacrosse *noun* a twelve-a-side ball game played with sticks having a shallow net at the end

lad *noun* a boy, a youth

ladder *noun* **1** a set of rungs or steps between two supports, for climbing up or down **2** damage to a stocking *etc* caused by a broken stitch

laden *adjective* loaded, burdened

ladies *noun singular* a women's public toilet

ladle *noun* a large spoon for lifting out liquid ▪ *verb* to lift with a ladle

lady *noun* (*plural* **ladies**) **1** a woman of good manners **2** a title for the wife of a knight, lord or baronet, or a daughter of a member of the aristocracy

ladybird *noun* a small beetle, usually red with black spots

ladyship *noun* used in talking to or about a titled lady: *your ladyship*

lag *verb* **1** to move slowly and fall behind **2** to cover (a boiler or pipes) with a warm covering ▪ *noun* a delay

| **lag** *verb* ▶ lags, lagging, lagged

lager *noun* a light beer

laggard *noun* someone who lags behind

lagging *noun* material for covering pipes *etc*

lagoon *noun* a shallow stretch of water separated from the sea by low sandbanks, rocks, *etc*

laid *past form of* lay¹

laid-back *adjective*, *informal* relaxed, easy-going

laid-up *adjective* ill in bed

lain *past participle of* lie²

lair *noun* the den of a wild beast

♦* Do not confuse with: **layer**

lake *noun* a large stretch of water surrounded by land

lamb *noun* **1** a young sheep **2** the meat of this animal

lambast *verb* to beat or reprimand severely

lame *adjective* **1** unable to walk **2** not very convincing or impressive: *a lame excuse* ▪ *verb* to make lame ▪ **lamely** *adverb*

lame duck an inefficient, useless person or organization

lament (*pronounced* la-ment) *verb* to mourn, feel or express grief for ▪ *noun* a mournful poem or piece of music

lamentable *adjective* **1** pitiful **2** very bad

laminated *adjective* made by putting layers together: *laminated glass*

lamp *noun* a device to give out light, containing an electric bulb, candle, *etc*

lampoon *noun* a piece of ridicule or satire directed at someone ▪ *verb* to make (someone) the target of ridicule or satire

lamppost *noun* a pillar supporting a street lamp

lamprey *noun* (*plural* **lampreys**) a type of fish like an eel

lance *noun* a long shaft of wood with a pointed metal end ▪ *verb* to cut open (a boil *etc*) with a knife

lance-corporal *noun* a soldier with rank just below a corporal

lancet *noun* a sharp surgical instrument

land *noun* 1 the solid portion of the earth's surface 2 ground 3 soil ■ *verb* 1 to arrive on land or on shore 2 to set (an aircraft, ship, *etc*) on land or on shore

landing *noun* 1 a coming ashore or to ground 2 the level part of a staircase between the flights of steps

landlocked *adjective* almost or completely shut in by land

landlord, **landlady** *noun* 1 the owner of land or accommodation for rent 2 the owner or manager of an inn *etc*

landlubber *noun* someone who works on land and knows little about the sea

landmark *noun* 1 an object on land that serves as a guide 2 an important event

land mine a bomb laid on or near the surface of the ground which explodes when someone passes over it

landscape *noun* 1 an area of land and the features it contains 2 a painting, photograph, *etc* of inland scenery

landslide *noun* a mass of land that slips down from the side of a hill

lane *noun* 1 a narrow street or passage 2 a part of the road, sea or air to which cars, ships, aircraft, *etc* must keep

language *noun* 1 human speech 2 the speech of a particular people or nation

languid *adjective* lacking liveliness

languish *verb* 1 to grow weak, droop 2 to pine: *the dog was languishing for its master*

languor *noun* a languid state, listlessness

lank *adjective* of hair: straight and limp

lanky *adjective* tall and thin

lantern *noun* a case for holding or carrying a light

lap *verb* 1 to lick up with the tongue 2 to wash or flow against 3 **lap up** to accept (praise *etc*) greedily ■ *noun* 1 the front part, from waist to knees, of someone seated 2 one round of a racecourse

| **lap** *verb* ► laps, lap**ping**, lap**ped** |

lapel *noun* the part of a coat joined to the collar and folded back on the chest

lapse *verb* 1 to fall into bad habits 2 to cease, be no longer valid ■ *noun* 1 a mistake, a failure 2 a period of time passing

laptop *noun* a compact portable computer combining screen, keyboard and processor in one unit

lapwing *noun* a type of bird of the plover family (*also called*: **peewit**)

larceny *noun* stealing, theft

larch *noun* (*plural* **larches**) a cone-bearing deciduous tree

lard *noun* the melted fat of a pig

larder *noun* **1** a room or place where food is kept **2** a stock of food

large *adjective* great in size, amount, *etc*

largely *adverb* mainly, to a great extent

largesse *noun* a generous giving away of money *etc*

lark *noun* **1** a general name for several kinds of singing bird **2** a piece of fun or mischief ▪ *verb* to fool about, behave mischievously

larva *noun* (*plural* **larvae**) an insect in its first stage after coming out of the egg, a grub

laryngitis *noun* inflammation of the larynx

larynx *noun* (*plural* **larynxes** or **larynges**) the upper part of the windpipe containing the vocal cords

lasagne *noun plural* flat sheets of pasta ▪ *noun singular* (also **lasagna**) a baked dish made with these

lascivious *adjective* lustful; indecent

laser *noun* **1** a very narrow powerful beam of light **2** an instrument that concentrates light into such a beam

lash *noun* (*plural* **lashes**) **1** a thong or cord of a whip **2** a stroke with a whip **3** an eyelash ▪ *verb* to strike with a whip ▪ **lash out 1** to kick or swing out without

thinking **2** to speak angrily **3** to spend extravagantly

lass *noun* (*plural* **lasses**) a girl

lasso *noun* (*plural* **lassoes** or **lassos**) a long rope with a loop that tightens when the rope is pulled, used for catching wild horses *etc*

last *adjective* **1** coming after all the others **2** the final one remaining **3** most recent: *my last employer* ▪ *adverb* **1** after all others **2** most recently **3** lastly ▪ *verb* **1** to continue, go on **2** to remain in good condition

lastly *adverb* finally

latch *noun* (*plural* **latches**) **1** a wooden or metal catch used to fasten a door **2** a light door-lock

late *adjective & adverb* **1** coming after the expected time **2** far on in time: *it's getting late* **3** recent **4** dead ▪ **lateness** *noun*

lately *adverb* recently

latent *adjective* hidden, undeveloped as yet: *latent ability*

lateral *adjective* of, at, to or from the side

latex *noun* the milky juice of plants, especially of the rubber tree

lathe *noun* a machine for turning and shaping articles of wood, metal, *etc*

lather *noun* a foam or froth, *eg* from soap and water ▪ *verb* to cover with lather

Latin *noun* the language of ancient Rome

latitude *noun* the distance,

measured in degrees, of a place north or south of the equator (*compare with*: **longitude**)

latrine *noun* a toilet in a camp, army barracks, *etc*

latter *adjective* (*contrasted with*: **former**) the last of two things mentioned: *between working and sleeping, I prefer the latter*

latter-day *adjective* of recent times

latterly *adverb* recently

lattice *noun* a network of crossed wooden *etc* strips

laudable *adjective* worthy of being praised ▪ **laudably** *adverb*

laugh *verb* to make sounds with the voice in showing amusement, scorn, *etc* ▪ *noun* the sound of laughing

laughable *adjective* comical, ridiculous

laughing jackass the Australian giant kingfisher (*also called*: **kookaburra**)

laughing stock an object of scornful laughter

laughter *noun* the act or noise of laughing

launch *verb* 1 to slide a boat or ship into water, especially on its first voyage 2 to fire off (a rocket *etc*) 3 to start off on a course 4 to put (a product) on the market with publicity 5 to throw, hurl ▪ *noun* (*plural* **launches**) 1 the act of launching 2 a large motor boat

launch pad the area for launching a spacecraft or missile

launder *verb* to wash and iron clothes *etc*

launderette *noun* a shop where customers may wash clothes *etc* in washing machines

laundry *noun* (*plural* **laundries**) 1 a place where clothes are washed 2 clothes to be washed

laurel *noun* the bay tree, from which ceremonial wreaths were made

lava *noun* molten rock *etc* thrown out by a volcano, becoming solid as it cools

lavatory *noun* (*plural* **lavatories**) a toilet

lavender *noun* 1 a sweet-smelling plant with small pale-purple flowers 2 a pale-purple colour

lavish *verb* to spend or give very freely ▪ *adjective* very generous

law *noun* 1 the official rules that apply in a country or state 2 one such rule 3 a scientific rule stating the conditions under which certain things always happen

law-abiding *adjective* obeying the law

lawful *adjective* allowed by law ▪ **lawfully** *adverb*

lawless *adjective* paying no attention to, and not observing, the laws

lawn *noun* an area of smooth grass, *eg* as part of a garden

lawnmower *noun* a machine for cutting grass

lawsuit *noun* a quarrel or dispute to be settled by a court of law

lawyer *noun* someone whose work it is to give advice in matters of law

lax *adjective* **1** not strict **2** careless, negligent

lay¹ *verb* **1** to place or set down **2** to put (eg a burden, duty) on (someone) **3** to set in order, arrange: *lay a trap* **4** of a hen: to produce eggs ∎ **lay down** to assert: *laying down the law* ∎ **lay off 1** to dismiss (workers) temporarily **2** *informal* to stop ∎ **lay up** to store for future use

│**lay** ► lays, laying, laid

◆* Do not confuse with: **lie**. It may help to remember that the verb **lay** always takes an object, while an object is not used with the verb **lie**

lay² *adjective* **1** not of the clergy **2** without special training in a particular subject

layabout *noun* a lazy idle person

lay-by *noun* a parking area at the side of a road

layer *noun* a thickness forming a covering or level

◆* Do not confuse with: **lair**. Layer comes from the verb 'to lay'

layman *noun* a man without special training in a subject

layout *noun* the way something, *eg* a printed page, is arranged

laze *verb* to be lazy; idle

lazy *adjective* not inclined to work; idle ∎ **lazily** *adverb*

│**lazy** ► lazier, laziest

lazybones *noun*, *informal* an idler

lb *abbreviation* pound(s) (in weight)

lead¹ (*pronounced* leed) *verb* **1** to show the way by going first **2** to direct, guide **3** to live (a busy, quiet, *etc* life) **4** of a road: to go (to) ∎ *noun* **1** the first or front place **2** a leash for a dog *etc*

│**lead** *verb* ► leads, leading, led

lead² (*pronounced* led) *noun* **1** a soft bluish-grey metal **2** the part of a pencil that writes, really made of graphite **3** a weight used for finding depths at sea *etc*

leaden *adjective* **1** made of lead **2** lead-coloured **3** dull, heavy

leader *noun* someone who leads or goes first; a chief

leadership *noun* **1** the state of being a leader **2** the ability to lead

lead-free *adjective* of petrol: containing no lead

leaf *noun* (*plural* **leaves**) **1** a part of a plant growing from the side of a stem **2** a page of a book **3** a hinged flap on a table *etc*

leaflet *noun* a small printed sheet

leafy *adjective* **1** of a plant or tree: having a lot of leaves **2** of a place:

having a lot of trees and plants

league *noun* **1** a union of people, nations, *etc* for the benefit of each other **2** an association of clubs for games

leak *noun* **1** a hole through which liquid passes **2** an escape of gas *etc* **3** a release of secret information ■ *verb* **1** to escape, pass out **2** to give (secret information) to the media *etc*

leakage *noun* a leaking

lean *verb* **1** to slope over to one side **2** to rest (against) ■ *adjective* **1** thin **2** of meat: not fat

| **lean** *verb* ▶ lea**ns**, lea**ning**, lea**nt**

leap *verb* **1** to move with jumps **2** to jump (over) ■ *noun* a jump

| **leap** *verb* ▶ lea**ps**, lea**ping**, lea**pt**

leapfrog *noun* a game in which one player leaps over another's bent back

leap year a year which has 366 days (February having 29), occurring every fourth year

learn *verb* **1** to get to know (something) **2** to gain skill

| **learn** ▶ lear**ns**, lear**ning**, lear**nt** or lear**ned**

learned (*pronounced* ler-nid) *adjective* having or showing great knowledge

learner *noun* someone who is learning something

learning *noun* knowledge

lease *noun* **1** an agreement

giving the use of a house *etc* in return for payment of rent **2** the period of this agreement ■ *verb* to let or rent

leash *noun* (*plural* leashes) a lead by which a dog *etc* is held

least *adjective* the smallest amount of anything ■ *adverb* (often **the least**) the smallest or lowest degree

leather *noun* the skin of an animal, prepared by tanning for use

leathery *adjective* like leather; tough

leave *noun* **1** permission to do something (*eg* to be absent) **2** a holiday ■ *verb* **1** to allow to remain **2** to abandon, forsake **3** to depart (from) **4** to hand down to someone in a will **5** to give over to someone's responsibility, care, *etc*: *leave the choice to her*

| **leave** *verb* ▶ lea**ves**, lea**ving**, **left**

leavened *adjective* raised with yeast

lecher *noun* a lustful man

lecherous *adjective* lustful ■ **lechery** *noun*

lectern *noun* a stand for a book to be read from

lecture *noun* **1** a formal talk on a certain subject given to an audience **2** a scolding ■ *verb* **1** to deliver a lecture **2** to scold

lecturer *noun* someone who lectures, especially to students

led *past form* of **lead**[1]

ledge noun a shelf or projecting rim

ledger noun the accounts book of an office or shop

lee noun the side away from the wind; the sheltered side

leech noun (plural **leeches**) a kind of blood-sucking worm

leek noun a long green and white vegetable of the onion family

leer noun a sly, sidelong or lustful look ■ verb to look sideways or lustfully (at)

leeway noun room to manoeuvre, latitude

left[1] adjective on or of the side of the body that in most people has the less skilful hand (contrasted with: **right**) ■ adverb on or towards the left side ■ noun 1 the left side 2 a political grouping with left-wing ideas etc

left[2] past form of **leave**

left-click verb to press and release the left-hand button on a computer mouse

left-handed adjective using the left hand rather than the right

left-wing adjective of or holding socialist or radical political views, ideas, etc

leg noun 1 one of the limbs by which humans and animals walk 2 a long slender support for a table etc 3 one stage in a journey, contest, etc

legacy noun (plural **legacies**) 1 something which is left by will 2 something left behind by the previous occupant of a house, job, etc

legal adjective 1 allowed by law, lawful 2 of law

legality noun (plural **legalities**) the state of being legal

legalize or **legalise** verb to make lawful

legate noun an ambassador, especially from the Pope

legend noun 1 a traditional story handed down, a myth 2 a caption

legendary adjective 1 of legend; famous 2 not to be believed

leggings noun plural close-fitting trousers for women

leggy adjective having long legs

legible adjective able to be read easily ■ **legibility** noun

legion noun 1 history a body of from three to six thousand Roman soldiers 2 a very great number

legionary noun (plural **legionaries**) a soldier of a legion

Legionnaires' disease a serious disease, similar to pneumonia, caused by a bacterium

legislate verb to make laws ■ **legislation** noun

legislative adjective law-making

legislator noun someone who makes laws

legislature noun the part of the government which has the powers of making laws

legitimate adjective 1 lawful

2 of a child: born of parents married to each other **3** correct, reasonable ▪ **legitimacy** *noun*

leisure *noun* time free from work, spare time

leisurely *adjective* unhurried

lemming *noun* **1** a small rat-like animal of the Arctic regions, said to follow others of its kind over sea cliffs *etc* when migrating **2** someone who follows others unquestioningly

lemon *noun* **1** an oval fruit with pale yellow rind and sour juice **2** the tree that bears this fruit

lemonade *noun* a soft drink flavoured with lemons

lemur *noun* an animal related to the monkey but with a pointed nose

lend *verb* **1** to give use of (something) for a time **2** to give, add (a quality) to someone or something: *his presence lent an air of respectability* ▪ **lend itself to** to be suitable for, adapt easily to

| **lend** ► lends, lending, lent

length *noun* **1** extent from end to end in space or time **2** the quality of being long **3** a great extent **4** a piece of cloth *etc*

lengthen *verb* to make or grow longer

lengthways *or* **lengthwise** *adverb* in the direction of the length

lengthy *adjective* **1** long **2** tiresomely long

lenient *adjective* merciful,

punishing only lightly ▪ **lenience** *or* **leniency** *noun*

lens *(plural* **lenses***)* **1** a piece of glass curved on one or both sides, used in spectacles, cameras, *etc* **2** a part of the eye

Lent *noun* in the Christian Church, a period of fasting before Easter lasting forty days

lent *past form of* **lend**

lentil *noun* the seed of a pod-bearing plant, used in soups *etc*

leopard *noun* an animal of the cat family with a spotted skin

leotard *noun* a tight-fitting garment worn for dancing, gymnastics, *etc*

leper *noun* **1** someone with leprosy **2** an outcast

leprechaun *noun* a creature in Irish folklore

leprosy *noun* a contagious skin disease causing thickening or numbness in the skin

lesion *noun* a wound

less *adjective* **1** not as much: *less time* **2** smaller: *a number less than 40* ▪ *adverb* not as much, to a smaller extent: *less often* ▪ *noun* a smaller amount: *he has less than I have* ▪ *preposition* minus: *5 less 2 equals 3*

lessen *verb* to make smaller

lesser *adjective* smaller

lesson *noun* **1** something which is learned or taught **2** a part of the Bible read in church **3** a period of teaching

lest *conjunction* for fear that, in case

let *verb* 1 to allow 2 to grant use of (*eg* a house, shop, farm) in return for payment ■ **let down** to fail to act as expected, disappoint ■ **let off** to excuse, not punish ■ **let up** to become less

| **let** ▶ lets, lett*ing*, let

lethal *adjective* causing death

lethargy *noun* a lack of energy or interest; sleepiness ■ **lethargic** *adjective*

let's *short for* let us

letter *noun* 1 a mark expressing a sound 2 a written message

lettering *noun* letters which have been drawn or painted, usually in a particular style

lettuce *noun* a kind of green plant whose leaves are used in a salad

leukaemia *or US* **leukemia** *noun* a cancerous disease of the white blood cells in the body

level *noun* 1 a flat, smooth surface 2 a height, position, *etc* in comparison with some standard: *water level* 3 an instrument for showing whether a surface is level: *spirit level* 4 personal rank or degree of understanding: *a bit above my level* ■ *adjective* 1 flat, even, smooth 2 horizontal ■ *verb* 1 to make flat, smooth or horizontal 2 to make equal

| **level** *verb* ▶ levels, level*ling*, level*led*

level crossing a place where a road crosses a railway track

level-headed *adjective* having good sense

lever *noun* 1 a bar of metal, wood, *etc* used to raise or shift something heavy 2 a handle for operating a machine

leverage *noun* 1 the use of a lever 2 power, influence

leveret *noun* a young hare

levitate *verb* to float in the air

levitation *noun* the illusion of raising a heavy body in the air without support

levy *verb* to collect by order (*eg* a tax, army conscripts) ■ *noun* (*plural* **levies**) money, troops, *etc* collected by order

| **levy** *verb* ▶ levies, levy*ing*, levi*ed*

lewd *adjective* taking pleasure in indecent thoughts or acts

liability *noun* (*plural* **liabilities**) 1 legal responsibility 2 a disadvantage

liable *adjective* 1 legally responsible (for) 2 likely or apt (to do something or happen)

liaise (*pronounced* lee-**eiz**) *verb* to make a connection (with), be in touch (with)

liaison (*pronounced* lee-**eiz**-on) *noun* contact, communication

liar *noun* someone who tells lies

lib *noun, informal* liberation: *women's lib*

libel *noun* something written to hurt another's reputation ■ *verb* to write something libellous about

libel *verb* ▶ libels, libell*ing*, libell*ed*

libellous *adjective* containing a written false statement which hurts a person's reputation

liberal *adjective* generous; broad-minded, tolerant ▪ *noun* (**Liberal**) a member of the former Liberal Party, which supported social and political reform

Liberal Democrats one of the chief political parties of Great Britain, formed in 1988 from the Liberal Party and the Social Democratic Party

liberate *verb* to set free ▪ **liberation** *noun*

liberty *noun* (*plural* **liberties**) freedom, especially of speech or action ▪ **take liberties** to behave rudely or impertinently

librarian *noun* a person employed in or in charge of a library

library *noun* (*plural* **libraries**) **1** a collection of books, records, *etc* **2** a building or room housing these

libretto *noun* (*plural* **libretti** or **librettos**) the words of an opera, musical show, *etc*

lice *plural* of **louse**

licence *noun* a form giving permission to do something, *eg* to keep a television set, drive a car, *etc*

◆* Do not confuse: **licence** and **license**. Licence/license and practice/practise follow the same pattern: you spell the verbs with an S (**licenSe, practiSe**), and the nouns with a C (**licenCe, practiCe**)

license *verb* to permit

licensee *noun* someone to whom a licence is given

lichen (*pronounced* **laik**-en) *noun* a large group of moss-like plants that grow on rocks *etc*

lick *verb* **1** to pass the tongue over **2** of flames: to reach up, touch ▪ *noun* **1** the act of licking **2** a tiny amount

licorice *another spelling of* **liquorice**

lid *noun* **1** a cover for a box, pot, *etc* **2** the cover of the eye

lie¹ *noun* a false statement meant to deceive ▪ *verb* to tell a lie

lie¹ *verb* ▶ lies, ly*ing*, lie*d*

lie² *verb* to rest in a flat position

lie² ▶ lies, ly*ing*, lay, lain

◆* Do not confuse with: **lay**. It may help to remember that an object is not used with the verb **lie**, while the verb **lay** always takes an object

lieutenant (*pronounced* lef-**ten**-ant *or US* loo-**ten**-ant) *noun* **1** an army officer below a captain **2** in the navy, an officer below a lieutenant-commander **3** a rank below a higher officer: *lieutenant-colonel*

life *noun* (*plural* **lives**) **1** the period between birth and death **2** the state of being alive

3 liveliness **4** manner of living

lifebelt *noun* a ring made of cork or filled with air for keeping someone afloat

lifeboat *noun* a boat for rescuing people in difficulties at sea

lifebuoy *noun* a float to support someone awaiting rescue at sea

life cycle the various stages through which a living thing passes

lifeguard *noun* an expert swimmer employed to save people in danger of drowning

life jacket a buoyant jacket for keeping someone afloat in water

lifeless *adjective* **1** dead **2** not lively, spiritless

lifelike *adjective* like a living person

lifeline *noun* a vital means of communication

lifelong *adjective* lasting the length of a life

life-size *adjective* full size, as in life

lifespan *noun* the length of someone's life

lifestyle *noun* the way in which someone lives

lifetime *noun* the period during which someone is alive

lift *verb* **1** to raise, take up **2** of fog: to disappear, disperse ▪ *noun* **1** a moving platform carrying goods or people between floors in a large building **2** a ride in someone's car *etc*

lift-off *noun* the take-off of a rocket, spacecraft, *etc*

ligament *noun* a tough substance that connects the bones of the body

light[1] *noun* **1** the brightness given by the sun, moon, lamps, *etc* that makes things visible **2** a source of light, *eg* a lamp **3** a flame on a cigarette lighter
▪ *adjective* **1** bright **2** of a colour: pale **3** having light, not dark
▪ *verb* **1** to give light to **2** to set fire to

| **light** *verb* ► lights, light*ing*, lit or light*ed*

light[2] *adjective* **1** not heavy **2** easy to bear or do: *light work* **3** easy to digest **4** nimble **5** lively **6** not grave, cheerful **7** not serious: *light reading* **8** of rain *etc*: little in quantity

lighten *verb* **1** to make less heavy **2** to make or become brighter

lighter *noun* a device with a flame *etc* for lighting

light-fingered *adjective* apt to steal

light-headed *adjective* dizzy

light-hearted *adjective* cheerful

lighthouse *noun* a tower-like building with a flashing light to warn or guide ships

lighting *noun* **1** a means of providing light **2** the combination of lights used, *eg* in a theatre or a disco

lightly *adverb* **1** gently **2** not seriously

lightning *noun* an electric flash in the clouds

lightning conductor a metal rod on a building *etc* which conducts electricity down to earth

lightweight *noun* a weight category in boxing

light-year *noun* the distance light travels in a year (6 billion miles)

like [1] *adjective* the same as or similar to ■ *adverb* in the same way as ■ *noun* something or someone that is the equal of another: *you won't see her like again*

like [2] *verb* **1** to be pleased with **2** to be fond of

likeable *or* **likable** *adjective* attractive, lovable

likelihood *noun* probability

likely *adjective* **1** probable **2** liable (to do something) ■ *adverb* probably

liken *verb* to think of as similar, compare

likeness *noun* **1** similarity, resemblance **2** a portrait, photograph, *etc* of someone

likewise *adverb* **1** in the same way **2** also

liking *noun* **1** fondness **2** satisfaction: *to my liking*

lilac *noun* a small tree with hanging clusters of pale purple or white flowers ■ *adjective* of pale purple colour

lilt *noun* a striking rhythm or

swing ■ *verb* to have this rhythm

lily *noun* (*plural* **lilies**) a tall plant grown from a bulb with large white or coloured flowers

lily-of-the-valley *noun* a plant with small white bell-shaped flowers

limb *noun* a leg or arm

limber *adjective* easily bent, supple ■ **limber up** to exercise so as to become supple

limbo [1] *noun* a place at the border of Hell, reserved for those unbaptized before death ■ **in limbo** forgotten, neglected

limbo [2] *noun* a W Indian dance in which the dancer passes under a low bar

lime *noun* **1** (*also called*: quicklime) a white, lumpy powder of calcium oxide, used in making glass and cement **2** a tree related to the lemon **3** the greenish-yellow fruit of this tree

limelight *noun* the glare of publicity

limerick *noun* a type of humorous poetry in five-line verses

limestone *noun* white, grey or black rock consisting mainly of calcium carbonate

limit *noun* **1** the farthest point or place **2** a boundary **3** the largest (or smallest) extent, degree, *etc* **4** a restriction ■ *verb* to set or keep to a limit

limitation *noun* **1** something which limits **2** a weak point, a flaw

limousine *noun* a kind of large car, especially one with a separate compartment for the driver

limp *adjective* 1 not stiff, floppy 2 weak ▪ *verb* to walk lamely ▪ *noun* 1 the act of limping 2 a limping walk

limpet *noun* a small cone-shaped shellfish that clings to rocks

limpid *adjective* clear, transparent

linchpin *noun* a pin-shaped rod used to keep a wheel on an axle

line *noun* 1 a cord, rope, *etc* 2 a long thin stroke or mark 3 a wrinkle 4 a row of people, printed words, *etc* 5 a service of ships or aircraft 6 a railway 7 a telephone connection 8 a short letter 9 a family from generation to generation 10 course, direction 11 a subject of interest, activity, *etc* 12 lines army trenches 13 lines a written school punishment exercise ▪ *verb* 1 to mark out with lines 2 (often **line up**) to place in a row or alongside of 3 to form lines along (a street) 4 to cover on the inside

lineage *noun* ancestors

linear *adjective* of lines

line graph a chart or graph which uses horizontal or vertical lines to show amounts

linen *noun* 1 cloth made of flax 2 articles made of linen: *bedlinen*

liner *noun* a ship or aeroplane working on a regular service

linesman, lineswoman *noun* an umpire at a boundary line

linger *verb* 1 to stay for a long time or for longer than expected 2 to loiter, delay

lingerie *noun* women's underwear

linguist *noun* 1 someone skilled in languages 2 someone who studies language

linguistic *adjective* to do with language

linguistics *noun singular* the scientific study of languages and of language in general

liniment *noun* an oil or ointment rubbed into the skin to cure stiffness in the muscles, joints, *etc*

lining *noun* a covering on the inside

link *noun* 1 a ring of a chain 2 a single part of a series 3 anything connecting two things 4 a hyperlink ▪ *verb* 1 to connect with a link 2 to join closely

links *noun plural* a seaside golf course

linnet *noun* a small songbird of the finch family

lino *noun, informal* linoleum

linoleum *noun* a type of smooth, hard-wearing covering for floors

linseed *noun* flax seed

linseed oil oil from flax seed

lint *noun* 1 a soft woolly material for putting over wounds 2 fine pieces of fluff

lintel noun a timber or stone over a doorway or window

lion noun a powerful animal of the cat family, the male of which has a shaggy mane

lioness noun a female lion

lip noun 1 either of the two fleshy flaps in front of the teeth forming the rim of the mouth 2 the edge of a container etc

lip-reading noun reading what someone says from the movement of their lips

lipstick noun a stick of red, pink, etc colouring for the lips

liquefy verb to make or become liquid

| **liquefy** ► lique**fies**, lique**fying**, lique**fied**

liqueur (pronounced lik-**yoor**) noun a strong alcoholic drink, strongly flavoured and sweet

♦* Do not confuse with: liquor

liquid noun a flowing, water-like substance ■ adjective 1 flowing 2 looking like water

liquidate verb to close down, wind up the affairs of (a bankrupt business company) ■ **liquidation** noun ■ **liquidator** noun

liquidize or **liquidise** verb 1 to make liquid 2 to make into a purée **liquidizer** or **liquidiser** noun a machine for liquidizing

liquor (pronounced **lik**-er) noun an alcoholic drink, especially a spirit (eg whisky)

♦* Do not confuse with: liqueur

liquorice or **licorice** noun 1 a plant with a sweet-tasting root 2 a black, sticky sweet flavoured with this root

lisp verb 1 to say th for s or z because of being unable to pronounce these letters correctly 2 to speak imperfectly, like a child ■ noun a speech disorder of this kind

list[1] noun a series of names, numbers, prices, etc written down one after the other ■ verb to write (something) down in this way

list[2] verb of a ship: to lean over to one side

listen verb to hear, pay attention to ■ **listener** noun

listless adjective weary, without energy or interest

lit past form of **light**[1]

literacy noun ability to read and write

literal adjective of a word or phrase: following the exact or most obvious meaning

literally adverb exactly as stated, not just as a figure of speech

literary adjective relating to books, authors, etc

literate adjective able to read and write

literature noun 1 the books etc that are written in any language 2 anything in written form on a subject

lithe *adjective* bending easily, supple, flexible

lithium *noun* a light metallic element used in batteries and alloys

litmus paper treated paper which changes colour when dipped in an acid or alkaline solution

litmus test something which indicates underlying attitudes *etc*

litre *or US* **liter** *noun* the basic unit for measuring liquids in the metric system

litter *noun* **1** an untidy mess of paper, rubbish, *etc* **2** a number of animals born at one birth ▪ *verb* to scatter rubbish carelessly about

little *adjective* small in quantity or size ▪ *adverb* **1** a little to a small extent or degree **2** not much ▪ *pronoun* a small amount, distance, *etc*: *have a little more*

live[1] (*pronounced* liv) *verb* **1** to have life **2** to dwell **3** to pass your life **4** to continue to be alive **5** to survive **6** to be lifelike or vivid ▪ **live down** to live until (an embarrassment *etc*) is forgotten by others ▪ **live on 1** to keep yourself alive **2** to be supported by ▪ **live up to** to be as good as expected from

live[2] (*pronounced* laiv) *adjective* **1** having life, not dead **2** full of energy **3** of a television broadcast *etc*: seen as the event takes place, not recorded **4** charged with

electricity and apt to give an electric shock

livelihood *noun* someone's means of living, *eg* their daily work

lively *adjective* full of life, high spirits ▪ **liveliness** *noun*

liven *verb* to make lively

liver *noun* a large gland in the body that carries out several important functions including purifying the blood

livery *noun* (*plural* **liveries**) the uniform of a servant *etc*

livestock *noun* farm animals

livewire *noun* a very lively, energetic person

livid *adjective* **1** of a bluish lead-like colour **2** very angry

living *adjective* **1** having life **2** active, lively **3** of a likeness: exact ▪ *noun* means of living

living room an informal sitting room

lizard *noun* a four-footed reptile

llama *noun* a S American animal of the camel family without a hump

lo *exclamation, old* look

load *verb* **1** to put on what is to be carried **2** to put the ammunition in (a gun) **3** to put a film in (a camera) ▪ *noun* **1** as much as can be carried at once **2** cargo **3** a heavy weight or task **4** the power carried by an electric circuit

loaf *noun* (*plural* **loaves**) a shaped mass of bread ▪ *verb* to pass time idly or lazily

loafer noun **1** an idler **2** loafers casual shoes

loam noun a rich soil

loan noun something lent, especially a sum of money ■ verb to lend

loath or **loth** (pronounced lohth) adjective unwilling (to)

> ●* Do not confuse: **loath** and **loathe**. Remember that loaTHE has an ending common to quite a few other verbs eg cloTHE and baTHE

loathe verb to dislike greatly

loathing noun great hate or disgust

loathsome adjective causing loathing or disgust, horrible

loaves plural of loaf

lob noun **1** cricket a slow, high ball bowled underhand **2** tennis a ball high overhead dropping near the back of the court ■ verb **1** to send such a ball **2** informal to throw

| **lob** verb ► lobs, lobbing, lobbed

lobby noun (plural lobbies) **1** a small entrance hall **2** a passage off which rooms open **3** a group of people who try to influence the government or another authority ■ verb **1** to try to influence (public officials) **2** to conduct a campaign to influence public officials

| **lobby** verb ► lobbies, lobbying, lobbied

lobe noun **1** the hanging-down part of an ear **2** a division of the brain, lungs, etc

lobotomy noun a surgical operation on the front lobes of the brain which has the effect of changing the patient's character

lobster noun a kind of shellfish with large claws, used for food

local adjective of or confined to a certain place ■ noun, informal **1** the public house nearest someone's home **2** locals the people living in a particular place or area

locale noun scene, location

locality noun a particular place and the area round about

localize or **localise** verb to confine to one area, keep from spreading

locate verb **1** to find **2** to set in a particular place: a house located in the Highlands

location noun **1** the act of locating **2** position, situation

loch noun **1** in Scotland, a lake **2** an arm of the sea

lock noun **1** a fastening for doors etc needing a key to open it **2** a part of a canal for raising or lowering boats **3** locks hair ■ verb **1** to fasten with a lock **2** to become fastened **3** lock up to shut in with a lock

locker noun a small cupboard

locket noun a little ornamental case hung round the neck

lockjaw noun a form of tetanus which stiffens the jaw muscles

lockout *noun* the locking out of workers by their employer during wage disputes

locksmith *noun* a person who makes locks

locomotion *noun* movement from place to place

locomotive *noun* a railway engine

locum *noun* (*plural* **locums**) a doctor, dentist, *etc* taking another's place for a time

locus *noun* (*plural* **loci**) *maths* a set of values that make an equation or conditions work

locust *noun* a large insect of the grasshopper family which destroys growing plants

lodge *noun* 1 a small house, often at the entrance to a larger building 2 a beaver's dwelling ■ *verb* 1 to live in rented rooms 2 to become fixed (in) 3 to make (a complaint, appeal, *etc*) officially

lodger *noun* someone who stays in rented rooms

lodging *noun* 1 a place to stay, sleep, *etc* 2 **lodgings** a room or rooms rented in someone else's house

loft *noun* a room just under a roof

lofty *adjective* 1 of great height 2 noble, proud

log *noun* 1 a thick, rough piece of wood, part of a felled tree 2 a logbook ■ *verb* to write down (events) in a logbook ■ **log in** *or* **on** to start a session on a computer, usually by typing in a password ■ **log out** *or* **off** to end a session on a computer, using a closing command

| **log** *verb* ▶ logs, log**g**ing, log**g**ed

loganberry *noun* a kind of fruit like a large raspberry

logbook *noun* 1 an official record of a ship's or aeroplane's progress 2 a record of progress, attendance, *etc* 3 the registration documents of a motor vehicle

loggerhead *noun*: **at loggerheads** quarrelling

logic *noun* 1 the study of reasoning correctly 2 correctness of reasoning

logical *adjective* according to the rules of logic or sound reasoning ■ **logically** *adverb*

logo *noun* (*plural* **logos**) a symbol of a business firm *etc* consisting of a simple picture or lettering

-logy *or* **-ology** *suffix* 1 forms words describing the scientific or serious study of something: *biology/psychology* 2 forms terms related to words or speaking: *tautology* (= a form of repetition using two words or phrases that say the same thing)/*eulogy*

loin *noun* 1 the back of an animal cut for food 2 **loins** the lower part of the back

loincloth *noun* a piece of cloth worn round the hips, especially in India and south-east Asia

loiter *verb* 1 to proceed, move

slowly **2** to linger **3** to stand around

loll *verb* to lie lazily about

lollipop *noun* a large boiled sweet on a stick

lollipop man, **lollipop woman** *Brit* a person employed to stop cars to allow children to cross the street, who carries a pole with a disc at the top

lollop *verb* to bound clumsily

lolly *noun* a lollipop

lone *adjective* alone; standing by itself

lonely *adjective* **1** lone **2** lacking or needing companionship **3** of a place: having few people ■ **loneliness** *noun*

lonesome *adjective* **1** lone **2** feeling lonely

long *adjective* **1** not short, measuring a lot from end to end **2** measuring a certain amount: *2 centimetres long* ■ *adverb* **1** for a great time **2** through the whole time: *all day long* ■ *verb* to wish very much (for)

longevity *noun* great length of life

longhand *noun* writing in full (*contrasted with*: **shorthand**)

longing *noun* a strong desire

longitude *noun* the distance, measured in degrees, of a place east or west of the Greenwich meridian (*compare with*: **latitude**)

long johns men's under-trousers reaching to the ankles

long jump an athletics contest

in which competitors jump as far as possible along the ground from a running start

long-range *adjective* **1** able to reach a great distance **2** looking a long way into the future

longship *noun*, *history* a Viking sailing ship

long-sighted *adjective* able to see things at a distance but not those close at hand

long-standing *adjective* begun a long time ago, having lasted a long time

long-suffering *adjective* putting up with troubles without complaining

long-term *adjective* **1** extending over a long time **2** taking the future, not just the present, into account

long-wave *adjective* of radio: using wavelengths over 1000 metres (*compare with*: **short-wave**)

long-winded *adjective* using too many words

loo *noun*, *informal* a toilet

loofah *noun* the fibrous fruit of a tropical plant, used as a rough sponge

look *verb* **1** to turn the eyes towards so as to see **2** to appear, seem: *you look tired* **3** to face: *his room looks south* ■ *noun* **1** the act of looking **2** the expression on someone's face **3** appearance **4** **looks** personal appearance

■ **look after** to take care of, take

responsibility for ■ **look down on** to think of as being inferior ■ **look for** to search for ■ **look forward to** to anticipate with pleasure ■ **look into** to investigate ■ **look on 1** to stand by and watch **2** to think of (as): *he looks on her as his mother* ■ **look out!** be careful! ■ **look over** to examine briefly

look-alike *noun* someone who looks physically like someone else

look-in *noun* a chance of doing something

looking-glass *noun* a mirror

lookout *noun* **1** (someone who keeps) a careful watch **2** concern, responsibility

loom *noun* a machine for weaving cloth ■ *verb* to appear indistinctly, often threateningly

loony *noun, informal* a lunatic, an insane person

loop *noun* **1** a doubled-over part in a piece of string *etc* **2** a U-shaped bend

loophole *noun* **1** a narrow slit in a wall **2** a way of avoiding a difficulty

loose (*pronounced* loos) *adjective* **1** not tight, slack **2** not tied, free **3** not closely packed **4** vague, not exact ■ *verb* **1** to make loose, slacken **2** to untie ■ **loosely** *adverb*

⚠ Do not confuse with: **lose**

loose-leaf *adjective* having a cover that allows pages to be inserted or removed

loosen *verb* to make loose or looser

loot *noun* goods stolen or plundered ■ *verb* to plunder, ransack

lop *verb* to cut off the top or ends of

|lop ► lops, lopping, lopped

lope *verb* to run with a long stride

lopsided *adjective* leaning to one side, not symmetrical

loquacious *adjective* talkative

lord *noun* **1** the owner of an estate **2** a title for a male member of the aristocracy, bishop, judge, *etc* **3 the Lord** God or Christ ■ **House of Lords** the upper (non-elected) house of the British parliament

lordly *adjective* **1** relating to a lord **2** noble, proud

lordship *noun* used in talking to or about a lord: *his lordship*

lore *noun* knowledge, beliefs, *etc* handed down

lorry *noun* (*plural* **lorries**) a motor vehicle for carrying heavy loads

lose (*pronounced* looz) *verb* **1** to cease to have, have no longer **2** to have (something) taken away from **3** to put (something) where it cannot be found **4** to waste (time) **5** to miss (a train, a chance, *etc*) **6** to not win (a game)

|lose ► loses, losing, lost

⚠ Do not confuse with: **loose**

loser *noun* **1** someone unlikely to succeed at anything **2** someone who loses a game or contest

loss *noun* (*plural* **losses**) **1** the act of losing **2** something which is lost **3** waste, harm, destruction

lost *adjective* **1** not able to be found **2** no longer possessed; thrown away **3** not won **4** ruined ▪ **lost in** completely taken up by, engrossed in: *lost in thought*

lot *noun* **1** a large number or quantity **2** someone's fortune or fate **3** a separate portion

loth another spelling of **loath**

lotion *noun* a liquid for treating or cleaning the skin or hair

lottery *noun* (*plural* **lotteries**) an event in which money or prizes are won through drawing lots

lotus *noun* (*plural* **lotuses**) **1** a kind of water lily **2** a mythical tree whose fruit caused forgetfulness

louche (*pronounced* loosh) *adjective* shady, disreputable

loud *adjective* **1** making a great sound; noisy **2** showy, over-bright ▪ *adverb* in a way that makes a great sound; noisily ▪ **loudly** *adverb* ▪ **loudness** *noun*

loudhailer *noun* a megaphone with microphone and amplifier

loudspeaker *noun* a device for converting electrical signals into sound

lounge *verb* to lie back in a relaxed way ▪ *noun* a sitting-room

lounger *noun* **1** a lazy person

2 an extending chair or light couch for relaxing on

lour another spelling of **lower**[2]

louse *noun* (*plural* **lice**) a small blood-sucking insect sometimes found on the bodies of animals and people

lousy *adjective*, *informal* inferior, of poor quality

lout *noun* a clumsy or bad-mannered man

lovable *adjective* worthy of love

love *noun* **1** a great liking or affection **2** a loved person **3** *tennis* no score, zero ▪ *verb* to be very fond of; like very much

lovely *adjective* beautiful; delightful ▪ **loveliness** *noun*

lover *noun* **1** someone who loves another **2** an admirer, an enthusiast: *an art lover*

lovesick *adjective* suffering with love

loving *adjective* full of love ▪ **lovingly** *adverb*

low *adjective* **1** not high; not lying or reaching far up **2** of a voice: not loud **3** cheap: *low air-fare* **4** feeling sad, depressed **5** humble **6** mean, unworthy ▪ *verb* to make the noise of cattle; bellow, moo ▪ *adverb* **1** in or to a low position **2** not loudly **3** cheaply

lower[1] (*pronounced* loh-er) *adjective* less high ▪ *verb* **1** to make less high **2** to let or come down

lower[2] or **lour** (*pronounced* low-er) *verb* **1** of the sky: to become dark and cloudy **2** to frown ▪ **lowering** *adjective*

lower-case *adjective* of a letter: not a capital, *eg a* as opposed to *A* (*contrasted with*: **upper-case**)

lowlands *noun plural* flat country, without high hills ▪ **lowland** *adjective*

lowly *adjective* low in rank, humble ▪ **lowliness** *noun*

loyal *adjective* faithful, true ▪ **loyally** *adverb*

loyalist *noun* someone loyal to their sovereign or country

loyalty *noun* (*plural* **loyalties**) **1** faithful support of *eg* your friends **2 loyalties** feelings of faithful friendship and support, especially for a particular person or thing

lozenge *noun* **1** a diamond-shaped figure **2** a small sweet for sucking

lubricant *noun* something which lubricates; an oil

lubricate *verb* to apply oil *etc* to (something) to overcome friction and make movement easier ▪ **lubrication** *noun*

lucid *adjective* **1** easily understood **2** clear in mind; not confused ▪ **lucidly** *adverb*

luck *noun* **1** fortune, either good or bad **2** chance: *as luck would have it* **3** good fortune: *have any luck?*

luckless *adjective* unfortunate, unhappy

lucky *adjective* **1** fortunate, having good luck **2** bringing good luck: *lucky charm* **3** happening as a result of good luck: *a lucky coincidence* ▪ **luckily** *adverb*

|**lucky** ▶ luck**ier**, luck**iest**

lucrative *adjective* profitable

lucre (*pronounced* **loo**-ker) *noun* gain; money

Luddite *noun* an opponent of technological innovation

ludicrous *adjective* ridiculous ▪ **ludicrously** *adverb*

ludo *noun* a game played with counters on a board

lug *verb* to pull or drag with effort

|**lug** ▶ lugs, lug**ging**, lug**ged**

luge *noun* a light toboggan

luggage *noun* suitcases and other travelling baggage

lugubrious *adjective* mournful, dismal

lukewarm *adjective* neither hot nor cold

lull *verb* to soothe or calm ▪ *noun* a period of calm

lullaby *noun* (*plural* **lullabies**) a song to lull children to sleep

lumbago *noun* a pain in the lower part of the back

lumber *verb* to move about clumsily

lumberjack *noun* someone who fells, saws and shifts trees

luminous *adjective* **1** giving light **2** shining; clear

lump *noun* **1** a small, solid mass of indefinite shape **2** a swelling ▪ *verb* **1** to form into lumps **2** to treat as being alike: *lumped all of us together*

lump sum an amount of money given all at once

lumpy *adjective* full of lumps

lunacy *noun* madness, insanity

lunar *adjective* of the moon

lunatic *noun* someone who is insane or crazy

lunch *noun* (*plural* **lunches**) a midday meal ▪ *verb* to eat lunch

luncheon *noun* lunch

lung *noun* either of the two bag-like organs which fill with and expel air in the course of breathing

lunge *noun* a sudden thrust or push ▪ *verb* to thrust or plunge forward suddenly

lupin *noun* a type of garden plant with flowers on long spikes

lurch *verb* to roll or pitch suddenly to one side; stagger ▪ *noun* a pitch to one side ▪ **leave in the lurch** to leave in a difficult position without help

lure *noun* something which entices; a bait ▪ *verb* to attract, entice away

lurid *adjective* glaring, garish

lurk *verb* 1 to keep out of sight; be hidden 2 to move or act secretly and slyly ▪ **lurker** *noun*

lurking *adjective* vague, hidden

luscious *adjective* sweet, delicious, juicy

lush *adjective* of grass *etc*: thick and plentiful

lust *noun* 1 a greedy desire for power, riches, *etc* 2 a strong physical desire ▪ *verb* to have a strong desire (for)

lustful *adjective* full of, or showing, strong sexual desire

lustre or US **luster** *noun* brightness, shine, gloss

◆※ This is one of a large number of words which is spelled with an **-re** ending in British English, but with an **-er** in American English, *eg* centre/center, calibre/caliber, metre/meter

lustrous *adjective* bright, shining

lusty *adjective* lively, strong ▪ **lustily** *adverb*

lute *noun* a stringed musical instrument with a pear-shaped, round-backed body and fretted neck

luxuriant *adjective* 1 thick with leaves, flowers, *etc*: *ornamental gardens full of luxuriant plants* 2 richly ornamented

◆※ Do not confuse with: luxurious

luxuriate *verb* 1 to be luxuriant 2 to enjoy; take delight (in)

luxurious *adjective* full of luxuries; very comfortable ▪ **luxuriously** *adverb*

◆※ Do not confuse with: luxuriant

luxury *noun* (*plural* **luxuries**)

1 something very pleasant or expensive but not necessary: *having a car is a luxury* **2** the use or enjoyment of such things

Lycra *noun, trademark* a lightweight synthetic elastic fabric

lying *see* **lie**[1] and **lie**[2]

lymph *noun* a colourless fluid in the body

lymph gland one of the glands carrying lymph

lynch *verb* to condemn and put to death without legal trial

lynx *noun* (*plural* **lynxes**) a wild animal of the cat family, noted for its keen sight

lyre *noun* an ancient stringed musical instrument, played like a harp

lyric *noun* **1** a short poem, often expressing the poet's feelings **2** **lyrics** the words of a song

lyrical *adjective* song-like

lyricist *noun* someone who writes the words for songs

M m

mac *short for* mackintosh

macabre *adjective* gruesome, horrible

macaroni *noun* pasta shaped into short hollow tubes

macaroon *noun* a sweet cake or biscuit made with ground almonds and sugar

macaw *noun* a long-tailed brightly-coloured parrot

mace *noun* a heavy staff with an ornamental head, carried as a sign of office

machete (*pronounced* ma-shet-i) *noun* a heavy knife used to cut through foliage *etc*

machine *noun* a working arrangement of wheels, levers, *etc* ▪ *verb* to sew *etc* with a machine

machine code a system of symbols that can be understood by a computer

machine-gun *noun* an automatic rapid-firing gun

machinery *noun* **1** machines in general **2** the working parts of a machine

machine tool a stationary, power-driven machine used for cutting and shaping metal *etc*

Mach number the ratio of the speed of an aircraft to the speed of sound (*eg* Mach 5 = 5 times the speed of sound)

macho (*pronounced* mach-oh) *adjective* aggressively masculine

Macintosh *noun, trademark* a type of personal computer

mackerel *noun* an edible seafish with wavy markings

mackintosh *noun* (*plural* **mackintoshes**) a waterproof overcoat

macro *noun, computing* a single instruction that prompts a computer to carry out a series of short tasks

mad *adjective* **1** out of your mind, insane **2** wildly foolish **3** furious with anger ▪ **madness** *noun*

madam *noun* a polite form of address to a woman

madcap *adjective* foolishly rash

madden *verb* to make angry or mad

maddening *adjective* extremely annoying

made *past form of* make

madhouse *noun* a place of confusion and noise

madly *adverb* **1** insanely

2 extremely: *madly in love* **3** with great energy: *waving her arms about madly*

madman, **madwoman** *noun* someone who is mad

Madonna *noun* the Virgin Mary as depicted in art

madrigal *noun* a medieval song for several voices

maelstrom (*pronounced* meilstrom) *noun* **1** a whirlpool **2** any place of great confusion

maestro (*pronounced* maistroh) *noun* (*plural* **maestros**) someone highly skilled in an art, especially music

magazine *noun* **1** a periodical paper containing articles, stories and pictures **2** a storage place for military equipment

magenta *noun* a reddish-purple colour ∎ *adjective* of this colour

maggot *noun* a small worm-like creature, the grub of a bluebottle *etc*

magic *noun* **1** a process which produces results which cannot be explained or which are remarkable **2** conjuring tricks **3** a sense of mysterious charm ∎ *adjective* **1** using magic **2** used in magic **3** magical

magical *adjective* **1** of or produced by magic **2** very wonderful or mysterious ∎ **magically** *adverb*

magician *noun* someone skilled in magic

magistrate *noun* someone with the power to enforce the law, *eg* a Justice of the Peace

magma *noun* molten rock

magnanimous *adjective* very generous

magnate *noun* someone with great power or wealth

magnesium *noun* a white metal which burns with an intense white light

magnet *noun* a piece of iron, steel, *etc* which has the power to attract other pieces of metal

magnetic *adjective* **1** having the powers of a magnet **2** strongly attractive: *magnetic personality*

magnetic field the area which is affected by a magnet

magnetic north the direction in which the magnetized needle of a compass points

magnetic pole 1 either of two areas on a magnet where the magnetic field is strongest **2** the two points on the earth's surface (**North Pole** and **South Pole**) towards which a compass needle points

magnetic tape tape on which sound, pictures, computer data, *etc* can be recorded

magnetism *noun* **1** the attractive power of a magnet **2** attraction, great charm

magnetize *or* **magnetise** *verb* to make magnetic

magnification *noun* **1** the process of making objects appear larger or closer, or the power that instruments such as microscopes and binoculars have to do this **2** a measure of how much larger or closer an object is made to appear than it is in reality

magnificent *adjective* **1** splendid in appearance or action **2** excellent, very fine
■ **magnificence** *noun*
■ **magnificently** *adverb*

magnify *verb* to make to appear larger by using special lenses

| **magnify** ► **magnifies**, **magnifying**, **magnified**

magnifying glass a hand-held lens through which things appear larger

magnitude *noun* size or importance

magnolia *noun* a tree which produces large white or purplish sweet-scented flowers

magpie *noun* a black-and-white bird of the crow family, known for its habit of collecting objects

mah-jong *noun* a Chinese table game played with small painted bricks

mahogany *noun* **1** a tropical American tree **2** its hard reddish-brown wood, often used for furniture

maid *noun* a female servant

maiden *noun, old* an unmarried girl ■ *adjective* **1** unmarried: *maiden aunt* **2** first, initial: *maiden voyage*

maiden name the surname of a married woman before her marriage

maiden over *cricket* an over in which no runs are scored

mail[1] *noun* letters, parcels, *etc* carried by post ■ *verb* to post

mail[2] *noun* body armour of steel rings or plates

mail order an order for goods to be sent by post

maim *verb* to disable

main *adjective* chief, most important

mainframe *noun* the central processing unit and storage unit of a computer ■ *adjective* of a computer: of the large, powerful type rather than the small-scale kind

mainland *noun* a large piece of land off whose coast smaller islands lie

mainly *adverb* chiefly, mostly

mainstay *noun* the chief support

maintain *verb* **1** to keep (something) as it is **2** to continue to keep in good working order **3** to support (a family *etc*) **4** to state (an opinion) firmly

maintenance *noun* **1** the act of maintaining; upkeep, repair **2** means of support, especially money for food, clothing, *etc*

maisonette *noun* a flat with two floors

maize *noun* a cereal crop grown in N and S America

majestic *adjective* stately, regal

majesty noun (plural **majesties**) a title used in addressing a king or queen: *Your Majesty*

major adjective great in size, importance, *etc* (contrasted with: **minor**) ■ noun a senior army officer

majority noun (plural **majorities**) 1 the greater number or quantity 2 the difference in amount between the greater and the lesser number 3 the age when someone becomes legally an adult (18 in the UK)

make verb 1 to form, construct 2 to cause to be: *he makes me mad at times* 3 to bring about: *make trouble* 4 to amount to: *2 plus 2 makes 4* 5 to earn 6 to force: *I made him do it* 7 to undergo (a journey *etc*) 8 to prepare (a meal *etc*) ■ noun 1 kind, shape, form 2 brand ■ **make believe** to pretend ■ **make off** to run away ■ **make out 1** to see in the distance or indistinctly 2 to declare, prove ■ **make up 1** to form a whole: *eleven players make up the side* 2 to put together, invent (a false story) 3 to put make-up on the face 4 to be friendly again after a quarrel ■ **make up for** to give or do something in return for damage done

| make verb ▶ makes, making, made

make-believe noun fantasy

maker noun the person or organization that has made something

makeshift adjective used for a time until something better can be found

make-up noun cosmetics

malady noun (plural **maladies**) illness, disease

malaise noun a feeling or general air of depression or despondency

malaria noun a fever caused by the bite of a particular mosquito

male adjective of the sex that is able to father children or young; masculine ■ noun a member of this sex

malevolent adjective wishing ill to others; spiteful ■ **malevolence** noun ■ **malevolently** adverb

malfunction verb to fail to work or operate properly ■ noun failure to operate

malice noun ill will; spite

malicious adjective intending harm; spiteful ■ **maliciously** adverb

malign verb to speak ill of

malignant adjective 1 wishing harm, spiteful 2 of a disease: likely to cause death ■ **malignantly** adverb

malinger verb to pretend to be ill to avoid work *etc* ■ **malingerer** noun

mall (pronounced mol) noun, originally US a shopping centre

malleable adjective 1 of metal: able to be beaten out by hammering 2 of people: easy to influence

mallet *noun* a heavy wooden hammer

malnutrition *noun* lack of sufficient or proper food; undernourishment

malpractice *noun* **1** doing what is wrong **2** professional misconduct

malt *noun* barley or other grain prepared for making beer or whisky

maltreat *verb* to treat roughly or unkindly ▪ **maltreatment** *noun*

mama *or* **mamma** *noun*, *informal* mother

mammal *noun* a member of the class of animals of which the female parent feeds the young with her own milk

mammoth *noun* a very large elephant, now extinct ▪ *adjective* enormous, huge

man *noun* (*plural* **men**) **1** a grown-up human male **2** a human being **3** the human race **4** a piece in chess or draughts ▪ *verb* to supply with workers, crew, *etc*

| **man** *verb* ▸ **mans**, **manning**, **manned**

manacles *noun plural*, *formal* handcuffs

manage *verb* **1** to have control or charge of **2** to deal with, cope: *can't manage on his own* **3** to succeed

manageable *adjective* easily managed or controlled

management *noun* **1** those in

charge of a business *etc* **2** the art of managing a business *etc*

manager *noun* someone in charge of a business *etc*

manageress *noun*, *old* a woman manager

mandarin *noun* **1** a small orange-like citrus fruit **2** *history* a senior Chinese official

mandate *noun* **1** power to act on someone else's behalf **2** a command

mandatory *adjective* compulsory

mandible *noun* the jaw or lower jawbone

mandolin *or* **mandoline** *noun* a round-backed stringed instrument similar to a lute

mane *noun* **1** long hair on the head and neck of a horse or male lion **2** a long or thick head of hair

manful *adjective* courageous and noble-minded ▪ **manfully** *adverb*

manganese *noun* a hard easily-broken metal of a greyish-white colour

mange *noun* a skin disease of dogs, cats, *etc*

manger *noun* a box or trough holding dry food for horses and cattle

mangle *noun* a machine for squeezing water out of clothes or for smoothing them ▪ *verb* to crush, tear, damage badly

mango *noun* (*plural* **mangoes**) **1** the fruit of a tropical Indian tree, with juicy orange flesh **2** the tree which produces mangoes

mangy *adjective* **1** shabby, squalid **2** of an animal: suffering from mange

manhandle *verb* to handle roughly

manhole *noun* a hole (into a drain, sewer, *etc*) large enough to let a man through

manhood *noun* the state of being a man

mania *noun* **1** a form of mental illness in which the sufferer is over-active, over-excited and unreasonably happy **2** extreme fondness or enthusiasm: *a mania for stamp-collecting*

maniac *noun* **1** a mad person **2** a very rash or over-enthusiastic person

manic *adjective* **1** suffering from mania **2** very energetic or excited

manicure *noun* **1** the care of hands and nails **2** a professional treatment for the hands and nails ■ *verb* to perform a manicure on

manicurist *noun* someone who performs manicures

manifest *verb* to show plainly

manifestation *noun* behaviour, actions or events which reveal or display something

manifesto *noun* (*plural* **manifestoes** *or* **manifestos**) a public announcement of intentions, *eg* by a political party

manifold *adjective* many and various

manipulate *verb* to handle so as to turn to your own advantage ■ **manipulation** *noun*

mankind *noun* the human race

manly *adjective* brave, strong ■ **manliness** *noun*

mannequin *noun* **1** someone who models clothes for prospective buyers **2** a display dummy

manner *noun* **1** the way in which something is done **2** the way in which someone behaves **3** **manners** polite behaviour towards others

mannerism *noun* an odd and obvious habit or characteristic

mannerly *adjective* polite

mannish *adjective* of a woman: behaving, looking like a man

manoeuvre *noun* **1** a planned movement of troops, ships or aircraft **2** a trick, a cunning plan ■ *verb* **1** to perform a manoeuvre **2** to manipulate

manor *noun* **1** a large house, usually attached to a country estate **2** *history* the land belonging to a lord or squire

manpower *noun* the number of people available for work

manse *noun* the house of a minister in certain Christian Churches

mansion *noun* a large house

manslaughter *noun* killing someone without deliberate intent

mantelpiece *noun* a shelf over a fireplace

mantis *noun* an insect of the cockroach family, with large spiny front legs (*also called:* **praying mantis**)

mantle *noun* a cloak or loose outer garment

mantra *noun* a word or phrase, chanted or repeated inwardly in meditation

manual *adjective* **1** of the hand or hands **2** worked by hand **3** working with the hands ■ *noun* a handbook giving instructions on how to use something ■ **manually** *adverb*

manufacture *verb* to make (articles or materials) in large quantities, usually by machine ■ **manufacturer** *noun*

manure *noun* a substance, especially animal dung, spread on soil to make it more fertile

manuscript *noun* **1** the prepared material for a book *etc* before it is printed **2** a book or paper written by hand

Manx *adjective* of or relating to the Isle of Man

Manx cat a tailless breed of cat

many *adjective* a large number of ■ *pronoun* a large number: *many survived*

Maori *noun* a member of a race of people who were first to arrive in New Zealand

map *noun* a flat drawing of all or part of the earth's surface, showing geographical features ■ *verb* **1** to make a map of **2** *maths* to correspond single members of a set with single members of another set **3 map something out** to plan it

| **map** *verb* ► maps, mapping, mapped

maple *noun* **1** a tree related to the sycamore, one variety of which produces sugar **2** its hard light-coloured wood used for furniture *etc*

mapping *noun, maths* a diagram showing the correspondence of single members of one set with those of another

mar *verb* to spoil, deface

| **mar** ► mars, marring, marred

maracas *noun plural* a pair of filled gourds shaken as a percussion instrument

marathon *noun* a long-distance foot-race, usually covering 26 miles 385 yards

maraud *verb* to plunder, raid

marauder *noun* a plundering robber

marble *noun* **1** limestone that can be highly polished, used for sculpture, decorating buildings, *etc* **2** a small glass ball used in a children's game

March *noun* the third month of the year

march *verb* **1** to (cause) to walk in time with regular steps **2** to go on steadily ■ *noun* (*plural* **marches**) **1** a marching movement **2** a piece of music for marching **3** the distance covered by marching

mare noun a female horse

margarine noun an edible spread similar to butter, made mainly of vegetable fats

margin noun **1** an edge, a border **2** the blank edge on the page of a book **3** additional space or room; allowance: *margin for error*

marginal adjective of little effect or importance

marginalize or **marginalise** verb to make less important or central

marigold noun a kind of plant with a yellow flower

marijuana noun a drug made from the plant hemp

marina noun a place with moorings for yachts, dinghies, *etc*

marinade noun a mixture of oil, wine, herbs, spices, *etc* in which food is steeped for flavour ■ verb to marinate

marinate verb to steep in a marinade

marine adjective of the sea ■ noun a soldier serving on board a ship

mariner (*pronounced* ma-rin-er) noun, *old* a sailor

marionette noun a puppet moved by strings

marital adjective of marriage

maritime adjective of the sea or ships

marjoram noun a sweet-smelling herb used in cooking

mark noun **1** a sign that can be

seen **2** a stain, spot, *etc* **3** a target aimed at **4** a trace **5** a point used to assess the merit of a piece of schoolwork *etc* **6** the starting-line in a race: *on your marks* ■ verb **1** to make a mark on; stain **2** to observe, watch **3** to stay close to (an opponent in football *etc*) **4** to award marks to (a piece of work, a test, *etc*) **5 mark off** to separate, distinguish

marked adjective easily noticed: *marked improvement*

markedly adverb noticeably

marker noun **1** a type of thick-nibbed pen **2** something used to show a position

market noun **1** a public place for buying and selling **2** (a country, place, *etc* where there is) a need or demand (for certain types of goods) ■ verb to put on sale

marketing noun the act or practice of advertising and selling

marksman, markswoman noun someone who shoots well

marmalade noun a jam made from citrus fruit, especially oranges

marmoset noun a type of small monkey found in America

maroon[1] noun a brownish-red colour ■ adjective brownish-red

maroon[2] verb **1** to abandon on an island *etc* without means of escape **2** to leave in a helpless or uncomfortable position

marquee (*pronounced* mah-kee*) noun a large tent used for large gatherings, *eg* a wedding reception or circus

marquess *or* **marquis** *noun* (*plural* **marquesses** *or* **marquises**) a nobleman of the rank below a duke

marriage *noun* the ceremony by which two people become husband and wife

marrow *noun* **1** the soft substance in the hollow part of bones **2** a long thick-skinned vegetable

marry *verb* to join, or be joined, together in marriage

| **marry** ▶ marri*es*, marry*ing*, marri*ed*

marsh *noun* (*plural* **marshes**) a piece of low-lying wet ground

marshal *noun* **1** a high-ranking officer in the army or air force **2** someone who directs processions *etc* **3** *US* a law-court official **4** *US* the head of a police force ■ *verb* to arrange (troops, facts, arguments, *etc*) in order

| **marshal** *verb* ▶ marshal*s*, marshal*ling*, marshal*led*

marshmallow *noun* a spongy jellylike sweet made from sugar and egg-whites *etc*

marshy *adjective* wet underfoot; boggy

marsupial *noun* an animal which carries its young in a pouch, *eg* the kangaroo

marten *noun* an animal related to the weasel

martial art a sport or method of

self-defence that involves fighting

martial law the government of a country by its army

Martian *noun* a potential or imaginary being from the planet Mars

martin *noun* a bird of the swallow family

martinet *noun* someone who keeps strict discipline

martyr *noun* someone who suffers death or hardship for their beliefs ■ *verb* to execute or make suffer for beliefs

martyrdom *noun* the death or suffering of a martyr

marvel *noun* something astonishing or wonderful ■ *verb* to feel amazement (at)

| **marvel** *verb* ▶ marvel*s*, marvel*ling*, marvel*led*

marvellous *adjective* **1** astonishing, extraordinary **2** *informal* excellent, very good

marzipan *noun* a mixture of ground almonds, sugar, *etc*, used in cake-making and confectionery

mascara *noun* a cosmetic paint used to colour the eyelashes

mascot *noun* a person, animal or thing believed to bring good luck

masculine *adjective* **1** of the male sex **2** manly ■ **masculinity** *noun*

mash *verb* to beat or crush into a pulp ■ *noun* mashed potato

mask *noun* a cover for the face for disguise or protection ■ *verb*

1 to hide, disguise **2** to cover the face with a mask

masochism *noun* an unnatural pleasure in being treated cruelly or made to suffer in any way
■ **masochist** *noun* ■ **masochistic** *adjective*

mason *noun* someone who carves stone

masonry *noun* things made out of stone

masquerade *noun* **1** a dance at which masks are worn **2** pretence ■ *verb* to pretend to be someone else: *masquerading as a journalist*

mass *noun* (*plural* **masses**) **1** *physics* the amount of matter that an object contains **2** a lump or quantity gathered together **3** a large quantity **4** the main part or body **5** **Mass** (in some Christian Churches) the celebration of Christ's last supper with his disciples ■ *adjective* of or consisting of large numbers or quantities ■ *verb* to form into a mass

massacre *noun* the merciless killing of a large number of people ■ *verb* to kill (a large number) in a cruel way

massage *noun* the rubbing of parts of the body to remove pain or tension ■ *verb* to perform massage on

masseur *noun* someone who performs massage

masseuse *noun* a female masseur

massive *adjective* bulky, heavy, huge

massively *adverb* enormously, heavily

mass production production in large quantities of articles all exactly the same

mast *noun* a long upright pole holding up the sails *etc* in a ship, or holding an aerial, flag, *etc*

master *noun* **1** someone who controls or commands **2** an owner of a slave *etc* **3** an employer **4** a male teacher **5** the commander of a merchant ship **6** someone who is very skilled in something; an expert **7** someone who has been awarded an advanced degree at a university: *Master of Arts* ■ *adjective* chief, controlling: *master switch* ■ *verb* **1** to overcome, defeat **2** to become able to do or use properly: *I've finally mastered this computer program*

masterful *adjective* strong-willed and expecting to be obeyed

masterly *adjective* showing the skill of an expert or master; clever

mastermind *verb* to plan, work out the details of (a scheme *etc*) ■ *noun* a person who organizes and plans a scheme

masterpiece *noun* the best example of someone's work, especially a very fine picture, book, piece of music, *etc*

mastery *noun* **1** control (of) **2** great skill (in)

mastiff noun a breed of large, powerful dog

mat noun 1 a piece of material (coarse plaited plant fibre, carpet, etc) for wiping shoes on, covering the floor, etc 2 a piece of material, wood, etc put below dishes on a table ■ adjective, another spelling of matt

matador noun the person who kills the bull in bullfights

match[1] noun (plural **matches**) a small stick of wood etc tipped with a substance which catches fire when rubbed against an abrasive surface

match[2] noun (plural **matches**) 1 a person or thing similar to or the same as another 2 a person or thing agreeing with or suiting another 3 an equal 4 someone suitable for marriage 5 a contest or game ■ verb 1 to be of the same make, size, colour, etc 2 to set (two things, teams, etc) against each other 3 to hold your own with, be equal to

matchbox noun a box for holding matches

matchless adjective having no equal

matchmaker noun someone who tries to arrange marriages or partnerships

matchstick noun the wooden stalk of a match

mate noun 1 a friend, a companion 2 an assistant worker: plumber's mate 3 a

husband or wife 4 the partner of an animal, bird, etc 5 a merchant ship's officer, next in rank to the captain ■ verb to bring or come together to breed

material noun 1 something out of which anything is, or may be, made 2 cloth, fabric

materialize or **materialise** verb 1 to appear in bodily form 2 to happen, come about

materially adverb 1 to a large extent, greatly 2 relating to objects, possessions or physical comfort, rather than to emotional or spiritual wellbeing

maternal adjective 1 of a mother 2 like a mother; motherly 3 related through your mother ■ maternally adverb

maternity noun the state of being a mother; motherhood ■ adjective of or for a woman having or about to have a baby

mathematical adjective of or done by mathematics

mathematician noun an expert in mathematics

mathematics noun singular the study of measurements, numbers and quantities

maths noun singular, informal mathematics

matinée noun an afternoon performance in a theatre or cinema

matins noun plural the morning service in certain churches

matriarch (pronounced meit-riahk) *noun* a woman who controls a family or community

matrimony *noun, formal* marriage

matrix *noun* (*plural* **matrices** *or* **matrixes**) a rectangular table of data in rows and columns

matron *noun* **1** a senior nurse in a hospital **2** *old* a woman in charge of housekeeping or nursing in a school, hostel, *etc*

matt *or* **mat** *adjective* having a dull surface; not shiny or glossy

matted *adjective* thickly tangled

matter *noun* **1** anything that takes up space, can be seen, felt, *etc*; material, substance **2** a subject written or spoken about **3** matters affairs, business **4** trouble, difficulty: *what is the matter?* **5** pus ■ *verb* to be of importance

matter-of-fact *adjective* keeping to the actual facts; unimaginative, uninteresting

mattress *noun* (*plural* **mattresses**) a thick layer of padding covered in cloth, usually as part of a bed

mature *adjective* **1** fully grown or developed **2** ripe, ready for use ■ *verb* to (cause to) become mature

maturity *noun* ripeness

maudlin *adjective* silly, sentimental

maul *verb* to hurt badly by rough or savage treatment

mausoleum *noun* a large or elaborate tomb

mauve *adjective* of a purple colour

maverick *noun* someone who refuses to act like other people

maxim *noun* a general truth or rule about behaviour *etc*

maximum *adjective* greatest, most ■ *noun* (*plural* **maxima**) **1** the greatest number or quantity **2** the highest point or degree

May *noun* the fifth month of the year

may *verb* **1** used with another verb to express permission or possibility: *you may watch the film* **2** used to express a wish: *may your wishes come true*

|may ► may, might

maybe *adverb* perhaps

mayday *noun* an international distress signal

mayfly *noun* a short-lived insect that appears in May

mayhem *noun* widespread chaos or confusion

mayonnaise *noun* a sauce made of eggs, oil and vinegar or lemon juice

mayor *noun* the chief elected public official of a city or town

mayoress *noun* a mayor's wife

maypole *noun* a decorated pole traditionally danced around on the first day of May

maze *noun* a series of winding paths in a park *etc*, planned to make it difficult to get out

me *pronoun* the word used by a speaker or writer in mentioning themselves: *she kissed me*

mead *noun* an alcoholic drink made with honey

meadow *noun* a field of grass

meagre *or US* **meager** *adjective* scanty, not enough

meal[1] *noun* the food taken at one time, *eg* breakfast or dinner

meal[2] *noun* grain ground to a coarse powder

mean[1] *adjective* 1 not generous with money *etc* 2 unkind, selfish ▪ **meanness** *noun*

mean[2] *noun, maths* average

mean[3] *verb* 1 to intend to express; indicate 2 to intend: *how do you mean to do that?*

| mean ▶ means, meaning, meant

meander *verb* of a river: to flow in a winding course

meaning *noun* 1 what is intended to be expressed or conveyed 2 purpose, intention

meaningful *adjective* full of significance; expressive

meaningless *adjective* 1 pointless 2 having no meaning

means *noun* 1 *singular* an action or instrument by which something is brought about 2 *plural* money, property, *etc*: *a woman of means*

meantime *noun*: **in the meantime** meanwhile

meanwhile *adverb* in the time between two happenings

measles *noun* an infectious disease causing red spots

measly *adjective, informal* mean, stingy

measure *noun* 1 size or amount (found by counting, weighing, *etc*) 2 **measures** a plan of action: *measures to prevent crime* ▪ *verb* 1 to find out the size, quantity, *etc* by using some form of measure 2 to be of a certain length, amount, *etc* 3 to indicate the measurement of 4 to mark (off) or weigh (out) in portions

measurement *noun* 1 the act of measuring 2 the size, amount, *etc* found by measuring

meat *noun* animal flesh used as food

meaty *adjective* 1 full of meat 2 tasting of meat

mechanic *noun* a skilled worker with tools or machines

mechanical *adjective* 1 of machinery: *mechanical engineering* 2 worked by machinery ▪ **mechanically** *adverb*

mechanics *noun* 1 *singular* the study and art of constructing machinery 2 *plural* the actual details of how something works: *the mechanics of the plan*

mechanism *noun* 1 a piece of machinery 2 the way a piece of machinery works

mechanize *or* **mechanise** *verb* to equip (a factory *etc*) with machinery

medal *noun* a metal disc stamped with a design, inscription, *etc*, made to commemorate an event or given as a prize

medallion *noun* a large medal or piece of jewellery like one

medallist *noun* someone who has gained a medal

meddle *verb* **1** to concern yourself with things that are not your business **2** to interfere or tamper (with) ▪ **meddler** *noun*

meddlesome *adjective* fond of meddling

media *noun plural* television, newspapers, *etc* as a form of communication

mediaeval *another spelling of* medieval

median *noun* **1** a straight line from an angle of a triangle to the centre of the opposite side **2** the middle value or point of a series

mediate *verb* to act as a peacemaker (between) ▪ **mediation** *noun*

mediator *noun* someone who tries to make peace between people who are quarrelling

medical *adjective* of doctors or their work ▪ *noun* a health check, a physical examination

medicate *verb* to give medicine to

medicated *adjective* including medicine or disinfectant

medication *noun* **1** medical treatment **2** a medicine

medicinal *adjective* **1** used in medicine **2** used as a medicine

medicine *noun* **1** something given to a sick person to make them better **2** the science of the treatment of illness

medieval *or* **mediaeval** *adjective* of or in the Middle Ages

mediocre *adjective* not very good, ordinary ▪ **mediocrity** *noun*

meditate *verb* **1** to think deeply and in quietness **2** to contemplate religious or spiritual matters **3** to consider, think about

meditation *noun* **1** deep, quiet thought **2** contemplation on a religious or spiritual theme

meditative *adjective* thinking deeply

medium *noun* (*plural* **media** *or* **mediums**) **1** a means or substance through which an effect is produced **2** (*plural* **mediums**) someone through whom spirits (of dead people) are said to speak ▪ *adjective* middle or average in size, quality, *etc*

medley *noun* (*plural* **medleys**) **1** a mixture **2** a piece of music put together from a number of other pieces

meek *adjective* gentle, uncomplaining ▪ **meekly** *adverb*

meet *verb* **1** to come face to face (with) **2** to come together, join **3** to make the acquaintance of **4** to be suitable for, satisfy: *able to meet the demand*

┃**meet** ▶ meets, meet*ing*, met

meeting noun a gathering of people for a particular purpose

mega- prefix **1** great, huge: megaphone **2** a million: megaton

megabyte noun a measure of computer data or memory, roughly equivalent to a million bytes

megaphone noun a portable cone-shaped device with microphone and amplifier to increase sound

meiosis noun a type of cell division that halves the number of chromosomes in reproductive cells

melancholy noun lowness of spirits, sadness ▪ adjective sad, depressed

melanin noun the dark pigment in human skin or hair

melanoma noun a skin tumour which usually develops from a mole

mêlée (pronounced mel-ei) noun a confused fight between two groups of people

mellifluous adjective sweet-sounding

mellow adjective **1** of fruit: ripe, juicy, sweet **2** having become pleasant or agreeable with age **3** of light, colour, etc: soft, not harsh ▪ verb to make or become mellow

melodic adjective of melody

melodious adjective pleasant sounding; tuneful

melodrama noun a type of play with a sensational or exaggerated plot

melodramatic adjective exaggerated, sensational, over-dramatic

melody noun (plural melodies) **1** a tune **2** pleasant music

melon noun a large round fruit with soft juicy flesh

melt verb to make or become liquid, eg by heating

meltdown noun the process in which the radioactive fuel in a nuclear reactor overheats and melts through the insulation into the environment

melting point the temperature at which a solid turns to liquid

member noun someone who belongs to a group or society

Member of Parliament (shortened to **MP**) noun someone elected to the House of Commons

membership noun **1** the group of people who are members, or the number of members, in a club etc **2** the state of being a member

membrane noun a thin skin or covering, especially as part of a human or animal body, plant, etc

memento noun (plural mementos) something by which an event is remembered

memo noun (plural memos) short for **memorandum**

memoirs noun plural a personal account of someone's life; an autobiography

memorable adjective worthy of being remembered; famous

▪ **memorably** adverb

memorandum noun (plural **memoranda**) (short form: **memo**) **1** a note which acts as a reminder **2** a brief note sent to colleagues in an office etc

memorial noun a monument commemorating a person or historical event

memorize or **memorise** verb to learn by heart

memory noun (plural **memories**) **1** the power to remember **2** the mind's store of remembered things **3** something remembered **4** computing a store of information

men plural of **man**

menace noun **1** potential harm or danger **2** someone persistently threatening or annoying

menacing adjective looking evil or threatening

menagerie noun a collection of wild animals

mend verb **1** to repair **2** to make or grow better

menial adjective of work: unskilled, unchallenging

meningitis noun an illness caused by inflammation of the covering of the brain

menopause noun the ending of menstruation in middle age

menstrual adjective of menstruation

menstruation noun the monthly discharge of blood from a woman's womb

mental adjective **1** of the mind **2** done, made, happening, etc in the mind **3** of illness: affecting the mind **4** informal suffering from an illness of the mind ■ **mentally** adverb

mentality noun (plural **mentalities**) a person's way of thinking

menthol noun a sharp-smelling substance obtained from peppermint oil

mention verb **1** to speak of briefly **2** to remark (that) ■ noun a mentioning, a remark

mentor noun someone who gives advice as a tutor or supervisor

menu noun (plural **menus**) **1** (a card with) a list of dishes to be served at a meal **2** computing a list of options

mercantile adjective of buying and selling; trading

mercenary adjective **1** working for money **2** influenced by the desire for money ■ noun (plural **mercenaries**) a soldier paid by a foreign country to fight in its army

merchandise noun goods to be bought and sold

merchant noun someone who carries on a business in the buying and selling of goods; a trader

merchant bank a bank specializing in providing services to commercial organizations

merchant navy ships and crews employed in trading

merciful *adjective* willing to forgive or be lenient

mercifully *adverb* fortunately, to one's great relief

merciless *adjective* showing no mercy; cruel ▪ **mercilessly** *adverb*

mercurial *adjective* changeable, volatile

mercury *noun* an element, a heavy, silvery liquid metal *(also called:* **quicksilver***)*

mercy *noun (plural* **mercies***)* lenience or forgiveness towards an enemy *etc*; pity

mere *adjective* nothing more than: *mere nonsense*

merely *adverb* only, simply

merge *verb* **1** to combine or join together **2** to blend, come together gradually

merger *noun* a joining together, *eg* of business companies

meridian *noun* an imaginary line around the globe passing through the North and South Poles

meringue *(pronounced me-rang) noun* a baked cake or shell made of sugar and egg-white

merit *noun* positive worth or value ▪ *verb* to deserve

meritorious *adjective, formal* deserving honour or reward

mermaid *noun* an imaginary sea creature with a woman's upper body and a fish's tail

merriment *noun* happy and cheerful behaviour

merry *adjective* full of fun; cheerful and lively ▪ **merrily** *adverb*

merry-go-round *noun, Brit* a roundabout at a fair with wooden horses *etc* for riding on

mesh *noun (plural* **meshes***)* a piece of netting

mesmeric *adjective* **1** hypnotic **2** commanding complete attention; fascinating

mesmerize *or* **mesmerise** *verb* **1** to hypnotize **2** to hold the attention of completely; fascinate

mess *noun (plural* **messes***)* **1** an untidy or disgusting sight **2** disorder, confusion ▪ **mess up** to make untidy, dirty or muddled ▪ **mess with** *US informal* to interfere with, fool with

message *noun* **1** a piece of news or information sent from one person to another **2** a lesson, a moral

messaging *noun* the sending of text or picture messages by mobile phone

messenger *noun* someone who carries a message

messiah *noun* a saviour, a deliverer

messy *adjective* **1** dirty **2** untidy, disordered

met *past form of* meet

metabolic *adjective* of metabolism

metabolism *noun* **1** the combined chemical changes in the cells of a living organism that provide energy for living processes and activity **2** the conversion of nourishment into energy

metal *noun* any of a group of substances (*eg* gold, silver, iron, *etc*) able to conduct heat and electricity

💧* Do not confuse with: **mettle**

metallic *adjective* **1** relating to or made of metal **2** shining like metal

metallurgy *noun* the study of metals ▪ **metallurgist** *noun*

metamorphose *verb* to change completely in appearance or character

metamorphosis *noun* (*plural* **metamorphoses**) a physical change that occurs during the growth of some creatures, *eg* from a tadpole into a frog

metaphor *noun* a way of describing something by suggesting that it is, or has the qualities of, something else, *eg the camel is the ship of the desert*

metaphorical *adjective* using a metaphor or metaphors

metaphorically *adverb* not in real terms, but as an imaginative way of describing something

mete *verb*: **mete out** *formal* to deal out (punishment *etc*)

meteor *noun* a small piece of matter moving rapidly through space, becoming bright as it enters the earth's atmosphere

meteoric *adjective* extremely rapid: *meteoric rise to fame*

meteorite *noun* a meteor which falls to the earth as a piece of rock

meteorologist *noun* someone who studies or forecasts the weather

meteorology *noun* the study of weather and climate

meter *noun* an instrument for measuring the amount of gas, electricity, *etc* used

methane *noun* a colourless gas produced by rotting vegetable matter

method *noun* **1** a planned or regular way of doing something **2** orderly arrangement

methodical *adjective* orderly, done or acting according to some plan

meths *noun, informal* methylated spirits

methylated spirits an alcohol with added violet dye, used as a solvent or fuel

meticulous *adjective* careful and accurate about small details ▪ **meticulously** *adverb*

metre *or US* **meter** *noun* **1** the chief unit of length in the metric system **2** the arrangement of syllables in poetry, or of musical notes, in a regular rhythm

💧* This is one of a large number of words which is spelled with an **-re** ending in British English, but with an **-er** in American English, *eg* centre/center, calibre/caliber, lustre/luster

metric *adjective* of the metric system

metrical *adjective* **1** of poetry: of or in metre **2** arranged in the form of verse

metric system the system of weights and measures based on tens, so that 1 metre = 10 decimetres = 100 centimetres *etc* (*compare with*: **avoirdupois**)

metronome *noun* an instrument that keeps a regular beat, used for music practice

metropolis *noun* (*plural* **metropolises**) a large city, usually the capital city of a country
■ **metropolitan** *adjective*

mettle *noun*, *formal* courage, spirit ■ **on your mettle** out to do your best

  ☀ Do not confuse with: **metal**

mew *noun* a whining cry made by a cat *etc* ■ *verb* to cry in this way

mews *noun* buildings (originally stables) built around a yard or in a lane

mezzanine *noun* a low storey between two main storeys

miaow *noun* the sound made by a cat ■ *verb* to make the sound of a cat

mica *noun* a mineral which glitters and divides easily into thin transparent layers

mice *plural* of **mouse**

mickey *noun*: **take the mickey** *informal* to tease, make fun of someone

micro- *prefix* very small: *microchip/microphone* (= an instrument which picks up and can amplify small sounds)

microbe *noun* a tiny living organism

microchip *noun* a tiny piece of silicon designed to act as a complex electronic circuit

microcomputer *noun* a small computer containing a microprocessor

microcosm *noun* a version on a small scale: *a microcosm of society*

microfiche (*pronounced* maik-roh-feesh) *noun* a sheet of microfilm suitable for filing

microfilm *noun* narrow photographic film on which books, newspapers, *etc* are recorded in miniaturized form

microorganism *noun* an organism that can only be seen through a microscope

microphone *noun* an instrument which picks up sound waves for broadcasting, recording or amplifying

microprocessor *noun* a computer unit consisting of one or more microchips

microscope *noun* a scientific instrument which magnifies very small objects placed under its lens

microscopic *adjective* tiny, minuscule

microsurgery *noun* delicate surgery carried out under a microscope

microwave *noun* 1 a microwave oven 2 a very short radio wave

microwave oven an oven which cooks food by passing microwaves through it

mid- *prefix* placed or occurring in the middle: *mid-morning*

midday *noun* noon

midden *noun* a rubbish or dung heap

middle *noun* the point or part of anything equally distant from its ends or edges; the centre ▪ *adjective* 1 occurring in the middle or centre 2 coming between extreme positions *etc*

middle-aged *adjective* between youth and old age

Middle Ages the time roughly between AD500 and AD1500

middle class the class of people between the working and upper classes

middle-of-the-road *adjective* bland, unadventurous

middle school a school for children from 8 or 9 to 12 or 13 years old

middling *adjective* neither good nor bad; mediocre

midge *noun* a small biting insect

midget *noun* an abnormally small person or thing

midlands *noun* the central, inland part of a country

midnight *noun* twelve o'clock at night ▪ *adjective* occurring at midnight

midriff *noun* the middle of the body, just below the ribs

midst *noun* the middle

midsummer *noun* the time around 21 June, which is the longest day in the year

midway *adverb* halfway

midwife *noun* (*plural* **midwives**) a nurse trained to assist women during childbirth

midwifery (*pronounced* mid-wif-*e*-ri *or* mid-**waif**-ri) *noun* the practice or occupation of being a midwife

midwinter *noun* the time around 21 December, the winter solstice and shortest day in the year

mien (*pronounced* meen) *noun*, *formal* look, appearance

might[1] *noun* power, strength

might[2] *past tense* of **may**

mightily *adverb* 1 extremely, greatly 2 with great strength or force

mighty *adjective* very great or powerful ▪ *adverb*, *US informal* very

| **mighty** *adjective* ▶ might**ier**, mighti**est**

migraine *noun* a severe form of headache

migrant *noun* someone migrating, or recently migrated, from another country

migrate *verb* **1** to change your home or move to another area or country **2** of birds: to fly to a warmer region for the winter ∎ **migration** *noun*

mike *noun*, *informal* a microphone

mild *adjective* **1** not harsh or severe; gentle **2** of taste: not sharp or bitter **3** of weather: not cold **4** of an illness: not serious

mildew *noun* a whitish mark on plants, fabric, *etc* caused by fungus

mildly *adverb* **1** in a mild or calm manner **2** slightly

mile *noun* a measure of length (1.61 kilometres or 1760 yards)

mileage *noun* **1** distance in miles **2** travel expenses (counted by the mile) **3** the amount of use or benefit you can get out of something

mileometer *or* **milometer** *noun* an instrument in a motor vehicle for recording the number of miles travelled

milestone *noun* **1** a stone beside the road showing the number of miles to a certain place **2** something which marks an important event

milieu (*pronounced* meel-**yer**) *noun* surroundings

militant *adjective* aggressive, favouring or taking part in forceful action ∎ *noun* someone who is militant

military *adjective* of soldiers or warfare ∎ **the military** the army

militate *verb* to fight or work (against): *her age will certainly militate against her finding employment*

⚫✳ Do not confuse with: **mitigate**. It may be helpful to remember that the idea of fighting is contained in the word **MILIT**ate (in common with 'military' and 'militia') but not in **mitigate**

militia *noun* a group of fighters, not regular soldiers, trained for emergencies

milk *noun* **1** a white liquid produced by female animals as food for their young **2** this liquid, especially from cows, used as a drink ∎ *verb* to draw milk from

milk float a vehicle that makes deliveries of milk to homes

milkmaid *noun*, *old* a woman who milks cows

milkman *noun* a man who sells or delivers milk

milkshake *noun* a drink of milk and a flavouring whipped together

milk tooth a tooth from the first set of teeth in humans and other mammals

milky *adjective* **1** like milk, creamy **2** white

Milky Way a bright band of stars seen in the night sky

mill *noun* **1** a machine for grinding or crushing grain, coffee, *etc* **2** a building where grain is ground ∎ *verb* to grind

millennium *noun* (*plural* **millennia**) a period of a thousand years

miller *noun* someone who grinds grain

millet *noun* a type of grain used for food

milligram *or* **milligramme** *noun* a thousandth of a gram

millilitre *noun* a thousandth of a litre

millimetre *noun* a thousandth of a metre

milliner *noun* someone who makes and sells women's hats

millinery *noun* the goods sold by a milliner

million *noun* a thousand thousands (1,000,000)

millionaire *noun* someone who has a million pounds (or dollars) or more

millionth *adjective* the last of a series of a million ∎ *noun* one of a million equal parts

millipede *noun* a small crawling insect with a long body and many pairs of legs

millisecond *noun* a thousandth of a second

millstone *noun* something felt as a burden or hindrance

mime *noun* a theatrical art using body movements and facial expressions in place of speech ∎ *verb* **1** to perform a mime **2** to express through mime

mimic *verb* to imitate, especially in a mocking way ∎ *noun* someone who mimics ∎ **mimicry** *noun*

| **mimic** *verb* ▶ **mimics**, **mimicking**, **mimicked**

mimosa *noun* a tree producing bunches of yellow, scented flowers

minaret *noun* a slender tower on an Islamic mosque

mince *verb* to cut or chop into small pieces ∎ *noun* meat chopped finely

mincemeat *noun* a chopped-up mixture of dried fruit, suet, *etc*

mince pie a pie filled with mincemeat

mincer *noun* a machine for mincing food

mind *noun* **1** consciousness, intelligence, understanding **2** intention: *I've a good mind to tell him so* ∎ *verb* **1** to see to, look after **2** to watch out for, be careful of: *mind the step* **3** to object to

minder *noun* **1** someone who looks after a child *etc* **2** a guard or adviser to a public figure

mindful *adjective*: mindful of paying attention to

mindless *adjective* foolish, unthinking; pointless

mine[1] *noun* **1** an underground pit or system of tunnels from which metals, coal, *etc* are dug **2** a heavy charge of explosive material ∎ *verb* to dig or work a mine

mine[2] *pronoun* a thing or things

belonging to me: *that drink is mine*

minefield *noun* an area covered with explosive mines

miner *noun* someone who works in a mine

mineral *noun* a natural substance mined from the earth, *eg* coal, metals, gems, *etc*
■ *adjective* of or containing minerals

mineralogy *noun* the study of minerals ■ **mineralogist** *noun*

mineral water 1 water containing small amounts of minerals **2** *informal* carbonated water

minestrone (*pronounced* min-is-**troh**-ni) *noun* a thick Italian vegetable soup containing rice or pasta

minesweeper *noun* a ship which removes explosive mines

mingle *verb* to mix

mingy (*pronounced* **min**-ji) *adjective*, *informal* stingy, mean

mini- *prefix* smaller than average; compact: *minibus/ minicab*

miniature *noun* a small-scale painting ■ *adjective* on a small scale

minibus *noun* (*plural* **minibuses**) a type of small bus

minim *noun*, *music* a note (♩) equal to two crotchets, or half a semibreve, in length

minimal *adjective* very little indeed: *minimal fuss*

minimize *or* **minimise** *verb* **1** to make seem small or unimportant **2** to make as small as possible

minimum *noun* (*plural* **minima**) the smallest possible quantity
■ *adjective* the least possible

minion *noun* a slave-like follower

minister *noun* **1** the head of a government department **2** a member of the clergy

ministry *noun* (*plural* **ministries**) **1** a government department or its headquarters **2** the work of a member of the clergy

mink *noun* a small weasel-like kind of animal or its fur

minnow *noun* a type of very small river or pond fish

minor *adjective* **1** of less importance, size, *etc* **2** small, unimportant (*contrasted with*: **major**) ■ *noun* someone not yet legally an adult (*i.e.* in the UK, under 18)

minority *noun* (*plural* **minorities**) **1** the smaller number or part **2** the state of being a minor

minster *noun* a large church or cathedral

minstrel *noun* a medieval travelling musician

mint¹ *noun* a plant with strong-smelling leaves, used as flavouring

mint² *noun* a place where coins are made

minuet noun 1 a kind of slow, graceful dance 2 the music for this

minus preposition used to show subtraction, represented by the sign (−): *five minus two equals three or 5 − 2 = 3* ■ adjective of a quantity less than zero

minuscule (pronounced min-is-kyool) adjective tiny, minute

minute[1] (pronounced min-it) noun 1 a sixtieth part of an hour 2 in measuring an angle, the sixtieth part of a degree 3 a very short time 4 minutes notes taken of what is said at a meeting

minute[2] (pronounced mai-nyoot) adjective very small

minx noun (plural minxes) a cheeky young girl

miracle noun 1 a wonderful act beyond normal human powers 2 a fortunate happening with no natural cause or explanation
■ miraculous adjective
■ miraculously adverb

mirage noun something imagined but not really there, eg an oasis seen by travellers in the desert

mire noun deep mud

mirror noun a backed piece of glass which shows the image of someone looking into it ■ verb to copy exactly

mirth noun merriment, laughter
■ mirthful adjective

mis- prefix wrong(ly), bad(ly): *mispronounce/misapply*

misadventure noun an unlucky happening

misappropriate verb to put to a wrong use, eg use (someone else's money) for yourself

misbehave verb to behave badly
■ misbehaviour noun

miscarriage noun 1 a going wrong, failure: *miscarriage of justice* 2 the accidental loss of a foetus during pregnancy

miscarry verb 1 to go wrong or astray 2 to have a miscarriage in pregnancy

| miscarry ► miscarries, miscarrying, miscarried

miscellaneous adjective assorted, made up of several kinds

miscellany noun (plural miscellanies) a mixture or collection of things, eg pieces of writing

mischance noun an unlucky accident

mischief noun naughtiness

mischievous adjective naughty, teasing; causing trouble
■ mischievously adverb

misconception noun a wrong idea, a misunderstanding

misconduct noun bad or immoral behaviour

misconstrue verb to misunderstand

miscreant noun a wicked person

misdeed noun a bad deed, a crime

misdemeanour *noun* a minor offence

miser *noun* someone who hoards money and spends very little

miserable *adjective* 1 very unhappy; wretched 2 having a tendency to be bad-tempered and grumpy 3 depressing

miserly *adjective* stingy, mean

misery *noun* (*plural* miseries) 1 great unhappiness, pain, poverty, *etc* 2 a person who is always sad or bad-tempered

misfit *noun* someone who cannot fit in happily in society *etc*

misfortune *noun* 1 bad luck 2 an unlucky accident

misgiving *noun* fear or doubt, *eg* about the result of an action

misguided *adjective* led astray, mistaken, unwise

mishandle *verb* to treat badly or roughly

mishap *noun* an unlucky accident

misinterpret *verb* to interpret wrongly

misjudge *verb* to judge unfairly or wrongly

mislay *verb* to put (something) aside and forget where it is; lose
| mislay ► mislays, mislaying, mislaid

mislead *verb* to give a false idea (to); deceive ▪ **misleading** *adjective*
| mislead ► misleads, misleading, misled

mismatch *noun* an unsuitable match

misnomer *noun* a wrong or unsuitable name

misplace *verb* to put in the wrong place; mislay

misprint *noun* a mistake in printing

misquote *verb* to make a mistake in repeating something written or said

misrepresent *verb* to give a wrong idea of (someone's words, actions, *etc*)

Miss *noun* (*plural* Misses) 1 a form of address used before the surname of an unmarried woman 2 miss a young woman or girl

miss *verb* 1 to fail to hit, see, hear, understand, *etc* 2 to discover the loss or absence of 3 to feel the lack of: *missing old friends* ▪ *noun* (*plural* misses) 1 the act of missing 2 a failure to hit a target ▪ **miss out** 1 to leave out 2 to be left out of something worthwhile or advantageous

missal *noun* the book containing the words used in the Mass of the Roman Catholic Church

misshapen *adjective* abnormally or badly shaped

missile *noun* a weapon or other object that is thrown or fired

missing *adjective* lost

mission *noun* 1 a task that someone is sent to do 2 a group of representatives sent to another country 3 a group sent to spread a religion **4** the headquarters of such groups **5** someone's chosen task or purpose

missionary noun (plural **missionaries**) someone sent abroad etc to spread a religion

missive noun something sent, eg a letter

misspell verb to spell wrongly ▪ **misspelling** noun

| **misspell** ▶ misspells, misspelling, misspelled or misspelt

misspent adjective spent unwisely, wasted: misspent youth

mist noun a cloud of moisture in the air; thin fog or drizzle ▪ **misty** adjective ▪ **mist up** or **mist over** to cover or become covered with mist

mistake verb **1** to misunderstand, be wrong or make an error about **2** to take (one thing or person) for another ▪ noun a wrong action or statement; an error

| **mistake** verb ▶ mistakes, mistaking, mistaken, mistook

mistaken adjective making an error, unwise

mister full form of **Mr**

mistletoe noun a plant with white berries, used as a Christmas decoration

mistreat verb to treat badly; abuse

mistress noun (plural **mistresses**) **1** a female teacher **2** a

female owner of a dog etc **3** a woman skilled in an art **4** a woman who is the lover though not the legal wife of a man **5** full form of **Mrs**

mistrust noun a lack of trust or confidence in ▪ verb to have no trust or confidence in

misunderstand verb to take a wrong meaning from what is said or done

misunderstanding noun **1** a mistake about a meaning **2** a slight disagreement

misuse noun bad or wrong use ▪ verb **1** to use wrongly **2** to treat badly

mite noun something very small, eg a tiny child

mitigate verb to make (punishment, anger, etc) less great or severe: reasonable efforts must be made to mitigate the risks to society ▪ **mitigation** noun

♦* Do not confuse with: **militate**. It may be helpful to remember that the idea of fighting is contained in the word **MILITate** (in common with 'military' and 'militia') but not in **mitigate**

mitosis noun the division of a cell nucleus to form two new nuclei

mitre noun **1** the pointed headdress worn by archbishops and bishops **2** a slanting joint between two pieces of wood

mitt or **mitten** noun a glove without separate divisions for the four fingers

mix verb 1 to unite or blend two or more things together 2 **mix up** to confuse, muddle 3 to have social contact with other people ▪ noun a mixture, a blending

mixed adjective 1 jumbled together 2 confused, muddled 3 consisting of different kinds 4 for both sexes

mixed number a number consisting of an integer and a vulgar fraction, eg $2\frac{3}{4}$

mixed-up adjective confused, bewildered, emotionally unstable

mixer noun 1 a machine that mixes food 2 someone who mixes socially

mixture noun 1 a number of things mixed together 2 a medicine

mnemonic (pronounced ni-mon-ik) noun a rhyme etc which helps you to remember something

moan noun a low sound of grief or pain ▪ verb to make this sound

moat noun a deep trench around a castle etc, often filled with water

mob noun a noisy crowd ▪ verb to crowd round, or attack, in disorder

| **mob** verb ► mobs, mobb**ing**, mobb**ed**

mobbed adjective, informal very busy, crowded

mobile adjective 1 able to move or be moved easily 2 not fixed, changing quickly 3 portable, not relying on fixed cables etc: mobile phone ▪ noun 1 a decoration or toy hung so that it moves slightly in the air 2 informal a mobile phone

mobility noun freedom or ease of movement, either in physical or career terms

mobilize or **mobilise** verb to gather (troops etc) together ready for active service ▪ **mobilization** noun

moccasin noun a soft leather shoe of the type originally worn by Native Americans

mocha (pronounced mok-a) noun 1 a fine coffee 2 coffee and chocolate mixed together 3 a deep brown colour

mock verb to laugh at, make fun of ▪ adjective false, pretended, imitation

mockery noun 1 the act of mocking 2 a ridiculous imitation

mode noun 1 a manner of doing or acting 2 kind, sort; fashion 3 maths the most frequent value in a set

model noun 1 a design or pattern to be copied 2 a small-scale copy of something: a model of the Titanic 3 a living person who poses for an artist 4 someone employed to wear and display new clothes ▪ adjective 1 acting as a model 2 fit to be copied, perfect: *model behaviour* ▪ *verb* **1** to make a model of **2** to shape according to a particular pattern **3** to wear and display (clothes)

| **model** *verb* ▸ models, modelling, modelled

modem *noun, computing* a device that allows data to be transferred from one computer to another via telephone lines

moderate *adjective* (*pronounced* mod-e-rat) **1** keeping within reason, not going to extremes **2** of medium or average quality, ability, *etc* ▪ *verb* (*pronounced* mod-e-reit) to make or become less great or severe

moderately *adverb* slightly, quite, fairly

moderation *noun* **1** a lessening or calming down **2** the practice of not going to extremes

modern *adjective* belonging to the present or to recent times; not old

modernize *or* **modernise** *verb* to bring up to date
▪ **modernization** *noun*

modest *adjective* **1** not exaggerating achievements; not boastful **2** not very large: *modest salary* **3** behaving decently; not shocking ▪ **modesty** *noun*

modicum *noun* (*plural* **modicums**) a small quantity or amount

modify *verb* **1** to make a change in **2** to make less extreme
▪ **modification** *noun*

| **modify** ▸ modifies, modifying, modified

module *noun* **1** a set course forming a unit in an educational scheme **2** a separate, self-contained section of a spacecraft

mogul *noun* an influential person; a magnate

mohair *noun* **1** the long silky hair of an Angora goat **2** fabric made from this

moist *adjective* damp, very slightly wet

moisten *verb* to make slightly wet or damp

moisture *noun* slight wetness; water or other liquid in tiny drops in the atmosphere or on a surface

moisturize *or* **moisturise** *verb* to add moisture to

moisturizer *or* **moisturiser** *noun* a cosmetic cream that restores moisture to the skin

molar *noun* a back tooth used for grinding food

molasses *noun singular* a thick dark syrup left when sugar is refined

mole[1] *noun* a small burrowing animal, with tiny eyes and soft fur

mole[2] *noun* a small dark spot on the skin, often raised

molecular *adjective* to do with a molecule or molecules

molecule *noun* a group of two or more atoms linked together

molehill *noun* a small heap of earth created by a burrowing mole

molest *verb* to annoy or torment

mollify *verb* to calm down; lessen the anger of

| **mollify** ► **mollifies**,
| **mollifying**, **mollified**

mollusc *noun* one of a group of boneless animals, usually with hard shells, *eg* shellfish and snails

mollycoddle *verb* to pamper, over-protect

molten *adjective* of metal *etc*: melted

moment *noun* a very short space of time; an instant

momentary *adjective* lasting for a moment ▪ **momentarily** *adverb*

momentous *adjective* of great importance

momentum *noun* (*plural* **momenta**) the force of a moving body

monarch *noun* a king, queen, emperor or empress

monarchist *noun* someone who believes in government by a monarch

monarchy *noun* (*plural* **monarchies**) **1** government by a monarch **2** an area governed by a monarch **3** the royal family

monastery *noun* (*plural* **monasteries**) a building housing a group of monks

monastic *adjective* of or like monasteries or monks

Monday *noun* the second day of the week

monetary (*pronounced* **mun**-it-ri) *adjective* of money or coinage

money *noun* **1** coins and banknotes used for payment **2** wealth

moneyed *or* **monied** *adjective* wealthy

mongoose *noun* (*plural* **mongooses**) a small weasel-like animal which kills snakes

mongrel *noun* an animal of mixed breed

monitor *noun* **1** an instrument used to check the operation of a system or apparatus **2** a screen in a television studio showing the picture being transmitted **3** a computer screen **4** a school pupil given certain responsibilities ▪ *verb* to keep a check on

monk *noun* a member of a male religious group living secluded in a monastery

monkey *noun* (*plural* **monkeys**) **1** a long-tailed mammal which walks on four legs **2** a mischievous child

monkey nut a peanut

mono- *or* **mon-** *prefix* one, single: *monarch* (= a person who is the sole ruler of a country)/ *carbon monoxide* (= a gas with only one oxygen atom in its molecule)

monochrome *adjective* **1** in one colour **2** black and white

monocle *noun* a single eyeglass

monogamy *noun* marriage to one spouse at a time ▪ **monogamous** *adjective*

monogram *noun* two or more letters, usually initials, made into a single design

monolithic *adjective* forming a single unmovable mass

monologue *noun* a long speech by one person

monopolize or **monopolise** *verb* 1 to have exclusive rights to 2 to take up the whole of: *monopolizing the conversation*

monopoly *noun* (*plural* **monopolies**) 1 an exclusive right to make or sell something 2 complete unshared possession, control, *etc*

monotonous *adjective* 1 in a single tone 2 unchanging, dull ▪ **monotonously** *adverb*

monotony *noun* lack of variety

monsoon *noun* 1 a wind that blows in the Indian Ocean 2 the rainy season caused by the south-west monsoon in summer

monster *noun* 1 something of unusual size or appearance 2 a huge terrifying creature 3 an evil person ▪ *adjective* huge

monstrosity *noun* (*plural* **monstrosities**) 1 something unnatural 2 something very ugly

monstrous *adjective* 1 huge, horrible 2 extremely cruel

montage (*pronounced* mon-tahsz) *noun* 1 a composite picture 2 a film made up of parts of other films

month *noun* a twelfth part of a year, approximately four weeks

monthly *adjective & adverb* happening once a month

monument *noun* a building, pillar, tomb, *etc* built in memory of someone or an event

monumental *adjective* 1 of a monument 2 huge, enormous ▪ **monumentally** *adverb* (meaning 2)

moo *noun* the sound made by a cow

mood *noun* the state of a person's feelings or temper

moody *adjective* 1 often changing in mood 2 ill-tempered, cross ▪ **moodily** *adverb*

moon *noun* the heavenly body which travels round the earth once each month and reflects light from the sun ▪ *verb* 1 to wander (about) 2 to gaze dreamily (at)

moonbeam *noun* a beam of light from the moon

moonlight *noun* the light of the moon

moonshine *noun* the shining of the moon

moor *noun* a large stretch of open ground, often covered with heather ▪ *verb* to tie up or anchor (a ship *etc*)

moorhen *noun* a kind of water bird

moorings *noun plural* 1 the place where a ship is moored 2 the anchor, rope, *etc* holding it

moorland *noun* a stretch of moor

moose noun (plural **moose**) a large deer-like animal, found in N America

mop noun 1 a pad of sponge or a bunch of short pieces of coarse yarn etc on a handle for washing or cleaning 2 a thick head of hair ■ verb 1 to clean with a mop 2 to clean or wipe: mopped his brow ■ **mop up** to clean up

| **mop** verb ▶ mops, mopping, mopped

mope verb to be unhappy and gloomy

moped noun a pedal bicycle with a motor

moral adjective 1 relating to standards of behaviour and character 2 of correct or acceptable behaviour or character ■ noun 1 the lesson of a story 2 **morals** principles and standards of behaviour

morale (pronounced mo-rahl) noun spirit and confidence

morality noun moral standards

moralize or **moralise** verb to draw a lesson from a story or event

morass noun (plural **morasses**) 1 a marsh or bog 2 a bewildering mass of something: a morass of regulations

moratorium noun (plural **moratoria**) an official suspension or temporary ban

morbid adjective too concerned with gloomy, unpleasant things, especially death ■ **morbidly** adverb

more adjective a greater number or amount of ■ adverb to a greater extent: more beautiful ■ noun 1 a greater proportion or amount 2 a further or additional matter: there are more where this came from

moreish adjective of food etc: enjoyable, making you want more

moreover adverb besides

morgue noun a place where dead bodies are laid, awaiting identification etc

moribund adjective 1 dying 2 stagnant

morn noun, formal morning

morning noun the part of the day before noon ■ adjective of or in the morning

moron noun someone of low mental ability; an idiot ■ **moronic** adjective

morose adjective bad-tempered, gloomy ■ **morosely** adverb

morphine noun a drug which causes sleep or deadens pain

morris dance a traditional English country dance in which male dancers carry sticks and wear bells

morse noun a signalling code with letters represented by dots and dashes (also called: **morse code**)

morsel noun a small piece, eg of food

mortal adjective 1 liable to die

2 causing death; deadly ■ *noun* a human being

mortality *noun* (*plural* **mortalities**) **1** the state of being mortal **2** death **3** frequency of death; death-rate

mortally *adverb* **1** fatally **2** very much, dreadfully: *mortally offended*

mortar *noun* **1** a short gun for firing shells **2** a mixture of lime, sand and water, used for fixing stones *etc*

mortarboard *noun* a university or college cap with a square flat top

mortgage *noun* a sum of money lent through a legal agreement for buying buildings, land, *etc* ■ *verb* to offer (buildings *etc*) as security for money borrowed

mortice *another spelling of* mortise

mortician *noun, US* an undertaker

mortify *verb* to make to feel ashamed or humble ■ **mortifying** *adjective*

| **mortify** ► **mortifies**, **mortifying**, **mortified**

mortise *or* **mortice** *noun* a hole in a piece of wood to receive the shaped end (**tenon**) of another piece

mortise lock *or* **mortice lock** a lock whose mechanism is sunk into the edge of a door

mortuary *noun* (*plural* **mortuaries**) a place where dead

bodies are kept before burial or cremation

mosaic *noun* a picture or design made up of many small pieces of coloured glass, stone, *etc*

Moslem *another spelling of* Muslim

mosque *noun* an Islamic place of worship

mosquito *noun* (*plural* **mosquitoes** *or* **mosquitos**) a biting or blood-sucking insect, often carrying disease

moss *noun* (*plural* **mosses**) a very small flowerless plant, found in moist places

mossy *adjective* covered with moss

most *adjective* the greatest number or amount of ■ *adverb* **1** very, extremely **2** to the greatest extent: *the most severely injured* ■ *noun* the greatest number or amount

mostly *adverb* mainly, chiefly

MOT *noun* a compulsory annual check on behalf of the Ministry of Transport on vehicles over a certain age

motel *noun* a hotel built to accommodate motorists and their vehicles

moth *noun* **1** a flying insect, seen mostly at night **2** the cloth-eating grub of the clothes-moth

mothball *noun* a small ball of chemical used to protect clothes from moths

moth-eaten *adjective* **1** full of

holes made by moths **2** tatty, shabby

mother *noun* **1** a female parent **2** the female head of a convent ■ *verb* **1** to be the mother of **2** to care for like a mother

motherboard *noun, computing* a printed circuit board into which other boards can be slotted

motherhood *noun* the state of being a mother

mother-in-law *noun* the mother of your husband or wife

motherland *noun* the country of your birth

motherly *adjective* of or like a mother

mother-of-pearl *noun* a hard shiny substance which forms inside certain shells

mother tongue a native language

motif (*pronounced* moh-**teef**) *noun* (*plural* **motifs**) a distinctive feature or idea in a piece of music, a play, *etc*

✳ Do not confuse with: **motive**

motion *noun* **1** the act or state of moving **2** a single movement **3** a suggestion put before a meeting for discussion ■ *verb* **1** to make a signal by a movement or gesture **2** to direct (someone) in this way

motionless *adjective* not moving

motivate *verb* to cause

(someone) to act in a certain way ■ **motivation** *noun*

motive *noun* the cause of someone's actions; a reason

✳ Do not confuse with: **motif**

motley *adjective* made up of different colours or kinds

motocross *noun* the sport of motorcycle racing across rough terrain

motor *noun* **1** an engine which causes motion **2** a car ■ *verb* to travel by motor vehicle

motorcade *noun* a procession of cars carrying a head of state *etc*

motorcycle or **motorbike** *noun* a bicycle with a petrol-driven engine ■ **motorcyclist** or **motorbiker** *noun*

motorist *noun* someone who drives a car

motorize or **motorise** *verb* to supply with an engine

motorway *noun* a road with several lanes on which traffic is allowed to drive faster than on other roads

mottled *adjective* marked with spots or blotches

motto *noun* (*plural* **mottoes**) a phrase which acts as a guiding principle or rule

mould[1] *noun* a shape into which a liquid is poured to take on that shape when it cools or sets ■ *verb* **1** to form in a mould **2** to shape

mould[2] *noun* **1** a fluffy growth on

stale food *etc* **2** soil containing rotted leaves *etc*

moulder *verb* to crumble away to dust

moulding *noun* a decorated border of moulded plaster around a ceiling *etc*

mouldy *adjective* affected by mould; stale

moult *verb* of an animal: to shed its feathers, hair, *etc*

mound *noun* **1** a bank of earth or stones **2** a pile; a heap

mount *verb* **1** to go up, ascend **2** to climb on to (a horse, bicycle, *etc*) **3** to fix (a picture *etc*) on to a backing or support **4** to fix (a precious stone) in a casing **5** to organize (an exhibition) ▪ *noun* **1** a support or backing for display **2** a horse, bicycle, *etc* to ride on **3** *old* a mountain

mountain *noun* **1** a large hill **2** a large quantity

mountaineer *noun* a mountain climber

mountainous *adjective* **1** having many mountains **2** huge

mounted *adjective* on horseback: *mounted police*

Mountie *noun*, *informal* a member of the Canadian horseback police

mourn *verb* **1** to grieve for **2** to be sorrowful ▪ **mourner** *noun*

mournful *adjective* sad

mourning *noun* **1** the showing of grief **2** the period during which someone grieves **3** dark-coloured clothes traditionally worn by mourners

mouse *noun* (*plural* **mice**) **1** a small gnawing animal, found in houses and fields **2** a shy, timid, uninteresting person **3** *computing* a device moved by hand which causes corresponding cursor movements on a screen

mousse *noun* a frothy set dish including eggs, cream, *etc*, either sweet or savoury

moustache *noun* unshaved hair above a man's upper lip

mousy *adjective* **1** of a light-brown colour **2** shy, timid, uninteresting

mouth *noun* (*pronounced* mowth) **1** the opening in the head through which an animal or person eats and makes sounds **2** the point of a river where it flows into the sea **3** an opening, an entrance ▪ *verb* (*pronounced* mowdh) **1** to speak **2** to shape (words) in an exaggerated way

mouthful *noun* (*plural* **mouthfuls**) as much as fills the mouth

mouth organ a small wind instrument, moved across the lips

mouthpiece *noun* the part of a musical instrument, tobacco-pipe, *etc* held in the mouth

movable *or* **moveable** *adjective* able to be moved, changed, *etc*

move *verb* **1** to (cause to) change place or position **2** to change your house **3** to rouse or affect the feelings of **4** to rouse into action **5** to propose, suggest ■ *noun* **1** an act of moving **2** a step, an action **3** a shifting of pieces in a game of chess *etc*

movement *noun* **1** the act or manner of moving **2** a change of position **3** a division of a piece of music **4** a group of people united in a common aim: *the peace movement*

movie *noun* a cinema film ■ **the movies** the cinema

moving *adjective* **1** in motion **2** causing emotion ■ **movingly** *adverb*

mow *verb* **1** to cut (grass, hay, *etc*) with a scythe or machine **2** **mow someone** *or* **something down** to destroy them in great numbers

mower *noun* a machine for mowing

MP *abbreviation* **1** Member of Parliament **2** Military Police

Mr *noun* (*short for* **mister**) the form of address used before a man's surname

Mrs *noun* (*short for* **mistress**) the form of address used before a married woman's surname

Ms *noun* a form of address used before the surname of a married or unmarried woman

much *adjective* a great amount of ■ *adverb* to or by a great extent: *much faster* ■ *pronoun* a great amount

muck *noun* dung, dirt, filth

mucus *noun* slimy fluid secreted from the nose *etc*

mud *noun* wet, soft earth

muddle *verb* **1** to confuse, bewilder **2** to mix up **3** to make a mess of ■ *noun* **1** a mess **2** a state of confusion

muddy *adjective* **1** covered with mud **2** unclear, confused ■ *verb* to make or become muddy

mudguard *noun* a shield or guard over wheels to catch mud splashes

muesli *noun* a mixture of grains, nuts and fruit eaten with milk

muff *noun* a tube of warm fabric to cover and keep the hands warm

muffin *noun* **1** a round, flat spongy cake, toasted and eaten hot with butter **2** *US* a small sweet cake made of flour, cornmeal, *etc*

muffle *verb* **1** to wrap up for warmth *etc* **2** to deaden (a sound)

muffler *noun* a scarf

mufti *noun* clothes worn by soldiers *etc* when off duty

mug¹ *noun* **1** a straight-sided cup **2** *informal* someone who is easily fooled **3** *informal* the face

mug² *verb* to attack and rob (someone) in the street ■ **mugger** *noun*

| **mug** ► mugs, mugg*ing*, mugg*ed*

muggy *adjective* of weather:

warm and damp ■ **mugginess** *noun*

mulberry *noun* **1** a tree on whose leaves silkworms are fed **2** its purple berry

mulch *noun* loose straw *etc* laid down to protect plant roots ■ *verb* to cover with mulch

mule[1] *noun* an animal bred from a horse and an ass

mule[2] *noun* a backless slipper

mull *verb*: **mull over** to think over, ponder over

mulled *adjective* of wine, *etc*: mixed with spices and served warm

mullet *noun* an edible small seafish

multi- *prefix* many

multi-coloured *adjective* many-coloured

multimedia *adjective* of a computer: able to run various sound and visual applications

multimillionaire *noun* someone who has property worth several million pounds (or dollars)

multinational *adjective* of a company: having branches in several different countries

multiple *adjective* **1** affecting many parts: *multiple injuries* **2** involving many things of the same sort: *vehicles in a multiple crash* ■ *noun* a number or quantity which contains another an exact number of times

multiple sclerosis a progressive nerve disease resulting in paralysis

multiplex *adjective* of a cinema: including several screens and theatres in one building

multiplicand *noun* a number which is to be multiplied by another (the **multiplier**)

multiplication *noun* the act of multiplying

multiplier *noun* the number by which another (the **multiplicand**) is to be multiplied

multiply *verb* **1** to increase **2** to increase a number by adding it to itself a certain number of times: *2 multiplied by 3 is 6*

| **multiply** ▶ multiplies, multiplying, multiplied

multitasking *noun*, *computing* the action of running several processes simultaneously

multitude *noun* a great number; a crowd

mum[1] *noun*, *informal* mother

mum[2] *adjective* silent

mumble *verb* to speak indistinctly

mummify *verb* to make into a mummy (meaning 2)

| **mummify** ▶ mummifies, mummifying, mummified

mummy[1] *noun* (*plural* **mummies**) *informal* mother

mummy[2] *noun* (*plural* **mummies**) a dead body preserved by wrapping in bandages and treating with wax, spices, *etc*

mumps *noun singular* an

infectious disease affecting glands at the side of the neck, causing swelling

munch *verb* to chew noisily

mundane *adjective* dull, ordinary

municipal *adjective* of or owned by a city or town

municipality *noun* a city or town; an area covered by local government

munitions *noun plural* weapons and ammunition used in war

mural *noun* a painting or design on a wall

murder *verb* to kill someone unlawfully and on purpose ▪ *noun* the act of murdering

murderer *noun* someone who commits murder

murderess *noun, old* a woman murderer

murderous *adjective* capable or guilty of murder; wicked

murky *adjective* dark, gloomy ▪ **murkiness** *noun*

murmur *noun* 1 a low indistinct continuous sound 2 a hushed speech or tone ▪ *verb* 1 to make a murmur 2 to complain, grumble

muscle *noun* 1 fleshy tissue which contracts and stretches to cause body movements 2 an area of this in the body 3 physical strength or power

muscular *adjective* 1 of muscles 2 strong

Muse *noun* one of the nine goddesses of poetry, music, dancing, *etc* in classical mythology

muse *verb* to think (over) in a quiet, leisurely way

museum *noun* (*plural* **museums**) a building for housing and displaying objects of artistic, scientific or historic interest

mush *noun* 1 something soft and wet 2 overly sentimental music, drama, *etc*

mushroom *noun* an edible fungus, usually umbrella-shaped ▪ *verb* to grow very quickly

mushy *adjective* 1 soft and wet 2 overly sentimental

music *noun* 1 the art of arranging, combining, *etc* certain sounds able to be produced by the voice, or by instruments 2 an arrangement of such sounds or its written form 3 a sweet or pleasant sound

musical *adjective* 1 of music 2 sounding sweet or pleasant 3 having a talent for music ▪ *noun* a light play or film with a lot of songs and dancing in it ▪ **musically** *adverb*

musician *noun* 1 a specialist in music 2 someone who plays a musical instrument

musk *noun* a strong perfume, obtained from certain animals or artificially

musket *noun* a kind of gun once used by soldiers

musketeer *noun* a soldier armed with a musket

Muslim or **Moslem** noun a follower of the Islamic religion ■ adjective Islamic

muslin noun a fine, soft cotton cloth

mussel noun an edible shellfish with two separate halves to its shell

must verb 1 used with another verb to express necessity: I must finish this today 2 expressing compulsion: you must do as you're told 3 expressing certainty or probability: that must be the right answer ■ noun something that must be done; a necessity

mustang noun a North American wild horse

mustard noun 1 a plant with sharp-tasting seeds 2 a hot yellow paste made from its seeds

muster verb to gather up or together (eg troops, courage)

musty adjective smelling old and stale

mutate verb 1 to undergo mutation 2 to change

mutation noun 1 change in the genes or chromosomes of an organism 2 any change

mute adjective 1 not able to speak; dumb 2 silent

muted adjective 1 of a sound: made quieter, hushed 2 of a colour: not bright

mutilate verb 1 to inflict great physical damage on; maim 2 to damage greatly ■ **mutilation** noun

mutineer noun someone who takes part in a mutiny

mutinous adjective rebellious; refusing to obey orders

mutiny verb 1 to rise against those in power 2 to refuse to obey the commands of military officers ■ noun (plural **mutinies**) refusal to obey commands; rebellion

| **mutiny** verb ▶ mutinies,
| mutinying, mutinied

mutt noun, slang 1 a dog 2 an idiot

mutter verb to speak in a low voice; mumble

mutton noun meat from a sheep, used as food

mutual adjective 1 given by each to the other(s): mutual help 2 shared by two or more: mutual friend

mutually adverb of a relationship between two people or things: each to the other, in both directions

muzzle noun 1 an animal's nose and mouth 2 a fastening placed over an animal's mouth to prevent it biting 3 the open end of a gun ■ verb 1 to put a muzzle on (a dog etc) 2 to prevent from speaking freely

muzzy adjective cloudy, confused

my adjective belonging to me: my book

myna or **mynah** noun a bird which can imitate human speech

myopic adjective short-sighted

myriad *noun* a very great number ▪ *adjective* very many, countless

myrrh *noun* a bitter-tasting resin used in medicines, perfumes, *etc*

myrtle *noun* a type of evergreen shrub

myself *pronoun* **1** used reflexively: *I can see myself in the mirror* **2** used for emphasis: *I wrote this myself*

mysterious *adjective* **1** puzzling, difficult to understand **2** secret, hidden, intriguing ▪ **mysteriously** *adverb*

mystery *noun* (*plural* **mysteries**) **1** something that cannot be or has not been explained; something puzzling **2** a deep secret

mystic *noun* someone who seeks knowledge of sacred or mystical things by going into a state of spiritual ecstasy

mystical *adjective* having a secret or sacred meaning beyond ordinary human understanding

mystify *verb* **1** to puzzle greatly **2** to confuse, bewilder

| **mystify** ▸ mysti*fies*, mystify*ing*, mysti*fied*

mystique (*pronounced* mis-**teek**) *noun* an atmosphere of mystery about someone or something

myth *noun* **1** a story about gods, heroes, *etc* of ancient times; a fable **2** something imagined or untrue

mythical *adjective* **1** of a myth **2** invented, imagined

mythological *adjective* of myth or mythology; mythical

mythology *noun* **1** the study of myths **2** a collection of myths

myxomatosis *noun* a contagious disease of rabbits

N*n*

N *abbreviation* **1** north **2** northern

nab *verb, informal* **1** to snatch, seize **2** to arrest

| **nab** ► nabs, nabb*ing*, nabb*ed*

nadir *noun* **1** the point of the heavens opposite the zenith **2** the lowest point of anything

naff *adjective, slang* inferior, crass, tasteless

nag *verb* to find fault with constantly ■ *noun* a horse

| **nag** *verb* ► nags, nagg*ing*, nagg*ed*

nail *noun* **1** a horny covering protecting the tips of the fingers and toes **2** a thin pointed piece of metal for fastening wood *etc*
■ *verb* **1** to fasten with nails **2** to enclose in a box *etc* with nails **3** *informal* to catch, trap

naive *or* **naïve** *adjective* **1** simple in thought, manner or speech **2** inexperienced and lacking knowledge of the world ■ **naiveté** *or* **naïveté** *noun*

naked *adjective* **1** without clothes **2** having no covering **3** bald, blatant: *naked lie* **4** of feelings: bad or unpleasant, and neither hidden nor controlled
■ **nakedly** *adverb* (meaning 4)

namby-pamby *adjective* childish, feeble

name *noun* **1** a word by which a person, place or thing is known **2** fame, reputation: *making a name for himself* **3** an offensive description: *call people names* **4** authority: *in the name of the king*
■ *verb* **1** to give a name to **2** to speak of by name, mention **3** to appoint

nameless *adjective* without a name, not named

namely *adverb* that is to say

namesake *noun* someone with the same name as another

nanny *noun* (*plural* **nannies**) a children's nurse

nanny goat a female goat

nano- *prefix* **1** a thousand millionth: *nanosecond* **2** microscopic in size

nap *noun* **1** a short sleep **2** a woolly or fluffy surface on cloth
■ *verb* to take a short sleep

| **nap** *verb* ► naps, napp*ing*, napp*ed*

nape *noun* the back of the neck

napkin *noun* a small piece of cloth or paper for wiping the lips at meals

nappy *noun* (*plural* **nappies**) a piece of cloth, or thick pad, put between a baby's legs to absorb urine and faeces

narcissism *noun* excessive admiration of yourself
■ **narcissistic** *adjective*

narcissus *noun* (*plural* **narcissi** or **narcissuses**) a plant like a daffodil with a white, star-shaped flower

narcotic *noun* a type of drug that brings on sleep or stops pain

nark *noun* a persistent complainer ■ *verb* to grumble

narrate *verb* to tell a story
■ **narration** *noun* ■ **narrator** *noun*

narrative *noun* a story
■ *adjective* telling a story

narrow *adjective* **1** of small extent from side to side, not wide **2** with little to spare: *a narrow escape* **3** lacking wide interests or experience: *narrow views* ■ *verb* to make or become narrow

narrowly *adverb* closely; barely

narrow-minded *adjective* unwilling to accept or tolerate new ideas

nasal *adjective* **1** of the nose **2** sounded through the nose

nascent *adjective* beginning to develop, in an early stage

nasturtium *noun* a climbing plant with brightly-coloured flowers

nasty *adjective* **1** very disagreeable or unpleasant **2** of a problem *etc*: difficult to deal with **3** of an injury: serious ■ **nastily** *adverb* (meaning 1)

nation *noun* **1** the people living in the same country, or under the same government **2** a race of people: *the French nation*

national *adjective* of, relating to or belonging to a nation or race
■ *noun* someone belonging to a nation: *a British national*
■ **nationally** *adverb*

nationalism *noun* the desire to bring the people of a nation together under their own government ■ **nationalist** *noun* & *adjective* ■ **nationalistic** *adjective*

nationality *noun* membership of a particular nation

nationwide *adjective* & *adverb* over the whole of a nation

native *adjective* **1** born in a person: *native intelligence* **2** of someone's birth: *my native land*
■ *noun* **1** someone born in a certain place: *a native of Peru* **2** an inhabitant of a country from earliest times before the discovery by explorers, settlers, *etc*

Native American a member of one of the peoples originating in America

Nativity *noun*: **the Nativity** the birth of Jesus Christ

natty *adjective* trim, tidy, smart
■ **nattily** *adverb*

natural *adjective* **1** of nature

2 produced by nature, not artificial **3** of a quality *etc*: present at birth, not learned afterwards **4** unpretentious, simple **5** of a result *etc*: expected, normal ■ *noun* **1** someone with a natural ability **2** *music* a note which is neither a sharp nor a flat, shown by the sign (♮)

natural gas gas suitable for burning found in the earth or under the sea

naturalist *noun* someone who studies animal and plant life

naturalize *or* **naturalise** *verb* to give the rights of a citizen to (someone born in another country)

naturally *adverb* **1** by nature **2** simply **3** of course

nature *noun* **1** the things which make up the physical world, *eg* animals, trees, rivers, mountains, *etc* **2** the qualities which characterize someone or something: *a kindly nature*

naturism *noun* the belief in nudity practised openly ■ **naturist** *noun*

naught *noun* nothing: *plans came to naught*

●* Do not confuse with: **nought**

naughty *adjective* bad, misbehaving ■ **naughtily** *adverb*

nausea *noun* a feeling of sickness

nauseate *verb* to make sick, fill

with disgust ■ **nauseating** *adjective* sickening

nauseous *adjective* sickening; disgusting

nautical *adjective* of ships or sailors

nautical mile 1.85 kilometres (6080 feet)

naval *adjective* of the navy

nave *noun* the middle or main part of a church

navel *noun* the small hollow in the centre of the front of the belly

navigable *adjective* able to be used by ships

navigate *verb* **1** to steer or pilot a ship, aircraft, *etc* on its course **2** to sail on, over or through **3** to use hyperlinks to move between the different parts of a Web site

navigation *noun* the art of navigating ■ **navigational** *adjective*

navigator *noun* someone who steers or sails a ship *etc*

navy *noun* (*plural* **navies**) **1** a nation's fighting ships **2** the men and women serving on these

navy blue dark blue

nay *adverb*, *old* no

Nazi *noun*, *history* a member of the National Socialist Party, a party ruling Germany in 1933–45 ■ **Nazism** *noun*

NB *or* **nb** *abbreviation* note well (from Latin *nota bene*)

NE *abbreviation* north-east; north-eastern

Neanderthal *adjective* **1** of a

primitive type of human living during the Stone Age **2** *informal* primitive or old-fashioned

neap tide a tide at the first and last quarters of the Moon, when there is least variation between high and low water

near *adjective* **1** not far away in place or time **2** close in relationship, friendship, *etc* **3** barely avoiding or almost reaching (something): *a near disaster* ■ *adverb* to or at a short distance; nearby ■ *preposition* close to ■ *verb* to approach

nearby *adverb* to or at a short distance

nearly *adverb* almost

nearside *adjective* of the side of a vehicle: furthest from the centre of the road (*contrasted with:* **offside**)

neat *adjective* **1** trim, tidy **2** skilfully done **3** of an alcoholic drink: not diluted with water *etc*

nebula *noun* (*plural* **nebulae**) a shining cloud-like appearance in the night sky, produced by very distant stars or by a mass of gas and dust

nebulous *adjective* hazy, vague

necessarily *adverb* for certain, definitely, inevitably

necessary *adjective* not able to be done without

necessitate *verb* to make necessary; force ■ **necessity** *noun* (*plural* **necessities**) **1**

something necessary **2** great need; want, poverty

neck *noun* **1** the part between the head and body **2** a narrow passage or area: *neck of a bottle* ■ **neck and neck** running side by side, staying exactly equal

necklace *noun* a string of beads or precious stones *etc* worn round the neck

nectar *noun* **1** the sweet liquid collected from flowers by bees to make honey **2** the drink of the ancient Greek gods

nectarine *noun* a kind of peach with a smooth skin

née (*pronounced* nei) *adjective* born (in stating a woman's surname before her marriage): *Mrs Rita Brown, née Stone*

need *verb* **1** to be without, be in want of **2** to require ■ *noun* **1** necessity, needfulness **2** difficulty, want, poverty

needful *adjective* necessary

needle *noun* **1** a small, sharp piece of steel used in sewing, with a small hole (**eye**) at the top for thread **2** a long thin piece of metal, wood, *etc* used *eg* in knitting **3** a thin hollowed-out piece of steel attached to a hypodermic syringe *etc* **4** the moving pointer in a compass **5** the long, sharp-pointed leaf of a pine, fir, *etc* **6** a stylus on a record-player

needless *adjective* unnecessary

needlework *noun* producing

things by sewing and embroidery

needy *adjective* poor

negate *verb* **1** to prove the opposite **2** to refuse to accept, reject (a proposal *etc*)

negative *adjective* **1** meaning or saying 'no', as an answer (*contrasted with*: **positive**) **2** of a person, attitude, *etc*: timid, lacking spirit or ideas **3** of a number: less than zero ▪ *noun* **1** a word or statement by which something is denied **2** the photographic film, from which prints are made, in which light objects appear dark and dark objects appear light

neglect *verb* **1** to treat carelessly **2** to fail to give proper attention to **3** to fail to do ▪ *noun* lack of care and attention

negligée *noun* a women's loose dressing-gown made of thin material

negligent *adjective* careless ▪ **negligence** *noun* ▪ **negligently** *adverb*

♦※ Do not confuse: **negligent** and **negligible**

negligible *adjective* not worth thinking about; very small

negotiable *adjective* able to be negotiated

negotiate *verb* **1** to discuss a subject (with) in order to reach agreement **2** to arrange (a treaty, payment, *etc*) **3** to get past (an obstacle or difficulty)

negotiation *noun* (meanings 1 and 2) ▪ **negotiator** *noun* (meanings 1 and 2)

Negro *noun* (*plural* **Negroes**) a Black African, or Black person of African descent

neigh *verb* to cry like a horse ▪ *noun* a horse's cry

neighbour *or US* **neighbor** *noun* someone who lives near another

neighbourhood *noun* surrounding district or area

neighbouring *adjective* near or next in position

neighbourly *adjective* friendly

neither *adjective & pronoun* not either: *neither bus goes that way* ▪ *conjunction* (sometimes with **nor**) used to show alternatives in the negative: *neither Bill nor David knew the answer*

neo- *prefix* new, recently

Neolithic *adjective* relating to the later Stone Age

neon *noun* a gas that glows red when electricity is passed through it

neonatal *adjective* of newly born babies

nephew *noun* the son of a brother or sister

nerd *noun, informal* a socially inept, irritating person

nerve *noun* **1** one of the fibres which carry feeling from all parts of the body to the brain **2** courage, coolness **3** *informal* impudence, cheek **4 nerves**

informal nervousness and stress
■ *verb* to strengthen the nerve or will of

nerve cell any of the cells in the nervous system (*also called:* neurone)

nerve-racking or **nerve-wracking** *adjective* causing nervousness or stress

nervous *adjective* **1** of the nerves **2** easily excited or frightened; timid **3** worried, frightened or uneasy ■ **nervously** *adverb* (meaning 3) ■ **nervousness** *noun* (meanings 2 and 3)

nervous system the brain, spinal cord and nerves of an animal or human being

nervy *adjective* excitable, jumpy

nest *noun* **1** a structure in which birds (and some animals and insects) live and rear their young **2** a shelter, a den ■ *verb* to build a nest and live in it

nestle *verb* **1** to lie close together as in a nest **2** to settle comfortably

nestling *noun* a young newly hatched bird

Net *noun*: **the Net** *informal* the Internet

net *noun* **1** a loose arrangement of crossed and knotted cord, string or thread, used for catching fish, wearing over the hair, *etc* **2** fine meshed material, used to make curtains, petticoats, *etc* **3** a flat figure made up of polygons which fold and join to form a polyhedron ■ *adjective* (*also:*

nett) **1** of profit *etc*: remaining after expenses and taxes have been paid **2** of weight: not including packaging ■ *verb* **1** to catch or cover with a net **2** to put (a ball) into a net **3** to make by way of profit

| **net** *verb* ► nets, net*ting*, net*ted*

netball *noun* a team game in which a ball is thrown into a high net

nether *adjective* lower

nethermost *adjective* lowest

nett *see* net

netting *noun* fabric of netted string, wire, *etc*

nettle *noun* a plant covered with hairs which sting sharply ■ *verb* to make angry, provoke

network *noun* **1** an arrangement of lines crossing one another **2** a widespread organization **3** a system of linked computers, radio stations, *etc*

neuralgia *noun* a pain in the nerves, especially in those of the head and face

neurone or **neuron** *see* **nerve cell**

neurosis *noun* a type of mental illness in which the patient suffers from extreme anxiety

neurotic *adjective* **1** suffering from neurosis **2** in a bad nervous state ■ *noun* someone suffering from neurosis ■ **neurotically** *adverb*

neuter *adjective* **1** *grammar*

neutral neither masculine nor feminine **2** of an animal: neither male nor female ∎ *verb* to sterilize (an animal)

neutral *adjective* **1** taking no side in a quarrel or war **2** of a colour: not strong or definite **3** of a substance: neither acid nor alkaline ∎ *noun* **1** someone or a nation that takes no side in a war *etc* **2** the gear position used when a vehicle is not moving

∎ **neutrality** *noun* (adjective, meaning I)

neutralize or **neutralise** *verb* **1** to make neutral **2** to make useless or harmless

neutron *noun* an uncharged particle which forms part of the nucleus of an atom (*see also* **electron**, **proton**)

never *adverb* **1** not ever; at no time **2** under no circumstances

nevertheless *adverb* in spite of that: *I hate opera, but I'll come with you nevertheless*

new *adjective* **1** recent; not seen or known before **2** not used or worn; fresh

newcomer *noun* someone lately arrived

newfangled *adjective* new and not thought very good

newly *adverb* (*used before past participles*) only recently

news *noun singular* **1** report of a recent event **2** new information

newsagent *noun* a shopkeeper who sells newspapers

newsgroup *noun* on the Internet, a group of individuals who share information, often on a particular subject

newspaper *noun* a paper printed daily or weekly containing news

newt *noun* a small lizard-like animal, living on land and in water

newton *noun* a unit used to measure force

next *adjective* nearest, closest in place, time, *etc* ∎ *adverb* in the nearest place or at the nearest time

nib *noun* a pen point

nibble *verb* to take little bites (of) ∎ *noun* a little bite

nice *adjective* **1** agreeable, pleasant **2** careful, precise, exact: *a nice distinction*

nicely *adverb* pleasantly; very well

niche (*pronounced* neesh) *noun* **1** a hollow in a wall for a statue, vase, *etc* **2** a suitable place in life: *she hasn't yet found her niche* **3** a gap in a market for a type of product

nick *noun* **1** a little cut, a notch **2** *slang* prison, jail ∎ *verb* **1** to cut notches in **2** *slang* to steal

nickel *noun* **1** a greyish-white metal used for mixing with other metals and for plating **2** *US* a 5-cent coin

nickname *noun* an informal name used instead of someone's real name, *eg* for fun or as an insult

nicotine *noun* a harmful substance contained in tobacco

niece *noun* the daughter of a brother or sister

nifty *adjective, slang* 1 fine, smart, neat 2 speedy, agile

niggardly *adjective* mean, stingy

niggle *verb* to irritate, rankle ▪ *noun* 1 an irritation 2 a minor criticism

niggling *adjective* 1 unimportant, trivial, fussy 2 of a worry or fear: small but always present

nigh *adjective, old* near

night *noun* 1 the period of darkness between sunset and sunrise 2 darkness ▪ *adjective* 1 of or for night 2 happening, active, *etc* at night

nightfall *noun* the beginning of night

nightingale *noun* a small bird, the male of which sings beautifully by night and day

nightly *adjective & adverb* 1 by night 2 every night

nightmare *noun* a frightening dream

nihilism *noun* belief in nothing ▪ **nihilist** *noun* ▪ **nihilistic** *adjective*

nil *noun* nothing

nimble *adjective* quick and neat, agile ▪ **nimbly** *adverb*

nimbus *noun* a rain cloud

nincompoop *noun* a weak, foolish person

nine *noun* the number 9 ▪ *adjective* 9 in number

nineteen *noun* the number 19 ▪ *adjective* 19 in number

nineteenth *adjective* the last of a series of nineteen ▪ *noun* one of nineteen equal parts

ninetieth *adjective* the last of a series of ninety ▪ *noun* one of ninety equal parts

ninety *noun* the number 90 ▪ *adjective* 90 in number

ninja *noun, history* a Japanese assassin, trained in martial arts

ninny *noun (plural* **ninnies)** a fool

ninth *adjective* the last of a series of nine ▪ *noun* one of nine equal parts

nip *verb* 1 to pinch, squeeze tightly 2 to be stingingly painful 3 to bite, cut (off) 4 to halt the growth of, damage (plants *etc*) 5 *informal* to go nimbly or quickly ▪ *noun* 1 a pinch 2 a sharp coldness in the weather: *a nip in the air* 3 a small amount: *nip of whisky*

| **nip** *verb* ► nips, nip*ping*, nip*ped*

nipper *noun, informal* 1 a child, a youngster 2 **nippers** pincers, pliers

nipple *noun* the pointed part of the breast from which a baby sucks milk

nippy *adjective, informal* 1

speedy, nimble **2** frosty, very cold

Nirvana *noun* the state to which a Buddhist or Hindu aspires as the best attainable ·

nit *noun* **1** the egg of a louse or other small insect **2** *informal* an idiot, a nitwit

nitrate *noun* a substance formed from nitric acid, often used as a soil fertilizer

nitric acid a strong acid containing nitrogen

nitrogen *noun* a gas forming nearly four-fifths of ordinary air

nitro-glycerine *noun* a powerful kind of explosive

nitwit *noun* a very stupid person

No *or* **no** *abbreviation* number

no *adjective* **1** not any: *they have no money* **2** not a: *she is no beauty* ▪ *adverb* not at all: *the patient is no better* ▪ *exclamation* expressing a negative: *are you feeling better today? No!* ▪ *noun* (*plural* **noes**) **1** a refusal **2** a vote against ▪ **no go** not possible, futile ▪ **no way** *informal* under no circumstances

no-ball *noun*, *cricket* a bowled ball disallowed by the rules

nobble *verb*, *slang* **1** get hold of **2** persuade, coerce **3** seize, arrest

noble *adjective* **1** great and good, fine **2** of aristocratic birth ▪ *noun* an aristocrat ▪ **nobility** *noun* **1** the aristocracy **2** goodness, greatness of mind or character ▪ **nobleman, noblewoman** *noun* ▪ **nobly** *adverb*

noble gas (*also called*: **inert gas**)

one of the gases helium, neon, argon, krypton, xenon and radon, that do not react with other substances

nobody *pronoun* not any person ▪ *noun* someone of no importance

nocturnal *adjective* happening or active at night

nod *verb* **1** to bend the head forward quickly, often as a sign of agreement **2** to let the head drop in weariness ▪ *noun* an action of nodding ▪ **nod off** to fall asleep

| **nod** *verb* ► nod*s*, nodd*ing*, nodd*ed*

node *noun* **1** the swollen part of a branch or twig where leaf-stalks join it **2** a swelling

nodule *noun* a small rounded lump

noise *noun* a sound, often one which is loud or harsh ▪ **noiseless** *adjective* ▪ **noisy** *adjective* making a loud sound

| **noisy** ► nois*ier*, nois*iest*

nomad *noun* **1** one of a group of people without a fixed home who wander with their animals in search of pasture **2** someone who wanders from place to place ▪ **nomadic** *adjective*

no-man's-land land owned by no one, especially that lying between two opposing armies

nomenclature *noun* **1** a system of naming **2** names

nominal *adjective* **1** in name only **2** very small: *a nominal fee*

nominate verb to propose (someone) for a post or for election; appoint ▪ **nomination** noun

nominee noun someone whose name is put forward for a post

non- prefix not (used with many words to change their meaning to the opposite): non-aggression/non-event/non-smoking

nonagon noun a nine-sided figure

nonchalant adjective not easily roused or upset, cool ▪ **nonchalance** noun ▪ **nonchalantly** adverb

non-commissioned adjective belonging to the lower ranks of army officers, below second-lieutenant

non-committal adjective unwilling to express, or not expressing, an opinion

nonconformist noun someone who does not agree with those in authority, especially in church matters ▪ adjective not agreeing with authority

nondescript adjective lacking anything noticeable or interesting

none adverb not at all: none the worse ▪ pronoun not one, not any

nonentity noun (plural **nonentities**) someone of no importance

non-existent adjective not existing, not real

nonplussed adjective taken aback, confused

nonsense noun **1** words that have no sense or meaning **2** foolishness ▪ **nonsensical** adjective

non sequitur a remark unconnected with what has gone before

non-stop adjective going on without a stop

noodle noun a long thin strip of pasta, eaten in soup or served with a sauce

nook noun **1** a corner **2** a small recess

noon noun twelve o'clock midday

no-one or **no one** pronoun not any person, nobody

noose noun a loop in a rope etc that tightens when pulled

nor conjunction used (often with **neither**) to show alternatives in the negative: neither Sean nor I can speak Swedish

Nordic adjective **1** relating to Finland or Scandinavia **2** of skiing: involving cross-country and jumping events

norm noun a pattern or standard to judge other things against

normal adjective ordinary, usual according to a standard ▪ **normality** noun ▪ **normally** adverb

north noun one of the four chief directions, that to the left of someone facing the rising sun

■ *adjective & adverb* in or to the north ■ **north-east** *noun* the point of the compass midway between north and east ■ **northerly** *adjective* **1** towards the north **2** of wind: from the north ■ **northern** *adjective* of, from or in the north ■ **northerner** *noun* someone living in a northern region or country ■ **northward** *or* **northwards** *adjective & adverb* towards the north ■ **north-west** *noun* the point of the compass midway between north and west

North Pole *see* pole

nose *noun* **1** the part of the face by which people and animals smell and breathe **2** a jutting-out part, *eg* the front of an aeroplane ■ *verb* **1** to track by smelling **2** *informal* to interfere in other people's affairs, pry (into)

nosedive *noun* a headfirst dive by an aeroplane ■ *verb* to dive headfirst

nosey *or* **nosy** *adjective* inquisitive, fond of prying

nostalgia *noun* **1** a longing for past times **2** a longing for home ■ **nostalgic** *adjective* ■ **nostalgically** *adverb*

nostril *noun* either of the two openings of the nose

not *adverb* expressing a negative, refusal or denial: *I am not going/give it to me, not to him/I did not break the window*

notable *adjective* worth taking notice of; important, remarkable ■ *noun* an important person ■ **notably** *adverb*

notary *noun* (*plural* **notaries**) an official who sees that written documents are drawn up in a way required by law

notation *noun* **1** the showing of numbers, musical sounds, *etc* by signs: *mathematical notation* **2** a set of such signs

notch *noun* (*plural* **notches**) a small V-shaped cut ■ *verb* to make a notch ■ **notched** *adjective*

note *noun* **1** a sign or piece of writing to draw someone's attention **2** **notes** details for a speech, from a talk, *etc* set down in a short form **3** a short explanation **4** a short letter **5** a piece of paper used as money: *£5 note* **6** a single sound or the sign standing for it in music **7** a key on the piano *etc* ■ *verb* **1** to make a note of **2** to notice ■ **of note** well-known, distinguished ■ **take note of** to notice particularly

notebook *noun* **1** a small book for taking notes **2** a small laptop computer

noted *adjective* well-known

notepaper *noun* writing paper

noteworthy *adjective* notable, remarkable

nothing *noun* **1** no thing, not anything **2** nought, zero **3** something of no importance ■ *adverb* not at all: *he's nothing like his father*

nothingness *noun* **1** non-

existence **2** space, emptiness
notice *noun* **1** a public
announcement **2** attention **3** a
period of warning given before
leaving, or before dismissing
someone from, a job ■ *verb* to see,
observe, take note of
noticeable *adjective* easily
noticed, standing out
■ **noticeably** *adverb*
notifiable *adjective* that must be
reported: *a notifiable disease*
notify *verb* **1** to inform **2** to give
notice of ■ **notification** *noun*

notify ► notif*ies*, notify*ing*,
notif*ied*

notion *noun* **1** an idea **2** a vague
belief or opinion
notorious *adjective* well known
because of badness ■ **notoriety**
noun
notwithstanding *preposition*
in spite of: *notwithstanding his
poverty, he refused all help*
nougat *noun* a sticky kind of
sweet containing nuts *etc*
nought *noun* the figure 0, zero

♣* Do not confuse with:
naught

noun *noun*, *grammar* the word
used as the name of someone or
something, *eg Ali* and *tickets* in
the sentence *Ali bought the tickets*
nourish *verb* **1** to feed **2** to
encourage the growth of
nourishing *adjective* giving the
body what is necessary for health
and growth

nourishment *noun* **1** food **2** an
act of nourishing
nouveau riche (*pronounced*
noo-voh **reesh**) someone who has
recently acquired wealth but not
good taste
nova *noun* (*plural* **novae** or
novas) a star that suddenly
increases in brightness for a time
novel *adjective* new and strange
■ *noun* a book telling a long story
novelist *noun* a writer of novels
novelty *noun* (*plural* **novelties**) **1**
something new and strange **2**
newness **3** a small, cheap
souvenir or toy
November *noun* the eleventh
month of the year
novice *noun* a beginner
now *adverb* **1** at the present time
2 immediately before the present
time: *I thought of her just now* **3** in
the present circumstances: *I can't
go now because my mother is ill*
■ *conjunction* (often **now that**)
because, since: *you can't go out
now that it's raining* ■ **now and
then** *or* **now and again**
sometimes, from time to time
nowadays *adverb* in present
times, these days
nowhere *adverb* not in, or to,
any place
noxious *adjective* harmful

♣* Do not confuse with:
obnoxious

nozzle *noun* a spout fitted to the
end of a pipe, tube, *etc*

nuance noun a slight difference in meaning or colour etc

nubile adjective of a young woman: attractive

nuclear adjective 1 of a nucleus, especially that of an atom 2 produced by the splitting of the nuclei of atoms

nuclear family the family unit made up of mother, father and children

nuclear fission the splitting of atomic nuclei

nuclear fusion the creation of a new nucleus by merging two lighter ones, with release of energy

nucleus noun (plural **nuclei**) 1 the central part of an atom 2 the central part round which something collects or from which it grows: the nucleus of my collection 3 the part of a plant or animal cell that controls its development

nude adjective without clothes, naked ■ noun 1 an unclothed human figure 2 a painting or statue of such a figure ■ **in the nude** naked

nudge noun a gentle push, eg with the elbow or shoulder ■ verb to give a gentle push

nudist noun someone who is in favour of going without clothes in public ■ **nudism** noun

nudity noun the state of being nude

nugget noun a lump, especially of gold

nuisance noun someone or something annoying or troublesome

null adjective: **null and void** having no legal force

nullify verb 1 to make useless or of no effect 2 to declare to be null and void

| **nullify** ► **nullifies**, **nullifying**, **nullified**

numb adjective having lost the power to feel or move ■ verb to make numb

number noun 1 a word or figure showing how many, or showing a position in a series 2 a collection of people or things 3 a single issue of a newspaper or magazine 4 a popular song or piece of music ■ verb 1 to count 2 to give numbers to 3 to amount to in number

numberless adjective more than can be counted

numeral noun a figure (eg 1, 2, etc) used to express a number

numerate adjective having some understanding of mathematics and science

numerator noun the number above the line in vulgar fractions, eg 2 in $\frac{2}{3}$ (compare with: **denominator**)

numerical adjective of, in, using or consisting of numbers

numerous adjective many

numskull noun a stupid person

nun noun a member of a female religious group living in a convent

nunnery noun (plural

nunneries) a house where a group of nuns live, a convent

nuptial *adjective* of marriage

nurse *noun* someone who looks after sick or injured people, or small children ■ *verb* **1** to look after sick people *etc* **2** to give (a baby) milk from the breast **3** to hold or look after with care: *he nurses his tomato plants* **4** to encourage (feelings) in yourself: *nursing her anger*

nursery *noun* (*plural* **nurseries**) **1** a room for young children **2** a place where young plants are reared

nursery school a school for very young children

nursing home a small private hospital

nurture *verb* to bring up, rear; to nourish ■ *noun* care, upbringing; food, nourishment

nut *noun* **1** a fruit with a hard shell which contains a kernel **2** a small metal block with a hole in it for screwing on the end of a bolt ■ **in a nutshell** expressed very briefly

nutcrackers *noun plural* an instrument for cracking nuts open

nutmeg *noun* a hard sweet-smelling seed used as a spice in cooking

nutrient *noun* a substance which provides nourishment

nutrition *noun* nourishment, food

nutritious *or* **nutritive** *adjective* valuable as food, nourishing

nutty *adjective* **1** containing, or having the flavour of nuts **2** *informal* mad, insane

nuzzle *verb* **1** to press, rub or caress with the nose **2** to lie close to, snuggle, nestle

NW *abbreviation* north-west; north-western

nylon *noun* **1** a synthetic material made from chemicals **2** **nylons** stockings made of nylon

nymph *noun* **1** a mythological female river or tree spirit **2** an insect not yet fully developed

NZ *abbreviation* New Zealand

O

O or **Oh** *exclamation* expressing surprise, admiration, pain, *etc*

oaf *noun* (*plural* **oafs**) a stupid or clumsy person ▪ **oafish** *adjective*

oak *noun* **1** a tree which produces acorns as fruit **2** its hard wood

OAP *abbreviation* **1** Old Age Pension **2** Old Age Pensioner

oar *noun* a pole for rowing, with a flat blade on the end

oarsman, **oarswoman** *noun* a person who rows

oasis *noun* (*plural* **oases**) a place in a desert where water is found and trees *etc* grow

oatcake *noun* a thin flat cake made of oatmeal

oath *noun* (*plural* **oaths**) **1** a solemn promise to speak the truth, keep your word, be loyal, *etc* **2** a swear-word

oatmeal *noun* meal made by grinding oats

oats *noun plural* a type of grassy plant or its grain, used as food

obbligato *noun* (*plural* **obbligatos** or **obbligati**) an accompaniment that is essential to a piece of music

obdurate *adjective* **1** hard-hearted **2** stubborn ▪ **obduracy** *noun*

obedience *noun* **1** the act of obeying **2** willingness to obey

obedient *adjective* obeying, ready to obey ▪ **obediently** *adverb*

obelisk *noun* a tall four-sided pillar with a pointed top

obese *adjective* very overweight ▪ **obesity** *noun*

obey *verb* to do what you are told to do

obituary *noun* (*plural* **obituaries**) a notice in a newspaper *etc* of someone's death, sometimes with a brief biography

object *noun* (*pronounced* ob-jekt) **1** something that can be seen or felt **2** an aim, a purpose: *the object of the exercise* **3** *grammar* the word in a sentence which stands for the person or thing on which the action of the verb is done, *eg me* in the sentence *He hit me* ▪ *verb* (*pronounced* ob-**jekt**): **object to something** to feel or show disapproval of it

objection *noun* **1** the act of

objecting **2** a reason for objecting

objectionable *adjective* nasty, disagreeable

objective *adjective* not influenced by personal interests, fair (*contrasted with:* **subjective**) ▪ *noun* aim, purpose, goal

objector *noun* someone who objects to something

obligation *noun* a promise or duty by which someone is bound

obligatory *adjective* required to be done with no exceptions by law, rule or custom

oblige *verb* **1** to force, compel **2** to do a favour or service to

obliged *adjective* owing or feeling gratitude for a favour or service done

obliging *adjective* ready to help others

oblique *adjective* **1** slanting **2** indirect, not straight or straightforward: *an oblique reference*

obliterate *verb* **1** to blot out (writing *etc*) **2** to destroy completely

oblivion *noun* **1** forgetfulness, unconsciousness **2** the state of being forgotten

oblivious *adjective* unaware, unconscious, forgetful

oblong *noun* a rectangle which is longer than it is wide ▪ *adjective* of this shape

obnoxious *adjective* offensive, causing dislike

♦* Do not confuse with: noxious

oboe *noun* (*plural* **oboes**) a high-pitched woodwind instrument

obscene *adjective* **1** indecent **2** disgusting, repellent

obscenity *noun* (*plural* **obscenities**) **1** the state or quality of being obscene **2** an obscene act or word

obscure *adjective* **1** dark **2** not clear or easily understood **3** unknown, not famous ▪ *verb* **1** to darken **2** to make less clear

obscurity *noun* **1** the state of being difficult to see or understand **2** the state of being unknown or forgotten

obsequious *adjective* submissive and fawning

observant *adjective* good at noticing

observation *noun* **1** the act of seeing and noting; attention **2** a remark

observatory *noun* (*plural* **observatories**) a place for making observations of the stars, weather, *etc*

observe *verb* **1** to notice **2** to watch with attention **3** to remark (that) **4** to obey (a law *etc*) **5** to keep, preserve: *observe a tradition* ▪ **observer** *noun*

obsess *verb* to fill the mind completely

obsession *noun* **1** a feeling or idea which someone cannot stop thinking about **2** the state of being obsessed

obsessive *adjective* **1** forming an obsession **2** having or likely to have an obsession

obsolescent *adjective* going out of date

obsolete *adjective* gone out of use

♠* Do not confuse: **obsolete** and **obsolescent**

obstacle *noun* something which stands in the way and hinders

obstacle race a race in which obstacles have to be passed, climbed, *etc*

obstetrician *noun* a doctor trained in obstetrics

obstetrics *noun singular* the branch of medicine and surgery dealing with pregnancy and childbirth

obstinacy *noun* stubbornness

obstinate *adjective* **1** of a person: rigidly sticking to decisions or opinions and unwilling to be influenced by persuasion **2** difficult to deal with, defeat or remove

obstreperous *adjective* noisy, unruly

obstruct *verb* **1** to block or close **2** to hold back or hinder
■ **obstruction** *noun*

obtain *verb* to get, gain

obtrusive *adjective* **1** too noticeable **2** pushy, impudent

obtuse *adjective* **1** of an angle: greater than a right angle

(*contrasted with*: **acute**) **2** stupid, slow to understand

obvious *adjective* easily seen or understood; plain, evident

obviously *adverb* in an obvious way; as is obvious, clearly

occasion *noun* **1** a particular time **2** a special event **3** a cause, a reason **4** opportunity

occasional *adjective* happening or used now and then
■ **occasionally** *adverb*

occult *adjective* **1** secret, mysterious **2** supernatural

occupancy *noun* (*plural* **occupancies**) the act, fact or period of occupying

occupant *noun* a person who occupies, has, or takes possession of something, not always the owner

occupation *noun* **1** the state of being occupied **2** something which occupies **3** someone's trade or job **4** possession of a house *etc*

occupier *noun* someone who has possession of a house *etc*

occupy *verb* **1** to dwell in **2** to keep busy **3** to take up, fill (space, time, *etc*)

| **occupy** ▶ occup**ies**, occup**ying**, occup**ied**

occur *verb* **1** to happen **2** to appear, be found **3 occur to someone** to come into their mind
■ **occurrence** *noun*

| **occur** ▶ occur**s**, occur**ring**, occur**red**

ocean *noun* **1** the expanse of salt water surrounding all the land masses of the earth **2** one of five main divisions of this, *ie* the Atlantic, Pacific, Indian, Arctic or Antarctic

ocelot *noun* a wild American cat like a small leopard

ochre *or US* **ocher** (*pronounced* oh-ker) *noun* a fine pale-yellow or red clay, used for colouring

o'clock *adverb* used after a number from one to twelve: specifying the time, indicating the number of hours after midday or midnight

octagon *noun* an eight-sided figure ■ **octagonal** *adjective*

octane *noun* a colourless liquid found in petroleum and used in petrol

octave *noun, music* a range of eight notes, *eg* from one C to the C next above or below it

octet *noun* a group of eight things which go together, *eg* a group of eight singers

October *noun* the tenth month of the year

octopus *noun* (*plural* **octopuses**) a sea creature with eight arms

odd *adjective* **1** of a number: leaving a remainder of one when divided by two, *eg* the numbers 3, 17, 31 (*contrasted with:* **even**) **2** unusual, strange **3** not one of a matching pair or group, left over

oddity *noun* (*plural* **oddities**) **1** queerness, strangeness

2 a strange person or thing

odd jobs jobs of different kinds, done occasionally and not part of regular employment

oddments *noun plural* scraps

odds *noun plural* the chances of something happening

ode *noun* a type of poem, often written to someone or something

odious *adjective* hateful

odium *noun* strong dislike, hatred

odour *noun* smell, either pleasant or unpleasant

odourless *adjective* without smell

odyssey *noun* a long, adventurous journey

oesophagus (*pronounced* ee-sof-ag-us) *or US* **esophagus** (*pronounced* i-**sof**-ag-us) *noun* the gullet

oestrogen (*pronounced* ees-tro-jen) *or US* **estrogen** (*pronounced* es-tro-jen) *noun* a female hormone which regulates the menstrual cycle, prepares the body for pregnancy, *etc*

of *preposition* **1** belonging to: *the house of my parents* **2** from (a place, person, *etc*): *within two miles of his home* **3** from among: *one of my pupils* **4** made from, made up of: *a house of bricks* **5** indicating an amount, a measurement, *etc*: *a gallon of petrol* **6** about, concerning: *talk of old friends* **7** with, containing: *a cup of coffee* **8** as a result of: *die of* *hunger* **9** indicating removal or taking away: *robbed her of her jewels* **10** indicating a connection between an action and its object: *the joining of the pieces* **11** indicating character, qualities, *etc*: *it was good of you to come*

off *adverb* **1** away from a place, or from a particular state, position, *etc*: *he walked off* **2** entirely, completely: *finish off your work* ▪ *adjective* **1** cancelled: *the holiday is off* **2** rotten, bad: *the meat is off* **3** not working, not on: *the control is in the off position* **4** not quite pure in colour: *off-white* ▪ *preposition* **1** not on, away from: *fell off the table* **2** taken away: *10% off the usual price* **3** below the normal standard: *off his game* ▪ **well off** rich

offal *noun* certain internal organs of an animal (heart, liver, *etc*), used as food

off-beat *adjective* not standard, eccentric

off-chance *noun* a slight chance

off-colour *adjective* not feeling well

offence *or US* **offense** *noun* **1** displeasure, hurt feelings **2** a crime, a sin

offend *verb* **1** to hurt the feelings of; insult, displease **2** to do wrong

offender *noun* a person who has committed an offence

offensive *noun* **1** the position of someone who attacks **2** an attack ▪ *adjective* **1** insulting, disgusting

2 used for attack or assault: *an offensive weapon*

offer *verb* **1** to put forward (a gift, payment, *etc*) for acceptance or refusal **2** to lay (a choice, chance, *etc*) before **3** to say that you are willing to do something ▪ *noun* **1** an act of offering **2** a bid of money **3** something proposed

offering *noun* **1** a gift **2** a collection of money in church

offhand *adjective* rude, curt ▪ *adverb* without preparation; impromptu

office *noun* **1** a place where business is carried on **2** the people working in such a place **3** a duty, a job **4** a position of authority, especially in the government

officer *noun* **1** someone who carries out a public duty **2** someone holding a commission in the armed forces

official *adjective* **1** done or given out by those in power **2** forming part of the tasks of a job or office **3** having full and proper authority ▪ *noun* someone who holds an office in the service of the government *etc*

🔸 Do not confuse with: **officious**. **Official** is a neutral adjective showing neither approval nor disapproval, and it is used most often with reference to position or authority rather than people's characters

officially adverb **1** as an official, formally **2** as announced or said in public (though not necessarily truthfully)

officiate verb to perform a duty or service, especially as a clergyman at a wedding etc

officious adjective fond of interfering, especially in a pompous way

> ●* Do not confuse with: **official**. **Officious** is a negative adjective showing disapproval, and it is used to describe people and their characters

offing noun: **in the offing** expected to happen soon, forthcoming

off-licence noun a shop selling alcohol which must not be drunk on the premises

off-line or **offline** adjective & adverb, computing **1** not under the control of the central processing unit **2** not switched on or connected

offload verb **1** to unload **2** to get rid of (something) by passing on to someone else

offpeak adjective not at the time of highest use or demand

off-putting adjective unpleasant, distracting

offset verb to weigh against, make up for: the cost was partly offset by a grant

offshoot noun **1** a shoot growing out of the main stem **2** a small business, project, etc created out of a larger one: an offshoot of an international firm

offshore adjective & adverb **1** in or on the sea close to the coast **2** at a distance from the shore **3** from the shore: offshore winds

offside adjective & adverb **1** sport illegally ahead of the ball, eg in football, in a position between the ball and the opponent's goal (contrasted with: **onside**) **2** of the side of a vehicle: nearest to the centre of the road (contrasted with: **nearside**)

offspring noun **1** someone's child or children **2** the young of animals etc

oft adverb, old often

often adverb many times

ogle verb to look at (someone) in an admiring or amorous way

ogre noun **1** a mythological man-eating giant **2** someone extremely frightening or threatening

Oh another spelling of **O**

ohm noun a unit of electrical resistance

-oholic see **-aholic**

-oid suffix forms technical terms containing the meaning 'like': anthropoid/android (= a humanlike robot)/tabloid (= originally a trademark for a medicine in tablet form)

oil noun **1** a greasy liquid obtained from plants (eg olive oil), from animals (eg whale oil), and from minerals (eg petroleum)

2 oils oil paints ■ verb to smear with oil, put oil on or in

oilfield noun an area where mineral oil is found

oil paint paint made by mixing a colouring substance with oil

oil painting a picture painted in oil colours

oil rig a structure set up for drilling an oil well

oilskin noun 1 cloth made waterproof with oil 2 a heavy coat made of this

oil well a hole drilled into the earth's surface or into the seabed to extract petroleum

oily adjective of or like oil

oink noun the noise of a pig ■ verb to make this noise

ointment noun a greasy substance rubbed on the skin to soothe, heal, etc

OK or **okay** exclamation, adjective & adverb all right

old adjective 1 advanced in age, aged 2 having a certain age: ten years old 3 not new, having existed a long time 4 belonging to the past 5 worn, worn-out 6 out-of-date, old-fashioned 7 of a person's past, replaced by something different in the present: my old school

olden adjective: the olden days past times

old-fashioned adjective in a style from the past, out-of-date

olive noun 1 a small oval fruit with a hard stone, which is pressed to produce a cooking oil 2 the Mediterranean tree that bears this fruit ■ adjective of a yellowish-green colour

olive branch a sign of a wish for peace

-ology see -logy

Olympic Games an international sporting competition held every four years (also called: **Olympics**)

ombudsman noun an official appointed to look into complaints against government departments

omega noun the last letter of the Greek alphabet

omelette or **omelet** noun beaten eggs fried in a single layer in a pan

omen noun a sign of future events

ominous adjective suggesting future trouble ■ **ominously** adverb

omission noun 1 something omitted 2 the act of omitting

omit verb 1 to leave out 2 to fail to do

| omit ► omits, omitting, omitted

omnibus noun (plural **omnibuses**) a book containing several connected items

omnibus edition a radio or TV programme made up of material from preceding editions of a series

omnipotent *adjective* having absolute, unlimited power

omniscient *adjective* knowing everything

omnivore *noun* an organism that feeds on both plants and animals ▪ **omnivorous** *adjective*

on *preposition* **1** touching or fixed to the outer or upper side: *on the table* **2** supported by: *standing on one foot* **3** receiving, taking, *etc*: *on antibiotics* **4** occurring in the course of a specified time: *on the following day* **5** about: *a book on Scottish history* **6** with: *do you have your cheque book on you?* **7** next to, near: *a city on the Rhine* **8** indicating membership of: *on the committee* **9** in the process or state of: *on sale* **10** by means of: *can you play that on the piano?* ▪ *adverb* **1** so as to be touching or fixed to the outer or upper side: *put your coat on* **2** onwards, further: *they carried on towards home* **3** at a further point: *later on* ▪ *adjective* **1** working, performing: *the television is on* **2** arranged, planned: *do you have anything on this afternoon?*

once *adverb* **1** at an earlier time in the past: *people once lived in caves* **2** for one time only: *I've been to Paris once* ▪ *noun* one time only: *just this once* ▪ *conjunction* when: *once you've finished, you can go* ▪ **at once** immediately

oncoming *adjective* approaching from the front

one *noun* **1** the number 1 **2** a particular member of a group: *the one I want to meet* ▪ *pronoun* **1** a single person or thing: *one of my cats* **2** in formal or pompous English used instead of **you**, meaning anyone: *one must do what one can* ▪ *adjective* **1** 1 in number, a single: *only one reply* **2** identical, the same: *we are all of one mind* **3** some, an unnamed (*time etc*): *one day soon* ▪ **one another** used when an action takes place between two or more people: *they looked at one another*

oneself *pronoun* **1** used reflexively: *wash oneself* **2** used for emphasis: *one prefers to feed the dogs oneself*

one-sided *adjective* with one person, side, *etc* having a great advantage over the other

one-way *adjective* for traffic moving in one direction only

ongoing *adjective* continuing

onion *noun* a bulb vegetable with a strong taste and smell

on-line *or* **online** *adjective*, *computing* **1** under the control of a central processing unit **2** switched on or connected

onlooker *noun* someone who watches an event, but does not take part in it

only *adverb* **1** not more than **2** alone, solely: *only you are invited* **3** not longer ago than: *only yesterday* **4** indicating an unavoidable result: *he'll only be*

offended if you ask ∎ *adjective*
single, solitary: *an only child*
∎ *conjunction, informal* but,
except that: *I'd like to go, only I
have to work*

onrush *noun* a rush forward

onset *noun* **1** beginning **2** an
attack

onside *see* offside

onslaught *noun* a fierce attack

onto *preposition* to a position on
or in

onus *noun* burden;
responsibility

onward *adjective* going forward
in place or time: *the onward
march of science* ∎ *adverb*
onwards

onwards *adverb* towards a point
further ahead: *from four o'clock
onwards*

onyx *noun* a precious stone with
layers of different colours

oodles *noun plural, informal* lots
(of), many

ooze *verb* **1** to flow gently or
slowly **2** to exude: *oozing charm*

opal *noun* a bluish-white
precious stone, with flecks of
various colours

opaque *adjective* not able to be
seen through

open *adjective* **1** not shut,
allowing entry or exit **2** not
enclosed or fenced **3** showing the
inside or inner part; uncovered **4**
not blocked **5** free for all to enter **6**
honest, frank ∎ *verb* **1** to make
open; unlock **2** to begin

open air any place not indoors
or underground

open-air *adjective* happening
outside

opener *noun* something that
opens: *tin opener*

opening *noun* **1** a hole, a gap **2**
an opportunity **3** a vacant job

openly *adverb* without trying to
hide or conceal anything

open-minded *adjective* ready
to take up new ideas

open-plan *adjective* with large
rooms, undivided by walls or
partitions

opera *noun* a play in which the
characters sing accompanied by
an orchestra

operand *noun* a number on
which a mathematical operation
is carried out

operate *verb* **1** to act, work **2** to
bring about an effect **3** to perform
an operation

operatic *adjective* of or for opera

operating system *computing* a
program which manages all other
software programs on a computer
and the hardware devices linked
to that computer, *eg* printer,
scanner, disk drives, *etc* (*compare
with*: application)

operation *noun* **1** action **2**
method or way of working **3** the
cutting of a part of the human
body to treat disease or repair
damage

operational *adjective* working

operative *adjective* **1** working, in

action **2** of a rule *etc*: in force, having effect

operator *noun* **1** someone who works a machine **2** someone who connects telephone calls **3** a mathematical symbol showing which operation is to be carried out, *eg* + for addition

operetta *noun* a play with music and singing

opinion *noun* **1** what someone thinks or believes **2** professional judgement or point of view: *he wanted another opinion on his son's case* **3** judgement of the value of someone or something: *a low opinion of her*

opinionated *adjective* having and expressing strong opinions

opinion poll a survey of what people think of something

opium *noun* a drug made from the dried juice of a type of poppy

opponent *noun* someone who opposes; an enemy, a rival

opportune *adjective* coming at the right or a convenient time

opportunist *noun* someone who takes advantage of a favourable situation
■ **opportunism** *noun*

opportunity *noun* (*plural* **opportunities**) a chance (to do something)

oppose *verb* **1** to struggle against, resist **2** to stand against, compete against

opposite *adjective* **1** facing, across from **2** lying on the other

side (of) **3** as different as possible ■ *preposition* **1** facing, across from **2** acting a role in a play, opera, *etc* in relation to another ■ *noun* something as different as possible (from something else)

opposition *noun* **1** resistance **2** those who resist **3** the political party which is against the governing party

oppress *verb* **1** to govern harshly like a tyrant **2** to treat cruelly **3** to distress, worry greatly
■ **oppression** *noun*

oppressive *adjective* **1** oppressing **2** cruel, harsh **3** of weather: close, tiring

opt *verb* **1** **opt for** to choose (something) **2** to decide (to do)
■ **opt out** to decide not to (do something)

optic *or* **optical** *adjective* relating to the eyes or sight

optical illusion an impression that something seen is different from what it is

optician *noun* someone who makes and sells spectacles

optics *noun singular* the science of light

optimism *noun* the habit of taking a positive, hopeful view of things (*contrasted with*: **pessimism**) ■ **optimist** *noun*
■ **optimistic** *adjective*
■ **optimistically** *adverb*

optimize *or* **optimise** *verb* to make the most of (a situation)

optimum *adjective* best, most

favourable: *optimum conditions*

option *noun* **1** choice; the right or power to choose **2** something chosen

optional *adjective* left to choice, not compulsory

opulence *noun* wealth and luxury ▪ **opulent** *adjective*

or *conjunction* **1** used (often with **either**) to show alternatives: *tea or coffee?* **2** because if not: *you'd better go or you'll miss your bus*

oracle *noun* **1** someone thought to be very wise or knowledgeable **2** a sacred place where a god is asked questions **3** someone through whom such answers are made known

oral *adjective* **1** spoken, not written **2** relating to the mouth ▪ *noun* an oral examination or test

♦* Do not confuse with: **aural**. Aural means 'relating to the ear'. It may help to think of the 'O' as looking like an open mouth

orally *adverb* by mouth

orange *noun* **1** a juicy citrus fruit, with a thick reddish-yellow skin **2** the colour of this fruit

orang-utan *noun* a large man-like ape, with long arms and long reddish hair

oration *noun* a public speech, especially one in fine formal language

orator *noun* a public speaker

orb *noun* anything in the shape of a ball, a sphere

orbit *noun* the path of a planet or moon round a sun, or of a space capsule round the earth ▪ *verb* to go round the earth *etc* in space

orchard *noun* a large garden of fruit trees

orchestra *noun* a group of musicians playing together under a conductor ▪ **orchestral** *adjective*

orchestrate *verb* **1** to arrange (a piece of music) for an orchestra **2** to organize so as to produce the best effect

orchid *noun* a plant with unusually shaped, often brightly coloured, flowers

ordain *verb* to receive (a member of the clergy) into the Church

ordeal *noun* **1** a hard trial or test **2** suffering, painful experience

order *noun* **1** an instruction to act made by someone in authority **2** a request or list of requests **3** an arrangement according to a system **4** an accepted way of doing things **5** a tidy or efficient state **6** peaceful conditions: *law and order* **7** rank, position, class **8** a society or brotherhood, *eg* of monks **9** one of the groups into which a class of animals, plants, *etc* is divided ▪ *verb* **1** to give an order to, to tell to do **2** to put in an order for **3** to arrange ▪ **in order to** for the purpose of

orderly *adjective* **1** in proper order **2** well-behaved, quiet ■ *noun* (*plural* **orderlies**) **1** a soldier who carries the orders and messages of an officer **2** a hospital attendant who does routine jobs

ordinal number a number which shows order in a series, *eg* first, second, third (*compare with*: **cardinal number**)

ordinance *noun* a command; a law

ordinarily *adverb* usually, normally

ordinary *adjective* **1** common, usual **2** normal; not exceptional

Ordnance Survey a government office which produces official detailed maps

ore *noun* a mineral from which a metal is obtained

oregano *noun* a Mediterranean herb used in cooking

organ *noun* **1** an internal part of the body, *eg* the liver **2** a large musical wind instrument with a keyboard

organdie *noun* a fine, thin, stiff muslin

organic *adjective* **1** of or produced by the bodily organs **2** of living things **3** of food: grown without the use of artificial fertilizers *etc* **4** of a chemical compound: containing carbon ■ **organically** *adverb*

organism *noun* any living thing

organist *noun* someone who plays the organ

organization *or* **organisation** *noun* **1** the act of organizing **2** a group of people working together for a purpose

organize *or* **organise** *verb* **1** to arrange, set up (an event *etc*) **2** to form into a whole ■ **organizer** *or* **organiser** *noun*

oriental *adjective* eastern; from the East

orientate *verb* **1** to find your position and sense of direction **2** to set or put facing a particular direction

orientation *noun* **1** the act or an instance of orientating or being orientated **2** a position relative to a fixed point

orienteering *noun* the sport of finding your way across country with the help of map and compass

origami *noun* the Japanese art of folding paper

origin *noun* **1** the starting point **2** the place from which someone or something comes

original *adjective* **1** first in time **2** not copied **3** able to think or do something new ■ *noun* **1** the earliest version **2** a model from which other things are made ■ **originality** *noun*

originally *adverb* in or from the beginning

originate *verb* **1** to bring or come into being **2** to produce

ornament *noun* something added to give or enhance beauty

ornamental *adjective* used for ornament; decorative

ornamentation *noun* decorating or the state of being decorated

ornate *adjective* richly decorated

ornithologist *noun* someone who studies or is an expert on birds

ornithology *noun* the scientific study of birds and their behaviour

orphan *noun* a child who has lost one or both parents

orphanage *noun* a home for orphans

orthodox *adjective* **1** agreeing with the prevailing or established religious, political, *etc* views **2** normal, generally practised and accepted

orthopaedic *or US*

orthopedic *adjective* relating to orthopaedics

orthopaedics *or US*

orthopedics *noun singular* the branch of medicine which deals with bone diseases and injuries

oscillate *verb* **1** to swing to and fro like the pendulum of a clock **2** to keep changing your mind
▪ **oscillation** *noun*

osmosis *noun* **1** diffusion of liquids through a membrane **2** gradual absorption or assimilation

osprey *noun* (*plural* **ospreys**) a type of eagle which eats fish

ostensible *adjective* of a reason *etc*: apparent, but not always real or true

ostentation *noun* pretentious display of wealth, knowledge, *etc*, especially to attract attention or admiration

ostentatious *adjective* showy, meant to catch the eye

osteopath *noun* someone who practises osteopathy

osteopathy *noun* a system of healing or treatment of bone and joint disorders, mainly involving manipulation and massage

osteoporosis *noun* a disease which makes bones porous and brittle, caused by lack of calcium

ostracize *or* **ostracise** *verb* to banish (someone) from the company of a group of people

ostrich *noun* (*plural* **ostriches**) a large African bird with showy plumage, which cannot fly but runs very fast

other *adjective* **1** the second of two: *the other sock* **2** remaining, not previously mentioned: *the other children* **3** different, additional: *some other reason* **4** recently past: *the other day*
▪ *pronoun* **1** the second of two **2** those remaining, those not previously mentioned: *the others arrived the next day* **3** the previous one: *one after the other*
▪ **every other** every second: *every other day*

otherwise *conjunction* or else
■ *adverb* **1** in a different way **2** in different circumstances: *he left, otherwise I'd have spoken to him*

otter *noun* a type of river animal living on fish

ought *verb* **1** used with other verbs to indicate duty or need: *we ought to set an example* **2** to indicate what can be reasonably expected: *the weather ought to be fine*

ounce *noun* a unit of weight, equal to one-sixteenth of a pound (about 28.35 grams)

our *adjective* belonging to us

ours *pronoun* something belonging to us: *the green car is ours*

ourselves *pronoun* **1** used reflexively: *we exhausted ourselves swimming* **2** used for emphasis: *we ourselves don't like it, but other people may*

oust *verb* to drive out (from)

out *adverb* **1** into or towards the open air: *go out for a walk* **2** from within: *take out a handkerchief* **3** not inside **4** far from here: *out in the Far East* **5** not at home, not in the office, *etc*: *she's out at the moment* **6** aloud: *shouted out* **7** inaccurate: *the total was five pounds out* **8** published, released (for viewing, hire or purchase): *the video is out next week* **9** dismissed from a game of cricket, baseball, *etc* **10** no longer in power or office

out-and-out *adjective* complete, total, thorough

outback *noun* the wild interior parts of Australia

outboard *adjective* on the outside of a ship or boat: *an outboard motor*

outbreak *noun* a beginning, a breaking out, *eg* of war or disease

outbuilding *noun* a building that is separate from the main buildings

outburst *noun* a bursting out, especially of angry feelings

outcast *noun* someone driven away from friends and home

outcome *noun* a result

outcrop *noun* the part of a rock formation that sticks out above the surface of the ground

outcry *noun* (*plural* **outcries**) a widespread show of anger, disapproval, *etc*

outdo *verb* to do better than

| **outdo** ▶ out**do**es, out**do**ing, out**did**, out**done**

outdoor *adjective* of or in the open air

outdoors *adverb* **1** outside the house **2** in or into the open air

outer *adjective* nearer the edge, surface, *etc*; further away

outermost *adjective* nearest the edge; furthest away

outfit *noun* a set of clothes worn together, often for a special occasion *etc*

outgrow *verb* to get too big or old for (clothes, toys, *etc*)

outgrow ► outgrows, outgrow*ing*, outgrew, outgrown

outhouse *noun* a shed

outing *noun* a trip, excursion

outlandish *adjective* looking or sounding very strange

outlaw *noun* someone put outside the protection of the law; a robber or bandit

outlay *noun* money paid out

outlet *noun* 1 a passage to the outside, *eg* for a water pipe 2 a means of expressing or getting rid of (a feeling, energy, *etc*) 3 a market for goods

outline *noun* 1 the outer line of a figure in a drawing *etc* 2 a sketch showing only the main lines 3 a rough sketch 4 a brief description ■ *verb* to draw or describe an outline of

outlive *verb* to live longer than

outlook *noun* 1 a view from a window *etc* 2 what is thought likely to happen: *the weather outlook*

outlying *adjective* far from the centre, distant

outnumber *verb* to be greater in number than

out-of-date *or* **out of date** *adjective* 1 old-fashioned 2 no longer valid: *an out-of-date ticket*

out-patient *noun* a patient who does not stay in a hospital while receiving treatment (*contrasted with*: **in-patient**)

outpost *noun* a military station

in front of or far from the main army; an outlying settlement

output *noun* 1 the goods produced by a machine, factory, *etc* 2 the amount of work done by a person 3 data produced by a computer program (*contrasted with*: **input**)

outrage *noun* 1 an act of great violence 2 an act which shocks or causes offence ■ *verb* 1 to injure, hurt by violence 2 to insult, shock

outrageous *adjective* 1 violent, very wrong 2 not moderate, extravagant

outright *adverb* completely ■ *adjective* complete, thorough

outset *noun* start, beginning

outside *noun* the outer surface or place ■ *adjective* 1 in, on or of the outer surface or place 2 relating to leisure rather than your full-time job: *outside interests* 3 slight: *an outside chance of winning* ■ *adverb* 1 not within a place: *they made us wait outside* 2 out-of-doors; in or into the open air: *let's eat outside* ■ *preposition* beyond the limits of; not within: *outside the building*

outsider *noun* someone not included in a particular social group

outsize *adjective* of a very large size

outskirts *noun plural* the outer borders of a city *etc*

outspoken *adjective* bold and frank in speech

outstanding *adjective* **1** well-known **2** excellent **3** of a debt: unpaid

outstretched *adjective* reaching out

out-tray *noun* an office tray for letters and work already dealt with (*contrasted with:* **in-tray**)

outvote *verb* to defeat by a greater number of votes

outward *adjective* towards or on the outside

outwardly *or* **outwards** *adverb* on the outside, externally

outweigh *verb* to be more important than: *the advantages outweigh the disadvantages*

outwit *verb* to defeat by cunning

| outwit ▶ outwits, outwitting, outwitted

oval *adjective* having the shape of an egg ■ *noun* an egg shape

ovary *noun* (*plural* **ovaries**) one of two organs in the female body in which eggs are formed

ovation *noun* an outburst of cheering, hand-clapping, *etc*

oven *noun* a covered place for baking; a small furnace

over *preposition* **1** higher than, above: *over thirty years* **2** across: *going over the bridge* **3** on the other side of: *the house over the road* **4** on top of: *threw his coat over the body* **5** here and there on: *paper scattered over the carpet* **6** about: *they quarrelled over their money* **7** by means of: *over the telephone* **8** during, throughout: *over the years* **9** while doing, having, *etc*: *fell asleep over his dinner* ■ *adverb* **1** above, higher up: *two birds flew over* **2** across a distance: *he walked over* **3** downwards: *did you fall over?* **4** above in number *etc*: *aged four and over* **5** as a remainder: *three left over* **6** through: *read the passage over* ■ *adjective* finished: *the sale is over* ■ *noun*, *cricket* a fixed number of balls bowled from one end of the wicket

over- *prefix* too much, to too great an extent: *overcook/over-excited*

overall *noun* **1** a garment worn over ordinary clothes to protect them against dirt **2** **overalls** hard-wearing trousers with a bib worn as work clothes ■ *adjective* **1** from one end to the other: *overall length* **2** including everything: *overall cost*

overarm *adjective* of bowling *etc*: with the arm above the shoulder

overawe *verb* to frighten or astonish into silence

overbalance *verb* to lose your balance and fall

overbearing *adjective* over-confident, domineering

overboard *adverb* out of a ship into the water

overcast *adjective* of the sky: cloudy

overcoat *noun* an outdoor coat worn over all other clothes

overcome verb to get the better of, defeat ∎ adjective helpless from exhaustion, emotion, etc

overdo verb 1 to do too much 2 to exaggerate 3 to cook (food) too long

overdose noun too great an amount (of medicine, a drug, etc)

overdraft noun the amount of money overdrawn from a bank

overdraw verb to draw more money from the bank than you have in your account

overdue adjective 1 later than the stated time 2 of a bill etc: still unpaid although the time for payment has passed

overflow verb 1 to flow or spill over: the river overflowed its banks 2 to be so full as to flow over

overgrown adjective 1 covered with plant growth 2 grown too large

overhang verb to jut out over

overhaul verb to examine carefully and carry out repairs ∎ noun a thorough examination and repair

overhead adverb directly above ∎ adjective placed high above the ground: overhead cables

overhear verb to hear what you were not meant to hear

overjoyed adjective filled with great joy

overland adverb & adjective on or by land, not sea

overlap verb 1 to extend over and partly cover: the two pieces of cloth overlapped 2 to cover a part of the same area or subject as another; partly coincide ∎ noun the amount by which something overlaps

overleaf adjective on the other side of a leaf of a book

overload verb to load or fill too much

overlook verb 1 to look down on from a higher point; have or give a view of 2 to fail to see, miss 3 to pardon, not punish

overlord noun, history a lord with power over other lords

overly adverb, excessively

overmuch adverb too much

overnight adverb 1 during the night: staying overnight with a friend 2 in a very short time: he changed completely overnight ∎ adjective 1 for the night: an overnight bag 2 got or made in a very short time: an overnight success

overpass noun a road going over above another road, railway, canal, etc

overpower verb 1 to defeat through greater strength 2 to overwhelm, make helpless ∎ overpowering adjective 1 unable to be resisted 2 overwhelming, very strong

overrate verb to value more highly than is deserved: his new film is overrated ∎ overrated adjective

overreach verb: overreach

yourself to try to do or get more than is possible and fail as a result

override verb **1** to ignore, set aside: *overriding the committee's decisions* **2** to take over control from: *override the automatic alarm signal*

overrule verb to go against or cancel an earlier judgement or request

overrun verb **1** to grow or spread over: *overrun with weeds* **2** to take possession of (a country)

overseas adjective & adverb abroad; beyond the sea

oversee verb to watch over, supervise

overseer noun a person who oversees workers, a supervisor

overshadow verb to lessen the importance of by doing better than

oversight noun **1** something left out or forgotten by mistake **2** failure to notice

overstep verb to go further than (a set limit, *etc*)

overt adjective not hidden or secret; openly done

overtake verb to catch up with and pass

overthrow verb to defeat

overtime noun **1** time spent working beyond the agreed normal hours **2** payment for this, usually at a higher rate

overtone noun an additional meaning or association, not directly stated

overture noun a piece of music played as an introduction to an opera

overweight adjective above an acceptable or healthy weight

overwhelm verb **1** to defeat completely **2** to load with too great an amount **3** to overcome, make helpless: *overwhelmed with grief*

overwhelming adjective physically or mentally crushing; intensely powerful

overwork verb to work more than is good for you

overwrought adjective excessively nervous or excited, agitated

ovule noun in flowering plants: the structure that develops into a seed when fertilized

ovum noun (*plural* **ova**) the egg from which the young of animals and people develop

owe verb **1** to be in debt to **2** to have (a person or thing) to thank for: *he owes his success to his family* ▪ **owing to** because of

owl noun a bird of prey which comes out at night

own verb **1** to have as a possession **2** to admit, confess to be true ▪ *adjective* belonging to the person mentioned: *is this all your own work?*

owner noun someone who possesses anything ▪ **ownership** noun

own goal a goal scored by

mistake against your own side

ox *noun* (*plural* **oxen**) a male cow, usually castrated, used for drawing loads *etc*

oxide *noun* a compound of oxygen and another element

oxidize *or* **oxidise** *verb* **1** to combine with oxygen **2** to become rusty ▪ **oxidation** *noun*

oxygen *noun* a gas with no taste, colour or smell, forming part of the air and of water

oyster *noun* a type of shellfish, often eaten raw

oz *abbreviation* ounce(s)

ozone *noun* a form of oxygen; O_3

ozone layer a layer of the upper atmosphere which protects the earth from the sun's ultraviolet rays

P p

pace *noun* **1** a step **2** rate of walking, running, *etc* ▪ *verb* to walk backwards and forwards

pacemaker *noun* **1** someone who sets the pace in a race **2** a device used to correct weak or irregular heart rhythms

pacifist *noun* someone who is against war

pacify *verb* to calm, soothe

| **pacify** ▶ pacif*ies*, pacify*ing*, pacif*ied*

pack *noun* **1** a bundle, especially one carried on the back **2** a set of playing-cards **3** a group of animals, especially dogs or wolves ▪ *verb* **1** to place (clothes *etc*) in a case or trunk for a journey **2** to press or crowd together closely ▪ **pack in** to cram in tightly

package *noun* a bundle, a parcel ▪ *verb* **1** to put into a container **2** to wrap

package holiday *or* **package tour** a holiday or tour arranged by an organizer with all travel and accommodation included in the price

packaging *noun* the wrappers or containers in which goods are packed

packet *noun* a container made of paper, cardboard, *etc*

packing *noun* **1** the act of putting things in cases, parcels, *etc* **2** material for wrapping goods to pack

pact *noun* **1** an agreement **2** a treaty, a contract

pad *noun* **1** a soft cushion-like object to prevent jarring or rubbing *etc* **2** a bundle of sheets of paper fixed together **3** the paw of certain animals **4** a rocket-launching platform ▪ *verb* **1** to stuff or protect with a soft material **2** (often **pad something out**) to fill it up with unnecessary material **3** to walk making a dull, soft noise

| **pad** *verb* ▶ pads, padd*ing*, padd*ed*

padding *noun* **1** stuffing material **2** words included in a speech, book, *etc* just to fill space or time

paddle *verb* **1** to move forward by the use of paddles; row **2** to wade in shallow water ▪ *noun* a short, broad, spoon-shaped oar

paddock *noun* a small closed-in field used for pasture

paddy field a muddy field in which rice is grown

padlock *noun* a removable lock with a hinged U-shaped bar

paediatrician *or US*

pediatrician *noun* a doctor specializing in studying and treating children's illnesses

pagan *noun* someone who does not believe in any religion; a heathen ▪ *adjective* heathen ▪ **paganism** *noun*

page *noun* **1** one side of a blank, written or printed sheet of paper **2** a boy servant a boy who carries the train of the bride's dress in a marriage service ▪ *verb* to contact someone using a pager

pageant *noun* **1** a show or procession made up of scenes from history **2** an elaborate parade or display ▪ **pageantry** *noun*

pager *noun* a small radio device that can be used to receive a signal, usually a beeping noise, from elsewhere

pagoda *noun* an Eastern temple, especially in China or India

paid *past form of* pay

pail *noun* an open vessel of tin, zinc, plastic, *etc* for carrying liquids; a bucket

pain *noun* **1** feeling caused by hurt to mind or body **2** pains care: *takes great pains with his work*

▪ *verb* to cause suffering to, distress

pained *adjective* showing pain or distress

painful *adjective* **1** causing pain **2** causing distress: *a painful duty* ▪ **painfully** *adverb*

painkiller *noun* a medicine taken to lessen pain

painless *adjective* without pain ▪ **painlessly** *adverb*

painstaking *adjective* very careful ▪ **painstakingly** *adverb*

paint *verb* to apply colour to in the form of liquid or paste ▪ *noun* a liquid substance used for colouring and applied with a brush, a spray, *etc*

painter *noun* **1** someone whose trade is painting **2** an artist who works in paint

painting *noun* **1** the act or art of creating pictures with paint **2** a painted picture

pair *noun* **1** two of the same kind **2** a set of two ▪ *verb* **1** to join to form a pair **2** to go in twos

pal *noun*, *informal* a friend

palace *noun* the house of a king, queen, or aristocrat

palatable *adjective* **1** pleasant to the taste **2** acceptable, pleasing

palate (*pronounced* **pal**-at) *noun* **1** the roof of the mouth **2** taste

◆✲ Do not confuse with: **palette** and **pallet**

palatial *adjective* like a palace, magnificent

pale¹ *noun* a wooden stake used in making a fence to enclose ground

pale² *adjective* **1** light or whitish in colour **2** not bright

palette (*pronounced* **pal**-et) *noun* a board or plate on which an artist mixes paints

✸ Do not confuse with: **pallet** and **palate**

palindrome *noun* a word or phrase that reads the same backwards as forwards, *eg* 'level'

paling *noun* a row of wooden stakes forming a fence

palisade *noun* a fence of pointed wooden stakes

pall (*pronounced* pawl) *noun* a dark covering or cloud: *a pall of smoke* ■ *verb* to become dull or uninteresting

pallbearer *noun* one of those carrying or walking beside the coffin at a funeral

pallet (*pronounced* **pal**-et) *noun* **1** a straw bed or mattress **2** a platform that can be lifted by a fork-lift truck for stacking goods

✸ Do not confuse with: **palette** and **palate**

palliative *adjective* making less severe or harsh ■ *noun* something which lessens pain, *eg* a drug

pallid *adjective* pale

pallor *noun* paleness

palm *noun* **1** a tall tree with broad fan-shaped leaves, which grows in hot countries **2** the inner surface of the hand between the wrist and the base of the fingers ■ **palm off** to give with the intention of cheating

palmistry *noun* the telling of fortunes from the lines and markings of the hand

palpable *adjective* **1** able to be touched or felt **2** easily noticed, obvious

palpate *verb* to examine by touch

palpitate *verb* of the heart: to beat rapidly, throb

palpitations *noun plural* uncomfortable rapid beating of the heart

palsy *noun* a loss of power and feeling in the muscles

paltry *adjective* of little value

pampas *noun plural* the vast treeless plains of South America

pampas grass a type of very tall, feathery grass

pamper *verb* to spoil (a child *etc*) by giving too much attention to

pamphlet *noun* a small book, stitched or stapled, often with a light paper cover

pan *noun* **1** a broad shallow pot used in cooking, a saucepan **2** the bowl of a toilet ■ *verb* to move a television or film camera so as to follow an object or give a wide view ■ **pan out** to turn out (well or badly)

pan *verb* ► pans, panning, panned

pan- *prefix* all, whole: *pan-African*

panacea (*pronounced* pan-*a*-see-*a*) *noun* a cure for all things

panache (*pronounced* pa-*nash*) *noun* a sense of style, swagger

pancake *noun* a thin cake of flour, eggs, sugar and milk, fried in a pan

pancreas *noun* a gland behind the stomach producing fluids that aid digestion

panda *noun* a large black-and-white bear-like animal found in Tibet *etc*

pandemonium *noun* a state of confusion and uproar

pander *verb*: **pander to** to indulge, easily comply with

pane *noun* a sheet of glass

panel *noun* **1** a flat rectangular piece of wood such as is set into a door or wall **2** a group of people chosen to judge a contest, take part in a television quiz, *etc*

pang *noun* a sudden sharp pain; a twinge

panic *noun* **1** a sudden fright and great fright **2** fear that spreads from person to person ■ *verb* **1** to throw into panic **2** to act wildly through fear

| **panic** *verb* ▶ **panics**,
| **panic**king, **panic**ked

pannier *noun* a light container attached to a bicycle *etc*

panorama *noun* a wide view of a landscape, scene, *etc*

pansy *noun* (*plural* **pansies**) a flower like the violet but larger

pant *verb* **1** to gasp for breath **2** to say breathlessly

pantechnicon *noun* a large van for transporting furniture

panther *noun* a large leopard

panties *noun plural* women's or children's knickers with short legs

pantomime *noun* a Christmas play, with songs, jokes, *etc*, based on a popular fairy tale *eg* Cinderella

pantry *noun* (*plural* **pantries**) a room for storing food

pants *noun plural* **1** underpants **2** women's short-legged knickers **3** US trousers

papacy *noun* the position or power of the Pope

papal *adjective* of, or relating to, the Pope or the papacy

paparazzo *noun* (*plural* **paparazzi**) a press photographer who hounds celebrities *etc*

papaya *noun* a green-skinned edible fruit from S America (*also called*: **pawpaw**)

paper *noun* **1** a material made from rags, wood, *etc* used for writing or wrapping **2** a single sheet of this **3** a newspaper **4** an essay on a learned subject **5** a set of examination questions **6** **papers** documents proving someone's identity, nationality, *etc* ■ *verb* to cover up (especially walls) with paper

paperback *noun* a book bound in a flexible paper cover (*compare with*: **hardback**)

paperweight *noun* a heavy glass, metal, *etc* object used to keep papers in place

papier-mâché (*pronounced* pap-yei-mash-ei) *noun* a substance consisting of paper pulp and some sticky liquid or glue, shaped into models, bowls, *etc*

paprika *noun* a type of ground red pepper

papyrus *noun* (*plural* **papyri** – *pronounced* pa-**pai**-rai – *or* **papyruses**) a reed used by the ancient Egyptians *etc* to make paper

par *noun* **1** an accepted standard, value, *etc* **2** *golf* the number of strokes allowed for each hole if the play is perfect

parable *noun* a story (*eg* in the Bible) which teaches a moral lesson

parabola *noun* **1** a curve **2** the intersection of a cone with a plane parallel to its side

paracetamol *noun* a pain-relieving drug

parachute *noun* an umbrella-shaped device made of light material and rope which supports someone or something dropping slowly to the ground from an aeroplane ■ *verb* to drop by parachute

parade *noun* **1** an orderly arrangement of troops for inspection or exercise **2** a procession of people, vehicles,

etc in celebration of some event ■ *verb* **1** to arrange (troops) in order **2** to march in a procession **3** to display in an obvious way

paradise *noun* **1** heaven **2** a place or state of great happiness

paradox *noun* (*plural* **paradoxes**) a saying which seems to contradict itself but which may be true

paradoxical *adjective* combining two apparently contradictory elements ■ **paradoxically** *adverb*

paraffin *noun* an oil which burns and is used as a fuel (for heaters, lamps, *etc*)

paragon *noun* a model of perfection or excellence: *a paragon of good manners*

paragraph *noun* a division of a piece of writing shown by beginning the first sentence on a new line

parakeet *noun* a type of small parrot

parallel *adjective* of lines: going in the same direction and never meeting, always remaining the same distance apart ■ *noun* something comparable in some way with something else

parallelogram *noun* a four-sided figure, the opposite sides of which are parallel and equal in length

parallel port *computing* a socket or plug for connecting a device such as a printer to a computer

paralyse *or US* **paralyze** *verb* **1** to affect with paralysis **2** to make helpless or ineffective **3** to bring to a halt

paralysis *noun* loss of the power to move and feel in part of the body

paramedic *noun* someone helping doctors and nurses, *eg* a member of an ambulance crew

paramedical *adjective* denoting personnel or services that are supplementary to and support the work of the medical profession

parameter *noun* (often **parameters**) the limiting factors or characteristics which affect the way in which something can be done or made

> ●✻ Do not confuse with: **perimeter**. Notice that words starting with peri- often relate to the idea of 'going around' and the **perimeter** of a figure or shape is the line that goes around it

paramilitary *adjective* **1** on military lines and intended to supplement the military **2** organized illegally as a military force ▪ *noun* a member of a paramilitary force

paramount *adjective* very greatest, supreme: *of paramount importance*

paranoia *noun* **1** a form of mental disorder characterized by delusions of grandeur, persecution, *etc* **2** intense, irrational fear or suspicion

paranoid *adjective* suffering from paranoia

paranormal *adjective* beyond what is normal in nature; supernatural, occult

parapet *noun* a low wall on a bridge or balcony to prevent people falling over the side

paraphernalia *noun plural* belongings; gear, equipment

paraphrase *verb* to express (a piece of writing) in other words ▪ *noun* an expression in different words

paraplegia *noun* paralysis of the lower part of the body and legs

paraplegic *adjective* of paraplegia ▪ *noun* someone who suffers from paraplegia

parasite *noun* an animal, plant or person living on another without being any use in return

parasol *noun* a light umbrella used to provide shade from the sun

paratrooper *noun* a soldier who is specially trained to drop from an aeroplane using a parachute

paratroops *noun plural* soldiers carried by air to be dropped by parachute into enemy country

parboil *verb* to partly cook (food) by boiling for a short time

parcel *noun* a wrapped and

sealed-up package to be sent by post ■ verb **1 parcel something out** to divide it into portions **2 parcel something up** to wrap it up as a package ■ **part and parcel** an absolutely necessary part

| **parcel** verb ▶ parcels, parcelling, parcelled

parch verb **1** to make hot and very dry **2** to make thirsty

parched adjective **1** very dry **2** very thirsty

parchment noun **1** the dried skin of a goat or sheep used for writing on **2** paper resembling this

pardon verb **1** to forgive **2** to free from punishment **3** to allow to go unpunished ■ noun **1** forgiveness **2** the act of pardoning

pardonable adjective able to be forgiven

pare verb to peel or cut off the edge or outer surface of

parent noun a father or mother

parentage noun descent from parents or ancestors

parental adjective **1** of parents **2** with the manner or attitude of a parent

parenthesis noun (plural **parentheses**) **1** a word or group of words in a sentence forming an explanation or comment, often separated by brackets or dashes, for instance so he said in 'he and his wife (so he said) were separated' **2 parentheses** brackets

parenthood noun the state of being a parent

pariah noun someone driven out from a community or group; an outcast

parish noun (plural **parishes**) a district with its own church and minister or priest

parishioner (pronounced pa-rish-on-er) noun a member of a parish

parity noun equality

park noun a public place for walking, with grass and trees ■ verb to stop and leave (a car etc) in a place

parka noun a type of thick jacket with a hood

Parkinson's disease a disease causing trembling in the hands etc and rigid muscles

parley verb to hold a conference, especially with an enemy ■ noun (plural **parleys**) a meeting between enemies to settle terms of peace etc

| **parley** verb ▶ parleys, parleying, parleyed

parliament noun **1** the chief law-making council of a nation **2 Parliament** Brit the House of Commons and the House of Lords

parliamentary adjective of, for or concerned with a parliament

parlour noun a sitting room in a house

parochial adjective **1** relating to a parish **2** interested only in local affairs; narrow-minded

parody noun (plural **parodies**) an amusing imitation of someone's writing style, subject matter, etc ■ verb to make a parody of

parody ▶ parod**ies**, parody**ing**, parod**ied**

parole noun the release of a prisoner before the end of a sentence on condition that they will have to return if they break the law ■ verb to release on parole

paroxysm noun a fit of pain, rage, laughter, etc

parrot noun a bird with a hooked bill and often brightly coloured feathers

parry verb to deflect, turn aside (a blow, question, etc)

parry ▶ parr**ies**, parry**ing**, parr**ied**

parsimonious adjective too careful in spending money; stingy

parsley noun a bright green leafy herb, used in cookery

parsnip noun a plant with an edible yellowish root shaped like a carrot

parson noun a member of the clergy, especially one in charge of a parish

parsonage noun a parson's house

part noun 1 a portion, a share 2 a piece forming part of a whole 3 a character taken by an actor in a play 4 a role in an action or event: *played a vital part in the campaign*

5 music the notes to be played or sung by a particular instrument or voice ■ verb 1 to divide 2 to separate, send or go in different ways 3 to put or keep apart ■ **part of speech** one of the grammatical groups into which words are divided, eg noun, verb, adjective, preposition ■ **part with** to let go, be separated from

partake verb: **partake of 1** to eat or drink some of something **2** to take a part in

partake ▶ partakes, partak**ing**, partook, partaken

partial adjective **1** in part only, not total or complete **2** having a liking for (someone or something): *partial to cheese*

partiality noun the favouring of one thing more than another, bias

partially adverb not completely or wholly; not yet to the point of completion

participant or **participator** noun someone who takes part in anything

participate verb **1** to take part (in) **2** to have a share in
■ **participation** noun

participle noun **1** a form of a verb which can be used with other verbs to form tenses, eg 'he was *eating*' or 'she has *arrived*' **2** used as an adjective, eg '*stolen* jewels' **3** used as a noun, eg '*running* makes me tired'

particle noun a very small piece

particular *adjective* **1** relating to a single definite person, thing, *etc* considered separately from others: *this particular colour* **2** special: *take particular care of the china* **3** fussy, difficult to please: *particular about her food* ■ *noun* (often **particulars**) the facts or details about someone or something

parting *noun* **1** the act of separating or dividing **2** a place of separation **3** a going away (from each other), a leave-taking **4** a line dividing hair on the head brushed in opposite directions

partisan *adjective* giving strong support or loyalty to a particular cause, theory, *etc*, often without considering other points of view

partition *noun* something which divides, *eg* a wall between rooms ■ *verb* **1** *maths* to split a number into component parts **2** to divide by making a wall *etc*

partly *adverb* in part, or in some parts; not wholly or completely

partner *noun* **1** someone who shares the ownership of a business *etc* with another or others **2** one of a pair in games, dancing, *etc* **3** a husband, wife or lover

partnership *noun* **1** a relationship in which two or more people or groups operate together as partners **2** the status of a partner: *she was offered a partnership* **3** a business or other enterprise jointly owned or run by two or more people *etc*

partridge *noun* a type of bird which is shot as game

part-time *adjective* for only part of the working week: *I went part-time in my job* (compare with: **full-time**)

party *noun* (*plural* **parties**) **1** a gathering of guests: *birthday party* **2** a group of people travelling together: *party of tourists* **3** a number of people with the same plans or ideas: *a political party* **4** someone taking part in, or approving, an action

pass *verb* **1** to go, move, travel, *etc* **2** to move on or along: *pass the salt* **3** to go by: *I saw the bus pass our house* **4** to overtake **5** of parliament: to put (a law) into force **6** to be successful in an examination **7** to be declared healthy or in good condition after an inspection **8** to come to an end: *the feeling of dizziness soon passed* **9** to hand on, give **10** to spend (time) **11** to make, utter (*eg* a remark) ■ *noun* **1** a narrow passage over or through a range of mountains **2** a ticket or card allowing someone to go somewhere **3** success in an examination ■ **pass away** to die ■ **pass off** to present (a forgery *etc*) as genuine ■ **pass on 1** to go forward, proceed **2** to hand on **3** to die ■ **pass out** to faint ■ **pass up** to fail to take up (an opportunity)

passable *adjective* **1** fairly good **2** of a river *etc*: able to be crossed ■ **passably** *adverb*

passage *noun* **1** the act of passing: *passage of time* **2** a journey in a ship **3** a corridor **4** a way through **5** a part of the text of a book

passageway *noun* a passage, a way through

passenger *noun* a traveller, not a member of the crew, in a train, ship, aeroplane, *etc*

passer-by *noun* (*plural* **passers-by**) someone who happens to pass by when something happens

passing *adjective* **1** going by: *a passing car* **2** not lasting long: *passing interest* ■ *noun* **1** the act of someone or something which passes **2** a going away, a coming to an end **3** death

passion *noun* strong feeling, especially anger or love

passionate *adjective* **1** easily moved to passion **2** full of passion ■ **passionately** *adverb*

passionfruit *noun* the edible, oblong fruit of a tropical flower

passive *adjective* **1** making no resistance **2** acted upon, not acting **3** *grammar* describing the form of a verb in which the subject undergoes, rather than performs, the action of the verb, *eg* 'the postman *was bitten* by the dog' (*compare with*: **active**) ■ **passively** *adverb* ■ **passivity** *noun*

passive smoking the involuntary inhaling of smoke from tobacco smoked by others

Passover *noun* a Jewish festival celebrating the exodus of the Israelites from Egypt

passport *noun* a card or booklet which gives someone's name and description, needed to travel in another country

password *noun* **1** a secret word which allows those who know it to pass **2** a word typed into a computer to allow access to restricted data

past *noun* **1 the past** the time gone by **2** someone's previous life or career **3** *grammar* the past tense ■ *adjective* **1** of an earlier time **2** just over, recently ended: *the past year* **3** gone, finished: *the time for argument is past* ■ *preposition* **1** after: *it's past midday* **2** up to and beyond, further than: *go past the traffic lights* ■ *adverb* by: *she walked past*

pasta *noun* **1** a dough used in making spaghetti, macaroni, *etc* **2** the prepared shapes of this, *eg* spaghetti

paste *noun* **1** pastry dough **2** a glue-like liquid for sticking paper *etc* together ■ *verb* **1** to stick something with paste **2** *computing* to insert text that has been cut or copied from another document *etc*

pastel *adjective* of a colour: soft,

pale ▪ *noun* a chalk-like crayon used for drawing

pasteurize or **pasteurise** *verb* to heat food (especially milk) in order to kill harmful germs in it

pastiche (*pronounced* pas-teesh*) noun* a humorous imitation, a parody

pastille *noun* a small sweet, sometimes sucked as a medicine

pastime *noun* a hobby, a spare-time interest

pastor *noun* a member of the clergy

pastoral *adjective* 1 relating to country life 2 of a pastor or the work of the clergy

past participle the form of a verb used after an auxiliary verb to indicate that something took place in the past, for instance *gone* in 'he has *gone*'

pastry *noun* (*plural* **pastries**) 1 a flour paste used to make the bases and crusts of pies, tarts, *etc* 2 a small cake

past tense the tense of a verb which indicates that something took place in the past

pasture *noun* ground covered with grass on which cattle graze

pasty[1] (*pronounced* **peis**-ti) *adjective* 1 like paste 2 pale

pasty[2] (*pronounced* **pas**-ti) *noun* a pie containing meat and vegetables in a covering of pastry

pat *noun* a light, quick blow or tap with the hand ▪ *verb* to strike gently, tap

pat *verb* ▶ pats, patting, patted

patch *verb* 1 to mend (clothes) by putting in a new piece of material to cover a hole 2 **patch something up** to mend it, especially hastily or clumsily 3 **patch something up** to settle (a quarrel) ▪ *noun* (*plural* **patches**) 1 a piece of material sewn on to mend a hole 2 a small piece of ground

patchwork *noun* fabric formed of small patches or pieces of material sewn together

patchy *adjective* uneven, mixed in quality

pâté or **paté** *noun* (*pronounced* pat*-ei) a paste made of finely minced meat, fish or vegetables, flavoured with herbs, spices, *etc*

patent *noun* an official written statement granting someone the sole right to make or sell something that they have invented ▪ *adjective* open, easily seen ▪ *verb* to obtain a patent for

patent leather leather with a very glossy surface

patently *adverb* openly, clearly: *patently obvious*

paternal *adjective* 1 of a father 2 like a father, fatherly 3 on the father's side of the family: *my paternal grandfather*

paternity *noun* the state or fact of being a father

path *noun* 1 a way made by people or animals walking on it, a track 2 the route to be taken by a person or vehicle: *in the lorry's path* **3** a course of action, a way of life

pathetic *adjective* **1** causing pity **2** causing contempt; feeble, inadequate ■ **pathetically** *adverb*

pathological *adjective* **1** relating to disease **2** *informal* compulsive, obsessive: *pathological liar*

pathologist *noun* **1** a doctor who studies the causes and effects of disease **2** a doctor who makes post-mortem examinations

pathology *noun* the study of diseases

pathos *noun* a quality that arouses pity

pathway *noun* a path

patience *noun* **1** the ability or willingness to be patient **2** (*also called*: **solitaire**) a card game played by one person

patient *adjective* suffering delay, discomfort, *etc* without complaint or anger ■ *noun* someone under the care of a doctor *etc* ■ **patiently** *adverb*

patio *noun* (*plural* **patios**) a paved open yard attached to a house

patriarch *noun* **1** the male head of a family or tribe **2** the head of the Greek Orthodox Church

patrician *noun* an aristocratic person

patriot *noun* someone who loves and is loyal to their country

patriotic *adjective* loyal or devoted to one's country
■ **patriotically** *adverb*

patriotism *noun* love of and loyalty to your country

patrol *verb* to keep guard or watch by moving regularly around an area *etc* ■ *noun* **1** the act of keeping guard in this way **2** the people keeping watch **3** a small group of Scouts or Guides

| **patrol** *verb* ▶ patrols, patrolling, patrolled

patrol car a police car used to patrol an area

patron *noun* **1** someone who protects or supports (an artist, a form of art, *etc*) **2** a customer of a shop *etc*

patronage *noun* the support given by a patron

patronize *or* **patronise** *verb* to treat (someone) as an inferior, look down on

patron saint a saint chosen as the protector of a country *etc*

patter [1] *verb* of rain, footsteps, *etc*: to make a quick tapping sound ■ *noun* the sound of falling rain, of footsteps, *etc*

patter [2] *noun* **1** chatter, rapid talk, especially that used by salesmen to encourage people to buy their goods **2** the jargon of a particular group

pattern *noun* **1** an example suitable to be copied **2** a model or guide for making something **3** a decorative design **4** *maths* a systematic arrangement of numbers, shapes, *etc*

patterned *adjective* having a design, not self-coloured

patty *noun* (*plural* **patties**) a small flat cake of chopped meat *etc*

paucity *noun* smallness of number or quantity

paunch *noun* (*plural* **paunches**) a fat stomach

pauper *noun* a very poor person

pause *noun* **1** a short stop, an interval **2** a break or hesitation in speaking or writing ▪ *verb* to stop for a short time

pave *verb* to lay (a street) with stone or concrete to form a level surface for walking on

pavement *noun* a hard path at the side of a road for pedestrians

pavilion *noun* **1** a building in a sports ground with facilities for changing clothes **2** a large ornamental building **3** a large tent

paw *noun* the foot of an animal ▪ *verb* **1** of an animal: to scrape with one of the front feet **2** to handle or touch roughly or rudely

pawn *verb* to put (an article of some value) in someone's keeping in exchange for a sum of money which, when repaid, buys back the article ▪ *noun* **1** *chess* a small piece of the lowest rank **2** someone who is used by a more powerful person for some purpose

pawnbroker *noun* someone who lends money in exchange for pawned articles

pawnshop *noun* a pawnbroker's place of business

pawpaw *another word for* papaya

pay *verb* **1** to give (money) in exchange for (goods *etc*) **2** to suffer the punishment (for) **3** to be advantageous or profitable: *it pays to be prepared* **4** to give (*eg* attention) ▪ *noun* money given or received for work; wages ▪ **pay off 1** to pay in full and discharge (workers) owing to lack of work **2** to have good results: *his hard work paid off* ▪ **pay out 1** to spend **2** to give out (a length of rope *etc*)

| **pay** *verb* ▸ pays, pay*ing*, paid

payable *adjective* requiring to be paid

payee *noun* someone to whom money is paid

payment *noun* **1** the act of paying **2** money paid for goods *etc*

payphone *noun* a coin- or card-operated public telephone

payroll *noun* a list of people entitled to receive pay

PC *abbreviation* **1** personal computer **2** police constable **3** political correctness

PE *abbreviation* physical education

pea *noun* **1** a climbing plant which produces round green seeds in pods **2** the seed itself, eaten as a vegetable

peace *noun* **1** quietness, calm **2** freedom from war or disturbance

💧✻ Do not confuse with: **piece**

peaceful *adjective* quiet; calm ▪ **peacefully** *adverb*

peach *noun* (*plural* **peaches**) **1** a juicy, velvet-skinned fruit **2** the tree that bears it **3** a pinkish-orange colour

peacock *noun* a large bird, the male of which has brightly coloured, patterned tail feathers

peahen *noun* a female peacock

peak *noun* **1** the pointed top of a mountain or hill **2** the highest point **3** the jutting-out part of the brim of a cap ▪ *verb* to reach the highest point: *prices peaked in May*

peaked *adjective* **1** pointed **2** of a cap: having a peak

peaky *adjective* looking pale and unhealthy

peal *noun* **1** a set of bells tuned to each other **2** the changes rung on such bells **3** a succession of loud sounds: *peals of laughter* ▪ *verb* to sound loudly

💧✻ Do not confuse with: **peel**

peanut *noun* a type of nut similar to a pea in shape (*also called*: **monkey nut**)

peanut butter a paste of ground roasted peanuts, spread on bread *etc*

pear *noun* a tree-growing fruit that is narrow at the top and widens at the bottom

pearl *noun* a gem formed in the shell of the oyster and several other shellfish

peasant *noun* someone who works and lives on the land, especially in an underdeveloped area

peat *noun* turf cut out of boggy places, dried and used as fuel

pebble *noun* a small, roundish stone

peck *verb* **1** to strike with the beak **2** to pick up with the beak **3** to eat little, nibble (at) **4** to kiss quickly and briefly ▪ *noun* **1** a sharp blow with the beak **2** a brief kiss

peckish *adjective* slightly hungry

peculiar *adjective* **1** strange, odd **2** peculiar to belonging to one person or thing only

peculiarity *noun* (*plural* **peculiarities**) that which marks someone or something off from others in some way; something odd

peculiarly *adverb* in a peculiar way

pedal *noun* **1** a lever worked by the foot on a bicycle, piano, *etc* **2** a key worked by the foot on an organ ▪ *verb* **1** to work the pedals of **2** to ride on a bicycle

| **pedal** *verb* ▶ pedals, pedalling, pedalled

pedant *noun* someone who is

very fussy about small details

pedantic *adjective* over-concerned with correctness

pedantry *noun* fussiness about unimportant details

peddle *verb* to travel from door to door selling goods

pedestal *noun* the foot or support of a pillar, statue, *etc*

pedestrian *adjective* **1** going on foot **2** for those on foot ■ *noun* someone who goes or travels on foot

pedestrian crossing a place where pedestrians may cross the road when the traffic stops

pedicure *noun* a treatment for the feet including treating corns, cutting nails, *etc*

pedigree *noun* the ancestry of a pure-bred animal ■ *adjective* of an animal: pure-bred, from a long line of ancestors of the same breed

pediment *noun* a triangular structure over the front of an ancient Greek building

pedlar *noun* someone who travels from door to door selling goods

pee *verb*, *informal* to urinate ■ *noun* **1** the act of urinating **2** urine

| **pee** *verb* ▶ pees, peeing, peed

peek *verb* to peep, glance, especially secretively ■ *noun* a secret look

peel *verb* **1** to strip off the outer covering or skin of **2** of skin, paint, *etc*: to come off in small pieces **3** to lose skin in small flakes, *eg* as a result of sunburn ■ *noun* skin, rind

● Do not confuse with: **peal**

peep *verb* **1** to look through a narrow opening, round a corner, *etc* **2** to look slyly or quickly (at) **3** to make a high, small sound ■ *noun* **1** a quick look, a glimpse, often from hiding **2** a high, small sound

peer *verb* to look at with half-closed eyes, as if with difficulty ■ *noun* **1** someone's equal in rank, merit or age **2** a nobleman of the rank of baron upwards **3** a member of the House of Lords

peerage *noun* **1** a peer's title **2** the peers as a group

peerless *adjective* without any equal, better than all others

peeve *verb*, *informal* to irritate

peeved *adjective* annoyed

peevish *adjective* cross, bad-tempered, irritable

peewit *noun* the lapwing

peg *noun* **1** a pin or stake of wood, metal, *etc* **2** a hook fixed to a wall for hanging clothes *etc* ■ *verb* to fasten with a peg

| **peg** *verb* ▶ pegs, pegging, pegged

pejorative *adjective* showing disapproval, scorn, *etc*: *a pejorative remark*

Pekinese or **Pekingese** *noun* a

breed of small dog with a long coat and flat face

pelican *noun* a large waterbird with a pouched bill for storing fish

pelican crossing a street-crossing where the lights are operated by pedestrians

pellet *noun* **1** a small ball of shot *etc* **2** a small pill

pell-mell *adverb* in great confusion; headlong

pelmet *noun* a strip or band hiding a curtain rail

pelt *noun* the untreated skin of an animal ▪ *verb* **1** to throw (things) at **2** to run fast **3** of rain: to fall heavily

pelvis *noun* the frame of bone which circles the body below the waist

pen[1] *noun* an instrument with a nib for writing in ink ▪ *verb* to write (*eg* a letter)

| pen *verb* ▶ pen*s*, pen*ning*, pen*ned*

pen[2] *noun* a small enclosure for sheep, cattle, *etc*

pen[3] *noun* a female swan

penalize or **penalise** *verb* to punish

penalty *noun* (*plural* **penalties**) **1** punishment **2** a disadvantage put on a player or team for having broken a rule of a game

penance *noun* punishment willingly suffered by someone to make up for a wrong

pence *plural* of penny

penchant *noun* an inclination (for), a bias

pencil *noun* an instrument containing a length of graphite or other substance for writing, drawing, *etc*

pendant *noun* **1** an ornament hung from a necklace *etc* **2** a necklace with such an ornament

pending *adjective* awaiting a decision or attention: *this matter is pending* ▪ *preposition* awaiting, until the coming of: *pending confirmation*

pendulum *noun* a swinging weight which drives the mechanism of a clock

penetrate *verb* to pierce or pass into or through ▪ **penetration** *noun*

penetrating *adjective* of a sound: piercing

pen friend or **pen pal** someone you have never seen (usually living abroad) with whom you exchange letters

penguin *noun* a large seabird of Antarctic regions, which cannot fly

penicillin *noun* a medicine obtained from mould, which kills many bacteria

peninsula *noun* a piece of land almost surrounded by water

penis *noun* the part of the body which a male human or animal uses in sexual intercourse and for urinating

penitent *adjective* sorry for doing something wrong

penitentiary *noun, US* a prison

penknife *noun* a pocket knife with folding blades

pen name a name adopted by a writer instead of their own name

pennant *noun* a long flag coming to a point at the end

penniless *adjective* having no money

penny *noun* **1** a coin worth $\frac{1}{100}$ of £1 **2** (*plural* **pence**) used to show an amount in pennies: *the newspaper costs sixty pence* **3** (*plural* **pennies**) used for a number of coins: *I need five pennies for the coffee machine*

penny-pinching *adjective* mean, stingy

pension *noun* a sum of money paid regularly to a retired person, a widow, someone wounded in war, *etc* ▪ **pension off** to dismiss or allow to retire with a pension

pensionable *adjective* having or giving the right to a pension: *pensionable age*

pensioner *noun* someone who receives a pension

pensive *adjective* thoughtful

pent *or* **pent-up** *adjective* **1** shut up, not allowed to go free **2** of emotions: not freely expressed

pentagon *noun* a five-sided figure ▪ **pentagonal** *adjective*

pentathlon *noun* a five-event contest in the Olympic Games *etc*

Pentecost *noun* **1** a Jewish festival held fifty days after Passover **2** a Christian festival held seven weeks after Easter

penthouse *noun* a luxurious flat at the top of a building

penultimate *adjective* last but one

penumbra *noun* a light shadow surrounding the main shadow of an eclipse

penury *noun* poverty, want

peony *noun* (*plural* **peonies**) a type of garden plant with large red, white or pink flowers

people *noun plural* **1** the men, women and children of a country or nation **2** persons generally ▪ *verb* **1** to fill with people **2** to inhabit, make up the population of

pep *noun, informal* spirit, verve ▪ *verb*: **pep up** to invigorate, enliven

pepper *noun* **1** a plant whose berries are dried, powdered and used as seasoning **2** the spicy powder it produces **3** a hot-tasting hollow fruit containing many seeds, eaten raw, cooked or pickled ▪ *verb* **1** to sprinkle with pepper **2** **pepper with** to throw at or hit: *peppered with bullets*

peppermint *noun* **1** a type of plant with a powerful taste and smell **2** a flavouring taken from this and used in sweets *etc*

pep talk a talk meant to encourage or arouse enthusiasm

per *preposition* **1** in, out of **2** for

each: *£2 per dozen* **3** in each: *six times per week*

perambulator *full form of* pram

perceive *verb* to become aware of through the senses

per cent *or US* **percent** (often written as **%**) out of every hundred: *five per cent* (= 5 out of every hundred)

percentage *noun* the number of parts per hundred, *eg* $\frac{1}{2}$ expressed as a percentage = 50 per cent

perceptible *adjective* able to be seen or understood ▪ **perceptibly** *adverb*

perception *noun* the ability to perceive; understanding

perceptive *adjective* able or quick to perceive or understand

perch[1] *noun* (*plural* **perches**) **1** a rod on which birds roost **2** a high seat or position ▪ *verb* to roost

perch[2] *noun* (*plural* **perches**) a type of freshwater fish

perchance *adverb, old* by chance; perhaps

percolate *verb* **1** of a liquid: to drip or drain through small holes **2** to cause (a liquid) to do this

percolator *noun* a device for percolating: *a coffee percolator*

percussion *noun* musical instruments played by striking, *eg* drums, cymbals, *etc*

perennial *adjective* **1** lasting through the year **2** everlasting, perpetual **3** of a plant: growing from year to year without

replanting or sowing ▪ *noun* a perennial plant

perfect *adjective* (*pronounced* per-fikt) **1** complete, finished **2** faultless **3** exact ▪ *verb* (*pronounced* pe-fekt) **1** to make perfect **2** to finish ▪ *noun*, *grammar* (*pronounced* per-fikt) a tense used to describe completed actions or states, *eg* 'he *has failed*'

perfection *noun* **1** the state of being perfect **2** the highest state or degree

perfectionist *noun* someone who is satisfied only by perfection

perforated *adjective* pierced with holes

perform *verb* **1** to do, act **2** to act (a part) on the stage **3** to provide entertainment for an audience **4** to play (a piece of music)

performance *noun* **1** an entertainment in a theatre *etc* **2** the act of doing something **3** the level of success of a machine, car, *etc*

performer *noun* someone who acts or performs

perfume *noun* **1** smell, fragrance **2** a fragrant liquid put on the skin, scent ▪ *verb* **1** to put scent on or in **2** to give a sweet smell to

perfumery *noun* a shop or factory where perfume is sold or made

perhaps *adverb* it may be (that), possibly

peril *noun* a great danger ▪ **at your peril** at your own risk

perilous *adjective* very dangerous ▪ **perilously** *adverb*

perimeter *noun* **1** the outside line enclosing a figure or shape **2** the outer edge of any area

◆* Do not confuse with: **parameter**. Notice that words starting with **peri-** often relate to the idea of 'going around' and the **perimeter** of a figure or shape is the line that goes around it

period *noun* **1** a stretch of time **2** a stage in the earth's development or in history **3** a time of menstruation

periodic *adjective* **1** happening at regular intervals, *eg* every month or year **2** happening every now and then

periodical *adjective* issued or done at regular intervals; periodic ▪ *noun* a magazine which appears at regular intervals

periodic table a table in which chemical elements are arranged by atomic number

peripatetic *adjective* moving from place to place; travelling

peripheral *adjective* **1** away from the centre **2** not essential, of little importance

periphery *noun* (*plural* **peripheries**) **1** the line surrounding something **2** an outer boundary or edge

periscope *noun* a tube with mirrors by which a viewer in a submarine *etc* is able to see objects on the surface

perish *verb* **1** to be destroyed, pass away completely; die **2** to decay, rot

perishable *adjective* liable to go bad quickly

periwinkle *noun* **1** a small shellfish, shaped like a small snail, eaten as food when boiled **2** a creeping evergreen plant with a small blue flower

perjure *verb*: **perjure yourself** *etc* to tell a lie when you have sworn to tell the truth, especially in a court of law

perjury *noun* the crime of lying while under oath in a court of law

perk[1] *noun* something of value allowed in addition to payment for work

perk[2] *verb*: **perk up** to recover energy or spirits

perky *adjective* jaunty, in good spirits

perm *noun* short for **permanent wave** ▪ *verb* to give a permanent wave to (hair)

permanence *or* **permanency** *noun* the state of continuing or remaining for a long time or for ever

permanent *adjective* lasting, not temporary ▪ **permanently** *adverb*

permanent wave a wave or curl put into the hair by a special process and usually lasting for some months

permeable *adjective* able to be permeated by liquids, gases, *etc*

permeate *verb* **1** to pass into through small holes, soak into **2** to fill every part of

permissible *adjective* allowable

permission *noun* freedom given to do something

permissive *adjective* **1** allowing something to be done **2** too tolerant ■ **permissiveness** *noun*

permit *verb* (*pronounced* pe-mit) **1** to agree to an action, allow **2** to make possible ■ *noun* (*pronounced* per-mit) a written order, allowing someone to do something: *a fishing permit*

permutation *noun* any of several different ways in which things, *eg* numbers, can be ordered or arranged

pernicious *adjective* destructive

pernickety *adjective* fussy about small details

peroxide *noun* a chemical (hydrogen peroxide) used for bleaching hair *etc*

perpendicular *adjective* **1** standing upright, vertical **2** at right angles (to) ■ *noun* a line at right angles to another

perpetrate *verb* to commit (a sin, error, *etc*)

●＊ Do not confuse with:
perpetuate

perpetrator *noun* a person who perpetrates; the one who is guilty

perpetual *adjective* everlasting, unending ■ **perpetually** *adverb*

perpetuate *verb* to make last for ever or for a long time

●＊ Do not confuse with:
perpetrate

perpetuity *noun*: **in perpetuity 1** for ever **2** for the length of someone's life

perplex *verb* to puzzle, bewilder

perplexity *noun* a puzzled state of mind

per se *adverb* in itself, essentially

persecute *verb* **1** to harass over a period of time **2** to cause to suffer, especially because of religious beliefs ■ **persecution** *noun*

●＊ Do not confuse with:
prosecute

perseverance *noun* the act of persevering

persevere *verb* to keep trying to do a thing (in spite of difficulties)

persist *verb* **1** to hold fast to (*eg* an idea) **2** to continue to do something in spite of difficulties **3** to survive, last

persistence *noun* **1** persisting **2** being persistent

persistent *adjective* **1** obstinate, refusing to be discouraged **2** lasting, not dying out ■ **persistently** *adverb*

person *noun* **1** a human being **2** someone's body: *jewels hidden on his person* **3** form, shape:

trouble arrived in the person of Gordon

persona *noun* the outward part of the personality presented to others; social image

personable *adjective* good-looking

personage *noun* a well-known person

personal *adjective* **1** your own; private **2** of a remark: insulting, offensive to the person it is aimed at

⚡ Do not confuse with: **personnel**

personality *noun* (*plural* **personalities**) **1** all of a person's characteristics as seen by others **2** a well-known person

personally *adverb* **1** speaking from your own point of view **2** by your own action, not using an agent or representative

personal stereo a small portable compact disc or cassette player with earphones

personification *noun* **1** giving human qualities to things or ideas **2** in art or literature, representing an idea or quality as a person **3** a person or thing that is seen as a perfect example of a quality: *the personification of patience*

personify *verb* to typify, be a perfect example of

| **personify** ► personifi*es*, personify*ing*, personifi*ed*

personnel (*pronounced* pers-o-

nel) *noun* the people employed in a firm *etc*

⚡ Do not confuse with: **personal**. **Personnel** is a noun coming from French company terminology, used to describe the 'person-assets' of a company (= the people who work for it) in contrast to its 'material-assets' (= all its non-human items of value)

perspective *noun* **1** a point of view **2** the giving of a sense of depth, distance, *etc* in a painting like that in real life

Perspex *noun*, *trademark* a transparent plastic which looks like glass

perspiration *noun* sweat

perspire *verb* to sweat

persuade *verb* to bring someone to do or think something, by arguing with them or advising them

persuasion *noun* **1** the act of persuading **2** a firm belief, especially a religious belief

persuasive *adjective* having the power to convince

pert *adjective* saucy, cheeky

pertain *verb*: **pertain to** to belong to, have to do with: *duties pertaining to the job*

pertinent *adjective* connected with the subject spoken about, to the point

perturb *verb* to disturb greatly; to make anxious or uneasy

perusal noun careful reading

peruse verb to read (with care)

pervade verb to spread through: *silence pervaded the room*

perverse adjective obstinate in holding to the wrong point of view; unreasonable

perverseness or **perversity** noun stubbornness

pervert verb (pronounced pe-vert) **1** to turn away from what is normal or right: *pervert the course of justice* **2** to turn (someone) to crime or evil; corrupt ■ noun (pronounced **per**-vert) someone who commits unnatural or abnormal acts

pessimism noun the habit of thinking that things will always turn out badly (contrasted with: optimism) ■ **pessimist** noun ■ **pessimistic** adjective ■ **pessimistically** adverb

pest noun **1** a troublesome person or thing **2** a creature that is harmful or destructive, *eg* a mosquito

pester verb to annoy continually

pesticide noun any substance which kills animal pests

pestilence noun a deadly, spreading disease

pestle noun a tool for pounding things to powder

pet noun **1** a tame animal kept in the home, such as a cat **2** a favourite ■ adjective **1** kept as a pet **2** favourite **3** chief: *my pet hate* ■ verb to fondle

pet verb ► pets, petting, petted

petal noun one of the leaf-like parts of a flower

peter verb: **peter out** to fade or dwindle away to nothing

petite adjective small and neat in appearance

petition noun a request or note of protest signed by many people and sent to a government or authority ■ verb to send a petition to

petrel noun a small, long-winged seabird

Petri dish a shallow circular container used for growing bacteria *etc*

petrify verb **1** to turn into stone **2** to turn (someone) stiff with fear

petrify ► petrifies, petrifying, petrified

petrochemical noun a chemical made from petroleum or natural gas

petrol noun petroleum when refined as fuel for use in cars *etc*

petroleum noun oil in its raw, unrefined form, extracted from natural wells below the earth's surface

petticoat noun an underskirt worn by women

petty adjective of little importance, trivial ■ **pettiness** noun

petty cash money paid or received in small sums

petty officer a rank of officer in

the navy (equal to a non-commissioned officer in the army)

petulance noun being petulant

petulant adjective **1** cross, irritable **2** unreasonably impatient

petunia noun a S American flowering plant related to tobacco

pew noun a seat or bench in a church

pewter noun a mixture of tin and lead

pH noun, chemistry a measure of the acidity or alkalinity of a solution

phantom noun a ghost

Pharaoh noun, history a ruler of ancient Egypt

pharmaceutical adjective relating to the making up of medicines and drugs

pharmacist noun someone who prepares and sells medicines

pharmacy noun (plural **pharmacies**) **1** the art of preparing medicines **2** a chemist's shop

phase noun **1** one in a series of changes in the shape or appearance of something (eg the moon) **2** a stage in the development of something (eg a war, a scheme, etc) ∎ **phase in** or **out** to introduce or end something in stages

pheasant noun a bird with brightly-coloured feathers which is shot as game

phenomenal adjective very unusual, remarkable
∎ **phenomenally** adverb

phenomenon noun (plural **phenomena**) **1** an event (especially in nature) that is observed by the senses: *the phenomenon of lightning* **2** something remarkable or very unusual, a wonder

phial noun a small glass bottle

philander verb to flirt, or have casual love affairs, with women

philanthropic adjective kind and generous

philanthropist noun someone who does good to others

philanthropy noun love of mankind, often shown by giving money for the benefit of others

philatelist noun a stamp-collector

philately noun the study and collecting of stamps

philistine noun someone ignorant of, or hostile to, culture and the arts

philosopher noun someone who studies philosophy

philosophical or **philosophic** adjective **1** of philosophy **2** calm, not easily upset

philosophy noun (plural **philosophies**) **1** the study of the nature of the universe, or of human behaviour **2** someone's personal view of life

philtre noun a love potion

phlegm (pronounced flem) noun

thick slimy matter brought up from the throat by coughing

phlegmatic (*pronounced* fleg-mat-ik) *adjective* not easily excited

-phobe *suffix* forms words describing people who suffer from particular phobias

phobia *noun* an intense, often irrational, fear or dislike

phoenix (*pronounced* fee-niks) *noun* a mythological bird believed to burn itself and to rise again from its ashes

phone *short for* telephone

phonecard *noun* a card that can be used instead of cash to operate certain public telephones

phonetic *adjective* relating to the sounds of language

phonetics *noun singular* 1 the study of the sounds of language 2 a system of writing according to sound

phoney *or* **phony** *adjective, informal* fake, not genuine

phosphorus *noun* a wax-like, poisonous substance that gives out light in the dark

photo *noun* (*plural* photos) *informal* a photograph

photocopier *noun* a machine that makes photocopies

photocopy *noun* a copy of a document made by a device which photographs and develops images ■ *verb* to make a photocopy of

photofit *noun, trademark* a method of making identification pictures by combining photographs of individual features

photogenic *adjective* photographing well

photograph *noun* a picture taken with a camera ■ *verb* to take a picture with a camera

photographer *noun* a person who takes photographs, especially professionally

photography *noun* the art of taking pictures with a camera ■ **photographic** *adjective*

photon *noun* the smallest unit of light

photosensitive *adjective* affected by light

photosynthesis *noun* the conversion of light into complex compounds by plants

phrase *noun* 1 a small group of words expressing a single idea, *eg* 'after dinner', 'on the water' 2 a short saying or expression ■ *verb* to express in words

phraseology *noun* someone's personal choice of words and phrases

phylum *noun* a division of natural objects below a kingdom and above a class

physical *adjective* 1 relating to the body 2 relating to things that can be seen or felt ■ **physically** *adverb*

physical education instruction in sports, games and

keeping fit (*short form:* PE)

physician *noun* a doctor specializing in medical rather than surgical treatment

physicist *noun* someone who specializes in physics

physics *noun singular* the science which includes the study of heat, light, sound, electricity, magnetism, *etc*

physiognomy *noun* the features or expression of the face

physiology *noun* the study of the way in which living bodies work, including blood circulation, food digestion, *etc*

physiotherapist *noun* a person skilled in treatment by physiotherapy

physiotherapy *noun* the treatment of disease by bodily exercise, massage, *etc* rather than by drugs

physique *noun* 1 the build of someone's body 2 bodily strength

pi *noun* a number that is the circumference of any circle divided by its diameter, approximately 3.142

pianist *noun* someone who plays the piano

piano *noun* (*plural* **pianos**) a large musical instrument played by striking keys

piazza *noun* a market-place or town square surrounded by buildings

piccolo *noun* (*plural* **piccolos**) a small, high-pitched flute

pick *verb* 1 to choose 2 to pluck, gather (flowers, fruit, *etc*) 3 to peck, bite, nibble (at) 4 to poke, probe (teeth *etc*) 5 to open (a lock) with a tool other than a key ▪ *noun* 1 choice: *take your pick* 2 the best or best part 3 a pickaxe ▪ **pick on** 1 to single out for criticism *etc* 2 to nag at ▪ **pick up** 1 to lift up 2 to learn (a language, habit, *etc*) 3 to give (someone) a lift in a car 4 to find or get by chance 5 to improve, gain strength

pickaxe *noun* a heavy tool for breaking ground, pointed at one end or both ends

picket *noun* a number of workers on strike who prevent others from going into work ▪ *verb* to place a guard or a group of strikers at (a place)

pickle *noun* 1 a liquid in which food is preserved 2 vegetables preserved in vinegar 3 *informal* an awkward, unpleasant situation ▪ *verb* to preserve with salt, vinegar, *etc*

pickpocket *noun* someone who robs people's pockets or handbags

picky *adjective* choosy, fussy

picnic *noun* a meal eaten out-of-doors, often during an outing *etc* ▪ *verb* to have a picnic

| **picnic** *verb* ► picnics, picnicking, picnicked

pictogram *noun* a chart or graph which uses pictures to show amounts, with one picture standing for a particular amount

pictorial *adjective* **1** having pictures **2** consisting of pictures **3** calling up pictures in the mind

picture *noun* **1** a painting or drawing **2** a portrait **3** a photograph **4** a film **5 the pictures** the cinema **6** a vivid description ▪ *verb* **1** to make a picture of **2** to see in the mind, imagine

picturesque *adjective* such as would make a good or striking picture; pretty, colourful

pidgin *noun* a distorted form of a language arising because of its combination with a different language

●✳ Do not confuse with:
pigeon

pie *noun* meat, fruit or other food baked in a casing or covering of pastry

piebald *adjective* white and black in patches

piece *noun* **1** a part or portion of anything **2** a single article or example: *a piece of paper* **3** an artistic work: *a piece of popular music* **4** a coin **5** a man in chess, draughts, *etc* ▪ *verb* to put (together)

●✳ Do not confuse with:
peace

piecemeal *adverb* by pieces, little by little

pie chart a circular diagram split into sections showing the

different percentages into which a whole amount is divided

pied *adjective* with two or more colours in patches

pier *noun* a platform stretching from the shore into the sea as a landing place for ships

pierce *verb* **1** to make a hole through **2** to force a way into **3** to move (the feelings) deeply

piercing *adjective* shrill, loud; sharp

piety *noun* respect for holy things

piffle *noun* nonsense

pig *noun* a farm animal, from whose flesh ham and bacon are made

pigeon *noun* a bird of the dove family

●✳ Do not confuse with:
pidgin

pigeonhole *noun* a small division in a case or desk for papers *etc* ▪ *verb* to classify, put into a category

piggyback *noun* a ride on someone's back with your arms round their neck

piggy bank a china pig with a slit along its back to insert coins for saving

pigheaded *adjective* stubborn

piglet *noun* a young pig

pigment *noun* **1** paint or other substance used for colouring **2** a substance in animals and plants that gives colour to the skin *etc* ▪ **pigmentation** *noun*

pigmy *another spelling of* **pygmy**

pigsty (*plural* **pigsties**) *or* **piggery** (*plural* **piggeries**) *noun* a place where pigs are kept

pigtail *noun* hair formed into a plait

pike *noun* a freshwater fish

pilchard *noun* a small seafish like a herring, often tinned

pile *noun* **1** a number of things lying one on top of another, a heap **2** a great quantity **3** the thick, soft surface on carpets and on cloth such as velvet ▪ *verb* (often **pile up** *or* **pile something up**) to make or form a pile or heap

pilfer *verb* to steal small things

pilgrim *noun* a traveller to a holy place

pilgrimage *noun* a journey to a holy place

pill *noun* a tablet of medicine

pillage *verb* to seize goods and money, especially as loot in war ▪ *noun* the act of plundering in this way

pillar *noun* an upright support for roofs, arches, *etc*

pillar box a tall box with a slot through which letters *etc* are posted

pillion *noun* a seat for a passenger on a motorcycle

pillory *noun* (*plural* **pillories**) *history* a wooden frame fitted over the head and hands of wrongdoers as a punishment ▪ *verb* to mock in public

pillory *verb* ▸ **pillories**, **pillory**ing, **pillori**ed

pillow *noun* a soft cushion for the head ▪ *verb* to rest or support on a pillow

pillowcase *or* **pillowslip** *noun* a cover for a pillow

pilot *noun* **1** someone who steers a ship in or out of a harbour **2** someone who flies an aeroplane ▪ *verb* to steer, guide

pilot light a small gas-light from which larger jets are lit

pimpernel *noun* a plant of the primrose family, with small pink or scarlet flowers

pimple *noun* a small round infected swelling on the skin

pimpled *or* **pimply** *adjective* having pimples

PIN (*pronounced* pin) *abbreviation* personal identification number (for automatic teller machines *etc*)

pin *noun* **1** a short pointed piece of metal with a small round head, used for fastening fabric **2** a wooden or metal peg **3** a skittle ▪ *verb* **1** to fasten with a pin **2** to hold fast, pressed against something

pin *verb* ▸ **pins**, **pin**ning, **pin**ned

pinafore *noun* **1** an apron to protect the front of a dress **2** a sleeveless dress worn over a jersey, blouse, *etc*

pinball *noun* a game played on a slot-machine in which a ball runs down a sloping board between obstacles

pincers *noun plural* the claw of a crab or lobster

pinch *verb* **1** to squeeze (especially flesh) between the thumb and forefinger, nip **2** to grip tightly, hurt by tightness **3** *informal* to steal ■ *noun* (*plural* **pinches**) **1** a squeeze, a nip **2** a small amount (*eg* of salt)

pinched *adjective* of a face: looking cold, pale or thin

pine *noun* **1** an evergreen tree with needle-like leaves which produces cones **2** the soft wood of such a tree used for furniture *etc* ■ *verb* **1** to waste away, lose strength **2** to long (for something)

pineapple *noun* a large tropical fruit shaped like a pine-cone

ping *noun* a whistling sound such as that of a bullet ■ *verb* to make a brief high-pitched sound

ping-pong *noun*, *trademark* table-tennis

pink *noun* **1** a pale red colour **2** a sweet-scented garden flower like a carnation **3** a healthy or good state: *in the pink*

pinkie *noun*, *informal* the little finger

pinnacle *noun* **1** a slender spire or turret **2** a high pointed rock or mountain **3** the highest point

pint *noun* a liquid measure equal to just over ½ litre

pioneer *noun* **1** an explorer **2** a person involved in the invention

or early use of something ■ *verb* to act as a pioneer

pious *adjective* respectful in religious matters

pip *noun* **1** a seed of a fruit **2** a spot or symbol on dice or cards **3** a short bleep as part of a time signal *etc* on the radio or telephone

pipe *noun* **1** a tube for carrying water, gas, *etc* **2** a tube with a bowl at the end, for smoking tobacco **3 pipes** a musical instrument made of several small pipes joined together **4 pipes** bagpipes ■ *verb* **1** to play (notes, a tune) on a pipe or pipes **2** to whistle, chirp **3** to speak in a shrill high voice **4** to convey (*eg* water) by pipe ■ **pipe down** to become silent, stop talking ■ **pipe up** to speak up, express an opinion

pipeline *noun* a long line of pipes, *eg* to carry oil from an oil-field ■ **in the pipeline** in preparation, soon to become available

piper *noun* someone who plays a pipe, especially the bagpipes

piping *adjective* high-pitched, shrill ■ *noun* a narrow ornamental cord for trimming clothes ■ **piping hot** very hot

pipsqueak *noun*, *informal* an insignificant, or very small, person

piquant (*pronounced* peek-ant) *adjective* **1** sharp-tasting, spicy **2** arousing interest ■ **piquancy** *noun*

pique (*pronounced* peek) *noun* anger caused by wounded pride, spite, resentment, *etc* ■ *verb* 1 to wound the pride of 2 to arouse (curiosity)

piracy *noun* the activity of pirates

piranha *noun* a S American river-fish which eats flesh

pirate *noun* someone who robs ships at sea

pirouette *noun* a rapid whirling on the toes in dancing ■ *verb* to twirl in a pirouette

pistachio *noun* (*plural* **pistachios**) a greenish nut, often used as a flavouring

pistil *noun* the seed-bearing part of a flower

pistol *noun* a small gun held in the hand

piston *noun* a round piece of metal that moves up and down inside a cylinder, *eg* in an engine

pit *noun* 1 a hole in the ground 2 a place from which coal and other minerals are dug ■ *verb* to set one thing or person against another: *pitting my wits against his*

| **pit** *verb* ▶ pits, pitt*ing*, pitt*ed*

pitch *verb* 1 to fix a tent *etc* in the ground 2 to throw 3 to fall heavily; lurch: *pitch forward* 4 to set the level or key of a tune ■ *noun* (*plural* **pitches**) 1 a thick dark substance obtained by boiling down tar 2 a throw 3 an attempt at selling or persuading: *sales pitch* 4 the height or depth of

a note 5 a peak, an extreme point: *fever pitch* 6 the field for certain sports 7 *cricket* the ground between wickets

pitch-dark *adjective* very dark

pitched battle a battle on chosen ground between sides arranged in position beforehand

pitcher *noun* a kind of large jug

pitchfork *noun* a fork for lifting and throwing hay

piteous *or* **pitiable** *adjective* deserving pity; wretched

pitfall *noun* a trap, a possible danger

pith *noun* the white substance under the rind of an orange, lemon, *etc*

pithy *adjective* 1 full of pith 2 full of meaning, to the point: *a pithy saying*

pitiable *see* piteous

pitiful *adjective* poor, wretched

pittance *noun* a very small wage or allowance

pituitary gland a gland in the brain affecting growth

pity *noun* 1 feeling for the sufferings of others, sympathy 2 a cause of grief 3 a regrettable fact ■ *verb* to feel sorry for

| **pity** *verb* ▶ piti*es*, pity*ing*, piti*ed*

pivot *noun* the pin or centre on which anything turns ■ *verb* to turn on a pivot

pivotal *adjective* 1 acting as a pivot 2 crucially important; critical

pixel *noun* the smallest element in an image on a TV or computer screen, consisting of a tiny dot

pixie *or* **pixy** *noun* (*plural* **pixies**) a kind of fairy

pizza *noun* a flat piece of dough spread with tomato, cheese, *etc* and baked

pizzicato *adverb, music* played by plucking the strings rather than bowing

placard *noun* a printed notice (as an advertisement *etc*) placed on a wall *etc*

placate *verb* to calm, make less angry, *etc*

place *noun* **1** a physical location; any area or building **2** a particular spot **3** an open space in a town: *market place* **4** a seat in a theatre, train, at a table, *etc* **5** a position in football *etc* **6** a position on a course, in a job, *etc* **7** rank ■ *verb* **1** to put in a particular place **2** to find a place for **3** to give (an order for goods *etc*) **4** to remember who someone is: *I can't place him at all*

| **place** *verb* ► plac*es*, plac*ing*,
| plac*ed*

placebo *noun* a substance resembling a drug but with no medicinal ingredients

placed *adjective* **1** having a place **2** among the first three in a competition

placenta *noun* a part of the womb that connects an unborn mammal to its mother, shed at birth

placid *adjective* calm, not easily disturbed

placidity *noun* being placid

plagiarism *noun* stealing or borrowing from the writings or ideas of someone else without permission

plagiarist *noun* a person who plagiarizes

plagiarize *or* **plagiarise** *verb* to steal or borrow from the writings or ideas of someone else without permission

plague *noun* **1** a fatal infectious disease carried by rat fleas **2** a great and troublesome quantity: *a plague of flies* ■ *verb* to pester or annoy continually

plaice *noun* a type of edible flatfish

plaid *noun* a long piece of cloth (especially tartan) worn over the shoulder

plain *adjective* **1** flat, level **2** simple, ordinary **3** without ornament or decoration **4** clear, easy to see or understand **5** not good-looking, not attractive ■ *noun* a level stretch of land

plain-clothes *adjective* of a police officer: wearing ordinary clothes, not uniform

plain text *computing* the format of most e-mail messages, using simple upper case and lower case letters

plaintiff *noun* someone who takes action against another in the law courts

plaintive *adjective* sad, sorrowful

plait *noun* 1 a length of hair arranged by intertwining three or more separate pieces 2 threads *etc* intertwined in this way ■ *verb* to form into a plait

plan *noun* 1 a diagram of a building, town, *etc* as if seen from above 2 a scheme or arrangement to do something ■ *verb* 1 to make a sketch or plan of 2 to decide or arrange to do (something)

| **plan** *verb* ▶ plans, planning, planned

plane[1] *short for* aeroplane

plane[2] *noun* 1 a level surface 2 a carpentry tool for smoothing wood ■ *adjective* flat, level ■ *verb* to smooth with a plane

plane[3] *noun* a type of tree with broad leaves

planet *noun* any of the bodies (*eg* the earth, Venus) which move round the sun or round another fixed star

planetary *adjective* relating to, consisting of or produced by planets

plank *noun* a long, flat piece of timber

plankton *noun* tiny living creatures floating in seas, lakes, *etc*

plant *noun* a living growth from the ground, with a stem, a root and leaves ■ *verb* 1 to put (something) into the ground so that it will grow 2 to put (an idea) into the mind 3 to put in position: *plant a bomb* 4 to set down firmly 5 *informal* to place (something) as false evidence

plantation *noun* 1 an area planted with trees 2 an estate for growing cotton, sugar, rubber, tobacco, *etc*

planter *noun* the owner of a plantation

plaque *noun* 1 a decorative plate of metal, china, *etc* for fixing to a wall 2 a film of saliva and bacteria which forms on the teeth

plasma *noun* the liquid part of blood and certain other fluids

plaster *noun* 1 a mixture of lime, water and sand which sets hard, for covering walls *etc* 2 (*also called:* plaster of Paris) a fine mixture used for moulding, making casts for broken limbs, *etc* 3 a small dressing that can be stuck over a wound ■ *adjective* made of plaster ■ *verb* 1 to apply plaster to 2 to cover too thickly (with)

plasterer *noun* someone whose trade is plastering walls

plastic *adjective* made of plastic ■ *noun* a chemically manufactured substance that can be moulded when soft, formed into fibres, *etc*

Plasticine *noun, trademark* a soft clay-like substance used for modelling

plastic surgery an operation to

plate 458 **play-off**

repair or replace damaged areas of skin, or to improve the appearance of a facial feature

plate *noun* **1** a shallow dish for holding food **2** a flat piece of metal, glass, china, *etc* **3** a book illustration ▪ *verb* to cover with a coating of metal

plateau *noun* (*plural* **plateaus** or **plateaux**) a broad level stretch of high land

plate glass glass in thick sheets, used for shop windows, mirrors, *etc*

platelet *noun* a cell fragment found in bone marrow that is responsible for blood clotting around bleeding

platform *noun* **1** a raised level surface for passengers at a railway station **2** a raised floor for speakers, entertainers, *etc*

platinum *noun* a heavy and very valuable steel-grey metal

platitude *noun* a dull, ordinary remark made as if it were important

platonic *adjective* of a relationship: not sexual

platoon *noun* a section of a company of soldiers

platter *noun* a large, flat plate

platypus *noun* (*plural* **platypuses**) a small water animal of Australia that has webbed feet and lays eggs (*also called*: **duck-billed platypus**)

plaudits *noun plural* applause, praise

plausibility *noun* a plausible quality

plausible *adjective* **1** seeming to be truthful or honest **2** seeming probable or reasonable

play *verb* **1** to amuse yourself **2** to take part in a game **3** to act (on a stage *etc*) **4** to perform on (a musical instrument) **5** to carry out (a trick) **6** to trifle or fiddle (with) ▪ *noun* **1** amusement, recreation **2** a story for acting, a drama **3** a way of behaving: *foul play* ▪ **play at** to treat in a light-hearted, not serious way ▪ **play off** to set off (one person) against another to gain some advantage for yourself ▪ **play on** to make use of (someone's feelings) to turn to your own advantage

player *noun* **1** an actor **2** someone who plays a game, musical instrument, *etc*

playful *adjective* **1** wanting to play: *a playful kitten* **2** fond of joking, not serious ▪ **playfully** *adverb* ▪ **playfulness** *noun*

playground *noun* an open area for playing at school, in a park, *etc*

playgroup *noun* a group of young children who play together supervised by adults

playing-card *noun* one of a pack of cards used in playing card games

playmate *noun* a friend with whom you play

play-off *noun* **1** a game to decide a tie **2** a game between the winners of other competitions

playschool *noun* a nursery school or playgroup

plaything *noun* a toy

playwright *noun* a writer of plays

plea *noun* **1** an excuse **2** an accused person's answer to a charge in a court of law **3** an urgent request

plead *verb* **1** to state your case in a lawcourt **2 plead with someone** to beg earnestly ■ **plead guilty** *or* **not guilty** to admit or deny guilt in a law court

pleasant *adjective* giving pleasure; agreeable

pleasantry *noun* (*plural* **pleasantries**) a good-humoured joke

please *verb* **1** to give pleasure or delight to **2** to satisfy **3** to choose, like (to do): *do as you please* ■ *exclamation* added for politeness to a command or request: *please keep off the grass*

pleasurable *adjective* delightful, pleasant

pleasure *noun* enjoyment, joy, delight

pleat *noun* a fold in cloth, which has been pressed or stitched down ■ *verb* to put pleats in

pleated *adjective* having pleats

plectrum *noun* a small piece of horn, metal, *etc* used for plucking the strings of a guitar

pledge *noun* a solemn promise ■ *verb* **1** to give as security, pawn **2** to promise solemnly

plentiful *or* **plenteous** *adjective* not scarce, abundant

plenty *noun* **1** a full supply, as much as is needed **2** a large number or quantity (of)

plethora *noun* too large a quantity of anything: *a plethora of politicians*

pleurisy *noun* an illness in which the covering of the lungs becomes inflamed

pliable *adjective* **1** easily bent or folded **2** easily persuaded

pliant *adjective* pliable

pliers *noun plural* a tool used for gripping, bending and cutting wire, *etc*

plight *noun* a bad state or situation

plimsoll *noun* a light rubber-soled canvas shoe for sports

Plimsoll line a line on a ship that indicates when it is not safe to increase its load any further

plinth *noun* **1** the square slab at the foot of a column **2** the base or pedestal of a statue, vase, *etc*

plod *verb* **1** to travel slowly and steadily **2** to work on steadily

| **plod** ► plods, plodding, plodded

plodder *noun* a dull but hard-working person

plonk *noun* **1** *informal* a sound made by something dropping heavily **2** *slang* cheap wine ■ *verb* to drop (something) heavily

plop *noun* the sound made by a small object falling into water

■ *verb* to make this sound

| **plop** *verb* ► plops, plop*ping*, plop*ped*

plot *noun* 1 a small piece of ground 2 a plan for an illegal or malicious action 3 the story of a play, novel, *etc* ■ *verb* 1 to plan secretly 2 to make a chart, graph, *etc* of 3 to mark points on one of these

| **plot** *verb* ► plots, plot*ting*, plot*ted*

plough *noun* a farm tool for turning over the soil ■ *verb* 1 to turn up the ground in furrows 2 to work through slowly

ploughshare *noun* the blade of a plough

plover (*pronounced* pluv-er) *noun* any of several kinds of bird that nest on the ground in open country

ploy *noun* an activity, an escapade

pluck *verb* 1 to pull out or off 2 to pick (flowers, fruit, *etc*) 3 to strip off the feathers of (a bird) before cooking ■ *noun* courage, spirit
■ **pluck up courage** to prepare yourself to face a danger or difficulty

plucky *adjective* brave, determined

plug *noun* 1 an object fitted into a hole to stop it up 2 a fitting on an appliance put into a socket to connect with an electric current 3 *informal* a brief advertisement
■ *verb* 1 to stop up with a plug

2 *informal* to advertise, publicize

| **plug** *verb* ► plugs, plug*ging*, plug*ged*

plum *noun* 1 a soft fruit, often dark red or purple, with a stone in the centre 2 the tree that produces this fruit

plumage (*pronounced* ploo-mij) *noun* the feathers of a bird

plumb *noun* a lead weight hung on a string (**plumbline**), used to test if a wall has been built straight up ■ *verb* to test the depth of (the sea *etc*)

plumber *noun* someone who fits and mends water, gas and sewage pipes

plumbing *noun* 1 the work of a plumber 2 the drainage and water systems of a building *etc*

plume *noun* a feather, especially an ornamental one

plummet *verb* to plunge

plump *adjective* fat, rounded, well filled out ■ *verb* 1 to beat or shake (cushions *etc*) back into shape 2 **plump for something** to choose, vote for it

plunder *verb* to carry off goods by force, loot, rob

plunge *verb* 1 to dive (into water *etc*) 2 to rush or lurch forward 3 to thrust suddenly (into) ■ *noun* a thrust; a dive

plural *adjective* more than one
■ *noun*, *grammar* the form which shows more than one, *eg* mice is the plural of *mouse*

plus *preposition* used to show

addition and represented by the sign (+): *five plus two equals seven* ■ *adjective* of a quantity more than zero ■ *adverb, informal* and a bit extra: *she earns £20,000 plus*

plush *noun* cloth with a soft velvety surface on one side ■ *adjective* luxurious

ply *verb* 1 to work at steadily 2 to keep supplying with (food, questions to answer, *etc*) ■ **two-** or **three-** *etc* **ply** having two or three *etc* layers or strands

┃**ply** ► plies, plying, plied

plywood *noun* a board made up of thin sheets of wood glued together

pm *abbreviation* after noon (from Latin *post meridiem*)

pneumatic (*pronounced* nyoo-mat-ik) *adjective* worked by air: *pneumatic drill*

pneumonia (*pronounced* nyoo-moh-ni-a) *noun* a disease in which the lungs become inflamed

poach *verb* 1 to cook gently in boiling water or stock 2 to catch fish or hunt game illegally

poacher *noun* someone who poaches or fishes illegally

pocket *noun* a small pouch or bag, especially as part of a garment ■ *verb* 1 to put in a pocket 2 to steal

pocket money an allowance of money for personal spending

pockmark *noun* a scar or small

hole in the skin left by disease

pod *noun* a long seed-case of the pea, bean, *etc*

podgy *adjective* short and fat

podium *noun* a low pedestal, a platform

poem *noun* a piece of imaginative writing set out in lines which often have a regular rhythm or rhyme

poet *noun* someone who writes poetry

poetic *adjective* of or like poetry ■ **poetically** *adverb*

poetry *noun* 1 the art of writing poems 2 poems

pogrom *noun* an organized killing or massacre of a group of people

poignant *adjective* very painful or moving; pathetic

point *noun* 1 a sharp end of anything 2 a headland 3 a dot: *decimal point* 4 a full stop in punctuation 5 an exact place or spot 6 an exact moment of time 7 the chief matter of an argument 8 the meaning of a joke 9 a mark in a competition 10 a purpose, an advantage: *there is no point in going* 11 an electrical wall socket 12 a mark of character: *he has many good points* ■ *verb* 1 to make pointed: *point your toes* 2 to direct, aim 3 to indicate with a gesture

point-blank *adjective* 1 of a shot: fired from very close range 2 of a question: direct

pointed *adjective* **1** having a point, sharp **2** of a remark: obviously aimed at someone

pointer *noun* **1** a rod for pointing **2** a type of dog used to show where game has fallen after it has been shot

pointless *adjective* having no meaning or purpose

point of view (*plural* **points of view**) someone's attitude towards something

poise *verb* to balance, keep steady ∎ *noun* **1** a state of balance **2** dignity, self-confidence

poised *adjective* **1** balanced, having poise **2** prepared, ready: *poised for action*

poison *noun* a substance which, when taken into the body, kills or harms ∎ *verb* to kill or harm with poison

poisonous *adjective* harmful because of containing poison

poke *verb* **1** to push (*eg* a finger or stick) into something **2** to prod, thrust at ∎ *noun* a nudge, a prod

poker *noun* **1** a rod for stirring up a fire **2** a card game in which players bet on their chance of winning

polar *adjective* **1** of the regions round the North or South Poles **2** of climate: very cold and dry

polar bear a type of large, white bear found in the Arctic

polarity *noun* the state of having two opposite poles

polarize *or* **polarise** *verb* **1** to give polarity to **2** to split into opposing sides

polaroid *noun*, *trademark* **1** a plastic through which light is seen less brightly **2** **polaroids** sunglasses **3** a camera that develops individual pictures in a few seconds

pole *noun* **1** a long rounded rod or post **2** the north or south end of the earth's axis (**the North** or **South Pole**) **3** either of the opposing points of a magnet or electric battery

polecat *noun* a large kind of weasel

Pole Star the star most directly above the North Pole

pole vault a sport in which an athlete jumps over a bar with the aid of a flexible pole

police *noun* the body of men and women whose work it is to see that laws are obeyed *etc* ∎ *verb* to keep law and order in (a place) by use of police

policeman *noun* a male police officer

police officer a member of a police force

police station the headquarters of the police in a district

policewoman *noun* a female police officer

policy *noun* (*plural* **policies**) **1** an agreed course of action **2** a written agreement with an insurance company

polio *short for* **poliomyelitis**

poliomyelitis *noun* a disease of the spinal cord, causing weakness or paralysis of the muscles

polish *verb* to make smooth and shiny by rubbing ▪ *noun* **1** a gloss on a surface **2** a substance used for polishing

polite *adjective* having good manners, courteous ▪ **politely** *adverb*

politic *adjective* wise, cautious

political *adjective* of government, politicians or politics

politician *noun* someone involved in politics, especially a member of parliament

politics *noun singular* the art or study of government

polka *noun* a lively dance or the music for it

poll *noun* **1** a counting of voters at an election **2** total number of votes **3** (*also called*: **opinion poll**) a test of public opinion by asking what people think of something

pollen *noun* the fertilizing powder of flowers

pollinate *verb* to fertilize with pollen

pollination *noun* fertilization with pollen

polling station a place where voting is done

pollutant *noun* something that pollutes

pollute *verb* **1** to make dirty or impure **2** to make (the environment) harmful to life

pollution *noun* **1** the act of polluting **2** dirt

polo *noun* a game like hockey played on horseback

polo neck 1 a close-fitting neck with a part turned over at the top **2** a jumper with a neck like this

poltergeist *noun* a kind of ghost believed to move furniture and throw objects around a room (literally, 'a ghost which makes a racket')

polyester *noun* a synthetic material often used in clothing

polygamy *noun* the fact of having more than one wife or husband at the same time

polygon *noun* a figure with many angles and sides
▪ **polygonal** *adjective*

polyhedron *noun* a solid body with four or more faces, all of which are polygons

polymer *noun* a chemical compound made up of linked smaller molecules

polyphonic *adjective* relating to polyphony

polyphony *noun* musical composition in parts, each with a separate melody

polystyrene *noun* a synthetic material which resists moisture, used for packing and disposable cups *etc*

polythene *noun* a type of plastic that can be moulded when hot

polyunsaturated *adjective* of oil: containing no cholesterol

pomegranate *noun* a fruit with a thick skin, many seeds and soft edible flesh

pommel *noun* **1** the knob on the hilt of a sword **2** the high part of a saddle

pomp *noun* solemn and splendid ceremony, magnificence

pompous *adjective* self-important, excessively dignified
■ **pomposity** *noun*

poncho *noun* (*plural* **ponchos**) a S American cloak made of a blanket with a hole for the head

pond *noun* a small lake or pool

ponder *verb* to think over, consider

ponderous *adjective* **1** weighty **2** clumsy **3** sounding very important

pontiff *noun* **1** a Roman Catholic bishop **2** the Pope

pontificate *verb* to speak in a pompous manner

pontoon[1] *noun* a flat-bottomed boat used to support a temporary bridge (a **pontoon bridge**)

pontoon[2] *noun* a card game in which players try to collect 21 points

pony *noun* (*plural* **ponies**) a small horse

ponytail *noun* a hairstyle in which the hair is drawn back and tied with a band at the back of the head

pony-trekking *noun* riding cross-country in small parties

poodle *noun* a breed of dog, with curly hair often clipped in a fancy way

pool *noun* **1** a small area of still water **2** a joint fund or stock (of money, typists, *etc*) ■ *verb* to put (money *etc*) into a joint fund

poop *noun* a ship's stern, or back part

poor *adjective* **1** having little money or property **2** not good: *this work is poor* **3** lacking (in) **4** deserving pity

poorly *adjective* in bad health, ill

pop *noun* **1** a sharp quick noise, *eg* that made by a cork coming out of a bottle **2** a fizzy soft drink **3** popular music ■ *verb* **1** to make a pop **2** to move quickly, dash: *pop in* ■ *adjective* of music: popular

| **pop** *verb* ► pops, popp*ing*, popp*ed* |

popadom or **popadum** *noun* a thin circle of dough fried in oil until crisp

popcorn *noun* a kind of maize that bursts open when heated

Pope or **pope** *noun* the bishop of Rome, head of the Roman Catholic Church

poplar *noun* a tall, narrow quick-growing tree

poppy *noun* (*plural* **poppies**) a scarlet flower growing wild in fields *etc*

populace *noun* the people of a country or area

popular *adjective* **1** of the people: *elected by popular vote* **2** liked by most people **3** widely held or believed: *popular belief*

popularity *noun* the state of being generally liked

popularize *or* **popularise** *verb* to make popular or widely known

popularly *adverb* in a popular way; in terms of most people: *a popularly held belief*

populate *verb* to fill (an area) with people ■ **populated** *adjective*

population *noun* the number of people living in a place

populous *adjective* full of people

porcelain *noun* a kind of fine china

porch *noun* (*plural* **porches**) a covered entrance to a building

porcupine *noun* a large gnawing animal, covered with sharp quills

pore *noun* the hole of a sweat gland in the skin

🔊 Do not confuse with: **pour**

pore over study closely or eagerly

pork *noun* the flesh of the pig, prepared for eating

pornographic *adjective* relating to pornography

pornography *noun* literature or art that is sexually explicit and often offensive

porous *adjective* **1** having pores **2** allowing fluid to pass through

porpoise *noun* a blunt-nosed sea animal of the dolphin family

porridge *noun* a food made from oatmeal boiled in water or milk

port *noun* **1** a harbour **2** a town with a harbour **3** the left side of a ship as you face the front **4** *computing* a socket or plug for connecting a hardware device to a computer

portable *adjective* ■ able to be lifted and carried ■ *noun* a computer, telephone, *etc* that can be carried around

portal *noun* a grand entrance or doorway

portcullis *noun* (*plural* **portcullises**) a grating which is let down quickly to close a gateway

portend *verb* to give warning of, foretell

portent *noun* a warning sign

portentous *adjective* **1** strange, wonderful **2** important, weighty

porter *noun* **1** someone employed to carry luggage, push hospital trolleys, *etc* **2** a doorkeeper

portfolio *noun* (*plural* **portfolios**) **1** a case for carrying papers, drawings, *etc* **2** the job of a government minister

porthole *noun* a small round window in a ship's side

portico *noun* (*plural* **porticoes** *or* **porticos**) a row of columns in front of a building forming a porch or covered walk

portion noun 1 a part 2 a share, a helping ▪ verb to divide into parts

portly adjective stout and dignified

portrait noun 1 a drawing, painting, or photograph of a person 2 a description of a person, place, etc

portray verb 1 to make a painting or drawing of 2 to describe in words 3 to act the part of ▪ **portrayal** noun

portray ▶ portrays, portraying, portrayed

pose noun 1 a position of the body 2 behaviour put on to impress others, a pretence ▪ verb 1 to position yourself for a photograph etc 2 **pose as someone** or **something** to pretend or claim to be what you are not 3 to put forward (a problem, question, etc)

poser noun 1 someone who poses to impress others 2 a difficult question

posh adjective, informal high-class; smart

position noun 1 place, situation 2 manner of standing, sitting, etc, posture 3 a rank or job ▪ verb to place

positive adjective 1 meaning or saying 'yes' (contrasted with: **negative**) 2 not able to be doubted: positive proof 3 certain, convinced 4 definite: a positive improvement 5 of a number: greater than zero 6 grammar of an

adjective or adverb: of the first degree of comparison, not comparative or superlative, eg big, not bigger or biggest

posse (pronounced pos-i) noun a body of police etc

possess verb 1 to own, have 2 to take hold of your mind

possessed adjective 1 in the power of an evil spirit 2 obsessed

possession noun 1 the state of possessing 2 the state of being possessed 3 something owned

possessive adjective 1 grammar of an adjective or pronoun: showing possession, for example my, mine, your, their, etc 2 over-protective and jealous in attitude

possibility noun (plural **possibilities**) something that may happen or that may be done

possible adjective 1 able to happen or to be done 2 not unlikely

possibly adverb perhaps

possum noun a small American animal that carries its young in a pouch ▪ **play possum** to pretend to be asleep or dead

post noun 1 an upright pole or stake 2 the service which delivers letters and other mail 3 a job ▪ verb 1 to put (a letter) in a postbox for collection 2 to send or station somewhere: posted abroad 3 to put (information etc) on an Internet site

post- prefix after: postgraduate/post-mortem

postage *noun* money paid for sending a letter *etc* by post

postage stamp a small printed label to show that postage has been paid

postal *adjective* of or by post

postal order a document bought at a post office which can be exchanged for a stated amount of money

postbox *noun* a box with an opening in which to post letters *etc*

postcard *noun* a card for sending a message by post

post code a short series of letters and numbers, used for sorting mail by machine

poster *noun* **1** a large notice or placard **2** a large printed picture

posterior *adjective* situated behind, coming after ▪ *noun* the buttocks

posterity *noun* **1** all future generations **2** someone's descendants

postgraduate *adjective* of study *etc*: following on from a first university degree ▪ *noun* someone continuing to study after a first degree

post-haste *adverb* with great speed

posthumous (*pronounced* pos-tyu-mus) *adjective* **1** of a book: published after the author's death **2** of a child: born after the father's death

Post-it *noun*, *trademark* a small sticky label for writing messages on

postman, postwoman *noun* someone who delivers letters

postmark *noun* a date stamp put on a letter at a post office

postmaster, postmistress *noun* a person in charge of a post office

post-mortem *noun* an examination of a dead body to find out the cause of death

post office an office for receiving and sending off letters by post *etc*

postpone *verb* to put off to a future time ▪ **postponement** *noun*

postscript *noun* an added remark at the end of a letter, after the sender's name

postulate *verb* to assume or take for granted (that)

posture *noun* **1** the manner in which someone holds themselves in standing or walking **2** a position, a pose

postwar *adjective* relating to the time after a war

posy *noun* (*plural* **posies**) a small bunch of flowers

pot *noun* a deep vessel used in cooking, as a container, or for growing plants ▪ *verb* to plant in a pot

| pot *verb* ► pots, pot*ting*, pot*ted* |

potash *noun* a chemical obtained from the ashes of wood

potassium *noun* a type of silvery-white metal

potato *noun* (*plural* **potatoes**) **1** a plant with round starchy roots which are eaten as a vegetable **2** the vegetable itself

pot belly a protruding stomach

potboiler *noun* a book with a sensational plot, written with the aim of selling a lot of copies

potency *noun* power

potent *adjective* powerful, strong

potentate *noun* a powerful ruler

potential *adjective* that may develop, possible ▪ *noun* the possibility of further development

pothole *noun* **1** a deep cave **2** a hole worn in a road surface

potholer *noun* someone who explores caves

potion *noun* a drink, often containing medicine or poison

pot plant a household plant kept in a pot

potpourri (*pronounced* poh-poo-ri) *noun* **1** a scented mixture of dried petals *etc* **2** a mixture or medley

pot shot a casual or random shot

potted *adjective* **1** of meat: pressed down and preserved in a jar **2** condensed and simplified: *potted history*

potter *noun* someone who makes articles of baked clay ▪ *verb* to do small odd jobs, dawdle

pottery *noun* **1** articles made of baked clay **2** (*plural* **potteries**) a place where such things are made **3** the art of making them

potty[1] *adjective*, *informal* mad, eccentric

potty[2] *noun*, *informal* a pot kept under a child's bed and used as a toilet

pouch *noun* (*plural* **pouches**) **1** a pocket or small bag **2** a bag-like fold on the front of a kangaroo, for carrying its young

pouffe *noun* a low, stuffed seat without back or arms

poultice *noun* a wet dressing spread on a bandage and put on inflamed skin

poultry *noun* farmyard fowls, *eg* hens, ducks, geese, turkeys

pounce *verb* to make a sudden leap or swoop

pound *noun* **1** the standard unit of money in Britain, shown by the sign (£), equal to 100 new pence **2** (*abbrev* **lb**) a measure of weight, equal to 16 ounces (about $\frac{1}{2}$ kilogram) **3** an enclosure for animals ▪ *verb* **1** to beat into powder **2** to beat heavily **3** to walk or run with heavy steps

pour *verb* **1** to flow in a stream **2** to make flow: *pour the tea* **3** to rain heavily

💧 Do not confuse with: **pore**

pout *verb* to push out the lips sulkily to show displeasure ▪ *noun* a sulky look

poverty noun the state of being poor

powder noun 1 a substance made up of very fine particles 2 cosmetic face powder ■ verb 1 to sprinkle or dab with powder 2 to grind down to powder

powdered adjective 1 in fine particles 2 covered with powder

powdery adjective 1 covered with powder 2 like powder

power noun 1 strength, force 2 ability to do things 3 authority or legal right 4 a strong nation 5 someone in authority 6 the force used for driving machines: electric power/steam power 7 maths the product obtained by multiplying a number by itself a given number of times (eg $2 \times 2 \times 2$ or 2^3 is the third power of 2)

powerful adjective having great power, strength, vigour, authority, influence, force or effectiveness

powerless adjective without power or ability

power station a building where electricity is produced

practical adjective 1 preferring action to thought 2 efficient 3 learned by practice, rather than from books: practical knowledge

practical joke a joke consisting of action, not words

practically adverb 1 in a practical way 2 in effect, in reality 3 almost

practice noun 1 habit: it is my practice to get up early 2 the actual doing of something: I always intend to get up early but in practice I stay in bed 3 repeated performance to improve skill 4 the business of a doctor, lawyer, etc

◆※ Do not confuse: **practice** and **practise**. To help you remember: 'ice' is a noun, 'ise' is not!

practise or US **practice** verb 1 to perform or exercise repeatedly to improve a skill 2 to make a habit of: practise self-control 3 to follow (a profession)

pragmatic adjective practical; matter-of-fact; realistic

pragmatism noun a practical, matter-of-fact approach to dealing with problems etc ■ **pragmatist** noun

prairie noun a stretch of level grassland in N America

praise verb 1 to speak highly of 2 to glorify (God) by singing hymns etc ■ noun an expression of approval

praiseworthy adjective deserving to be praised

pram noun a small wheeled carriage for a baby, pushed by hand

prance verb 1 to strut or swagger about 2 to dance about

prank noun a trick played for mischief

prattle verb to talk or chatter meaninglessly ■ noun meaningless talk

prawn *noun* a type of shellfish like the shrimp

pray *verb* **1** to ask earnestly, beg **2** to speak to God in prayer

◆* Do not confuse with: **prey**

prayer *noun* a request, or thanks, given to God

praying mantis *see* mantis

pre- *prefix* **1** before: *prehistoric* **2** to the highest degree: *pre-eminent*

preach *verb* **1** to give a sermon **2** to teach, speak in favour of: *preach caution*

preacher *noun* a religious teacher

preamble *noun* something said as an introduction

prearrange *verb* to arrange beforehand

precarious *adjective* uncertain, risky, dangerous

precaution *noun* care taken beforehand to avoid an accident *etc*

precede *verb* to go before in time, rank or importance

◆* Do not confuse with: **proceed**

precedence *noun* the right to go before; priority

precedent *noun* a past action which serves as an example or rule for the future

preceding *adjective* going before; previous

precept *noun* a guiding rule, a commandment

precinct *noun* **1** an area enclosed by the boundary walls of a building **2 precincts** the area closely surrounding any place

precious *adjective* **1** highly valued or valuable **2** over-fussy or precise

precipice *noun* a steep cliff

precipitate *verb* (*pronounced* pri-**sip**-it-eit) to force hastily ■ *adjective* (*pronounced* pri-**sip**-it-at) **1** headlong **2** hasty, rash ■ *noun* (*pronounced* pri-**sip**-it-at) sediment at the bottom of a liquid

precipitation *noun* **1** great hurry **2** rainfall

precipitous *adjective* very steep

précis (*pronounced* **prei**-see) *noun* (plural **précis** – *pronounced* **prei**-seez) a summary of a piece of writing

precise *adjective* **1** definite **2** exact, accurate ■ **precisely** *adverb*

◆* Do not confuse with: **concise**

precision *noun* **1** preciseness **2** exactness, accuracy

preclude *verb* to prevent, make impossible

precocious *adjective* of a child: unusually advanced or well-developed

preconceive *verb* to form (ideas *etc*) before having actual knowledge or experience

preconception *noun* an idea formed without actual knowledge

precursor *noun* a person or thing which goes before, an early form of something

predate *verb* to happen before in time

predator *noun* a bird or animal that kills others for food
- **predation** *noun*

predatory *adjective* **1** of a predator **2** using other people for your own advantage

predecessor *noun* the previous holder of a job or office

predestine *verb* to destine beforehand, preordain
- **predestination** *noun*

predetermine *verb* to settle beforehand

predicament *noun* an unfortunate or difficult situation

predicate *noun*, *grammar* something said about the subject of a sentence, *eg has green eyes* in the sentence *Anne has green eyes*

predict *verb* to foretell, forecast

predictable *adjective* able to be foretold

prediction *noun* an act of predicting; something predicted

predilection *noun* a preference, a liking for something

predispose *verb* **1** to make (someone) in favour of something beforehand: *we were predisposed to believe her* **2** to make liable (to): *predisposed to colds*
- **predisposition** *noun*

predominance *noun* being predominant

predominant *adjective* **1** ruling **2** most noticeable or outstanding

predominantly *adverb* mostly, mainly

predominate *verb* to be the strongest or most numerous

pre-eminent *adjective* outstanding, excelling all others

pre-empt *verb* to block or stop by making a first move ∎ **pre-emptive** *adjective*

preen *verb* **1** of a bird: to arrange its feathers **2** to smarten your appearance in a conceited way

prefabricated *adjective* made of parts made beforehand, ready to be fitted together

preface (*pronounced* **pref**-is) *noun* an introduction to a book *etc*

prefect *noun* a senior pupil in some schools with certain powers

prefer *verb* to like better

| **prefer** ▶ prefers, preferring, preferred

preferable (*pronounced* **pref**-ra-bl) *adjective* more desirable

preference *noun* **1** greater liking **2** something preferred

preferential *adjective* giving preference

prefix *noun* (*plural* **prefixes**) a syllable or word at the beginning of a word which adds to its meaning, *eg dis-, un-, re-,* in *dislike, unhappy, regain*

pregnancy *noun* (*plural* **pregnancies**) the state of being pregnant or the time during which a female is pregnant

pregnant *adjective* carrying a foetus in the womb

prehistoric *adjective* relating to the time before history was written down

prehistory *noun* the period before historical records

prejudge *verb* to decide (something) before hearing the facts of a case

prejudice *noun* **1** an unfair feeling for or against anything **2** an opinion formed without careful thought ■ *verb* to fill with prejudice

prejudiced *adjective* showing prejudice

prejudicial *adjective* damaging, harmful

preliminary *adjective* going before, preparatory

prelude *noun* **1** a piece of music played as an introduction to the main piece **2** a preceding event: *a prelude to war*

premature *adjective* coming, born, *etc* before the right, proper or expected time

premeditated *adjective* thought out beforehand, planned: *premeditated murder*

premier (*pronounced* prem-i-er) *adjective* first, leading, foremost ■ *noun* a prime minister

♣* Do not confuse: **premier** and **première**

première (*pronounced* prem-i-eir) *noun* a first performance of a play, film, *etc*

premise *or* **premiss** *noun* (*plural* **premises** *or* **premisses**) something assumed from which a conclusion is drawn

premises *noun plural* a building and its grounds

premium *noun* (*plural* **premiums**) a payment on an insurance policy

premonition *noun* a feeling that something is going to happen; a forewarning

preoccupation *noun* **1** being preoccupied **2** something that preoccupies: *a preoccupation with death*

preoccupied *adjective* deep in thought

preoccupy *verb* to completely engross the attention of (someone)

preordain *verb* to decide beforehand

prep *noun, informal* preparation

preparation *noun* **1** an act of preparing **2** study for a lesson **3** something prepared for use, *eg* a medicine

preparatory *adjective* acting as an introduction to or preparation for

preparatory school a private school educating children of primary-school age

prepare *verb* **1** to make or get ready **2** to train, equip

prepared *adjective* **1** ready **2** willing

preponderance *noun* greater

amount or number: *a preponderance of young people in the audience*

preposition *noun, grammar* a word placed before a noun or pronoun to show its relation to another word, *eg 'through the door'*, *'in the town'*, *'written by me'*

♦* Do not confuse with: **proposition**

prepossessing *adjective* pleasant, making a good impression

preposterous *adjective* very foolish, absurd

prep school a preparatory school

prerequisite *noun* something necessary before another thing can happen

prerogative *noun* a right enjoyed by someone because of rank or position

prescribe *verb* to order the use of (a medicine)

prescription *noun* **1** a doctor's written instructions for preparing a medicine **2** something prescribed

prescriptive *adjective* laying down rules

presence *noun* **1** the state of being present **2** someone's personal appearance, manner, *etc*

present[1] *adjective* **1** here, in this place **2** happening or existing now ▪ *noun* **1** the time now

2 *grammar* the tense describing events happening now, *eg 'we are on holiday'*

present[2] *noun* (pronounced **prez**-ent) a gift ▪ *verb* (pronounced pri-**zent**) **1** to hand over (a gift) formally **2** to offer, put forward **3** to introduce (someone) to another

presentation *noun* **1** the giving of a present **2** something presented **3** a formal talk or demonstration **4** a showing of a play *etc*

presentiment *noun* a feeling that something is about to happen

presently *adverb* soon

present participle the form of a verb used after an auxiliary verb to indicate that something is taking place in the present, for instance *going* in 'I am *going*'

preservation *noun* preserving or being preserved

preservative *noun* a substance added to food to prevent it from going bad

preserve *verb* **1** to keep safe from harm **2** to keep in existence, maintain **3** to treat (food) so that it will not go bad ▪ *noun* **1** a place where game animals, birds, *etc* are protected **2** jam

preside *verb* to be in charge at a meeting *etc*

presidency *noun* (*plural* **presidencies**) the position of president

president noun 1 the leading member of a society etc 2 the head of a republic

press verb 1 to push on, against or down 2 to urge, force 3 to iron (clothes etc) ■ noun 1 a printing machine 2 the news media, journalists

pressgang noun, history a group of men employed to carry off people by force into the army or navy

pressing adjective requiring immediate action, insistent

press-up noun an exercise performed by raising and lowering the body on the arms while face down

pressure noun 1 force on or against a surface 2 strong persuasion, compulsion 3 stress, strain 4 urgency

pressure cooker a pan in which food is cooked quickly by steam under pressure

pressurize or **pressurise** verb 1 to fit (an aeroplane etc) with a device that maintains normal air pressure 2 to force (someone) to do something

prestige noun reputation, influence due to rank, success, etc

prestigious adjective having or giving prestige

presumably adverb I suppose

presume verb to take for granted, assume (that)

presumption noun a strong likelihood

presumptuous adjective unsuitably bold

presuppose verb to take for granted

pretence noun 1 the act of pretending 2 a false claim

pretend verb 1 to make believe, imagine 2 to make a false claim: pretending to be ill

pretender noun someone who lays claim to something (especially to the crown)

pretension noun 1 a claim (whether true or not) 2 self-importance

pretentious adjective self-important; showy

pretext noun an excuse

pretty adjective pleasing or attractive to see, listen to, etc ■ adverb fairly, quite: pretty good ■ prettiness noun

prevail verb 1 prevail against or over to gain control over 2 to win, succeed 3 prevail on to persuade: she prevailed on me to stay

prevailing adjective most common: the prevailing mood

prevalent adjective common, widespread ■ prevalence noun

prevaricate verb to avoid telling the truth

prevent verb to hinder, stop happening ■ prevention noun the act of preventing

preventive or **preventative** adjective of medicine: helping to prevent illness

preview noun a view of a

performance, exhibition, *etc* before its official opening

previous *adjective* earlier; former; prior ▪ **previously** *adverb*

prey *noun* an animal killed by others for food ▪ **prey on someone** *or* **something 1** to seize and eat them **2** to stalk and harass them

🖋 Do not confuse with: **pray**

price *noun* **1** the money for which something is bought or sold, the cost **2** something that must be given up in order to gain something: *the price of fame*

priceless *adjective* **1** very valuable **2** *informal* very funny

pricey *adjective*, *informal* expensive

prick *verb* **1** to pierce slightly **2** to give a sharp pain to **3** to stick up (the ears) ▪ *noun* a pricking feeling on the skin

prickle *noun* a sharp point on a plant or animal ▪ *verb* **1** to be prickly **2** to feel prickly

prickly *adjective* **1** full of prickles **2** stinging, pricking

pride *noun* **1** too great an opinion of yourself **2** pleasure in having done something well **3** dignity **4** a group of lions ▪ *verb*: **pride yourself on** to feel or show pride in

priest *noun* **1** a member of the clergy in the Roman Catholic and Anglican Churches **2** an official in a non-Christian religion

priestess *noun* a female, non-Christian priest

priesthood *noun* those who are priests

prim *adjective* unnecessarily formal and correct

prima donna 1 a leading female opera singer **2** a woman who is over-sensitive and temperamental

primary *adjective* **1** first **2** most important, chief

primary colour one of the colours from which all others can be made, that is red, blue and yellow

primary school a school for the early stages of education

primate *noun* **1** a member of the highest order of mammals including humans, monkeys and apes **2** an archbishop

prime *adjective* **1** first in time or importance **2** best quality, excellent **3** of a number: having only two factors, itself and 1, *eg* 3 which has the factors 1 and 3 but no others ▪ *noun* the time of greatest health and strength: *the prime of life* ▪ *verb* **1** to prepare the surface of for painting: *prime a canvas* **2** to prepare by supplying detailed information: *she was well primed before the meeting*

prime minister the head of a government

primer *noun* **1** a simple introductory book on a subject **2** a substance for preparing a surface for painting

primeval or **primaeval** adjective **1** relating to the beginning of the world **2** primitive, instinctive

primitive adjective **1** belonging to very early times **2** old-fashioned **3** not skilfully made, rough

primogeniture noun **1** the fact of being born first **2** the rights of a first-born child

primrose noun a pale-yellow spring flower common in woods and hedges

prince noun **1** the son of a king or queen **2** a ruler of certain states

princely adjective splendid, impressive: *a princely reward*

princess noun (plural **princesses**) the daughter of a king or queen

principal adjective most important, chief ▪ noun **1** the head of a school or university **2** money in a bank on which interest is paid

♦* Do not confuse: **principal** and **principle**. It may help to remember that the adjective **principAL** means 'first or most important', and that it also contains an A, the first letter of the alphabet

principality noun (plural **principalities**) a state ruled by a prince

principally adverb chiefly, mostly

principle noun **1** a general truth or law **2 principles** someone's personal rules of behaviour, sense of right and wrong, *etc*

print verb **1** to mark letters on paper with type **2** to write in capital letters **3** to publish in printed form **4** to stamp patterns on (cloth *etc*) **5** to make a finished photograph ▪ noun **1** a mark made by pressure: *footprint* **2** printed lettering **3** a photograph made from a negative **4** a printed reproduction of a painting *etc* **5** cloth printed with a design

printed circuit a wiring circuit, formed by printing a design on copper foil bonded to a flat base

printer noun **1** someone who prints books, newspapers, *etc* **2** a machine that prints, attached to a computer system

printout noun the printed information produced by a computer

prior adjective **1** earlier **2** previous (to)

priority noun (plural **priorities**) **1** first position **2** the right to be first **3** something that must be done first

prise verb to force open or off with a lever

♦* Do not confuse with: **prize**

prism noun **1** a glass tube with triangular ends that breaks light into different colours **2** maths a solid body with faces joined by two identical, parallel polygons at either end (the **bases**)

prison *noun* a building for holding criminals

prisoner *noun* someone held under arrest or locked up

prisoner of war someone captured by the enemy forces during war

pristine *adjective* in the original or unspoilt state

privacy *noun* freedom from observation; secrecy

private *adjective* **1** relating to an individual, not to the general public; personal **2** not open to the public **3** secret, not generally known ▪ *noun* the lowest rank of ordinary soldier (not an officer)

private eye *informal* a private detective

privately *adverb* in a private way

privatize or **privatise** *verb* to transfer from state ownership to private ownership ▪ **privatization** *noun*

privet *noun* a type of shrub used for hedges

privilege *noun* a right available to one person or to only a few people

privileged *adjective* having privileges

prize *noun* **1** a reward **2** something won in a competition **3** something highly valued ▪ *adjective* very fine, worthy of a prize ▪ *verb* to value highly

💧* Do not confuse with: **prise**

pro *short for* **professional**

pro- *prefix* in favour of: *pro-devolution* ▪ **pros and cons** the arguments for and against anything

probability *noun* (*plural* **probabilities**) likelihood

probable *adjective* **1** likely to happen **2** likely to be true

probably *adverb* very likely

probation *noun* **1** a trial period in a new job *etc* **2** a system of releasing prisoners on condition that they commit no more offences and report regularly to the authorities

probe *noun* **1** a long, thin instrument used to examine a wound **2** a thorough investigation **3** a spacecraft for exploring space ▪ *verb* **1** to examine very carefully **2** to investigate thoroughly to find out information

problem *noun* **1** a question to be solved **2** a matter which is difficult to deal with

problematic or **problematical** *adjective* doubtful, uncertain

procedure *noun* **1** method of doing business **2** a course of action

proceed *verb* **1** to go on with, continue **2** to begin (to do something)

💧* Do not confuse with: **precede**

proceeding noun 1 a step forward 2 **proceedings** a record of the meetings of a society etc

proceeds noun plural profit made from a sale etc

process noun (plural **processes**) 1 a series of operations in manufacturing goods 2 a series of events producing change or development ■ verb to perform a series of operations on

procession noun a line of people or vehicles moving forward in order

processor noun, computing a central processing unit or microprocessor

proclaim verb to announce publicly, declare openly

proclamation noun an official announcement made to the public

procrastinate verb to put things off, delay doing something till a later time ■ **procrastination** noun

procure verb to obtain; to bring about

prod verb to poke; urge on

| prod ► prods, prodding, prodded

prodigal adjective spending money recklessly, wasteful

prodigious adjective 1 strange, astonishing 2 enormous

prodigy noun (plural **prodigies**) someone astonishingly clever for their age: child prodigy

produce verb (pronounced pro-dyoos) 1 to bring into being 2 to

bring about, cause 3 to prepare (a play etc) for the stage 4 to make, manufacture ■ noun (pronounced **prod** yoos) food grown or produced on a farm or in a garden

producer noun someone who produces a play, film, etc

product noun 1 something produced 2 a result 3 maths the number that results from the multiplication of two or more numbers

production noun 1 the act of producing; the process of producing or being produced 2 the quantity produced or rate of producing it 3 a particular presentation of a play, opera, ballet, etc

productive adjective fruitful, producing results

productivity noun the rate of work done

profane adjective 1 not sacred 2 treating holy things without respect

profess verb to pretend, claim: he professes to be an expert

profession noun an occupation requiring special training, eg that of a doctor, lawyer, teacher, etc

professional adjective 1 of a profession 2 earning a living from a game or an art (contrasted with: **amateur**) 3 skilful, competent ■ noun 1 someone who works in a profession 2 someone who earns money from a game or art

professionalism noun a

professional status **2** professional expertise or competence

professionally *adverb* in a professional way; in terms of one's profession

professor *noun* a teacher of the highest rank in a university

proffer *verb* to offer

proficiency *noun* skill

proficient *adjective* skilled, expert

profile *noun* **1** an outline **2** a side view of a face, head, *etc* **3** a short description of someone's life, achievements, *etc*

profit *noun* **1** gain, benefit **2** money earned by selling an article for a higher price than was paid for it ■ *verb* to gain (from), benefit

profitable *adjective* bringing profit or gain

profligate *adjective* very extravagant

profound *adjective* **1** very deep **2** deeply felt **3** showing great knowledge or understanding

profuse *adjective* abundant, lavish, extravagant

prognosis *noun* a prediction of the course of a disease

program *noun* a set of instructions telling a computer to carry out certain actions ■ *verb* **1** to give instructions to **2** to prepare instructions to be carried out by a computer

┃ **program** *verb* ▶ programs, ┃ programming, programmed

programme *or US* **program** *noun* **1** a booklet with details of an entertainment, ceremony, *etc* **2** a scheme, a plan **3** a TV or radio broadcast

progress *noun* **1** advance, forward movement **2** improvement ■ *verb* **1** to go forward **2** to improve

progression *noun* **1** the process of moving forward or advancing in stages **2** *maths* a sequence of numbers, each of which bears a specific relationship to the preceding one

progressive *adjective* **1** going forward **2** favouring reforms

prohibit *verb* **1** to forbid **2** to prevent

prohibition *noun* the forbidding or prevention of something

prohibitive *adjective* **1** prohibiting **2** of price: too expensive, discouraging

project *noun* (*pronounced* proj-ekt) **1** a plan, a scheme **2** a task **3** a piece of study or research ■ *verb* (*pronounced* pro-jekt) **1** to throw out or up **2** to jut out **3** to cast (an image, a light, *etc*) on to a surface **4** to plan, propose

projectile *noun* a missile

projection *noun* **1** an act of projecting **2** something projected **3** something which juts out

projectionist *noun* someone who operates a film projector

projector *noun* a machine for

projecting cinema pictures on a screen

proletariat *noun* the ordinary working people

proliferate *verb* to grow or increase rapidly

prolific *adjective* producing a lot, fruitful

prologue *noun* a preface or introduction to a play *etc*

prolong *verb* to make longer

prom *noun, informal, short for* **1** promenade **2** promenade concert

promenade *noun* a level roadway or walk, especially by the seaside

promenade concert a concert at which a large part of the audience stands instead of being seated

prominence *noun* being prominent

prominent *adjective* **1** standing out, easily seen **2** famous, distinguished

promise *verb* **1** to give your word (to do or not do something) **2** to show signs for the future: *the weather promises to improve*
■ *noun* **1** a statement of something promised **2** a sign of something to come **3** a sign of future success: *his painting shows great promise*

promising *adjective* showing signs of being successful

promontory *noun* (*plural* **promontories**) a headland jutting out into the sea

promote *verb* **1** to raise to a higher rank **2** to help onwards, encourage **3** to advertise, encourage the sales of

promotion *noun* **1** advancement in rank or honour **2** encouragement **3** advertising, or an effort to publicize and increase sales of a particular brand

promotional *adjective* relating to or involving promotion

prompt *adjective* **1** quick, immediate **2** punctual ■ *verb* **1** to move to action **2** to supply words to an actor who has forgotten their lines ■ **prompter** *noun*

promptly *adverb* **1** without delay **2** punctually

promptness *noun* being prompt

promulgate *verb* to make widely known

prone *adjective* **1** lying face downward **2 prone to** inclined to

prong *noun* the spike of a fork

pronged *adjective* having prongs

pronoun *noun* a word used instead of a noun, *eg* I, you, who

pronounce *verb* **1** to speak (words, sounds) **2** to announce (an opinion), declare

pronounced *adjective* noticeable, marked

pronouncement *noun* a statement, an announcement

pronto *adverb, informal* quickly

pronunciation *noun* the way a word is said

proof *noun* evidence that makes something clear beyond doubt

-proof *suffix* protected against: *waterproof*

prop *noun* **1** a support **2** *short for* stage property (= an item needed on stage for a play) ▪ *verb* to hold up, support

| prop *verb* ▶ props, propping, propped

propaganda *noun* **1** the spreading of ideas to influence public opinion **2** material used for this, *eg* posters, leaflets

propagate *verb* **1** to spread **2** to produce seedlings or young

propel *verb* to drive forward

| propel ▶ propels, propelling, propelled

propeller *noun* a shaft with revolving blades which drives forward a ship, aircraft, *etc*

propensity *noun* (plural **propensities**) a natural inclination: *a propensity for bumping into things*

proper *adjective* **1** right, correct **2** full, thorough **3** prim, well-behaved

properly *adverb* **1** in the right way **2** thoroughly

proper noun *or* **proper name** *grammar* a name for a particular person, place or thing, *eg* *Shakespeare, the Parthenon*

property *noun* (plural **properties**) **1** land or buildings owned **2** a quality **3** properties the furniture *etc* required by actors in a play

prophecy (*pronounced* prof-es-i) *noun* (plural **prophecies**) **1** foretelling the future *etc* **2** something prophesied

---

♦* Do not confuse: **prophecy** and **prophesy**. The spelling with the 'c' is the noun, the spelling with the 's' the verb. It may help to remember that this is a common pattern, seen also in such pairs as practice/practise, licence/license and advice/advise

---

prophesy (*pronounced* prof-es-ai) *verb* to foretell the future, predict

| prophesy ▶ prophesies, prophesying, prophesied

prophet *noun* **1** someone who claims to foretell events **2** someone who tells what they believe to be the will of God

proponent *noun* someone in favour of a thing

proportion *noun* **1** a part of a total amount **2** relation in size, number, *etc* compared with something else

proportional *or* **proportionate** *adjective* in proportion

proposal *noun* **1** an act of proposing **2** anything proposed **3** an offer of marriage

propose *verb* **1** to put forward for

consideration, suggest **2** to intend **3** to make an offer of marriage (to)

proposition *noun* **1** a proposal, a suggestion **2** a statement **3** a situation that must be dealt with: *a tough proposition*

✷ Do not confuse with: preposition

propound *verb* to state, put forward for consideration

proprietor, **proprietress** *noun* an owner, especially of a hotel

propriety *noun* (*plural* **proprieties**) **1** fitness, suitability **2** correct behaviour, decency

propulsion *noun* an act of driving forward

prose *noun* **1** writing which is not in verse **2** ordinary written or spoken language

prosecute *verb* to bring a lawcourt action against

✷ Do not confuse with: persecute

prosecution *noun* **1** an act of prosecuting **2** *law* those bringing the case in a trial (*contrasted with*: *defence*)

prospect *noun* (*pronounced* **pros**-pekt) **1** a view, a scene **2** a future outlook or expectation: *the prospect of a free weekend* ■ *verb* (*pronounced* pros-**pekt**) to search for gold or other minerals

prospective *adjective* soon to be, likely to be: *the prospective election*

prospector *noun* someone who prospects for minerals

prospectus *noun* (*plural* **prospectuses**) a booklet giving information about a school, organization, *etc*

prosper *verb* to get on well, succeed

prosperity *noun* success, good fortune

prosperous *adjective* successful, wealthy

prostate *noun* a gland in a man's bladder

prostitute *noun* someone who offers sexual intercourse for payment

prostrate *adjective* lying flat face downwards

protagonist *noun* a chief character in a play *etc*

protect *verb* to shield from danger, keep safe ■ **protection** *noun*

protective *adjective* giving protection; intended to protect

protector *noun* a guardian, a defender

protégé *or feminine* **protégée** *noun* a pupil or employee who is taught or helped in their career by someone important or powerful

protein *noun* a substance present in milk, eggs, meat, *etc* which is a necessary part of a human or animal diet

protest *verb* (*pronounced* pro-**test**) **1** to object strongly **2** to declare solemnly ■ *noun* (*pronounced* **pro**-test) a strong objection

Protestant *noun* a member of one of the Christian Churches that broke away from the Roman Catholic Church at the time of the Reformation

protocol *noun* correct procedure

proton *noun* a particle with a positive electrical charge, forming part of the nucleus of an atom (*see also* **electron**, **neutron**)

prototype *noun* the original model from which something is copied

protract *verb* to lengthen in time

protractor *noun* an instrument for drawing and measuring angles on paper

protrude *verb* to stick out, thrust forward

proud *adjective* **1** thinking too highly of yourself, conceited **2** feeling pleased at an achievement *etc* **3** dignified, self-respecting: *too proud to accept the money*

prove *verb* **1** to show to be true or correct **2** to try out, test **3** to turn out (to be): *his prediction proved correct*

provenance *noun* source, origin

proverb *noun* a well-known wise saying, *eg* 'nothing ventured, nothing gained'

proverbial *adjective* well-known, widely spoken of

provide *verb* to supply

■ **providing that** on condition that

providence *noun* foresight; thrift

provident *adjective* thinking of the future; thrifty

providential *adjective* fortunate, coming as if by divine help

province *noun* **1** a division of a country **2** **provinces** all parts of a country outside the capital

provincial *adjective* of a province or provinces

provision *noun* **1** an agreed arrangement **2** a rule or condition **3** **provisions** a supply of food

provisional *adjective* used for the time being; temporary

proviso *noun* (*plural* **provisos**) a condition laid down beforehand

provocative *adjective* tending to rouse anger

provoke *verb* **1** to cause, result in **2** to rouse to anger or action ■ **provocation** *noun*

prow *noun* the front part of a ship

prowess *noun* skill, ability

prowl *verb* to go about stealthily

proximity *noun* nearness

proxy *noun* (*plural* **proxies**) someone who acts or votes on behalf of another

prude *noun* someone who is easily shocked by improper behaviour ■ **prudery** *noun* ■ **prudish** *adjective*

prudent *adjective* wise and cautious ■ **prudence** *noun* ■ **prudently** *adverb*

prune[1] *verb* to trim (a tree) by cutting off unneeded twigs

prune[2] *noun* a dried plum

pry *verb* to look closely into things that are not your business ∎ **prying** *adjective*

|**pry** ▶ pri*es*, pry*ing*, pri*ed*

PS *abbreviation* postscript

psalm *noun* a sacred song

psalter *noun* a book of psalms

p's and q's correct social manners

pseudo (*pronounced* **sood**-oh) *adjective, informal* false, fake, pretended

pseudonym (*pronounced* **sood**-o-nim) *noun* a false name used by an author

psychedelic *adjective* bright and multi-coloured

psychiatrist *noun* someone who treats mental illness

psychiatry *noun* the treatment of mental illness ∎ **psychiatric** (*pronounced* sai-ki-**at**-rik) *adjective*

psychic (*pronounced* **sai**-kik) *adjective* 1 relating to the mind 2 able to read other people's minds, or tell the future

psychoanalyse *or US* **psychoanalyze** *verb* to treat by psychoanalysis

psychoanalysis *noun* a method of treating mental illness by discussing with the patient its possible causes in their past ∎ **psychoanalyst** *noun*

psychological *adjective* of psychology or the mind

psychology *noun* the science which studies the human mind ∎ **psychologist** *noun*

ptarmigan (*pronounced* **tah**-mig-*an*) *noun* a mountain-dwelling bird of the grouse family, which turns white in winter

pterodactyl (*pronounced* te-ro-**dak**-til) *noun* an extinct flying reptile

pub *short for* public house

puberty (*pronounced* **pyoob**-et-i) *noun* the time during youth when the body becomes mature

public *adjective* 1 relating to or shared by the people of a community or nation in general 2 generally or widely known ∎ *noun* people in general

publican *noun* the keeper of an inn or public house

publication *noun* 1 the act of making news *etc* public 2 the act of publishing a book, newspaper, *etc* 3 a published book, magazine, *etc*

public house a building where alcoholic drinks are sold and consumed, a pub

publicity *noun* advertising; bringing to public notice or attention

publicize *or* **publicise** *verb* to make public, advertise

publish *verb* 1 to make generally known 2 to prepare and put out (a book *etc*) for sale

publisher *noun* someone who publishes books

puce *adjective* of a brownish-purple colour

puck *noun* a thick disc of rubber that is struck in ice hockey

pucker *verb* to wrinkle ■ *noun* a wrinkle, a fold

pudding *noun* **1** the sweet course of a meal **2** a sweet dish made with eggs, flour, milk, *etc*

puddle *noun* a small, often muddy, pool

puerile (*pronounced* pyoor-rail) *adjective* childish, silly

puff *verb* **1** to blow out in small gusts **2** to breathe heavily, *eg* after running **3** to blow up, inflate **4** to swell (up or out) ■ *noun* **1** a short, sudden gust of wind, breath, *etc* **2** a light biscuit

puffin *noun* a type of sea bird, with a short, thick, brightly-coloured beak

puff pastry a light, flaky kind of pastry

puffy *adjective* swollen, flabby

pug *noun* a breed of small dog with a snub nose

pugnacious *adjective* quarrelsome, fond of fighting

puke *noun & verb, slang* (to) vomit

pull *verb* **1** to move or try to move (something) towards yourself by force **2** to drag, tug **3** to stretch, strain: *pull a muscle* **4** to tear: *pull to pieces* ■ *noun* **1** the act of pulling **2** a pulling force, *eg* of a magnet ■ **pull out** to withdraw from a competition *etc* **2** of a

driver or vehicle: to move into the centre of the road ■ **pull through** to get safely to the end of a difficult or dangerous experience ■ **pull yourself together** to regain self-control or self-possession ■ **pull up** to stop, halt

pull-down menu a computer menu displayed on screen by moving the cursor or pressing a key (*also called*: **drop-down menu**)

pullet *noun* a young hen

pulley *noun* (*plural* **pulleys**) a grooved wheel fitted with a cord and set in a block, used for lifting weights *etc*

pullover *noun* a knitted garment for the top half of the body, a jersey

pulp *noun* **1** the soft fleshy part of a fruit **2** a soft mass of wood *etc* which is made into paper **3** any soft mass

pulpit *noun* an enclosed platform in a church for the minister or priest

pulsate *verb* to beat, throb

pulse *noun* the beating or throbbing of the heart and blood vessels as blood flows through them ■ *verb* to throb, pulsate

pulses *noun plural* beans, peas, lentils and other edible seeds of this family

pulverize or **pulverise** *verb* to make or crush into powder

puma *noun* an American wild animal like a large cat

pumice or **pumice stone** noun a piece of light solidified lava used for smoothing skin and for rubbing away stains

pummel verb to beat with the fists

| **pummel** ► pummels, pummelling, pummelled

pump noun **1** a machine used for making water rise to the surface **2** a machine for drawing out or forcing in air, gas, etc: bicycle pump **3** a kind of thin- or soft-soled shoe for dancing, gymnastics, etc ■ verb to raise or force with a pump

pumpkin noun a large, roundish, thick-skinned, yellow fruit, with stringy edible flesh

pun noun a play upon words which sound similar but have different meanings, eg 'two pears make a pair' ■ verb to make a pun

| **pun** verb ► puns, punning, punned

punch¹ verb **1** to hit with the fist **2** to make a hole in with a tool ■ noun (plural **punches**) **1** a blow with the fist **2** a tool for punching holes

punch² noun a drink made of spirits or wine, water, sugar, etc

punchline noun the words that give the main point to a joke

punctilious adjective paying attention to details, especially in behaviour; fastidious

punctual adjective **1** on time, not late **2** strict in keeping the time of appointments ■ **punctuality** noun

punctuate verb to divide up sentences by commas, full stops, etc

punctuation noun the use of punctuation marks

punctuation mark one of the symbols used in punctuating sentences, eg full stop, comma, colon, question mark, etc

puncture noun **1** an act of pricking or piercing **2** a small hole made with a sharp point **3** a hole in a tyre

pundit noun an expert

pungent adjective sharp-tasting or sharp-smelling

punish verb **1** to make (someone) suffer for a fault or crime **2** to inflict suffering on **3** to treat roughly or harshly

punishment noun pain or constraints inflicted for a fault or crime

punitive adjective inflicting punishment or suffering

punk noun **1** a type of loud and aggressive rock music **2** a young person who dresses in a shocking way and listens to punk music

punnet noun a small basket for fruit

punt noun a flat-bottomed boat with square ends ■ verb to move (a punt) by pushing a pole against the bottom of a river

punter noun **1** a professional gambler **2** a customer, a client **3** an ordinary person

puny adjective little and weak

pup noun 1 (also: **puppy**) a young dog 2 the young of certain other animals, eg a seal

pupa noun (plural **pupae**) the stage in the growth of an insect in which it changes from a larva to its mature form, eg from a caterpillar into a butterfly

pupil noun 1 someone who is being taught by a teacher 2 the round opening in the middle of the eye through which light passes

puppet noun 1 a doll which is moved by strings or wires 2 a doll that fits over the hand and is moved by the fingers

puppeteer noun someone who operates puppets

puppy see pup

purchase verb to buy ■ noun something which is bought

purdah noun the seclusion of Hindu or Islamic women from strangers, behind a screen or under a veil

pure adjective 1 clean, spotless 2 free from dust, dirt, etc 3 not mixed with other substances 4 free from faults or sin, innocent 5 utter, absolute, nothing but

purée noun food made into a pulp by being put through a sieve or liquidizing machine ■ verb to make into a purée, pulp

purely adverb 1 wholly, entirely: purely on merit 2 merely, only

purgatory noun in the Roman Catholic Church, a place where souls are made pure before entering heaven

purge verb 1 to make clean, purify 2 to clear (something) of anything unwanted ■ noun 1 a removal of impurities 2 a removal of something unwanted

purify verb to make pure
■ **purification** noun

| **purify** ► purifies, purifying, purified

purist noun someone who insists on correctness

puritan noun 1 someone of strict, often narrow-minded, morals 2 **Puritan** history one of a group believing in strict simplicity in worship and daily life
■ **puritanical** adjective
■ **puritanism** noun

purity noun the state of being pure

purl verb to knit in stitches made with the wool in front of the work

purloin verb to steal

purple noun a dark colour formed by the mixture of blue and red

purport verb to seem, pretend: he purports to be a film expert

purpose noun 1 aim, intention 2 use, function (of a tool etc) ■ verb to intend ■ **on purpose** intentionally

purposeful adjective determined ■ **purposefully** adverb

purposely adverb intentionally

purr noun the low, murmuring sound made by a cat when pleased ▪ verb of a cat: to make this sound

purse noun a small bag for carrying money ▪ verb to close (the lips) tightly

purser noun the officer who looks after a ship's money

pursue verb 1 to follow after (in order to overtake or capture), chase 2 to be engaged in, carry on (studies, an enquiry, etc)

pursuer noun someone who pursues

pursuit noun 1 the act of pursuing 2 an occupation or hobby

purvey verb to supply (food etc) as a business ▪ **purveyor** noun

pus noun a thick yellowish liquid produced from infected wounds

push verb 1 to press hard against 2 to thrust (something) away with force, shove 3 to urge on 4 to make a big effort ▪ noun 1 a thrust 2 effort 3 informal energy and determination

pushchair noun a folding chair on wheels for a young child

pushy adjective aggressively assertive

pussy or **puss** noun, informal a cat, a kitten

pussyfoot verb to act timidly or non-committally

put verb 1 to place, lay, set 2 to bring to a certain position or state: put the light on 3 to express: put the question more clearly ▪ **put about** to spread (news) ▪ **put by** to set aside, save up ▪ **put down** to defeat ▪ **put in for** to make a claim for, apply for ▪ **put off 1** to delay 2 to turn (someone) away from their plan or intention ▪ **put out 1** to extinguish (a fire, light, etc) 2 to annoy, embarrass ▪ **put up 1** to build 2 to propose, suggest (a plan, candidate, etc) 3 to let (someone) stay in your house etc ▪ **put up with** to bear patiently, tolerate

|put ▶ puts, putt**ing**, put

putrid adjective rotten; stinking

putt verb, golf to send a ball gently forward ▪ **putter** noun a golf club used for this

putty noun a cement made from ground chalk, used in putting glass in windows etc

puzzle verb 1 to present with a difficult problem or situation etc 2 to be difficult (for someone) to understand 3 **puzzle something out** to consider long and carefully in order to solve (a problem) ▪ noun 1 a difficulty which needs a lot of thought 2 a toy or riddle to test knowledge or skill

PVC noun, short for polyvinyl chloride, a kind of tough plastic

pygmy or **pigmy** (plural **pygmies** or **pigmies**) noun one of a race of very small human beings

pyjamas noun plural a sleeping

suit consisting of trousers and a jacket

pylon *noun* a high, steel tower supporting electric power cables

pyramid *noun* **1** a solid shape with flat sides which come to a point at the top **2** *history* a building of this shape used as a tomb in ancient Egypt

pyre *noun* a pile of wood on which a dead body is burned

pyromaniac *noun* someone who gets pleasure from starting fires

pyrotechnics *noun plural* a display of fireworks

python *noun* a large, non-poisonous snake which crushes its victims

quack *noun* **1** the cry of a duck **2** someone who falsely claims to have medical knowledge or training ▪ *verb* to make the noise of a duck

quad *short for* **1** quadruplet **2** quadrangle

quadrangle *noun* a four-sided courtyard surrounded by buildings in a school, college, *etc* (*short form:* **quad**)

quadrant *noun* **1** one quarter of the circumference or area of a circle **2** one of the four areas into which a plane is divided by axes

quadratic equation *maths* an equation that involves the square of a variable or unknown quantity

quadrilateral *noun* a four-sided figure or area ▪ *adjective* four-sided

quadruped *noun* a four-footed animal

quadruple *adjective* **1** four times as much or many **2** made up of four parts ▪ *verb* to make or become four times greater

quadruplet *noun* one of four children born to the same mother at one birth (*short form:* **quad**)

quaff (*pronounced* kwof) *verb* to drink up eagerly

quagmire *noun* wet, boggy ground

quail[1] *verb* to shrink back in fear

quail[2] *noun* a type of small bird like a partridge

quaint *adjective* pleasantly odd, especially because of being old-fashioned

quake *verb* to shake, tremble with fear ▪ *noun, informal* an earthquake

| **quake** *verb* ▶ quake*s*, quak*ing*, quak*ed*

Quaker *noun* a member of a religious group opposed to violence and war, founded in the 17th century

qualification *noun* **1** a qualifying statement **2** a skill that makes someone suitable for a job

qualified *adjective* having the necessary qualifications for a job

qualify *verb* **1** to be suitable for a job or position **2** to pass a test **3** to lessen the force of (a statement) by adding or changing words

| **qualify** ▶ qualif*ies*, qualify*ing*, qualif*ied*

quality *noun* (*plural* **qualities**) **1** an outstanding feature of someone or thing **2** degree of worth: *cloth of poor quality*

qualm *noun* doubt about whether something is right

quandary *noun* (*plural* **quandaries**) **1** a state of uncertainty **2** a situation in which it is difficult to decide what to do

quango *noun* (*plural* **quangos**) an official body, funded and appointed by government, that supervises some national activity *etc*

quantify *verb* to state the quantity of
| **quantify** ► **quantifies**, **quantifying**, **quantified**

quantity *noun* (*plural* **quantities**) **1** amount **2** a symbol which represents an amount

quantum *noun*, *physics* the smallest amount of energy, charge, *etc* that can exist on its own

quantum leap a huge, dramatic jump

quarantine *noun* the isolation of people or animals who might be carrying an infectious disease
■ *verb* to put in quarantine

quark *noun*, *physics* a sub-atomic particle

quarrel *noun* an angry disagreement or argument ■ *verb* **1** to disagree violently or argue angrily (with) **2** to find fault (with)

| **quarrel** *verb* ► **quarrels**, **quarrelling**, **quarrelled**

quarrelsome *adjective* fond of quarrelling, inclined to quarrel

quarry *noun* (*plural* **quarries**) **1** a pit from which stone is taken for building **2** a hunted animal **3** someone or something eagerly looked for ■ *verb* to dig (stone *etc*) from a quarry

| **quarry** *verb* ► **quarries**, **quarrying**, **quarried**

quart *noun* a measure of liquids, 1.136 litres (2 pints)

quarter *noun* **1** one of four equal parts of something **2** a fourth part of a year, three months **3** direction: *no help came from any quarter* **4** a district **5** **quarters** lodgings, accommodation ■ *verb* to divide into four equal parts

quarter-final *noun* a match in a competition immediately before a semi-final

quarterly *adjective* happening every three months ■ *adverb* every three months ■ *noun* (*plural* **quarterlies**) a magazine *etc* published every three months

quartet *noun* **1** a group of four players or singers **2** a piece of music written for such a group

quartz *noun* a hard substance often in crystal form, found in rocks

quasar *noun* an extremely distant, star-like object in the sky

quash *verb* **1** to crush, put down (*eg* a rebellion) **2** to wipe out, annul (*eg* a judge's decision)

quasi- *prefix* to some extent, but not completely: *quasi-historical*

quaver *verb* 1 to shake, tremble 2 to speak in a shaking voice ■ *noun* 1 a trembling of the voice 2 *music* a note (♪) equal to half a crotchet in length

quay (*pronounced* kee) *noun* a solid landing place for loading and unloading boats

queasy *adjective* 1 feeling nauseous 2 easily shocked or disgusted ■ **queasiness** *noun*

queen *noun* 1 a female monarch 2 the wife of a king 3 the most powerful piece in chess 4 a high value playing-card with a picture of a queen 5 an egg-laying female bee, ant or wasp

queen bee 1 an egg-laying female bee 2 a woman who is the centre of attention

queen mother the mother of the reigning king or queen who was once queen herself

queer *adjective* odd, strange

quell *verb* 1 to crush (a rebellion *etc*) 2 to remove (fears, suspicions, *etc*)

quench *verb* 1 to drink and so satisfy (thirst) 2 to put out (eg a fire)

query *noun* (*plural* **queries**) 1 a question 2 a question mark (?) ■ *verb* to question (eg a statement)

| **query** *verb* ► queries, querying, queried

quest *noun* a search

question *noun* 1 something requiring an answer, eg 'where do you live?' 2 a subject, matter, *etc*: *the energy question* 3 a matter for dispute or doubt: *there's no question of him leaving* ■ *verb* 1 to ask questions of (someone) 2 to express doubt about

questionable *adjective* doubtful

question mark a symbol (?) put after a question in writing

questionnaire *noun* a written list of questions to be answered by several people to provide information for a survey

queue *noun* a line of people waiting, eg for a bus ■ *verb* to stand in, or form, a queue

quibble *verb* to avoid the important part of an argument by quarrelling over details ■ *noun* a petty argument or complaint

quiche (*pronounced* keesh) *noun* an open pastry case filled with beaten eggs, cheese, *etc* and baked

quick *adjective* 1 done or happening in a short time 2 acting without delay, fast-moving: *a quick brain* ■ *noun* a tender area of skin under the nails ■ *adverb*, *informal* quickly

quicken *verb* to speed up, become or make faster

quickly *adverb* without delay, rapidly

quicksand *noun* sand that sucks in anyone who stands on it

quicksilver *noun* mercury

quickstep *noun* a ballroom dance like a fast foxtrot

quick-tempered *adjective* easily made angry

quid *noun, slang* a pound (£1)

quiet *adjective* 1 making little or no noise 2 calm: *a quiet life* ▪ *noun* 1 the state of being quiet 2 lack of noise, peace ▪ *verb* to make or become quiet

●* Do not confuse with: **quite**

quieten *verb* to make or become quiet

quietly *adverb* in a quiet way; with little or no sound

quietness *noun* being quiet

quiff *noun* a tuft of hair brushed up and back from the forehead

quill *noun* 1 a large feather of a goose or other bird made into a pen 2 one of the sharp spines of a porcupine

quilt *noun* a bedcover filled with down, feathers, *etc*

quilted *adjective* made of two layers of material with padding between them

quin *short for* **quintuplet**

quince *noun* a pear-like fruit with a sharp taste, used to make jams *etc*

quintessential *adjective* central, essential

quintet *noun* 1 a group of five players or singers 2 a piece of music written for such a group

quintuplet *noun* one of five children born to a mother at the same time (*short form*: **quin**)

quip *noun* a witty remark or reply ▪ *verb* to make a witty remark

| **quip** *verb* ▶ quips, quipping, quipped

quirk *noun* 1 an odd feature of someone's behaviour 2 a trick, a sudden turn: *quirk of fate* ▪ **quirky** *adjective*

quisling *noun* someone who collaborates with an enemy, especially a puppet ruler

quit *verb* 1 to give up, stop 2 *informal* to leave, resign from (a job)

| **quit** ▶ quits, quitting, quit or quitted

quite *adverb* 1 completely, entirely 2 fairly, moderately

●* Do not confuse with: **quiet**

quiver[1] *noun* a tremble, a shake ▪ *verb* to tremble, shake

quiver[2] *noun* a carrying case for arrows

quiz *verb* to question ▪ *noun* (*plural* **quizzes**) a competition to test knowledge

| **quiz** *verb* ▶ quizzes, quizzing, quizzed

quizzical *adjective* of a look: as if asking a question, especially mockingly

quoits *noun singular* a game in which heavy flat rings (**quoits**) are thrown on to small rods

quota *noun* a part or share to be given or received by each member of a group

quotation *noun* **1** the act of repeating something said or written **2** the words repeated **3** a price stated

quotation marks marks used in writing to show that someone's words are being repeated exactly, *eg* 'he said, "I'm going out"'

quote *verb* **1** to repeat the words of (someone) exactly as said or written **2** to state (a price for something)

quotient *noun, maths* the result obtained by dividing one number by another, *eg* 4 is the quotient when 12 is divided by 3

R r

rabbi *noun* (*plural* **rabbis**) a Jewish priest or teacher of the Jewish law

rabbit *noun* a small, burrowing, long-eared animal

rabble *noun* a disorderly, noisy crowd

rabid *adjective* of a dog: suffering from rabies

rabies *noun* a disease transmitted by the bite of an infected animal, causing fear of water and madness

raccoon *or* **racoon** *noun* a small furry animal of N America

race[1] *noun* a group of people with the same ancestors and physical characteristics

race[2] *noun* a competition to find the fastest person, animal, vehicle, *etc* ■ *verb* **1** to run fast **2** to take part in a race

racecourse *or* **racetrack** *noun* a course over which races are run

racehorse *noun* a horse bred and used for racing

racial *adjective* of or according to race

racism *or* **racialism** *noun* **1** the belief that some races of people are superior to others **2** prejudice

on the grounds of race ■ **racist** *or* **racialist** *noun & adjective*

rack *noun* **1** a framework for holding letters, plates, coats, *etc* **2** *history* an instrument for torturing victims by stretching their joints

racket[1] *or* **racquet** *noun* a bat made up of a strong frame strung with gut or nylon for playing tennis, badminton, *etc*

racket[2] *noun* **1** a great noise, a din **2** *informal* a dishonest way of making a profit

racoon *another spelling of* raccoon

racquet *another spelling of* racket[1]

radar *noun* a method of detecting solid objects using radio waves which bounce back off the object and form a picture of it on a screen

radiance *noun* brightness, splendour

radiant *adjective* **1** sending out rays of light, heat, *etc* **2** showing joy and happiness: *a radiant smile*

radiate *verb* **1** to send out rays of light, heat, *etc* **2** to spread or send out from a centre

radiation noun 1 the giving off of rays of light, heat, etc or of those from radioactive substances 2 radioactivity

radiator noun 1 a device (especially a series of connected hot-water pipes) which sends out heat 2 the part of a car which cools the engine

radical adjective 1 thorough: a radical change 2 basic, deep-seated: radical differences 3 proposing dramatic changes in the method of government ■ noun someone who has radical political views

radio noun (plural radios) a device for sending and receiving signals by means of electromagnetic waves ■ verb to send a message to (someone) in this way

| **radio** verb ▶ radios, radioing, radioed

radioactive adjective giving off rays which are often dangerous but which can be used in medicine ■ **radioactivity** noun

radiology noun 1 the study of radioactive substances and radiation 2 the branch of medicine involving the use of X-rays

radiotherapy noun the treatment of certain diseases by X-rays or radioactive substances

radish noun (plural radishes) a plant with a sharp-tasting root, eaten raw in salads

radium noun a radioactive metal used in radiotherapy

radius noun (plural radii) 1 a straight line from the centre to the circumference of a circle 2 an area within a certain distance from a central point

radon noun a colourless radioactive gas

raffia noun strips of fibre from the leaves of a palm tree, used in weaving mats etc

raffle noun a way of raising money by selling numbered tickets, one or more of which wins a prize ■ verb to give as a prize in a raffle

raft noun a number of logs etc fastened together and used as a boat

rafter noun one of the sloping beams supporting a roof

rag noun 1 a torn or worn piece of cloth 2 **rags** worn-out, shabby clothes

ragamuffin noun a ragged, dirty child

rag doll a floppy doll made of scrap material

rage noun great anger, fury ■ verb 1 to be violently angry 2 of a storm, battle, etc: to be violent

ragged adjective 1 in torn, shabby clothes 2 torn and tattered

ragtime noun a style of jazz music with a highly syncopated rhythm

raid noun 1 a short, sudden

attack **2** an unexpected visit by the police to catch a criminal, recover stolen goods, *etc* ▪ *verb* to make a raid on

raider *noun* a person who raids

rail *noun* **1** a bar of metal used in fences **2 rails** strips of steel which form the track on which trains run **3** the railway: *travel by rail*

railing *noun* a fence or barrier of rails

railway *or US* **railroad** *noun* a track laid with steel rails on which trains run

rain *noun* water falling from the clouds in drops ▪ *verb* to pour or fall in drops

rainbow *noun* **1** the brilliant coloured bow or arch sometimes to be seen in the sky opposite the sun when rain is falling **2** a member of the most junior branch of the Guides

raincoat *noun* a waterproof coat to keep out the rain

rainfall *noun* the amount of rain that falls in a certain time

rainforest *noun* a tropical forest with very heavy rainfall

rainy *adjective* showery, wet

| **rainy** ▸ rain*ier*, rain*iest*

raise *verb* **1** to lift up **2** to make higher: *raise the price* **3** to bring up (a subject) for consideration **4** to bring up (a child, family, *etc*) **5** to breed or grow (*eg* pigs, crops) **6** to collect, get together (a sum of money)

raisin *noun* a dried grape

rake *noun* a tool, like a large comb with a long handle, for smoothing earth, gathering hay, *etc* ▪ *verb* **1** to draw a rake over **2** to scrape (together)

rally *verb* **1** to gather again **2** to come together for a joint action or effort **3** to recover from an illness ▪ *noun* (*plural* **rallies**) **1** a gathering **2** a political mass meeting **3** an improvement in health after an illness **4** *tennis* a long series of shots before a point is won or lost **5** a competition to test driving skills over an unknown route

| **rally** *verb* ▸ rall*ies*, rally*ing*, rall*ied*

ram *noun* a male sheep ▪ *verb* **1** to press or push down hard **2** of a ship, car, *etc*: to run into and cause damage to

| **ram** *verb* ▸ rams, ram*ming*, ram*med*

Ramadan *noun* **1** the ninth month of the Islamic calendar, a period of fasting by day **2** the fast itself

ramble *verb* **1** to walk about for pleasure, especially in the countryside **2** to speak in an aimless or confused way ▪ *noun* a country walk for pleasure

rambler *noun* **1** someone who goes walking in the country for pleasure **2** a climbing rose or other plant

ramification *noun* **1** a branch or part of a subject, plot, *etc* **2** a consequence, usually indirect and one of several

ramp noun a sloping surface (eg of a road)

rampage verb to rush about angrily or violently ▪ noun an angry or violent attack

rampant adjective widespread and uncontrolled

rampart noun a mound or wall built as a defence

ramshackle adjective badly made, falling to pieces

ran past form of **run**

ranch noun (plural **ranches**) a large farm in North America for rearing cattle or horses

rancid adjective of butter: smelling or tasting stale

rancour noun ill-will, hatred

random adjective done without any aim or plan; chance

rang past form of **ring**[2]

range noun 1 a line or row: a range of mountains 2 extent, number 3 a piece of ground with targets for shooting or archery practice 4 the distance which an object can be thrown, or across which a sound can be heard 5 the distance between the top and bottom notes of a singing voice ▪ verb 1 to set in a row or in order 2 to wander (over) 3 to stretch, extend

ranger noun a keeper who looks after a forest or park

Ranger Guide an older member of the Guide movement

rank noun 1 a row or line (eg of soldiers) 2 class, order: the rank of captain ▪ verb 1 to place in order of importance, merit, etc 2 to have a place in an order: apes rank above dogs in intelligence ▪ adjective 1 having a strong, unpleasant taste or smell 2 absolute: rank nonsense

rankle verb to cause lasting annoyance, bitterness, etc

ransack verb to search thoroughly; plunder

ransom noun the price paid for the freeing of a captive ▪ verb to pay money to free (a captive)

rant verb to talk foolishly and angrily for a long time

rap[1] noun a sharp blow or knock ▪ verb (often **rap on something**) to strike it with a quick, sharp blow

| **rap** verb ▶ raps, rapping, rapped

rap[2] noun 1 informal an informal talk or discussion 2 a style of music accompanied by a rhythmic monologue

rape[1] verb to have sexual intercourse with (someone) against their will, usually by force ▪ noun 1 the act of raping 2 the act of seizing and carrying off by force

rape[2] noun a plant related to the turnip, whose seeds give oil

rapid adjective quick, fast: a rapid rise to fame

rapidity noun swiftness

rapidly adverb quickly

rapids noun plural a part in a river where the current flows swiftly

rapier noun a type of light sword with a narrow blade

rapport (pronounced ra-**pawr**) noun a good relationship, sympathy

rapt adjective having the mind fully occupied, engrossed

rapture noun great delight

rapturous adjective experiencing or demonstrating rapture

rare adjective 1 seldom found, uncommon 2 of meat: lightly cooked

♦* Do not confuse with: **unique**. You can talk about something being **rare**, quite **rare**, very **rare** etc. It would be incorrect, however, to describe something as very **unique**, since things either are or are not **unique** – there are no levels of this quality

raring adjective: **raring to go** very keen to go, start, etc

rarity noun (plural **rarities**) 1 something uncommon 2 uncommonness

rascal noun a naughty or wicked person

rash adjective acting, or done, without thought ▪ noun redness or outbreak of spots on the skin

rasher noun a thin slice (of bacon or ham)

rashness noun the state of being rash

rasp noun a rough, grating sound ▪ verb to make a rough, grating noise

raspberry noun 1 a type of red berry similar to a blackberry 2 the bush which bears this fruit

rasping adjective of a sound: rough and unpleasant

rat noun a gnawing animal, larger than a mouse ▪ **rat on** to inform against

|rat verb ▸ rats, ratting, ratted

ratchet noun a toothed wheel, eg in a watch

rate noun 1 the frequency with which something happens or is done 2 speed 3 level of cost, price, etc ▪ verb 1 to work out the value of for taxation etc 2 to value

rather adverb 1 somewhat, fairly 2 more willingly 3 more correctly speaking: he agreed, or rather he didn't say no

ratification noun ratifying or being ratified

ratify verb to approve officially and formally: ratified the treaty

|ratify ▸ ratifies, ratifying, ratified

rating noun a sailor below the rank of an officer

ratio noun (plural **ratios**) the proportion of one thing to another

ration noun 1 a measured amount of food given out at

intervals **2** an allowance ▪ *verb* **1** to deal out (*eg* food) in measured amounts **2** to allow only a certain amount to (someone)

rational *adjective* **1** able to reason **2** sensible; based on reason **3** *maths* denoting a number that can be expressed as a fraction whose denominator is not zero, *eg* 1 or $\frac{1}{3}$

rationalize or **rationalise** *verb* **1** to think up a good reason for (an action or feeling) so as not to feel guilty about it **2** to make (an industry or organization) more efficient and profitable by reorganizing it to get rid of unnecessary costs and labour ▪ **rationalization** *noun*

rationally *adverb* in a rational way

rat-race *noun* a fierce, unending competition for success or wealth

rattle *verb* **1** to give out short, sharp, repeated sounds **2** to fluster or irritate (someone) ▪ *noun* **1** a sharp noise, quickly repeated **2** a toy or instrument which makes such a sound ▪ **rattle off** to go through (a list of names *etc*) quickly

rattlesnake *noun* a poisonous snake with bony rings on its tail which rattle when shaken

ratty *adjective* irritable

| **ratty** ▶ rattier, rattiest

raucous *adjective* hoarse, harsh

raunchy *adjective* sexually suggestive, lewd

| **raunchy** ▶ raunchier, raunchiest

ravage *verb* to cause destruction or damage to; plunder ▪ **ravages** *noun plural* damaging effects

rave *verb* **1** to talk very wildly, as if mad **2** *informal* to talk very enthusiastically (about) ▪ *noun* a large party held in a warehouse *etc* with electronic music

raven *noun* a type of large black bird of the crow family ▪ *adjective* of hair: black and glossy

ravenous *adjective* very hungry

ravine *noun* a deep, narrow valley between hills

raving *adjective* mad, crazy

ravishing *adjective* filling with delight

raw *adjective* **1** not cooked **2** not prepared or refined, in its natural state **3** of weather: cold **4** sore

ray *noun* **1** a line of light, heat, *etc* **2** a small degree or amount: *a ray of hope* **3** one of several lines going outwards from a centre **4** a kind of flat-bodied fish

rayon *noun* a type of artificial silk

razor *noun* a sharp-edged instrument for shaving

re *preposition* concerning, about

re- *prefix* again, once more: *recreate/redo*

reach *verb* **1** to arrive at: *reach the summit* **2** to stretch out (the hand) so as to touch: *I couldn't reach the top shelf* **3** to extend ▪ *noun* **1** a distance that can be travelled easily: *within reach of home* **2** the distance someone can stretch their arm

react *verb* **1** to act or behave in response to something done or said **2** to undergo a chemical change

reaction *noun* **1** behaviour as a result of action **2** a chemical change **3** a movement against a situation or belief

read *verb* **1** to look at and understand, or say aloud written or printed words **2** to study a subject in a university or college: *reading law*

| read ▸ reads, reading, read

readable *adjective* quite interesting to read

reader *noun* **1** someone who reads books *etc* **2** someone who reads manuscripts for a publisher **3** a senior university lecturer **4** a reading book for children

readily *adverb* easily; willingly

readiness *noun* **1** the state of being ready and prepared **2** willingness

ready *adjective* **1** prepared **2** willing **3** quick: *too ready to find fault* **4** available for use

ready-made *adjective* of clothes: made for general sale, not made specially for one person

reagent *noun* any substance involved in a chemical reaction (*compare with:* **agent**)

real *adjective* **1** actually existing,

not imagined **2** not imitation, genuine **3** sincere: *a real love of music*

realism *noun* the showing or viewing of things as they really are

realist *noun* someone who claims to see life as it really is

realistic *adjective* **1** lifelike **2** viewing things as they really are
- **realistically** *adverb*

reality *noun* (*plural* **realities**) that which is real and not imaginary; truth

realization *or* **realisation** *noun* realizing or being realized

realize *or* **realise** *verb* to come to understand, know

really *adverb* **1** in fact **2** very: *really dark*

realm *noun* **1** a kingdom, a country **2** an area of activity or interest

reap *verb* **1** to cut and gather (corn *etc*) **2** to gain: *reap the benefits of hard work*

reaper *noun* **1** someone who reaps **2** a machine for reaping

rear *noun* **1** the back part of anything **2** the last part of an army or fleet ▪ *verb* **1** to bring up (children) **2** to breed (animals) **3** of an animal: to stand on its hindlegs

rearguard *noun* troops who protect the rear of an army

reason *noun* **1** cause, excuse **2** purpose **3** the power of the mind to form opinions, judge right and truth, *etc* **4** common sense ■ *verb* **1** to think out (opinions *etc*) **2** **reason with someone** to try to persuade them by arguing

reasonable *adjective* **1** sensible **2** fair

reassurance *noun* something which reassures, or the feeling of being reassured

reassure *verb* to take away (someone's) doubts or fears

reassuring *adjective* that reassures

rebate *noun* a part of a payment or tax which is given back to the payer

rebel *noun* (*pronounced* **reb**-el) someone who opposes or fights against those in power ■ *verb* (*pronounced* ri-**bel**) to take up arms against or oppose those in power

| **rebel** *verb* ► rebels, rebelling, rebelled

rebellion *noun* **1** an open or armed fight against those in power **2** a refusal to obey

rebellious *adjective* rebelling or likely to rebel ■ **rebelliousness** *noun*

reboot *verb* to restart (a computer) using its start-up programs

rebound *verb* (*pronounced* ri-**bownd**) to bounce back ■ *noun* (*pronounced* **ree**-bownd) **1** the act of rebounding **2** a reaction following an emotional situation or crisis

rebuff *noun* a blunt refusal or rejection ■ *verb* to reject bluntly

rebuke *verb* to scold, blame ■ *noun* a scolding

rebut *verb* to deny (what has been said)

| **rebut** ► rebuts, rebutting, rebutted

recall *verb* **1** to call back **2** to remember ■ *noun* **1** a signal or message to return **2** the act of recalling or remembering

recap *noun*, *short for* **recapitulation** ■ *verb*, *short for* **recapitulate**

| **recap** *verb* ► recaps, recapping, recapped

recapitulate *verb* to go over again quickly the chief points of anything (*eg* a discussion)

recapitulation *noun* an act or instance of recapitulating or summing up

recapture *verb* to capture (what has escaped or been lost)

recede *verb* **1** to go back **2** to become more distant **3** to slope backwards

receding *adjective* **1** going or sloping backwards **2** becoming more distant

receipt *noun* **1** the act of receiving (especially money or goods) **2** a written note saying that money has been received

receive *verb* **1** to have something given or brought to you **2** to meet and welcome

receiver *noun* **1** the part of a

telephone through which words are heard and into which they are spoken **2** an apparatus through which television or radio broadcasts are received

recent *adjective* happening, done or made only a short time ago

recently *adverb* a short time ago

receptacle *noun* an object to receive or hold things, a container

reception *noun* **1** a welcome **2** a large meeting to welcome guests **3** the quality of radio or television signals

receptionist *noun* someone employed in an office or hotel to answer the telephone *etc*

receptive *adjective* quick to take in or accept ideas *etc*

recess *noun* (*plural* **recesses**) **1** part of a room set back from the rest, an alcove **2** the time during which parliament or the law courts do not work

recession *noun* **1** the act of moving back **2** a temporary fall in a country's or the world's business activities

recessive *adjective* tending to recede

recipe *noun* instructions on how to prepare or cook a certain kind of food

recipient *noun* someone who receives

reciprocal *adjective* both given and received ■ *noun* one of a pair

of numbers whose product is 1, *eg* 4 is the reciprocal of $\frac{1}{4}$

reciprocate *verb* to feel or do the same in return

recital *noun* **1** the act of reciting **2** a musical performance **3** the facts of a story told one after the other

recitation *noun* a poem *etc* recited

recite *verb* to repeat aloud from memory

reckless *adjective* rash, careless ■ **recklessly** *adverb*

reckon *verb* **1** to count **2** to consider, believe

reckoning *noun* **1** the settling of debts, grievances, *etc* **2** a sum, calculation

reclaim *verb* **1** to claim back **2** to win back (land from the sea) by draining, building banks, *etc* **3** to make waste land fit for use

recline *verb* to lean or lie on your back or side

recluse *noun* someone who lives alone and avoids other people

reclusive *adjective* preferring to stay away from other people

recognition *noun* the act of recognizing someone or something

recognizable *or* **recognisable** *adjective* capable of being recognized

recognize *or* **recognise** *verb* **1** to know from a previous meeting *etc* **2** to admit, acknowledge **3** to show appreciation of

recoil verb **1** to shrink back in horror or fear **2** of a gun: to jump back after a shot is fired ▪ noun a shrinking back

recollect verb to remember

recollection noun **1** the act or power of remembering **2** a memory, something remembered

recommend verb **1** to urge, advise **2** to speak highly of

recommendation noun **1** the act of recommending **2** a point in favour of someone or something

recompense verb to pay money to or reward (a person) to make up for loss, inconvenience, etc ▪ noun payment in compensation

reconcile verb **1** to bring together in friendship, after a quarrel **2** to show that two statements, facts, etc do not contradict each other ▪ **be reconciled to** or **reconcile oneself to something** to agree to accept an unwelcome fact or situation patiently

reconciliation noun the fact of being friendly with someone again, after an argument, dispute or conflict

reconnaissance (pronounced ri-kon-is-ens) noun a survey to obtain information, especially before a battle

reconnoitre (pronounced rek-o-noi-ter) verb to make a reconnaissance of

reconstitute verb to put back into its original form

reconstruct verb **1** to rebuild **2** to create an impression of (a past event etc) using what is known **3** to re-enact (a crime)

▪ **reconstruction** noun

record verb (pronounced ri-kawd) **1** to write down for future reference **2** to put (music, speech, etc) on tape or disc so that it can be listened to later **3** to show in writing (eg a vote) **4** to show, register: the thermometer recorded 30°C yesterday ▪ noun (pronounced rek-awd) **1** a written report of facts **2** a round, flat piece of plastic on which sounds are recorded for playing on a record player **3** the best known performance: the school record for the mile

recorder noun **1** someone who records **2** a type of simple musical wind instrument

recording noun **1** the act of recording **2** recorded music, speech, etc

record player a machine for playing records

recount verb **1** (pronounced ree-kownt) to count again **2** (pronounced ri-kownt) to tell (the story of) ▪ noun (pronounced ree-kownt) a second count, especially of votes in an election

recoup (pronounced ri-koop) verb to make good, recover (expenses, losses, etc)

◆* Do not confuse with: **recuperate**

◆* Do not confuse with: **recoup**

recover *verb* **1** to get possession of again **2** to become well again after an illness

recovery *noun* (*plural* **recoveries**) **1** a return to health **2** the regaining of something lost *etc*

recreation *noun* a sport, hobby, *etc* done in your spare time

recriminations *noun plural* angry remarks made during an argument

recruit *noun* a newly-enlisted soldier, member, *etc* ■ *verb* to enlist (someone) in an army, political party, *etc*

recruitment *noun* recruiting

rectangle *noun* a four-sided figure with all its angles right angles and its opposite sides equal in length, an oblong

rectangular *adjective* of or like a rectangle

rectify *verb* to put right

| **rectify** ▶ **rectifies**, rectify*ing*, rectif*ied*

rectitude *noun* honesty; correctness of behaviour

rector *noun* a member of the clergy in the Church of England in charge of a parish

rectory *noun* (*plural* **rectories**) the house of a rector

rectum *noun* the part of the bowels below the colon

recuperate *verb* to recover strength or health

recuperation *noun* recovery

recur *verb* to happen again

| **recur** ▶ recurs, recurr*ing*, recurr*ed*

recurrent *adjective* happening often or regularly ■ **recurrence** *noun*

recycle *verb* **1** to remake into something different **2** to treat (material) by some process in order to use it again

red *adjective* of the colour of blood ■ *noun* this colour

redden *verb* to make or grow red

redeem *verb* **1** to buy back (*eg* articles from a pawnbroker) **2** to save from sin or condemnation

redeemer *noun* **1** a person who redeems **2 the Redeemer** Jesus Christ

redeeming *adjective* making up for other faults: *a redeeming feature*

redemption *noun* the act of redeeming or state of being redeemed, especially the freeing of humanity from sin by Christ

red-handed *adverb* in the act of doing wrong: *caught red-handed*

red herring something mentioned to lead a discussion away from the main subject; a false clue

red-hot *adjective* having reached a degree of heat at which metals glow with a red light

red-letter *adjective* of a day: especially important or happy for some reason

red light 1 a danger signal **2** a signal to stop

redolent *adjective* **1** sweet-smelling **2** smelling (of) **3** suggestive, making one think (of): *redolent of earlier times*

redouble *verb* to make twice as great: *redouble your efforts*

redoubtable *adjective* brave, bold

redress *verb* to set right, make up for (a wrong *etc*) ▪ *noun* something done or given to make up for a loss or wrong, compensation

red tape unnecessary and troublesome rules about how things are to be done

reduce *verb* **1** to make smaller **2** to lessen **3** to bring to the point of by force of circumstances: *reduced to begging* **4** to change into other terms: *reduce pounds to pence*

reduction *noun* **1** an act or instance of reducing; the state of being reduced **2** the amount by which something is reduced **3** a reduced copy of a picture, document, *etc* **4** *chemistry* a reaction in which an atom or ion gains electrons

redundancy *noun* (*plural* **redundancies**) **1** being redundant, or an instance of this **2** a dismissal or a person dismissed because they are no longer needed

redundant *adjective* **1** more than what is needed **2** of a worker: no longer needed because of the lack of a suitable job

reed *noun* **1** a tall stiff grass growing in moist or marshy places **2** a part (originally made of reed) of certain wind instruments which vibrates when the instrument is played

reef *noun* a chain of rocks lying at or near the surface of the sea

reef knot a square, very secure knot

reek *noun* a strong, unpleasant smell ▪ *verb* to smell strongly

reel *noun* **1** a cylinder of plastic, metal or wood on which thread, film, fishing lines, *etc* may be wound **2** a length of cinema film **3** a lively Scottish or Irish dance ▪ *verb* **1** to stagger **2** reel in to draw, pull in (a fish on a line) ▪ **reel off** to repeat or recite quickly, without pausing

ref *noun*, short for **1** referee **2** reference

refer *verb*: **refer to 1** to mention **2** to turn to for information **3** to relate to, apply to **4** to direct to for information, consideration, *etc*

| **refer** ▶ refers, referring, referred |

referee *noun* **1** someone to whom a matter is taken for settlement **2** a judge in a sports match **3** someone willing to provide a note about someone's character, work record, *etc*

reference *noun* **1** the act of referring **2** a mention **3** a note about a person's character, work, *etc*

reference book a book to be consulted for information, *eg* an encyclopedia

referendum *noun* (*plural* **referenda** *or* **referendums**) a vote given by the people of a country about some important matter

refine *verb* **1** to purify **2** to improve, make more exact, *etc*

refined *adjective* **1** purified **2** polite in manners, free of vulgarity

refinement *noun* **1** good manners, taste, learning **2** an improvement

refinery *noun* (*plural* **refineries**) a place where sugar, oil, *etc* are refined

refit *verb* to repair damages (especially to a ship)

| **refit** ▶ refits, refitt*ing*, refitt*ed*

reflect *verb* **1** to throw back (light or heat) **2** to give an image of **3** **reflect on someone** to be an indication of their worth: *her behaviour reflects well on her mother* **4** **reflect on something** to think it over carefully

reflection *noun* **1** the act of throwing back **2** the image of someone *etc* reflected in a mirror **3** *maths* a transformation that

produces a mirror image on the other side of a line of symmetry (*compare with*: **enlargement**, **rotation**, **translation**) **4** careful thought

reflective *adjective* thoughtful

reflector *noun* something (*eg* a piece of shiny metal) which throws back light

reflex *noun* (*plural* **reflexes**) an action which is automatic, not intended, *eg* jerking the leg when the kneecap is struck ■ *adjective* **1** done as an automatic response, unthinking **2** of an angle: greater than 180°

reflexive *adjective*, *grammar* showing that the object (**reflexive pronoun**) of the verb (**reflexive verb**) is the same as its subject, *eg* in 'he cut himself', *himself* is a *reflexive pronoun* and *cut* a *reflexive verb*

reform *verb* **1** to improve, remove faults from **2** to give up bad habits, evil, *etc* ■ *noun* an improvement

reformation *noun* **1** a change for the better **2** **the Reformation** the religious movement in the Christian Church in the 16th century from which the Protestant Church arose

reformer *noun* someone who wishes to bring about improvements

refract *verb* to change the direction of (a wave of light, sound, *etc*)

refraction noun a change in the direction of (a wave of light, sound, etc)

refrain noun a chorus coming at the end of each verse of a song ▪ verb to stop yourself (from doing something)

refresh verb to give new strength, power or life to ▪ **refresh your memory** to go over facts again so that they are clear in your mind

refreshing adjective 1 bringing back strength 2 cooling

refreshments noun plural food and drink

refrigerate verb to make or keep (food) cold or frozen to prevent it from going bad

refrigeration noun the process whereby a cabinet or room and its contents are kept at a low temperature, especially in order to prevent food from going bad

refrigerator noun a storage machine which keeps food cold and so prevents it from going bad

refuel verb to supply with, or take in, fresh fuel

| **refuel** ▸ refuels, refuelling, refuelled

refuge noun a place of safety (from attack, danger, etc)

refugee noun someone who seeks shelter from persecution in another country

refund verb (pronounced ri-**fund**) to pay back ▪ noun (pronounced **ree**-fund) a payment returned, eg for unsatisfactory goods

refusal noun an act of refusing

refuse[1] (pronounced ri-**fyooz**) verb 1 to say that you will not do something 2 to withhold, not give (eg permission)

refuse[2] (pronounced **ref**-yoos) noun something which is thrown aside as worthless, rubbish

refute verb to prove wrong (something that has been said or written)

regain verb 1 to win back again 2 to get back to

regal adjective kingly, royal

regale verb to entertain lavishly

regalia noun plural symbols of royalty, eg a crown and sceptre

regard verb 1 to look upon, consider: I regard you as a nuisance 2 to look at carefully 3 to pay attention to ▪ noun 1 concern 2 affection 3 respect 4 regards good wishes ▪ **with regard to** or **in regard to** concerning

regarding preposition concerning, to do with

regardless adverb not thinking or caring about costs, problems, dangers, etc; in spite of everything

regatta noun a meeting for yacht or boat races

regenerate verb to make new and good again ▪ **regeneration** noun

regent noun someone who governs in place of a king or queen

reggae noun a strongly rhythmic type of music, originally from Jamaica

regime or **régime** (both pronounced rei-**zeem**) noun method or system of government or administration

regiment noun a body of soldiers, commanded by a colonel ▪ verb to organize or control too strictly

regimental adjective of a regiment

region noun an area, a district

regional adjective of a region

register noun 1 a written list (eg of attendances at school, of those eligible to vote, etc) 2 the distance between the highest and lowest notes of a voice or instrument ▪ verb 1 to write down in a register 2 to record, cast (a vote etc) 3 to show, record: a thermometer registers temperature

registrar noun a public official who keeps a register of births, deaths and marriages

registry noun (plural **registries**) an office where a register is kept

registry office a place where records of births, marriages and deaths are kept and where marriages may be performed

regret verb 1 to be sorry about 2 to be sorry (to have to say something) ▪ noun sorrow for anything

regret verb ► regrets, regretting, regretted

regretful adjective feeling or showing regret ▪ **regretfully** adverb

regrettable adjective to be regretted, unwelcome ▪ **regrettably** adverb

regular adjective 1 done according to rule or habit; usual 2 arranged in order; even 3 happening at certain fixed times 4 maths of a polygon: with all its sides and angles equal ▪ noun a person who does something or goes somewhere on a regular basis

regularity noun being regular

regularly adverb in a regular way or at a regular time

regulate verb 1 to control by rules 2 to adjust to a certain order or rate

regulation noun a rule, an order

regurgitate verb to bring back into the mouth after swallowing

regurgitation noun regurgitating

rehabilitate verb 1 to give back rights, powers or health to 2 to train or accustom (a disabled person etc) to live a normal life

rehabilitation noun rehabilitating or being rehabilitated

rehash verb to express in different words, do again

rehearsal noun 1 a private practice of a play, concert, etc before performance in public 2 a practice for a future event or action

rehearse *verb* 1 to practise beforehand 2 to recount (facts, events, *etc*) in order

reign *noun* 1 rule 2 the time during which a king or queen rules ■ *verb* 1 to rule 2 to prevail: *silence reigned*

reimburse *verb* to pay (someone) an amount to cover expenses

rein *noun* 1 one of two straps attached to a bridle for guiding a horse 2 **reins** a simple device for controlling a child when walking

reincarnation *noun* the rebirth of the soul in another body after death

reindeer *noun* (*plural* **reindeer**) a type of deer found in the far North

reinforce *verb* to strengthen (*eg* an army with men, concrete with iron)

reinforcement *noun* 1 the act of reinforcing 2 something which strengthens 3 **reinforcements** additional troops

reinstate *verb* to put back in a former position

reiterate *verb* to repeat several times

reiteration *noun* reiterating

reject *verb* (*pronounced* ri-**jekt**) 1 to throw away, cast aside 2 to refuse to take 3 to turn down (*eg* an application, request) ■ *noun* (*pronounced* **ree**-jekt) something discarded or refused

rejection *noun* 1 rejecting or

being rejected 2 something that is rejected

rejig *verb* to rearrange, especially in an unexpected way

| **rejig** ▸ rejigs, rejigg*ing*, rejig*ged*

rejoice *verb* to feel or show joy

rejoicing *noun* 1 being joyful 2 festivities, celebrations, merrymaking

rejoinder *noun* an answer to a reply

rejuvenate *verb* to make young again

relapse *verb* to fall back (*eg* into ill health, bad habits) ■ *noun* a falling back

relate *verb* 1 to show a connection between (two or more things) 2 to tell (a story)

related *adjective* 1 (often **related to someone**) of the same family (as) 2 connected

relation *noun* 1 someone who is of the same family, either by birth or marriage 2 a connection between two or more things

relationship *noun* 1 a connection between things or people 2 an emotional partnership

relative *noun* someone who is of the same family *etc* ■ *adjective* comparative

relatively *adverb* more or less

relativity *noun* the state of being relative

relax *verb* 1 to become or make less tense 2 to slacken (*eg* your grip or control) **3** to make (laws or rules) less severe

relaxation *noun* **1** a slackening **2** rest from work, leisure

relay *verb* to receive and pass on (eg a message, a television programme) ▪ *noun* the sending out of a radio or television broadcast received from another station

| **relay** *verb* ▶ relays, relaying, relayed

relay race a race in which members of each team take over from each other, each running a set distance

release *verb* **1** to set free; let go **2** to allow (news *etc*) to be made public ▪ *noun* a setting free

relegate *verb* **1** to put down (to a lower position, group, *etc*) **2** to leave (a task *etc*) to someone else ▪ **relegation** *noun*

relent *verb* to treat (someone) less severely or strictly

relentless *adjective* **1** without pity **2** refusing to be turned from a purpose ▪ **relentlessly** *adverb*

relevance *noun* being relevant

relevant *adjective* having to do with what is being spoken about

reliable *adjective* able to be trusted or counted on ▪ **reliability** *noun*

reliance *noun* trust (in), dependence (on)

reliant *adjective* relying on or having confidence in

relic *noun* something left over from a past time; an antiquity

relief *noun* **1** a lessening of pain or anxiety **2** release from a post or duty **3** people taking over someone's duty *etc* **4** help given to those in need: *famine relief* **5** a way of carving or moulding in which the design stands out from its background

relief map a map in which variations in the height of the land are shown by shading

relieve *verb* **1** to lessen (pain or anxiety) **2** to take over a duty from (someone else) **3** to come to the help of (a town *etc* under attack)

religion *noun* belief in, or worship of, a god

religious *adjective* **1** of or relating to religion **2** following the rules of worship of a particular religion very closely

relinquish *verb* to give up, abandon

relish *verb* **1** to enjoy **2** to like the taste of ▪ *noun* (*plural* relishes) **1** enjoyment **2** flavour **3** something which adds flavour

relocate *verb* to move to another position, residence, *etc*

reluctance *noun* unwillingness; lack of enthusiasm

reluctant *adjective* unwilling

rely *verb* to have full trust in, depend (on)

| **rely** ▶ relies, relying, relied

remain *verb* **1** to stay, not leave

2 to be left: *only two tins of soup remained* **3** to be still the same: *the problem remains unsolved*

remainder *noun* **1** something which is left behind after removal of the rest **2** *maths* the number left after subtraction or division

remains *noun plural* **1** that which is left **2** a dead body

remake *noun* (pronounced ree-meik) a second making of a film *etc* ■ *verb* (pronounced ree-**meik**) to make again

remand *verb* to put (someone) back in prison until more evidence is found

remark *verb* **1** to say **2** to comment (on) **3** to notice ■ *noun* something said

remarkable *adjective* deserving notice, unusual ■ **remarkably** *adverb*

remedial *adjective* **1** remedying **2** relating to the teaching of slow-learning children

remedy *noun* (plural **remedies**) a cure for an illness, evil, *etc* ■ *verb* **1** to cure **2** to put right

| **remedy** *verb* ► **remedies**, **remedying**, **remedied**

remember *verb* **1** to keep in mind **2** to recall after having forgotten **3** to send your best wishes (to): *remember me to your mother* **4** to reward, give a present to: *he remembered her in his will*

remembrance *noun* **1** the act of remembering **2** memory **3** something given to remind

someone of a person or event, a keepsake

remind *verb* **1** to bring (something) back to a person's mind **2** to cause (someone) to think about (someone or something) by resemblance

reminder *noun* something which reminds

reminisce *verb* to think and talk about things remembered from the past

reminiscence *noun* **1** something remembered from the past **2** **reminiscences** memories, especially told or written

reminiscent *adjective* reminding (of): *reminiscent of Paris*

remiss *adjective* careless, unthinking

remission *noun* **1** a shortening of a prison sentence **2** a lessening of a disease or illness

remnant *noun* a small piece or number left over

remonstrate *verb* to protest (about)

remorse *noun* regret about something done in the past

remorseful *adjective* full of remorse, sorrowful

remorseless *adjective* having no remorse; cruel

remote *adjective* **1** far away in time or place **2** isolated, far from other people **3** slight: *a remote chance*

remote control 1 the control of devices from a distance, using electrical signals or radio waves **2** a device for transmitting remote control signals

removal noun the act of removing, especially of moving furniture to a new home

remove verb **1** to take (something) from its place **2** to dismiss from a job **3** to take off (clothes etc) **4** to get rid of: remove a stain

remuneration noun pay, salary

renaissance noun **1** a rebirth **2** a period of cultural revival and growth

renal adjective of the kidneys

rend verb to tear (apart), divide

| **rend** ▸ rends, rending, rent

render verb **1** to give (eg thanks) **2** to perform (music etc) **3** to cause to be: his words rendered me speechless

rendering noun a performance

rendezvous (pronounced ron-dei-voo) noun (plural rendezvous – pronounced ron-dei-vooz) **1** a meeting place fixed beforehand **2** an arranged meeting

renegade noun someone who deserts their own side, religion or beliefs

renew verb **1** to make as if new again **2** to begin again: renew your efforts **3** to make valid for a further period (eg a driving licence) **4** to replace ▪ **renewable** adjective

renewal noun renewing or being renewed

renounce verb to give up publicly or formally

renovate verb to make (something) like new again, mend

renovation noun renovating or being renovated

renown noun fame

renowned adjective famous

rent noun payment made for the use of property or land ▪ verb **1** to pay rent for (a house etc) **2** (also **rent something out**) to receive rent for (a house etc)

rental noun money paid as rent

reorganize or **reorganise** verb to put in a different order ▪ **reorganization** noun

rep noun, short for **1** representative: sales rep **2** repertory

repair verb **1** to mend **2** to make up for (a wrong) ▪ noun **1** state, condition: in bad repair **2** mending: in need of repair **3** a mend, a patch

repartee noun an exchange of witty remarks

repatriate verb to send (someone) back to their own country

repay verb **1** to pay back **2** to give or do something in return: he repaid her kindness with a gift

| **repay** ▸ repays, repaying, repaid

repayment noun repaying

repeal verb to do away with, cancel (especially a law)

repeat *verb* **1** to say or do over again **2** to say from memory **3** to pass on (someone's words) ▪ *noun* a musical passage, television programme, *etc* played or shown for a second time
repeatedly *adverb* again and again
repel *verb* **1** to drive back or away **2** to disgust
| **repel** ▸ repels, repelling, repelled
repellent *adjective* disgusting ▪ *noun* something that repels: *insect repellent*
repent *verb* **1** to be sorry for your actions **2** repent of something to regret it
repentance *noun* sorrow and regret for your actions
repentant *adjective* feeling or showing sorrow and regret for your actions
repercussion *noun* an indirect or resultant effect of something which has happened
repertoire *noun* the range of works performed by a musician, theatre company, *etc*
repertory *noun* (*plural* **repertories**) repertoire
repertory theatre a theatre with a permanent company which performs a series of plays
repetition *noun* **1** the act of repeating or being repeated **2** a thing which is repeated
repetitive *adjective* repeating too often, predictable

replace *verb* **1** to put (something) back where it was **2** to put in place of another ▪ **replacement** *noun*
replay *noun* (*pronounced* **ree**-play) **1** a repeat of a contest or game, because there was no winner the first time **2** the playing again of a recording, piece of film, *etc* ▪ *verb* (*pronounced* ree-**play**) to play (a game, recording, *etc*) again
replenish *verb* to refill (a stock, supply)
replete *adjective* full
replica *noun* an exact copy of a work of art
reply *verb* to speak or act in answer to something ▪ *noun* (*plural* **replies**) an answer
| **reply** *verb* ▸ replies, replying, replied
report *verb* **1** to pass on news **2** to give a description of (an event) **3** to give information about events for a newspaper **4** to make a formal complaint against ▪ *noun* **1** a statement of facts **2** an account, a description **3** a news article **4** a rumour **5** a written description of a school pupil's work
reporter *noun* a news journalist
repose *noun*, *formal* sleep, rest ▪ *verb* to rest
repository *noun* (*plural* **repositories**) a storage place for safe keeping
repossess *verb* to take back

(goods, property), especially because of non-payment

reprehensible *adjective* deserving blame

represent *verb* 1 to speak or act on behalf of others 2 to stand for, be a symbol of 3 to claim to be

representation *noun* 1 an image, a picture 2 a strong claim or appeal

representative *adjective* 1 typical, characteristic 2 standing or acting for others ▪ *noun* 1 someone who acts or speaks on behalf of others 2 a travelling salesman for a company

repress *verb* 1 to keep down by force 2 to keep under control

repression *noun* the strict controlling of people, not allowing them to do things such as vote in elections or attend religious worship

repressive *adjective* severe; harsh

reprieve *verb* 1 to pardon (a criminal) 2 to relieve from trouble or difficulty ▪ *noun* a pardon, a relief

reprimand *verb* to scold severely, censure ▪ *noun* scolding, censure

reprint *verb* to print more copies of (a book *etc*) ▪ *noun* another printing of a book

reprisal *noun* a return of wrong for wrong, a repayment in kind

reproach *verb* to scold, blame ▪ *noun* 1 blame, discredit 2 a cause of blame or censure

reproachful *adjective* expressing or full of reproach

reprobate *noun* someone of evil or immoral habits

reproduce *verb* 1 to produce a copy of 2 to produce (children or young)

reproduction *noun* 1 a copy or imitation (especially of a work of art) 2 the act or process of producing (children or young)

reproductive *adjective* involving, or required for, reproduction

reproductive system the system of organs involved with reproduction

reproof *noun* a scolding, criticism for a fault

reprove *verb* to scold, blame

reptile *noun* a creeping, cold-blooded animal, such as a snake, lizard, *etc*

republic *noun* a form of government in which power is in the hands of elected representatives with a president at its head

Republican *adjective* belonging to the more conservative of the two main political parties in the United States

repudiate *verb* to refuse to acknowledge or accept: *repudiate a suggestion*

repugnant *adjective* hateful, distasteful

repulse *verb* 1 to drive back 2 to reject, snub

repulsion *noun* disgust

repulsive *adjective* causing disgust, loathsome

reputable (*pronounced* **rep**-yut-a-bl) *adjective* having a good reputation, well thought of

reputation *noun* **1** opinion held by people in general of a particular person **2** good name

repute *noun* reputation

reputed *adjective* **1** considered, thought (to be something) **2** supposed: *the reputed author of the book*

reputedly *adverb* in the opinion of most people

request *verb* to ask for ▪ *noun* **1** an asking for something **2** something asked for

requiem *noun* a hymn or mass sung for the dead

require *verb* **1** to need **2** to demand, order

requirement *noun* **1** something needed **2** a demand

requisite *adjective* required; necessary

requisition *noun* a formal request for supplies, *eg* for a school or army ▪ *verb* to put in a formal request for

rerun *verb* (*pronounced* ree-**run**) to run again ▪ *noun* (*pronounced* **ree**-run) a repeated television programme

rescue *verb* **1** to save from danger **2** to free from capture ▪ *noun* an act of saving from danger or capture ▪ **rescuer** *noun*

research *noun* (*plural* **researches**) close and careful scientific study to try to find out new facts ▪ *verb* to study carefully ▪ **researcher** *noun*

resemblance *noun* likeness

resemble *verb* to look like or be like

resent *verb* to feel injured, annoyed or insulted by

resentful *adjective* full of or caused by resentment

resentment *noun* annoyance, bitterness

reservation *noun* **1** the act of reserving, booking **2** an exception or condition **3** doubt, objection **4** an area of land set aside by treaty for Native American people in the United States

reserve *verb* **1** to set aside for future use **2** to book, have kept for you (*eg* a seat, a table) ▪ *noun* **1** something reserved **2** an extra person or thing kept to replace or help others **3** a piece of land set apart for some reason: *nature reserve* **4** shyness, reluctance to speak or act openly

reserved *adjective* **1** shy, reluctant to speak openly **2** kept back for a particular person or purpose

reservoir *noun* an artificial lake where water is kept in store

reshuffle *verb* to give people different jobs within (a government cabinet) ▪ *noun* a rearrangement of a cabinet

reside verb to live, stay (in)

residence noun 1 the building where someone lives 2 living, or time of living, in a place

resident noun someone who lives in a particular place ▪ adjective 1 living in (a place) 2 living in a place of work

residential adjective 1 of an area: containing houses rather than shops, offices, etc 2 providing accommodation

residual adjective remaining; left over

residue noun what is left over

resign verb to give up (a job, position, etc) ▪ **resign yourself to** to accept (a situation) patiently and calmly

resignation noun 1 the act of resigning 2 a letter to say you are resigning 3 patient, calm acceptance of a situation

resigned adjective patient, not actively complaining

resilience noun being resilient

resilient adjective able to recover easily from misfortune, hurt, etc

resin noun a sticky substance produced by certain plants (eg firs, pines)

resist verb 1 to struggle against, oppose 2 to stop yourself from (doing something)

resistance noun 1 the act of resisting 2 an organized opposition, especially to an occupying force 3 ability to turn a

passing electrical current into heat 4 physics a force that prevents or slows down motion

resistant adjective able to resist or remain unaffected or undamaged by something

resit verb (pronounced ree-sit) to sit (an examination) again ▪ noun (pronounced ree-sit) a retaking of an examination

| **resit** verb ► resits, resitting, resat

resolute adjective determined, with mind made up ▪ **resolutely** adverb

resolution noun 1 determination of mind or purpose 2 a firm decision (to do something) 3 a proposal put before a meeting 4 a decision expressed by a public meeting

resolve verb 1 to decide firmly (to do something) 2 to solve (a difficulty) 3 to break up into parts ▪ noun a firm purpose

resonance noun a deep, echoing tone

resonant adjective echoing, resounding

resonate verb to echo

resort verb 1 to begin to use 2 to turn (to) in a difficulty ▪ noun a popular holiday destination

resound verb 1 to sound loudly 2 to echo

resounding adjective 1 echoing 2 thorough: a resounding victory

resourceful adjective good at finding ways out of difficulties

resources *noun plural* **1** a source of supplying what is required **2** the natural sources of wealth in a country *etc* **3** money or other property

respect *verb* **1** to feel a high regard for **2** to treat with consideration: *respect his wishes* ∎ *noun* **1** high regard, esteem **2** consideration **3** a detail, a way: *alike in some respects*

respectability *noun* being respectable

respectable *adjective* **1** worthy of respect **2** having a good reputation **3** considerable, fairly good: *a respectable score*

respectful *adjective* showing respect

respective *adjective* belonging to each (person or thing mentioned) separately: *my brother and his friends went to their respective homes* (that is, each went to their own home)

respectively *adverb* in the order given: *Mina, Sonja and Inge finished first, second and third respectively*

respiration *noun* the process by which organisms exchange gases with the environment, *eg* breathing is a form of respiration

respirator *noun* a device to help people breathe when they are too ill to do so naturally

respire *verb* to breathe

respite (*pronounced* res-pait *or* res-pit) *noun* a pause, a rest

resplendent *adjective* very bright or splendid in appearance

respond *verb* **1** to answer **2** to react in response to: *I waved but he didn't respond* **3** to show a positive reaction to: *responding to treatment*

response *noun* **1** a reply **2** an action, feeling, *etc* in answer to another

responsibility *noun* (*plural* **responsibilities**) **1** something or someone for which one is responsible **2** the state of being responsible or having important duties for which one is responsible

responsible *adjective* **1** (sometimes **responsible for something**) being the cause of **2** liable to be blamed (for) **3** involving making important decisions *etc* **4** trustworthy

responsive *adjective* quick to react, to show sympathy, *etc*

rest *noun* **1** a break in work **2** a sleep **3** a support, a prop: *book rest* **4** what is left, the remainder **5** the others, those not mentioned ∎ *verb* **1** to stop working for a time **2** to be still **3** to sleep **4** to lean or place on a support ∎ **rest with** to be the responsibility of: *the choice rests with you*

restaurant *noun* a place where meals may be bought and eaten

restful *adjective* **1** relaxing **2** relaxed

restitution *noun* **1** the return of

what has been lost or taken away **2** compensation for harm or injury done

restive *adjective* restless, impatient

restless *adjective* **1** unable to keep still **2** agitated

restoration *noun* **1** the act of giving back something lost or stolen **2** a model or reconstruction (*eg* of a ruin)

restorative *adjective* curing, giving strength

restore *verb* **1** to put or give back **2** to repair (a building, a painting, *etc*) so that it looks as it used to **3** to cure (a person)

restrain *verb* **1** to hold back (from) **2** to keep under control

restraint *noun* **1** the act of restraining **2** self-control **3** a tie or bond used to restrain

restrict *verb* **1** to limit, keep within certain bounds **2** to open only to certain people

restriction *noun* **1** an act or instance of restricting **2** a regulation or rule which restricts or limits

restrictive *adjective* restricting

result *noun* **1** a consequence of something already done or said **2** the answer to a sum **3** a score in a game ■ *verb* **1** result from something to be the result or effect of it **2** result in something to have it as a result: *result in a draw*

resultant *adjective* happening as a result

resume *verb* **1** to begin again after an interruption **2** to take again: *he resumed his seat*

résumé (*pronounced* rez-yoo-mei) *noun* a summary

resumption *noun* the act of resuming

resurgence *noun* the act of returning to life, to a state of activity, *etc* after a period of decline

resurgent *adjective* rising again, becoming prominent again

resurrect *verb* to bring back to life or into use

resurrection *noun* **1** a rising from the dead **2** Resurrection the rising of Christ from the dead **3** the act of bringing back into use

resuscitate *verb* to bring back to consciousness, revive
■ **resuscitation** *noun*

retail *verb* to sell goods to someone who is going to use them, rather than to another seller (*compare with*: **wholesale**)
■ *noun* the sale of goods to the actual user

retailer *noun* a shopkeeper, a trader

retain *verb* **1** to keep possession of **2** to keep (something) in mind **3** to reserve (someone's services) by paying a fee in advance **4** to hold back, keep in place

retainer *noun* a fee for services paid in advance

retake *verb* to take or capture

again ■ noun the filming of part of a film again

retaliate verb to return like for like, hit back ■ **retaliation** noun

retard verb to keep back, hinder

retarded adjective slow in mental or physical growth

retch verb to make the actions and sound of vomiting, without actually vomiting

retention noun the act of holding in or keeping

retentive adjective able to hold or retain well: retentive memory

reticence noun being reticent

reticent adjective unwilling to speak openly and freely, reserved

retina noun (plural **retinas** or **retinae**) the part of the back of the eye that receives the image of what is seen

retinue noun the attendants of someone important

retire verb 1 to give up work permanently, usually because of age 2 to go to bed 3 to draw back, retreat

retired adjective 1 having given up work 2 out-of-the-way, quiet

retirement noun 1 the act of retiring from work 2 someone's life after they have given up work

retiring adjective shy, avoiding being noticed

retort verb to make a quick and witty reply ■ noun a quick, witty reply

retrace verb to go over again: retrace your steps

retract verb to take back (something said or given)

retractable adjective able to be retracted

retraction noun a retracting (especially of something one has said, agreed or promised)

retreat verb 1 to draw back, withdraw 2 to go away ■ noun 1 a movement backwards corresponding to the advance of an enemy 2 a withdrawal 3 a quiet, peaceful place

retribution noun punishment

retrieve verb 1 to get back, recover (something lost) 2 to search for and fetch

retriever noun a breed of dog trained to find and fetch shot birds

retro adjective recreating the past for effect

retrograde adjective 1 going backwards 2 going from a better to a worse stage

retrospect noun: in retrospect considering or looking back on the past

retrospective adjective 1 looking back on past events 2 of a law: applying to the past as well as the present and the future

return verb 1 to go or come back 2 to give, send, pay, etc back ■ noun 1 the act of returning 2 a profit: a return on your investment 3 a statement of income for calculating income tax

return ticket a ticket which

covers a journey both to and from a place

reunion noun a meeting of people who have been apart for some time

reunite verb to join after having been separated

Rev or **Revd** abbreviation Reverend

rev noun a revolution of an engine ■ verb (often **rev up**) to increase the speed of (an engine)

| **rev** verb ► revs, rev**ving**, rev**ved**

revamp verb to renovate, renew the appearance of

reveal verb 1 to make known 2 to show

reveille (pronounced ri-**val**-i) noun a bugle call at dawn to waken soldiers

revel verb 1 to take great delight (in) 2 to celebrate ■ noun (often **revels**) festivities

| **revel** verb ► revels, revel**ling**, revel**led**

revelation noun 1 the act of revealing 2 something unexpected which is made known

reveller noun a merrymaker, a partygoer

revelry noun noisy lively enjoyment, festivities, or merrymaking

revenge noun 1 harm done to someone in return for harm they themselves have committed 2 the desire to do such harm ■ verb 1 to inflict punishment in return for harm done 2 **revenge oneself** to take revenge: revenged himself on his enemies

revenue noun money received as payment

reverberate verb to echo and re-echo, resound

reverberation noun reverberating

revere verb to look upon with great respect

reverence noun great respect

reverend adjective 1 worthy of respect 2 **Reverend** a title given to a member of the clergy (short form: **Rev** or **Revd**)

reverent or **reverential** adjective showing respect

reverie (pronounced **rev**-e-ri) noun a daydream

reversal noun the act of reversing or being reversed

reverse verb 1 to turn upside down or the other way round 2 to move backwards 3 to undo (a decision, policy, etc) ■ noun 1 the opposite (of) 2 the other side (of a coin etc) 3 a defeat

reversible adjective of clothes: able to be worn with either side out

revert verb to go back to an earlier topic

review verb 1 to give an opinion or criticism of (an artistic work) 2 to consider again ■ noun 1 a critical opinion of a book etc 2 a magazine consisting of reviews 3 a second look, a reconsideration

♠* Do not confuse with: **revue**

reviewer noun someone who reviews, a critic

revile verb to say harsh things about

revise verb 1 to correct faults in and make improvements 2 to study notes etc in preparation for an examination 3 to change (eg an opinion)

revision noun 1 the act of revising 2 a revised version of a book etc

revival noun 1 a return to life, use, etc 2 a fresh show of interest

revive verb to bring or come back to life, use or fame

revoke verb to cancel (a decision etc)

revolt verb 1 to rise up (against), rebel 2 to feel disgust (at) 3 to disgust ■ noun a rising, a rebellion

revolting adjective causing disgust

revolution noun 1 a full turn round a centre 2 the act of turning round a centre 3 a general uprising against those in power 4 a complete change in ideas, way of doing things, etc

revolutionary adjective 1 relating to a revolution 2 bringing about great changes ■ noun (plural **revolutionaries**) someone who is involved in, or is in favour of, revolution

revolutionize or **revolutionise** verb to bring about a complete change in

revolve verb to roll or turn round

revolver noun a kind of pistol

revue noun a light-hearted theatre show, with short topical plays or sketches

♠* Do not confuse with: **review**

revulsion noun disgust

reward noun 1 something given in return for work done or for good behaviour etc 2 a sum of money offered for helping to find a criminal, lost property, etc ■ verb 1 to give a reward to 2 to give a reward for (a service)

rewarding adjective giving pleasure or satisfaction

rewind verb to wind back (a spool, cassette, etc) to the beginning

rewrite verb to write again

rhapsody noun music or poetry which expresses strong feeling

rhesus factor a substance present in most people's blood

rhetoric noun the art of good speaking or writing

rhetorical adjective relating to or using rhetoric

rheumatic adjective relating to or caused by rheumatism

rheumatism noun a disease which causes stiffness and pain in the joints

rhinestone *noun* an artificial diamond

rhino *noun* (*plural* **rhinos**) *short for* **rhinoceros**

rhinoceros *noun* (*plural* **rhinoceros** *or* **rhinoceroses**) a large, thick-skinned animal, with a horn (or two) on its nose (often shortened to **rhino**)

rhododendron *noun* a flowering shrub with thick evergreen leaves and large flowers

rhombus *noun* (*plural* **rhombi** *or* **rhombuses**) a geometrical figure with four equal straight sides

rhubarb *noun* a plant with long red-skinned stalks, edible when cooked

rhyme *noun* **1** a similarity in sounds between words or their endings, *eg humble* and *crumble*, or *convention* and *prevention* **2** a word which sounds like another **3** a short poem ■ *verb* (sometimes **rhyme with**) to sound like, be rhymes: *harp rhymes with carp*

rhythm *noun* **1** a regular repeated pattern of sounds or beats in music or poetry **2** a regularly repeated pattern of movements

rhythmic *or* **rhythmical** *adjective* of or with rhythm

rib *noun* **1** any of the bones which curve round and forward from the backbone, enclosing the heart and lungs **2** a spar of wood in the framework of a boat, curving up from the keel **3** a ridged knitting pattern

ribald *adjective* of a joke *etc*: coarse, vulgar

ribbed *adjective* arranged in ridges and furrows

ribbon *noun* a narrow strip of silk or other material, used for decoration, tying hair, *etc*

rice *noun* the seeds of a plant, grown for food in well-watered ground in tropical countries

rice paper thin edible paper often put under baking to prevent it sticking

rich *adjective* **1** having a lot of money or valuables, wealthy **2** **rich in something** having a lot of it **3** of food: containing a lot of fat, eggs, *etc*

riches *noun plural* wealth

richly *adverb* **1** in a rich or elaborate way **2** fully and suitably: *richly deserved*

richness *noun* being rich

Richter scale (*pronounced* rikh-ter) a scale for measuring the intensity of earthquakes

rickets *noun singular* a children's disease caused by lack of calcium, with softening and bending of the bones

rickety *adjective* unsteady: *a rickety table*

rickshaw *noun* a two-wheeled carriage pulled by a man, used in Japan *etc*

ricochet (*pronounced* rik-osh-ei)

verb of a bullet: to rebound at an angle from a surface

| **ricochet** ► ricochets, ricochet*ing*, ricochet*ed*

rid *verb* to free from, clear of ■ **get rid of** to free yourself of

| **rid** ► ri*ds*, ridd*ing*, rid

riddance *noun*: **good riddance to** I am happy to have got rid of

riddle[1] *noun* **1** a puzzle in the form of a question which describes something in a misleading way **2** something difficult to understand

riddle[2] *verb*: **riddled with** covered with small holes made by: *riddled with woodworm*

ride *verb* **1** to travel on a horse or bicycle, or in a vehicle **2** to travel on and control (a horse) ■ *noun* a journey on horseback, bicycle, *etc* ■ **ride up** of a skirt *etc*: to work itself up out of position

| **ride** *verb* ► rides, rid*ing*, rode, ridden

rider *noun* **1** someone who rides **2** something added to what has already been said

ridge *noun* **1** a raised part between furrows **2** a long crest of high ground

ridicule *verb* to laugh at, mock ■ *noun* mockery

ridiculous *adjective* deserving to be laughed at, very silly

rife *adjective* very common

riff *noun* a short, repeated pattern in a piece of music

riff-raff *noun* worthless people

rifle[1] *verb* **1** to search through and rob **2** to steal

rifle[2] *noun* a gun fired from the shoulder

rift *noun* **1** a crack **2** a disagreement between friends

rig *verb* **1** **rig someone out** to clothe or dress them **2** to fix (an election result) illegally or dishonestly

| **rig** ► rigs, rigg*ing*, rigg*ed*

rigging *noun* ship's spars, ropes, *etc*

right *adjective* **1** on or belonging to the side of the body which in most people has the more skilful hand (*contrasted with:* **left**[1]) **2** correct, true **3** just, good **4** straight ■ *adverb* **1** to or on the right side **2** correctly **3** straight **4** all the way: *right along the pier and back* ■ *noun* **1** something good which ought to be done **2** something you are entitled to **3** the right-hand side, direction, *etc* **4** the conservative side in politics ■ *verb* to mend, set in order

right angle an angle like one of those in a square, an angle of 90°

right-click *verb* to press and release the right-hand button on a computer mouse

righteous *adjective* living a good life; just

rightful *adjective* by right, proper: *the rightful owner*

right-handed *adjective* using

the right hand more easily than the left

right-of-way *noun* a road or path over private land along which people may go as a right

right-wing *adjective* of conservative views in politics

rigid *adjective* 1 not easily bent, stiff 2 strict

rigidity *noun* a rigid state or quality

rigmarole *noun* a long, rambling speech

rigor mortis the stiffening of the body after death

rigorous *adjective* very strict

rigour *noun* strictness; harshness

rile *verb* to anger or annoy

rim *noun* an edge or border, *eg* the top edge of a cup

rind *noun* a thick firm covering, *eg* fruit peel, bacon skin, the outer covering of cheese

ring¹ *noun* 1 a small hoop worn on the finger, on the ear, *etc* 2 a hollow circle 3 an enclosed space for boxing, circus performances, *etc* 4 a small group of people formed for business or criminal purposes ▪ *verb* to encircle, go round

| **ring** *verb* ▶ rings, ringing, ringed

ring² *verb* 1 to make the sound of a bell 2 to strike (a bell *etc*) 3 to telephone ▪ *noun* the sound of a bell being struck

ring *verb* ▶ rings, ringing, rang, rung

ringleader *noun* someone who takes the lead in mischief *etc*

ringlet *noun* a long curl of hair

ringmaster *noun* someone who is in charge of the performance in a circus ring

ring road a road that circles a town *etc* avoiding the centre

rink *noun* a sheet of ice, often artificial, for skating or curling

rinse *verb* 1 to wash lightly to remove soap *etc* 2 to clean (a cup, your mouth, *etc*) by swilling with water ▪ *noun* 1 the act of rinsing 2 liquid colour for the hair

riot *noun* 1 a noisy disturbance by a crowd 2 a striking display: *a riot of colour* 3 a hilarious event ▪ *verb* to take part in a riot ▪ **rioter** *noun*

riotous *adjective* noisy, uncontrolled

rip *verb* 1 to tear apart or off 2 to come apart ▪ *noun* a tear ▪ **rip off** to cheat or swindle

| **rip** *verb* ▶ rips, ripping, ripped

ripe *adjective* 1 of fruit *etc*: ready to be picked or eaten 2 fully developed, mature

ripen *verb* to make or become ripe

ripeness *noun* being ripe

rip-off *noun*, *slang* a cheat, a swindle

riposte *noun* a quick return or reply

ripple *noun* **1** a little wave or movement on the surface of water **2** a soft sound *etc* that rises and falls quickly and gently

rise *verb* **1** to get up from bed **2** to stand up **3** to move upwards **4** of a river: to have its source (in) ▪ *noun* **1** a slope upwards **2** an increase in wages, prices, *etc*

| **rise** *verb* ▸ rises, rising, rose, risen

risible *adjective* laughable

rising *noun* **1** an act of rising **2** a rebellion

risk *noun* a chance of loss or injury; a danger ▪ *verb* **1** to take the chance of **2** to take the chance of losing

risky *adjective* possibly resulting in loss or injury

| **risky** ▸ riskier, riskiest

rissole *noun* a fried cake or ball of minced meat, fish, *etc*

rite *noun* a solemn ceremony, especially a religious one

ritual *noun* a traditional way of carrying out religious worship *etc* ▪ *adjective* relating to a rite or ceremony

ritualistic *adjective* done in a set, unchanging way

rival *noun* someone who tries to equal or beat another ▪ *verb* to try to equal

| **rival** *verb* ▸ rivals, rivalling, rivalled

rivalry *noun* (*plural* **rivalries**) the state of being a rival or rivals

river *noun* a large stream of water flowing across land

rivet *noun* a bolt for fastening plates of metal together ▪ *verb* **1** to fasten with a rivet **2** to fix firmly (someone's attention *etc*)

roach *noun* (*plural* **roaches**) a type of freshwater fish

road *noun* **1** a hard, level surface for vehicles and people **2** a way of getting to (somewhere), a route

road hog a reckless or selfish driver

road movie a film showing the travels of a character or characters

road rage anger directed at other road users by a driver

roadway *noun* the part of a road used by cars *etc*

roadworthy *adjective* (of a vehicle) fit to be used on the road

roam *verb* to wander about

roan *noun* a horse with a dark coat spotted with grey or white

roar *verb* **1** to give a loud, deep sound **2** to laugh loudly **3** to say (something) loudly ▪ *noun* a loud, deep sound or laugh

roast *verb* to cook or be cooked in an oven or over a fire ▪ *adjective* roasted: *roast beef* ▪ *noun* **1** meat roasted **2** meat for roasting

rob *verb* to steal from

| **rob** ▸ robs, robbing, robbed

robber *noun* a person who robs; a thief

robbery noun (plural **robberies**) the act of stealing

robe noun 1 a long loose garment 2 US a dressing-gown 3 **robes** the official dress of a judge etc

robin noun a type of small bird, known by its red breast

robot noun 1 a mechanical man or woman 2 a machine that can do the work of a person

robotic adjective relating to or characteristic of robots

robust adjective strong, healthy

rock noun 1 a large lump of stone 2 a hard sweet made in sticks 3 music music with a heavy beat and simple melody (also called: **rock music**) ▪ verb to sway backwards and forwards or from side to side

rock-and-roll or **rock'n'roll** noun a simpler, earlier form of rock music

rock cake a small rough-textured cake

rocker noun a curved support on which a chair, cradle, etc rocks

rockery noun (plural **rockeries**) a collection of stones amongst which small plants are grown

rocket noun 1 a tube containing inflammable materials, used for launching a spacecraft, signalling and as a firework 2 a spacecraft ▪ verb to move upwards rapidly: prices are rocketing

rocking chair a chair which rocks backwards and forwards on rockers

rocking horse a toy horse which rocks backwards and forwards on rockers

rocky adjective 1 full of rocks 2 inclined to rock, unsteady

|**rocky** ► rockier, rockiest

rod noun 1 a long thin stick 2 a fishing rod

rode past form of ride

rodent noun a gnawing animal, such as a rat, beaver, etc

rodeo noun (plural **rodeos**) 1 a round-up of cattle for marking 2 a show of riding by cowboys

roe noun 1 the eggs of fishes 2 (also **roe deer**) a small kind of deer

rogue noun a dishonest or mischievous person, a rascal

roguery noun dishonesty; mischief

roguish adjective characteristic of a rogue; mischievous, dishonest

role or **rôle** noun a part played by an actor

roll verb 1 to move along by turning over like a wheel 2 of a ship: to rock from side to side 3 of thunder etc: to rumble 4 to wrap round and round: roll up a carpet ▪ noun 1 a sheet of paper, length of cloth, etc rolled into a cylinder 2 a very small loaf of bread 3 a rocking movement 4 a list of names 5 a long, rumbling sound

rollcall noun the calling of names from a list

roller noun 1 a cylindrical tool for flattening 2 a tube over which hair is rolled and styled 3 a small solid wheel 4 a long heavy wave on the sea

rollerblades noun plural rollerskates with the wheels in a single line

rollerskates noun plural skates with wheels at each corner of the shoe

rollicking adjective noisy and full of fun

rolling pin a roller for flattening dough

rolling stock the stock of engines, carriages, etc that run on a railway

Roman adjective of a number: written in letters, as I, II, III, IV, etc for 1, 2, 3, 4, etc

Roman Catholic Church the Church whose head is the Pope, with its headquarters in Rome

romance noun 1 a love affair 2 a love story 3 an atmosphere of excitement, adventure and mystery

romantic adjective 1 of romance 2 full of feeling and imagination 3 relating to love

Romany noun (plural **Romanies**) 1 a Gypsy 2 the Gypsy language

romp verb 1 to play in a lively way 2 to move quickly and easily ▪ noun a lively game

rompers noun plural a short suit for a baby

roof noun (plural **roofs**) 1 the top

covering of a building, car, etc 2 the upper part of the mouth

rook noun 1 a kind of crow 2 chess the castle

room noun 1 an inside compartment in a house 2 space: room for everybody

roomy adjective having plenty of space

| **roomy** ► roomi**er**, roomi**est**

roost noun a perch on which a bird rests at night ▪ verb to sit or sleep on a roost

rooster noun a farmyard cock

root noun 1 the underground part of a plant 2 the base of anything, eg a tooth 3 a cause, a source 4 a word from which other words have developed ▪ verb 1 to form roots and begin to grow 2 to be fixed 3 of an animal: to turn up ground in a search for food 4 to search (about) ▪ **root out** or **root up** 1 to tear up by the roots 2 to get rid of completely

rope noun 1 a thick cord, made by twisting strands together 2 anything resembling a thick cord ▪ verb 1 to fasten or catch with a rope 2 to enclose, mark off with a rope

ropy adjective, informal bad, not well

| **ropy** ► ropi**er**, ropi**est**

rosary noun (plural **rosaries**) 1 a set of prayers 2 a string of beads used in saying prayers

rose¹ past form of **rise**

rose² noun 1 a type of flower,

often scented, usually growing on a prickly bush **2** a deep pink colour

rosé noun a pink-coloured wine produced by removing red grape-skins during fermentation

rosehip noun the fruit of the rose

rosemary noun an evergreen sweet-smelling shrub, used as a cooking herb

rosette noun a badge shaped like a rose, made of ribbons

roster noun a list showing a repeated order of duties *etc*

rostrum noun (plural **rostrums** or **rostra**) a platform for public speaking

rosy adjective **1** red, pink **2** (of the future *etc*) bright, hopeful

| **rosy** ▶ rosier, rosiest

rot verb to go bad, decay ■ noun **1** decay **2** informal nonsense

| **rot** verb ▶ rots, rotting, rotted

rota noun a list of duties *etc* to be repeated in a set order

rotary adjective turning round like a wheel

rotate verb **1** to turn round like a wheel **2** to go through a repeating series of changes

rotation noun **1** an act of rotating or state of being rotated **2** maths a transformation involving a turn around an axis (compare with: **enlargement**, **reflection**, **translation**) **3** a regular and recurring sequence

rote noun: **by rote** off by heart, automatically

rotor noun a turning part of a motor, dynamo, *etc*

rotten adjective **1** decayed, bad **2** worthless, disgraceful

rotter noun, informal a very bad, worthless person

rotund adjective round; plump

rouble or **ruble** noun a standard unit of Russian coinage

rouge noun a powder or cream used to add colour to the cheeks

rough adjective **1** not smooth **2** uneven **3** coarse, harsh **4** boisterous, wild **5** not exact: *a rough guess* **6** stormy ■ noun **1** a hooligan, a bully **2** rough ground

roughage noun bran or fibre in food

roughen verb to make rough

roulette noun a gambling game, played with a ball which is placed on a wheel

round adjective **1** shaped like a circle **2** plump **3** even, exact: *a round dozen* ■ adverb & preposition **1** on all sides (of), around **2** in a circle (about) **3** from one (person, place, *etc*) to another ■ noun **1** a circle, something round in shape **2** a single bullet or shell **3** a burst of firing, cheering, *etc* **4** a usual route: *a postman's round* **5** a series of regular activities **6** each stage of a contest ■ verb **1** to make or become round **2** to go round (*eg* a headland) ■ **round on** to make a sudden attack on

■ **round up** to gather or drive together

roundabout noun 1 a revolving machine for children to ride on in a park etc 2 a meeting place of roads, where traffic must move in a circle ■ adjective not straight or direct

rounders noun singular a ball game played with a bat in which players run around a series of stations

Roundhead noun a supporter of Parliament during the English Civil War

roundly adverb boldly, plainly

round trip a journey to a place and back

rouse verb 1 to awaken 2 to stir up, excite

rousing adjective stirring, exciting

rout noun a complete defeat ■ verb to defeat utterly

route noun the course to be followed, a way of getting to somewhere

routine noun a fixed, unchanging order of doing things ■ adjective regular, usual

rove verb to wander or roam

rover noun a wanderer; an unsettled person

Rover Scout an older member of the Scout Association

row[1] (pronounced roh) noun a line of people or things ■ verb to drive (a boat) by oars

row[2] (pronounced row) noun 1 a noisy quarrel 2 a noise

rowan noun a tree with clusters of bright red berries

rowdy adjective noisy, disorderly

| **rowdy** ► rowdier, rowdiest

rower noun someone who rows a boat

rowing boat a boat rowed by oars

royal adjective relating to a king or queen

royal blue a deep, bright blue

royalty noun (plural royalties) 1 the state of being royal 2 royal people as a whole 3 a sum paid to the author of a book for each copy sold

RSVP abbreviation please reply (from French répondez, s'il vous plaît)

rub verb 1 to move one thing against the surface of another 2 to clean, polish (something) 3 rub out to remove (a mark) ■ noun 1 the act of rubbing 2 a wipe ■ rub in 1 to work into (a surface) by rubbing 2 to keep reminding someone of (something unpleasant)

| **rub** verb ► rubs, rubbing, rubbed

rubber noun 1 a tough elastic substance made from plant juices 2 a piece of rubber used for erasing pencil marks

rubber stamp an instrument with rubber figures or letters for stamping dates etc on paper

rubbish *noun* **1** waste material, litter **2** nonsense

rubble *noun* small rough stones, bricks, *etc* left from a building

rubella *noun* German measles

ruble *another spelling of* **rouble**

ruby *noun* (*plural* **rubies**) a type of red precious stone

ruck *noun* a wrinkle, a crease

rucksack *noun* a bag carried on the back by walkers, climbers, *etc*

ruckus *noun*, *US* an uproar, a rumpus

ructions *noun plural* a row, a disturbance

rudder *noun* a device fixed to the stern of a boat, or tail of an aeroplane, for steering

ruddy *adjective* **1** red **2** of the face: rosy, in good health

rude *adjective* **1** showing bad manners, not polite **2** roughly made **3** rough, not refined **4** startling and sudden: *a rude awakening* **5** coarse, vulgar, lewd ■ **rudely** *adverb*

rudimentary *adjective* in an early stage of development

rudiments *noun plural* the first simple rules or facts of anything

rue *verb* to be sorry for, regret

rueful *adjective* sorrowful, regretful

ruff *noun* **1** in the past, a pleated frill worn round the neck **2** a band of feathers round a bird's neck

ruffian *noun* a rough, brutal person

ruffle *verb* **1** to make unsmooth, crumple (*eg* hair, a bird's feathers) **2** to annoy, offend

rug *noun* **1** a floor mat **2** a blanket

rugby *or* **Rugby** *noun* a form of football using an oval ball which can be handled

rugged *adjective* **1** having a rough, uneven appearance **2** strong, robust

ruin *noun* **1** complete loss of money *etc* **2** a downfall **3** ruins broken-down remains of buildings ■ *verb* **1** to destroy **2** to spoil completely: *ruin your chances* **3** to make very poor

ruination *noun* the act of ruining or state of being ruined

ruined *adjective* in ruins, destroyed

ruinous *adjective* likely to cause ruin

rule *noun* **1** government **2** a regulation **3** what usually happens **4** a guiding principle **5** *maths* a procedure **6** a measuring ruler ■ *verb* **1** to govern, be in power **2** to decide (that) **3** to mark with lines ■ **rule out** to leave out, not consider

ruler *noun* **1** someone who rules **2** a marked tool for measuring length and drawing straight lines

ruling *adjective* governing; most important ■ *noun* a decision, a rule

rum¹ *noun* an alcoholic spirit made from sugar cane

rum² *adjective*, *informal* strange, odd

rumble verb to make a low rolling noise like that of thunder etc ■ noun a low rolling noise

ruminate verb to be deep in thought

rummage verb to turn things over in search ■ noun a thorough search

rummy noun a card game played with hands each of seven cards

rumour noun 1 general talk 2 a story passed from person to person which may not be true ■ verb 1 to spread a rumour of 2 to tell widely

rump noun 1 the hind part of an animal 2 the meat from this part

rumple verb 1 to make untidy 2 to crease

rumpus noun an uproar, a clamour

run verb 1 to move swiftly, hurry 2 to race 3 to travel: the train runs every day 4 of water: to flow 5 to follow a certain route: the main road running between Liverpool and Manchester 6 of a machine: to work 7 to spread (rapidly): this colour is running 8 to continue, extend 9 to operate (machinery etc) 10 to organize, conduct (a business etc) ■ noun 1 a trip 2 a distance run 3 a spell of running 4 a continuous period 5 a ladder in a stocking etc 6 free use of: the run of the house 7 a single score in cricket 8 an enclosure for hens etc ■ **run down 1** to knock (someone) down 2 to speak ill of

■ **run into 1** to bump into, collide with 2 to meet accidentally ■ **run out of** to become short of ■ **run over** to knock down or pass over with a car

┃run verb ▶ runs, running, ran, run

runaway noun a person who runs away ■ adjective of an animal or vehicle: out of control and moving very fast

run-down adjective in poor health or condition

rune noun a letter of an early alphabet used in ancient writings

rung[1] noun a step of a ladder

rung[2] past participle of **ring**[2]

runner noun 1 someone who runs 2 a blade of a skate or sledge

runner-up noun (plural **runners-up**) someone who comes second in a race or competition

running noun 1 the act of moving fast 2 management, control ■ adjective 1 for use in running 2 giving out fluid: running sore 3 carried on continuously: running commentary ■ adverb one after another

runny adjective 1 running with liquid 2 too watery 3 of the nose: discharging mucus

┃runny ▶ runnier, runniest

run-of-the-mill adjective ordinary

runway noun a path for aircraft to take off from or land on

rupee noun the standard

currency of India, Pakistan and Sri Lanka

rupture *noun* **1** a breaking, *eg* of a friendship **2** a tear in a part of the body ■ *verb* to break, burst

rural *adjective* of the country (*contrasted with*: **urban**)

ruse *noun* a trick, a cunning plan

rush[1] *verb* **1** to move quickly, hurry **2** to make (someone) hurry **3** to take (a fort *etc*) by a sudden attack ■ *noun* (*plural* **rushes**) **1** a quick forward movement **2** a hurry

rush[2] *noun* (*plural* **rushes**) a tall grasslike plant growing near water

rusk *noun* a hard dry biscuit like toast

russet *adjective* reddish-brown ■ *noun* a type of apple of russet colour

rust *noun* a reddish-brown coating on metal, caused by air and moisture ■ *verb* to form rust

rustic *adjective* **1** relating to the country **2** roughly made **3** simple, unsophisticated ■ *noun* someone who lives in the country

rustle *verb* **1** of silk *etc*: to make a soft, whispering sound **2** to steal (cattle) **3** **rustle something up** *informal* to prepare it quickly ■ *noun* a soft, whispering sound

rustler *noun* someone who steals cattle

rusty *adjective* **1** covered with rust **2** *informal* showing lack of practice

rut *noun* a deep track made by a wheel *etc* ■ **in a rut** having a dull, routine way of life

ruthless *adjective* without pity, cruel

rye *noun* a kind of grain

S

Sabbath *noun* the day of the week regularly set aside for religious services and rest (among Muslims, Friday; Jews, Saturday; Christians, Sunday)

sable *noun* a small weasel-like animal with dark brown or blackish fur ▪ *adjective* black or dark brown in colour

sabotage (*pronounced* sab-ot-ahsz) *noun* deliberate destruction of machinery, of an organization, *etc* by enemies or dissatisfied workers ▪ *verb* to destroy or damage deliberately

saboteur *noun* someone who carries out sabotage

sabre *noun*, *history* a curved sword used by cavalry

saccharin *or* **saccharine** *noun* a very sweet substance used as a sugar substitute

sachet (*pronounced* sash-ei) *noun* a small sealed packet containing powder or liquid, *eg* shampoo

sack *noun* **1** a large bag of coarse cloth for holding flour *etc* **2 the sack** *informal* dismissal from your job ▪ *verb*, *informal* to dismiss from a job

sacrament *noun* a religious ceremony, *eg* baptism or communion

sacred *adjective* **1** holy **2** religious

sacrifice *noun* **1** the offering of an animal killed for the purpose to a god **2** an animal *etc* offered to a god **3** the giving up of something for the benefit of another person, or to gain something more important **4** something given up for this purpose ▪ *verb* **1** to offer (an animal *etc*) as a sacrifice to a god **2** to give up (something) for someone or something else

sacrificial *adjective* of or for sacrifice

sacrilege *noun* the use of something holy in a disrespectful way ▪ **sacrilegious** *adjective*

sacrosanct *adjective* **1** very sacred **2** not to be harmed or touched

sad *adjective* **1** sorrowful, unhappy **2** showing sorrow **3** causing sorrow **4** *informal* pitiful, feeble

sadden *verb* to make or become sad

saddle noun a seat for a rider on the back of a horse or bicycle ▪ verb to put a saddle on (an animal) ▪ **saddle with** to burden with

sadist noun someone who gets pleasure from inflicting pain and suffering on others

safari noun an expedition for observing or hunting wild animals

safari park an enclosed area where wild animals are kept outdoors and on view to visitors

safe adjective 1 unharmed 2 free from harm or danger 3 reliable, trustworthy ▪ noun a box that can be locked for keeping money and valuables

safeguard noun anything that gives protection or security ▪ verb to protect

safety noun freedom from harm or danger

safety belt a seat belt

safety pin a curved pin in the shape of a clasp, with a guard covering its point

saffron noun a type of crocus from which is obtained a yellow food dye and flavouring agent

sag verb to droop or sink in the middle

| sag ▶ sags, sagging, sagged

saga noun 1 an ancient story about heroes etc 2 a novel or series of novels about several generations of a family 3 a long detailed story

sage noun 1 a type of herb with grey-green leaves which are used for flavouring 2 a wise man ▪ adjective wise ▪ **sagely** adverb

sago noun a white starchy substance obtained from a palm-tree, often used in puddings

said adjective mentioned before: the said shopkeeper ▪ verb, past form of say

sail noun 1 a sheet of canvas spread out to catch the wind and drive forward a ship or boat 2 a journey in a ship or boat 3 an arm of a windmill ▪ verb 1 to travel in a ship or boat (with or without sails) 2 to navigate or steer a ship or boat 3 to begin a sea voyage 4 to glide along easily

sailor noun 1 someone who sails 2 a member of a ship's crew

saint noun 1 a very good or holy person 2 a title conferred after death on a holy person by the Roman Catholic Church (short form: **St**)

Saint Bernard or **St Bernard** a breed of large dog, famous for its use in mountain rescues

saintly adjective 1 relating to a saint or the saints 2 very good or holy

sake noun 1 cause, purpose: for the sake of making money 2 benefit, advantage: for my sake

salaam noun a low bow with the right palm on the forehead, a form of greeting in the Arab world

salad noun a dish of raw vegetables, eg lettuce, cucumber, etc

salamander noun a kind of small lizard-like animal

salami noun a type of highly seasoned sausage

salary noun (plural **salaries**) fixed wages regularly paid for work

salat noun the prayers said by Muslims five times daily

sale noun **1** the exchange of anything for money **2** a selling of goods at reduced prices **3** an auction

salesman, **saleswoman** noun someone who sells or shows goods to customers

saline adjective containing salt; salty: saline solution

saliva noun the liquid that forms in the mouth to help digestion

sallow adjective of complexion: pale, yellowish

sally noun (plural **sallies**) **1** a sudden rush forward **2** a trip, an excursion **3** a witty remark or retort ▪ verb to rush out suddenly

▪ **sally forth** to go out, emerge

| **sally** verb ▶ sallies, sallying, sallied

salmon noun a large fish with yellowish-pink flesh

salmonella noun a bacterium which causes food poisoning

salon noun **1** a shop in which hairdressing etc is done **2** a large room for receiving important guests **3** a gathering of such people

saloon noun **1** a passengers' dining-room in a ship **2** a covered-in car **3** a public house, a bar

salt noun **1** a substance used for seasoning, either mined from the earth or obtained from sea water **2** a substance formed from a metal and an acid ▪ adjective **1** containing salt: salt water **2** tasting of salt **3** preserved in salt: salt herring ▪ verb **1** to sprinkle with salt **2** to preserve with salt

salt cellar a small container for salt

salty adjective tasting of salt

salute verb **1** to greet with words, an embrace, etc **2** military to raise the hand to the forehead to show respect to **3** to honour someone by a firing of guns etc ▪ noun an act or way of saluting

salvage noun **1** goods saved from destruction or waste **2** the act of saving a ship's cargo, goods from a fire, etc **3** payment made for this act ▪ verb to save from loss or ruin

salvation noun **1** an act, means or cause of saving **2** the saving of humanity from sin

salve noun an ointment for healing or soothing ▪ verb to soothe (pride, conscience, etc)

same adjective **1** exactly alike, identical **2** not different, unchanged **3** mentioned before:

the same person came again
■ *pronoun* the thing just mentioned

sameness *noun* lack of change or variety

sample *noun* a small part extracted to show what the whole is like ■ *verb* **1** to test a sample of **2** *music* to mix (a short extract) from one recording into a different backing track

sampler *noun* **1** someone who samples **2** a piece of needlework *etc* showing skill in different techniques

sanatorium *noun* **1** a hospital, especially for people suffering from lung diseases **2** a sick-room in a school *etc*

sanction *noun* **1** permission, approval **2** a penalty for breaking a law or rule **3 sanctions** measures applied to force another country *etc* to stop a course of action

sanctity *noun* holiness; sacredness

sanctuary *noun* (*plural* **sanctuaries**) **1** a sacred place **2** the most sacred part of a temple or church **3** a place of safety from arrest or violence **4** a protected reserve for birds or animals

sand *noun* **1** a mass of tiny particles of crushed rocks *etc* **2 sands** a stretch of sand on the seashore ■ *verb* **1** to sprinkle with sand **2** to add sand to **3** to smooth or polish with sandpaper

sandal *noun* a shoe with straps to hold the sole onto the foot

sandalwood *noun* a fragrant E Indian wood

sand dune a ridge of sand blown up by the wind

sandpaper *noun* paper with a layer of sand glued to it for smoothing and polishing

sandshoe *noun* a light shoe with a rubber sole

sandstone *noun* a soft rock made of layers of sand pressed together

sandwich *noun* (*plural* **sandwiches**) two slices of bread, or a split roll, stuffed with a filling ■ *verb* to fit between two other objects

sandy *adjective* **1** covered with sand **2** like sand **3** of hair: yellowish-red in colour

sane *adjective* **1** of sound mind, not mad **2** sensible ■ **sanely** *adverb*

sang *past form of* sing

sanguine *adjective* **1** hopeful, cheerful **2** of a complexion: red, ruddy

sanitary *adjective* **1** promoting good health, especially by having good drainage and sewage disposal **2** free from dirt, infection, *etc*

sanitation *noun* arrangements for protecting health, especially drainage and sewage disposal

sanity *noun* **1** soundness of mind **2** mental health **3** good sense or judgement

sank *past form* of **sink**

Sanskrit *noun* the ancient literary language of India

sap *noun* **1** the juice in plants, trees, *etc* **2** *informal* a weakling, a fool ■ *verb* to weaken (someone's strength *etc*)

| **sap** *verb* ► saps, sapp*ing*, sapp*ed*

sapling *noun* a young tree

sapphire *noun* a precious stone of a deep blue colour

sarcasm *noun* **1** scornful humour, characterized by the use of a mocking tone to say the exact opposite of what you really think **2** a hurtful remark made in scorn

sarcastic *adjective* **1** of a remark: containing sarcasm **2** often using sarcasm, scornful ■ **sarcastically** *adverb*

sardine *noun* a young pilchard, often tinned in oil ■ **like sardines** crowded closely together

sardonic *adjective* bitter, mocking, scornful

sari *noun* a long cloth wrapped round the waist and brought over the shoulder, traditionally worn by Indian women

sarong *noun* a skirt traditionally worn by Malay men and women

sash[1] *noun* (*plural* **sashes**) a decorative band worn round the waist or over the shoulder

sash[2] *noun* (*plural* **sashes**) a sliding frame for window panes

sat *past form* of **sit**

Satan *noun* the Devil

Satanic *adjective* of Satan, devilish

satchel *noun* a small bag for carrying schoolbooks *etc*

satellite *noun* **1** a moon orbiting a larger planet **2** a man-made object launched into space to orbit a planet **3** a state controlled by a more powerful neighbour

satellite television the broadcasting of television programmes via satellite

satin *noun* a closely woven silk with a glossy surface

satire *noun* **1** a piece of writing *etc* which makes fun of particular people or events **2** ridicule, scorn

satirical *adjective* containing or using satire to attack or criticize someone or something

satisfaction *noun* **1** the act of satisfying or being satisfied **2** a feeling of pleasure or comfort **3** something that satisfies **4** compensation for damage *etc*

satisfactory *adjective* **1** satisfying **2** fulfilling the necessary requirements ■ **satisfactorily** *adverb*

satisfy *verb* **1** to give enough (of something) to **2** to please, make content **3** to give enough to lessen or quieten: *satisfied her curiosity* **4** to convince **5** to fulfil: *satisfy all our requirements*

| **satisfy** ► satisf*ies*, satisf*ying*, satisf*ied*

satsuma *noun* a small seedless orange

saturate *verb* **1** to soak or immerse in water **2** to cover or fill completely (with): *saturated with information*

saturated *adjective* **1** soaked in water **2** of a compound: unable to be combined with any other atoms **3** of a solution: unable to dissolve any more of a solute (*contrasted with:* **unsaturated**)

saturation *noun* saturating or being saturated: *the market has reached saturation point*

Saturday *noun* the seventh day of the week

sauce *noun* **1** a liquid seasoning added to food to improve flavour **2** *informal* cheek, impudence

saucepan *noun* a deep-sided cooking pan with a long handle

saucer *noun* a small, shallow dish for placing under a cup

saucy *adjective* impudent, cheeky

sauna *noun* a room filled with dry steam to induce sweating

saunter *verb* to stroll about without hurrying ■ *noun* a leisurely stroll

sausage *noun* minced meat seasoned and stuffed into a tube of animal gut *etc*

savage *adjective* **1** wild, untamed **2** fierce and cruel **3** uncivilized **4** very angry ■ *noun* **1** an uncivilized person **2** someone fierce or cruel ■ *verb* to attack very fiercely ■ **savagely** *adverb*

savagery *noun* extreme cruelty or fierceness

savanna or **savannah** *noun* a grassy, treeless plain

save *verb* **1** to bring out of danger, rescue **2** to protect from harm, damage or loss **3** to keep from spending or using: *saving money/ saves time* **4** to put money aside for the future ■ **save up** to put money aside for future use

savings *noun plural* money put aside for the future

saviour *noun* **1** someone who saves others from harm or evil **2** **the Saviour** Jesus Christ

savour *noun* **1** characteristic taste or flavour **2** an interesting quality ■ *verb* **1** to taste or smell of **2** to taste with enjoyment

savoury *adjective* **1** having a pleasant taste or smell **2** salt or sharp in flavour; not sweet ■ *noun* (*plural* **savouries**) a savoury dish or snack

savoy *noun* a type of winter cabbage

saw¹ *noun* a tool with a toothed edge for cutting wood *etc* ■ *verb* to cut with a saw

| **saw** *verb* ▶ saws, sawing, sawed, sawn

saw² *past form of* **see**

sawdust *noun* a dust of fine fragments of wood, made in sawing

Saxon *noun*, *history* one of a Germanic people who invaded Britain in the 5th century

saxophone *noun* a wind instrument with a curved metal tube and keys for the fingers

saxophonist *noun* a player of the saxophone

say *verb* **1** to speak, utter **2** to express in words, state ▪ *noun* **1** the right to speak: *no say in the matter* **2** the opportunity to speak: *I've had my say*

| **say** *verb* ► says, saying, said

saying *noun* something often said; a proverb

scab *noun* **1** a crust formed over a sore **2** *informal* a blackleg

scabbard *noun* the sheath in which the blade of a sword is kept

scabby *adjective* **1** covered in scabs **2** *informal* disgusting, revolting

scabies *noun* an itchy skin disease

scaffold *noun* a platform on which people are put to death

scaffolding *noun* a framework of poles and platforms used by people doing repairs on a building *etc*

scalar *noun*, *maths* a quantity, *eg* mass, length or speed, that has magnitude but not direction (*compare with:* **vector**)

scald *verb* to burn with hot liquid or steam ▪ *noun* a burn caused by hot liquid or steam

scale *noun* **1** a set of regularly spaced marks for measurement on a thermometer *etc* **2** a series or system of increasing values **3** *music* a group of notes going up or down in order **4** the measurements of a map compared with the actual size of the area shown **5** the size of a business *etc* **6** a small thin flake on the skin of a fish or snake **7 scales** a weighing machine ▪ *verb* **1** to climb up **2** to remove the scales from (*eg* a fish) **3** to remove in thin layers

scalene *adjective* of a triangle: having each side of a different length

scallop *noun* a shellfish with a pair of hinged fan-shaped shells

scalloped *adjective* of an edge: cut into curves or notches

scallywag *noun* a rogue

scalp *noun* **1** the outer covering of the skull **2** the skin and hair on top of the head ▪ *verb* to cut the scalp from

scalpel *noun* a small, thin-bladed knife, used in surgery

scaly *adjective* having scales; flaky

scamp *noun* a rascal

scamper *verb* **1** to run about playfully **2** to run off in haste

scampi *noun plural* large prawns cooked for eating

scan *verb* **1** to count the beats in a line of poetry **2** of poetry: to have the correct number of beats **3** to examine carefully **4** *informal* to read quickly, skim over **5** to create an image of part of the body as an aid to medical examination

■ *noun* an act of scanning

|scan *verb* ► scans, scanning, scanned

scandal *noun* **1** something disgraceful or shocking **2** talk or gossip about people's (supposed) misdeeds

scandalize *or* **scandalise** *verb* to shock, horrify

scandalous *adjective* **1** shameful, disgraceful **2** containing scandal

■ **scandalously** *adverb*

scanner *noun* a machine which scans, eg a device for scanning and recording graphic images so that they can be edited or viewed on a computer

scant *adjective* not plentiful, hardly enough: *pay scant attention*

scanty *adjective* little or not enough in amount ■ **scantily** *adverb*

scapegoat *noun* someone who bears the blame for the wrongdoing of others

scar *noun* **1** the mark left by a wound or sore **2** a mark, a blemish ■ *verb* to mark with a scar

|scar *verb* ► scars, scarring, scarred

scarce *adjective* **1** not plentiful, not enough **2** rare, seldom found

scarcely *adverb* **1** only just, barely **2** surely not: *you can scarcely expect me to eat that*

scarcity *noun* (*plural* **scarcities**) want, shortage

scare *verb* **1** to drive away with fear **2** to startle, frighten ■ *noun* a sudden fright or alarm

scarecrow *noun* a figure set up to scare birds away from crops

scarey *another spelling of* **scary**

scarf *noun* (*plural* **scarves** *or* **scarfs**) a strip of material worn round the neck, shoulders or head

scarlet *noun* a bright red colour ■ *adjective* bright red

scarlet fever an infectious illness, causing a rash

scarper *verb, slang* to run away

scary *or* **scarey** *adjective* frightening

scathing *adjective* cruel, hurtful: *scathing remark*

scatter *verb* **1** to throw loosely about; sprinkle **2** to spread widely **3** to flee in all directions

scatterbrain *noun* someone who frequently forgets things

scattered *adjective* thrown or spread about widely

scattering *noun* a small amount thinly spread or scattered

scavenge *verb* to search among waste for useful or valuable items

scavenger *noun* an animal which feeds on dead flesh

scenario (*pronounced* si-**nah**-ri-oh) *noun* **1** a scene-by-scene outline of a play, film, *etc* **2** an outline of a plan or project

♦* Do not confuse with: **scene**

scene noun 1 the place where something happens 2 a view, a landscape 3 a division of a play or opera 4 an area of activity: *the music scene* 5 a show of bad temper: *don't make a scene*

🔸 Do not confuse with: **scenario**

scenery noun 1 the painted background on a theatre stage 2 the general appearance of a stretch of country

scenic adjective 1 of scenery 2 picturesque

scent verb 1 to discover by the smell 2 to have a suspicion of, sense: *scent danger* 3 to give a pleasant smell to ▪ noun 1 perfume 2 an odour, a smell 3 the trail of smell used to track an animal *etc*

sceptic (pronounced skep-tik) noun someone who doubts what they are told

🔸 Do not confuse with: **septic**

sceptical (pronounced skep-tik-al) adjective unwilling to believe, doubtful

sceptre (pronounced sep-ter) noun an ornamental rod carried by a monarch on ceremonial occasions

schedule (pronounced shed-yool or sked-yool) noun 1 the time set for doing something 2 a written statement of details 3 a form for filling in information

▪ verb 1 to form into a schedule 2 to plan, arrange

scheme noun 1 a plan, a systematic arrangement 2 a dishonest or crafty plan ▪ verb to make schemes, plot

scheming adjective crafty, cunning

schism (pronounced si-zm or ski-zm) noun a breaking away from the main group

scholar noun 1 someone of great learning 2 someone who has been awarded a scholarship 3 a pupil, a student

scholarly adjective showing or having knowledge, high intelligence and love of accuracy

scholarship noun 1 learning 2 a sum of money given to help a student to carry on further studies

scholastic adjective of schools or scholars

school noun 1 a place for teaching, especially children 2 a group of artists *etc* who share the same ideas 3 a large number of fish, whales, *etc* ▪ verb 1 to educate in a school 2 to train by practice

schooling noun 1 education in a school 2 training

schoolmaster, **schoolmistress** noun a teacher at a school

schooner noun a two-masted sailing ship

science noun 1 knowledge obtained by observation and

experiment **2** a branch of this knowledge, *eg* chemistry, physics, biology, *etc* **3** these sciences considered together

science fiction stories dealing with future life on earth, space travel, other planets, *etc*

scientific *adjective* **1** of science **2** done according to the methods of science ▪ **scientifically** *adverb*

scientist *noun* someone who studies one or more branches of science

sci-fi *abbreviation* science fiction

scimitar *noun* a sword with a curved blade

scissors *noun plural* a cutting instrument with two hinged blades

scoff¹ *verb* to express scorn

scoff² *verb, slang* to eat greedily

scold *verb* to tell off; blame or rebuke with angry words

scolding *noun* a telling-off

scone *noun* a small plain cake made with flour, milk and a little fat

scoop *noun* **1** a hollow instrument used for lifting loose material, water, *etc* **2** an exclusive news story ▪ *verb* to lift or dig out with a scoop

scooter *noun* **1** a two-wheeled toy vehicle pushed along by foot **2** a low-powered motorcycle

scope *noun* **1** opportunity or room to do something **2** extent, range

scorch *verb* **1** to burn slightly,

singe **2** to dry up with heat

scorching *adjective* **1** burning, singeing **2** very hot **3** harsh, severe

score *noun* **1** a gash, a notch **2** an account, a debt: *settle old scores* **3** the total number of points gained in a game **4** a written piece of music showing separate parts for voices and instruments **5** a set of twenty **6** scores a great many **7** a reason, account: *don't worry on that score* ▪ *verb* **1** to mark with lines or notches **2** to gain (points) **3** to keep a note of points gained in a game ▪ **score out** to cross out

scorn *verb* **1** to look down on, despise **2** to refuse (help *etc*) because of pride ▪ *noun* mocking contempt

scornful *adjective* full of scorn ▪ **scornfully** *adverb*

scorpion *noun* an eight-legged creature with a poisonous sting in its tail

scot-free *adjective* unhurt; unpunished

scoundrel *noun* a rascal

scour *verb* **1** to clean by hard rubbing; scrub **2** to search thoroughly

scourge *noun* a cause of great suffering

Scouse *noun, Brit* a native or inhabitant of Liverpool

scout *noun* **1** a guide or spy sent ahead to bring back information **2** Scout a member of the Scout Association

scowl *verb* to wrinkle the brows in displeasure or anger ▪ *noun* a frown

Scrabble *noun*, *trademark* a word-building game

scrabble *verb* to scratch or grope about

scraggy *adjective* **1** long and thin **2** uneven, rugged

scram *exclamation* go away!

scramble *verb* **1** to struggle against other people to get or do something **2** to wriggle along on hands and knees **3** to mix or toss together: *scrambled eggs* **4** to jumble up (a message) to make it unintelligible without decoding ▪ *noun* **1** a rush and struggle to get something **2** a motorcycle race over rough country

scrap *noun* **1** a small piece, a fragment **2** a picture for pasting in a scrapbook **3** *informal* a fight **4** parts of a car *etc* no longer required **5 scraps** small pieces, odds and ends ▪ *verb* **1** to abandon as useless **2** *informal* to fight, quarrel

| **scrap** *verb* ▸ scraps, scrapping, scrapped

scrapbook *noun* a blank book in which to stick pictures *etc*

scrape *verb* **1** to rub and mark with something sharp **2** to drag or rub against or across a surface with a harsh grating sound **3 scrape together** to collect (money *etc*) with difficulty ▪ *noun* **1** an act of scraping **2** a mark or sound

made by scraping **3** *informal* a difficult situation ▪ **scrape through** to only just avoid failure

scrapheap *noun* a heap of old metal *etc*, a rubbish heap ▪ **on the scrapheap** no longer needed

scrap metal metal for melting and re-using

scrappy *adjective* made up of odd scraps, not well put together

scratch *verb* **1** to draw a sharp point across the surface of **2** to mark by doing this **3** to tear or dig with claws, nails, *etc* **4** to rub with the nails to relieve or stop itching **5** to withdraw from a competition ▪ *noun* (*plural* **scratches**) **1** a mark or sound made by scratching **2** a slight wound ▪ *adjective* **1** *golf* too good to be allowed a handicap **2** of a team: made up of players hastily got together ▪ **scratchy** *adjective*

scrawl *verb* to write or draw untidily or hastily ▪ *noun* **1** untidy, hasty or bad writing **2** something scrawled

scrawny *adjective* thin, skinny

scream *verb* to utter a shrill, piercing cry as in fear *etc*; shriek ▪ *noun* a shrill cry

screech *verb* to utter a harsh, shrill and sudden cry ▪ *noun* a harsh shrill cry

screen *noun* **1** a flat covered framework to shelter from view or protect from heat, cold, *etc* **2** something that shelters from wind, danger, difficulties, *etc*

3 the surface on which cinema films are projected **4** the surface on which a television picture, or computer data, appears ■ *verb* **1** to shelter, hide **2** to make a film of **3** to show on a screen **4** to sift, sieve **5** to sort out (the good from the bad) by testing **6** to conduct examinations on someone to test for disease ■ **screen off** to hide behind, or separate by, a screen

screenplay *noun* the written text for a film, with dialogue and descriptions of characters and setting

screen saver an animated image displayed on a computer screen when the computer is not in use

screw *noun* **1** a nail with a slotted head and a winding groove or ridge (called the **thread**) on its surface **2** a kind of propeller (a **screw-propeller**) with spiral blades, used in ships and aircraft **3** a turn or twist (of a screw *etc*) ■ *verb* **1** to fasten or tighten with a screw **2** to fix (*eg* a stopper) in place with a twisting movement **3** to twist, turn round (your head *etc*) **4** to twist up, crumple, pucker

screwdriver *noun* a tool for turning screws

scribble *verb* **1** to write carelessly **2** to make untidy or meaningless marks with a pencil *etc* ■ *noun* **1** careless writing **2** meaningless marks on a piece of paper

scribe *noun, history* **1** a clerk who copied out manuscripts **2** a teacher of the Jewish law

scrimp *verb* to be sparing or stingy with money

script *noun* **1** the text of a play, talk, *etc* **2** handwriting like print

scripture *noun* **1** sacred writings **2** Scripture the Christian Bible

scroll *noun* **1** a piece of paper rolled up **2** an ornament shaped like this ■ *verb, computing* to move text up or down on a screen to see more of a document

scroll bar a strip at the side of a computer screen, to which the mouse is pointed to scroll down or up

scrounge *verb, slang* **1** to cadge **2** to get by begging ■ *noun* an attempt to beg or cadge: *on the scrounge*

scrounger *noun* a person who scrounges

scrub *verb* to rub hard in order to clean ■ *noun* countryside covered with low bushes

scrub *verb* ► scrubs, scrub*bing*, scrub*bed*

scruff *noun* the back of the neck

scruffy *adjective* untidy

scrum *noun, rugby* a struggle for the ball by the forwards of the opposing sides bunched together

scrumptious *adjective, informal* delicious

scrunch *verb* to crumple

scruple *noun* doubt over what is right or wrong that keeps someone from doing something ■ *verb* to hesitate because of a scruple

scrupulous *adjective* careful over the smallest details

scrutinize or **scrutinise** *verb* to examine very closely

scrutiny *noun* (*plural* **scrutinies**) careful examination, a close look

scuba *noun* breathing apparatus used by skin-divers

scuba diving swimming underwater using a device consisting of a breathing tube attached to a cylinder of air

scuff *verb* to graze or scrape

scuffle *noun* a confused fight

sculpt *verb* to carve or model

sculptor, **sculptress** *noun* an artist who carves or models figures in wood, stone, clay, *etc*

sculpture *noun* **1** the art of the sculptor or sculptress **2** a piece of their work

scum *noun* **1** foam that rises to the surface of liquids **2** the most worthless part of anything

scupper *verb* to put an end to, ruin: *scupper his chances*

scurry *verb* to hurry along, scamper

| **scurry** ► **scurries**, **scurry***ing*, **scurr***ied*

scurvy *noun* a type of disease caused by a lack of fresh fruit and vegetables

scuttle *noun* a fireside container for coal ■ *verb* **1** to make a hole in

(a ship) in order to sink it **2** to hurry along, scamper

scythe *noun* a large curved blade, on a long handle, for cutting grass *etc* by hand ■ *verb* to cut with a scythe

sea *noun* **1** the mass of salt water covering most of the earth's surface **2** a great stretch of water of less size than an ocean **3** a great expanse or number

seabed *noun* the bottom of the sea

seaboard *noun* land along the edge of the sea

seafarer *noun* a traveller by sea, a sailor

seafaring *adjective* travelling by or working at sea

seafront *noun* a promenade with its buildings facing the sea

seagull *noun* a type of web-footed sea bird

seahorse *noun* a type of small fish with a horse-like head and neck

seal[1] *noun* a furry sea animal living partly on land

seal[2] *noun* **1** a piece of wax with a design pressed into it, attached to a document to show that it is legal or official **2** a piece of wax used to keep a parcel closed **3** anything that closes tightly ■ *verb* **1** to mark or fasten with a seal **2** to close up completely **3** to make (legally) binding and definite: *seal a bargain*

sea level the level of the surface of the sea

sealing wax a hard kind of wax for sealing letters, documents, *etc*

sea lion a large kind of seal, the male of which has a mane

seam *noun* **1** the line formed by the sewing together of two pieces of cloth **2** a line or layer of metal, coal, *etc* in the earth

seaman *noun* a sailor, especially a member of a ship's crew who is not an officer

seamanship *noun* the art of steering and looking after ships at sea

seamstress *noun* a woman who sews for a living

seamy *adjective* sordid; disreputable

séance (*pronounced* sei-ons) *noun* a meeting of people to receive messages from the spirits of the dead

sear *verb* to scorch, burn

search *verb* **1** to look over in order to find something **2 search for something** to look for it ■ *noun* (*plural* **searches**) **1** an act of searching **2** an attempt to find

search engine on the Internet, a program that compares search requests against items in its index and returns search results to the user

searching *adjective* examining closely and carefully

searchlight *noun* a strong beam of light used for picking out objects at night

seashore *noun* the land next to the sea

seasick *adjective* made ill by the rocking movement of a ship

seaside *noun* the land beside the sea

season *noun* **1** one of the four divisions of the year (spring, summer, autumn, winter) **2** the proper time for anything **3** a time associated with a particular activity: *football season* ■ *verb* to add (salt *etc*) to improve the flavour of (food)

seasonable *adjective* **1** happening at the proper time **2** of weather: suitable for the season

seasonal *adjective* **1** of the seasons or a season **2** of work *etc*: taking place in one particular season only

seasoned *adjective* **1** of food: flavoured **2** trained, experienced: *a seasoned traveller*

seasoning *noun* something (eg salt, pepper) added to food to give it more taste

season ticket a ticket that can be used repeatedly for a certain period of time

seat *noun* **1** a piece of furniture for sitting on **2** the part of a chair on which you sit **3** the buttocks **4** a place in parliament, on a council, *etc* **5** the centre of some activity: *the seat of government* ■ *verb* **1** to make to sit down **2** to have seats for (a certain number)

seat belt a belt fixed to a seat in

a car *etc* to prevent an occupant from being thrown violently forward in the event of a crash

sea urchin a type of small sea creature with a spiny shell

seaward *adjective & adverb* towards the sea

seaweed *noun* any of many kinds of plants growing in the sea

seaworthy *adjective* in a good enough condition to go to sea

secateurs *noun plural* a tool like scissors, for trimming bushes *etc*

seclude *verb* to keep (yourself) apart from people's notice or company

secluded *adjective* of a place: private and quiet

seclusion *noun* the state of being secluded; peacefulness and privacy

second *adjective* **1** next after the first in time, place, *etc* **2** other, alternate: *every second week* **3** another of the same kind as: *they thought him a second Mozart* ■ *noun* **1** someone or something that is second **2** an attendant to someone who boxes or fights a duel **3** the 60th part of a minute of time, or of a degree (in measuring angles) **4** an article not quite perfectly made ■ *verb* **1** to support, back up **2** (*pronounced se-***kond**) to transfer temporarily to a special job

secondary *adjective* second in position or importance

secondary school a school between primary school and university *etc*

second-hand *adjective* not new; having been used by another

secondly *adverb* in the second place

second nature a firmly fixed habit

second-rate *adjective* not of the best quality, inferior

secrecy *noun* the state of being secret, mystery

secret *adjective* **1** hidden from, or not known by, others **2** secretive ■ *noun* a fact, plan, *etc* that is not told or known

secretarial *adjective* of a secretary or their work

secretary *noun* (*plural* **secretaries**) **1** someone employed to write letters, keep records, *etc* in an office **2** someone elected to deal with the written business of a club *etc*

secrete *verb* **1** to hide, conceal in a secret place **2** of a part of the body: to store up and give out (a fluid)

secretion *noun* **1** a substance secreted **2** the process of secreting

secretive *adjective* inclined to hide or conceal your feelings, activities, *etc*

secret service a government department dealing with spying

sect *noun* a group of people who hold certain views, especially in religious matters

sectarian *adjective* **1** of a sect **2** loyal to a sect **3** narrow-minded **4** of a crime, especially a murder: committed as a result of hatred between rival religious groups

section *noun* **1** a part, a division **2** a thin slice of a specimen for examination under a microscope **3** the view of the inside of anything when it is cut right through or across **4** *maths* the surface formed when a plane cuts through a solid

sector *noun* **1** a three-sided part of a circle whose sides are two radii and a part of the circumference **2** a part, a section

secure *adjective* **1** safe, free from danger or fear **2** confident **3** firmly fixed or fastened ■ *verb* **1** to make safe, firm or established **2** to seize, get hold of **3** to fasten

security *noun* safety

sedate *adjective* calm, serious, dignified

sedation *noun* the use of sedatives to calm a patient

sedative *adjective* calming, soothing ■ *noun* a medicine with this effect

sedge *noun* a type of coarse grass growing in swamps and rivers

sediment *noun* **1** the grains or solid parts which settle at the bottom of a liquid **2** sand, rocks, *etc* carried and deposited by wind, water or ice

seduce *verb* to tempt (someone) away from right or moral behaviour

seductive *adjective* attractive, tempting

see *verb* **1** to have sight **2** to be aware of, notice by means of the eye **3** to form a picture of in the mind **4** to understand **5** to find out **6** to make sure **7** to accompany **8** to meet ■ **see through 1** to take part in to the end **2** to not be deceived by (a person, trick, *etc*) ■ **see to** to take charge of (the preparation of)

| **see** *verb* ► sees, seeing, saw, seen

seed *noun* **1** the part of a tree, plant, *etc* from which a new plant may grow **2** a seed-like part of a grain or a nut **3** the beginning from which anything grows **4** a seeded player in a tournament ■ *verb* **1** of a plant: to produce seed **2** to sow **3** to remove the seeds from (*eg* a fruit) **4** to arrange (good players) in a tournament so that they do not compete against each other till the later rounds

seedling *noun* a young plant just sprung from a seed

seedy *adjective* **1** shabby **2** sickly, not very well

seek *verb* **1** to look or search for **2** to try (to do something) **3** to try to get (advice *etc*)

seek ► seeks, seeking, sought

seem *verb* 1 to appear to be: *he seems kind* 2 to appear: *she seems to like it*

seeming *adjective* apparent but not actual or real ■ **seemingly** *adverb*

seemly *adjective* suitable; decent

seen *past participle* of **see**

seep *verb* to flow slowly through a small opening, leak

seesaw *noun* a plank balanced across a stand so that one end of it goes up when the other goes down ■ *verb* to move with a seesaw-like movement

seethe *verb* 1 to boil 2 to be very angry

seething *adjective* 1 boiling 2 furious

see-through *adjective* able to be seen through

segment *noun* 1 a part cut off 2 a part of a circle cut off by a straight line

segregate *verb* to separate (someone or a group) from others ■ **segregation** *noun*

seize *verb* 1 to take suddenly by force 2 to overcome: *seized with fury* 3 **seize up** of machinery: to become stuck, break down

seizure *noun* 1 sudden capture 2 a sudden attack of illness, rage, *etc*

seldom *adverb* not often, rarely

select *verb* to pick out from several according to your preference, choose ■ *adjective* 1 picked out, chosen 2 very good 3 exclusive, allowing only certain people in

selection *noun* 1 the act of choosing 2 things chosen 3 a number of things from which to choose

selective *adjective* selecting carefully

self *noun* (*plural* **selves**) 1 someone's own person 2 someone's personality, character

self-assured *adjective* trusting in your own power or ability, confident

self-centred *adjective* concerned with your own affairs, selfish

self-confident *adjective* believing in your own powers or abilities

self-conscious *adjective* too aware of your faults *etc* and therefore embarrassed in the company of others

self-contained *adjective* 1 of a house: complete in itself, not sharing any part with other houses 2 of a person: self-reliant

self-control *noun* control over yourself, your feelings, *etc*

self-defence *noun* the defence of your own person, property, *etc*

self-esteem *noun* respect for yourself; conceit

self-expression *noun* expressing your own personality in your activities

self-important *adjective* having a mistakenly high sense of your importance

self-indulgent *adjective* too ready to satisfy your own inclinations and desires

self-interest *noun* a selfish desire to consider only your own interests or advantage

selfish *adjective* caring only for your own pleasure or advantage ■ **selfishly** *adverb*

selfless *adjective* thinking of others before yourself, unselfish

self-made *adjective* owing success *etc* to your own efforts

self-possessed *adjective* calm in mind or manner, quietly confident

self-raising flour flour already containing an ingredient to make it rise

self-reliant *adjective* trusting in your own abilities *etc* ■ **self-reliance** *noun*

self-respect *noun* respect for yourself and concern for your own character and reputation

self-righteous *adjective* thinking highly of your own goodness and virtue

self-sacrifice *noun* the act of giving up your own life, possessions, *etc* in order to do good to others

selfsame *adjective* the very same

self-service *adjective* of a restaurant: where customers help or serve themselves

self-sufficient *adjective* needing no help or support from anyone else

sell *verb* **1** to give or hand over for money **2** to have or keep for sale **3** to be sold for, cost ■ **seller** *noun*
| **sell** ▸ sells, sell*ing*, sold

Sellotape *noun, trademark* transparent adhesive tape, especially for use on paper

semaphore *noun* a form of signalling using the arms to form different positions for each letter

semblance *noun* an outward, often false, appearance: *a semblance of listening*

semi- *prefix* **1** half: *semicircle* **2** *informal* partly

semibreve *noun, music* a whole-note (○), equal to four crotchets in length

semicircle *noun* half of a circle

semicolon *noun* the punctuation mark (;) indicating a pause stronger than a pause marked by a comma

semiconductor *noun* a substance, *eg* silicon, which can conduct electricity less easily than a conductor

semi-detached *adjective* of a house: joined to another house on one side but not on the other

semi-final *noun* the stage or match of a contest immediately before the final

seminar *noun* a group of students working on, or meeting to discuss, a particular subject

semi-precious *adjective* of a stone: having some value, but not considered a gem

Semitic *adjective* Jewish

semitone *noun, music* **1** half a tone **2** the interval between notes on a keyboard instrument

semolina *noun* the hard particles of wheat sifted from flour, used for puddings *etc*

senate *noun* **1** the upper house of parliament in the USA, Australia, *etc* **2** the governing council of some universities **3** *history* the law-making body in ancient Rome

senator *noun* a member of a senate

send *verb* **1** to make (someone) go **2** to have (something) carried or delivered to a place ∎ **send for** to order to be brought

|send ▶ sends, sending, sent

sender *noun* a person who sends something, especially by post

senile *adjective* **1** of old age **2** showing the mental feebleness of old age

senior *adjective* older in age or higher in rank ∎ *noun* someone older or in a senior position

senior citizen an elderly person

seniority *noun* the state of being senior

sensation *noun* **1** a feeling through any of the five senses **2** a vague effect: *a floating sensation* **3** a state of excitement: *causing a sensation*

sensational *adjective* causing great excitement, horror, *etc*

sense *noun* **1** one of the five powers by which humans feel or notice (hearing, taste, sight, smell, touch) **2** a feeling: *a sense of loss* **3** an ability to understand or appreciate: *a sense of humour* **4** **senses** right mind, common sense: *to take leave of your senses* **5** wisdom, ability to act in a reasonable way **6** ability to be understood: *the last paragraph does not make sense* **7** meaning: *to what sense of this word are your referring?* ∎ *verb* to feel, realize: *sense disapproval*

senseless *adjective* **1** stunned, unconscious **2** foolish

sensible *adjective* **1** wise **2** able to be felt or noticed **3** sensible of aware of

sensitive *adjective* **1** feeling, especially strongly or painfully **2** strongly affected by light, movements, *etc*

sensitivity *noun* the quality or condition of being sensitive

sensor *noun* a device that detects and measures physical changes

sensual *adjective* **1** driven by, or affecting, the senses rather than the mind **2** indulging too much in bodily pleasures

sensuality *noun* **1** the quality of being sensual **2** indulgence in physical pleasures

sent *past form* of **send**

sentence noun 1 a number of words which together make a complete statement 2 a judgement announced by a judge or court ■ verb to condemn to a particular punishment

sentiment noun 1 a thought expressed in words 2 a show of feeling or emotion, often excessive

sentimental adjective having or showing too much feeling or emotion ■ **sentimentality** noun

sentry noun a soldier posted to guard an entrance

separable adjective able to be separated

separate verb (pronounced sep-a-reit) 1 to set or keep apart 2 to divide into parts 3 to disconnect 4 to go different ways 5 to live apart by choice ■ adjective (pronounced sep-a-rat) 1 placed, kept, etc apart 2 divided 3 not connected 4 different ■ **separation** noun

September noun the ninth month of the year

septet noun a group of seven musicians etc

septic adjective of a wound: full of germs that are poisoning the blood

   💠 Do not confuse with: sceptic

sequel noun 1 a result, a consequence 2 a story that is a continuation of an earlier story

sequence noun 1 the order (of events) in time 2 a number of things following in order, a connected series

sequin noun a small round sparkling ornament sewn on a dress etc

serenade noun music played or sung in the open air at night, especially under a woman's window ■ verb to sing or play a serenade (to)

serene adjective 1 calm 2 not worried, happy, peaceful

serenity noun calmness, peacefulness

serf noun, history a slave bought and sold with the land on which he worked

serfdom noun slavery

sergeant noun 1 an army rank above corporal 2 a rank in the police force above a constable

sergeant-major noun an army rank above sergeant

serial noun a story which is published, broadcast or televised in instalments

serial port computing a socket or plug for connecting a device such as a mouse or a scanner to a computer

series noun (plural series) 1 a number of things following each other in order 2 a set of things of the same kind

serious adjective 1 grave, thoughtful 2 not joking, in earnest 3 important, needing careful thought **4** likely to have dangerous results ∎ **seriously** *adverb*

sermon *noun* a serious talk, especially one given in church

serpent *noun*, *old* a snake

serrated *adjective* having notches or teeth like a saw

serum *noun* **1** a clear watery fluid in blood that helps fight disease **2** a fluid injected into the body to help fight disease

servant *noun* **1** someone paid to work for another, especially in helping to run a house **2** a government employee: *civil servant*

serve *verb* **1** to work for and obey **2** to attend or wait upon at table **3** to give out food, goods, *etc* **4** to be able to be used (as) **5** to be suitable for: *serve a purpose* **6** to carry out duties as a member of the armed forces **7** to undergo (a sentence in prison *etc*) **8** *tennis* to throw up the ball and hit it with the racket to start play

server *noun* a computer that stores and manages data from several other smaller computers on a network

service *noun* **1** an act of serving **2** the duty required of a servant or other employee **3** a performance of (public) worship **4** use: *bring the new machine into service* **5** time spent in the armed forces **6** **services** the armed forces **7** **services** help: *services to refugees*

8 a regular supply: *bus service* **9** **services** public supply of water, gas, electricity, *etc* **10** a set of dishes: *dinner service* ∎ *verb* to keep (a car, machine, *etc*) in good working order by regular checks and repairs

service station a petrol station providing facilities such as a shop, car-washing, *etc*

serviette *noun* a table napkin

servile *adjective* slave-like; showing lack of spirit: *a servile attitude to his employer*

sesame (*pronounced* **ses**-am-i) *noun* a SE Asian plant whose seeds produce an edible oil

session *noun* **1** a meeting of a court, council, *etc* **2** the period of the year when classes are held in a school *etc* **3** a period of time spent on a particular activity

set *verb* **1** to place or put **2** to fix in the proper place (*eg* broken bones) **3** to arrange (a table for a meal, jewels in a necklace, *etc*) **4** to fix (a date, a price, *etc*) **5** to fix hair (in waves or curls) **6** to adjust (a clock or a machine *etc*) so that it is ready to work or perform some function **7** to give (a task *etc*) **8** to put in a certain state or condition: *set free* **9** of a jelly *etc*: to become firm or solid **10** to compose music for: *he set the poem to music* **11** of the sun: to go out of sight below the horizon ∎ *adjective* **1** fixed or arranged beforehand; ready: *all set* **2** fixed, stiff: *a set expression* on his face ■ *noun* **1** a group of people **2** a number of things of a similar kind, or used together **3** *maths* a group of objects or elements with something in common **4** an apparatus **5** scenery made ready for a play *etc* **6** a series of six or more games in tennis **7** a fixing of hair in waves or curls **8** (*also called*: **sett**) a badger's burrow ■ **set about 1** to begin (doing something) **2** to attack ■ **set in** to begin ■ **set off** *or* **out** *or* **forth** to start (on a journey *etc*) ■ **set on** *or* **upon** to attack

|**set** *verb* ▶ **sets, setting, set**

setback *noun* a movement in the wrong direction, a failure

set square *noun* a triangular drawing instrument, with one right angle

sett *another spelling* of **set** (noun sense 8)

settee *noun* a sofa

setter *noun* a dog trained to point out game in hunting

setting *noun* **1** the act of someone who or something that sets **2** an arrangement **3** a background

settle *verb* **1** to place in a position or at rest **2** to come to rest **3** to agree over (a matter) **4** (sometimes **settle down**) to become calm or quiet **5** (sometimes **settle down**) to make your home in a place **6** to pay (a bill) **7** to fix, decide (on) **8** to bring

(a quarrel *etc*) to an end **9** to sink to the bottom

settlement *noun* **1** the act of settling **2** a decision, an agreement **3** payment of a bill **4** money given to a woman on her marriage **5** a number of people who have come to live in a country

settler *noun* someone who goes to live in a new area or country

seven *noun* the number 7 ■ *adjective* 7 in number

seventeen *noun* the number 17 ■ *adjective* 17 in number

seventeenth *adjective* the last of a series of seventeen ■ *noun* one of seventeen equal parts

seventh *adjective* the last of a series of seven ■ *noun* one of seven equal parts

seventieth *adjective* the last of a series of seventy ■ *noun* one of seventy equal parts

seventy *noun* the number 70 ■ *adjective* 70 in number

sever *verb* **1** to cut apart or away, break off **2** to separate, part

several *adjective* **1** more than one or two, but not many **2** various **3** different: *going their several ways* ■ *pronoun* more than one or two people, things, *etc*, but not a great many

severe *adjective* **1** serious **2** harsh, strict **3** very plain and simple, not fancy

severity *noun* strictness, harshness

sew *verb* **1** to join together with a needle and thread **2** to make or mend in this way

sew ► sews, sewing, sewed, sewn

sewage *noun* water and waste matter

sewer *noun* an underground drain for carrying off water and waste matter

sex *noun* **1** either of the two classes (male or female) into which animals are divided according to the part they play in producing children or young **2** sexual intercourse

sexism *noun* discrimination against someone on the grounds of their sex

sexist *noun* someone who treats the opposite sex unfairly or thinks that they are inferior ■ *adjective* relating to or characteristic of sexism

sextet *noun* a group of six musicians *etc*

sexual *adjective* **1** of sex or gender **2** relating to sexual intercourse ■ **sexually** *adverb*

sexual intercourse physical union between a man and a woman involving the insertion of the penis into the vagina

sexual reproduction reproduction involving the union of male and female reproductive cells

SF *abbreviation* science fiction

shabby *adjective* **1** worn-looking **2** poorly dressed **3** of behaviour: mean, unfair ■ **shabbily** *adverb*

shack *noun* a roughly-built hut

shackle *verb* **1** to fasten with a chain **2** to hold back, prevent, hinder

shackles *noun plural* chains fastening a prisoner's legs or arms

shade *noun* **1** slight darkness caused by cutting off some light **2** a place not in full sunlight **3** a screen from the heat or light **4** **shades** *informal* sunglasses **5** the deepness or a variation of a colour **6** the dark parts in a picture ■ *verb* **1** to shelter from the sun or light **2** to make parts of a picture darker **3** to change gradually, *eg* from one colour into another

shading *noun* the marking of the darker places in a picture

shadow *noun* **1** shade caused by some object coming in the way of a light **2** the dark shape of that object on the ground **3** a dark part in a picture **4** a very small amount: *a shadow of doubt* ■ *verb* **1** to shade, darken **2** to follow someone about secretly and watch them closely

shadow cabinet leading members of the opposition in parliament

shady *adjective* **1** sheltered from light or heat **2** *informal* dishonest, underhand

shaft *noun* **1** anything long and straight **2** the rod on which the head of an axe, arrow, *etc* is fixed **3** an arrow **4** a revolving rod which turns a machine or engine **5** the deep, narrow passageway leading to a mine **6** a deep vertical hole for a lift **7** a ray (of light)

shaggy *adjective* rough, hairy, or woolly

shake *verb* **1** to move backwards and forwards or up and down with quick, jerky movements **2** to make or be made unsteady **3** to shock, disturb ■ *noun* **1** the act of shaking or trembling **2** a shock **3** a drink mixed by shaking or stirring quickly: *milk shake*

| **shake** *verb* ▸ shakes, shak*ing*, shook, shaken

shaky *adjective* unsteady; trembling ■ **shakily** *adverb*

shale *noun* a kind of rock from which oil can be obtained

shall *verb* **1** used to form future tenses of other verbs when the subject is *I* or *we* **2** used for emphasis, or to express a promise, when the subject is *you, he, she, it* or *they*: *you shall go if I say you must/you shall go if you want to* (*see also* **will, should**)

shallot *noun* a kind of small onion

shallow *adjective* **1** not deep **2** not capable of thinking or feeling deeply ■ *noun* (often **shallows**) a place where the water is not deep

sham *noun* something which is not what it appears to be, a

pretence ■ *adjective* false, imitation, pretended ■ *verb* to pretend falsely

| **sham** *verb* ▸ shams, sham*ming*, shamm*ed*

shaman *noun* a tribal healer or medicine man

shamble *verb* to walk in a shuffling or awkward manner

shambles *noun singular, informal* a mess, confused disorder

shame *noun* **1** an uncomfortable feeling caused by realization of guilt or failure **2** disgrace, dishonour **3** *informal* bad luck, a pity ■ *verb* **1** to make to feel shame or ashamed **2 shame into** to cause (someone to do something) by making them ashamed: *they shamed him into paying his share*

shamefaced *adjective* showing shame or embarrassment

shameful *adjective* disgraceful

shameless *adjective* feeling or showing no shame

shammy *another spelling of* chamois

shampoo *verb* to wash (the hair and scalp) ■ *noun* **1** an act of shampooing **2** a soapy liquid used for cleaning the hair **3** a similar liquid used for cleaning carpets or upholstery

shamrock *noun* a plant like clover with leaves divided in three

shank *noun* the part of the leg

between the knee and the foot

shan't *short for* shall not

shanty *noun* (*plural* **shanties**) **1** a roughly-made hut **2** a sailors' song

shantytown *noun* an area of makeshift, squalid housing

shape *noun* **1** the form or outline of anything **2** condition: *in good shape* ■ *verb* **1** to make into a certain form **2** to model, mould **3** to develop (in a particular way): *our plans are shaping well*

shapeless *adjective* having no shape or regular form

shapely *adjective* having an attractive shape

share *noun* **1** one part of something that is divided among several people **2** one of the parts into which the money of a business firm is divided ■ *verb* **1** to divide out among a number of people **2** to allow others to use (your possessions *etc*) **3** to have or use in common with someone else

shareholder *noun* someone who owns shares in a business company

shareware *noun*, *computing* software programs distributed on a trial basis for which the user must pay after the trial period ends

shark *noun* **1** a large, very fierce, flesh-eating fish **2** *informal* a swindler

sharp *adjective* **1** cutting, piercing **2** having a thin edge or

fine point **3** hurting, stinging, biting: *sharp words* **4** alert, quick-witted **5** sensitive, perceptive, able to pick up faint signals **6** severe, inclined to scold **7** *music* of a note: raised half a tone in pitch **8** of an outline: clear ■ *adverb* punctually: *at ten o'clock sharp* ■ *noun*, *music* a sign (♯) showing that a note is to be raised half a tone

sharpen *verb* to make or grow sharp

sharpener *noun* an instrument for sharpening

shatter *verb* to break in pieces; to upset, ruin (hopes, health, *etc*)

shave *verb* **1** to cut away hair with a razor **2** to scrape away the surface of (wood *etc*) **3** to touch lightly, or just avoid touching, in passing ■ *noun* **1** the act of shaving **2** a narrow escape: *a close shave*

shaven *adjective* shaved

shaver *noun* an electric device for shaving

shavings *noun plural* very thin slices of wood *etc*

shawl *noun* a loose covering for the shoulders

she *pronoun* a woman, girl or female animal, *etc* already spoken about (used only as the subject of a verb): *when the girl saw us, she waved*

sheaf *noun* (*plural* **sheaves**) a bundle (*eg* of corn, papers) tied together

shear *verb* to clip, cut (especially wool from a sheep)

| **shear** ► shears, shearing, sheared, shorn

♦* Do not confuse with:
sheer

shears *noun plural* large scissors

sheath *noun* **1** a case for a sword or dagger **2** a long close-fitting covering

sheathe *verb* to put into a sheath

shed *noun* a building for storage or shelter ■ *verb* **1** to throw or cast off (leaves, a skin, clothing) **2** to pour out (tears, blood) **3** to give out (light *etc*)

| **shed** *verb* ► sheds, shedding, shed

sheen *noun* brightness, gloss

sheep *noun* an animal whose flesh is used as food and whose fleece is used for wool

sheepdog *noun* a dog trained to look after sheep

sheepish *adjective* shy; embarrassed, shamefaced

sheepskin *noun* **1** the skin of a sheep **2** a kind of leather made from this

sheer *adjective* **1** very steep **2** pure, not mixed: *sheer delight* **3** of cloth: very thin or fine ■ *adverb* straight up and down, very steeply: *rock face rising sheer* ■ *verb* to turn aside from a straight line, swerve

♦* Do not confuse with:
shear

sheet *noun* **1** a large piece of linen, cotton, nylon, *etc* for a bed **2** a large thin piece of metal, glass, ice, *etc* **3** a piece of paper

sheikh *noun* an Arab chief

shelf *noun* (*plural* **shelves**) a board fixed on a wall, for laying things on

shell *noun* **1** a hard outer covering (of a shellfish, egg, nut, *etc*) **2** a husk or pod (*eg* of peas) **3** a metal case filled with explosive fired from a gun **4** a framework, *eg* of a building not yet completed or burnt out ■ *verb* to take the shell from (a nut, egg, *etc*)

shellfish *noun* a water creature covered with a shell, *eg* an oyster, limpet or mussel

shelter *noun* **1** a building which acts as a protection from harm, rain, wind, *etc* **2** the state of being protected from any of these ■ *verb* **1** to give protection to **2** to put in a place of safety or protection **3** to go to, or stay in, a place of safety

shelve *verb* **1** to put up shelves in **2** to put aside (a problem *etc*) for later consideration **3** of land: to slope gently

shepherd *noun* a man who looks after sheep ■ *verb* to watch over carefully, guide

shepherdess *noun* a woman who looks after sheep

shepherd's pie a dish of minced meat covered with mashed potatoes

sherbet *noun* **1** a fizzy drink **2** powder for making this

sheriff *noun* **1** the chief representative of a monarch in a county, whose duties include keeping the peace **2** in Scotland, the chief judge of a county **3** *US* the chief law-enforcement officer of a county

sherry *noun* a strong kind of wine, often drunk before a meal

shied *past form of* shy

shield *noun* **1** anything that protects from harm **2** a broad piece of metal carried by a soldier *etc* as a defence against weapons **3** a shield-shaped trophy won in a competition ▪ *verb* to protect, defend, shelter

shift *verb* **1** to move, change the position of **2** to change position or direction: *the wind shifted* **3** to get rid of ▪ *noun* **1** a change: *shift of emphasis* **2** a change of position, transfer **3** a group of workers on duty at the same time **4** a specified period of work or duty: *night shift* **5** a loose-fitting lightweight dress

shifty *adjective* not to be trusted, looking dishonest

shilling *noun* a silver-coloured coin used before decimal currency, worth $\frac{1}{20}$ of £1

shillyshally *verb* to hesitate in making up your mind, waver

| shillyshally ▶ shillyshallies, shillyshallying, shillyshallied |

shimmer *verb* to shine with a quivering or unsteady light

shin *noun* the front part of the leg below the knee ▪ **shin up** to climb

shine *verb* **1** to give out or reflect light **2** to be bright **3** to polish (shoes *etc*) **4** to be very good at: *he shines at arithmetic* ▪ *noun* **1** brightness **2** an act of polishing

| shine *verb* ▶ shines, shining, shone |

shingle *noun* coarse gravel or rounded stones on the shores of rivers or of the sea

shingles *noun singular* an infectious disease causing a painful rash

shining *adjective* **1** very bright and clear **2** admired, distinguished: *a shining example*

shiny *adjective* glossy, polished

ship *noun* a large vessel for journeys across water ▪ *verb* **1** to take onto a ship **2** to send by ship **3** to go by ship

| ship *verb* ▶ ships, shipping, shipped |

-ship *suffix* a state or condition: *friendship*

shipment *noun* **1** an act of putting on board ship **2** a load of goods sent by ship

shipping *noun* **1** ships as traffic: *a gale warning to shipping* **2** the business of transporting goods and freight, especially by ship

shipshape *adjective* in good order, neat, trim

shipwreck *noun* **1** the sinking or destruction of a ship (especially by accident) **2** a wrecked ship

shipyard *noun* the yard in which ships are built or repaired

shire *noun* a county

shirk *verb* to avoid or evade (doing your duty *etc*)

shirker *noun* a person who avoids work or responsibilities

shirt *noun* **1** a garment worn by men on the upper part of the body, having a collar, sleeves and buttons down the front **2** a similar garment for a woman

shiver *verb* **1** to tremble with cold or fear **2** to break into small pieces, shatter ■ *noun* **1** the act of shivering **2** a small broken piece

shoal *noun* a group of fishes, moving and feeding together

shock *noun* **1** a sudden forceful blow **2** a feeling of fright, horror, dismay, *etc* **3** a state of weakness or illness following such feelings **4** the effect on the body of an electric current passing through it **5** an earthquake **6** a bushy mass (of hair) ■ *verb* **1** to give a shock to **2** to upset or horrify

shock absorber a device in an aircraft, car, *etc* for lessening the impact or force of bumps

shocking *adjective* causing horror or dismay; disgusting

shod *adjective* wearing shoes ■ *verb, past form of* **shoe**

shoddy *adjective* **1** of poor material or quality **2** mean, low: *a shoddy trick*

shoe *noun* **1** a stiff outer covering for the foot, not reaching above the ankle **2** a rim of iron nailed to the hoof of a horse ■ *verb* to put shoes on (a horse)

| **shoe** *verb* ▶ shoes, shoe*ing*, shod

shoehorn *noun* a curved piece of horn, metal, *etc* for making a shoe slip easily over your heel

shoelace *noun* a cord or string used for fastening a shoe

shoemaker *noun* someone who makes and mends shoes

shone *past form of* **shine**

shoo *exclamation* used to scare away birds, animals, *etc* ■ *verb* to drive or scare away

| **shoo** *verb* ▶ shoos, shoo*ing*, shoo*ed*

shook *past form of* **shake**

shoot *verb* **1** to send a bullet from a gun, or an arrow from a bow **2** to hit or kill with an arrow, bullet, *etc* **3** to kick for a goal **4** to score (a goal) **5** to photograph, film **6** to move very swiftly or suddenly ■ *noun* a new sprout on a plant

| **shoot** *verb* ▶ shoots, shoot*ing*, shot

shooting star a meteor

shop *noun* **1** a place where goods are sold **2** a workshop ■ *verb* **1** to visit shops and buy goods **2** *slang* to betray (someone) to the police

| **shop** *verb* ▶ shops, shopping, shopped

shopkeeper *noun* someone who owns and keeps a shop

shoplifter *noun* someone who steals goods from a shop
- **shoplifting** *noun*

shopper *noun* someone who shops, a customer

shopping *noun* **1** visiting shops to buy goods **2** goods bought

shore *noun* the land bordering on a sea or lake

shorn *past form of* shear

short *adjective* **1** not long **2** not tall **3** brief, not lasting long **4** not enough, less than it should be **5** rude, sharp, abrupt **6** of pastry: crisp and crumbling easily
- *adverb* **1** suddenly, abruptly **2** not as far as intended: *the shot fell short* • *noun* **1** a short film **2** a short circuit **3** a drink of an alcoholic spirit **4** shorts short trousers

shortage *noun* a lack

shortbread *noun* a thick biscuit made of butter and flour *etc*

short circuit the missing out of a major part of an intended electric circuit, sometimes causing blowing of fuses • *verb* (**short-circuit**) of an electrical appliance: to have a short circuit

shortcoming *noun* a fault, a defect

short cut a short way of going

somewhere or doing something

shorten *verb* to make less in length

shorthand *noun* a method of swift writing using strokes and dots to show sounds (*contrasted with*: **longhand**)

short list a list of candidates selected from the total number of applicants or contestants

short-lived *adjective* living or lasting only a short time

shortly *adverb* **1** soon **2** curtly, abruptly **3** briefly

short-sighted *adjective* **1** seeing clearly only things which are near **2** taking no account of what may happen in the future

short-tempered *adjective* easily made angry

short-term *adjective* intended to last only a short time

short-wave *adjective* of a radio wave: using wavelengths between 10 and 100 metres (*compare with*: **long-wave**)

shot *noun* **1** something which is shot or fired **2** small lead bullets, used in cartridges **3** a single act of shooting **4** the sound of a gun being fired **5** the distance covered by a bullet, arrow, *etc* **6** a marksman **7** a throw or turn in a game **8** an attempt at doing something, guessing, *etc* **9** a photograph **10** a scene in a motion picture • *adjective* **1** of silk: showing changing colours **2** streaked or mixed with (a colour *etc)* ∎ *verb, past form* of **shoot**

shotgun *noun* a light type of gun which fires shot

should *verb* **1** the form of the verb **shall** used to express a condition: *I should go if I had time* **2** used to mean 'ought to': *you should know that already*

shoulder *noun* the part of the body between the neck and upper arm ∎ *verb* **1** to bear the full weight of (a burden *etc*) **2** to push with the shoulder

shoulder blade the broad flat bone of the shoulder

shout *noun* a loud cry or call ∎ *verb* to make a loud cry

shove *verb* to push roughly, thrust, push aside ∎ *noun* a rough push

shovel *noun* a spade-like tool used for lifting coal, gravel, *etc* ∎ *verb* to lift or move with a shovel

show *verb* **1** to allow, or cause, to be seen **2** to be able to be seen **3** to exhibit, display (an art collection *etc*) **4** to point out (the way *etc*) **5** to direct, guide: *show her to a seat* **6** to make clear, demonstrate ∎ *noun* **1** the act of showing **2** a display, an exhibition **3** a performance, an entertainment ∎ **show off 1** to show or display (something) **2** to try to impress others with your talents *etc* ∎ **show up 1** to make to stand out clearly **2** to expose, make obvious (especially someone's faults)

| **show** *verb* ► **show**s, **show**ing, **show**ed, **show**n

show business the branch of the theatre concerned with variety entertainments

showdown *noun, informal* a confrontation to settle a long-running dispute

shower *noun* **1** a short fall of rain **2** a large quantity: *a shower of questions* **3** a bath in which water is sprayed from above **4** the apparatus which sprays water for this ∎ *verb* **1** to pour (something) down on **2** to bathe under a shower

showerproof *adjective* of material, a coat, *etc*: able to withstand light rain

showery *adjective* raining from time to time

shown *past participle* of **show**

showroom *noun* a room where goods are laid out for people to see

showy *adjective* bright, gaudy; (too) obvious, striking

shrank *past form* of **shrink**

shrapnel *noun* **1** a shell containing bullets *etc* which scatter on explosion **2** splinters of metal, a bomb, *etc*

shred *noun* **1** a long, narrow piece, cut or torn off **2** a scrap, a very small amount: *not a shred of evidence* ∎ *verb* to cut or tear into shreds

| **shred** *verb* ► **shred**s, **shred**ding, **shred**ded

shrew noun a small mouse-like type of animal with a long nose

shrewd adjective clever, cunning

shriek verb to make a shrill scream or laugh ■ noun a shrill scream or laugh

shrift noun: **give someone short shrift** to dismiss them quickly

shrill adjective of a sound or voice: high in tone, piercing ■ **shrilly** adverb

shrimp noun a small, long-tailed edible shellfish

shrine noun a holy or sacred place

shrink verb 1 to make or become smaller 2 to draw back in fear and disgust (from)

| shrink verb ► shrinks,
| shrinking, shrank, shrunk

shrinkage noun the amount by which something grows smaller

shrivel verb to dry up, wrinkle, wither

| shrivel ► shrivels,
| shrivelling, shrivelled

shroud noun 1 a cloth covering a dead body 2 something which covers: a shroud of mist ■ verb to wrap up, cover

Shrove Tuesday in the Christian Church, the last day before Lent, when pancakes are traditionally eaten

shrub noun a small bush or plant

shrubbery noun (plural **shrubberies**) a place where shrubs grow

shrug verb to show doubt, lack of interest, etc by drawing up the shoulders ■ noun a movement of the shoulders to show doubt, lack of interest, etc ■ **shrug off** to dismiss, treat as being unimportant

| shrug verb ► shrugs,
| shrugging, shrugged

shrunk past participle of shrink

shrunken adjective shrunk

shudder verb to tremble from fear, cold, disgust ■ noun a trembling

shuffle verb 1 to mix, rearrange (eg playing-cards) 2 to move by dragging or sliding the feet along the ground without lifting them 3 to move (the feet) in this way ■ noun 1 a rearranging 2 a dragging movement of the feet

shun verb to avoid, keep clear of

| shun ► shuns, shunning,
| shunned

shut verb 1 to move (a door, window, lid, etc) so that it covers an opening 2 to close, lock (a building etc) 3 to become closed 4 to confine, restrain in a building etc ■ **shut down** to close (a factory etc) ■ **shut up 1** to close completely 2 informal to stop speaking or making other noise

| shut ► shuts, shutting, shut

shutter noun 1 a cover for a window 2 a cover which closes over a camera lens as it takes a picture

shuttle noun the part of a weaving loom which carries the cross thread from side to side
■ adjective of a transport service: going to and fro between two places

shuttlecock noun a rounded cork stuck with feathers, used in the game of badminton

shy adjective 1 of a wild animal: easily frightened, timid 2 lacking confidence in the presence of others 3 not wanting to attract attention ■ verb 1 to jump or turn suddenly aside in fear 2 to throw, toss ■ noun a try, an attempt
■ shyly adverb

| shy verb ► shies, shying, shied

Siamese cat a fawn-coloured domestic cat

sibling noun a brother or sister

sick adjective 1 wanting to vomit 2 vomiting 3 not well, ill 4 sick of tired of (someone or something)

sicken verb to make or become sick

sickening adjective 1 causing sickness 2 disgusting, revolting

sickle noun a hooked knife for cutting or reaping grain, hay, etc

sickly adjective 1 unhealthy 2 feeble

sickness noun 1 an illness 2 vomiting or nausea

side noun 1 an edge, border or boundary line 2 a surface that is not the top, bottom, front or back 3 either surface of a piece of paper, cloth, etc 4 the right or left part of the body 5 a division, a part: the north side of the town 6 an aspect, point of view 7 a team or party which is opposing another ■ adjective 1 on or towards the side: side door 2 indirect, additional but less important: side issue ■ side with to support (one person, group, etc against another)

sideboard noun a piece of furniture in a dining-room for holding dishes etc

side effect an additional (often bad) effect of a drug

sideline noun an extra bit of business outside regular work

sidelong adjective & adverb from or to the side: sidelong glance

sideshow noun a less important show that is part of a larger one

sidestep verb to avoid by stepping to one side

sidetrack verb to turn (someone) away from what they were going to do or say

sideways adverb 1 with the side foremost 2 towards the side

siding noun a short line of rails on which trucks are shunted off the main line

sidle verb 1 to go or move sideways 2 to move stealthily, sneak

siege noun 1 an attempt to capture a town etc by keeping it surrounded by an armed force 2 a constant attempt to gain control

siesta *noun* a short sleep or rest taken in the afternoon

sieve (*pronounced* siv) *noun* a container with a mesh used to separate liquids from solids, or fine pieces from coarse pieces, *etc* ▪ *verb* to put through a sieve

sift *verb* 1 to separate by passing through a sieve 2 to consider and examine closely

sigh *noun* a long, deep-sounding breath, showing tiredness, longing, *etc* ▪ *verb* to give out a sigh

sight *noun* 1 the act or power of seeing 2 a view, a glimpse: *catch sight of her* 3 (often *sights*) something worth seeing 4 something or someone unusual, ridiculous, shocking, *etc* 5 a guide on a gun for taking aim ▪ *verb* 1 to get a view of, see suddenly 2 to look at through the sight of a gun

♦* Do not confuse with: **site** and **cite**

sight-reading *noun* playing or singing from music that has not been seen previously

sightseeing *noun* visiting the chief buildings, monuments, *etc* of a place ▪ **sightseer** *noun*

sign *noun* 1 a mark with a special meaning, a symbol 2 a gesture (*eg* a nod, wave of the hand) to show your meaning 3 an advertisement or notice giving information 4 something which

shows what is happening or is going to happen: *signs of irritation* ▪ *verb* 1 to write your name on (a document, cheque, *etc*) 2 to make a sign or gesture to 3 to show (your meaning) by a sign or gesture ▪ **sign off** 1 to bring a broadcast to an end 2 to stop work *etc* ▪ **sign on** *or* **up** to enter your name on a list for work, the army, *etc*

signal *noun* 1 a gesture, light or sound giving a command, warning etc 2 something used for this purpose: *railway signals* 3 the wave of sound received or sent out by a radio *etc* set ▪ *verb* 1 to make signals (to) 2 to send (information) by signal

| **signal** *verb* ▶ signals, signalling, signalled

signalman *noun* someone who works railway signals, or who sends signals

signature *noun* 1 a signed name 2 an act of signing 3 *music* the flats or sharps at the beginning of a piece which show its key, or figures showing its timing

signature tune a tune used to identify a particular radio or television series *etc* played at the beginning or end of the programme

signet *noun* a small seal, usually bearing someone's initials

♦* Do not confuse with: **cygnet**

significance *noun* **1** meaning **2** importance

significant *adjective* meaning much; important ▪ **significantly** *adverb*

signify *verb* **1** to mean, be a sign of **2** to show, make known by a gesture **3** to have meaning or importance

| **signify** ► signifies, signifying, signified

sign language communication, especially with the deaf, using gestures to represent words and ideas

signpost *noun* a post with a sign, especially one showing direction and distances to certain places

Sikhism *noun* a religion whose followers observe the teachings of its ten gurus ▪ **Sikh** *noun & adjective*

silage *noun* green fodder preserved in a silo

silence *noun* **1** absence of sound or speech **2** a time of quietness ▪ *verb* to cause to be silent

silencer *noun* a device (on a car engine, gun, *etc*) for making noise less

silent *adjective* **1** free from noise **2** not speaking ▪ **silently** *adverb*

silhouette *noun* **1** an outline drawing of someone, often in profile, filled in with black **2** a dark outline seen against the light

silicon *noun* a chemical element used to make computer components

silk *noun* **1** very fine, soft fibres spun by silkworms **2** thread or cloth made from this ▪ *adjective* **1** made of silk **2** soft, smooth

silken *adjective* **1** made of silk **2** smooth like silk

silkworm *noun* the caterpillar of certain moths which spins silk

silky *adjective* like silk

sill *noun* a ledge of wood, stone, *etc* below a window or a door

silly *adjective* foolish, not sensible

silo *noun* (*plural* **silos**) **1** a tower for storing grain *etc* **2** a pit or airtight chamber for holding silage

silt *noun* sand or mud left behind by flowing water

silver *noun* **1** a white precious metal, able to take on a high polish **2** money made of silver or of a metal alloy resembling it **3** objects (especially cutlery) made of, or plated with, silver ▪ *adjective* made of, or looking like, silver ▪ *verb* **1** to cover with silver **2** to become like silver

silver medal a medal given to a competitor who comes second

silversmith *noun* someone who makes or sells articles of silver

silver wedding the 25th anniversary of a wedding

silvery *adjective* **1** like silver **2** of sound: ringing and musical

SIM card a removable electronic card inside a mobile phone that stores information about the user

similar adjective alike, almost the same

similarity noun (plural **similarities**) 1 being similar, likeness 2 resemblance

similarly adverb 1 in the same, or a similar, way 2 likewise, also

simile noun an expression using 'like' or 'as', in which one thing is likened to another that is well-known for a particular quality (eg 'as black as night', 'to swim like a fish')

simmer verb to cook gently just below or at boiling point

simper verb 1 to smile in a silly manner 2 to say with a simper ■ noun a silly smile

simple adjective 1 easy, not difficult or complicated 2 plain, not fancy 3 ordinary: simple, everyday objects 4 of humble rank: a simple peasant 5 mere, nothing but: the simple truth 6 too trusting, easily cheated 7 foolish, half-witted

simple fraction a vulgar fraction

simpleton noun a foolish person

simplicity noun the state of being simple

simplification noun 1 an act of making simpler 2 a simple form of anything

simplify verb to make simpler

simplify ► simplifies, simplifying, simplified

simply adverb 1 in a simple manner 2 only, merely: I do it simply for the money 3 completely, absolutely

simulate verb 1 to pretend, feign 2 to have the appearance of, look like

simulated adjective 1 pretended 2 having the appearance of

simulation noun 1 the act of simulating something or the methods used to simulate something 2 something that has been created artificially to reproduce a real event or real set of conditions

simultaneous adjective happening, or done, at the same time ■ **simultaneously** adverb

sin noun 1 a wicked act, especially one which breaks religious laws 2 wrongdoing 3 informal a shame, pity ■ verb to commit a sin, to do wrong

sin verb ► sins, sinning, sinned

since adverb 1 (often **ever since**) from that time onwards 2 at a later time 3 ago: long since ■ prep from the time of ■ conjunction 1 after the time when 2 because

sincere adjective 1 honest in word and deed, meaning what you say or do, true 2 truly felt ■ **sincerely** adverb

sincerity noun the state or quality of being truthful and genuine in what you believe and say

sinew *noun* a tough cord that joins a muscle to a bone

sinewy *adjective* having strong sinews, tough

sinful *adjective* wicked

sing *verb* 1 to make musical sounds with your voice 2 to utter (words, a song, *etc*) by doing this

| **sing** ► sings, singing, sang, sung

singe *verb* to burn slightly on the surface, scorch ■ *noun* a surface burn

singer *noun* someone who sings or whose voice has been specially trained for singing

single *adjective* 1 one only 2 not double 3 not married 4 for one person: *a single bed* 5 for one direction of a journey: *a single ticket* ■ **single out** to pick out, treat differently in some way

single-handed *adjective* working *etc* by yourself

single-minded *adjective* having one aim only

singlet *noun* a vest, an undershirt

singly *adverb* one by one, separately

sing-song *noun* a gathering of people singing informally together ■ *adjective* of a speaking voice *etc*: having a fluctuating rhythm

singular *adjective* 1 *grammar* the opposite of **plural**, showing one person, thing, *etc* 2 exceptional 3 unusual, strange

singularly *adverb* strangely, exceptionally

sinister *adjective* suggesting evil, evil-looking

sink *verb* 1 to go down below the surface of the water *etc* 2 to go down or become less 3 of a very ill person: to become weaker 4 to lower yourself (into) ■ *noun* a basin in a kitchen, bathroom, *etc*, with a water supply connected to it and a drain for carrying off dirty water *etc*

| **sink** *verb* ► sinks, sinking, sank, sunk

sinner *noun* a person who has committed a sin or sins

sinus *noun* (*plural* **sinuses**) an air cavity in the head connected with the nose

sip *verb* to drink in very small quantities ■ *noun* a taste of a drink, a swallow

| **sip** *verb* ► sips, sipping, sipped

siphon *or* **syphon** *noun* 1 a bent tube for drawing off liquids from one container into another 2 a glass bottle, for soda water *etc*, containing such a tube ■ *verb* 1 to draw (off) through a siphon 2 **siphon off** to take (part of something) away gradually

sir *noun* 1 a polite form of address used to a man 2 **Sir** the title of a knight or baronet

sire *noun* a male parent, especially of a horse ■ *verb* of an animal: to be the male parent of

siren *noun* 1 an instrument that gives out a whole hooting noise as a warning 2 a mythical sea nymph whose singing enchanted sailors and tempted them into danger 3 an attractive but dangerous woman

sirloin *noun* the upper part of the loin of beef

sister *noun* 1 a female born of the same parents as yourself 2 a senior nurse, often in charge of a hospital ward 3 a nun ■ *adjective* of similar design or structure: *a sister ship*

sisterhood *noun* 1 the state of being a sister 2 a religious community of women

sister-in-law *noun* 1 the sister of your husband or wife 2 the wife of your brother or of your brother-in-law

sisterly *adjective* like a sister

sit *verb* 1 to rest on the buttocks, be seated 2 of a bird: to perch 3 to be an official member: *sit on a committee* 4 of a court *etc*: to meet officially 5 to pose for a photographer, painter, *etc* 6 to take (an examination *etc*) ■ **sit up** 1 to sit with your back straight 2 to stay up instead of going to bed

| **sit** *verb* ▸ sits, sit*ting*, sat

sitcom *noun* a television comedy series with a running theme

site *noun* a place where a building, town, *etc* is or is to be placed ■ *verb* to select a place for (a building *etc*)

✦ ❋ Do not confuse with: **sight** and **cite**

sitter *noun* 1 someone who poses for a portrait *etc* 2 a babysitter

sitting *noun* the state or time of sitting ■ *adjective* 1 seated 2 for sitting in or on

sitting-room *noun* a room chiefly for sitting in

situation *noun* 1 the place where anything stands 2 a job, employment 3 a state of affairs, circumstances

six *noun* the number 6 ■ *adjective* 6 in number

sixteen *noun* the number 16 ■ *adjective* 16 in number

sixteenth *adjective* the last of a series of sixteen ■ *noun* one of sixteen equal parts

sixth *adjective* the last of a series of six ■ *noun* one of six equal parts

sixtieth *adjective* the last of a series of sixty ■ *noun* one of sixty equal parts

sixty *noun* the number 60 ■ *adjective* 60 in number

size *noun* 1 space taken up by anything 2 measurements, dimensions 3 largeness 4 a class into which shoes and clothes are grouped according to size ■ **size up** to form an opinion of a person, situation, *etc*

sizeable *or* **sizable** *adjective* fairly large

sizzle *verb* **1** to make a hissing sound **2** to fry, scorch

skate *noun* **1** a steel blade attached to a boot for gliding on ice **2** one of a pair of rollerskates **3** a type of large flatfish ■ *verb* to move on skates ■ **skater** *noun*

skateboard *noun* a narrow board on four small wheels, ridden in a standing or crouching position ■ **skateboarding** *noun*

skeleton *noun* **1** the bony framework of an animal or person, without the flesh **2** any framework or outline ■ *adjective* of staff *etc*: reduced to a very small or minimum number

skeleton key a key from which the inner part has been cut away so that it can open many different locks

sketch *noun* (*plural* **sketches**) **1** a rough plan or drawing **2** a short or rough account **3** a short play, dramatic scene, *etc* ■ *verb* **1** to draw roughly **2** to give the chief points of **3** to draw in pencil or ink

sketchy *adjective* **1** roughly done **2** not thorough, incomplete

skew *adjective & adverb* off the straight, slanting ■ *verb* to set at a slant

skewer *noun* a long pin of wood or metal for holding meat together while roasting *etc* ■ *verb* to fix with a skewer or with something sharp

ski *noun* (*plural* **skis**) one of a pair of long narrow strips of wood or metal that are attached to boots for gliding over snow ■ *verb* to move or travel on skis

| **ski** *verb* ► skis, skiing, skied or ski'd

skid *noun* a slide sideways ■ *verb* **1** of a wheel: to slide along without turning **2** to slip sideways

| **skid** *verb* ► skids, skidding, skidded

ski-jump *noun* **1** a steep, snow-covered track ending in a platform from which a skier jumps **2** a jump made by a skier from such a platform ■ **ski-jumping** *noun*

skilful *adjective* having or showing skill ■ **skilfully** *adverb*

skill *noun* cleverness at doing a thing, either from practice or as a natural gift

skilled *adjective* **1** having skill, especially through training **2** of a job: requiring skill

skim *verb* **1** to remove cream, scum, *etc* from the surface of (something) **2** to move lightly and quickly over (a surface) **3** to read quickly, missing parts

| **skim** ► skims, skimming, skimmed

skimmed *adjective* of milk: with some of the fat removed

skimp *verb* **1** to give (someone) hardly enough **2** to do (a job) imperfectly **3** to spend too little money (on)

skimpy *adjective* **1** too small **2** of clothes: too short or tight

skin *noun* **1** the natural outer covering of an animal or person **2** a thin outer layer on a fruit **3** a thin film that forms on a liquid ∎ *verb* to strip the skin from

| **skin** *verb* ▶ skin**s**, skinn**ing**, skinn**ed**

skin-deep *adjective* as deep as the skin only, on the surface

skin-diver *noun* a diver who wears simple equipment (originally someone who dived naked for pearls)

skinflint *noun* a very mean person

skinny *adjective* very thin

| **skinny** ▶ skinn**ier**, skinn**iest**

skint *adjective*, *Brit informal* broke, without much money

skip *verb* **1** to go along with a rhythmic step and hop **2** to jump over a turning rope **3** to leap, especially lightly or joyfully **4** to leave out (parts of a book, a meal, *etc*) ∎ *noun* **1** an act of skipping **2** a large metal container for transporting refuse

| **skip** *verb* ▶ skip**s**, skipp**ing**, skipp**ed**

skipper *noun* the captain of a ship, aeroplane or team ∎ *verb* to act as captain for (a ship, team, *etc*)

skipping rope a rope used in skipping

skirmish *noun* (plural skirmishes) **1** a fight between small parties of soldiers **2** a short sharp contest or disagreement

skirt *noun* **1** a garment, worn by women, that hangs from the waist **2** the lower part of a dress ∎ *verb* to pass along, or lie along, the edge of

skirting *or* **skirting-board** *noun* the narrow board next to the floor round the walls of a room (*also called*: **wainscot**)

skit *noun* a piece of writing, a short play, *etc* that makes fun of a person, event, *etc*

skittle *noun* **1** a bottle-shaped object used as a target in some games **2** **skittles** a game in which skittles are knocked over by a ball

skive *verb*, *informal* (often **skive off**) to avoid doing a duty ∎ **skiver** *noun*

skulk *verb* to wait about, stay hidden

skull *noun* the bony case which encloses the brain

skunk *noun* a small American animal which defends itself by giving off a bad smell

sky *noun* (plural **skies**) the upper atmosphere, the heavens

sky-diving *noun* jumping with a parachute as a sport

skylark *noun* the common lark which sings while hovering far overhead

skylight *noun* a window in a roof or ceiling

skyline *noun* the horizon

skyscraper *noun* a high building of very many storeys

slab *noun* a thick flat slice or piece of anything

slack *adjective* 1 not firmly stretched 2 not firmly in position 3 not strict 4 lazy and careless 5 not busy ■ *noun* 1 the loose part of a rope 2 **slacks** loose, casual trousers ■ *verb* to do less work than you should, be lazy

slacken *verb* 1 to make or become looser 2 to make or become less active, less busy or less fast, *etc*

slag *noun* waste left from metal-smelting ■ *verb, slang* to criticize, make fun of cruelly

| **slag** *verb* ▶ slags, slagging, slagged

slain *past participle* of **slay**

slalom *noun* a downhill, zigzag ski run among posts or trees

slam *verb* 1 to shut (a door, lid, *etc*) with a loud noise 2 to put down with a loud noise ■ *noun* the act of slamming

| **slam** *verb* ▶ slams, slamming, slammed

slander *noun* an untrue statement (in England, a spoken one) aimed at harming someone's reputation ■ *verb* to speak slander against (someone)

slanderous *adjective* of a statement: untrue and therefore unfairly damaging someone's reputation

slang *noun* 1 popular words and phrases that are used in informal, everyday speech or writing 2 the special language of a particular group: *Cockney slang*

slant *verb* 1 to slope 2 to lie or move diagonally or in a sloping position 3 to give or present (facts or information) in a distorted way that suits your own purpose ■ *noun* 1 a slope 2 a diagonal direction 3 a point of view

slap *noun* a blow with the palm of the hand or anything flat ■ *verb* to give a slap to

| **slap** *verb* ▶ slaps, slapping, slapped

slapdash *adjective* hasty, careless

slapstick *adjective* of comedy: boisterous, funny in a very obvious way ■ *noun* comedy in this style

slash *verb* 1 to make long cuts in 2 to strike at violently ■ *noun* (*plural* **slashes**) 1 a long cut 2 a sweeping blow

slat *noun* a thin strip of wood, metal or other material

slate *noun* an easily split blue-grey rock, used for roofing, or at one time for writing upon ■ *adjective* made of slate ■ *verb* 1 to cover with slate 2 to say or write harsh things to or about

slaughter *noun* 1 the killing of animals, especially for food 2 cruel killing of great numbers of people ■ *verb* 1 to kill (an animal) for food 2 to kill brutally

slaughterhouse *noun* a place where animals are killed in order to be sold for food

slave *noun* **1** someone forced to work for a master and owner **2** someone who serves another devotedly **3** someone who works very hard ▪ *verb* to work like a slave

slavery *noun* **1** the state of being a slave **2** the system of owning slaves

slavish *adjective* thinking or acting exactly according to rules or instructions

slay *verb*, *formal* to kill
| slay ▶ slays, slay*ing*, slew, slain

sleazy *adjective* squalid, disreputable ▪ **sleaze** *noun*

sled *or* **sledge** *noun* a vehicle with runners, made for sliding upon snow ▪ *verb* to ride on a sledge

sleek *adjective* **1** smooth, glossy **2** of an animal: well-fed and well-cared for **3** elegant, well-groomed

sleep *verb* to rest with your eyes closed in a state of natural unconsciousness ▪ *noun* **1** the state of sleeping **2** a spell of sleeping ▪ **sleep with** *informal* to have sexual intercourse with
| sleep *verb* ▶ sleeps, sleep*ing*, slept

sleeper *noun* **1** someone who sleeps **2** a beam of wood or metal supporting railway lines **3** a

sleeping car or sleeping berth on a railway train

sleeping bag a large warm bag for sleeping in, used by campers *etc*

sleepless *adjective* unable to sleep, without sleep

sleepwalker *noun* someone who walks *etc* while asleep

sleepy *adjective* **1** drowsy, wanting to sleep **2** looking as if needing sleep **3** quiet, not bustling

sleet *noun* rain mixed with snow or hail

sleeve *noun* the part of a garment which covers the arm

sleeveless *adjective* without sleeves

sleigh *noun* a large horse-drawn sledge

slender *adjective* **1** thin, narrow **2** slim **3** small in amount: *a slender margin*

sleuth *noun* someone who tracks down criminals, a detective

slew *past form of* slay

slice *noun* **1** a thin, broad piece of something **2** a broad-bladed utensil for serving fish *etc* ▪ *verb* **1** to cut into slices **2** to cut through **3** to cut (off from *etc*) **4** *golf* to hit (a ball) in such a way that it curves away to the right

slick *adjective* **1** smart, clever, often too much so **2** smooth ▪ *noun* a thin layer of spilt oil

slide *verb* **1** to move smoothly

over a surface **2** to slip **3** to pass quietly or secretly ■ *noun* **1** an act of sliding **2** a smooth, slippery slope or track **3** a chute **4** a picture for showing on a screen

| **slide** *verb* ► slides, slid*ing*, slid

slide rule an instrument used for calculating, made up of one ruler sliding against another

slight *adjective* **1** of little amount or importance **2** small, slender ■ *verb* to treat as unimportant, insult by ignoring ■ *noun* an insult, an offence

slightly *adverb* a little

slim *adjective* **1** slender, thin **2** small, slight: *slim chance* ■ *verb* **1** to make slender **2** to use means (such as eating less) to become slender

| **slim** *verb* ► slims, slimm*ing*, slimm*ed*

slime *noun* sticky, half-liquid material, especially thin, slippery mud

slimy *adjective* **1** covered with slime **2** *informal* behaving in an excessively attentive manner

sling *noun* **1** a bandage hanging from the neck or shoulders to support an injured arm **2** a strap with a string attached to each end, for flinging stones ■ *verb* **1** to hang loosely **2** *informal* to throw

| **sling** *verb* ► slings, sling*ing*, slung

slink *verb* to sneak away, move stealthily

| **slink** ► slinks, slink*ing*, slunk

slip *verb* **1** to slide accidentally and lose footing or balance **2** to fall out of place, or out of your control **3** to move quickly and easily **4** to move quietly, quickly and secretly **5** to escape from: *slip your mind* ■ *noun* **1** the act of slipping **2** an error, a slight mistake **3** a strip or narrow piece of anything (*eg* paper) **4** a thin undergarment worn under a dress, an underskirt **5** *cricket* a fielding position ■ **slip up** to make a mistake

| **slip** *verb* ► slips, slipp*ing*, slipp*ed*

slipper *noun* a loose indoor shoe

slippery *adjective* causing skidding or slipping

slipshod *adjective* untidy, careless

slipstream *noun* the stream of air driven back by an aircraft propeller *etc*

slip-up *noun* a mistake

slit *verb* **1** to make a long narrow cut in **2** to cut into strips ■ *noun* a long narrow cut or opening

| **slit** *verb* ► slits, slitt*ing*, slit

slither *verb* **1** to slide or slip about (*eg* on mud) **2** to move with a gliding motion

sliver *noun* a thin strip or slice

slobber *verb* to let saliva dribble from the mouth

slog *verb* to work or plod on steadily, especially against difficulty ■ *noun* a difficult spell of work

| **slog** *verb* ▶ slogs, slogging, slogged

slogan *noun* an easily remembered and frequently repeated phrase, used in advertising *etc*

slop *verb* 1 to flow over, spill 2 to splash ■ *noun* 1 spilt liquid 2 slops dirty water 3 slops thin, tasteless food

| **slop** *verb* ▶ slops, slopping, slopped

slope *noun* 1 a position or direction that is neither level nor upright, a slant 2 a surface with one end higher than the other, *eg* a hillside ■ *verb* to be in a slanting, sloping position

sloppy *adjective* 1 wet, muddy 2 careless, untidy 3 silly, sentimental

slosh *verb* 1 to splash 2 *informal* to hit

slot *noun* 1 a small, narrow opening, *eg* to insert coins 2 a position ■ *verb* 1 to make a slot in 2 (sometimes **slot into**) to find a position or place for

| **slot** *verb* ▶ slots, slotting, slotted

sloth *noun* 1 laziness 2 a slow-moving S American animal that lives in trees

slothful *adjective* lazy

slot machine a vending machine worked by putting a coin in a slot

slouch *noun* a hunched-up body position ■ *verb* to walk with shoulders rounded and head hanging

slovenly *adjective* untidy, careless, dirty

slow *adjective* 1 not fast 2 not hasty or hurrying 3 of a clock: behind in time 4 not quick in learning, dull ■ *verb* (often **slow down**) to make or become slower ■ **slowly** *adverb*

slowcoach *noun* someone who moves, works, *etc* slowly

slow-motion *adjective* 1 slower than normal movement 2 of a film: slower than actual motion

sludge *noun* soft, slimy mud

slug *noun* 1 a snail-like animal with no shell 2 a small piece of metal used as a bullet

sluggish *adjective* moving slowly

sluice *noun* 1 (*also called*: **sluicegate**) a sliding gate for controlling a flow of water in an artificial channel 2 the stream which flows through this ■ *verb* to clean out with a strong flow of water

slum *noun* 1 an overcrowded part of a town where the houses are dirty and unhealthy 2 a house in a slum

slumber *verb* to sleep ■ *noun* sleep

slump verb 1 to fall or sink suddenly and heavily 2 to lose value suddenly ▪ noun a sudden fall in values, prices, *etc*

slung past form of **sling**

slunk past form of **slink**

slur verb 1 to pronounce indistinctly 2 to damage (a reputation *etc*), speak evil of ▪ noun 1 a blot or stain (on someone's reputation) 2 a criticism, an insult

| **slur** *verb* ▶ slurs, slur*ring*, slur*red*

slurp verb to drink or gulp noisily ▪ noun a noisy gulp

slurry noun 1 thin, liquid cement 2 liquid waste

slush noun 1 watery mud 2 melting snow 3 something very sentimental 4 sentimentality

slushy adjective 1 covered with, or like, slush 2 sentimental

sly adjective cunning; wily; deceitful ▪ **slyly** adverb

smack verb 1 to strike smartly, slap 2 to have a trace or suggestion (of) ▪ noun 1 an act of smacking 2 the sound made by smacking 3 a boisterous kiss 4 a taste, a flavour 5 a trace, a suggestion ▪ adverb with sudden violence: *run smack into the door*

small adjective 1 little, not big or much 2 not important 3 not operating on a large scale: *a small businessman* 4 of a voice: soft ▪ noun the most slender or narrow part: *the small of the back*

▪ adverb into small pieces: *cut the carrots up small*

smallholding noun a small farm

small hours the hours just after midnight

small-minded adjective having narrow opinions, ungenerous

smallpox noun a serious infectious illness, causing a rash of large pimples (**pocks**)

small talk polite conversation about nothing very important

smarmy adjective smooth in manner; ingratiating

smart adjective 1 clever and quick in thought or action 2 well-dressed 3 brisk ▪ verb 1 to feel a sharp, stinging pain 2 to feel annoyed, resentful, *etc* after being insulted

smarten verb to make smarter

smash verb 1 to break in pieces, shatter 2 to strike with force 3 to crash (into *etc*): *the car smashed into the wall* ▪ noun (plural smashes) 1 an act of smashing 2 a crash, a collision (of vehicles)

smashing adjective, informal excellent

smattering noun a very slight knowledge of a subject

smear verb 1 to spread (something sticky or oily) 2 to spread, smudge with (something sticky *etc*) 3 to become smeared 4 to slander, insult ▪ noun a smudge of something sticky

smell noun 1 the sense or power of being aware of things through your nose **2** an act of using this sense **3** something sensed through the nose, a scent ▪ *verb* **1** to notice by the sense of smell **2** to use your sense of smell on **3** to give off a smell ▪ **smell out** to find out by prying or inquiring closely

| **smell** *verb* ► smells, smell*ing*, smelt or smell*ed*

smelly *adjective* having a bad smell

smile *verb* to show pleasure by drawing up the corners of the lips ▪ *noun* an act of smiling

smirk *verb* to smile in a self-satisfied or foolish manner ▪ *noun* a self-satisfied smile

smith *noun* a worker in metals; a blacksmith

smock *noun* a loose shirt-like garment, sometimes worn over other clothes as a protection

smog *noun* thick, smoky fog

smoke *noun* **1** the cloud-like gases and particles of soot given off by anything burning **2** an act of smoking (a cigarette *etc*) ▪ *verb* **1** to give off smoke **2** to inhale and exhale tobacco smoke from a cigarette, pipe, *etc* **3** to cure or preserve (ham, fish, *etc*) by applying smoke

smokeless *adjective* **1** burning without smoke **2** where the emission of smoke is prohibited: *a smokeless zone*

smoker *noun* **1** someone who smokes **2** a railway compartment in which smoking is allowed

smokescreen *noun* anything (originally smoke) meant to confuse or mislead

smoky *adjective* **1** full of smoke **2** tasting of smoke

smooth *adjective* **1** not rough **2** having an even surface **3** without lumps **4** hairless **5** without breaks, stops or jolts **6** too agreeable in manner ▪ *verb* **1** to make smooth **2** to calm, soothe **3** to free from difficulty

smother *verb* **1** to kill by keeping air from, *eg* by covering over the nose and mouth **2** to die by this means **3** to cover up, conceal (feelings *etc*) **4** to put down, suppress (a rebellion *etc*)

smoulder *verb* **1** to burn slowly without bursting into flame **2** to exist in a hidden state **3** to show otherwise hidden emotion, *eg* anger, hate

smudge *noun* a smear ▪ *verb* to make dirty with spots or smears

smug *adjective* well-satisfied, too obviously pleased with yourself

smuggle *verb* **1** to take (goods) into, or out of, a country without paying the required taxes **2** to send or take secretly

smuggler *noun* someone who smuggles goods

smut *noun* a spot of dirt or soot

smutty *adjective* dirty, grimy

snack *noun* a light, hasty meal

snag *noun* a difficulty, an

obstacle ■ *verb* to catch or tear on something sharp

snag *verb* ▶ snags, snagg*ing*, snagg*ed*

snail *noun* a soft-bodied, small, crawling animal with a shell

snake *noun* a legless reptile with a long body, which moves along the ground with a winding movement

snap *verb* 1 to make a sudden bite 2 snap something up to eat it up, or grab it, eagerly 3 to break or shut suddenly with a sharp noise 4 to cause (the fingers) to make a sharp noise 5 to speak sharply 6 to take a photograph of ■ *noun* 1 the noise made by snapping 2 a sudden spell (*eg* of cold weather) 3 a card game in which players try to match cards 4 a photograph

snap *verb* ▶ snaps, snapp*ing*, snapp*ed*

snappy *adjective* irritable, inclined to speak sharply ■ **snappily** *adverb*

snapshot *noun* a quickly taken photograph

snare *noun* 1 a noose or loop that draws tight when pulled, for catching an animal 2 a trap 3 a hidden danger or temptation ■ *verb* to catch in or with a snare

snarl *verb* 1 to growl, showing the teeth 2 to speak in a furious, spiteful tone 3 to become tangled ■ *noun* 1 a growl, a furious noise 2 a tangle, a knot 3 a muddled or confused state

snatch *verb* 1 to seize or grab suddenly 2 to take quickly when you have time ■ *noun* (*plural* **snatches**) 1 an attempt to seize 2 a small piece or quantity: *a snatch of music*

sneak *verb* 1 to creep or move in a stealthy, secretive way 2 to tell tales, tell on others ■ *noun* 1 someone who tells tales 2 a deceitful, underhand person

sneaky *adjective* underhand, deceitful ■ **sneakily** *adverb*

sneer *verb* to show contempt by a scornful expression, words, *etc* ■ *noun* a scornful expression or remark

sneeze *verb* to make a sudden, unintentional and violent blowing noise through the nose and mouth ■ *noun* an involuntary blow through the nose

snide *adjective* mean, malicious

sniff *verb* 1 to draw in air through the nose with a slight noise, *eg* when having a cold, or showing disapproval 2 sniff at something to treat it with scorn or suspicion ■ *noun* a quick drawing in of air through the nose

sniffle *noun* a light sniff, a snuffle ■ *verb* to sniff lightly

snigger *verb* to laugh in a quiet, sly manner ■ *noun* a quiet, sly laugh

snip *verb* to cut off sharply, especially with a single cut ■ *noun* 1 a cut with scissors 2 a small piece snipped off 3 *informal* a bargain: *a snip at the price*

| **snip** *verb* ► snips, snipp*ing*, snipp*ed*

snipe *noun* a bird with a long straight beak, found in marshy places ■ **snipe at 1** to shoot at (someone) from a place of hiding **2** to attack (someone) with critical remarks

sniper *noun* someone who shoots at a single person from cover

snippet *noun* a little piece, especially of information or gossip

snivel *verb* **1** to have a running nose, *eg* because of a cold **2** to whine or complain tearfully

| **snivel** *verb* ► snivels, snivell*ing*, snivell*ed*

snob *noun* someone who looks down on those in a lower social class

snobbery *noun* the behaviour that is typical of a snob or snobs

snobbish *adjective* admiring things associated with the higher social classes and despising things associated with the lower classes

snooker *noun* a game like billiards, using 22 coloured balls

snoop *verb* to spy or pry in a sneaking secretive way ■ *noun* someone who pries

snooty *adjective* haughty, snobbish

snooze *verb* to sleep lightly, doze ■ *noun* a light sleep

snore *verb* to make a snorting noise in your sleep while breathing ■ *noun* a snorting sound made in sleep

snorkel *noun* a tube with one end above the water, to enable an underwater swimmer to breathe

snort *verb* **1** to force air noisily through the nostrils **2** to make such a noise to express disapproval, anger, laughter, *etc* ■ *noun* a loud noise made through the nostrils

snout *noun* the projecting nose and mouth of an animal, *eg* of a pig

snow *noun* frozen water vapour which falls in light white flakes ■ *verb* to fall down in, or like, flakes of snow

snowball *noun* a ball made of snow pressed hard together ■ *verb* **1** to throw snowballs **2** to grow increasingly quickly

snowboard *noun* a single board used as a ski on snow

snowdrift *noun* a bank of snow blown together by the wind

snowdrop *noun* a small white flower growing from a bulb in early spring

snowflake *noun* a flake of snow

snowman *noun* a figure shaped like a human being, made of snow

snowplough *noun* a large vehicle for clearing snow from roads *etc*

snowshoe *noun* a long broad frame with a mesh, one of a pair for walking on snow

snowy *adjective* covered with snow

snub *verb* to treat or speak to in an abrupt, scornful way, insult ■ *noun* an act of snubbing ■ *adjective* of a nose: short and turned up at the end

| **snub** *verb* ▶ snub*s*, snubb*ing*, snubb*ed*

snuff *verb* to put out or trim the wick of (a candle)

snuffle *verb* to make a sniffing noise through the nose, *eg* because of a cold ■ *noun* a sniffling through the nose

snug *adjective* **1** lying close and warm **2** cosy, comfortable **3** closely fitting; neat and trim

snuggle *verb* **1** to curl up comfortably **2** to draw close to for warmth, affection, *etc*

so *adverb* **1** as shown, *eg* by a hand gesture **2** to such an extent, to a great extent: *that is so true* **3** in this or that way **4** correct: *is that so?* ■ *conjunction* therefore

soak *verb* **1** to let stand in a liquid until wet through **2** to drench (with) **3** soak something up to suck it up, absorb it

soaking *adjective* wet through ■ *noun* a wetting, drenching ■ **soaking wet** thoroughly wet, drenched

so-and-so *noun, informal* **1** this or that person or thing **2** *euphemistic* used instead of a stronger insult: *she's a real so-and-so, saying that to you!*

soap *noun* **1** a mixture containing oils or fats and other substances, used in washing **2** *informal* a soap opera ■ *verb* to use soap on

soap opera a television series about a group of characters and their daily lives

soapsuds *noun plural* soapy water worked into a froth

soapy *adjective* **1** like soap **2** full of soap

soar *verb* **1** to fly high into the air **2** of prices: to rise high and quickly

sob *verb* to weep noisily ■ *noun* a noisy weeping

| **sob** *verb* ▶ sob*s*, sobb*ing*, sobb*ed*

sober *adjective* **1** not drunk **2** serious, staid ■ *verb* (sometimes **sober up**) to make or become sober ■ **soberly** *adverb*

soberness or **sobriety** *noun* the state of being sober

sob story a story told to arouse sympathy

so-called *adjective* called by such a name, often mistakenly

soccer *noun* football

sociable *adjective* fond of the company of others, friendly

social *adjective* **1** relating to society, or to a community **2** living in communities: *social insects* **3** of companionship: *social gathering* **4** of rank or level in society: *social class*

socialism *noun* the belief that a

country's wealth should belong to the people as a whole, not to private owners

socialist noun someone who believes in socialism ▪ adjective relating to or characteristic of socialism

social security the system, paid for by taxes, of providing insurance against old age, illness, unemployment, etc

social work work which deals with the care of the people in a community, especially of the poor or underprivileged

social worker a person who is employed to do social work

society noun (plural **societies**) 1 humanity considered as a whole 2 a community of people 3 a social club, an association 4 the class of people who are wealthy, fashionable, etc

sociologist noun someone who studies the structure and organization of human societies and human behaviour in society

sociology noun the study of human society

sock noun a short stocking

socket noun a hollow into which something is fitted

sod noun a piece of earth with grass growing on it, a turf

soda noun 1 the name of several substances formed from sodium 2 soda water

soda water water through

which gas has been passed, making it fizzy

sodden adjective soaked through and through

sodium noun a metallic element from which many substances are formed, including common salt

sofa noun a kind of long, stuffed seat with back and arms

soft adjective 1 easily put out of shape when pressed 2 not hard or firm 3 not loud 4 of a colour: not bright or glaring 5 not strict enough 6 lacking strength or courage 7 lacking common sense, weak in the mind 8 of a drink: not alcoholic 9 of water: containing little calcium etc

soften verb to make or grow soft

soft-hearted adjective kind and generous

softly adverb gently, quietly

software noun, computing programs etc as opposed to the machines (contrasted with: **hardware**)

soggy adjective 1 soaked 2 soft and wet

soil noun 1 the upper layer of the earth in which plants grow 2 loose earth; dirt ▪ verb to make dirty

solace noun something which makes pain or sorrow easier to bear, comfort

solar adjective 1 relating to the sun 2 influenced by the sun 3 powered by energy from the sun's rays

solar energy 1 energy produced by the sun **2** energy derived from the sun's radiation, eg in a solar cell

solar system the sun with the planets (including the earth) going round it

sold past form of **sell**

solder noun melted metal used for joining metal surfaces ▪ verb to join (with solder)

soldering-iron noun an electric tool for soldering joints

soldier noun someone in military service, especially someone who is not an officer

sole[1] noun **1** the underside of the foot **2** the underside of a shoe etc ▪ verb to put a sole on (a shoe etc)

sole[2] adjective **1** only **2** belonging to one person or group only

sole[3] noun a small type of flatfish

solely adverb only, alone

solemn adjective **1** serious, earnest **2** of an occasion: celebrated with special ceremonies

sol-fa noun, music a system of syllables (do, ray, me, etc) to be sung to the notes of a scale

solicit verb to ask earnestly for: solicit advice

solicitor noun a lawyer who advises people about legal matters

solid adjective **1** fixed in shape, not in the form of gas or liquid **2** in three dimensions, with length,

breadth and height **3** not hollow **4** firm, strongly made **5** made or formed completely of one substance: solid silver **6** reliable, sound: solid business **7** informal without a break: three solid hours' work ▪ noun **1** a substance that is solid **2** a figure that has three dimensions

solidarity noun a sense of togetherness, unity, etc

solidify verb to make or become firm or solid

| solidify ▸ solidifies,
| solidifying, solidified

solidity noun the state of being solid

soliloquy noun (plural soliloquies) a speech made by an actor etc to themselves

solitaire noun a card game for one player (also called: **patience**)

solitary adjective **1** lone, alone **2** single: not a solitary crumb remained

solitude noun the state of being alone; lack of company

solo noun (plural solos) a musical piece for one singer or player ▪ adjective performed by one person alone

soloist noun someone who plays or sings a solo

solstice noun the time of longest daylight (**summer solstice** about 21 June) or longest night (**winter solstice** about 21 December)

soluble adjective able to be dissolved or made liquid

solute *noun* a substance that is dissolved in a liquid

solution *noun* **1** a liquid with something dissolved in it **2** the act of solving a problem *etc* **3** an answer to a problem, puzzle, *etc*

solve *verb* **1** to clear up or explain (a mystery) **2** to discover the answer or solution to

solvent *noun* anything that dissolves another substance

sombre *adjective* gloomy, dark, dismal

sombrero *noun* (*plural* **sombreros**) a broad-brimmed Mexican hat

some *adjective* **1** several **2** a few: *some oranges, but not many* **3** a little: *some bread, but not much* **4** certain: *some people prefer bananas* ■ *pronoun* **1** a number or part out of a quantity: *please try some* **2** certain people: *some won't be happy*

somebody or **someone** *noun* **1** an unknown or unnamed person **2** an important person

somehow *adverb* in some way or other

somersault *noun* a forward or backward roll in which the heels go over the head ■ *verb* to perform a somersault

something *pronoun* **1** a thing not known or not stated **2** a thing of importance

sometime *adverb* at a time not known or stated definitely

sometimes *adverb* at times, now and then

somewhat *adverb* rather

somewhere *adverb* in some place

son *noun* a male child

sonar *noun* a system using reflected sound waves to locate underwater objects

sonata *noun* a piece of music with three or more movements, usually for one instrument

song *noun* **1** singing **2** a piece of music to be sung

songbird *noun* a bird that sings

sonic *adjective* of sound waves

son-in-law *noun* a daughter's husband

sonnet *noun* a type of poem in fourteen lines

soon *adverb* **1** in a short time from now or from the time mentioned **2** early

sooner *adverb* more willingly, rather

soot *noun* the black powder left by smoke

soothe *verb* **1** to calm or comfort (a person, feelings, *etc*) **2** to help or ease (a pain *etc*)

soothing *adjective* that soothes

sophisticated *adjective* **1** of a person: full of experience, accustomed to an elegant, cultured way of life **2** of ways of thought, or machinery *etc*: highly developed, complicated, elaborate

sopping *adjective* wet through

soppy *adjective* overly sentimental

soprano *noun* (*plural* **sopranos**) **1** a singing voice of high pitch **2** a singer with this voice

sorcerer *noun* someone who works magic spells; a witch or wizard

sorcery *noun* magic, witchcraft

sordid *adjective* **1** dirty, filthy **2** mean, selfish **3** contemptible

sore *adjective* painful ▪ *noun* a painful, inflamed spot on the skin

sorely *adverb* very greatly: *sorely in need*

sorrow *noun* sadness caused by a loss, disappointment, *etc*

sorrowful *adjective* full of sadness

sorry *adjective* **1** feeling regret for something you have done **2** feeling sympathy or pity (for) **3** miserable: *in a sorry state*

sort *noun* a kind of (person or thing) ▪ *verb* to separate things, putting each in its place

SOS *noun* **1** a code signal calling for help **2** any call for help

so-so *adjective* not particularly good

sought *past form of* seek

soul *noun* **1** the spirit, the part of someone which is not the body **2** a person **3** a perfect example (of): *the soul of kindness*

soulful *adjective* full of feeling

sound *noun* **1** anything that can be heard, a noise **2** a distance from which something may be heard: *within the sound of Bow Bells* **3** a narrow passage of water ▪ *verb* **1** to strike you as being **2** **sound like** to resemble in sound **3** to make a noise with: *sound a horn* **4** to examine by listening carefully to: *sound a patient's chest* **5** to measure (the depths of water) **6** to try to find out someone's opinions: *I'll sound him out tomorrow* ▪ *adjective* **1** healthy, strong **2** of sleep: deep **3** thorough: *a sound beating* **4** reliable: *sound opinions*

sound barrier a sudden increase in drag experienced by aircraft flying close to the speed of sound

soundproof *adjective* built or made so that sound cannot pass in or out ▪ *verb* to make soundproof

soundtrack *noun* the strip on a film where the speech and music are recorded

soup *noun* a liquid food made from meat, vegetables, *etc*

sour *adjective* having an acid or bitter taste, often as a stage in going bad: *sour milk*

source *noun* **1** the place where something has its beginning or is found **2** a spring, especially one from which a river flows

south *noun* one of the four chief directions, that to the left of someone facing the setting sun ▪ *adjective & adverb* in or to the south ▪ **south-east** *noun* the point of the compass midway between south and east ■ **southerly** *adjective* **1** towards the south **2** of wind: *from the south* ■ **southern** *adjective* of, from or in the south ■ **southerner** *noun* someone living in a southern region or country ■ **southward** or **southwards** *adjective* & *adverb* towards the south ■ **south-west** *noun* the point of the compass midway between south and west

South Pole *see* **pole**

souvenir *noun* something bought or given as a reminder of a person, place or occasion

sou'wester *noun* a kind of waterproof hat

sovereign *noun* **1** a king or queen **2** an old British gold coin worth £1 ■ *adjective* **1** supreme, highest: *sovereign lord* **2** having its own government: *sovereign state*

sovereignty *noun* highest power

sow[1] (*pronounced* sow) *noun* a female pig

sow[2] (*pronounced* soh) *verb* **1** to scatter (seeds) so that they may grow **2** to cover (an area) with seeds

| **sow** ► sows, sowing, sowed, sown or sowed

soya bean or **soy bean** a kind of bean, rich in protein, used as a substitute for meat

soya sauce or **soy sauce** a

sauce made from soya beans used in Chinese cooking

spa *noun* a place where people go to drink or bathe in the water from a natural spring

space *noun* **1** a gap, an empty place **2** the distance between objects **3** an uncovered part on a sheet of paper **4** length of time: *in the space of a day* **5** the empty region in which all stars, planets, *etc* are situated ■ *verb* to put things apart from each other, leaving room between them

spacecraft *noun* a machine for travelling in space

spaceman, **spacewoman** *noun* a traveller in space

spaceship *noun* a manned spacecraft

space suit a sealed suit designed for space travel

spacious *adjective* having plenty of room

spade *noun* **1** a tool with a broad blade for digging in the earth **2** **spades** one of the four suits in playing-cards

spaghetti *noun* a type of pasta made into long sticks

span *noun* **1** the distance between the tips of the little finger and the thumb when the hand is spread out (about 23 centimetres, 9 inches) **2** the full time anything lasts **3** an arch of a bridge ■ *verb* to stretch across

| **span** *verb* ► spans, spanning, spanned

spangle noun a thin sparkling piece of metal used as an ornament

spaniel noun a breed of dog with large, hanging ears

spank verb to strike with the flat of the hand ■ noun a slap with the hand, especially on the buttocks

spanking noun a beating with the hand ■ adjective fast: a spanking pace

spanner noun a tool used to tighten or loosen nuts, screws, etc

spar noun a long piece of wood or metal used as a ship's mast or to support a sail ■ verb 1 to fight with the fists 2 to engage in an argument

spar verb ▶ spars, sparring, sparred

spare verb 1 to do without 2 to afford, set aside 3 to treat with mercy, hold back from injuring 4 to avoid causing (trouble etc) ■ adjective extra, not yet in use ■ noun another of the same kind (eg a tyre, part of a machine) kept for emergencies

sparing adjective careful, economical

spark noun 1 a small red-hot part thrown off from something burning 2 a trace: a spark of humanity 3 a lively person ■ verb to make sparks

sparkle noun 1 a little spark 2 brightness, liveliness ■ verb 1 to shine in a glittering way 2 to be lively or witty 3 to bubble

sparkling adjective 1 glittering 2 witty 3 of a drink: bubbling, fizzy

spark plug or **sparking-plug** a device in a car engine that produces a spark to set on fire explosive gases

sparrow noun a type of small dull-coloured bird

sparse adjective 1 thinly scattered 2 not much, not enough

spartan adjective of conditions etc: hard, without luxury

spasm noun a sudden involuntary jerk of the muscles

spasmodic adjective 1 occurring in spasms 2 coming now and again, not regularly
■ **spasmodically** adverb

spastic adjective suffering from brain damage which has resulted in extreme muscle spasm and paralysis

spat past form of spit

spate noun 1 flood: the river is in spate 2 a sudden rush: a spate of new books

spatial adjective of or relating to space

spatter verb to splash (eg with mud)

spatula noun a tool with a broad, blunt blade

spawn noun a mass of eggs of fish, frogs, etc ■ verb 1 of fish etc: to lay eggs 2 to cause, produce

speak verb 1 to say words, talk 2 to hold a conversation (with) 3 to make a speech 4 to be able to talk (a certain language) ■ **speak up**

1 to speak more loudly or clearly **2** to give your opinion openly

| **speak** ► speaks, speaking, spoke, spoken

speaker noun **1** someone who speaks, especially giving formal speeches **2** a device attached to a radio etc which converts audio signals into sound

spear noun a long weapon, with an iron or steel point

special adjective **1** not ordinary, exceptional **2** put on for a particular purpose: special train **3** belonging to one person or thing and not to others: special tool for drilling holes in tiles

specialist noun someone who studies one branch of a subject or field: heart specialist

speciality noun (plural specialities) something for which a person is well known

specialize or **specialise** verb to work in, or study, a particular job, subject, etc

specially adverb for a special purpose: specially written for younger children

💧 Do not confuse with: especially

species noun (plural species) **1** a group of plants or animals which are alike in most ways **2** a kind (of anything)

specific adjective giving all the details clearly; particular, exactly stated

specifically adverb **1** particularly or for the purpose stated and no other **2** exactly and clearly: I specifically told you not to leave the gate open

specification noun **1** the act of specifying **2** a full description of details (eg in a plan or contract)

specify verb **1** to set down or say clearly (what is wanted) **2** to make particular mention of

| **specify** ► specifies, specifying, specified

specimen noun something used as a sample of a group or kind of anything, especially for study or for putting in a collection

speck noun **1** a small spot **2** a tiny piece (eg of dust)

speckle noun a spot on a different-coloured background

speckled adjective dotted with speckles

spectacle noun **1** a striking or wonderful sight **2** spectacles glasses which someone wears to improve eyesight

spectacular adjective **1** very impressive to see or watch **2** remarkable or dramatic: a spectacular success

■ spectacularly adverb

spectator noun someone who watches an event eg a football match

spectre noun a ghost

spectrum noun (plural spectra or spectrums) **1** the band of colours as seen in a rainbow, sometimes formed when light passes through water or glass **2** the range or extent of anything

speculate verb **1** to guess **2** to wonder (about) ■ **speculation** noun

speculative adjective speculating

sped past form of **speed**

speech noun **1** the power of making sounds which have meaning for other people **2** a way of speaking: his speech is always clear **3** (plural **speeches**) a formal talk given to an audience

speechless adjective so surprised etc that you cannot speak

speed noun quickness of, or rate of, movement or action ■ verb **1** (past form **sped**) to (cause to) move along quickly, hurry **2** (past form **speeded**) to drive very fast in a car etc (especially faster than is allowed by law)

| **speed** verb ▶ speeds, speeding, sped or speeded

speeding noun driving at (an illegally) high speed

speed limit the greatest speed permitted on a particular road

speedometer noun an instrument that shows how fast you are travelling

speedway noun a motorcycle racing track

speedy adjective going quickly

spell noun **1** words which, when spoken, are supposed to have

magic power **2** magic or other powerful influence **3** a (short) space of time **4** a turn (at work, rest, play) ■ verb **1** to give or write correctly the letters which make up a word **2** to mean, imply: this defeat spells disaster for us all

■ **spell out** to say (something) very frankly or clearly

| **spell** verb ▶ spells, spelling, spelt or spelled

spellbound adjective charmed, held by a spell

spellcheck or **spellchecker** noun a computer program that checks the accuracy of spelling ■ **spell-check** verb to run a spellcheck over (a document)

spelling noun **1** the ability to spell words correctly **2** the study of spelling words correctly

spelt past form of **spell**

spend verb **1** to use (money) for buying **2** to use (energy etc) **3** to pass (time)

| **spend** ▶ spends, spending, spent

spendthrift noun someone who spends money freely and carelessly

spent adjective exhausted; having lost force or power: a spent bullet

sperm noun (the fluid in a male carrying) the male sex cell that fertilizes the female egg

spew verb to vomit

sphere noun **1** a ball or similar perfectly round object **2** range (of influence or action)

spherical *adjective* having the shape of a sphere

spheroid *noun*, *geometry* a figure that is almost a sphere

Sphinx *noun* **1** a mythological monster with the head of a woman and the body of a lioness **2** the large stone model of the Sphinx in Egypt

spice *noun* **1** any substance used for flavouring, *eg* pepper, nutmeg **2** anything that adds liveliness, interest ▪ *verb* to flavour with spice

spick-and-span *adjective* neat, clean and tidy

spicy *adjective* **1** full of spices **2** lively and sometimes slightly indecent

spider *noun* a kind of small, insect-like creature with eight legs, that spins a web

spidery *adjective* **1** like a spider **2** of handwriting: having fine, sprawling strokes

spike *noun* **1** a pointed piece of rod (of wood, metal, *etc*) **2** a type of large nail

spiky *adjective* having spikes or a sharp point

spill *verb* to (allow liquid to) run out or overflow ▪ *noun* **1** a fall **2** a thin strip of wood or twisted paper for lighting a candle, a pipe, *etc*

| **spill** *verb* ▶ spills, spilling, spilt or spilled

spillage *noun* an act of spilling or what is spilt

spin *verb* **1** to draw out (cotton, wood, silk, *etc*) and twist into threads **2** to (cause to) whirl round quickly **3** to produce a fine thread as a spider does ▪ *noun* **1** a whirling motion **2** a ride (especially on wheels) ▪ **spin out** to make to last a long or longer time

| **spin** *verb* ▶ spins, spinning, spun

spinach *noun* a type of plant whose leaves are eaten as vegetables

spinal *see* spine

spinal cord a cord of nerve cells in the spine

spindle *noun* the pin from which the thread is twisted in spinning wool or cotton

spindly *adjective* long and thin

spin dryer a machine for taking water out of clothes by whirling them round

spine *noun* **1** the line of linked bones running down the back in animals and humans, the backbone **2** a ridge **3** a stiff, pointed spike which is part of an animal's body (*eg* a porcupine) **4** a thorn ▪ **spinal** *adjective*

spineless *adjective* having no spine; weak

spinning wheel a machine for spinning thread, consisting of a wheel which drives spindles

spinster *noun* a woman who is not married

spiny *adjective* containing pointed spines

spiral *adjective* **1** coiled round like a spring **2** winding round and round, getting further and further away from the centre ▪ *noun* **1** anything with a spiral shape **2** a spiral movement **3** an increase which gets ever more rapid ▪ *verb* **1** to move in a spiral **2** to increase ever more rapidly

| **spiral** *verb* ▶ spirals, spiral*ling*, spiral*led*

spire *noun* a tall, sharp-pointed tower (especially on the roof of a church)

spirit *noun* **1** the soul **2** a being without a body, a ghost **3** liveliness, boldness **4** a feeling or attitude: *a spirit of kindness* **5** **spirits** strong alcoholic drinks in general (*eg* whisky) **6** **spirits** state of mind, mood: *in high spirits* ▪ *verb* (especially **spirit away**) to remove, as if by magic

spirited *adjective* lively

spiritual *adjective* having to do with the soul or with ghosts ▪ *noun* an emotional, religious song of a kind originally developed by the African American slaves

spiritualism *noun* the belief that living people can communicate with the souls of dead people

spiritualist *noun* someone who believes in spiritualism

spit *noun* **1** the liquid which forms in a person's mouth **2** a metal bar on which meat is roasted ▪ *verb* (*past form* **spat**) **1** to throw liquid out from the mouth **2** to rain slightly

| **spit** *verb* ▶ spits, spit*ting*, spat or spit*ted*

spite *noun* the wish to hurt (especially feelings) ▪ *verb* to annoy out of spite

spiteful *adjective* motivated by spite; malicious

spitting image an exact likeness

splash *verb* **1** to spatter with water, mud, *etc* **2** to move or fall with a splash or splashes ▪ *noun* (*plural* **splashes**) **1** the sound made by, or the scattering of liquid caused by, something hitting water *etc* **2** a mark made by splashing (*eg* on your clothes) **3** a bright patch: *a splash of colour*

splay *verb* to turn out at an angle

spleen *noun* a spongy, blood-filled organ inside the body, near the stomach

splendid *adjective* **1** magnificent, brilliant **2** *informal* excellent ▪ **splendidly** *adverb*

splendour *noun* the state or quality of being very grand and beautiful in appearance or style

splice *verb* to join (two ends of a rope) by twining the threads together

splint *noun* a piece of wood *etc* tied to a broken limb to keep it in a fixed position

splinter *noun* a sharp, thin,

broken piece of wood, glass, *etc*
■ *verb* to split into splinters
split *verb* **1** to cut or break
lengthways **2** to crack, break **3** to
divide into pieces or groups *etc*
■ *noun* a crack, a break
splitting *adjective* of a
headache: severe, intense
splutter *verb* **1** to make spitting
noises **2** to speak hastily and
unclearly
spoil *verb* **1** to make useless;
damage, ruin **2** to give in to the
wishes of (a child *etc*) and so ruin
its character **3** of food: to become
bad or useless

| **spoil** *verb* ► spoils, spoil*ing*,
spoil*ed* or spoil*t*

spoilsport *noun* someone who
won't join in other people's fun
spoke *noun* one of the ribs or
bars from the centre to the rim of
a wheel ■ *verb, past form of* **speak**
spoken *past participle of* **speak**
spokesman, **spokeswoman**
noun someone who speaks on
behalf of others
sponge *noun* **1** a sea animal **2** its
soft, elastic skeleton which can
soak up water and is used for
washing **3** an artificial object like
this used for washing **4** a light
cake or pudding ■ *verb* to wipe
with a sponge
spongy *adjective* soft like a
sponge
sponsor *noun* **1** someone who
takes responsibility for
introducing something, a

promoter **2** someone who
promises to pay a sum of money if
another person completes a set
task (*eg* a walk, swim, *etc*) **3** a
business firm which pays for a
radio or television programme
and advertises its products
during it ■ *verb* to act as a sponsor
to
sponsorship *noun* the act of
sponsoring
spontaneity *noun* being
spontaneous
spontaneous *adjective* **1** not
planned beforehand **2** natural,
not forced
spoof *noun* a trick played as a
joke, a hoax
spook *noun* a ghost
spooky *adjective* frightening
spool *noun* a reel for thread, film,
etc
spoon *noun* a piece of metal *etc*
with a hollow bowl at one end,
used for lifting food to the mouth
■ *verb* to lift with a spoon
sporadic *adjective* happening
here and there, or now and again
■ **sporadically** *adverb*
spore *noun* the seed of certain
plants (*eg* ferns, fungi)
sporran *noun* a small pouch
worn hanging in front of a kilt
sport *noun* **1** games such as
football, tennis, skiing, *etc* in
general **2** any one game of this
type **3** a good-natured, obliging
person ■ *verb* **1** to have fun, play **2**
to wear

sporting *adjective* 1 fond of sport 2 believing in fair play, good-natured

sporting chance a reasonably good chance

sports car a small, fast car with only two seats

sportsman, **sportswoman** *noun* 1 someone who plays sports 2 someone who shows fair play in sports

sportsmanlike *adjective* fair, sporting

spot *noun* 1 a small mark or stain (of mud, paint, *etc*) 2 a round mark as part of a pattern on material *etc* 3 a pimple 4 a place ▪ *verb* 1 to mark with spots 2 to catch sight of

| **spot** *verb* ▶ spots, spott*ing*, spott*ed*

spotless *adjective* very clean

spotlight *noun* a bright light that is shone on an actor on the stage ▪ *verb* 1 to show up clearly 2 to draw attention to

spotted *or* **spotty** *adjective* covered with spots

spouse *noun* a husband or wife

spout *noun* 1 the part of a kettle, teapot, *etc* through which liquid is poured out 2 a strong jet of liquid ▪ *verb* to pour or spurt out

sprain *noun* a painful twisting (eg of an ankle) ▪ *verb* to twist painfully

sprang *past form of* **spring**

sprat *noun* a small fish similar to a herring

sprawl *verb* 1 to sit, lie or fall with the limbs spread out widely 2 of a town *etc*: to spread out in an untidy, irregular way

spray *noun* 1 a fine mist of liquid like that made by a waterfall 2 a device with many small holes (*eg* on a watering-can or shower) for producing spray 3 a liquid for spraying 4 a shoot spreading out in flowers ▪ *verb* to cover with a mist or fine jets of liquid

spread *verb* 1 to put more widely or thinly over an area: *spread the butter on the bread* 2 to cover: *spread the bread with jam* 3 to open out (eg your arms, a map) 4 to scatter or distribute over a wide area, length of time, *etc* ▪ *noun* 1 the act of spreading 2 the extent or range (of something) 3 a food which is spread on bread 4 *informal* a large meal laid out on a table

| **spread** *verb* ▶ spreads, spread*ing*, spread

spread-eagled *adjective* with limbs spread out

spreadsheet *noun* a computer program with which data can be viewed on screen and manipulated

spree *noun* a careless spell of some activity: *a spending spree*

sprig *noun* a small twig or shoot

sprightly *adjective* lively, brisk

spring *verb* 1 to jump, leap 2 to move swiftly 3 spring back to return suddenly to an earlier position when released **4** to come from: *his bravery springs from his love of adventure* ■ *noun* **1** a leap **2** a coil of wire used in a mattress **3** the ability to stretch and spring back **4** bounce, energy **5** a small stream flowing out from the ground **6** the season which follows winter, when plants begin to grow again ■ **spring up** to appear suddenly

| **spring** *verb* ▶ springs, springing, sprang, sprung

springboard *noun* a springy board from which swimmers may dive

spring-cleaning *noun* a thorough cleaning of a house, especially in the spring

springy *adjective* able to spring back into its former position *etc*, elastic

sprinkle *verb* to scatter or cover in small drops or pieces

sprinkler *noun* something which sprinkles water

sprinkling *noun* a few, a small amount: *a sprinkling of snow*

sprint *verb* to run at full speed ■ *noun* a short running race

sprinter *noun* someone who is good at running fast over short distances

sprite *noun* **1** a supernatural spirit **2** *computing* an icon which can be moved about a screen

sprocket *noun* one of a set of teeth on the rim of a wheel

sprout *verb* **1** to begin to grow

2 to put out new shoots ■ *noun* **1** a young bud **2 sprouts** Brussels sprouts

spruce *adjective* neat, smart ■ *noun* a kind of fir tree

sprung *past participle* of **spring**

spry *adjective* lively, active

spud *noun*, *informal* a potato

spun *past form* of **spin**

spur *noun* **1** a sharp point worn by a horse-rider on the heel and used to urge on a horse **2** anything that urges someone on ■ *verb* **1** to use spurs on (a horse) **2** to urge on

| **spur** *verb* ▶ spurs, spurring, spurred

spurn *verb* to cast aside, reject with scorn

spurt *verb* to pour out in a sudden stream ■ *noun* **1** a sudden stream pouring or squirting out **2** a sudden increase of effort: *put a spurt on*

sputter *verb* to make a noise as of spitting and throw out moisture in drops

spy *noun* (*plural* **spies**) someone who secretly collects (and reports) information about another person, country, firm, *etc* ■ *verb* **1** to catch sight of **2 spy on someone** to watch them secretly

| **spy** *verb* ▶ spies, spying, spied

squabble *verb* to quarrel noisily ■ *noun* a noisy quarrel

squad *noun* **1** a group of soldiers, workmen, *etc* doing a particular job **2** a group of people

squadron noun a division of a regiment, section of a fleet or group of aeroplanes

squalid adjective 1 very dirty, filthy 2 contemptible

squall noun a sudden violent storm

squally adjective stormy

squalor noun dirty or squalid living conditions

squander verb to waste (money, goods, strength, etc)

square noun 1 a figure with four equal sides and four right angles, of this shape: □ 2 an open space enclosed by buildings in a town 3 the answer when a number is multiplied by itself (eg the square of 3 is 9) ■ adjective 1 shaped like a square 2 in area: one metre square 3 equal in scores in a game 4 of two or more people: not owing one another anything 5 straight, level ■ verb 1 to make like a square 2 to straighten (the shoulders) 3 to multiply a number by itself 4 to fit, agree: that doesn't square with what you said earlier 5 **square up** to settle a debt ■ adverb 1 in a straight or level position 2 directly; exactly: hit square on the nose

square deal fair treatment

square meal a large, satisfying meal

square root the number which, multiplied by itself, gives a certain other number (eg 3 is the square root of 9)

squash verb 1 to crush flat or to a pulp 2 to put down, defeat (rebellion etc) ■ noun 1 a crushing or crowding 2 a mass of people crowded together 3 a drink made from the juice of crushed fruit 4 a game with rackets and a rubber ball played in a walled court

squat verb 1 to sit down on the heels 2 to settle without permission in property which you do not pay rent for ■ adjective short and thick

| squat verb ► squats, squatting, squatted

squatter noun someone who squats in a building, on land, etc

squawk verb to give a harsh cry ■ noun a harsh cry

squeak verb to give a short, high-pitched sound ■ noun a high-pitched sound

squeaky adjective 1 high-pitched 2 tending to squeak: a squeaky floorboard

squeal verb to give a loud, shrill cry ■ noun a shrill cry

squeamish adjective 1 easily sickened or shocked 2 feeling sick

squeegee noun a sponge for washing windows etc

squeeze verb 1 to press together 2 to grasp tightly 3 to force out (liquid or juice from) by pressing 4 to force a way: squeeze through the hole in the wall ■ noun 1 a squeezing or pressing 2 a few drops got by squeezing: a squeeze of lemon juice **3** a crowd of people crushed together

squelch noun a sound made, eg by walking through marshy ground ■ verb to make this sound

squid noun a sea animal with long tentacles

squiggle noun a curly or wavy mark

squint verb **1** to screw up the eyes in looking at something **2** to have the eyes looking in different directions ■ noun **1** a fault in eyesight which causes squinting **2** informal a quick, close glance

squire noun, history **1** a country landowner **2** a knight's servant

squirm verb to wriggle or twist the body, especially in pain or embarrassment

squirrel noun a small gnawing animal, either reddish-brown or grey, with a bushy tail

squirt verb to shoot out a narrow jet of liquid ■ noun a narrow jet of liquid

St abbreviation **1** saint **2** street

stab verb **1** to wound or pierce with a pointed weapon **2** to poke (at) ■ noun **1** the act of stabbing **2** a wound made by stabbing **3** a sharp pain **4** informal an attempt

| **stab** verb ▶ stabs, stabbing, stabbed

stability noun steadiness

stabilize or **stabilise** verb to make steady

stable noun a building for

keeping horses ■ adjective firm, steady

staccato adjective **1** of sounds: sharp and separate, like the sound of tapping **2** music with each note sounded separately and clearly

stack noun a large pile (of straw, hay, wood, etc) ■ verb to pile in a stack

stadium noun (plural **stadiums** or **stadia**) a large sports-ground or race-course with seats for spectators

staff noun **1** a stick or pole carried in the hand **2** music a stave **3** workers employed in a business, school, etc ■ verb to supply (a school etc) with staff

stag noun a male deer

stage noun **1** a platform for performing or acting on **2** the stage the theatre; the job of working as an actor **3** a step in development: the first stage of the plan **4** a part of a journey ■ verb **1** to prepare and put on a performance of (a play etc) **2** to arrange (an event, eg an exhibition)

stagecoach noun, history a coach running every day with passengers

stage fright an actor's fear when acting in public, especially for the first time

stage whisper a loud whisper

stagger verb **1** to walk unsteadily, totter **2** to astonish

3 to arrange (people's hours of work *etc*) so that they do not begin or end together

staggered *adjective* of two or more things: arranged to begin and end at different times

staggering *adjective* astonishing

staging *noun* putting on the stage

stagnant *adjective* of water: standing still, not flowing and therefore not pure

stagnate *verb* **1** of water: to remain still and so become impure **2** to remain for a long time in the same situation and so become bored, inactive, *etc*

stagnation *noun* **1** stagnating **2** being stagnant

stag party a party for men only, held shortly before one of them gets married

staid *adjective* set in your ways, sedate

stain *verb* **1** to give a different colour to (wood *etc*) **2** to mark or make dirty by accident ▪ *noun* **1** a liquid which dyes or colours something **2** a mark which is not easily removed **3** something shameful in someone's character or reputation

stained glass coloured glass cut in shapes and used for decoration

stainless steel a mixture of steel and chromium which does not rust

stair *noun* **1** one or all of a number of steps one after the other **2** stairs a series or flight of steps

staircase *noun* a stretch of stairs with rails on one or both sides

stake *noun* **1** a strong stick pointed at one end **2** money invested or put down as a bet **3** *history* a post to which people were tied to be burned ▪ *verb* to bet (money)

stalactite *noun* a spike of limestone hanging from the roof of a cave, formed by the dripping of water containing lime

stalagmite *noun* a spike of limestone, like a stalactite, rising from the floor of a cave

stale *adjective* **1** of food: no longer fresh **2** no longer interesting because heard, done, *etc* too often before **3** not able to do your best (because of overworking, boredom, *etc*)

stalemate *noun* **1** *chess* a position in which a player cannot move without putting their king in danger **2** a position in an argument in which neither side can win

stalk *noun* the stem of a plant or of a leaf or flower ▪ *verb* **1** to walk stiffly or proudly **2** to go quietly up to animals being hunted to shoot at close range

stall *noun* **1** a division for one animal in a cowshed *etc* **2** a table on which things are laid out for sale **3** an open-fronted shop **4** a seat in a church (especially for choir or clergy) **5 stalls** theatre seats on the ground floor ▪ *verb* **1** of a car engine: to come to a halt without the driver intending it to do so **2** *informal* to avoid action or decision for the time being

stallion *noun* a male horse, especially one kept for breeding purposes

stalwart *adjective* brave, stout-hearted ▪ *noun* a loyal supporter

stamen *noun* one of the thread-like spikes in the middle of a flower which bear the pollen

stamina *noun* strength, power to keep going

stammer *verb* **1** to have difficulty in saying the first letter of words in speaking **2** to stumble over words ▪ *noun* a speech difficulty of this kind

stamp *verb* **1** to bring the foot down firmly on the ground **2** to stick a (postage stamp) on **3** to mark with a design cut into a mould and inked **4** to fix or mark deeply: *forever stamped in my memory* ▪ *noun* **1** the act of stamping **2** a design *etc* made by stamping **3** a cut or moulded design for stamping **4** a postage stamp ▪ **stamp out 1** to put out (a fire) by stamping **2** to suppress, crush

stampede *noun* **1** a wild rush of frightened animals **2** a sudden, wild rush of people ▪ *verb* to rush wildly

stance *noun* someone's manner of standing

stanchion *noun* an upright iron bar used as a support (*eg* in windows, ships)

stand *verb* **1** to be on your feet (not lying or sitting down) **2** to rise to your feet **3** of an object: to (cause to) be in a particular place: *it stood by the door* **4** to bear: *I cannot stand this heat* **5** to be a candidate (for) **6** to be short (for) ▪ *noun* **1** something on which anything is placed **2** an object made to hold, or for hanging, things: *a hat-stand* **3** lines of raised seats from which people may watch games *etc* **4** an effort made to support, defend, resist, *etc*: *a stand against violence* ▪ **stand by** to be ready or available to be used or help in an emergency *etc* ▪ **stand down** to withdraw (from a contest) or resign (from a job) ▪ **stand in (for)** to take another's place, job, *etc* for a time ▪ **stand out** to stick out, be noticeable ▪ **stand up for** to defend strongly ▪ **stand up to** to face or oppose bravely

| **stand** *verb* ► stands, standing, stood

stand-alone *noun & adjective, computing* (of) a system, device, *etc* that can operate unconnected to any other

standard *noun* **1** a level against which things may be judged **2** a level of excellence aimed at **3** a

large flag *etc* on a pole ■ *adjective*
1 normal, usual **2** ordinary,
without extras: *standard model*
standardize *or* **standardise**
verb to make all of one kind or size
standard lamp a kind of tall
lamp which stands on the floor of
a room *etc*
standby *noun* something that is
kept ready for use, especially in
an emergency
stand-in *noun* someone who
takes another's place, job, *etc* for
a time
standing *noun* social position or
reputation ■ *adjective* **1** on your
feet **2** placed on end **3** not moving
4 lasting, permanent
standoffish *adjective*
unfriendly
standpoint *noun* the position
from which you look at
something (*eg* a question,
problem), point of view
standstill *noun* a complete stop
stank *past form of* **stink**
stanza *noun* a group of lines
making up a part of a poem, a
verse
staple *noun* **1** a U-shaped iron
nail **2** a piece of wire driven
through sheets of paper to fasten
them together ■ *verb* to fasten with
a staple ■ *adjective* chief, main
stapler *noun* a hand-held device
for attaching staples
star *noun* **1** any of the bodies in
the sky appearing as points of
light **2** the fixed bodies which are

really distant suns, not the
planets **3** an object, shape or
figure with a number of pointed
rays (often five) **4** a leading actor
or actress or other well-known
performer ■ *adjective* for or of a
star (in a film *etc*) ■ *verb* **1** to act
the chief part (in a play or film) **2**
of a play *etc*: to have as its star

| **star** *verb* ▶ stars, starring,
| starred

starboard *noun* the right side of
a ship, as you look towards the bow
(or front)
starch *noun* (*plural* **starches**) **1** a
white carbohydrate (found in
flour, potatoes, bread, biscuits,
etc) **2** a form of this used for
stiffening clothes
starchy *adjective* of food:
containing starch
stardom *noun* the state of being
a leading performer
stare *verb* to look with a fixed
gaze ■ *noun* a fixed gaze
starfish *noun* a type of small sea
creature with five points or arms
stark *adjective* **1** barren, bare **2**
harsh, severe ■ *adverb*
completely: *stark naked*
starling *noun* a common bird
with dark, glossy feathers
starry *adjective* full of stars;
shining like stars
start *verb* **1** to begin (an action) **2**
to get (a machine *etc*) working **3**
to jump or jerk (*eg* in surprise)
■ *noun* **1** the act of starting (*eg* on
a task, journey) **2** a sudden

movement of the body **3** a sudden shock **4** in a race *etc* the advantage of beginning before, or farther forward than, others, or the amount of this

startle *verb* to give a shock or fright to

startling *adjective* that startles, surprising

starvation *noun* a potentially fatal form of malnutrition caused by eating insufficient quantities of food over a long period, or by total lack of food

starve *verb* **1** to die for want of food **2** to suffer greatly from hunger **3** to deprive (of something needed or wanted badly): *starved of company*

state *noun* **1** the condition (of something) **2** the people of a country under a government **3** *US* an area and its people with its own laws forming part of the whole country **4** a government and its officials **5** great show, pomp: *the king drove by in state* ■ *adjective* **1** of the government **2** national and ceremonial: *state occasions* **3** *US* of a certain state of America: *the state capital of Texas* ■ *verb* to tell, say or write (especially clearly and fully)

stately *adjective* noble-looking; dignified

stately home a large, grand old house

statement *noun* that which is said or written

state-of-the-art *adjective* most up-to-date

statesman *noun* someone skilled in government

static *adjective* not moving ■ *noun* **1** atmospheric disturbances causing poor reception of radio or television programmes **2** (*also called*: **static electricity**) electricity on the surface of objects, *eg* hair, nylon, *etc*, which will not conduct it

station *noun* **1** a building with a ticket office, waiting rooms, *etc* where trains, buses or coaches stop to pick up or set down passengers **2** a place which is the centre for work or duty of any kind: *fire station* **3** rank, position: *lowly station* ■ *verb* **1** to assign to a position or place **2** to take up a position

stationary *adjective* standing still, not moving

♦* Do not confuse:
stationary and **stationery**.
Remember that a stationER's
shop sells **stationERy**

stationer *noun* someone who sells writing paper, envelopes, pens, *etc*

stationery *noun* writing paper, envelopes, pens, *etc*

statistic *noun* **1** one of a series of figures and facts set out in order: *statistics of road accidents for last year* **2** **statistics** the study of such facts and figures: *statistics is not an easy subject*

statistical *adjective* of or shown by statistics ■ **statistically** *adverb*

statue *noun* a likeness of someone or an animal carved in stone, metal, *etc*

statuesque *adjective* like a statue in dignity *etc*

statuette *noun* a small statue

stature *noun* **1** height **2** importance, reputation

status *noun* position, rank (of a person) in the eyes of others

statute *noun* a written law of a country

statutory *adjective* according to law

staunch *adjective* firm, loyal; trustworthy

stave *noun* a set of spaced lines on which music is written ■ **stave off** to keep (something) away

| **stave** ▶ staves, staving, stove or staved

stay *verb* **1** to continue to be: *stayed calm* **2** to live (for a time) ■ *noun* time spent in a place

St Bernard *see* Saint Bernard

stead *noun* place: *she went in my stead*

steadfast *adjective* **1** steady, fixed **2** faithful, loyal

steady *adjective* **1** firm, not moving or changing **2** not easily upset or put off **3** even, regular, unchanging: *a steady pace* ■ *verb* to make or become steady ■ **steadily** *adverb*

| **steady** *verb* ▶ steadies, steadying, steadied

steak *noun* a thick slice of meat *etc* for cooking

steal *verb* **1** to take (something not belonging to you) without permission **2** to move quietly **3** to take quickly or secretly: *stole a look at him*

| **steal** ▶ steals, stealing, stole, stolen

stealth *noun* a secret way of doing, acting, *etc*

stealthy *adjective* of movement: slow, quiet and secretive ■ **stealthily** *adverb*

steam *noun* **1** vapour from hot liquid, especially from boiling water **2** power produced by steam ■ *verb* **1** to give off steam **2** to cook by steam **3** to open or loosen by putting into steam: *steam open the envelope* ■ **steam up** of glass: to become covered with condensed steam in the form of small drops of water

steam engine an engine (especially a railway engine) worked by steam

steamer *noun* a ship driven by steam

steamroller *noun* a steam-driven engine with large and very heavy wheels, used for flattening the surfaces of roads

steamy *adjective* **1** full of steam **2** *informal* passionate

steel *noun* a very hard mixture of iron and carbon

steep *adjective* **1** of a slope: rising nearly straight up **2** *informal* of a price: too great ■ *verb* to soak in a liquid

steeple *noun* a tower of a church *etc* rising to a point, a spire

steeplechase *noun* **1** a race run across open country, over hedges, *etc* **2** a race over a course on which obstacles (*eg* walls) have been made

steeplejack *noun* someone who climbs steeples or other high buildings to make repairs

steer *noun* a young ox raised for its beef ■ *verb* to control the course of (a car, ship, discussion, *etc*)

steering *noun* the parts of a ship, car, *etc* which have to do with controlling its course

steering wheel the wheel in a car used by the driver to steer it

stellar *adjective* of the stars

stem *noun* **1** the part of a plant from which the leaves and flowers grow **2** the thin support of a wine-glass ■ *verb* **1** to stop, halt **2** to start, spring (from)

| **stem** *verb* ▶ stems, stemm*ing*, stemm*ed*

stench *noun* a strong unpleasant smell

stencil *noun* **1** a sheet of metal, cardboard, *etc* with a pattern cut out **2** the drawing or design made by rubbing ink or brushing paint *etc* over a cut-out pattern **3** a piece of waxed paper on which words are cut with a typewriter, and which is then used to make copies ■ *verb* to make a design or copy in one of these ways

| **stencil** *verb* ▶ stencils, stencil*ling*, stencil*led*

step *noun* **1** a movement of the leg in walking, running, *etc* **2** the distance covered by this **3** a particular movement of the feet, as in dancing **4** the sound made by the foot in walking *etc* **5** a riser on a stair, or rung on a ladder **6** one of a series of moves in a plan, career, *etc* **7** a way of walking **8** **steps** a flight of stairs **9** **steps** a stepladder ■ *verb* **1** to take a step **2** to walk, move ■ **step up** to increase (*eg* production)

| **step** *verb* ▶ steps, step*ping*, step*ped*

stepladder *noun* a ladder with a support on which it rests

steppe *noun* a dry, grassy treeless plain in SE Europe and Asia

stepping-stone *noun* **1** a stone rising above water or mud, used to cross on **2** anything that helps you to advance

stereo *adjective*, *short for* **stereophonic** ■ *noun* (*plural* **stereos**) stereophonic equipment, especially a record-player and/or tape recorder, with amplifier and loudspeakers

stereophonic *adjective* of sound: giving a lifelike effect, with different instruments, voices, *etc* coming from different directions

stereotype *noun* a characteristic type of person ■ *verb* to treat (someone) as a stereotype

stereotyped *or* **stereotypical** *adjective* fixed, not changing: *stereotyped ideas*

sterile *adjective* **1** unable to have children or reproduce **2** producing no ideas *etc*: *sterile imagination* **3** free from germs

sterility *noun* the state of being sterile

sterilization *or* **sterilisation** *noun* **1** a surgical operation that is performed on humans or animals so that offspring can no longer be produced **2** the treatment of food *etc* in order to destroy germs

sterilize *or* **sterilise** *verb* **1** to make sterile **2** to free from germs by boiling *etc*

sterling *noun* British money, when used in international trading: *the value of sterling fell today* ■ *adjective* **1** of silver: of a certain standard of purity **2** worthy, good: *sterling qualities*

stern[1] *adjective* **1** looking or sounding angry or displeased **2** severe, strict, harsh ■ **sternly** *adverb*

stern[2] *noun* the back part of a ship

steroid *noun* any of a number of substances, including certain hormones (*see also* **anabolic steroids**)

stethoscope *noun* an instrument by means of which a doctor listens to someone's heartbeats, breathing, *etc*

stew *verb* to cook by boiling slowly ■ *noun* **1** a dish of stewed food, often containing meat and vegetables **2** *informal* a state of worry; a flap

steward *noun* **1** a flight attendant on an aircraft **2** someone who shows people to their seats at a meeting *etc* **3** an official at a race meeting *etc*

stewardess *noun* a female flight attendant (*also called*: **air hostess**)

stick *noun* **1** a long thin piece of wood; a branch or twig from a tree **2** a piece of wood shaped for a special purpose: *hockey-stick* **3** a long piece (*eg* of rhubarb) ■ *verb* **1** to push or thrust (something): *stick the knife in your belt* **2** to fix with glue *etc* **3** to be or become caught, fixed or held back: *stuck in the ditch* **4** to hold fast to, keep to (*eg* a decision) ■ **stick up for** to speak in defence of

> **stick** *verb* ▶ sticks, stick*ing*, stuck

sticker *noun* a label, small poster, *etc* with an adhesive back

sticking-plaster *noun* a kind of tape with a sticky surface, used to protect slight cuts *etc*

stick insect a long, thin, tropical insect with legs that look like twigs

stick-in-the-mud *noun*

someone who is against new ideas, change, *etc*

stickler *noun* someone who attaches great importance to a particular (often small) matter: *stickler for punctuation*

sticky *adjective* **1** clinging closely (like glue, treacle, *etc*) **2** covered with something sticky **3** difficult: *a sticky problem*

stiff *adjective* **1** not easily bent or moved **2** of a mixture, dough, *etc*: thick, not easily stirred **3** cold and distant in manner **4** hard, difficult **5** severe: *stiff penalty* **6** strong: *stiff drink*

stiffen *verb* to make or become stiff

stifle *verb* **1** to suffocate **2** to put out (flames) **3** to keep back (tears, a yawn, *etc*)

stifling *adjective* very hot and stuffy

stigma *noun* **1** (*plural* **stigmata**) a mark of disgrace **2** (*plural* **stigmas**) in a flower, the top of the pistil

stigmatize *or* **stigmatise** *verb* to mark, describe as something bad

stile *noun* a step or set of steps for climbing over a wall or fence

stiletto *noun* (*plural* **stilettos**) (a shoe with) a stiletto heel

stiletto heel a high, thin heel on a shoe

still *adjective* **1** not moving **2** calm, without wind; quiet **3** of drinks: not fizzy ■ *verb* to make

calm or quiet ■ *adverb* **1** up to the present time or the time spoken of **2** even so, nevertheless **3** even: *still more people*

stillborn *adjective* of a child: dead at birth

still life a picture of something that is not living (as a bowl of fruit *etc*)

stilted *adjective* stiff, not natural

stilts *noun plural* long poles with footrests on which someone may walk clear of the ground

stimulant *noun* something which makes a part of the body more active or which makes you feel livelier

stimulate *verb* **1** to make more active **2** to encourage **3** to excite

stimulus *noun* (*plural* **stimuli**) **1** something that brings on a reaction in a living thing **2** something that rouses (someone *etc*) to action or greater effort

sting *noun* **1** the part of some animals and plants (*eg* the wasp, the nettle) which can prick the skin and cause pain or irritation **2** the act of piercing with a sting **3** the wound, swelling or pain caused by a sting ■ *verb* **1** to pierce with a sting or cause pain like that of a sting **2** to be painful, smart **3** to hurt the feelings of: *stung by his words*

| **sting** *verb* ► stings, sting*ing*, stung

stingy (*pronounced* stin-ji)

adjective mean, not generous
■ **stinginess** *noun*

stink *noun* a bad smell ■ *verb* to give out a bad smell

| **stink** *verb* ▶ stinks, stink*ing*, stank or stunk, stunk

stint *verb* to allow (someone) very little: *don't stint on the sugar*

stipulate *verb* to state as a condition (of doing something)

stipulation *noun* something stipulated, a condition

stir *verb* **1** to set (liquid) in motion, especially with a spoon *etc* moved circularly **2** to move slightly **3** to arouse (a person, a feeling, *etc*) ■ *noun* disturbance, fuss ■ **stir up** to rouse, cause (*eg* trouble)

| **stir** *verb* ▶ stirs, stir*ring*, stir*red*

stirring *adjective* exciting

stirrup *noun* a metal loop hung from a horse's saddle as a support for the rider's foot

stitch *noun* (*plural* **stitches**) **1** the loop made in a thread, wool, *etc* by a needle in sewing or knitting **2** a sharp, sudden pain in your side ■ *verb* to put stitches in, sew

stoat *noun* a type of small fierce animal similar to a weasel, sometimes called an ermine when in its white winter fur

stock *noun* **1** family, race: *of ancient stock* **2** goods in a shop, warehouse, *etc* **3** the capital of a business company divided into shares **4** liquid (used for soup)

obtained by boiling meat, bones, *etc* **5** **stocks** *history* a wooden frame, with holes for the ankles and wrists, in which criminals *etc* were fastened as a punishment ■ *verb* **1** to keep a supply of (for sale) **2** to supply (a farm with animals *etc*) ■ *adjective* usual, known by everyone: *a stock joke*

stockade *noun* a fence of strong posts set up round an area or building for defence

stockbroker *noun* someone who buys and sell shares in business companies on behalf of others

stock car a car that has been strengthened to take part in races where colliding is allowed

stock exchange 1 a place where stocks and shares are bought and sold **2** an association of people who do this

stocking *noun* a close-fitting covering in a knitted fabric (wool, nylon, *etc*) for the leg and foot

stock market the stock exchange; dealings in stocks and shares

stockpile *noun* a store, a reserve supply ■ *verb* to build up a store

stock-still *adjective* perfectly still

stocktaking *noun* a regular check of the goods in a shop or warehouse

stocky *adjective* short and stout
■ **stockiness** *noun*

stodgy *adjective* of food: heavy,

not easily digested ■ **stodginess** *noun*

stoic *noun* someone who bears pain, hardship, *etc* without showing any sign of feeling it ■ **stoical** *adjective*

stoke *verb* to put coal, wood, or other fuel on (a fire)

stole[1] *noun* a length of silk, linen or fur worn over the shoulders

stole[2] and **stolen** see **steal**

stomach *noun* 1 the bag-like part of the body into which the food passes when swallowed 2 desire or courage (for something): *no stomach for a fight* ■ *verb* to put up with, bear

stomp *verb* to stamp the feet, especially noisily

stone *noun* 1 the material of which rocks are composed 2 a (small) loose piece of this 3 a piece of this shaped for a certain purpose: *tombstone* 4 a precious stone (*eg* a diamond) 5 the hard shell around the seed of some fruits (*eg* peach, cherry) 6 a measure of weight (14 pounds, 6.35 kilograms) ■ *verb* 1 to throw stones at 2 to take the stones out of fruit ■ *adjective* made of stone

Stone Age human culture before the use of metal

stone-cold *adjective* very cold

stony *adjective* 1 like stone 2 covered with stones 3 hard, cold in manner

stood past form of **stand**

stooge *noun* someone who is used by another to do a (usually humble or unpleasant) job

stool *noun* a seat without a back

stoop *verb* 1 to bend the body forwards and downwards 2 to be low or wicked enough to do a certain thing: *I wouldn't stoop to stealing* ■ *noun* 1 the act of stooping 2 a forward bend of the body

stop *verb* 1 to bring to a halt 2 to prevent from doing 3 to put an end to 4 to come to an end 5 **stop something up** to block (a hole *etc*) ■ *noun* 1 the state of being stopped 2 a place where something stops 3 a full stop

| **stop** *verb* ► stops, stopping, stopped

stopgap *noun* something which is used in an emergency until something better is found

stoppage *noun* something which blocks up (*eg* a tube or a passage in the body) 2 a halt (*eg* in work in a factory)

stopper *noun* something that stops up an opening (especially in the neck of a bottle, jar, *etc*)

stopwatch *noun* a watch that can be stopped and started, used in timing races

storage *noun* 1 the act of storing 2 the state of being stored: *our furniture is in storage*

store *noun* 1 a supply (*eg* of goods) from which things are taken when needed 2 a place where goods are kept 3 a shop 4 a

collected amount or number
■ *verb* to put aside for future use

storey *noun* (*plural* **storeys**) all that part of a building on the same floor

> ♦* Do not confuse with:
> **story**

stork *noun* a wading bird with a long bill, neck and legs

storm *noun* **1** a sudden burst of bad weather (especially with heavy rain, lightning, thunder, high wind) **2** a violent outbreak (*eg* of anger) ■ *verb* **1** to be in a fury **2** to rain, blow, *etc* violently ■ **stormy** *adjective*

story *noun* (*plural* **stories**) an account of an event or events, real or imaginary

> ♦* Do not confuse with:
> **storey**

stout *adjective* **1** fat, stocky **2** strong: *stout walking-stick*

stove *noun* an apparatus using coal, gas or electricity, *etc*, used for heating, cooking, *etc* ■ *verb*, *past form of* **stave**

stow *verb* **1** to pack or put away **2** to fill, pack

stowaway *noun* someone who hides in a ship in order to travel without paying a fare

straddle *verb* **1** to stand or walk with legs apart **2** to sit with one leg on each side of (*eg* a chair or horse)

straggle *verb* **1** to wander from

the line of a march *etc* **2** to lag behind

straggler *noun* a person or animal that wanders or lags behind

straggly *adjective* spread out untidily

straight *adjective* **1** not bent or curved **2** direct, frank, honest **3** in the proper position or order **4** of a hanging picture *etc*: placed level with ceiling or floor **5** of a drink: without anything added: *a straight vodka* **6** expressionless: *he kept a straight face* ■ *adverb* **1** by the shortest way, directly **2** at once, without delay **3** fairly, frankly: *he's not playing straight with you*

> ♦* Do not confuse with:
> **strait**

straighten *verb* to make straight

straightforward *adjective* **1** without any difficulties **2** honest, frank

strain *verb* **1** to hurt (a muscle or other part of the body) by overworking or misusing it **2** to work or use to the fullest: *he strained his ears to hear the whisper* **3** to make a great effort: *he strained to reach the rope* **4** to stretch too far, to the point of breaking (a person's patience *etc*) **5** to separate liquid from a mixture of liquids and solids by passing it through a sieve ■ *noun* **1** the act of straining **2** a hurt to a muscle *etc* caused by straining it **3** (the effect of) too much work, worry, *etc*: *suffering from strain* **4** too great a demand: *a strain on my patience* **5** a kind, breed: *a strain of fowls*

strained *adjective* **1** not natural, done with effort **2** unfriendly: *strained relations*

strainer *noun* a sieve

strait *noun* **1** a narrow strip of sea between two pieces of land **2 straits** difficulties, hardships: *dire straits*

◆* Do not confuse with: **straight**

straitjacket *noun* a jacket with long sleeves tied behind to prevent a violent or insane person from using their arms

straitlaced *adjective* strict in attitude and behaviour

strand *noun* a length of something soft and fine (*eg* hair, thread)

stranded *adjective* **1** of a ship: run aground on the shore **2** left helpless without money or friends

strange *adjective* **1** unusual, odd **2** not known, seen, heard, *etc* before, unfamiliar **3** not accustomed (to) ▪ **strangely** *adverb*

stranger *noun* someone who is unknown to you

strangle *verb* to kill by gripping or squeezing the throat tightly ▪ **strangulation** *noun*

stranglehold *noun* a tight control over something which prevents it from escaping, growing, *etc*

strap *noun* a narrow strip of leather, cloth, *etc* used to hold things in place or together ▪ *verb* **1** to bind or fasten with a strap *etc* **2** to beat with a strap

| **strap** *verb* ▶ strap*s*, strapp*ing*, strapp*ed*

strapping *adjective* tall and strong

stratagem *noun* a cunning act, meant to deceive and outwit an enemy

strategic *adjective* **1** of strategy **2** done according to a strategy: *a strategic retreat* **3** giving an advantage: *a strategic position*

strategy *noun* (*plural* **strategies**) the art of guiding, forming or carrying out a plan

straw *noun* **1** the stalk on which corn grows **2** a paper or plastic tube for sucking up a drink

strawberry *noun* a type of small, juicy, red fruit or the low creeping plant which bears it

strawberry blonde a woman with reddish blond hair

stray *verb* **1** to wander **2** to lose your way, become separated (from companions *etc*) ▪ *adjective* **1** wandering, lost **2** happening *etc* here and there: *a stray example* ▪ *noun* a wandering animal which has been abandoned or lost

streak noun 1 a line or strip different in colour from that which surrounds it 2 a smear of dirt, polish, etc 3 a flash (eg of lightning) 4 a trace of some quality in one's character: a streak of selfishness ■ verb 1 to mark with streaks 2 informal to move very fast

streaked adjective having streaks

streaky adjective marked with streaks

stream noun 1 a flow (of water, air, light, etc) 2 a small river, a brook 3 any steady flow of people or things: a stream of traffic ■ verb to flow or pour out

streamer noun 1 a long strip, usually of paper, used for decorating rooms etc (especially at Christmas) 2 a narrow flag blowing in the wind

streamline verb 1 to shape (a vehicle etc) so that it may cut through the air or water as easily as possible 2 to make more efficient

street noun a road lined with houses etc

strength noun 1 the state of being strong 2 an available number or force (of soldiers, volunteers, etc) 3 an area of high performance or particular ability

strengthen verb to make, or become, strong or stronger

strenuous adjective performed with or needing great effort

stress noun (plural **stresses**) 1 force, pressure, pull, etc of one thing on another 2 physical or nervous pressure or strain 3 emphasis, importance 4 extra weight laid on a part of a word (as in **but**ter) ■ verb to put stress, pressure, emphasis or strain on

stretch verb 1 to draw out to greater length, or too far, or from one point to another 2 to be able to be drawn out to a greater length or width: that material stretches 3 to (cause to) exert (yourself): the work stretched him to the full 4 to hold (out) ■ noun (plural **stretches**) 1 the act of stretching 2 the state of being stretched 3 a length in distance or time: a stretch of bad road ■ **stretchy** adjective

stretcher noun a light folding bed with handles for carrying the sick or wounded

strew verb 1 to scatter 2 to cover, sprinkle (with)

| **strew** ► strews, strewing, strewed, strewn or strewed

stricken adjective 1 wounded 2 deeply affected (eg by illness)

strict adjective 1 insisting on exact obedience to rules 2 exact: the strict meaning of a word 3 allowing no exception: strict orders 4 rather severe ■ **strictly** adverb

stride verb 1 to walk with long steps 2 to take a long step 3 to walk over, along, etc ■ noun 1 a long step **2** the distance covered by a step **3** a step forward

| **stride** verb ▶ strides, striding, strode, stridden

strident adjective **1** of a sound: harsh, grating **2** forceful; assertive: *their demands for reform became more and more strident*

strife noun quarrelling; fighting

strike verb **1** to hit with force **2** to give, deliver (a blow) **3** to knock: *to strike your head on the beam* **4** to attack: *the enemy struck at dawn* **5** to light (a match) **6** to make (a musical note) sound **7** of a clock: to sound (*eg* at ten o'clock with ten chimes) **8** (often **strike something off** *or* **out**) to cross it out, cancel it **9** to stop working (in support of a claim for more pay *etc*) **10** to give (someone) the impression of being: *did he strike you as lazy?* **11** to affect, impress: *I am struck by her beauty* ■ noun **1** a refusal to work in support of a claim for more pay *etc* **2** a sudden swift attack ■ **strike up 1** to begin to play or sing (a tune) **2** to begin (a friendship, conversation, *etc*)

| **strike** verb ▶ strikes, striking, struck

striker noun **1** someone participating in a strike **2** in football, a player whose main role is to score goals

striking adjective **1** noticeable **2** impressive

string noun **1** a long narrow cord

for binding, tying, *etc* made of threads twisted together **2** a piece of wire or gut producing a note on a musical instrument **3 strings** the stringed instruments in an orchestra **4** a line of objects threaded together: *string of pearls* **5** a number of things coming one after another ■ verb **1** to put on a string **2** to stretch out in a line ■ **string along** to give false expectations to, deceive ■ **string up** to hang

| **string** verb ▶ strings, stringing, strung

stringed adjective having strings

stringent adjective strictly enforced: *stringent rules*

stringy adjective **1** like string **2** of meat: tough and fibrous

strip noun a long narrow piece (*eg* of paper) ■ verb **1** to pull (off) in strips **2** to remove (*eg* leaves, fruit) from **3** to remove the clothes from **4** to deprive: *stripped of his disguise* **5** to make bare or empty: *strip the bed*

| **strip** verb ▶ strips, stripping, stripped

strip cartoon a line of drawings which tell a story

stripe noun a band of colour different from the background on which it lies ■ verb to make stripes on

stripy or **striped** adjective patterned with stripes

strive verb to try hard

strive ► strives, striving, strove, striven

strobe noun a light which produces a flickering beam

strode past form of **stride**

stroke noun 1 the act of striking 2 a blow (eg with a sword, whip) 3 something unexpected: a stroke of good luck 4 one movement (of a pen, an oar) 5 one chime of a clock 6 one complete movement of the arms and legs in swimming 7 a particular style of swimming: breast stroke 8 a way of striking the ball (eg in tennis, cricket) 9 a sudden attack of illness causing paralysis ▪ verb to rub gently, especially as a sign of affection

stroll verb to walk slowly in a leisurely way ▪ noun a leisurely walk; an amble

strong adjective 1 not easily worn away 2 not easily defeated etc 3 forceful, not easily resisted 4 very healthy and robust, with great muscular strength 5 forceful, commanding respect or obedience 6 of a smell, colour, etc: striking, very noticeable 7 of a feeling: intense 8 in number: a workforce 500 strong

stronghold noun a place built to withstand attack, a fortress

strongly adverb 1 in a strong way 2 to a strong degree

stroppy adjective, informal quarrelsome, disobedient, rowdy

strove past form of **strive**

struck past form of **strike**

structural adjective of or relating to structure, or a basic structure or framework

▪ **structurally** adverb

structure noun 1 a building; a framework 2 the way the parts of anything are arranged

struggle verb 1 to try hard (to do something) 2 to twist and fight to escape 3 to fight (with or against someone) 4 to move with difficulty ▪ noun 1 a great effort 2 a fight

strum verb to play (a guitar etc) in a relaxed way

strum ► strums, strumming, strummed

strung past form of **string**

strut verb to walk in a proud manner ▪ noun a proud way of walking

strut verb ► struts, strutting, strutted

stub noun a small stump (eg of a pencil, cigarette) ▪ verb 1 to put out (eg a cigarette) by pressure against something 2 to knock (your toe) painfully against something

stub verb ► stubs, stubbing, stubbed

stubble noun a short growth of beard

stubborn adjective 1 unwilling to give way, obstinate 2 of resistance etc: strong, determined 3 difficult to manage or deal with ▪ **stubbornly** adverb

▪ **stubbornness** noun

stubby *adjective* short, thick and strong

stuck *past form of* stick

stud *noun* **1** a nail with a large head **2** a decorative knob on a surface ■ *verb* to cover or fit with studs

| **stud** *verb* ▸ stud*s*, stud*ding*, stud*ded*

student *noun* someone who studies, especially at college, university, *etc*

studio *noun* (*plural* **studios**) **1** the workshop of an artist or photographer **2** a building or place in which cinema films are made **3** a room from which television or radio programmes are broadcast

studious *adjective* **1** studying carefully and much **2** careful: *his studious avoidance of quarrels*
■ **studiously** *adverb*

study *verb* **1** to gain knowledge of (a subject) by reading, experiment, *etc* **2** to look carefully at a ■ *noun* (*plural* **studies**) **1** the gaining of knowledge of a subject **2** a room where someone reads and writes

| **study** *verb* ▸ studi*es*, study*ing*, studi*ed*

stuff *noun* **1** the material of which anything is made **2** cloth, fabric **3** substance or material of any kind ■ *verb* **1** to pack full **2** to fill the skin of (a dead animal) to preserve it **3** to fill (a prepared bird) with stuffing before cooking

stuffing *noun* **1** feathers, scraps of material, *etc* used to stuff a cushion, chair, *etc* **2** breadcrumbs, onions, *etc* packed inside a fowl or other meat and cooked with it

stuffy *adjective* **1** full of stale air, badly ventilated **2** *informal* dull, having old-fashioned ideas

stumble *verb* **1** to trip in walking **2** to walk unsteadily, as if blind **3** to make mistakes or hesitate in speaking **4** **stumble on something** to find it by chance
■ *noun* the act of stumbling

stump *noun* **1** the part of a tree, leg, tooth, *etc* left after the main part has been cut away **2** *cricket* one of the three wooden stakes which make up a wicket ■ *verb* **1** *cricket* to put out (a batsman) by touching the stumps with the ball **2** to puzzle completely ■ **stump up** *informal* to pay up

stumpy *adjective* short and thick

stun *verb* **1** to knock senseless (by a blow *etc*) **2** to surprise or shock very greatly: *stunned by the news*

| **stun** ▸ stun*s*, stun*ning*, stun*ned*

stung *past form of* sting

stunk *past form of* stink

stunt *noun* **1** a daring trick **2** something done to attract attention ■ *verb* to stop the growth of

stunted *adjective* small and badly shaped

stupefy *verb* **1** to make stupid, deaden the feelings of **2** to astonish

| **stupefy** ► stupefies, stupefying, stupefied

stupendous *adjective* wonderful, amazing (*eg* because of size and power)

stupid *adjective* **1** foolish **2** dull, slow at learning

stupidity *noun* the quality or condition of being stupid

stupor *noun* the state of being only partly conscious

sturdy *adjective* strong, well built; healthy ▪ **sturdily** *adverb*

sturgeon *noun* a type of large fish from which caviare is taken

stutter *verb* to speak in a halting, jerky way; stammer ▪ *noun* a stammer

sty[1] *noun* (*plural* **sties**) a pen in which pigs are kept

sty[2] or **stye** *noun* (*plural* **sties** or **styes**) an inflamed swelling on the eyelid

style *noun* **1** manner of acting, writing, speaking, *etc* **2** fashion: *in the style of the late 19th century* **3** an air of elegance

stylesheet *noun, computing* a set of specifications used as a template for documents or web pages

stylish *adjective* smart, elegant, fashionable

suave (*pronounced* swahv) *adjective* of a person: superficially polite and sophisticated, smooth

sub- *prefix* **1** under, below **2** less than **3** lower in rank or importance

subconscious *noun* the contents of the mind of which someone is not themselves aware ▪ *adjective* of the subconscious, not conscious or aware

subdirectory *noun, computing* a directory contained within another

subdivide *verb* to divide into smaller parts

subdivision *noun* a part made by subdividing

subdue *verb* **1** to conquer (an enemy *etc*) **2** to keep under control (*eg* a desire) **3** to make quieter: *he seemed subdued after the fight* ▪ **subdued** *adjective*

subject *adjective* (*pronounced* sub-jekt) **1** under the power of another: *a subject nation* **2** **subject to something** liable to suffer from it (*eg* colds) **3** **subject to something** depending on it: *subject to your approval* ▪ *noun* (*pronounced* sub-jekt) **1** someone under the power of another: *the king's subjects* **2** a member of a nation with a monarchy: *a British subject* **3** something or someone spoken about, studied, *etc* **4** *grammar* the word in a sentence or clause which stands for the person or thing doing the action of the verb (*eg* cat is the subject in 'the *cat* drank the milk') ■ *verb* (*pronounced* sub-**jekt** – often **subject someone to something**) to force them to submit to it

subjective *adjective* based on personal feelings, thoughts, *etc*, not impartial (*contrasted with*: **objective**)

sublime *adjective* very noble, great or grand

submarine *noun* a type of ship which can travel under water ■ *adjective* under the surface of the sea

submerge *verb* to cover with water; sink

submission *noun* 1 the act of submitting 2 readiness to yield, meekness 3 an idea, statement, *etc* offered for consideration

submissive *adjective* meek, yielding easily

submit *verb* 1 to give in, yield 2 to place (a matter) before someone for making a judgement

| **submit** ► submits, submitting, submitted

subordinate *adjective* (often **subordinate to someone**) lower in rank or importance ■ *noun* someone who is subordinate

subpoena (*pronounced* su-**pee-na**) *noun* an order for someone to appear in court ■ *verb* to order to appear in court

subscribe *verb* 1 to make a contribution (especially of money) towards a charity 2 to

promise to take and pay for a number of issues of a magazine *etc* 3 **subscribe to something** to agree with (an idea, statement, *etc*)

subscription *noun* a payment for *eg* a club membership fee or a number of issues of a magazine for a given period

subsequent *adjective* following, coming after

subside *verb* 1 to settle down, sink lower 2 of noise *etc*: to get less and less

subsidence *noun* a sinking down, especially into the ground

subsidize or **subsidise** *verb* to give money as a help

subsidy *noun* (*plural* **subsidies**) money paid by a government *etc* to help an industry

substance *noun* a material that can be seen and felt

substantial *adjective* 1 solid, strong 2 large 3 able to be seen and felt

substitute *verb* to put (something) in place or instead of another ■ *noun* someone or thing used instead of another

substitution *noun* 1 the process of substituting or being substituted 2 something that is substituted

subtitle *noun* a translation of a foreign-language film, appearing at the bottom of the screen

subtle (*pronounced* su-tl) *adjective* difficult to describe or explain ■ **subtly** *adverb*

subtlety (*pronounced* su-tl-ti) *noun* the quality of being subtle

subtotal *noun* a total of one set of figures within a larger group

subtract *verb* 1 to take away (a part from) 2 to take away (one number from another)

subtraction *noun* the process of subtracting

suburb *noun* a residential area on the outskirts of a town

suburban *adjective* of suburbs

subversive *adjective* likely to overthrow (government, discipline, *etc*)

subway *noun* 1 an underground crossing for pedestrians *etc* 2 an underground railway

succeed *verb* 1 to succeed in **something** to manage to do what you have been trying to do 2 to get on well 3 to take the place of, follow 4 (often **succeed to**) to follow in order (to the throne *etc*)

success *noun* (*plural* **successes**) 1 the achievement of something you have been trying to do 2 someone who succeeds 3 something that turns out well

successful *adjective* 1 having achieved what was aimed at 2 having achieved wealth, importance, *etc* 3 turning out as planned

succession *noun* 1 the act of following after 2 the right of becoming the next holder (of a throne *etc*) 3 a number of things coming one after the other

successive *adjective* following one after the other

successor *noun* someone who comes after, follows in a post, *etc*

succinct *adjective* in a few words, brief, concise: *a succinct reply*

succulent *adjective* juicy

succumb *verb* to yield (to): *succumbed to temptation*

such *adjective* 1 of a kind previously mentioned 2 similar: *doctors, nurses and such people* 3 so great: *his excitement was such that he shouted out loud* 4 used for emphasis: *such a disappointment!*
■ *pronoun* thing, people, *etc* of a kind already mentioned: *such as these are not to be trusted*

such-and-such *adjective* & *pronoun* any given (person or thing): *such-and-such a book*

suck *verb* 1 to draw into the mouth 2 to draw milk from with the mouth 3 to hold in the mouth and lick hard (*eg* a sweet) 4 (often **suck up** or **in**) to draw in, absorb
■ *noun* 1 a sucking action 2 the act of sucking

sucker *noun* 1 a side shoot rising from the root of a plant 2 a part of an animal's body by which it sticks to objects 3 a pad (of rubber *etc*) which can stick to a surface 4 *informal* someone easily fooled

suckle *verb* of a woman or female animal: to give milk from the breast or teat

suction noun **1** the act of sucking **2** the process of reducing the air pressure, and so producing a vacuum, on the surface or between surfaces

sudden adjective happening all at once without being expected ■ **suddenly** adverb ■ **suddenness** noun

suds noun plural frothy, soapy water

sue verb to start a law case against

suede noun a kind of leather with a soft, dull surface

suet noun a kind of hard animal fat

suffer verb **1** to feel pain or punishment **2** to bear, endure **3** to go through, undergo (a change etc)

suffering noun pain or distress

suffice verb to be enough, or good enough

sufficient adjective enough ■ **sufficiency** noun ■ **sufficiently** adverb

suffix noun (plural **suffixes**) a small part added to the end of a word to make another word, such as -ness to good to make goodness, -ly to quick to make quickly etc

suffocate verb **1** to kill by preventing the breathing of **2** to die from lack of air **3** to feel unable to breathe freely: suffocating in this heat

suffocation noun suffocating or being suffocated

sugar noun a sweet substance obtained mostly from sugar cane and sugar beet

sugary adjective **1** tasting of sugar **2** too sweet

suggest verb **1** to put forward, propose (an idea etc) **2** to put into the mind, hint

suggestion noun **1** an act of suggesting **2** an idea put forward **3** a slight trace

suggestive adjective that suggests something particular, especially sexually improper: suggestive remarks

suicidal adjective **1** of or considering suicide **2** likely to cause your death or ruin

suicide noun the taking of your own life

suit noun **1** a set of clothes to be worn together **2** a case in a law court **3** one of the four divisions (spades, hearts, diamonds, clubs) of playing-cards ■ verb **1** to be convenient or suitable for **2** to look well on: that dress suits you

suitability noun being suitable

suitable adjective **1** fitting the purpose **2** just what is wanted, convenient

suitcase noun a travelling case for carrying clothes etc

suite (pronounced sweet) noun a number of things in a set, eg rooms, furniture, pieces of music

suitor noun a man who tries to gain the love of a woman

sulk *verb* to keep silent because of being displeased

sulky *adjective* sulking; inclined to sulk

sullen *adjective* angry and silent, sulky ∎ **sullenness** *noun*

sulphur *noun* a yellow substance found in the ground which gives off a choking smell when burnt, used in matches, gunpowder, *etc*

sultan *noun* 1 *history* the head of the Turkish Ottoman empire 2 an Islamic ruler

sultana *noun* 1 a sultan's wife 2 a light-coloured raisin

sultry *adjective* 1 of weather: very hot and close 2 passionate, steamy

sum *noun* 1 the amount made by two or more things added together 2 a quantity of money 3 a problem in arithmetic ∎ **sum up** to give the main points of (a discussion, evidence in a trial, *etc*)

summarize *or* **summarise** *verb* to state briefly, make a summary of

summary *noun* (*plural* **summaries**) a shortened form (of a story, statement, *etc*) giving only the main points ∎ *adjective* 1 short, brief 2 done without wasting time or words

summer *noun* the warmest season of the year

summit *noun* the highest point of a hill *etc*

summon *verb* 1 to order (someone) to come to you, appear in a court of law, *etc* 2 **summon up** to gather up (courage, strength, *etc*)

summons *noun* (*plural* **summonses**) an order to appear in court

sumo *noun* a Japanese form of wrestling

sumptuous *adjective* costly, splendid

sun *noun* 1 the round body in the sky which gives light and heat to the earth 2 sunshine ∎ **sun yourself** to lie in the sunshine, sunbathe

| **sun** *verb* ▶ **suns**, **sun**n*ing*, **sun**n*ed*

sunbathe *verb* to lie or sit in the sun to acquire a suntan

sunbeam *noun* a ray of light from the sun

sunburn *noun* a burning or redness caused by over-exposure to the sun

sunburned *or* **sunburnt** *adjective* affected by sunburn

sundae *noun* a sweet dish of ice-cream served with fruit, syrup, *etc*

Sunday *noun* the first day of the week, the Christian Sabbath

sundial *noun* an instrument for telling the time from the shadow of a rod on its surface cast by the sun

sundry *adjective* several, various

sunflower *noun* a large yellow

flower with petals like rays of the sun

sung *past participle* of **sing**

sunglasses *noun plural* spectacles with tinted lenses that shield the eyes from sunlight

sunk *adjective* on a lower level than the surroundings; sunken

sunken *adjective* **1** that has been sunk **2** of cheeks *etc*: hollow

sunlight *noun* the light from the sun

sunlit *adjective* lighted up by the sun

sunny *adjective* **1** full of sunshine **2** cheerful

sunrise *noun* the rising of the sun in the morning

sunset *noun* the setting of the sun in the evening

sunshine *noun* bright sunlight

sunstroke *noun* a serious illness caused by over-exposure to very hot sunshine

suntan *noun* a browning of the skin caused by exposure to the sun

sup *verb* to eat or drink in small mouthfuls

| **sup** ▶ sups, supp*ing*, supp*ed*

super *adjective*, *informal* extremely good

super- *prefix* above, beyond, very, too: *superannuate* (= make someone retire because they are 'beyond the years')/*superhuman* (= beyond what a normal person is capable of)

superannuate *verb* to make

(someone) retire from their job because of old age

superb *adjective* magnificent, very fine, excellent

supercilious *adjective* belittling or looking down on other people

superficial *adjective* **1** of a wound: affecting the surface of the skin only, not deep **2** not thorough or detailed **3** apparent at first glance, not actual **4** of a person: not capable of deep thoughts or feelings

■ **superficially** *adverb*

💧* Do not confuse:
superficial and **superfluous**

superfluous (*pronounced* soo-**per**-floo-*us*) *adjective* beyond what is enough or necessary

💧* Do not confuse:
superficial and **superfluous**

superhuman *adjective* **1** divine, godly **2** greater than would be expected of an ordinary person

superintendent *noun* **1** someone who is in charge of an institution, building, *etc* **2** a police officer above a chief inspector

superior *adjective* **1** higher in place or rank **2** better or greater than others **3** having an air of being better than others ■ *noun* someone better than, or higher in rank than, others

superiority *noun* **1** a superior state **2** advantage

superlative *adjective* **1** better than, or going beyond, all others

2 *grammar* an adjective or adverb of the highest degree of comparison, not positive or comparative, *eg* kind*est*, *worst*, *most* quickly

supermarket *noun* a large self-service store selling food *etc*

supernatural *adjective* not happening in the ordinary course of nature, miraculous

supernova *noun* an exploding star surrounded by a bright cloud of gas

supersede *verb* to take the place of: *superseded by a newer model*

supersonic *adjective* faster than the speed of sound

superstition *noun* **1** belief in magic and in things which cannot be explained by reason **2** an example of such belief (*eg* not walking under ladders)

superstitious *adjective* having superstitions

supervise *verb* to be in charge of work and see that it is properly done

supervision *noun* the act of supervising; control, inspection

supervisor *noun* a person who is responsible for making sure that other people's work is done correctly

supper *noun* a meal taken in the evening

supplant *verb* to take the place of somebody or of something: *the baby supplanted the dog in her affections*

supple *adjective* **1** bending easily, flexible **2** of an object: bending easily without breaking

supplement *noun* **1** something added to supply a need or lack **2** a special section added to the main part of a newspaper or magazine ▪ *verb* to make or be an addition to

supplementary *adjective* added to supply a need; additional

supply *verb* **1** to provide (what is wanted or needed) **2** to provide (someone with something) ▪ *noun* (*plural* **supplies**) **1** an act of supplying **2** something supplied **3** a stock or store **4** **supplies** a stock of essentials, *eg* food, equipment, money, *etc* ▪ *adjective* of a teacher: filling another's place or position for a time

| **supply** *verb* ► supplies, supplying, supplied

support *verb* **1** to hold up, take part of the weight of **2** to help, encourage **3** to supply with a means of living: *support a family* ▪ *noun* **1** an act of supporting **2** something that supports

supporter *noun* someone who supports (especially a football club)

suppose *verb* **1** to take as true, assume for the sake of argument **2** to believe, think probable **3** used to give a polite order: *suppose you leave now* ▪ **be supposed to** to be required or expected to (do)

supposed *adjective* believed (often mistakenly) to be so: *her supposed generosity*

supposedly *adverb* according to what is supposed

supposing *conjunction* in the event that: *supposing it rains*

supposition *noun* 1 the act of supposing 2 something supposed

suppress *verb* 1 to crush, put down (a rebellion *etc*) 2 to keep back (a yawn, a piece of news, *etc*)

suppression *noun* the act of suppressing

supremacy *noun* highest power or authority

supreme *adjective* 1 highest, most powerful 2 greatest

sure *adjective* 1 having no doubt 2 certain (to do, happen, *etc*) 3 reliable, dependable

surely *adverb* 1 certainly, without doubt 2 sometimes expressing a little doubt: *surely you won't tell him?* 3 without hesitation, mistake, *etc*

surf *noun* the foam made by the breaking of waves ■ *verb* 1 to ride over the surf on a long, narrow board 2 to look for information on the Internet

surface *noun* the outside or top part of anything (*eg* of the earth, of a road, *etc*) ■ *verb* 1 to come up to the surface of (water *etc*) 2 to put a (smooth) surface on ■ *adjective* 1 on the surface 2 travelling on the surface of land or water: *surface mail*

surfboard *noun* a long, narrow board on which someone can ride over the surf

surfeit *noun* too much of anything

surfer *noun* someone who surfs

surfing *noun* 1 the sport of riding on a surfboard 2 the activity of looking for information on the Internet

surge *verb* 1 to move (forward) like waves 2 to rise suddenly or excessively ■ *noun* 1 the swelling of a large wave 2 a swelling or rising movement like this 3 a sudden rise or increase (of pain *etc*)

surgeon *noun* a doctor who performs operations, often cutting the body open to examine or remove a diseased part

surgery *noun* (*plural* **surgeries**) 1 treatment of diseases *etc* by operation 2 a doctor's or dentist's consulting room

surgical *adjective* of, for use in, or by means of surgery: *a surgical mask* ■ **surgically** *adverb*

surly *adjective* gruff, rude, ill-mannered

surmise *verb* to suppose, guess

surmount *verb* 1 to overcome (a difficulty *etc*) 2 to climb over, get over

surname *noun* a person's last name or family name

surpass *verb* to go beyond, be more or better than

surplus (*pronounced* **ser**-plus)

noun the amount left over after what is needed has been used up ■ *adjective* left over, extra

surprise *noun* **1** the feeling caused by an unexpected happening **2** an unexpected happening ■ *verb* **1** to cause someone to feel surprise **2** to come upon (someone) suddenly and without warning

surprised *adjective* experiencing feelings of surprise

surreal *adjective* dreamlike, using images from the subconscious

surrealism *noun* the use of surreal images in art

surrealist *noun* an adherent of surrealism ■ *adjective* relating to or characteristic of surrealism

surrender *verb* **1** to give up, give in, yield **2** to hand over ■ *noun* an act of surrender, especially in a war

surreptitious *adjective* done in a secret, underhand way

surrogate *adjective* used or acting as a substitute for another person or thing: *a surrogate mother* ■ *noun* a substitute

surround *verb* **1** to be all round (someone or something) **2** to enclose, put round ■ *noun* a border

surroundings *noun plural* **1** the country lying round a place **2** the people and places with which you have to deal in daily life

surveillance *noun* a close watch or constant guard

survey *verb* **1** to look over **2** to inspect, examine **3** to make careful measurements of (a piece of land *etc*) ■ *noun* (*plural* **surveys**) **1** a general view **2** a detailed examination or inspection **3** a piece of writing giving results of this **4** a careful measuring of land *etc* **5** a map made with the measurements obtained

| **survey** *verb* ▶ **surveys**, **surveying**, **surveyed**

surveyor *noun* someone who makes surveys of land, buildings, *etc*

survival *noun* the state of surviving

survive *verb* **1** to remain alive, continue to exist (after an event *etc*) **2** to live longer than

survivor *noun* someone who remains alive: *the only survivor of the crash*

susceptibility *noun* the state or degree of being susceptible to something

susceptible *adjective* **1** **susceptible to something** liable to be affected by it **2** easily affected or moved

suspect *verb* (*pronounced* sus-**pekt**) **1** to be inclined to think (someone) guilty **2** to distrust, have doubts about **3** to guess: *I suspect that we're wrong* ■ *noun* (*pronounced* **sus**-pekt) someone

thought to be guilty of a crime *etc*
▪ *adjective* (*pronounced* **sus**-pekt)
arousing doubt, suspected
suspend *verb* **1** to hang **2** to keep
from falling or sinking: *particles
suspended in a liquid* **3** to stop for
a time **4** to take away a job,
privilege, *etc* from for a time
suspender *noun* an elastic strap
to keep up socks or stockings
suspense *noun* **1** a state of being
undecided **2** a state of
uncertainty or worry
suspension *noun* **1** the act of
suspending **2** the state of being
suspended **3** the state of a solid
which is mixed with a liquid or gas
and does not sink or dissolve in it
suspension bridge a bridge
which is suspended from cables
hanging from towers
suspicion *noun* **1** a feeling of
doubt or mistrust **2** an opinion, a
guess
suspicious *adjective* **1** inclined
to suspect or distrust **2** arousing
suspicion ▪ **suspiciously** *adverb*
sustain *verb* **1** to hold up, support
2 to bear (an attack *etc*) without
giving way **3** to suffer (an injury
etc) **4** to give strength to **5** to keep
up, keep going
sustenance *noun* food,
nourishment
svelte *adjective* slender, trim
swab *noun* a piece of cotton
wool used for cleaning, absorbing
blood, *etc* ▪ *verb* to clean with a
swab

| **swab** *verb* ► swab**s**,
| swab**bing**, swab**bed**

swagger *verb* **1** to walk proudly,
swinging the arms and body **2** to
boast ▪ *noun* a proud walk or
attitude
swallow[1] *verb* **1** to pass (food or
drink) down the throat into the
stomach **2 swallow something up**
to make it disappear ▪ *noun* an
act of swallowing
swallow[2] *noun* a bird with
pointed wings and a forked tail
swam *past form of* **swim**
swamp *noun* wet, marshy
ground ▪ *verb* to overwhelm
swan *noun* a large, stately water
bird, with white feathers and a
long neck
swan song the last work of a
musician, writer, *etc*
swap *or* **swop** *verb* to give one
thing in exchange for another:
swap addresses

| **swap** *or* **swop** ► swap**s** or
| swop**s**, swap**ping** or
| swop**ping**, swap**ped** or
| swop**ped**

swarm *noun* **1** a large number of
insects flying or moving together
2 a dense moving crowd ▪ *verb* **1**
of insects: to gather together in
great numbers **2** to move in
crowds **3** to be crowded with
swarthy *adjective* dark-skinned
swashbuckling *adjective* bold,
swaggering
swastika *noun* an ancient
design of a cross with bent arms,

taken up as a symbol of Nazism

swat *verb* to squash (a fly *etc*)
■ *noun* an instrument for squashing insects

| **swat** *verb* ▶ swat*s*, swat*ting*, swat*ted*

swathe *verb* to wrap round with clothes or bandages

sway *verb* **1** to swing or rock to and fro **2** to bend in one direction or to one side **3** to influence: *sway opinion* ■ *noun* a swaying movement

swear *verb* **1** to promise or declare solemnly **2** to vow **3** to curse, using the name of God or other sacred things without respect **4** to make (someone) take an oath: *to swear someone to secrecy* ■ **swear by** to rely on, have complete faith in

| **swear** ▶ swear*s*, swear*ing*, swore, sworn

swear-word *noun* a word used in swearing or cursing

sweat *noun* moisture secreted by the skin, perspiration ■ *verb* to give out sweat

sweater *noun* a jersey, a pullover

sweatshirt *noun* a long-sleeved jersey made of thick fabric

sweaty *adjective* wet, or stained with, sweat

swede *noun* a kind of large yellow turnip

sweep *verb* **1** to clean (a floor *etc*) with a brush or broom **2** (often **sweep up** *or* **sweep something up**) to gather up (dust *etc*) by

sweeping **3** to carry (away, along, off) with a long brushing movement **4** to travel over quickly, move with speed: *a new fad which is sweeping the country* **5** to move quickly in a proud manner (*eg* from a room) ■ *noun* **1** a sweeping movement **2** a curve, a stretch **3** a chimney sweeper **4** a sweepstake

| **sweep** *verb* ▶ sweep*s*, sweep*ing*, swept

sweeper *noun* **1** a device for sweeping **2** *football* a player positioned behind the defenders

sweeping *adjective* **1** that sweeps of a victory *etc*: great, overwhelming **2** of a statement *etc*: too general, allowing no exceptions, rash

sweepstake *noun* a gambling system in which those who take part stake money which goes to the holder of the winning ticket

sweet *adjective* **1** having the taste of sugar, not salty, sour or bitter **2** pleasing to the taste **3** pleasant to hear or smell **4** kindly, agreeable, charming ■ *noun* **1** a small piece of sweet substance, *eg* chocolate, toffee, *etc* **2** something served towards the end of a meal, a pudding

sweetcorn *noun* maize

sweeten *verb* to make or become sweet

sweetener *noun* an artificial substance used to sweeten food or drinks

sweetheart *noun* a lover

sweetly *adverb* in a sweet way

sweetness *noun* a sweet quality

sweet pea a sweet-smelling climbing flower grown in gardens

sweet talk flattery, persuasion

sweet tooth a liking for sweet-tasting things

swell *verb* **1** to grow in size or volume **2** of the sea: to rise into waves ▪ *noun* **1** an increase in size or volume **2** large, heaving waves **3** a gradual rise in the height of the ground

| **swell** *verb* ▶ swells, swelling, swelled, swollen

swelling *noun* a swollen part of the body, a lump

sweltering *adjective* very hot

swept *past form of* sweep

swerve *verb* to turn quickly to one side ▪ *noun* a quick turn aside

swift *adjective* moving quickly; rapid ▪ *noun* a bird rather like the swallow ▪ **swiftly** *adverb*

swig *noun, informal* a mouthful of liquid, a large drink ▪ *verb, informal* to gulp down

| **swig** *verb* ▶ swigs, swigging, swigged

swill *verb* to wash out ▪ *noun* **1** partly liquid food given to pigs **2** *informal* a big drink

swim *verb* **1** to move on or in water, using arms, legs, fins, *etc* **2** to cross by swimming **3** to move with a gliding motion **4** to be dizzy **5** to be covered (with liquid)

▪ *noun* an act of swimming

| **swim** *verb* ▶ swims, swimming, swam, swum

swimmer *noun* someone or something that swims

swimming costume *or* **swimsuit** a brief close-fitting garment for swimming in

swimmingly *adverb* smoothly, easily, successfully

swimming pool a large water-filled tank for swimming, diving, *etc* in

swindle *verb* to cheat, defraud ▪ *noun* a fraud, a deception ▪ **swindler** *noun*

swine *noun* (*plural* **swine**) **1** *old* a pig **2** *informal* a contemptible person

swing *verb* **1** to move to and fro, sway **2** to turn or whirl round **3** to walk quickly, moving the arms to and fro ▪ *noun* **1** a swinging movement **2** a seat for swinging, hung on ropes *etc* from a support

| **swing** *verb* ▶ swings, swinging, swung

swipe *verb* to strike with a sweeping blow ▪ *noun* a sweeping blow

swirl *verb* to sweep along with a whirling motion ▪ *noun* a whirling movement

swish *verb* **1** to strike or brush against with a rustling sound **2** to move making such a noise ▪ *noun* a rustling sound or movement

switch *noun* (*plural* **switches**) **1** a

small lever or handle, *eg* for turning an electric current on and off **2** an act of switching **3** a change ▪ *verb* **1** to strike with a switch **2** to turn (off or on) by means of a switch **3** to change, turn

switchback *noun* a road or railway with steep slopes or sharp turns

switchblade *noun* a flick-knife

switchboard *noun* a board with equipment for making telephone connections

swivel *noun* a joint that turns on a pin or pivot ▪ *verb* to turn on a swivel, pivot

swivel *verb* ▶ swivels, swivelling, swivelled

swollen *adjective* increased in size by swelling ▪ *verb, past participle* of **swell**

swoon *verb, old* to faint ▪ *noun* a fainting fit

swoop *verb* to come down with a sweep, like a bird of prey ▪ *noun* a sudden downward rush

swop *another spelling* of **swap**

sword *noun* a type of weapon with a long blade for cutting or piercing

swordfish *noun* a large type of fish with a long pointed upper jaw like a sword

swore *past form* of **swear**

sworn *past participle* of **swear**

swot *verb, informal* to study hard ▪ *noun* someone who studies hard

swot *verb* ▶ swots, swotting, swotted

swum *past participle* of **swim**

swung *past form* of **swing**

sycamore *noun* a name given to several different types of tree, the maple, plane, and a kind of fig tree

sycophant *noun* someone who flatters others in order to gain favour or personal advantage ▪ **sycophantic** *adjective*

syllable *noun* a word or part of a word spoken with one breath (*cheese* has one syllable, *but-ter* two, *mar-gar-ine* three)

syllabus *noun* (*plural* **syllabuses** or **syllabi**) a programme or list of lectures, classes, *etc*

symbol *noun* **1** something that stands for or represents another thing, *eg* the red cross, which stands for first aid **2** a character used as a short form of something, *eg* the signs + meaning plus, and O meaning oxygen

symbolic or **symbolical** *adjective* standing as a symbol of

symbolism *noun* the use of symbols to express ideas in art and literature

symbolize or **symbolise** *verb* to be a symbol of

symmetrical *adjective* having symmetry; not lopsided in appearance ▪ **symmetrically** *adverb*

symmetry *noun* the equality in

size, shape and position of two halves on either side of a dividing line (*contrasted with*: **asymmetry**)
sympathetic *adjective* feeling or showing sympathy: *sympathetic to the scheme*
■ **sympathetically** *adverb*
sympathize or **sympathise** *verb*: **sympathize with** to express or feel sympathy for
sympathy *noun* (*plural* **sympathies**) **1** a feeling of pity or sorrow for someone in trouble **2** agreement with, or understanding of, the feelings, attitudes, *etc* of others
symphony *noun* (*plural* **symphonies**) a long piece of music written for an orchestra of many different instruments
symptom *noun* an outward sign indicating the presence of a disease *etc*
synagogue *noun* a Jewish place of worship
synchronize or **synchronise** *verb* **1** to cause to happen at the same time **2** to set to the same time: *synchronize watches*
syncopate *verb, music* to change the beat by accenting beats not usually accented
syndicate *noun* a number of persons who join together to manage some piece of business
syndrome *noun* a pattern of behaviour, events, *etc* characteristic of some problem or condition
synonym *noun* a word which

has the same, or nearly the same, meaning as another, *eg* 'ass' and 'donkey', or 'brave' and 'courageous'
syntax *noun* rules for the correct combination of words to form sentences
synthesis *noun* **1** the act of making a whole by putting together its separate parts **2** the making of a substance by combining chemical elements
synthesize or **synthesise** *verb* to make (*eg* a drug) by synthesis
synthesizer or **synthesiser** *noun* a computerized instrument which creates electronic musical sounds
synthetic *adjective* **1** made artificially to look like a natural product **2** not natural, pretended
syphon *another spelling of* **siphon**
syringe *noun* a tubular instrument with a needle and plunger, used to extract blood, inject drugs, *etc* ■ *verb* to clean out with a syringe
syrup *noun* **1** a thick sticky liquid made by boiling water or fruit juice with sugar **2** a purified form of treacle
system *noun* **1** an arrangement of several parts which work together **2** a way of organizing **3** a regular method of doing something **4** the body, or its parts, considered as a whole
systematic *adjective* following a system; methodical
■ **systematically** *adverb*

T t

tab *noun* a small tag or flap attached to something

tabard *noun* a short sleeveless tunic

tabby (*plural* **tabbies**) *or* **tabby-cat** *noun* (*plural* **tabby-cats**) a striped (usually female) cat

tabernacle *noun* a place of worship for some Christian groups

table *noun* 1 a flat-topped piece of furniture, supported by legs 2 a flat surface, a plateau 3 facts or figures set out in columns: *multiplication tables* ■ *verb* to make into a list or table

tableau *noun* (*plural* **tableaux**) a striking group or scene

tablecloth *noun* a cloth for covering a table

tablespoon *noun* a large size of spoon

tablet *noun* 1 a small flat plate on which to write, paint, *etc* 2 a small flat piece, *eg* of soap or chocolate 3 a pill

table tennis a form of tennis played across a table with small bats and a light ball

tabloid *noun* a small-sized newspaper giving news in shortened and often simplified form (*compare with*: **broadsheet**)

taboo *adjective* forbidden by common consent; not approved by social custom ■ *noun* a taboo subject or behaviour

tabulate *verb* to set out (information *etc*) in columns or rows

tacit (*pronounced* **tas**-it) *adjective* understood but not spoken aloud, silent: *tacit agreement*

taciturn (*pronounced* **tas**-it-ern) *adjective* not inclined to talk

tack *noun* 1 a short sharp nail with a broad head 2 a direction, a course 3 a rough stitch to keep material in place while sewing ■ *verb* 1 to fasten with tacks 2 to sew with tacks

tackle *verb* 1 to come to grips with, deal with 2 *football etc* to try to stop, or take the ball from, another player ■ *noun* 1 the ropes and rigging of a ship 2 equipment, gear: *fishing tackle* 3 an act of tackling

tacky[1] *adjective* sticky, glue-like

tacky[2] *adjective*, *informal* shabby; vulgar, in bad taste

tact *noun* skill in dealing with people so as to avoid giving offence

tactful *adjective* using tact; avoiding giving offence ▪ **tactfully** *adverb*

tactical *adjective* **1** involving clever and successful planning **2** diplomatic, politic: *tactical withdrawal*

tactics *noun plural* **1** a way of acting in order to gain advantage **2** the art of coordinating military forces in action

tactile *adjective* of or perceived through touch

tactless *adjective* giving offence through lack of thought ▪ **tactlessly** *adverb*

tadpole *noun* a young frog or toad in its first stage of life

tae kwon do (*pronounced* tei kwon **doh**) a Korean martial art similar to karate

taffeta *noun* a thin, glossy fabric made mainly of silk

tag *noun* **1** a label **2** a chasing game played by children ▪ *verb* to put a tag or tags on ▪ **tag on to** or **tag after** to follow closely and continually

| **tag** *verb* ► **tags**, **tagging**, **tagged**

tail *noun* **1** a part of the body sticking out from the end of the spine on an animal, bird or fish **2** a part at the back of a machine *etc*: *tail of an aeroplane* **3** **tails** the side of a coin opposite to the head

4 **tails** a tail-coat ▪ *verb, informal* to follow closely ▪ **tail off** to become less, fewer or worse

tailcoat *noun* a coat with a divided tail, part of a man's evening dress

tail-end *noun* the very end of a procession *etc*

tailor *noun* someone who cuts out and makes clothes ▪ *verb* **1** to make and fit (clothes) **2** to make to fit the circumstances, adapt

tailor-made *adjective* exactly suited to requirements

taint *verb* **1** to spoil by contact with something bad or rotten **2** to corrupt

take *verb* **1** to lay hold of, grasp **2** to choose: *take a card!* **3** to accept, agree to have: *please take a biscuit* **4** to have room for: *my car only takes four people* **5** to eat, swallow **6** to get or have regularly: *doesn't take sugar* **7** (*also*: **take away**) to subtract: *take two from eight* **8** to lead, carry, drive: *take the children to school* **9** to use, make use of: *take care!* **10** to require: *it'll take too much time* **11** to travel by: *took the train* **12** to experience, feel: *takes pride in his work* **13** to photograph: *took some shots inside the house* **14** to understand: *took what I said the wrong way* ▪ **take after** to be like in appearance or behaviour

▪ **take down** to write, note down

▪ **take for** to believe (mistakenly)

to be ■ **take in 1** to include **2** to receive **3** to understand: *didn't take in what you said* **4** to make smaller: *take in a dress* **5** to cheat, deceive ■ **take off 1** to remove (clothes *etc*) **2** to imitate unkindly **3** of an aircraft: to leave the ground ■ **take on 1** to undertake (work *etc*) **2** to accept (as an opponent): *take you on at tennis* ■ **take over** to take control of ■ **take to 1** to be attracted by **2** to begin to do or use regularly ■ **take up 1** to lift, raise **2** to occupy (space, time, *etc*) **3** to begin to learn, show interest in

|take ► takes, tak*ing*, took, taken

takeaway *noun* **1** a meal prepared and bought in a restaurant or shop but taken away and eaten somewhere else **2** a restaurant or shop providing such meals

take-off *noun* **1** the act of an aircraft leaving the ground **2** an act of imitating or mimicking

takeover *noun* the act of taking control of something, especially a company by buying the majority of its shares

taking *adjective* pleasing, attractive ■ *noun* **1** an act of taking **2 takings** money received from things sold

talc *noun* **1** a soft mineral, soapy to the touch **2** *informal* talcum powder

talcum powder a fine powder

made from talc, used for rubbing on the body

tale *noun* **1** a story **2** an untrue story, a lie

talent *noun* a special ability or skill

talented *adjective* skilled, gifted

talisman *noun* (*plural* **talismans**) an object believed to have magic powers; a charm

talk *verb* **1** to speak **2** to gossip **3** to give information ■ *noun* **1** conversation **2** gossip **3** the subject of conversation: *the talk is of revolution* **4** a discussion or lecture ■ **talk over 1** to discuss **2** to persuade ■ **talk round 1** to discuss without coming to the main point **2** to persuade

talkative *adjective* inclined to chatter

tall *adjective* **1** high or higher than average **2** hard to believe: *tall story*

tally *noun* (*plural* **tallies**) an account ■ *verb* to agree (with): *his story doesn't tally with yours*

|tally *verb* ► tallies, tally*ing*, tallied

Talmud *noun* the body of Jewish law

talon *noun* a hooked claw

tambourine *noun* a small one-sided drum with tinkling metal discs set into the sides

tame *adjective* **1** of an animal: not wild, used to living with humans **2** dull, not exciting ■ *verb* to make tame, subdue

tamper *verb*: **tamper with** to meddle with so as to damage or alter

tan *verb* **1** to make (animal skin) into leather by treating with tannin **2** to make or become brown, *eg* by exposure to the sun ■ *noun* **1** a yellowish-brown colour **2** a suntan

| **tan** *verb* ► tans, tann*ing*, tann*ed*

tandem *noun* a long bicycle with two seats and two sets of pedals one behind the other

tandoori *noun* a style of Indian cookery in which food is baked over charcoal in a clay oven

tang *noun* a strong taste, flavour or smell

tangent *noun* a straight line which touches a circle or curve without crossing it ■ **go off at a tangent** to go off suddenly in another direction or line of thought

tangerine *noun* a small type of orange

tangible *adjective* **1** able to be felt by touching **2** real, definite: *tangible profits*

tangle *verb* **1** to twist together in knots **2** to make or become difficult or confusing ■ *noun* **1** a twisted mass of knots **2** a confused situation

tango *noun* (*plural* tangos) a ballroom dance with long steps and pauses, originally from South America

tank *noun* **1** a large container for water, petrol, *etc* **2** a heavy armoured vehicle which moves on caterpillar wheels

tankard *noun* a large drinking mug

tanker *noun* **1** a ship or large lorry for carrying liquids, *eg* oil **2** an aircraft carrying fuel

tanner *noun* someone who works at tanning leather

tannin *noun* a bitter-tasting substance found in tea, red wine, *etc*, also used in tanning and dyeing

tantalize *or* **tantalise** *verb* to torment by offering something and keeping it out of reach

tantalizing *or* **tantalising** *adjective* teasing; tormenting

tantamount *adjective*: **tantamount to** coming to the same thing as, equivalent to: *tantamount to stealing*

tantrum *noun* a fit of rage or bad temper

tap *noun* **1** a light touch or knock **2** a device with a valve for controlling the flow of liquid, gas, *etc* ■ *verb* to knock or strike lightly ■ **on tap** ready, available for use

| **tap** *verb* ► taps, tapp*ing*, tapp*ed*

tapdance *noun* a dance done with special shoes that make a tapping sound ■ *verb* to perform a tapdance

tape *noun* **1** a narrow band or strip used for tying **2** a piece of string over the finishing line on a racecourse **3** a tape measure **4** a strip of magnetic material for recording sound or pictures ■ *verb* **1** to fasten with tape **2** to record on tape

tape measure a narrow strip of paper, plastic, *etc* used for measuring distance

taper *noun* **1** a long, thin kind of candle **2** a long waxed wick used for lighting oil lamps *etc* ■ *verb* to make or become thinner at one end

tape recorder a kind of instrument for recording sound *etc* on magnetic tape

tapering *adjective* becoming gradually thinner at one end

tapestry *noun* (*plural* **tapestries**) a cloth with designs or figures woven into it, used to decorate walls or cover furniture

tapeworm *noun* a type of long worm sometimes found in the intestines of humans and animals

tapioca *noun* a starchy food obtained from the root of the cassava plant

tapir *noun* a kind of wild animal something like a large pig

tar *noun* a thick, black, sticky liquid derived from wood or coal, used in roadmaking *etc*

tarantula *noun* a type of large, poisonous spider

tardy *adjective* slow; late

| **tardy** ▶ tardi**er**, tardi**est**

target *noun* **1** a mark to aim at in

shooting, darts, *etc* **2** a result or sum that is aimed at: *a target of £3000* **3** someone at whom unfriendly remarks are aimed

tariff *noun* **1** a list of prices **2** a list of taxes payable on goods brought into a country

tarmac *noun* the surface of a road or airport runway, made of tarmacadam

tarmacadam *noun* a mixture of small stones and tar used to make road surfaces *etc*

tarn *noun* a small mountain lake

tarnish *verb* **1** of metal: to (cause to) become dull or discoloured **2** to spoil (a reputation *etc*)

tarot (*pronounced* ta-roh) *noun* a system of fortune-telling using special cards divided into suits

tarpaulin *noun* **1** strong waterproof cloth **2** a sheet of this material

tarragon *noun* a herb used in cooking

tarry (*pronounced* ta-ri) *verb* **1** to stay behind, linger **2** to be slow or late

tart *noun* a small pie containing fruit, vegetables, *etc* ■ *adjective* sharp, sour

tartan *noun* **1** fabric patterned with squares of different colours, traditionally used by Scottish Highland clans **2** one of these patterns: *Macdonald tartan* ■ *adjective* with a pattern of tartan

tartar *noun* a substance that gathers on the teeth

task noun a set piece of work to be done

tassel noun a hanging bunch of threads, used to decorate a hat etc

taste verb 1 to try by eating or drinking a sample 2 to eat or drink some of 3 to recognize (a flavour): can you taste the chilli in it? 4 to have a particular flavour: tasting of garlic 5 to experience: taste success ■ noun 1 the act or sense of tasting 2 a flavour 3 a small quantity of something 4 a liking: taste for literature 5 ability to judge what is suitable in behaviour, dress, etc, or what is fine or beautiful

tasteful adjective showing good taste and judgement

tasteless adjective 1 without flavour 2 not tasteful; vulgar

tasty adjective having a good flavour

| tasty ► tastier, tastiest

tattered adjective ragged

tatters noun plural torn, ragged pieces

tattoo noun 1 a coloured design on the skin, made by pricking with needles 2 a pattern of sound made by drumming 3 an outdoor military display with music etc ■ verb to prick coloured designs into the skin

| tattoo verb ► tattoos,
| tattooing, tattooed

tattooed adjective marked with tattoos

tatty adjective shabby, tawdry

taught past form of teach

taunt verb to tease or jeer at unkindly ■ noun a jeer

taut adjective 1 pulled tight 2 tense, strained

tautology noun a form of repetition in which the same thing is said in different ways, eg 'he looked anxious and worried'

tavern noun, old a public house, an inn

tawdry adjective cheap-looking and gaudy

tawny adjective yellowish-brown

tax noun (plural taxes) a charge made by the government on income, certain types of goods, etc ■ verb 1 to make to pay a tax 2 to put a strain on: taxing her strength

taxation noun 1 the act or system of taxing 2 taxes

taxi noun (plural taxis) a vehicle which may be hired, with a driver ■ verb of an aeroplane: to travel on the runway before or after take-off

| taxi verb ► taxies, taxiing,
| taxied

taxidermist noun someone who prepares and stuffs the skins of dead animals

taxidermy noun the art of preparing and stuffing the skins of animals to make them lifelike

taxpayer noun someone who pays taxes

TB abbreviation tuberculosis

tea *noun* **1** a plant grown in India, China, *etc*, or its dried and prepared leaves **2** a drink made by infusing its dried leaves **3** an afternoon or early evening meal

teabag *noun* a small sachet of tea to which boiling water is added

teacake *noun* a light, flat bun

teach *verb* to give (someone) skill or knowledge

| **teach** ▶ teaches, teaching, taught

teacher *noun* someone employed to teach others in a school, or in a particular subject

teaching *noun* **1** the work of a teacher **2** guidance, instruction

teacup *noun* a medium-sized cup for drinking tea

teak *noun* **1** a hardwood tree from the East Indies **2** its very hard wood

teal *noun* **1** a small water bird like a duck **2** a dark greenish-blue colour

team *noun* **1** a group of people working together **2** a side in a game ■ **team up with** to join together with, join forces with

◆* Do not confuse with: teem

teapot *noun* a pot with a spout, for making and pouring tea

tear[1] (*pronounced* teer) *noun* a drop of liquid from the eye

tear[2] (*pronounced* teir) *verb* **1** to pull with force **2** to make a hole or split in (material *etc*) **3** *informal* to rush ■ *noun* a hole or split made by tearing

| **tear** *verb* ▶ tears, tearing, tore, torn

tearful *adjective* **1** inclined to weep **2** in tears, crying ■ **tearfully** *adverb*

tear gas gas which causes the eyes to stream with tears

tease *verb* **1** to annoy, irritate on purpose **2** to pretend to upset or annoy for fun

teasel *noun* a type of prickly plant

teaser *noun* a problem, a puzzle

teaspoon *noun* a small spoon

teat *noun* **1** the part of an animal through which milk passes to its young **2** a rubber object shaped like this attached to a baby's feeding bottle

tea towel a cloth for drying dishes

technical *adjective* relating to a particular art or skill, especially a mechanical or industrial one

technicality *noun* (*plural* technicalities) a technical detail or point

technically *adverb* according to the rules, strictly speaking

technician *noun* someone trained in the practical side of an art

technique *noun* the way in which a process is carried out; a method

techno- *prefix* of or relating to technology

technological *adjective* relating to or involving technology ∎ **technologically** *adverb*

technology *noun* science applied to practical (especially industrial) purposes

teddy *or* **teddy bear** *noun* (*plural* **teddies** *or* **teddy bears**) a stuffed toy bear

tedious *adjective* long and tiresome ∎ **tediously** *adverb*

tedium *noun* boredom

tee *noun* **1** the square of level ground from which a golfball is driven **2** the peg or sand heap on which the ball is placed for driving

teem *verb* **1** to be full: *teeming with people* **2** to rain heavily

◆* Do not confuse with: team

teenage *adjective* suitable for, or typical of, those in their teens

teenager *noun* someone in their teens

teens *noun plural* the years of age from thir*teen* to nine*teen*

teeny *adjective*, *informal* tiny, minute

tee-shirt *or* **T-shirt** *noun* a short-sleeved shirt pulled on over the head

teeter *verb* **1** to wobble **2** to hesitate

teeth *plural* of tooth

teethe *verb* of a baby: to grow its first teeth

teetotal *adjective* never drinking alcohol

teetotaller *noun* a person who never drinks alcohol

telecommunications *noun singular* the sending of information by telephone, radio, television, *etc*

telegram *noun* a message sent by telegraph

telegraph *noun* an instrument for sending messages to a distance using electrical impulses ∎ *verb* to send (a message) by telegraph

telepathic *adjective* relating to or involving telepathy

telepathy *noun* communication between people without using sight, hearing, *etc*

telephone *noun* (*short form*: **phone**) an instrument for speaking over distances, which uses an electric current travelling along a wire, or radio waves

telephonist *noun* an operator on a telephone switchboard

telephoto *adjective* of a lens: used to photograph enlarged images of distant objects

teleprinter *noun* a typewriter which receives and prints out messages sent by telegraph

telescope *noun* a tubular instrument fitted with lenses which magnify distant objects ∎ **telescopic** *adjective*

teletext *noun* news and general information that can be received through a television set

televise *verb* to broadcast on television

television *noun* **1** the reproduction on a small screen of pictures sent from a distance **2** an apparatus for receiving these pictures

tell *verb* **1** to say or express in words **2** to give the facts of (a story) **3** to inform, give information **4** to order, command **5** to make out, distinguish: *I can't tell one wine from the other* **6** to give away a secret ▪ **tell off** *informal* to scold ▪ **tell on 1** to have an effect on **2** to give information about

| **tell** ▶ tells, telling, told

teller *noun* a bank clerk who receives and pays out money

telling *adjective* having a marked effect: *telling remark*

tell-tale *noun* someone who spreads gossip about others ▪ *adjective* revealing: *tell-tale signs of illness*

telly *noun* (*plural* **tellies**) *informal* (a) television

temerity *noun* rashness, boldness

temp *noun*, *informal* a temporarily employed worker ▪ *verb*, *informal* to work as a temp

temper *noun* **1** habitual state of mind: *of an even temper* **2** a passing mood: *in a good temper*

3 a tendency to get angry easily **4** a fit of anger

temperament *noun* someone's nature as it affects the way they feel and act; disposition

temperamental *adjective* **1** of temperament **2** excitable, emotional

temperate *adjective* **1** moderate in temper, eating or drinking, *etc* **2** of climate: neither very hot nor very cold

temperature *noun* **1** degree of heat or cold **2** a body heat higher than normal

tempest *noun* a storm, with great wind

tempestuous *adjective* **1** very stormy and windy **2** passionate, violently emotional

template *noun* a thin plate cut in a design for drawing round

temple[1] *noun* a building used for public worship; a church

temple[2] *noun* a small flat area on each side of the forehead

tempo *noun* (*plural* **tempos** or **tempi**) the speed at which music is played

temporary *adjective* lasting only for a time, not permanent

tempt *verb* **1** to try to persuade or entice **2** to attract **3** to make inclined (to): *tempted to phone him*

temptation *noun* **1** the act of tempting **2** the feeling of being tempted **3** something which tempts

tempting *adjective* attractive

ten *noun* the number 10
■ *adjective* 10 in number

tenable *adjective* able to be defended; justifiable

tenacious *adjective* 1 keeping a firm hold or grip 2 obstinate, persistent, determined

tenacity *noun* persistence, determination

tenancy *noun* (*plural* **tenancies**) 1 the holding of a house, farm, *etc* by a tenant 2 the period of this holding

tenant *noun* someone who pays rent for the use of a house, land, *etc*

tend *verb* 1 to be likely or inclined to do something 2 to move or slope in a certain direction 3 to take care of, look after

tendency *noun* (*plural* **tendencies**) a leaning or inclination (towards)

tender *adjective* 1 soft, not hard or tough 2 easily hurt or damaged 3 hurting when touched 4 loving, gentle ■ *verb* 1 to offer (a resignation *etc*) formally 2 to make a formal offer for a job ■ *noun* an offer to take on work, supply goods, *etc* for a fixed price

tendon *noun* a tough cord joining a muscle to a bone

tendril *noun* 1 a thin curling stem of a climbing plant which attaches itself to a support 2 a curling strand of hair *etc*

tenement *noun* a block of flats

tenet *noun* a belief, opinion

tenner *noun*, *informal* a ten-pound note; ten pounds

tennis *noun* a game for two or four players using rackets to hit a ball to each other over a net

tennis court a place made level and prepared for tennis

tenon *see* mortise

tenor *noun* 1 a singing voice of the highest normal pitch for an adult male 2 a singer with this voice

tenpin bowling a game played by bowling a ball at ten skittles standing at the end of a bowling lane

tense[1] *noun* the form of a verb that shows time of action, *eg* '*I was*' (**past tense**), '*I am*' (**present tense**), '*I shall be*' (**future tense**)

tense[2] *adjective* 1 tightly stretched 2 nervous, strained

tension *noun* 1 the state of being stretched 2 strain, anxiety

tent *noun* a movable shelter of canvas or other material, supported by poles and pegged to the ground

tentacle *noun* a long thin flexible part of an animal used to feel or grasp, *eg* the arm of an octopus

tentative *adjective* 1 experimental, initial 2 uncertain, hesitating ■ **tentatively** *adverb*

tenterhooks *noun plural*: on tenterhooks uncertain and very

anxious about what will happen
tenth *adjective* the last of ten
items ■ *noun* one of ten equal
parts
tenuous *adjective* slight, weak:
tenuous connection
tenure *noun* **1** the holding of
property or a position of
employment **2** the period, or
terms or conditions, of this
tepee *noun* a traditional Native
American tent made of animal
skins
tepid *adjective* lukewarm
term *noun* **1** a length of time:
term of imprisonment **2** a division
of an academic or school year **3** a
word, an expression **4 terms** the
rules or conditions of an
agreement **5 terms** fixed charges
6 terms footing, relationship: *on
good terms with his neighbours*
■ *verb* to name, call
terminal *adjective* of an illness:
fatal, incurable ■ *noun* **1** an end **2**
a point of connection in an
electric circuit **3** a computer
monitor connected to a network **4**
a terminus **5** an airport building
containing arrival and departure
areas **6** a bus station in a town
centre running a service to a
nearby airport
terminate *verb* to bring or come
to an end
termination *noun* an act of
ending or the state of being
brought to an end
terminology *noun* the special

words or expressions used in a
particular field, science, *etc*
terminus *noun* (*plural* **termini** or
terminuses) **1** the end **2** an end
point on a railway, bus route, *etc*
termite *noun* a pale-coloured
wood-eating insect, like an ant
tern *noun* a type of sea bird like a
small gull
terrace *noun* **1** a raised level
bank of earth **2** a raised flat place
3 a connected row of houses
■ *verb* to form into a terrace or
terraces
terracotta *noun* a brownish-red
mixture of clay and sand used for
tiles, pottery, *etc*
terrain *noun* an area of land
considered in terms of its
physical features
terrapin *noun* a small turtle
living in ponds or rivers
terrestrial *adjective* of or living
on the earth
terrible *adjective* **1** causing great
fear **2** causing great hardship or
distress **3** *informal* very bad: *a
terrible writer*
terribly *adverb*, *informal* **1** badly:
sang terribly **2** extremely: *terribly
tired*
terrier *noun* a breed of small dog
terrific *adjective* **1** powerful,
dreadful **2** huge, amazing **3**
informal attractive, enjoyable, *etc*:
a terrific party
terrify *verb* to frighten greatly
| **terrify** ▶ terri*fies*, terrif*ying*,
| terrif*ied*

territorial *adjective* of, belonging to a territory

territory *noun* (*plural* **territories**) **1** an area of land, a region **2** land under the control of a ruler or state **3** an area allocated to a salesman *etc* **4** a field of activity or interest

terror *noun* **1** very great fear **2** something which causes great fear **3** *informal* an uncontrollable child

terrorism *noun* the organized use of violence or intimidation for political or other ends

terrorist *noun* someone who practises terrorism

terrorize *or* **terrorise** *verb* to frighten very greatly

terse *adjective* using few words ▪ **tersely** *adverb*

tessellate *verb* of identical shapes: to fit together exactly, leaving no spaces between them ▪ **tessellation** *noun*

test *noun* **1** a short examination **2** something done to check soundness, reliability, *etc*: *ran tests on the new model* **3** a means of finding the presence of: *test for radioactivity* **4** an event that shows up a good or bad quality: *a test of courage* ▪ *verb* to carry out tests on

testament *noun* **1** a written statement **2** a will

testicle *noun* one of two sperm-producing glands in the male body

testify *verb* **1** to give evidence in a law court **2** to make a solemn declaration of **3 testify to something** to show, give evidence of it

| **testify** ▶ testif*ies*, testify*ing*, testif*ied*

testimonial *noun* a personal statement about someone's character, abilities, *etc*

testimony *noun* (*plural* **testimonies**) **1** the statement made by someone who testifies **2** evidence

test match *cricket* a game between two countries

testosterone *noun* a hormone secreted by the testicles

test pilot a pilot who tests new aircraft

test tube a glass tube closed at one end, used in chemical tests

testy *adjective* easily angered, irritable ▪ **testily** *adverb* ▪ **testiness** *noun*

| **testy** ▶ testi*er*, testi*est*

tetanus *noun* a disease, caused especially by an infected wound, that can cause stiffening and spasms in the jaw muscles

tetchy *adjective* irritable, testy ▪ **tetchily** *adverb*

| **tetchy** ▶ tetchi*er*, tetchi*est*

tether *noun* a rope or chain for tying an animal to restrict its movement ▪ *verb* to tie with a tether

tetrahedron *noun* a solid body

with four faces, all of which are polygons

text *noun* **1** the written or printed part of a book, not the pictures, notes, *etc* **2** a printed or written version of a speech, play, *etc* **3** a Biblical passage used as the basis for a sermon ■ *verb* to send a text message

textbook *noun* a book used for teaching, giving the main facts about a subject

textile *adjective* of weaving; woven ■ *noun* a woven cloth or fabric

text message a short message typed into and sent by a mobile phone

textual *adjective* of or in a text

texture *noun* **1** the quality of cloth resulting from weaving: *loose texture* **2** the quality of a substance in terms of how it looks or feels: *rough texture*

than *conjunction & preposition* used in comparisons: *easier than I expected*

thank *verb* to express gratitude to (someone) for a favour, gift, *etc* ■ **thank you** *or* **thanks** a polite expression used to thank someone (*see also* **thanks**)

thankful *adjective* grateful; relieved and glad ■ **thankfully** *adverb*

thankless *adjective* neither worthwhile nor appreciated: *thankless task*

thanks *noun plural* gratitude;

appreciation ■ **thanks to 1** with the help of: *we arrived on time, thanks to our friends* **2** owing to: *we were late, thanks to our car breaking down*

thanksgiving *noun* **1** a church service giving thanks to God **2 Thanksgiving** *US* the fourth Thursday of November, a national holiday commemorating the first harvest of the Puritan settlers

that *adjective & pronoun* (*plural* **those**) used to point out a thing or person *etc* (contrasted with: **this**): *that woman over there/don't say that* ■ *relative pronoun* referring to the person or thing just named: *the man that I spoke to* ■ *adverb* to such an extent or degree: *why were you that late?* ■ *conjunction* **1** used in reporting speech: *she said that she was there* **2** used to connect clauses: *I heard that you were ill*

thatch *noun* straw *etc* used to make the roof of a house ■ *verb* to cover with thatch

thaw *verb* **1** to melt **2** of frozen food: to defrost, become unfrozen **3** to become friendly ■ *noun* **1** the melting of ice and snow by heat **2** a change in the weather that causes this

the *adjective* **1** referring to a particular person or thing: *the boy in the park* **2** referring to all or any of a general group: *the horse is of great use to man*

theatre *or US* **theater** *noun* **1** a

place for the public performance of plays *etc* **2** a room in a hospital for surgical operations **3** the acting profession

theatrical *adjective* **1** of theatres or acting **2** over-dramatic, overdone

thee *pronoun, old* you as the object of a sentence

theft *noun* stealing

their *adjective* belonging to them: *their car*

⬥※ Do not confuse with:
there. Remember that the 'y' in the pronoun 'they' turns into an 'i' in **their** and that **there** is spelt the same as 'here' except for the first letter

theirs *pronoun* the one(s) belonging to them: *the red car is theirs*

them *pronoun plural* **1** people or things already spoken about (as the object of a verb): *we've seen them* **2** those: *one of them over in the corner* ■ *pronoun singular* used to avoid giving the gender of the person being referred to: *if anyone phones, ask them to leave their number*

theme *noun* **1** the subject of a discussion, essay, *etc* **2** *music* a main melody which is often repeated

theme park a large park with rides and attractions based on a single theme

theme song *or* **theme tune** a

tune that is repeated often in a film, television series, *etc*

themselves *pronoun plural* **1** used reflexively: *they tired themselves out* **2** used for emphasis: *they'll just have to do it themselves*

then *adverb* **1** at that time **2** after that: *and then where did you go?* ■ *conjunction* in that case, therefore: *if you're busy, then don't come*

thence *adverb, old* from that time or place

thenceforth *adverb* from that time onwards

theologian *noun* someone who studies theology

theological *adjective* relating to or involving theology

theology *noun* the study of God and religion

theorem *noun* a proposition to be proved in mathematics *etc*

theoretical *adjective* of theory, not experience or practice

■ **theoretically** *adverb*

theorize *or* **theorise** *verb* to form theories

theory *noun* (*plural* **theories**) **1** an explanation that has not been proved or tested **2** the underlying ideas in an art, science, *etc*, compared to practice or performance

therapeutic *adjective* healing, curing

therapist *noun* someone who gives therapeutic treatment: *speech therapist*

therapy *noun* (*plural* **therapies**) treatment of disease or disorders

there *adverb* at, in or to that place: *what did you do there?*
■ *pronoun* used (with *be*) as a subject of a sentence or clause when the real subject follows the verb: *there is nobody at home*

> ✲ Do not confuse with: **their**. Remember that **there** is spelt the same as 'here' except for the first letter and that the 'y' in the pronoun 'they' turns into an 'i' in **their**

thereabouts *adverb* approximately

thereafter *adverb* after that

thereby *adverb* by that means

therefore *adverb* for this or that reason

thereof *adverb* of that

therm *noun* a unit of heat used in measuring gas

thermal *adjective* 1 of heat 2 of hot springs

thermometer *noun* an instrument for measuring temperature

Thermos *noun, trademark* a kind of vacuum flask

thermostat *noun* a device for automatically controlling temperature in a room

thesaurus *noun* (*plural* **thesauri** *or* **thesauruses**) 1 a reference book listing words and their synonyms 2 a dictionary or encyclopedia

these *see* **this**

thesis *noun* (*plural* **theses**) a long piece of written work on a topic, often part of a university degree

thespian *noun, formal* an actor

they *pronoun plural* some people or things already mentioned (used only as the subject of a verb): *they followed the others*
■ *pronoun singular* used to avoid giving the gender of the person being referred to: *anyone can come if they like*

thick *adjective* 1 not thin, of reasonable width 2 of a mixture: containing solid matter, stiff 3 dense, difficult to see or pass through: *thick fog* 4 *informal* stupid ■ *noun* the thickest, most crowded or active part: *in the thick of the fight*

thicken *verb* to make or become thick

thicket *noun* a group of close-set trees and bushes

thickness *noun* 1 the quality of being thick 2 the distance between opposite sides 3 a layer

thickset *adjective* 1 closely set or planted 2 having a thick sturdy body

thick-skinned *adjective* not sensitive or easily hurt

thief *noun* (*plural* **thieves**) someone who steals

thieve *verb* to steal

thieving *noun* stealing
■ *adjective* that thieves

thigh *noun* the thick, fleshy part

of the leg between the knee and the hip

thimble *noun* a small cap worn over a fingertip, used to push a needle while sewing

thin *adjective* **1** not very wide between its two sides: *thin slice* **2** slim, not fat **3** not dense or crowded **4** poor in quality **5** of a voice: weak, not resonating **6** of a mixture: not stiff, watery ■ *verb* to make or become thin or thinner

| **thin** *verb* ► thins, thin*ning*, thin*ned*

thine *adjective*, *old* belonging to you (used before words beginning with a vowel or a vowel sound): *thine enemies* ■ *pronoun*, *old* something belonging to you: *my heart is thine*

thing *noun* **1** an object that is not living **2** *informal* a person: *you poor thing!* **3** things belongings **4** an individual object, quality, idea, *etc* that may be referred to: *several things must be taken into consideration*

think *verb* **1** to work things out, reason **2** to form ideas in the mind **3** to believe, judge or consider: *I think we should go* **4** think of doing something to intend to do it: *she is thinking of resigning* ■ think out to work out in the mind

| **think** ► thinks, think*ing*, thought

third *adjective* the last of a series

of three ■ *noun* one of three equal parts

Third World *see* **Developing World**

thirst *noun* **1** a dry feeling in the mouth caused by lack of fluid **2** an eager desire (for) ■ *verb* **1** to feel thirsty **2** thirst for something to desire it eagerly

thirsty *adjective* **1** having thirst **2** eager (for)

| **thirsty** ► thirst*ier*, thirst*iest*

thirteen *noun* the number 13 ■ *adjective* 13 in number

thirteenth *adjective* the last of a series of thirteen ■ *noun* one of thirteen equal parts

thirtieth *adjective* the last of a series of thirty ■ *noun* one of thirty equal parts

thirty *noun* the number 30 ■ *adjective* 30 in number

this *adjective & pronoun* (*plural* these) **1** used to point out someone or something, especially one nearby (*contrasted with:* that): *look at this letter/take this instead* **2** to such an extent or degree: *this early*

thistle *noun* a prickly plant with purple flowers

thither *adverb* to that place

-thon *see* **-athon**

thong *noun* a thin strap of leather to fasten anything

thorax *noun* (*plural* thoraxes or thoraces) **1** the chest in the human or animal body **2** the middle section of an insect's body

thorn noun a sharp prickle sticking out from the stem of a plant

thorny adjective 1 full of thorns; prickly 2 difficult, causing arguments

thorough adjective 1 complete, absolute 2 very careful, attending to every detail

thoroughbred noun an animal of pure breed

thoroughfare noun a public street

thoroughly adverb 1 completely, absolutely 2 very carefully

those see that

thou pronoun, old you (as the subject of a sentence)

though conjunction although ■ adverb, informal however: I wish I'd never said it, though

thought noun 1 the act of thinking 2 something which you think, an idea 3 an opinion 4 consideration: after much thought ■ verb, past form of think

thoughtful adjective 1 full of thought 2 thinking of others, considerate

thoughtless adjective showing lack of thought; inconsiderate

thousand noun the number 1000 ■ adjective 1000 in number

thousandth adjective the last of a series of a thousand ■ noun one of a thousand equal parts

thrash verb 1 to beat severely 2 to move or toss violently (about)

3 thrash something out to discuss a problem etc thoroughly

thrashing noun a flogging, a beating

thread noun 1 a very thin line of cotton, wool, silk, etc, often twisted and drawn out 2 the ridge which goes in a spiral round a screw 3 a connected series of details in correct order in a story ■ verb 1 to put a thread through a needle etc 2 to make (your way) in a narrow space

threadbare adjective of clothes: worn thin

threat noun 1 a warning that you intend to hurt or punish someone 2 a warning of something bad that may come: a threat of war 3 something likely to cause harm: a threat to our plans

threaten verb 1 to make a threat 2 to suggest the approach of something unpleasant 3 to be a danger to

three noun the number 3 ■ adjective 3 in number

3-D short for three-dimensional

three-dimensional adjective having height, width and depth (short form: **3-D**)

thresh verb to beat out (grain) from straw

threshold noun 1 a piece of wood or stone under the door of a building 2 a doorway 3 an entry or beginning: on the threshold of a new era

threw past form of throw

thrice *adverb* three times

thrift *noun* careful management of money in order to save

thrifty *adjective* careful about spending

thrill *noun* an excited feeling ■ *verb* **1** to feel excitement **2** to make excited

thriller *noun* an exciting story, often about crime and detection

thrilling *adjective* very exciting

thrive *verb* **1** to grow strong and healthy **2** to get on well, be successful

throat *noun* **1** the back part of the mouth **2** the front part of the neck

throb *verb* **1** of a pulse *etc*: to beat, especially more strongly than normal **2** to beat or vibrate rhythmically and regularly

| **throb** ► **throbs**, **throb***bing*, **throb***bed*

throes *noun plural* great suffering or struggle ■ **in the throes of** in the middle of (a struggle, doing a task, *etc*)

thrombosis *noun* the forming of a clot in a blood vessel

throne *noun* **1** the seat of a monarch or bishop **2** a monarch or their power

throng *noun* a crowd ■ *verb* **1** to move in a crowd **2** to crowd, fill (a place)

throttle *noun* the part of an engine through which steam or petrol can be turned on or off ■ *verb* to choke by gripping the throat

through *preposition* **1** entering from one direction and out the other **2** from end to end, or side to side, of: *all through the performance* **3** by way of: *related through his grandmother* **4** as a result of: *through his expertise* ■ *adverb* **1** into and out, from beginning to end: *go straight through* **2** connected by telephone: *I couldn't get through* ■ *adjective* without break or change: *through train*

through-and-through *adverb* completely, entirely

throughout *preposition* **1** in all parts of: *throughout Europe* **2** from start to finish of: *throughout the journey*

throw *verb* **1** to send through the air with force **2** of a horse: to make (a rider) fall to the ground **3** to shape (pottery) on a wheel **4** to give (a party) ■ *noun* **1** the act of throwing **2** the distance a thing is thrown: *within a stone's throw of the house* ■ **throw away** to get rid of

| **throw** *verb* ► **throws**, **throw***ing*, threw, thrown

throwback *noun* something that goes back to an earlier form

thrush *noun* (*plural* **thrushes**) a type of singing bird with a speckled breast

thrust *verb* **1** to push with force **2** to make a sudden push forward with a pointed weapon ■ *noun* **1** a stab **2** a pushing force ■ **thrust**

on *or* **upon** to force to accept

| **thrust** *verb* ► thrusts, thrusting, thrust

thud *noun* a dull, hollow sound like that made by a heavy body falling ■ *verb* to move or fall with such a sound

| **thud** *verb* ► thuds, thudding, thudded

thug *noun* a violent, brutal person

thumb *noun* the short, thick finger of the hand ■ *verb* to turn over (the pages of a book) with the thumb or fingers

thumbscrew *noun, history* an instrument of torture which worked by squashing the thumbs

thump *noun* a heavy blow ■ *verb* **1** to beat heavily **2** to move or fall with a dull, heavy noise

thunder *noun* **1** the deep, rumbling sound heard after a flash of lightning **2** any loud, rumbling noise ■ *verb* **1** to produce the sound of, or a sound like, thunder **2** to shout out angrily

thunderbolt *noun* **1** a flash of lightning followed by thunder **2** a very great and sudden surprise

thunderclap *noun* a sudden roar of thunder

thunderous *adjective* like thunder; very angry

thunderstruck *adjective* overcome by surprise

thundery *adjective* of weather: sultry, bringing thunder

Thursday *noun* the fifth day of the week

thus *adverb* **1** in this or that manner **2** to this degree or extent: *thus far* **3** because of this, therefore: *thus, we must go on*

thwart *verb* **1** to hinder (someone) from carrying out a plan, intention, *etc* **2** to prevent (an attempt *etc*)

thy *adjective, old* belonging to you: *thy wife and children*

thyme *noun* a small sweet-smelling herb used for seasoning food

tiara *noun* a jewelled ornament for the head like a crown

tic *noun* a twitching motion of certain muscles, especially of the face

tick [1] *noun* **1** a light mark (✓) used to mark as correct, or mark off in a list **2** a small quick noise, made regularly by a clock or watch **3** *informal* a moment ■ *verb* **1** to mark with a tick **2** of a clock *etc*: to produce regular ticks

tick [2] *noun* a tiny blood-sucking animal

ticket *noun* **1** a card entitling the holder to admittance to a show, travel on public transport, *etc* **2** a notice that a traffic offence has been committed **3** a label on an item showing price, size, *etc*

ticking *noun* the noise made by a clock *etc*

tickle *verb* **1** to excite the surface nerves of a part of the body by touching lightly **2** to please or amuse

ticklish *adjective* **1** sensitive to tickling **2** not easy to deal with: *ticklish problem*

tickly *adjective* ticklish

tidal *adjective* of the tide

tidal wave an enormous wave in the sea often caused by an earthquake *etc*

tiddler *noun, informal* **1** a small fish **2** a small person or thing

tiddlywinks *noun singular* a game in which small plastic discs (**tiddlywinks**) are flipped into a cup

tide *noun* **1** the rise and fall of the sea which happens regularly twice each day **2** *old* time, season: *Christmastide* ■ **tide over** to get over a difficulty for a time

tidings *noun plural* news

tidy *adjective* **1** in good order, neat **2** *informal* fairly big: *a tidy sum of money* ■ *verb* to make neat ■ **tidily** *adverb*

|**tidy** *verb* ▶ tidies, tidy*ing*, tidi*ed*

tie *verb* **1** to fasten with a cord, string, *etc* **2** to knot or put a bow in (string, shoelaces, *etc*) **3** to join, unite **4** to limit, restrict: *tied to a tight schedule* **5** to score the same number of points (in a game *etc*), draw ■ *noun* **1** a band of fabric worn round the neck, tied with a knot or bow **2** something that connects: *ties of friendship* **3** something that restricts or limits

4 an equal score in a competition **5** a game or match to be played

|**tie** *verb* ▶ ties, ty*ing*, tie*d*

tie-breaker *noun* an extra question or part of a tied contest to decide a winner

tier (*pronounced* teer) *noun* a row of seats in a theatre *etc*, with others above or below it

tiff *noun* a slight quarrel

tiger *noun* a large animal of the cat family with a tawny coat striped with black

tight *adjective* **1** packed closely **2** firmly stretched, not loose **3** fitting too closely

tighten *verb* to make or become tight or tighter

tight-fisted *adjective* stingy

tightrope *noun* a tightly stretched rope on which acrobats perform

tights *noun plural* a close-fitting garment covering the feet, legs and body as far as the waist

tigress *noun* a female tiger

tile *noun* a piece of baked clay *etc* used in covering floors or roofs ■ *verb* to cover with tiles

till[1] *noun* a container or drawer for money in a shop ■ *verb* to cultivate (land); plough

till[2] *another word for* **until**

tiller *noun* the handle of a boat's rudder

tilt *verb* to fall into, or place in, a sloping position ■ *noun* a slant

timber *noun* wood for building *etc*

time noun **1** the hour of the day **2** the period at which something happens **3** (often **times**) a particular period: *in modern times* **4** opportunity: *no time to listen* **5** a suitable or right moment **6** one of a number of occasions **7** times multiplied by ▪ verb **1** to measure the minutes, seconds, *etc* taken to do anything **2** to choose the time for (well, badly, *etc*): *time your entrance well*

time bomb a bomb designed to go off at a particular time

timeless adjective **1** not belonging to any particular time **2** never ending

timely adjective coming at the right moment

timescale noun the time envisaged for the completion of a project

time-sharing noun **1** a system of using a computer so that it can deal with several programs at the same time **2** a scheme by which someone buys the right to use a holiday home for a specified period each year

timetable noun a list showing times of classes, arrivals or departures of trains, *etc*

timid adjective easily frightened; shy

timidity noun nervousness, shyness

timidly adverb shyly

timing noun the co-ordination of when actions or events happen to achieve the best possible effect

timorous adjective very timid

timpani or **tympani** noun plural kettledrums

tin noun **1** a silvery-white kind of metal **2** a box or can made of tinplate, thin iron covered with tin or other metal ▪ verb to pack (food *etc*) in tins

| **tin** verb ▸ tins, tinn*ing*, tinn*ed*

tinder noun dry material easily set alight by a spark

tinfoil noun a very thin sheet of tin, aluminium, *etc* used for wrapping

tinge verb **1** to tint, colour slightly **2** **tinge with something** to add a slight amount of it to ▪ noun a slight amount; a hint: *tinge of sadness*

tingle verb **1** to feel a sharp prickling sensation **2** to feel a thrill of excitement ▪ noun a sharp prickle

tinker verb **1** to work clumsily or unskilfully **2** to meddle (with)

tinkle verb to (cause to) make a light, ringing sound; clink, jingle ▪ noun a light, ringing sound

tinny adjective **1** like tin **2** of a sound: thin, high-pitched

tinsel noun a sparkling, glittering material used for decoration

tint noun a variety or shade of a colour ▪ verb to give slight colour to

tiny adjective very small

tiny ► tin*ier*, tini*est*

tip *noun* **1** the top or point of something thin or tapering **2** a piece of useful information **3** a small gift of money to a waiter *etc* **4** a rubbish dump ■ *verb* **1** to slant **2 tip something over** to overturn it **3** to empty (out or into) **4** (also **tip off**) to give a hint to **5** to give a small gift of money

tip *verb* ► tips, tipp*ing*, tipp*ed*

Tipp-Ex *noun, trademark* correcting fluid for covering over mistakes in typing or writing

tipple *verb, informal* to drink small amounts of alcohol regularly ■ *noun* an alcoholic drink

tipsy *adjective* rather drunk

tiptoe *verb* to walk on your toes in order to go very quietly ■ **on tiptoe** standing or walking on your toes

tirade *noun* a long, bitter, scolding speech

tire *verb* **1** to make or become weary **2 tire of something** to lose patience with or interest in it

tired *adjective* **1** weary **2 tired of** bored with

tireless *adjective* **1** never becoming weary **2** never resting

tiresome *adjective* **1** making weary **2** long and dull **3** annoying

tiring *adjective* causing tiredness or weariness: *a tiring journey*

tissue *noun* **1** the substance of

which body organs are made **2** a paper handkerchief

tissue paper thin, soft paper used for wrapping

tit *noun* a type of small bird: *blue tit* ■ **tit for tat** blow for blow, repayment of injury with injury

titanic *adjective* huge, enormous

titbit *noun* a tasty piece of food *etc*

tithe *noun, history* a tax paid to the church, a tenth part of someone's income or produce

titillate *verb* to gently stimulate or arouse

title *noun* **1** the name of a book, poem, *etc* **2** a word in front of a name to show rank or office (*eg Sir, Lady, Major*), or in addressing anyone formally (*eg Mr, Mrs, Ms*)

titled *adjective* having a title which shows noble rank

titter *verb* to giggle ■ *noun* a giggle

to *preposition* **1** showing the place or direction aimed for: *going to the cinema* **2** showing the indirect object in a phrase, sentence, *etc*: *show it to me* **3** used before a verb to indicate the infinitive: *to err is human* **4** showing that one thing belongs with another in some way: *key to the door* **5** compared with: *nothing to what happened before* **6** showing a ratio, proportion, *etc*: *odds are six to one against* **7** showing the purpose or result of an action: *tear it to pieces* ■ *adverb* almost closed: *pull the door to*

toad *noun* a type of amphibian like a frog

toadstool *noun* a mushroom-like fungus, often poisonous

toady *verb* to give way to someone's wishes, or flatter them, to gain favour ■ *noun* (*plural* **toadies**) someone who acts in this way

toast *verb* 1 to brown (bread) by heating at a fire or grill 2 to drink to the success or health of (someone) ■ *noun* 1 bread toasted 2 the drinking of a toast

toaster *noun* an electric machine for toasting bread

toast rack a stand with partitions for slices of toast

tobacco *noun* a type of plant whose dried leaves are used for smoking

tobacconist *noun* someone who sells tobacco, cigarettes, *etc*

toboggan *noun* a long, light sledge ■ *verb* to go in a toboggan

today *adverb & noun* 1 (on) this day 2 (at) the present time

toddle *verb* to walk unsteadily, with short steps

toddler *noun* a young child just able to walk

to-do *noun* (*plural* **to-dos**) a bustle, commotion

toe *noun* 1 one of the five finger-like parts of the foot 2 the front part of a shoe, golf club, *etc*

toffee *noun* a kind of sweet made of sugar and butter

toffee-nosed *adjective*, *informal* snobbish, conceited

toga *noun*, *history* the loose outer garment worn by a citizen of ancient Rome

together *adverb* 1 with each other, in place or time: *we must stay together* 2 in or into union or connection: *glue the pages together* 3 by joint action: *together we can afford it*

toggle *noun* a cylindrical fastening for a coat

toil *verb* 1 to work hard and long 2 to walk, move, *etc* with effort ■ *noun* hard work

toilet *noun* 1 a receptacle for waste matter from the body, with a water-supply for flushing this away 2 a room containing this

toiletries *noun plural* soaps, cosmetics, *etc*

toilet water a lightly perfumed, spirit-based liquid for the skin

token *noun* 1 a mark, a sign: *a token of my friendship* 2 a stamped piece of plastic *etc*, or a voucher, for use in place of money: *book token* ■ *adjective* done for show only, insincere: *token gesture*

told *past form of* **tell**

tolerable *adjective* able to be endured; bearable

tolerance *noun* putting up with and being fair to people with different beliefs, manners, *etc* from your own

tolerant *adjective* fair towards other people and accepting their right to have different political and religious beliefs

tolerate *verb* to bear, endure; put up with

toleration *noun* the act of tolerating

toll [1] *noun* **1** a tax charged for crossing a bridge *etc* **2** loss, damage

toll [2] *verb* **1** to sound (a large bell) slowly, as for a funeral **2** of a bell: to be sounded slowly

tomahawk *noun*, *history* a Native American light axe used as a weapon and tool

tomato *noun* (*plural* **tomatoes**) a juicy red-skinned fruit, used in salads, sauces, *etc*

tomb *noun* **1** a grave **2** a burial vault or chamber

tombola *noun* a kind of lottery

tomboy *noun* a high-spirited active girl who enjoys the rough, boisterous activities which people tend to associate with boys

tombstone *noun* a stone placed over a grave in memory of the dead person

tomcat *noun* a male cat

tome *noun* a large heavy book

tomorrow *adverb & noun* **1** (on) the day after today **2** (in) the future: *the children of tomorrow*

tomtom *noun* a type of drum beaten with the hands

ton *noun* a measure of weight equal to 2240 pounds, about 1016 kilograms ■ **metric ton** *or* **metric tonne** 1000 kilograms

tone *noun* **1** sound **2** quality of sound: *harsh tone* **3** *music* one of the larger intervals in a scale, *eg* between C and D **4** the quality of a voice expressing the mood of the speaker **5** a shade of colour ■ *verb* **1** (sometimes **tone in**) to blend, fit in well **2 tone down** to make or become softer **3 tone up** to give strength to (muscles *etc*)

tongs *noun plural* an instrument for lifting and grasping coals, sugar lumps, *etc*

tongue *noun* **1** the fleshy organ inside the mouth, used in tasting, speaking, and swallowing **2** a flap in a shoe **3** the tongue of an animal served as food **4** a language: *his mother tongue*

tongue-tied *adjective* not able to speak freely

tongue-twister *noun* a phrase, sentence, *etc* not easy to say quickly, *eg* 'she sells sea shells'

tonic *noun* **1** a medicine which gives strength and energy **2** *music* the keynote of a scale **3 tonic water** ■ *adjective* **1** of tones or sounds **2** of a tonic

tonic water *noun* a type of flavoured, slightly fizzy, water

tonight *adverb & noun* (on) the night of the present day

tonne *noun* a metric ton

tonsil *noun* one of a pair of soft,

fleshy lumps at the back of the throat

tonsillitis noun reddening and painfulness of the tonsils

too adverb 1 to a greater extent, in a greater quantity, etc than is wanted: too hot to go outside 2 (with a negative) very, particularly: not feeling too well (ie not feeling very well) 3 also, as well: I'm feeling cold, too

took past form of **take**

tool noun an instrument for doing work, especially by hand

toolbar noun, computing a bar with a list of features and functions which appears at the top of a computer screen

toot noun the sound of a car horn etc

tooth noun (plural **teeth**) 1 any of the hard, bony objects projecting from the gums, arranged in two rows in the mouth 2 any of the points on a saw, cogwheel, comb, etc

toothache noun pain in a tooth

toothpaste noun paste for cleaning the teeth

toothpick noun a small sharp instrument for picking out food from between the teeth

top noun 1 the highest part of anything 2 the upper surface 3 the highest place or rank 4 a lid 5 a kind of spinning toy ■ adjective highest, chief ■ verb 1 to cover on the top 2 to rise above 3 to do better than 4 to reach the top

of 5 to take off the top of

| **top** verb ► tops, topping, topped

topaz noun a type of precious stone, of various colours

top hat a man's tall silk hat

top-heavy adjective having the upper part too heavy for the lower

topic noun a subject spoken or written about

topical adjective of current interest, concerned with present events

topmost adjective highest, uppermost

topple verb to become unsteady and fall

top-secret adjective (of information etc) very secret

topsy-turvy adjective & adverb turned upside down

Torah noun the book of Jewish law

torch noun (plural **torches**) a small hand-held light with a switch and electric battery

tore past form of **tear**²

torment verb 1 to treat cruelly and make suffer 2 to worry greatly 3 to tease ■ noun 1 great pain, suffering 2 a cause of these

tormentor noun a person who torments

torn past participle of **tear**²

tornado noun (plural **tornadoes**) a violent whirling wind that causes great damage

torpedo noun (plural **torpedoes**) a large cigar-shaped type of missile fired by ships, planes, *etc* ■ *verb* to hit or sink (a ship) with a torpedo

| **torpedo** *verb* ▶ torpedo*es*, torpedo*ing*, torpedo*ed*

torrent *noun* **1** a rushing stream **2** a heavy downpour of rain **3** a violent flow of words *etc*

torrential *adjective* like a torrent; rushing violently

torrid *adjective* **1** parched by heat; very hot **2** very intense: *torrid love affair*

torso *noun* (*plural* **torsos**) the body, excluding the head and limbs

tortilla *noun* **1** a type of flat Mexican bread **2** a Spanish omelette

tortoise *noun* a four-footed, slow-moving kind of reptile, covered with a hard shell

tortoiseshell *noun* the shell of a kind of sea turtle, used in making ornamental articles ■ *adjective* **1** made of this shell **2** mottled brown, yellow and black: *a tortoiseshell cat*

tortuous *adjective* winding, roundabout, not straightforward

torture *verb* **1** to treat someone cruelly as a punishment or to force them to confess something **2** to cause to suffer ■ *noun* **1** the act of torturing **2** great suffering

Tory *noun* (*plural* **Tories**) a member of the British Conservative Party

toss *verb* **1** to throw up in the air **2** to throw up (a coin) to see which side falls uppermost **3** to turn restlessly from side to side **4** of a ship: to be thrown about by rough water ■ **toss off** to produce quickly ■ **toss up** to toss a coin

toss-up *noun* an equal choice or chance

tot[1] *noun* **1** a little child **2** a small amount of alcoholic spirits

tot[2] *verb*: **tot up** to add up

total *adjective* **1** whole: *total number* **2** complete: *total wreck* ■ *noun* **1** the entire amount **2** the sum of amounts added together ■ *verb* **1** to add up **2** to amount to

| **total** *verb* ▶ totals, totall*ing*, totall*ed*

totalitarian *adjective* governed by a single party that allows no rivals

totally *adverb* completely

totem *noun* an image of an animal or plant used as the badge or sign of a Native American tribe

totem pole a pole on which totems are carved and painted

totter *verb* **1** to shake as if about to fall **2** to stagger

toucan *noun* a type of S American bird with a heavy curved beak

touch *verb* **1** to feel (with the hand) **2** to come or be in contact (with) **3** to move, affect the feelings of **4** to reach the standard of: *I can't touch him at chess* **5** to have anything to do with: *I wouldn't touch a job like that* **6** to eat or drink: *he won't touch meat* **7** to concern (someone) ■ *noun* **1** the act of touching **2** the physical sense of touch **3** a small quantity or degree: *a touch of salt* **4** of an artist, pianist, *etc*: skill or style **5** *football* the ground beyond the edges of the pitch marked off by **touchlines** ■ **touch down** of an aircraft: to land ■ **touch off** to cause to happen ■ **touch on** to mention briefly ■ **touch up** to improve (a drawing or photograph *etc*) by making details clearer *etc*

touch-and-go *adjective* very uncertain: *it's touch-and-go whether we'll get it done on time*

touché (*pronounced* too-**shei**) *exclamation* acknowledging a point scored in a game or argument

touching *preposition* about, concerning ■ *adjective* causing emotion, moving

touchy *adjective* **1** easily offended **2** needing to be handled with care and tact: *a touchy subject*

tough *adjective* **1** strong, not easily broken **2** of meat *etc*: hard to chew **3** of strong character, able to stand hardship or strain **4** difficult to cope with or overcome: *tough opposition*

toughen *verb* to (cause to) become tough

tour *noun* a journey in which you visit various places; a pleasure trip ■ *verb* to make a tour (of)

tourism *noun* the activities of tourists and of those who cater for their needs

tourist *noun* someone who travels for pleasure, and visits places of interest

tournament *noun* **1** a competition involving many contests and players **2** *history* a meeting at which knights fought together on horseback

tourniquet (*pronounced* toorn-ik-ei) *noun* a bandage tied tightly round a limb to prevent loss of blood from a wound

tousled *adjective* of hair: untidy, tangled

tout *verb* to go about looking for support, votes, buyers, *etc* ■ *noun* someone who does this

tow (*pronounced* toh) *verb* to pull (a car *etc*) with a rope attached to another vehicle ■ *noun* **1** the act of towing **2** the rope used for towing

towards or **toward** *preposition* **1** moving in the direction of (a place, person, *etc*): *walking towards the house* **2** to (a person, thing, *etc*): *his attitude towards his son* **3** as a help or contribution to: *I gave £5 towards the cost* **4** near, about (a time *etc*): *towards four o'clock*

towel *noun* a cloth for drying or wiping (*eg* the skin after washing) ■ *verb* to rub dry with a towel

towel verb ▸ **towels**, **towelling**, **towelled**

towelling noun a cotton cloth often used for making towels

tower noun 1 a high narrow building 2 a high narrow part of a castle etc ▪ verb to rise high (over, above)

towering adjective rising high

town noun a place, larger than a village, which includes many buildings, houses, shops, etc

town hall the building where the official business of a town is done

towpath noun a path alongside a canal used by horses which tow barges

toxic adjective 1 poisonous 2 caused by poison

toxin noun a naturally-occurring poison

toy noun an object for a child to play with ▪ **toy with** to play or trifle with

trace noun 1 a mark or sign left behind 2 a footprint 3 a small amount ▪ verb 1 to follow the tracks or course of 2 to copy (a drawing etc) on transparent paper placed over it

traceable adjective able to be traced (to)

tracery noun ornamental stone holding the glass in some church windows

trachea (pronounced tra-ki-a) noun (plural tracheae – pronounced tra-ki-ai) the windpipe

tracing noun a traced copy

tracing paper semi-transparent paper used for tracing drawings etc

track noun 1 a mark left 2 **tracks** footprints 3 a path or rough road 4 a racecourse for runners, cyclists, etc 5 a railway line 6 an endless band on which wheels of a tank etc travel ▪ verb to follow (an animal) by its footprints and other marks left ▪ **track down** to search for (someone or something) until caught or found

tracksuit noun a warm suit worn while jogging, before and after an athletic performance, etc

tract noun 1 a stretch of land 2 a short pamphlet, especially on a religious subject

tractable adjective easily made to do what is wanted

traction noun 1 the act of pulling or dragging 2 the state of being pulled

tractor noun a motor vehicle for pulling loads, ploughs, etc

trade noun 1 the buying and selling of goods 2 someone's occupation, craft, job ▪ verb 1 to buy and sell 2 to have business dealings (with) 3 to deal (in) 4 to exchange, swap ▪ **trade in** to give as part-payment for something else (eg an old car for a new one) ▪ **trade on** to take advantage of, often unfairly

trademark noun a registered mark or name put on goods to show that they are made by a certain company

trader noun someone who buys and sells

tradesman noun 1 a shopkeeper 2 a workman in a skilled trade

trade union a group of workers of the same trade who join together to bargain with employers for fair wages etc

trade unionist a member of a trade union

trade wind a wind which blows towards the equator (from the north-east and south-east)

tradition noun 1 the handing-down of customs, beliefs, stories, etc from generation to generation 2 a custom, belief, etc handed down in this way

traditional adjective of customs: having existed for a long time without changing

traditionalist noun someone who believes in maintaining traditions

traffic noun the cars, buses, boats, etc which use roads or waterways ■ verb 1 to trade 2 to deal (in)

┃ **traffic** verb ▶ traffics,
┃ trafficking, trafficked

traffic lights lights of changing colours for controlling traffic at road junctions or street crossings

tragedy noun (plural **tragedies**) 1 a very sad event 2 a play about unhappy events and with a sad ending (contrasted with: **comedy**)

tragic adjective of tragedy; very sad ■ **tragically** adverb

trail verb 1 to draw along, in or through 2 to hang down (from) or be dragged loosely behind 3 to hunt (animals) by following footprints etc 4 to walk wearily 5 of a plant: to grow over the ground or a wall ■ noun 1 an animal's track 2 a pathway through a wild region 3 something left stretching behind: a trail of dust

trailer noun 1 a vehicle pulled behind a car 2 a short film advertising a longer film to be shown at a later date

train noun 1 a railway engine with carriages or trucks 2 a part of a dress which trails behind the wearer 3 a line (of thought, events, etc) ■ verb 1 to prepare yourself by practice or exercise for a sporting event, job, etc 2 to educate 3 to exercise (animals or people) in preparation for a race etc 4 to tame and teach (an animal) 5 to make (a tree or plant) grow in a certain direction

trainee noun someone who is being trained

trainer noun someone who trains people or animals for a sport, circus, etc

training noun 1 preparation for a sport 2 experience or learning of the practical side of a job

trait noun a point that stands out in a person's character

traitor noun 1 someone who goes over to the enemy's side, or gives away secrets to the enemy 2 someone who betrays trust

trajectory noun (plural **trajectories**) the curved path of something (eg a bullet) moving through the air or through space

tram noun a long car running on rails and driven by electric power for carrying passengers (also called: **tramcar**)

tramline noun 1 a rail of tramway 2 **tramlines** tennis the parallel lines marked at the sides of the court

tramp verb 1 to walk with heavy footsteps 2 to walk along, over, etc: tramping the streets in search of a job ■ noun 1 someone with no fixed home and no job, who lives by begging 2 a journey made on foot 3 the sound of marching feet

trample verb 1 to tread under foot, stamp on 2 (usually **trample on**) to treat roughly or unfeelingly

trampoline noun a bed-like framework holding a sheet of elastic material for bouncing on, used by gymnasts etc

tramway noun a system of tracks on which trams run

trance noun a sleep-like or half-conscious state

tranquil adjective quiet, peaceful

tranquillity noun the state of being quiet, calm and peaceful

tranquillize or **tranquillise**, or

US **tranquilize** verb to make calm

tranquillizer or **tranquilliser**, or US **tranquilizer** noun a drug to calm the nerves or cause sleep

trans- prefix across, through: transatlantic/translate (= to carry across into a different language)

transact verb to do (a piece of business)

transaction noun a piece of business, a deal

transatlantic adjective 1 crossing the Atlantic Ocean: transatlantic yacht race 2 across or over the Atlantic: transatlantic friends

transcend verb 1 to be, or rise, above 2 to be, or do, better than

transcribe verb to copy from one book into another or from one form of writing (eg shorthand) into another

transcript noun a written copy

transfer verb 1 to remove to another place 2 to hand over to another person ■ noun 1 the act of transferring 2 a design or picture which can be transferred from one surface to another

| **transfer** verb ▶ transfer**s**, transfer**ring**, transfer**red**

transferable adjective able to be transferred

transference noun the act of moving or transferring something from one person, place or group to another

transfix verb to make unable to move or act (eg because of surprise): *transfixed by the sight*

transform *verb* to change in shape or appearance completely and often dramatically

transformation *noun* 1 transforming or being transformed 2 *maths* a change of size or position of a figure

transformer *noun* an apparatus for changing electrical energy from one voltage to another

transfusion *noun* (*in full* **blood transfusion**) the introduction of blood into a person's body by allowing it to drip through a needle inserted in a vein

transgress *verb* to break a rule, law, *etc*

transgression *noun* the act of breaking a rule, law, *etc*

transient *adjective* not lasting, passing

transistor *noun* a small device, made up of a crystal enclosed in plastic or metal, which controls the flow of an electrical current

transit *noun* the carrying or movement of goods, passengers, *etc* from place to place

transition *noun* a change from one form, place, appearance, *etc* to another

transitional *adjective* involving transition; temporary

transitive *adjective*, *grammar* of a verb: having an object, *eg* the verb '*hit*' in 'he *hit* the ball'

transitory *adjective* lasting only for a short time

translate *verb* to turn (something said or written) into another language

translation *noun* 1 the act of translating 2 something translated 3 *maths* a transformation with a sliding movement but no turning (*compare with*: **enlargement**, **reflection**, **rotation**)

translator *noun* someone who translates

translucent *adjective* allowing light to pass through, but not transparent

transmission *noun* 1 the act of transmitting 2 a radio or television broadcast

transmit *verb* 1 to pass on (a message, news, heat) 2 to send out signals which are received as programmes

| transmit ▶ transmits, transmitt*ing*, transmitt*ed*

transmitter *noun* an instrument for transmitting (especially radio signals)

transom *noun* a beam across a window or the top of a door

transparency *noun* (*plural* **transparencies**) 1 the state of being transparent 2 a photograph printed on transparent material and viewed by shining light through it

transparent *adjective* 1 able to be seen through 2 easily seen to be true or false

transpire *verb* 1 to happen: *tell*

me what transpired **2** to let out (moisture *etc*) through pores of the skin or through the surface of leaves

transplant *verb* **1** to lift and plant (a growing plant) in another place **2** to remove (skin) and graft it on another part of the same body **3** to remove (an organ) and graft it in another person or animal ▪ *noun* **1** the act of transplanting **2** a transplanted organ, plant, *etc*

transplantation *noun* the transfer of an organ or tissue from one person to another, or from one part of the body to another

transport *verb* to carry from one place to another ▪ *noun* **1** the act of transporting **2** any means of carrying persons or goods: *rail transport*

transportation *noun* **1** the act of transporting **2** means of transport

transporter *noun* a vehicle that carries other vehicles, heavy objects, *etc*

transpose *verb* to cause (two things) to change places

transverse *adjective* lying, placed, *etc* across: *transverse beams in the roof*

trap *noun* **1** a device for catching animals *etc* **2** a plan or trick for taking someone by surprise **3** a bend in a pipe which is kept full of water, for preventing the escape of air or gas ▪ *verb* to catch in a

trap, or in such a way that escape is not possible

| **trap** *verb* ▸ traps, trapp*ing*, trapp*ed*

trapdoor *noun* a door in a floor or ceiling

trapeze *noun* a swing used in performing gymnastic exercises or feats

trapezium *noun* a figure with four sides, two of which are parallel

trapezoid *noun* a figure with four sides, none of which are parallel

trapper *noun* someone who makes a living by catching animals for their skins and fur

trappings *noun plural* clothes or ornaments suitable for a particular person or occasion

trash *noun* something of little worth, rubbish

trashy *adjective* worthless

trauma *noun* **1** injury to the body **2** a very violent or distressing experience which has a lasting effect **3** a condition (of a person) caused in this way

traumatic *adjective* very upsetting, unpleasant or frightening

travel *verb* **1** to go on a journey **2** to move **3** to go along, across **4** to visit foreign countries ▪ *noun* the act of travelling

| **travel** *verb* ▸ travels, travel*ling*, travel*led*

traveller *noun* **1** someone who

travels **2** a travelling representative of a business firm who tries to obtain orders for his firm's products

traverse *verb* to go across, pass through ▪ *noun* **1** something that crosses or lies across **2** a going across a rock face *etc*

travesty *noun* (*plural* **travesties**) a poor or ridiculous imitation

trawl *verb* to fish by dragging a trawl along the bottom of the sea ▪ *noun* a wide-mouthed, bag-shaped net

trawler *noun* a boat used for trawling

tray *noun* a flat piece of wood, metal, *etc* with a low edge, for carrying dishes

treacherous *adjective* **1** likely to betray **2** dangerous

treachery *noun* (*plural* **treacheries**) the act of betraying those who have trusted you

treacle *noun* a thick, dark syrup produced from sugar when it is being refined

tread *verb* **1** to walk on or along **2** **tread on something** to put your foot on it **3** to crush, trample under foot ▪ *noun* **1** a step **2** a way of walking **3** the part of a tyre which touches the ground

| **tread** *verb* ▶ treads, treading, trod, trodden

treadle *noun* part of a machine which is worked by the foot

treadmill *noun* **1** *history* a mill turned by the weight of people

who were made to walk on steps fixed round a big wheel **2** any tiring, routine work

treason *noun* disloyalty to your own country or its government, *eg* by giving away its secrets to an enemy

treasure *noun* **1** a store of money, gold, *etc* **2** anything of great value or highly prized ▪ *verb* **1** to value greatly **2** to keep carefully because of its personal value

treasurer *noun* someone who has charge of the money of a club

Treasury *or* **treasury** *noun* (*plural* **treasuries**) the part of a government which has charge of the country's money

treat *verb* **1** to deal with, handle, act towards **2** to try to cure (someone) of a disease **3** to try to cure (a disease) **4** to write or speak about **5** to buy (someone) a meal, drink, *etc* ▪ *noun* something special (*eg* an outing) that gives much pleasure

treatise *noun* a long, detailed essay *etc* on some subject

treatment *noun* **1** the act of treating (*eg* a disease) **2** remedy, medicine **3** the way in which someone or something is dealt with

treaty *noun* (*plural* **treaties**) an agreement made between countries

treble *adjective* **1** three times the normal amount **2** *music* high in pitch ▪ *verb* to become three times as great ▪ *noun* **1** the highest part in singing **2** a child who sings the treble part of a song

treble clef a sign (𝄢) at the beginning of a written piece of music placing the note G on the second line of the stave

tree *noun* the largest kind of plant with a thick, firm wooden stem and branches

trek *noun* a long or wearisome journey ▪ *verb* to make a long hard journey

| **trek** *verb* ▸ tre**ks**, tre**kking**, tre**kked**

trellis *noun* (*plural* **trellises**) a network of strips for holding up growing plants

tremble *verb* **1** to shake with cold, fear, weakness **2** to feel fear (for another person's safety *etc*) ▪ *noun* **1** the act of trembling **2** a fit of trembling

tremendous *adjective* **1** very great or strong **2** *informal* very good, excellent

tremendously *adverb*, *informal* very

tremolo *noun* (*plural* **tremolos**), *music* a trembling effect produced by the quick succession of the same note

tremor *noun* a shaking or quivering

tremulous *adjective* shaking

trench *noun* (*plural* **trenches**) a long narrow ditch dug in the ground (*eg* by soldiers as a protection against enemy fire)

trenchant *adjective* of a remark, policy, *etc*: forceful, vigorous

trenchcoat *noun* a kind of waterproof overcoat with a belt

trend *noun* a general direction: *the trend of events*

trendy *adjective*, *informal* fashionable

| **trendy** ▸ trend**ier**, trend**iest**

trepidation *noun* fear, nervousness

trespass *verb* to go illegally on private land *etc*

trespasser *noun* someone who trespasses

tress *noun* (*plural* **tresses**) **1** a lock of hair **2 tresses** hair, especially long

trestle *noun* a wooden support with legs, used for holding up a table, platform, *etc*

tri- *prefix* three: *triangle/tricycle*

trial *noun* **1** the act of testing or trying (*eg* something new) **2** a test **3** the judging (of a prisoner) in a court of law **4** suffering

triangle *noun* **1** a figure with three sides and three angles: △ **2** a triangular metal musical instrument, played by striking with a small rod

triangular *adjective* having the shape of a triangle

triathlon *noun* a sporting contest consisting of three events, often swimming, running and cycling

tribal *adjective* belonging to or done by a tribe or tribes

tribe *noun* **1** a people who are all descended from the same ancestor **2** a group of families, especially of a wandering people ruled by a chief

tribesman, tribeswoman *noun* someone who belongs to a particular tribe

tribulation *noun* great hardship or sorrow

tribunal *noun* **1** a group of people appointed to give judgement, especially on an appeal **2** a court of justice

tributary *noun* (*plural* **tributaries**) a stream that flows into a river or other stream

tribute *noun* an expression, in word or deed, of praise, thanks, *etc*

triceps *noun* a muscle at the back of the arm that straightens the elbow

trick *noun* **1** a cunning or skilful action to puzzle, amuse, *etc* **2** in card games, the cards picked up by the winner when each player has played a card ▪ *adjective* meant to deceive: *trick photography* ▪ *verb* to cheat by some quick or cunning action

trickery *noun* cheating

trickle *verb* **1** to flow in small amounts **2** to arrive or leave slowly and gradually ▪ *noun* a slow, gradual flow

trickster *noun* someone who deceives by tricks

tricky *adjective* not easy to do

tricky ▶ trick**ier**, trick**iest**

tricolour *noun* a flag consisting of three upright stripes of different colours, especially the red, white and blue flag of France

tricycle *noun* a three-wheeled bicycle

trident *noun* a three-pronged spear

tried *past form of* try

tries *see* try

trifle *noun* **1** anything of little value **2** a small amount **3** a pudding of whipped cream, sponge-cake, wine, *etc* ▪ *verb* **1** **trifle with someone** to act towards them without sufficient respect **2** to amuse yourself in an idle way (with): *he trifled with her affections*

trifling *adjective* very small in value or amount

trigger *noun* a small lever on a gun which, when pulled with the finger, causes the bullet to be fired ▪ *verb* (often **trigger off**) to start, be the cause of, an important event, chain of events, *etc*

trigonometry *noun* the branch of mathematics which has to do chiefly with the relationship between the sides and angles of triangles

trilby *noun* a man's hat with an indented crown and narrow brim

trill *verb* to sing, play or utter in a quivering or bird-like way ▪ *noun* a trilled sound; in music, a rapid repeating of two notes several times

trillion noun **1** (originally US) a million millions **2** old a million million millions

trilogy noun (plural **trilogies**) a group of three related plays, novels, etc by the same author, meant to be seen or read as a whole

trim verb **1** to clip the edges or ends of **2** to decorate (eg a hat) ▪ noun the act of trimming ▪ adjective tidy, in good order, neat

| **trim** verb ▶ trims, trimming, trimmed

trimming noun **1** a decoration added to a dress, cake, etc **2** a piece of cloth, hair, etc cut off while trimming

trinket noun a small ornament (especially one of little value)

trio noun (plural **trios**) **1** three performers **2** three people or things

trip verb **1** (often **trip up**) to stumble, fall over **2 trip up** to make a mistake ▪ noun a journey for pleasure or business

| **trip** verb ▶ trips, tripping, tripped

tripe noun **1** part of the stomach of the cow or sheep used as food **2** informal rubbish, nonsense

triple adjective **1** made up of three **2** three times as large (as something else) ▪ verb to make or become three times as large

triplet noun one of three children or animals born of the same mother at one time

triplicate noun: **in triplicate** in three copies

tripod noun a three-legged stand (especially for a camera)

tripper noun someone who goes on a short pleasure trip

triptych noun three painted panels forming a whole work of art

trite adjective of a remark: used so often that it has little force or meaning

triumph noun **1** a great success or victory **2** celebration after a success ▪ verb **1** to win a victory **2** to rejoice openly because of a victory

triumphal adjective used in celebrating a triumph

triumphant adjective victorious; showing joy because of, or celebrating, triumph

▪ **triumphantly** adverb

trivia noun plural unimportant matters or details

trivial adjective of very little importance

trod and **trodden** see tread

troll noun a mythological creature, giant or dwarf, who lives in a cave

trolley noun (plural **trolleys**) **1** a small cart (eg as used by porters at railway stations) **2** a supermarket basket on wheels **3** a hospital bed on wheels for transporting patients **4** a table on wheels, used for serving tea *etc*

trombone *noun* a brass wind instrument with a sliding tube which changes the notes

troop *noun* 1 a collection of people or animals 2 **troops** soldiers 3 a unit in cavalry *etc* ▪ *verb* 1 to gather in numbers 2 to go in a group

trooper *noun* a horse-soldier

trophy *noun* (*plural* **trophies**) 1 something taken from an enemy and kept in memory of the victory 2 a prize such as a silver cup won in a sports competition *etc*

tropic *noun* 1 either of two imaginary circles running round the earth at about 23° north (**Tropic of Cancer**) or south (**Tropic of Capricorn**) of the equator 2 **tropics** the hot regions near or between these circles

tropical *adjective* 1 of the tropics 2 growing in hot countries: *tropical fruit* 3 of climate: very hot and wet

trot *verb* 1 of a horse: to run with short, high steps 2 of a person: to run slowly with short steps ▪ *noun* the pace of a horse or person when trotting

| trot *verb* ▶ trots, trotting, trotted

trotters *noun plural* the feet of pigs or sheep, especially when used as food

troubadour *noun*, *history* a travelling singer, especially in medieval France

trouble *verb* 1 to cause worry or sorrow to 2 to cause inconvenience to 3 to make an effort, bother (to) ▪ *noun* 1 worry, uneasiness 2 difficulty; disturbance 3 something which causes worry, difficulty, *etc* 4 a disease 5 care and effort put into doing something

troubleshooter *noun* someone whose job is to solve difficulties (*eg* in a firm's business activities)

troublesome *adjective* causing difficulty or inconvenience

trough *noun* 1 a long, open container for holding animals' food and water 2 an area of low atmospheric pressure

trounce *verb* 1 to punish or beat severely 2 to defeat heavily

troupe *noun* a company of actors, dancers, *etc*

trouser *adjective* of a pair of trousers: *trouser leg*

trousers *noun plural* an outer garment for the lower part of the body which covers each leg separately

trousseau *noun* (*plural* **trousseaux** *or* **trousseaus** – *both pronounced* troos-ohz) a bride's outfit for her wedding

trout *noun* a freshwater or sea fish, used as food

trowel *noun* 1 a small spade used in gardening 2 a similar tool with a flat blade, used for spreading mortar

truancy *noun* the practice of

being absent from school without permission

truant *noun* someone who stays away from school *etc* without permission

truce *noun* a rest from fighting or quarrelling agreed to by both sides

truck *noun* **1** a wagon for carrying goods on a railway **2** a strong lorry for carrying heavy loads

truculent *adjective* fierce and threatening, aggressive

trudge *verb* to walk with heavy steps, as if tired

true *adjective* **1** of a story *etc*: telling of something which really happened **2** correct, not invented or wrong: *it's true that the earth is round* **3** accurate **4** faithful: *a true friend* **5** real, properly so called: *the spider is not a true insect* **6** rightful: *the true heir*

truffle *noun* a round fungus found underground and much valued as a flavouring for food

truism *noun* a statement which is so clearly true that it is not worth making

truly *adverb* **1** really: *is that truly what he said?* **2** genuinely; honestly **3** completely, utterly

trump *noun* **1** a suit having a higher value than cards of other suits **2** a card of this suit ■ *verb* to play a card which is a trump

■ **trump up** to make up, invent

trump card 1 a card which is a

trump **2** something kept in reserve as a means of winning an argument *etc*

trumpet *noun* **1** a brass musical instrument with a clear, high-pitched tone **2** the cry of an elephant ■ *verb* **1** to announce (*eg* news) so that all may hear **2** to blow a trumpet **3** of elephants: to make a long, loud cry

truncheon *noun* a short heavy staff or baton such as that used by police officers

trundle *verb* to wheel or roll along

trunk *noun* **1** the main stem of a tree **2** the body (not counting the head, arms or legs) of a person or animal **3** the long nose of an elephant **4** a large box or chest for clothes *etc* **5 trunks** short pants worn by boys and men for swimming

trunk road a main road

truss *noun* (*plural* **trusses**) **1** a bundle (*eg* of hay, straw) **2** a kind of supporting bandage ■ *verb* to bind, tie tightly (up)

trust *noun* **1** belief in the power, truth or goodness of a thing or person **2** something (*eg* a task or an item of value) handed over to someone in the belief that they will do it, guard it, *etc* **3** charge, keeping: *the child was put in my trust* **4** arrangement by which something (*eg* money) is given to someone for use in a particular way **5** a number of business firms working closely together ■ *verb* **1** to have faith or confidence (in) **2** to give (someone something) in the belief that they will use it well *etc* **3** to feel confident (that): *I trust that you can find your way here*

trustee *noun* someone who keeps something in trust for another

trustful *or* **trusting** *adjective* ready to trust, not suspicious

trustworthy *adjective* able to be trusted or depended on

trusty *adjective* able to be trusted or depended on

truth *noun* **1** the state of being true **2** a true statement **3** the facts

truthful *adjective* **1** telling the truth, not lying **2** of a statement: true ■ **truthfully** *adverb*

try *verb* **1** to attempt, make an effort (to do something) **2** to test by using **3** to test severely, strain: *you're trying my patience* **4** to attempt to use, open, *etc*: *I tried the door but it was locked* **5** to judge (a prisoner) in a court of law ■ *noun* (*plural* **tries**) **1** an effort, an attempt **2** one of the ways of scoring in rugby football ■ **try on** to put on (clothing) to see if it fits *etc* ■ **try out** to test by using

| **try** *verb* ► tries, try*ing*, tri*ed*

trying *adjective* hard to bear; testing

tsar *or* **tzar** *or* **czar** *noun, history* the emperor of Russia before the Revolution

tsarina *or* **tzarina** *or* **czarina**

noun, history **1** the wife of a tsar **2** an empress of Russia before the Revolution

T-shirt *another spelling of* **tee-shirt**

tsunami *noun* a very large wave caused by an underwater earthquake or volcanic eruption

tub *noun* **1** a round wooden container used for washing *etc*; a bath **2** a round container for ice-cream *etc*

tuba *noun* a large brass musical instrument giving a low note

tubby *adjective* fat and round

tube *noun* **1** a hollow, cylinder-shaped object through which liquid may pass **2** an organ of this kind in humans, animals, *etc* **3** a container from which something may be squeezed **4** an underground railway system

tuber *noun* a swelling on the underground stem of a plant (*eg* a potato)

tuberculosis *noun* an infectious disease affecting the lungs

tubular *adjective* shaped like a tube

tuck *noun* **1** a fold stitched in a piece of cloth **2** *informal* sweets, cakes, *etc* ■ *verb* **1** to gather (cloth) together into a fold **2** to fold or push (into or under a place) ■ **tuck in** *informal* **1** to eat with enjoyment or greedily **2** to push bedclothes closely round (someone in bed)

tuck shop a shop in a school

where sweets, cakes, *etc* are sold

Tuesday *noun* the third day of the week

tuft *noun* a bunch or clump of grass, hair, *etc*

tug *verb* 1 to pull hard 2 to pull along ▪ *noun* 1 a strong pull 2 a tugboat

| **tug** *verb* ► tugs, tug*ging*, tug*ged*

tugboat *noun* a small but powerful ship used for towing larger ones

tug-of-war *noun* a contest in which two teams, holding the ends of a strong rope, pull against each other

tuition *noun* 1 teaching 2 private coaching or teaching

tulip *noun* a type of flower with cup-shaped flowers grown from a bulb

tumble *verb* 1 to fall or come down suddenly and violently 2 to roll, toss (about) ▪ *noun* a fall

tumbledown *adjective* falling to pieces

tumbler *noun* a large drinking glass

tummy *noun* (*plural* **tummies**) *informal* the stomach

tumour *noun* an abnormal growth on or in the body

tumult *noun* 1 a great noise made by a crowd 2 excitement, agitation

tumultuous *adjective* with great noise or confusion: *a tumultuous welcome*

tuna *noun* (*plural* **tuna** or **tunas**) a large sea fish, used as food

tundra *noun* a level treeless plain in Arctic regions

tune *noun* 1 notes put together to form a melody 2 the music of a song ▪ *verb* 1 to put (a musical instrument) in tune 2 to adjust a radio set to a particular station 3 (sometimes **tune up**) to improve the working of an engine

tuneful *adjective* having a pleasant or recognizable tune

tungsten *noun* an element, a grey metal

tunic *noun* 1 a soldier's or police officer's jacket 2 *history* a loose garment reaching to the knees, worn in ancient Greece and Rome 3 a similar modern garment: *gym tunic*

tuning fork a steel fork which, when struck, gives a note of a certain pitch

tunnel *noun* an underground passage (*eg* for a railway train) ▪ *verb* 1 to make a tunnel 2 of an animal: to burrow

| **tunnel** *verb* ► tunnels, tunnel*ling*, tunnel*led*

turban *noun* 1 a long piece of cloth wound round the head, worn by Muslim and Sikh men 2 a kind of hat resembling this

turbine *noun* an engine with curved blades, turned by the action of water, steam, hot air, *etc*

turbot *noun* a type of large flat sea fish, used as food

turbulence *noun* irregular movement of air currents, especially when affecting the flight of aircraft

turbulent *adjective* 1 disturbed, in a restless state 2 likely to cause a disturbance or riot

tureen *noun* a large dish for holding soup at table

turf *noun* grass and the soil below it ∎ **turf out** *informal* to throw out

turgid *adjective* 1 swollen 2 of language: pompous

turkey *noun* (*plural* **turkeys**) a large farmyard bird, used as food

Turkish bath a type of hot air or steam bath in which someone is made to sweat heavily, is massaged and then slowly cooled

turmoil *noun* a state of wild, confused movement or disorder

turn *verb* 1 to go round 2 to face or go in the opposite direction 3 to change direction: *the road turns sharply to the left* 4 to direct (*eg* attention) 5 of milk: to go sour 6 to become: *his hair turned white* 7 of leaves: to change colour 8 to pass (the age of) ∎ *noun* 1 the act of turning 2 a point where someone may change direction, *eg* a road junction 3 a bend (*eg* in a road) 4 a spell of duty: *your turn to wash the dishes* 5 a fit of dizziness, shock, *etc* ∎ **turn against** to become hostile to ∎ **turn down 1** to say no to, refuse (*eg* an offer, a request) 2 to

reduce, lessen (heat, volume of sound, *etc*) ∎ **turn in 1** to go to bed 2 to hand over to those in authority ∎ **turn off 1** to stop the flow of (a tap) 2 to switch off the power for (a television *etc*) ∎ **turn on 1** to set running (*eg* water from a tap) 2 to switch on power for (a television *etc*) 3 to depend (on) 4 to become angry with (someone) unexpectedly ∎ **turn out 1** to make to leave, drive out 2 to make, produce 3 to empty: *turn out your pockets* 4 of a crowd: to come out, gather for a special purpose 5 to switch off (a light) 6 to prove (to be) ∎ **turn to 1** to set to work 2 to go to for help *etc* ∎ **turn up 1** to appear, arrive 2 to be found 3 to increase (*eg* heat, volume of sound, *etc*)

turncoat *noun* someone who betrays their party, principles, *etc*

turning *noun* 1 the act of turning 2 a point where a road *etc* joins another

turning-point *noun* a crucial point of change

turnip *noun* a plant with a large round root used as a vegetable

turnover *noun* 1 rate of change or replacement (*eg* of workers in a firm *etc*) 2 the total amount of sales made by a firm during a certain time

turnpike *noun* US a road on which a toll is paid

turnstile *noun* a gate which

turns, allowing only one person to pass at a time

turntable *noun* a revolving platform for turning a railway engine round

turpentine *noun* an oil from certain trees used for mixing paints, cleaning paint brushes, *etc*

turquoise *noun* a greenish-blue precious stone

turret *noun* 1 a small tower on a castle or other building 2 a structure for supporting guns on a warship

turreted *adjective* having turrets

turtle *noun* a kind of large tortoise which lives in water

tusk *noun* a large tooth (one of a pair) sticking out from the mouth of certain animals (*eg* an elephant, a walrus)

tussle *noun* a struggle ▪ *verb* to struggle, compete

tutor *noun* 1 a teacher of students in a university *etc* 2 a teacher employed privately to teach individual pupils ▪ *verb* to teach

tutorial *noun* a meeting for study or discussion between tutor and students

tutu *noun* a ballet dancer's short, stiff, spreading skirt

TV *abbreviation* television

twaddle *noun*, *informal* nonsense

twain *noun*, *old* two

twang *noun* 1 a tone of voice in which the words seem to come through the nose 2 a sound like that of a tightly-stretched string being plucked ▪ *verb* to make such a sound

tweak *verb* to pull with a sudden jerk, twitch ▪ *noun* a sudden jerk or pull

tweed *noun* 1 a woollen cloth with a rough surface 2 **tweeds** clothes made of this cloth ▪ *adjective* made of tweed

tweezers *noun plural* small pincers for pulling out hairs, holding small things, *etc*

twelfth *adjective* the last of a series of twelve ▪ *noun* one of twelve equal parts

twelve *noun* the number 12 ▪ *adjective* 12 in number

twentieth *adjective* the last of a series of twenty ▪ *noun* one of twenty equal parts

twenty *noun* the number 20 ▪ *adjective* 20 in number

twice *adverb* two times

twiddle *verb* to play with, twirl idly

twig *noun* a small branch of a tree

twilight *noun* the faint light between sunset and night, or before sunrise

twill *noun* a kind of strong cloth with a ridged appearance

twin *noun* one of two children or animals born of the same mother at the same birth ▪ *adjective*

1 born at the same birth **2** made up of two parts or things which are alike

twine *noun* a strong kind of string made of twisted threads ▪ *verb* **1** to wind or twist together **2** to wind (about or around something)

twinge *noun* a sudden, sharp pain

twinkle *verb* **1** of a star *etc*: to shine with light which seems to vary in brightness **2** of eyes: to shine with amusement *etc*

twirl *verb* **1** to turn or spin round quickly and lightly **2** to turn round and round with the fingers ▪ *noun* a spin round and round

twist *verb* **1** to wind (threads) together **2** to wind round or about something **3** to make (*eg* a rope) into a coil **4** to bend out of shape **5** to bend or wrench painfully (*eg* your ankle) **6** to make (*eg* facts) appear to have a meaning which is really false ▪ *noun* **1** the act of twisting **2** a painful wrench

twister *noun, informal* a dishonest and unreliable person

twitch *verb* **1** to pull with a sudden light jerk **2** to jerk slightly and suddenly: *a muscle in his face twitched* ▪ *noun* **1** a sudden jerk **2** a muscle spasm

twitter *noun* **1** high, rapidly repeated sounds, as are made by small birds **2** slight nervous excitement ▪ *verb* **1** of a bird: to make a series of high quivering

notes **2** of a person: to talk continuously

two *noun* the number 2 ▪ *adjective* 2 in number

two-dimensional *adjective* having height and width, but not depth (*short form:* **2-D**)

two-faced *adjective* deceitful, insincere

twofold *adjective* double

two-time *verb* to have a love affair with two people at the same time

tycoon *noun* a business man of great wealth and power

tympani *another spelling of* timpani

type *noun* **1** kind **2** an example which has all the usual characteristics of its kind **3** a small metal block with a raised letter or sign, used for printing **4** a set of these **5** printed lettering ▪ *verb* **1** to print with a typewriter **2** to use a typewriter **3** to identify or classify as a particular type

typecast *verb* to give (an actor) parts very similar in character

typeface *noun* a set of printed letters and characters in a particular style

typewriter *noun* a machine with keys which, when struck, print letters on a sheet of paper

typhoid *noun* an infectious disease caused by germs in infected food or drinking water

typhoon *noun* a violent storm of wind and rain in Eastern seas

typhus *noun* a dangerous fever carried by lice

typical *adjective* having or showing the usual characteristics: *typical of her to be late* ∎ **typically** *adverb*

typify *verb* to be a good example of

| **typify** ▶ typif*ies*, typify*ing*, typif*ied*

typist *noun* someone who works with a typewriter and does other secretarial or clerical tasks

tyrannical *or* **tyrannous** *adjective* like a tyrant, cruel

tyrannize *or* **tyrannise** *verb* to act as a tyrant, rule over harshly

tyranny *noun* (*plural* **tyrannies**) the rule of a tyrant

tyrant *noun* a ruler who governs cruelly and unjustly

tyre *noun* a thick rubber cover round a motor or cycle wheel

tzar *another spelling of* tsar

tzarina *another spelling of* tsarina

U u

ubiquitous (*pronounced* yoo-bik-wit-*us*) *adjective* **1** being everywhere at once **2** found everywhere

udder *noun* a bag-like part of a cow, goat, *etc* with teats which supply milk

UFO *abbreviation* unidentified flying object

ugliness *noun* being ugly

ugly *adjective* unpleasant to look at or hear: *ugly sound*

ukelele (*pronounced* yook-e-lei-li) *noun* a small, stringed musical instrument played like a banjo

ulcer *noun* an open sore on the inside or the outside of the body

ulterior *adjective* beyond what is admitted or seen: *ulterior motive*

ultimate *adjective* last, final

ultimately *adverb* finally, in the end

ultimatum *noun* a final demand sent with a threat to break off discussion, declare war, *etc* if it is not met

ultra- *prefix* **1** very: *ultra-careful* **2** beyond: *ultramicroscopic*

ultraviolet *adjective* having rays of slightly shorter wavelength than visible light

umbrage *noun* a feeling of offence or hurt: *took umbrage at my suggestion*

umbrella *noun* an object made up of a folding covered framework on a stick which protects against rain

umpire *noun* a sports official who sees that a game is played according to the rules ■ *verb* to act as an umpire

umpteen *adjective* many, lots

un- *prefix* **1** not: *unequal* **2** (with verbs) used to show the reversal of an action: *unfasten*

unabashed *adjective* shameless, blatant

unable *adjective* lacking enough strength, power, skill, *etc*

unaccompanied *adjective* **1** alone, not escorted by another person **2** not having a musical accompaniment

unaccountable *adjective* not able to be explained ■ **unaccountably** *adverb*

unaccustomed *adjective* not used (to)

unanimous (*pronounced* yoo-nan-im-*us*) *adjective* **1** all of the same opinion **2** agreed to by all ■ **unanimously** *adverb*

unapproachable *adjective* unfriendly and stiff in manner

unassuming *adjective* modest

unattached *adjective* **1** not attached **2** single, not married or having a partner

unaware *adjective* not knowing, ignorant (of)

unawares *adverb* **1** without warning **2** unintentionally

unbalanced *adjective* **1** mad **2** lacking balance: *unbalanced view*

unbearable *adjective* too painful or bad to be endured

unbeliever *noun* someone who does not follow a certain religion

unbridled *adjective* not kept under control: *unbridled fury*

unburden *verb*: **unburden yourself** to tell your secrets or problems to someone else

uncalled *adjective*: **uncalled for** quite unnecessary: *your remarks were uncalled for*

uncanny *adjective* strange, mysterious ■ **uncannily** *adverb*

uncared *adjective*: **uncared for** not looked after properly

uncertain *adjective* **1** not certain, doubtful **2** not definitely known **3** of weather: changeable

uncharted *adjective* **1** not shown on a map or chart **2** little known

uncle *noun* **1** the brother of your father or mother **2** the husband of

your father's or mother's sister

unclean *adjective* dirty, impure

uncoil *verb* to unwind

uncomfortable *adjective* not comfortable

uncommon *adjective* not common, strange

uncommonly *adverb* very: *uncommonly talented*

uncompromising *adjective* not willing to give in or make concessions to others

unconditional *adjective* with no conditions attached; absolute

unconscious *adjective* **1** senseless, stunned (*eg* by an accident) **2** not aware (of) **3** not recognized by the person concerned ■ *noun* the deepest level of the mind

uncouth *adjective* **1** clumsy, awkward **2** rude

uncover *verb* **1** to remove a cover from **2** to disclose

undaunted *adjective* fearless; not discouraged

undecided *adjective* not yet decided

undeniable *adjective* not able to be denied, clearly true

under *preposition* **1** directly below or beneath **2** less than: *under £5* **3** within the authority or command of **4** having, using: *under a false name* **5** in accordance with: *under our agreement* ■ *adverb* in or to a lower position, condition, *etc*

under- *prefix* **1** below, beneath:

underachieve/underarm **2** lower in position or rank: *underdog/ underling* **3** too little: *underdeveloped/underrate*

underachieve *verb* to achieve less than your potential

underarm *adverb* of bowling *etc*: with the arm kept below the shoulder

undercarriage *noun* the wheels of an aeroplane and their supports

underclothes *noun plural* clothes worn next to the skin under other clothes

undercover *adjective* acting or done in secret: *an undercover policeman*

undercurrent *noun* **1** a flow or movement under the surface **2** a half-hidden feeling or tendency: *an undercurrent of despair in her voice*

undercut *verb* to sell at a lower price than someone else

underdeveloped *adjective* **1** not fully grown **2** of a country: lacking modern agricultural and industrial systems, and with a low standard of living

underdog *noun* the weaker side, or the loser in any conflict or fight

underdone *adjective* of food: not quite cooked

underestimate *verb* to estimate at less than the real worth, value, *etc*

underfoot *adjective* under the feet

undergo *verb* **1** to suffer, endure **2** to receive (*eg* as medical treatment)

undergraduate *noun* a university student who has not yet passed final examinations

underground *adjective* **1** below the surface of the ground **2** secret, covert ■ *noun* a railway which runs in a tunnel beneath the surface of the ground

undergrowth *noun* shrubs or low plants growing amongst trees

underhand *adjective* sly, deceitful

underlie *verb* to be the hidden cause or source of

underline *verb* **1** to draw a line under **2** to stress the importance of, emphasize

underling *noun* someone of lower rank

underlying *adjective* **1** lying under or beneath **2** fundamental, basic: *the underlying causes*

undermine *verb* to do damage to, weaken gradually (health, authority, *etc*)

underneath *adverb & preposition* in a lower position (than), beneath: *look underneath the table/wearing a jacket underneath his coat*

underpants *noun plural* underwear covering the buttocks and upper legs

underpass *noun* a road passing under another one

underpin verb to support from beneath, prop up

underprivileged adjective not having normal living standards or rights

underrate verb to think too little of, underestimate

undersigned noun: **the undersigned** the people whose names are written at the end of a letter or statement

undersized adjective below the usual or required size

underskirt noun a thin skirt worn under another skirt

understand verb 1 to see the meaning of 2 to appreciate the reasons for: I don't understand your behaviour 3 to have a thorough knowledge of: do you understand economics? 4 to have the impression that: I understood that you weren't coming 5 to take for granted as part of an agreement

understandable adjective 1 reasonable, natural or normal: he reacted with understandable fury 2 capable of being understood: his speech was barely understandable

understanding noun 1 the ability to see the full meaning of something 2 an agreement 3 condition: on the understanding that we both pay half 4 appreciation of other people's feelings, difficulties, etc
■ adjective able to understand other people's feelings, sympathetic

understatement noun a statement which does not give the whole truth, making less of certain details than is actually the case

understudy noun (plural **understudies**) an actor who learns the part of another actor and is able to take their place if necessary

undertake verb 1 to promise (to do something) 2 to take upon yourself (a task, duty, etc): I undertook responsibility for the food

undertaker noun someone whose job is to organize funerals

undertaking noun 1 something which is being attempted or done 2 a promise

undertone noun 1 a soft voice 2 a partly hidden meaning, feeling, etc: an undertone of discontent

undervalue verb to value (something) below its real worth

underwater adjective under the surface of the water

underwear noun underclothes

underweight adjective under the usual or required weight

underworld noun 1 the criminal world or level of society 2 the place where spirits go after death

undesirable adjective not wanted

undivided adjective not split, complete, total: undivided attention

undo *verb* 1 to unfasten (a coat, parcel, *etc*) 2 to wipe out the effect of, reverse: *undoing all the good I did*

undoubted *adjective* not to be doubted

undoubtedly *adverb* without doubt, certainly

undreamt-of *adjective* more *etc* than could have been imagined

undress *verb* to take your clothes off

undue *adjective* too much, more than is necessary: *undue expense*

undulate *verb* 1 to move as waves do 2 to have a rolling, wavelike appearance
■ **undulating** *adjective*
■ **undulation** *noun*

unduly *adverb* excessively; unreasonably

undying *adjective* unending, never fading: *undying love*

unearth *verb* to bring or dig out from the earth, or from a place of hiding

unearthly *adjective* 1 strange, as if not of this world 2 *informal* absurd, especially absurdly early: *at this unearthly hour*

uneasiness *noun* an uneasy state: *feelings of uneasiness*

uneasy *adjective* anxious, worried

unemployed *adjective* without a job ■ **the unemployed** unemployed people as a group

unemployment *noun* the state of being unemployed

unenviable *adjective* not arousing envy: *unenviable task*

unequal *adjective* 1 not equal; unfair: *unequal distribution* 2 lacking enough strength or skill: *unequal to the job*

unequalled *adjective* without an equal, unique

unequivocal (*pronounced* un-i-kwiv-ok-al) *adjective* clear, not ambiguous: *unequivocal orders*

uneven *adjective* 1 not smooth or level 2 not all of the same quality *etc*: *this work is very uneven*

unexceptionable *adjective* not causing objections or criticism

♦* Do not confuse: **unexceptionable** and **unexceptional**

unexceptional *adjective* not exceptional, ordinary

unexpected *adjective* not expected, sudden

unfailing *adjective* never failing, never likely to fail

unfair *adjective* not just

unfaithful *adjective* not true to your marriage vows

unfasten *verb* to loosen, undo (*eg* a buttoned coat)

unfathomable *adjective* not understandable, not clear

unfavourable *adjective* not helpful: *unfavourable conditions for sailing*

unfeeling *adjective* harsh, hard-hearted

unfettered adjective not restrained

unfit adjective 1 not suitable 2 not good enough, or not in a suitable state (to, for): *unfit for drinking*/*unfit to travel* 3 not in good health

unfold verb 1 to spread out 2 to give details of (a story, plan) 3 of details of a plot *etc*: to become known

unforgettable adjective unlikely to ever be forgotten; memorable

unfortunate adjective 1 unlucky 2 regrettable: *unfortunate turn of phrase* ▪ **unfortunately** adverb

unfurl verb to unfold (eg a flag)

ungainly adjective clumsy, awkward

ungracious adjective rude, not polite

ungrateful adjective not showing thanks for kindness

unguarded adjective 1 without protection 2 thoughtless, careless: *unguarded remark*

unhappy adjective 1 miserable, sad 2 unfortunate ▪ **unhappily** adverb

unhealthy adjective 1 not well, ill 2 harmful to health: *unhealthy climate* 3 showing signs of not being well: *unhealthy complexion*

unheard-of adjective very unusual, unprecedented

unhinged adjective mad, crazy

unholy adjective 1 evil 2 outrageous

uni- prefix one, a single: *unilateral*

unicorn noun a mythological animal like a horse, but with one straight horn on its forehead

unification noun the act of unifying or the state of being unified

uniform adjective the same in all parts or times, never varying ▪ noun the form of clothes worn by people in the armed forces, children at a certain school, *etc*

uniformity noun sameness: *the uniformity of modern architecture*

unify verb to combine into one

| **unify** ▶ unif*ies*, unify*ing*, unif*ied*

unilateral adjective 1 one-sided 2 involving one person or group out of several

uninhibited adjective not inhibited, unrestrained

uninitiated adjective not knowing, ignorant

uninterested adjective not interested

🔺 Do not confuse with: **disinterested**. It is generally a negative thing to be **uninterested** (= bored). It is generally a positive thing to be **disinterested** (= fair), especially if you are trying to make an unbiased decision

uninterrupted *adjective* **1** continuing without a break **2** of a view: not blocked by anything

union *noun* **1** the act of joining together **2** partnership; marriage **3** countries or states joined together **4** a trade union

unique *adjective* without a like or equal

◆* Do not confuse with: **rare**. You can talk about something being **rare**, quite **rare**, very **rare** *etc*. It would be incorrect, however, to describe something as 'very **unique**', since things either are or are not **unique** – there are no levels of this quality

unisex *adjective* suitable for either men or women

unison *noun* **1** exact sameness of musical pitch **2** agreement, accord

unit *noun* **1** a single thing, person or group, especially when considered as part of a larger whole **2** a fixed amount or length used as a standard by which others are measured (*eg* metres, litres, centimetres, *etc*) **3** the number one

unite *verb* **1** to join together; become one **2** to act together

united *adjective* **1** in agreement about something: *united in their opposition* **2** joined together: *a united Ireland*

unity *noun* **1** complete

agreement **2** the state of being one or a whole

universal *adjective* **1** relating to the universe **2** relating to, or coming from, all people: *universal criticism* ▪ **universally** *adverb*

universe *noun* all known things, including the earth and planets

university *noun* (*plural* **universities**) a college which teaches a wide range of subjects to a high level, and which awards degrees to students who pass its examinations

unkempt *adjective* untidy

unkind *adjective* not kind; harsh, cruel

unknown *adjective* **1** not known; unfamiliar **2** not at all famous ▪ *noun* **the unknown** things that are unexplained, undiscovered, *etc*

unleaded *adjective* of petrol: not containing lead compounds

unleash *verb* **1** to set free (a dog *etc*) **2** to let loose (*eg* anger)

unleavened (*pronounced* un-lev-end) *adjective* of bread: not made to rise with yeast

unless *conjunction* if not, except in a case where: *unless he's here soon, I'm going* (= if he's not here soon)

unlike *adjective* different, not similar ▪ *preposition* **1** different from **2** not characteristic of: *it was unlike her not to phone*

unlikely *adjective* **1** not probable: *it's unlikely that it will* *rain today* **2** probably not true: *an unlikely tale*

unload *verb* **1** to take the load from **2** to remove the charge from a gun

unlucky *adjective* **1** not lucky or fortunate **2** unsuccessful
■ **unluckily** *adverb*

unmentionable *adjective* not fit to be spoken of, scandalous, indecent

unmistakable *or* **unmistakeable** *adjective* very clear; impossible to confuse with any other

unmoved *adjective* not affected, unsympathetic: *unmoved by my pleas*

unnatural *adjective* not natural, perverted

unnecessary *adjective* not necessary; avoidable

unobtrusive *adjective* not obvious or conspicuous; modest

unpack *verb* to open (a piece of luggage) and remove the contents

unpalatable *adjective* **1** not pleasing to the taste **2** not pleasant to have to face up to: *unpalatable facts*

unparalleled *adjective* not having an equal, unprecedented

unpick *verb* to take out sewing stitches from

unpleasant *adjective* not pleasant, nasty

unprecedented *adjective* never having happened before

unprepossessing *adjective* not attractive

unprincipled *adjective* without (moral) principles

unquestionable *adjective* undoubted, certain

unravel *verb* **1** to unwind, take the knots out of **2** to solve (a problem or mystery)

unravel ▸ unravels, unravelling, unravelled

unreal *adjective* not real, imaginary

unreasonable *adjective* not reasonable, unfair

unremitting *adjective* never stopping; unending: *unremitting rain*

unrequited *adjective* of love: not given in return, one-sided

unrest *noun* a state of trouble or discontent, especially among a group of people

unrivalled *adjective* without an equal

unruly *adjective* **1** badly behaved **2** not obeying laws or rules ■ **unruliness** *noun*

unsaturated *adjective* **1** of a compound: unable to combine with any other atoms **2** of a solution: unable to dissolve any more of a solute (*contrasted with*: **saturated**)

unsaturated fat a fat that can raise the amount of cholesterol in the blood

unsavoury *adjective* very

unpleasant, causing a feeling of disgust

unscathed *adjective* not harmed

unscrew *verb* to loosen (something screwed in)

unscrupulous *adjective* having no scruples or principles

unseemly *adjective* unsuitable, improper: *unseemly haste*

unseen *adjective* not seen

unselfish *adjective* 1 showing concern for others 2 generous

unsettle *verb* to disturb, upset

unsettled *adjective* 1 disturbed 2 of weather: changeable

unsettling *adjective* disturbing, upsetting

unsightly *adjective* ugly

unsociable *adjective* not willing to mix with other people

unsophisticated *adjective* 1 simple, uncomplicated 2 naive, inexperienced

unsound *adjective* 1 incorrect, unfounded 2 not sane

unspeakable *adjective* too bad to describe in words

unsteady *adjective* 1 not secure or firm 2 not regular or constant 3 of movement: unsure

unstinting *adjective* unrestrained, generous

unstoppable *adjective* not able to be stopped

unsuspecting *adjective* not aware of coming danger

unswerving *adjective* solid, unwavering

untenable *adjective* unjustifiable: *the government's position is untenable*

unthinkable *adjective* 1 very unlikely 2 too bad to be thought of

untidy *adjective* not neat or well-organized

untie *verb* 1 to release from bonds 2 to loosen (a knot)

until *preposition* up to the time of: *can you wait until Tuesday?*
■ *conjunction* up to the time that: *keep walking until you come to the corner*

untimely *adjective* 1 happening too soon: *untimely arrival* 2 not suitable to the occasion: *untimely remark*

unto *preposition*, *old* to

untold *adjective* 1 not yet told: *the untold story* 2 too great to be counted or measured: *untold riches*

untoward *adjective* 1 unlucky, unfortunate 2 inconvenient

untrue *adjective* 1 not true, false 2 unfaithful

untruth *noun* a lie

untruthful *adjective* lying or dishonest

unusual *adjective* 1 not usual 2 rare, remarkable

unusually *adverb* to an unusual degree

unveil *verb* 1 to remove a veil from 2 to remove a cover from (a memorial *etc*)

unwarranted *adjective* uncalled for, unnecessary

unwell *adjective* not in good health

unwieldy *adjective* not easily moved or handled

unwind *verb* **1** to wind off from a ball or reel **2** to relax

unwitting *adjective* unintended: *unwitting insult* ■ **unwittingly** *adverb*

unworthy *adjective* **1** not worthy **2** low, worthless, despicable **3 unworthy of something** not deserving of: *unworthy of attention* **4** below someone's usual standard, out of character: *that remark is unworthy of you*

up *adverb* **1** towards or in a higher or more northerly position: *going camping up in the Highlands* **2** completely, so as to finish: *drink up your tea* **3** to a larger size: *blow up a balloon* **4** as far as: *he came up to me* ■ *preposition* **1** towards or in the higher part of: *climbed up the ladder* **2** along: *walking up the road* ■ *adjective* **1** ascending, going up: *the up escalator* **2** ahead in score: *2 goals up* **3** better off, richer: *£50 up on the deal* **4** risen: *the sun is up* **5** of a given length of time: ended: *your time is up* **6** *informal* wrong: *what's up with her today?*

up-and-coming *adjective* likely to succeed

upbeat *adjective*, *informal* cheerful, optimistic

upbraid *verb* to scold

upbringing *noun* the rearing of, or the training given to, a child

update *verb* to bring up to date ■ *noun* **1** the act of updating **2** new information

upend *verb* to turn upside down

upfront *or* **up-front** *adjective* **1** candid, frank **2** foremost

upgrade *verb* **1** to raise to a more important position **2** to improve the quality of ■ *noun, computing* a newer version of a software program

upheaval *noun* a violent disturbance or change

uphill *adjective* **1** going upwards **2** difficult: *uphill struggle* ■ *adverb* upwards

uphold *verb* **1** to defend, give support to **2** to maintain, keep going (*eg* a tradition)

upholster *verb* to fit (furniture) with springs, stuffing, covers, *etc*

upholstery *noun* **1** covers, cushions, *etc* **2** the skill of upholstering

upkeep *noun* **1** the act of keeping (*eg* a house or car) in a good state of repair **2** the cost of this

upland *noun* **1** high ground **2 uplands** a hilly or mountainous region

uplift *verb* to raise the spirits of, cheer up

up-market *adjective* of high quality or price, luxury

upon *preposition* **1** on the top of: *upon the table* **2** at or after the time of: *upon completion of the task*

upper *adjective* higher, further up ▪ *noun* the part of a shoe *etc* above the sole

upper-case *adjective* of a letter: capital, *eg* A not a (contrasted with: **lower-case**)

upper-class *adjective* belonging to the highest social class, aristocratic

uppermost *adjective* highest, furthest up

upright *adjective* 1 standing up, vertical 2 honest, moral ▪ *noun* an upright post, piano, *etc*

uprising *noun* a revolt against a government *etc*

uproar *noun* a noisy disturbance

uproarious *adjective* very noisy

uproot *verb* 1 to tear up by the roots 2 to leave your home and go to live in another place

upset *verb* (pronounced up-**set**) 1 to make unhappy, angry, worried, *etc* 2 to overturn 3 to disturb, put out of order 4 to ruin (plans *etc*) ▪ *adjective* (pronounced up-**set**) distressed, unhappy, *etc*, ill ▪ *noun* (pronounced up-set) 1 distress, unhappiness, worry, *etc* 2 something that causes distress

| **upset** *verb* ▶ upsets, upsett*ing*, upset

upshot *noun* a result or end of a matter

upside down 1 with the top part underneath 2 in confusion

upstage *adverb* away from the footlights on a theatre stage ▪ *verb* to divert attention from (someone) to yourself

upstairs *adverb* in or to the upper storey of a house *etc* ▪ *noun* the upper storey or storeys of a house ▪ *adjective* in the upper storey or storeys: *upstairs bedroom*

upstanding *adjective* honest, respectable

upstart *noun* someone who has risen quickly from a low to a high position in society, work, *etc*

upstream *adverb* higher up a river or stream, towards the source

upsurge *noun* a rising, a swelling up

uptake *noun* the taking up or accepting of something ▪ **quick on the uptake** quick to understand

uptight *adjective* nervous, tense

up-to-date *adjective* 1 modern, in touch with recent ideas, *etc* 2 belonging to the present time 3 containing all recent facts *etc*: *an up-to-date account*

upturn *noun* a positive change, an improvement

upward *adjective* moving up, ascending ▪ **upwards** *adverb* from lower to higher, up

uranium *noun* a radioactive metal

urban *adjective* relating to a town or city (contrasted with: **rural**)

urbane *adjective* polite in a smooth way

urchin *noun* a dirty, ragged child

urge *verb* 1 to drive (on) 2 to try to persuade 3 to advise, recommend ▪ *noun* a strong desire or impulse

urgency *noun* an urgent state or condition

urgent *adjective* 1 requiring immediate attention 2 asking for immediate action ▪ **urgently** *adverb*

urinate *verb* to pass urine from the bladder

urine *noun* the waste liquid passed out of the body of animals and humans from the bladder

urn *noun* 1 a vase for the ashes of the dead 2 a metal drum with a tap, used for heating water for tea or coffee

US *or* **USA** *abbreviation* United States (of America)

us *pronoun* used by a speaker or writer in referring to themselves together with other people (as the object in a sentence): *when would you like us to come?*

usage *noun* 1 the act or manner of using 2 the established way of using a word *etc* 3 custom, habit 4 treatment: *rough usage*

use *verb* 1 to put to some purpose 2 to bring into action: *use your common sense* 3 (often **use up**) to spend, exhaust (*eg* patience, energy) ▪ *noun* 1 the act of using 2

value or suitability for a purpose: *no use to anybody* 3 the fact of being used: *it's in use at the moment* ▪ **used to 1** accustomed to 2 was or were in the habit of (doing something)

used *adjective* 1 employed, put to a purpose 2 not new

useful *adjective* serving a purpose; helpful ▪ **usefully** *adverb*

useless *adjective* having no use or effect

user *noun* someone who uses anything (especially a computer)

user-friendly *adjective* easily understood, easy to use

username *or* **user ID** *noun*, *computing* in e-mail addresses, the name or alias of an individual, usually appearing before the @ sign

usher *noun* someone who shows people to their seats in a theatre *etc* ▪ *verb* **usher someone in** *or* **out** to lead or convey them into or out of a room, building, *etc*

usherette *noun* a woman who shows people to their seats in a theatre *etc*

usual *adjective* 1 done or happening most often: *usual method* 2 customary: *with his usual cheerfulness* 3 ordinary ▪ *noun* a customary event, order, *etc*

usually *adverb* on most occasions

usurp (*pronounced* yoo-**zerp**)

verb to take possession of (*eg* a throne) by force

utensil *noun* an instrument or container used in the home (*eg* a ladle, knife, pan)

uterus *noun* (*plural* uteri – *pronounced* yoo-te-rai) the womb

utility *noun* (*plural* **utilities**) **1** usefulness **2** a public service supplying water, gas, *etc*

utilize *or* **utilise** *verb* to make use of

utmost *adjective* **1** the greatest possible: *utmost care* **2** furthest

utopia *noun* a perfect place, a paradise

utopian *adjective* unrealistically ideal

utter[1] *verb* to produce with the voice (words, a scream, *etc*)

utter[2] *adjective* complete, total

utterance *noun* something said

utterly *adverb* completely, absolutely

uttermost *adjective* most complete, utmost

U-turn *noun* a complete change in direction, policy, *etc*

V v

vacancy *noun* (*plural* **vacancies**) **1** a job that has not been filled **2** a room not already booked in a hotel *etc*

vacant *adjective* **1** empty, not occupied **2** of an expression: showing no interest or intelligence ■ **vacantly** *adverb*

vacate *verb* to leave empty, cease to occupy

vacation *noun* **1** the act of vacating **2** a holiday

vaccinate *verb* to give a vaccine to, *eg* by injection into the skin

vaccination *noun* the act or process of injecting someone with a vaccine

vaccine *noun* a substance made from the germs that cause a disease, given to people and animals to try to prevent them catching that disease

vacillate *verb* to move from one opinion to another; waver

vacuous *adjective* **1** empty **2** empty-headed, stupid

vacuum *noun* a space from which all, or almost all, the air has been removed

vacuum cleaner a machine which cleans carpets *etc* by sucking up dust

vacuum flask a container with double walls enclosing a vacuum, for keeping liquids hot or cold

vagabond *noun* **1** someone with no permanent home; a wanderer **2** a rascal, a rogue

vagaries *noun plural* strange, unexpected behaviour: *vagaries of human nature*

vagina *noun* the passage connecting a woman's genitals to her womb

vagrancy *noun* the state of being a tramp

vagrant *noun* a wanderer or tramp, with no settled home

vague *adjective* **1** not clear; not definite **2** not practical or efficient; forgetful ■ **vaguely** *adverb*

vain *adjective* **1** conceited, self-important **2** useless: *vain attempt* **3** empty, meaningless: *vain promises* ■ **vainly** *adverb* ■ **in vain** without success

valance *noun* a decorative frill round the edge of a bed

vale *noun*, *formal* a valley

valentine *noun* **1** a greetings

card sent on St Valentine's Day, 14 February **2** a sweetheart, a lover
valet (*pronounced* val-et *or* val-ei) *noun* a male personal servant
valiant *adjective* brave
■ **valiantly** *adverb*
valid *adjective* **1** sound, acceptable: *valid reason for not going* **2** legally in force: *valid passport*
validate *verb* **1** to make (a document) *etc* valid with a mark, stamp, *etc* **2** to confirm that (something) is true or sound **3** *computing* to check (a file) has been input according to certain rules ■ **validation** *noun*
validity *noun* **1** the state of being valid or acceptable for use **2** soundness of an argument or proposition
valley *noun* (*plural* **valleys**) low land between hills, often with a river flowing through it
valour *noun* courage, bravery
valuable *adjective* of great value
valuables *noun plural* articles of worth
valuation *noun* **1** the act of valuing **2** an estimated price or value
value *noun* **1** worth; price **2** purchasing power (of a coin *etc*) **3** importance **4** usefulness **5** *algebra* a number or quantity put as equal to an expression ■ *verb* **1** to put a price on **2** to think highly of
value-added tax a

government tax raised on the selling-price of an article, or charged on certain services
valueless *adjective* worthless
valve *noun* **1** a device allowing air, steam or liquid to flow in one direction only **2** a small flap controlling the flow of blood in the body **3** an electronic component found in older television sets, radios, *etc*
vampire *noun* a dead person supposed to rise at night and suck the blood of sleeping people
vampire bat a South American bat that sucks blood
van[1] *noun* a covered or closed-in vehicle or wagon for carrying goods by road or rail
van[2] *short for* **vanguard**
vandal *noun* someone who pointlessly destroys or damages public buildings *etc*
vandalism *noun* the activity of a vandal
vandalize *or* **vandalise** *verb* to damage by vandalism
vane *noun* **1** a weathercock **2** the blade of a windmill, propeller, *etc*
vanguard *noun* **1** the leading group in a movement *etc* **2** the part of an army going in front of the main body
vanilla *noun* a sweet-scented flavouring obtained from the pods of a type of orchid
vanish *verb* **1** to go out of sight **2** to fade away to nothing
vanity *noun* (*plural* **vanities**)

1 conceit **2** worthlessness **3** something vain and worthless

vanquish *verb* to defeat

vantage point a position giving an advantage or a clear view

vapid *adjective* dull, uninteresting

vaporize *or* **vaporise** *verb* to change into vapour

vapour *noun* **1** the air-like or gas-like state of a substance that is usually liquid or solid **2** mist or smoke in the air

variable *adjective* changeable; that may be varied ▪ *noun* something that varies *eg* in value

variance *noun* a state of differing or disagreement

variant *noun* a different form or version ▪ *adjective* in a different form

variation *noun* **1** a varying, a change **2** the extent of a difference or change

varicose vein a swollen or enlarged vein, usually on the leg

varied *adjective* having variety, diverse

variegated *adjective* marked with different colours; multicoloured

variety *noun* (*plural* **varieties**) **1** the quality of being of many kinds, or of being different **2** a mixed collection **3** a sort, a type: *a variety of potato* **4** mixed theatrical entertainment including songs, comedy, *etc*

various *adjective* **1** of different kinds **2** several: *various attempts*

variously *adverb* in different ways or at different times

varnish *noun* a sticky liquid which gives a glossy surface to paper, wood, *etc* ▪ *verb* **1** to cover with varnish **2** to cover up (faults)

vary *verb* **1** to make, be, or become different **2** to make changes in (a routine *etc*) **3** to differ, disagree

| **vary** ► varies, varying, varied

vase (*pronounced* vahz) *noun* a jar of pottery, glass, *etc* used as an ornament or for holding cut flowers

Vaseline *noun, trademark* a type of ointment made from petroleum

vast *adjective* of very great size or amount

vastly *adverb* greatly or to a considerable extent

vastness *noun* immensity

VAT *abbreviation* value-added tax

vat *noun* a large tub or tank, used *eg* for fermenting liquors and dyeing

vaudeville *noun* theatrical entertainment of dances and songs, usually comic

vault *noun* **1** an arched roof **2** an underground room, a cellar ▪ *verb* to leap, supporting your weight on your hands, or on a pole

vaunt *verb* to boast

VDU *abbreviation* visual display unit

veal *noun* the flesh of a calf, used as food

vector *noun*, *maths* **1** a description of horizontal and vertical motion, shown in a pair of brackets with the horizontal value above the vertical value **2** a quantity, *eg* velocity or change of position, that has both magnitude and direction (*compare with*: scalar)

Veda *noun* one, or all, of four ancient books of the Hindus

veer *verb* **1** to change direction or course **2** to change mood, opinions, *etc*

veg (*pronounced* vedj) *verb*, *informal*: **veg out** to relax, laze about

vegan *noun* a vegetarian who uses no animal products

vegetable *noun* a plant, especially one grown for food ▪ *adjective* **1** of plants **2** made from or consisting of plants

vegetarian *noun* someone who eats no meat, only vegetable or dairy foods ▪ *adjective* consisting of, or eating, only vegetable or dairy foods

vegetate *verb* **1** to grow as a plant does **2** to lead a dull, aimless life

vegetation *noun* **1** plants in general **2** the plants growing in a particular area

vehemence *noun* strong and forceful feeling

vehement *adjective* emphatic and forceful in expressing opinions *etc* ▪ **vehemently** *adverb*

vehicle *noun* a means of transport used on land, especially one with wheels

veil *noun* **1** a piece of cloth or netting worn to shade or hide the face **2** something that hides or covers up ▪ *verb* to cover with a veil

vein *noun* **1** one of the tubes which carry the blood back to the heart **2** a small rib of a leaf **3** a thin layer of mineral in a rock **4** a streak in wood, stone, *etc*

Velcro *noun*, *trademark* a fastening material consisting of one surface of tiny hooks, and another of tiny loops

vellum *noun* **1** a fine parchment, made from the skins of calves, kids or lambs **2** paper made in imitation of this

velocity *noun* rate or speed of movement

velvet *noun* a fabric made from silk *etc*, with a thick, soft surface ▪ *adjective* **1** made of velvet **2** soft or smooth as velvet; silky

velvety *adjective* soft, like velvet

vendetta *noun* a bitter, long-lasting quarrel or feud

vending machine a machine with sweets *etc* for sale, operated by putting coins in a slot

vendor *noun* someone who sells

veneer *verb* **1** to cover a piece of wood with another thin piece of finer quality **2** to give a good appearance to what is really bad ■ *noun* **1** a thin surface layer of fine wood **2** a false outward show hiding some bad quality

venerable *adjective* worthy of respect because of age or wisdom

veneration *noun* great respect

Venetian blind a window blind formed of thin movable strips of metal or plastic hung on tapes

vengeance *noun* punishment given, harm done in return for wrong or injury, revenge

vengeful *adjective* seeking revenge ■ **vengefully** *adverb*

venison *noun* the flesh of a deer, used as food

Venn diagram *maths* a diagram showing the relationship between sets using overlapping circles and other figures

venom *noun* **1** poison **2** hatred, spite

venomous *adjective* **1** poisonous **2** spiteful

vent *noun* **1** a small opening **2** a hole to allow air or smoke to pass through **3** an outlet **4** a slit at the bottom of the back of a coat *etc* ■ *verb* to express (strong emotion) in some way

ventilate *verb* to allow fresh air to pass through (a room *etc*)

ventilation *noun* circulation of fresh air

ventilator *noun* a grating or other device for allowing in fresh air

ventriloquism *noun* the art of speaking in a way that makes the sound appear to come from elsewhere, especially a puppet's mouth

ventriloquist *noun* someone who can speak without appearing to move their lips and can project their voice on to a puppet *etc*

venture *noun* an undertaking which involves some risk ■ *verb* **1** to risk, dare **2** to do or say something at the risk of causing annoyance

venue *noun* the scene of an event, *eg* a sports contest or conference

veracity *noun* truthfulness

veranda *or* **verandah** *noun* a kind of terrace with a roof supported by pillars, extending along the side of a house

verb *noun* the word that tells what someone or something does in a sentence, *eg* 'I *sing*'/'he *had* no idea'

verbal *adjective* **1** of words **2** spoken, not written **3** of verbs

verbatim *adjective* in the exact words, word for word

verbose *adjective* using more words than necessary

verdant *adjective* green with grass or leaves

verdict *noun* **1** the judge's decision at the end of a trial

2 someone's personal opinion on a matter

verge noun **1** the grassy border along the edge of a road etc **2** edge, brink ▪ **verge on** to be close to: verging on the absurd

verger noun a church caretaker, or church official

verifiable adjective able to be verified

verify verb to prove, show to be true, confirm ▪ **verification** noun

| **verify** ▸ veri*fies*, veri*fying*, veri*fied*

veritable adjective **1** true **2** real, genuine

vermicelli noun a type of food like spaghetti but in much thinner pieces

vermilion noun a bright red colour

vermin noun plural animals or insects that are considered pests, eg rats, mice, fleas, etc

vernacular noun the ordinary spoken language of a country or district

verruca noun a wart, especially on the foot

versatile adjective **1** able to turn easily from one subject or task to another **2** useful in many different ways

versatility noun the ability to be adaptable

verse noun **1** a number of lines of poetry forming a planned unit **2** poetry as opposed to prose **3** a short division of a chapter of the Bible

version noun **1** an account from one point of view **2** a form: another version of the same tune

versus preposition against (short form: **v**)

vertebra noun (plural **vertebrae**) one of the bones of the spine

vertebrate noun an animal with a backbone

vertex noun (plural **vertices**) **1** the top or summit **2** the point of a cone, pyramid or angle **3** a point where two or more lines meet

vertical adjective **1** standing upright **2** straight up and down ▪ **vertically** adverb

vertigo noun giddiness, dizziness

verve noun lively spirit, enthusiasm

very adverb **1** to a great extent or degree: walk very quietly **2** exactly: the very same person ▪ adjective **1** same, identical: the very people who claimed to support him voted against him **2** ideal, exactly what is wanted: the very man for the job **3** actual: in the very act of stealing **4** mere: the very thought of blood

vessel noun **1** a ship **2** a container for liquid **3** a tube carrying fluids in the body: blood vessels

vest noun an undergarment for the top half of the body

vestibule noun an entrance hall; a lobby

vestige noun a trace, an

indication of something's existence

vestment *noun* a ceremonial garment, worn *eg* by a religious officer during a service

vestry *noun* (*plural* **vestries**) a room in a church in which vestments are kept

vet[1] *noun, informal* a veterinary surgeon

vet[2] *verb* to examine, check | vet ▶ vets, vetting, vetted

vetch *noun* a plant of the pea family

veteran *adjective* old, experienced ■ *noun* 1 someone who has given long service 2 an old soldier 3 *US* anyone who has served in the armed forces

veterinary surgeon a doctor who treats animals

veto *noun* (*plural* **vetoes**) 1 the power to forbid or block (a proposal) 2 an act of forbidding or blocking ■ *verb* to forbid, block | veto *verb* ▶ vetos, vetoing, vetoed

vex *verb* to annoy; cause trouble to

vexation *noun* 1 the state of being vexed 2 something that vexes

via *preposition* by way of: *travelling to Paris via London*

viable *adjective* able to be managed: *viable proposition*

viaduct *noun* a long bridge taking a railway or road over a river *etc*

vibrant *adjective* full of energy; lively, sparkling

vibrate *verb* 1 to shake, tremble 2 to swing to and fro rapidly 3 of sound: to resound, ring ■ **vibration** *noun*

vicar *noun* an Anglican member of the clergy who is in charge of a parish

vicarage *noun* the house of a vicar

vice *noun* 1 a bad habit, a serious fault 2 wickedness, immorality 3 a tool with two jaws for gripping objects firmly

vice- *prefix* second in rank to: *vice-president*

vice versa the other way round: *I needed his help and vice versa* (= he needed mine)

vicinity *noun* 1 nearness 2 neighbourhood

vicious *adjective* wicked; spiteful ■ **viciously** *adverb*

vicious circle a bad situation whose results cause it to get worse

victim *noun* someone who is killed or harmed, intentionally or by accident: *victim of a brutal attack*

victimize or **victimise** *verb* to treat unjustly; make a victim of

victor *noun* a winner of a contest *etc*

victorious *adjective* successful in a battle or other contest

victory *noun* (*plural* **victories**)

success in any battle, struggle or contest

video *adjective* **1** relating to the recording and broadcasting of TV pictures and sound **2** relating to recording by video ■ *noun* (*plural* **videos**) **1** a video cassette recorder **2** a recording on videotape ■ *verb* to make a recording by video

| **video** *verb* ► video*s*, video*ing*, video*ed*

video camera a portable camera that records images onto videotape

video cassette a cassette containing videotape

video cassette recorder a tape recorder using video cassettes for recording and playing back TV programmes

videotape *noun* magnetic tape for carrying pictures and sound

vie *verb*: **vie with** to compete with, try to outdo

| **vie** ► vie*s*, vy*ing*, vie*d*

view *noun* **1** a range or field of sight: *a good view* **2** a scene **3** an opinion ■ *verb* **1** to look at **2** to watch (television) **3** to consider

viewpoint *noun* **1** a place from which a scene is viewed **2** a personal opinion (*also*: **point of view**)

vigil *noun* a time of watching or of keeping awake at night, often before a religious festival

vigilance *noun* watchfulness, alertness

vigilant *adjective* watchful, alert

vigilante (*pronounced* vij-i-**lan**-tei) *noun* a private citizen who assumes the task of keeping order in a community

vigorous *adjective* strong, healthy; forceful: *vigorous defence* ■ **vigorously** *adverb*

vigour *noun* strength of body or mind; energy

Viking *noun*, *history* a Norse invader of Western Europe

vile *adjective* **1** very bad **2** disgusting, revolting ■ **vilely** *adverb*

vilify *verb* to say bad things about

| **vilify** ► vilif*ies*, vilify*ing*, vilif*ied*

villa *noun* a house in the country *etc* used for holidays

village *noun* a collection of houses, not big enough to be called a town

villager *noun* someone who lives in a village

villain *noun* a scoundrel, a rascal

villainous *adjective* wicked

villainy *noun* (*plural* **villainies**) wickedness

vindicate *verb* **1** to clear from blame **2** to justify

vindictive *adjective* revengeful; spiteful

vine *noun* **1** a grapevine **2** any climbing or trailing plant

vinegar *noun* a sour-tasting liquid made from wine, beer, *etc*, used for seasoning or pickling

vineyard (*pronounced* vin-yad) *noun* an area planted with grapevines

vintage *noun* 1 the gathering of ripe grapes 2 the grapes gathered 3 wine of a particular year, especially when of very high quality 4 time of origin or manufacture ■ *adjective* 1 of a vintage 2 of wine: of a particular year 3 very characteristic of an author, style, *etc*: *vintage Monty Python*

vintage car one of a very early type, still able to run

viola (*pronounced* vi-oh-la) *noun* a stringed instrument like a large violin

violate *verb* 1 to break (a law, a treaty, *etc*) 2 to treat with disrespect

violation *noun* the act or process of violating

violence *noun* great roughness and force

violent *adjective* 1 acting with great force 2 extremely; severely; ardently: *violently opposed to our involvement*

violently *adverb* 1 in a violent or aggressive way 2 extremely; severely; ardently: *violently opposed to our involvement*

violet *noun* a kind of small bluish-purple flower

violin *noun* a musical instrument with four strings, held under the chin and played with a bow

violinist *noun* someone who plays the violin

violoncello *see* cello

VIP *abbreviation* very important person

viper *noun* an adder

viral *adjective* of a virus

virgin *noun* someone who has had no sexual intercourse

virile *adjective* manly; strong, vigorous

virility *noun* manhood; manliness; strength, vigour

virtual *adjective* 1 in effect, though not in strict fact 2 *computing* any system that behaves or functions in the same way as a real person or thing

virtually *adverb* almost, nearly

virtual reality a computer-created environment that the person operating the computer is able to be a part of

virtue *noun* 1 goodness of character and behaviour 2 a good quality, *eg* honesty, generosity, *etc* 3 a good point: *one virtue of plastic crockery is that it doesn't break*

virtuosity *noun* brilliance of technique

virtuoso *noun* (*plural* virtuosos) a highly skilled artist, especially a musician

virtuous *adjective* good, just, honest ■ **virtuously** *adverb*

virulent *adjective* 1 full of poison 2 bitter, spiteful 3 of a disease: dangerous

virus noun (plural **viruses**) **1** a germ that is smaller than any bacteria, and causes diseases such as mumps, chickenpox, etc **2** a piece of computer code that can corrupt other data and be unknowingly passed to other users

visa noun a permit given by the authorities of a country to allow someone to stay for a time in that country

viscount (pronounced vai-kownt) noun a title of nobility next below an earl

viscous adjective of a liquid: sticky, not flowing easily

visibility noun **1** the clearness with which objects may be seen **2** the extent or range of vision as affected by fog, rain, etc

visible adjective able to be seen ■ **visibly** adverb

vision noun **1** the act or power of seeing **2** something seen in the imagination **3** a strange, supernatural sight **4** the ability to foresee likely future events

visionary noun (plural **visionaries**) someone who dreams up imaginative plans

visit verb **1** to go to see; call on **2** to stay with as a guest ■ noun **1** a call at a person's house or at a place of interest etc **2** a short stay

visitation noun a visit of an important official

visitor noun someone who makes a visit

visor noun **1** a part of a helmet covering the face **2** a movable shade on a car's windscreen **3** a peak on a cap for shading the eyes

vista noun a view, especially one seen through a long, narrow opening

visual adjective relating to, or received through, sight: visual aids

visual display unit a device like a television set, on which data from a computer's memory can be displayed

visualize or **visualise** verb to form a clear picture of in the mind

vital adjective **1** of the greatest importance **2** necessary to life **3** of life **4** vigorous, energetic

vitality noun life; liveliness, strength; ability to go on living

vitally adverb essentially; urgently

vitamin noun one of a group of substances necessary for health, occurring in different natural foods

vitriolic adjective biting, scathing

vivacious adjective lively, sprightly ■ **vivaciously** adverb

vivacity noun liveliness, spark

vivid adjective **1** lifelike **2** brilliant, striking

vividly adverb brightly, clearly, intensely

vivisection noun the carrying out of experiments on living animals

vixen noun 1 a female fox 2 an ill-tempered woman

vizier noun, history a minister of state in some Eastern countries

vocabulary noun (plural **vocabularies**) 1 the range of words used by an individual or group 2 the words of a particular language 3 a list of words in alphabetical order, with their meanings

vocal adjective 1 of the voice 2 expressing your opinions loudly and fully

vocalist noun a singer

vocation noun 1 an occupation or profession to which someone feels called to dedicate themselves 2 a strong inclination or desire to follow a particular course of action or work

vociferous adjective loud in speech, noisy

vodka noun an alcoholic spirit made from grain or potatoes

vogue noun the fashion of the moment; popularity

voice noun 1 the sound produced from the mouth in speech or song 2 ability to sing 3 an opinion ■ verb to express (an opinion)

voice mail or **voicemail** a telephone-answering system by which telephone messages can be stored to be picked up later

voice recognition the ability of a computer or other machine to receive and interpret spoken language and commands

void adjective 1 empty, vacant 2 not valid ■ noun an empty space

volatile adjective 1 of a liquid: quickly turning into vapour 2 of a person: changeable in mood or behaviour, fickle

volcanic adjective 1 relating to volcanoes 2 caused or produced by heat within the earth

volcano noun (plural **volcanoes**) a mountain with an opening through which molten rock, ashes, etc are periodically thrown up from inside the earth

vole noun any of a group of small rodents, including the water rat

volition noun an act of will or choice: he did it of his own volition

volley noun (plural **volleys**) 1 a number of shots fired or missiles thrown at the same time 2 an outburst of abuse or criticism 3 tennis a return of a ball before it reaches the ground ■ verb 1 to shoot or throw in a volley 2 to return (a ball) before it reaches the ground

volt noun the unit used in measuring the force of electricity

voltage noun electrical force measured in volts

voluble adjective speaking with a great flow of words

volume noun 1 a book, often one of a series 2 the amount of space taken up by anything 3 amount: volume of trade 4 loudness or fullness of sound

voluminous *adjective* bulky, of great volume

voluntary *adjective* **1** done or acting by choice, not under compulsion **2** working without payment

volunteer *noun* someone who offers to do something of their own accord, often for no payment ▪ *verb* **1** to act as a volunteer **2** to give (information, an opinion, *etc*) unasked

voluptuous *adjective* full of, or too fond of, the pleasures of life

vomit *verb* to throw up the contents of the stomach through the mouth

voracious *adjective* very greedy, difficult to satisfy: *voracious appetite*

voracity *noun* extreme greed or eagerness

vortex *noun* (*plural* **vortices** *or* **vortexes**) **1** a whirlpool **2** a whirlwind

vote *verb* **1** to give your support to (a particular candidate, a proposal, *etc*) in a ballot or show of hands **2** to decide by voting ▪ *noun* **1** an expression of opinion or support by voting **2** the right to vote

voter *noun* someone who votes

vouch *verb*: **vouch for something** to say that you are sure of it or can guarantee it

voucher *noun* a paper which can be exchanged for money or goods

vow *noun* a solemn promise or declaration, especially one made to God ▪ *verb* **1** to make a vow **2** to threaten (revenge *etc*)

vowel *noun* **1** a sound made by the voice that does not require the use of the tongue, teeth or lips **2** the letters *a*, *e*, *i*, *o*, *u* (or various combinations of them), and sometimes *y*, which represent those sounds

voyage *noun* a journey, usually by sea ▪ *verb* to make a journey

vulgar *adjective* **1** coarse, ill-mannered **2** indecent **3** of the common people

vulgar fraction a fraction not written as a decimal, *eg* $\frac{1}{3}$, $\frac{4}{5}$ (*also called*: **common fraction**, **simple fraction**)

vulgarity *noun* coarseness in speech or behaviour

vulgarly *adverb* in a vulgar or coarse way

vulnerability *noun* a state of being vulnerable or easily harmed

vulnerable *adjective* **1** exposed to, or in danger of, attack **2** liable to be hurt physically or emotionally

vulture *noun* a large bird that feeds mainly on the flesh of dead animals

Ww

wad *noun* **1** a lump of loose material (*eg* wool, cloth, paper) pressed together **2** a bunch of banknotes

wadding *noun* soft material (*eg* cotton wool) used for packing or padding

waddle *verb* to walk with short, unsteady steps, moving from side to side as a duck does ■ *noun* the act of waddling

wade *verb* **1** to walk through deep water or mud **2** to get through with difficulty: *still wading through this book*

wader *noun* **1** a long-legged bird that wades in search of food **2 waders** high waterproof boots worn by anglers for wading

wafer *noun* a very thin, light type of biscuit, as that eaten with ice-cream

waffle *noun* **1** *US* a light, crisp cake made from batter, cooked in a waffle-iron **2** pointless, long-drawn-out talk ■ *verb* to talk long and meaninglessly

waft *verb* to carry or drift lightly through the air or over water

wag *verb* to move from side to side or up and down ■ *noun* **1** an

act of wagging **2** someone who is always joking

| **wag** *verb* ▸ wags, wag*ging*, wag*ged*

wage *verb* to carry on (a war *etc*) ■ *noun* (often **wages**) payment for work

wager *noun* a bet ■ *verb* to bet

waggle *verb* to move from side to side in an unsteady manner ■ *noun* an unsteady movement from side to side

wagon *or* **waggon** *noun* **1** a four-wheeled vehicle for carrying loads **2** an open railway carriage for goods

waif *noun* an uncared-for or homeless child or animal

wail *verb* to cry or moan in sorrow ■ *noun* a sorrowful cry

wainscot *see* **skirting board**

waist *noun* the narrow part of the body, between ribs and hips

waistcoat *noun* a short, sleeveless jacket, often worn under an outer jacket

wait *verb* **1** to put off or delay action **2 wait for something** to remain in expectation or readiness for it ■ *noun* a delay

■ **wait on 1** to serve (someone) at table **2** to act as a servant to

waiter *noun* a man whose job it is to serve people at table in a restaurant

waiting list a list of people waiting for something in order of priority

waiting room a room in which to wait at a railway station, clinic, *etc*

waitress *noun* a woman whose job it is to serve people at table in a restaurant

waive *verb* to give up (a claim or right)

💧 Do not confuse with: **wave**

waiver *noun* **1** the act of waiving **2** a document indicating this

💧 Do not confuse with: **waver**

wake[1] *verb* (often **wake up**) to stop sleeping ■ *noun* a night of watching beside a dead body

| **wake** *verb* ▶ wak*es*, wak*ing*, woke or wak*ed*, woken

wake[2] *noun* a streak of foamy water left in the track of a ship ■ **in the wake of** immediately behind or after

wakeful *adjective* not sleeping, unable to sleep

waken *verb* to wake, arouse or be aroused

waking *adjective* being or becoming awake

walk *verb* **1** to move along on foot **2** to travel along (streets *etc*) on foot ■ *noun* **1** an act of walking **2** a manner of walking **3** a distance to be walked over: *a short walk from here*

walkie-talkie *noun* a portable radio set for sending and receiving messages

walking stick a stick used for support when walking

Walkman *noun*, *trademark* a personal stereo

walk-over *noun* an easy victory

wall *noun* **1** a structure built of stone, brick, *etc* used to separate or enclose **2** the side of a building ■ **wall in** or **off** *etc* to enclose or separate with a wall

wallaby *noun* (*plural* **wallabies**) a small kind of kangaroo

wallet *noun* a small folding case for holding banknotes, credit cards, *etc*

wallflower *noun* **1** a sweet-smelling spring flower **2** someone who is continually without a partner at a dance *etc*

wallop *verb*, *informal* to beat, hit ■ *noun* a violent hit or smack

wallow *verb* to roll about with enjoyment in water, mud, *etc*

wallpaper *noun* **1** paper used in house decorating for covering walls **2** a background pattern on a computer screen ■ *verb* to cover with wallpaper

walnut *noun* **1** a tree whose wood is used for making furniture **2** the nut it produces

walrus *noun* (*plural* **walruses**) a large sea animal, like a seal, with two long tusks

waltz *noun* (*plural* **waltzes**) **1** a ballroom dance for couples with a circling movement **2** music for this dance, with three beats to each bar ▪ *verb* to dance a waltz

wan (*pronounced* won) *adjective* pale and sickly looking

wand *noun* a long slender rod used by a conjuror, magician, *etc*

wander *verb* **1** to roam about with no definite purpose; roam **2** to go astray **3** to be mentally confused because of illness *etc* ▪ *noun* an aimless walk

wanderer *noun* a person or animal that wanders

wanderlust *noun* a keen desire for travel

wane *verb* **1** to become smaller (*contrasted with:* **wax**) **2** to lose power, importance, *etc*

wangle *verb* to get or achieve through craftiness, skilful planning, *etc*

want *verb* **1** to wish for **2** to need, lack ▪ *noun* **1** poverty **2** scarcity, lack

wanted *adjective* looked for, especially by the police

wanting *adjective* **1** absent, missing; without **2** not good enough **3 wanting in something** lacking it: *wanting in good taste*

wanton *adjective* thoughtless, pointless, without motive

war *noun* an armed struggle, especially between nations ▪ **war against** to fight in a war, make war against

war *verb* ▸ wars, warring, warred

warble *verb* to sing like a bird, trill

warbler *noun* a type of songbird

ward *noun* **1** a hospital room containing a number of beds **2** one of the parts into which a town is divided for voting **3** someone who is in the care of a guardian ▪ **ward off** to keep off, defend yourself against (a blow *etc*)

warden *noun* **1** someone who guards a game reserve **2** someone in charge of a hostel or college

warder *noun* a prison guard

wardrobe *noun* **1** a cupboard for clothes **2** someone's personal supply of clothes

-ware *suffix* manufactured material: *earthenware/glassware*

warehouse *noun* a building where goods are stored

wares *noun plural* goods for sale

warfare *noun* the carrying on of war

warhead *noun* the part of a missile containing the explosive

warlike *adjective* **1** fond of war **2** threatening war

warm *adjective* **1** fairly hot **2** of clothes: keeping the wearer warm **3** of a person: friendly, loving ■ *verb* to make or become warm

warm-blooded *adjective* having a blood temperature higher than that of the surrounding atmosphere

warm-hearted *adjective* kind, generous

warmth *noun* 1 pleasant or comfortable heat, or the condition or quality of being warm 2 affection, friendliness or enthusiasm

warn *verb* 1 to tell (someone) beforehand about possible danger, misfortune, *etc* 2 to give cautionary advice to: *I warned him not to be late*

warning *noun* a remark, notice, *etc* that warns

warp *verb* 1 to become twisted out of shape 2 to distort, make unsound: *his previous experiences had warped his judgement* ■ *noun* the threads stretched lengthwise on a loom, which are crossed by the weft

warpath *noun* the march to a battle ■ **on the warpath** in a fighting or angry mood

warrant *noun* a certificate granting someone a right or authority: *search warrant* ■ *verb* to justify, be a good enough reason for

warren *noun* 1 a collection of rabbit burrows 2 a building with many rooms and passages; a maze

warrior *noun* a great fighter

warship *noun* a ship armed with guns *etc*

wart *noun* a small hard growth on the skin

wary *adjective* cautious, on guard ■ **warily** *adverb*

was *past form* of **be**

wash *verb* 1 to clean with water, soap, *etc* 2 to clean yourself with water *etc* 3 of water: to flow over or against 4 to sweep (away, along, *etc*) by force of water ■ *noun* (*plural* **washes**) 1 a washing 2 a streak of foamy water left behind by a moving boat 3 a thin coat of paint *etc* ■ **wash up** to wash the dishes

washer *noun* 1 someone or something that washes 2 a flat ring of metal, rubber, *etc* for keeping joints tight

washing *noun* 1 the act of cleaning by water 2 clothes to be washed

washing machine an electric machine for washing clothes

washing-up *noun* dishes to be washed

wasp *noun* a stinging, winged insect, with a slender, yellow and black striped body

wastage *noun* 1 an amount wasted 2 loss through decay or squandering

waste *adjective* 1 thrown away, rejected as useless 2 of land: uncultivated, barren and desolate ■ *verb* 1 to spend (money, time, energy) extravagantly, without result or profit **2** to decay or wear away gradually ■ *noun* **1** extravagant use, squandering **2** rubbish, waste material **3** an expanse of water, snow, *etc*

wasteful *adjective* causing waste, extravagant

wastepaper basket a basket for paper rubbish

wastepipe *noun* a pipe for carrying away dirty water or semi-liquid waste

waster or **wastrel** *noun* an idle, good-for-nothing person

watch *verb* **1** to look at, observe closely **2** (often **watch over**) to look after, mind ■ *noun* (*plural* **watches**) **1** the act of keeping guard **2** someone who keeps, or those who keep, guard **3** a sailor's period of duty on deck **4** a small clock worn on the wrist or kept in a pocket

watchdog *noun* **1** a dog which guards a building **2** an organization which monitors business practices *etc*

watchful *adjective* alert, cautious ■ **watchfully** *adverb*

watchman *noun* a man who guards a building *etc* at night

watchword *noun* a motto, a slogan

water *noun* **1** a clear, tasteless liquid which falls as rain **2** a collection of this liquid in a lake, river, *etc* **3** urine ■ *verb* **1** to supply

with water **2** to dilute or mix with water **3** of the mouth: to fill with saliva **4** of the eyes: to fill with tears

water closet a toilet, a lavatory (*short form:* **WC**)

watercolour *noun* **1** a paint which is mixed with water, not oil **2** a painting done with this paint

watercress *noun* a plant which grows beside streams, with hot-tasting leaves which are eaten in salads

waterfall *noun* a place where a river falls from a height, often over a ledge of rock

water lily a plant which grows in ponds *etc*, with flat floating leaves and large flowers

waterlogged *adjective* **1** filled with water **2** soaked with water

watermark *noun* a faint design on writing paper showing the maker's name, crest, *etc*

watermelon *noun* a large melon with red juicy flesh and a thick, green rind

watermill *noun* a mill driven by water

water polo a ball game played in a pool between teams of swimmers

waterproof *adjective* not allowing water to pass through ■ *noun* an overcoat made of waterproof material

water rat a kind of vole

watershed *noun* a ridge separating the valleys of two rivers

water-skiing *noun* the sport of being towed very fast on skis behind a boat

watertight *adjective* so closely fitted that water cannot leak through

waterway *noun* a channel along which ships can sail

waterwheel *noun* a wheel moved by water

waterworks *noun plural* **1** a place which purifies and stores a town's water supply **2** *informal* tears

watery *adjective* **1** full of water **2** too liquid, textureless

watt *noun* (*abbrev* **W**) a unit of electric power

wattle *noun* **1** interwoven twigs and branches used for fences *etc* **2** an Australian acacia tree **3** a fleshy part hanging from the neck of a turkey

wave *noun* **1** a moving ridge on the surface of the water **2** a ridge or curve of hair **3** a vibration travelling through the air carrying light, sound, *etc* **4** a hand gesture for attracting attention, or saying hello or goodbye **5** a rush of an emotion (*eg* despair, enthusiasm, *etc*) ▪ *verb* **1** to make a wave with the hand **2** to move to and fro, flutter **3** to curl, curve

🔸 Do not confuse with:
waive

wavelength *noun* the distance from one point on a wave or

vibration to the next similar point

waver *verb* **1** to be unsteady, wobble **2** to be uncertain or undecided

🔸 Do not confuse with:
waiver

wavy *adjective* having waves

wax *noun* **1** the sticky, fatty substance of which bees make their cells **2** a fatty substance in the ear **3** a quickly hardening substance used for sealing letters *etc* ▪ *adjective* made of wax ▪ *verb* **1** to rub with wax **2** to grow, increase (*contrasted with*: **wane**)

waxen *adjective* **1** of or like wax **2** pale

waxworks *noun singular* a museum displaying wax models of famous people

waxy *adjective* of, or like, wax

way *noun* **1** an opening, a passage **2** road, path **3** room to go forward or pass **4** direction: *he went that way* **5** distance: *do you know the way?* **6** distance: *a long way* **7** condition: *in a bad way* **8** means, method **9** manner: *in a clumsy way* **10** someone's own wishes or choice: *he always gets his own way*

wayfarer *noun*, *old* a traveller on foot

waylay *verb* to wait for and stop (someone)

wayside *noun* the edge of a road or path ▪ *adjective* located by the side of a road

wayward *adjective* wilful, following your own way

WC *abbreviation* water closet

we *pronoun* used by a speaker or writer in mentioning themselves together with others (as the subject of a verb): *we are having a party this weekend*

weak *adjective* **1** not strong, feeble **2** lacking determination, easily persuaded **3** easily overcome: *weak opposition*

weaken *verb* to make or become weak

weakling *noun* a person or animal that is lacking in strength

weakness *noun* (*plural* **weaknesses**) **1** lack of strength **2** a fault **3** a special fondness (for): *a weakness for ice cream*

weal *noun* a raised mark on the skin caused by a blow from a whip

wealth *noun* **1** riches **2** a large quantity: *wealth of information*

wealthy *adjective* rich

wealthy ► wealth*ier*, wealth*iest*

wean *verb* **1** to make (a child or young animal) used to food other than the mother's milk **2** wean someone from *or* off something to make them gradually give up (a bad habit *etc*)

weapon *noun* **1** an instrument used for fighting, *eg* a sword, gun, *etc* **2** any means of attack

wear *verb* **1** to be dressed in, have on the body **2** to arrange in a particular way: *she wears her hair*

long **3** to have (a beard, moustache) on the face **4** to damage or weaken by use, rubbing, *etc* **5** to be damaged in this way ■ *noun* **1** use by wearing: *for my own wear* **2** damage by use **3** ability to last **4** clothes *etc*: *school wear* ■ **wear off** to pass away gradually ■ **wear on** to become later: *the afternoon wore on* ■ **wear out 1** to make or become unfit for further use **2** to exhaust

wear *verb* ► wears, wear*ing*, wore, worn

wearing *adjective* tiring, exhausting

wearisome *adjective* causing tiredness, boredom or impatience

weary *adjective* **1** tired, having used up your strength or patience **2** tiring, boring ■ *verb* to make or become tired, bored or impatient

weary *verb* ► wear*ies*, wear*ying*, wear*ied*

weasel *noun* a small wild animal with a long and slender body, that lives on mice, birds, *etc*

weather *noun* the state of the atmosphere, *eg* heat, coldness, cloudiness, *etc* ■ *verb* **1** to dry or wear away (rock *etc*) through exposure to the air **2** to come safely through (a storm, difficulty, *etc*)

weatherbeaten *adjective* showing signs of having been out in all weathers

weathercock *or*
weathervane *noun* a flat piece of metal that swings in the wind to show its direction

weave *verb* 1 to pass threads over and under each other on a loom *etc* to form cloth 2 to plait cane *etc* for basket-making 3 to put together (a story, plan, *etc*) 4 to move in and out between objects, or move from side to side

| weave ► weaves, weaving, wove, woven

weaver *noun* someone who weaves

Web *noun*: **the Web** the World Wide Web

web *noun* 1 the net made by a spider, a cobweb 2 the skin between the toes of ducks, swans, frogs, *etc*

webbed *adjective* of feet: having the toes joined by a web

web-footed *or* **web-toed** *adjective* having webbed feet or toes

Web page one of the linked pages or files that make up a Web site

Web site a linked collection of Web pages or files with a home page from which the other pages can be accessed

wed *verb* to marry

| wed ► weds, wedding, wed

we'd *short for* 1 we would; we should 2 we had

wedding *noun* 1 marriage 2 a marriage ceremony

wedge *noun* 1 a piece of wood, metal, *etc* thick at one end with a thin edge at the other, used in splitting wood, forcing two surfaces apart, *etc* 2 anything shaped like a wedge ■ *verb* 1 to fix or become fixed with a wedge 2 to push or squeeze (in): *wedged in amongst the crowd*

wedlock *noun* the state of being married

Wednesday *noun* the fourth day of the week

wee *adjective*, *Scottish* small, tiny

weed *noun* 1 a useless, troublesome plant 2 a weak, worthless person ■ *verb* to clear (a garden *etc*) of weeds

weedy *adjective* 1 full of weeds 2 thin and puny, unmanly

week *noun* 1 the space of seven days from Sunday to Saturday 2 the working days of the week, not Saturday and Sunday

weekday *noun* any day except Saturday and Sunday

weekend *noun* Saturday and Sunday

weekly *adjective* happening, or done, once a week ■ *adverb* once a week ■ *noun* (*plural* **weeklies**) a newspaper, magazine, *etc* coming out once a week

weep *verb* 1 to shed tears 2 to ooze, drip: *a weeping wound*

| weep ► weeps, weeping, wept

weeping willow a willow tree with drooping branches

weevil *noun* a small beetle that destroys grain, flour, *etc*

weft *noun* the threads on a loom which cross the warp

weigh *verb* 1 to find out how heavy (something) is by putting it on a scale *etc* 2 to have a certain heaviness: *weighing 10 kilograms* 3 of burdens *etc*: to press down, be heavy or troublesome 4 to consider (a matter, a point) carefully ▪ **weigh in** to test your weight before a boxing match ▪ **weigh out** to measure out a quantity by weighing it on a scale

weight *noun* 1 the amount that anything weighs 2 *physics* the force put on an object by the pull of gravity 3 a piece of metal weighing a certain amount: *a 100 gram weight* 4 a load, a burden 5 importance ▪ *verb* to make heavy by adding or attaching a weight

weightless *adjective* 1 weighing nothing or almost nothing 2 not affected by gravity, so able to float about ▪ **weightlessness** *noun*

weighty *adjective* 1 heavy 2 important

weir *noun* a dam across a stream

weird *adjective* 1 mysterious, supernatural 2 odd, strange

welcome *verb* 1 to receive with warmth or pleasure 2 to accept gladly: *I welcome the challenge* ▪ *noun* a welcoming, a warm reception ▪ *adjective* received with pleasure

weld *verb* 1 to join (pieces of metal) by pressure, with or without heating 2 to join closely ▪ *noun* a joint made by welding

welfare *noun* comfort, good health

welfare state a country with a health service, insurance against unemployment, pensions for those who cannot work, *etc*

well *noun* 1 a spring of water 2 a shaft in the earth to extract water, oil, *etc* 3 an enclosed space round which a staircase winds ▪ *verb* (often **well up**) to rise up and gush ▪ *adjective* in good health ▪ *adverb* 1 in a good and correct manner 2 thoroughly: *well beaten* 3 successfully: *do well* 4 conveniently: *it fits in well with my plans* ▪ *exclamation* expressing surprise, or used in explaining, narrating, *etc*

|**well** *adverb* ▶ better, best

we'll *short for* we will; we shall

well-advised *adjective* wise

well-behaved *adjective* with good manners

wellbeing *noun* welfare; contentment

well-disposed *adjective* inclined to be friendly or sympathetic

well-informed *adjective* having or showing knowledge

wellingtons *noun plural* high rubber boots covering the lower part of the legs

well-known *adjective* 1 familiar 2 celebrated, famous

well-meaning *adjective* having good intentions

well-meant *adjective* rightly, kindly intended

well-off *adjective* rich

well-read *adjective* having read many good books

well-to-do *adjective* rich

well-wisher *noun* someone who wishes someone success

welt *noun* **1** a firm edging or band, *eg* on the wrist or waist of a garment **2** a weal

welter *noun* a muddled mass, a jumble: *a welter of information*

wench *noun* (plural **wenches**) *old* a young woman, a girl

wend *verb*, *old* to go ▪ **wend your way** to make your way slowly

went *past form of* **go**

wept *past form of* **weep**

were *past form of* **be**

we're *short for* we are

werewolf *noun* a mythical creature which changes periodically from a human into a wolf

west *noun* one of the four chief directions, that in which the sun sets ▪ *adjective* in the west ▪ *adverb* to or towards the west

westerly *adjective* **1** lying or moving towards the west **2** of wind: from the west

western *adjective* relating to, or in, the west ▪ *noun* a film or story about life among the early settlers in the western United States

westward *adjective & adverb* towards the west

westwards *adverb* towards the west

wet *adjective* **1** soaked or covered with water or other liquid **2** rainy: *a wet day* ▪ *verb* to make wet

| **wet** *verb* ▸ wets, wetting, wet *or* wetted

wet suit a suit that allows water to pass through but retains body heat

whack *noun* a loud, violent slap or blow ▪ *verb* to slap or hit violently

whale *noun* a very large mammal living in the sea ▪ *verb* to catch whales

whaler *noun* a ship engaged in catching whales

wharf *noun* (plural **wharfs** *or* **wharves**) a landing stage for loading and unloading ships

what *adjective & pronoun* used to indicate something about which a question is being asked: *what day is this?/what are you doing?* ▪ *adjective* any that: *give me what money you have*
▪ *conjunction* anything that: *I'll take what you can give me*
▪ *adjective, adverb & pronoun* used for emphasis in exclamations: *what terrible ties he wears!/what rubbish!*

whatever *adjective & pronoun* **1** anything (that): *show me whatever you have* **2** no matter what: *whatever happens*

whatsoever *adjective* at all: *nothing whatsoever*

wheat *noun* a grain from which the flour used for making bread *etc* is made

wheaten *adjective* **1** made of wheat **2** wholemeal

wheatgerm *noun* the vitamin-rich embryo of wheat

wheedle *verb* to beg or coax, often by flattery

wheel *noun* **1** a circular frame or disc turning on an axle, used for transporting things **2** a steering wheel of a car *etc* ▪ *verb* **1** to move or push on wheels **2** to turn like a wheel or in a wide curve **3** to turn round suddenly

wheelbarrow *noun* a hand-pushed cart with one wheel in front, two handles and legs behind

wheelchair *noun* a chair on wheels for an invalid

wheeze *verb* to breathe with difficulty, making a whistling or croaking sound ▪ *noun* **1** the sound of difficult breathing **2** *informal* a joke

whelk *noun* a type of small shellfish, used as food

when *adverb* at what time: *when did you arrive?* ▪ *adverb & conjunction* the time at which: *I know when you left/I fell when I was coming in* ▪ *relative pronoun* at which: *at the time when I saw him* ▪ *conjunction* seeing that, since: *why walk when you have a car?*

whence *adverb, old* from what place: *whence did you come?* ▪ *conjunction* to the place from which: *he's gone back whence he came*

whenever *adverb & conjunction* **1** at any given time: *come whenever you're ready* **2** at every time: *I go whenever I get the chance*

where *adverb & conjunction* to or in what place: *where are you going?/I wonder where we are* ▪ *relative pronoun & conjunction* (in the place) in which, (to the place) to which: *go where he tells you to go/it's still where it was*

whereabouts *adverb & conjunction* near or in what place: *whereabouts is it?/I don't know whereabouts it is* ▪ *noun* the place where someone or something is: *I don't know her whereabouts*

whereas *conjunction* **1** when in fact: *they thought I was lying, whereas I was telling the truth* **2** but, on the other hand: *he's tall, whereas I'm short*

whereby *conjunction* by means of which

whereupon *adverb & conjunction* at or after which time, event, *etc*

wherever *adverb* to what place: *wherever did you go?* ▪ *conjunction* to any place: *wherever you may go*

wherewithal *noun* **1** the means of doing something **2** money

whet *verb* **1** to sharpen (a knife *etc*) by rubbing **2** to make (desire, appetite, *etc*) keener

| **whet** ▸ whet*s*, whett*ing*, whett*ed*

whether *conjunction* **1** either if: *whether you come or not* **2** if: *I don't know whether it's possible*

which *adjective & pronoun* **1** used to refer to a particular person or thing from a group: *which colour do you like best?* **2** the one that: *show me which dress you would like* ■ *relative pronoun* referring to the person or thing just named: *I bought the chair which you are sitting on*

whichever *adjective & pronoun* any (one), no matter which: *I'll take whichever you don't want/I saw trees whichever way I turned*

whiff *noun* a sudden puff or scent

while *conjunction* (*also*: *whilst*) **1** during the time that: *while I'm at the office* **2** although: *while I sympathize, I can't really help* ■ *noun* a space of time: *I'll join you in a while* ■ **while away** to pass (time) without boredom: *he whiled away the time by reading*

whim *noun* a sudden thought or desire

whimper *verb* to cry with a low, whining voice ■ *noun* a low, whining cry

whimsical *adjective* **1** full of whims, fanciful **2** humorous

whine *verb* **1** to make a high-pitched, complaining cry **2** to complain unnecessarily ■ *noun* an unnecessary complaint

whinge *verb* to whine, complain ■ *noun* a complaint

| **whinge** *verb* ▸ whinge*s*, whinge*ing* or whing*ing*, whinge*d*

whinny *verb* of a horse: to neigh ■ *noun* (*plural* **whinnies**) a neighing sound

| **whinny** *verb* ▸ whinnie*s*, whinny*ing*, whinnie*d*

whip *noun* **1** a lash with a handle, for punishing, urging on animals, *etc* **2** a member of parliament who sees that the members of their own party attend to give their vote when needed ■ *verb* **1** to hit or drive with a lash **2** to beat (eggs, cream, *etc*) into a froth **3** to snatch (away, off, out, up, *etc*): *whipped out a revolver* **4** to move fast, like a whip

| **whip** *verb* ▸ whip*s*, whipp*ing*, whipp*ed*

whippet *noun* a breed of racing dog, like a small greyhound

whipping *noun* a beating with a whip

whir *or* **whirr** *noun* a sound of fast, continuous whirling ■ *verb* to move or whirl with a buzzing noise

| **whir** *verb* ▸ whir*s*, whirr*ing*, whirr*ed*

whirl *verb* **1** to turn round quickly **2** to carry (off, away, *etc*) quickly

■ *noun* **1** a fast circling movement **2** great excitement, confusion

whirlpool *noun* a place in a river or sea where the current moves in a circle

whirlwind *noun* a violent current of wind with a whirling motion

whisk *verb* **1** to move quickly and lightly, sweep: *their car whisked past* **2** to beat or whip (a mixture) ■ *noun* **1** a quick sweeping movement **2** a kitchen utensil for beating eggs or mixtures

whisker *noun* **1** a long bristle on the upper lip of a cat *etc* **2 whiskers** hair on the sides of a man's face, sideburns

whisky *or Irish & US* **whiskey** *noun* (*plural* **whiskies** *or* **whiskeys**) an alcoholic spirit made from grain

whisper *verb* **1** to speak very softly, using the breath only, not the voice **2** to make a soft, rustling sound ■ *noun* a soft sound made with the breath

whist *noun* a type of card game for four players

whistle *verb* **1** to make a high-pitched sound by forcing breath through the lips or teeth **2** to make such a sound with an instrument **3** to move with such a sound, like a bullet ■ *noun* **1** the sound made by whistling **2** any instrument for whistling

white *adjective* **1** of the colour of pure snow **2** pale or light-coloured: *white wine* **3** of a pale-coloured complexion ■ *noun* **1** something white **2** someone with a pale-coloured complexion **3** the part of an egg surrounding the yolk

white elephant something useless and costly or troublesome to maintain

white-hot *adjective* having reached a degree of heat at which metals glow with a white light (hotter than **red-hot**)

whiten *verb* to make or become white or whiter

whiteness *noun* a white state or quality

whitewash *noun* a mixture of ground chalk and water, or lime and water, for whitening walls *etc* ■ *verb* **1** to put whitewash on **2** to cover up the faults of, give a good appearance to

whither *adverb & conjunction, old* to what place?

whiting *noun* a small type of fish related to the cod

Whitsun *noun* the week beginning with the seventh Sunday after Easter

whittle *verb* **1** to pare or cut (wood *etc*) with a knife **2 whittle away** *or* **down** to make gradually less: *whittled away his savings*

whiz[1] *or* **whizz** *verb* **1** to move with a hissing sound, like an arrow **2** to move very fast

| whiz ► whizzes, whizzing, whizzed

whiz[2] *or* **whizz kid** *noun* someone who achieves rapid success while relatively young

who *pronoun* used to refer to someone or some people unknown or unnamed (only as the subject of a verb): *who is that woman in the green hat?* ■ *relative pronoun* referring to the person or people just named: *do you know who those people are?*

whoever *pronoun* any person or people

whole *adjective* **1** complete **2** all, with nothing or no one missing **3** not broken ■ *noun* the entire thing

wholefood *noun* unprocessed food produced without the aid of artificial fertilizers

wholehearted *adjective* enthusiastic, generous

wholemeal *noun* flour made from the entire wheat grain

whole number a positive integer or zero

wholesale *noun* the sale of goods in large quantities to a shop from which they can be bought in small quantities by ordinary buyers (*compare with*: **retail**) ■ *adjective* **1** buying or selling in large quantities **2** on a large scale: *wholesale killing*

wholesaler *noun* a person who buys goods on a large scale and sells them in smaller quantities to shopkeepers for sale to the public

wholesome *adjective* giving health, healthy

who'll *short for* who will; who shall

wholly *adverb* entirely, altogether

whom *pronoun* **1** used to refer to someone or some people unknown or unnamed (only as the object of a sentence): *whom did you see?/to whom am I speaking?* **2** which person: *do you know to whom I gave it?* ■ *relative pronoun* referring to the person or people just named: *the person whom I liked best*

whoop *noun* a loud cry, rising in pitch ■ *verb* to give a whoop

whooping-cough *noun* an infectious disease in which violent bouts of coughing are followed by a whoop as the breath is drawn in

whose *adjective & pronoun* belonging to whom?: *whose handwriting is this?* ■ *relative pronoun* of whom: *the man whose wife I know*

why *adverb & pronoun* for which reason?: *why did you not stay?*

wick *noun* the twisted threads in a candle or lamp which draw up the oil or grease to the flame

wicked *adjective* **1** evil, sinful **2** mischievous, spiteful ■ **wickedly** *adverb*

wicker *adjective* of a chair: made of woven willow twigs

wicket *noun, cricket* the set of three stumps, or one of these, at which the ball is bowled

wide *adjective* **1** broad, not narrow **2** stretching far: *a wide grin* **3** general, big: *a wide selection* **4** measuring a certain amount from side to side: *5 centimetres wide* ■ *adverb* **1** off the target: *the shots went wide* **2** (often **wide apart**) far apart: *hold your arms wide*

wide-awake *adjective* fully awake; alert

wide-eyed *adjective* with eyes wide open in surprise *etc*

widely *adverb* **1** over a wide area; among many **2** far apart

widen *verb* to make or become wide

wide-open *adjective* opened to the full extent

widespread *adjective* spread over a large area or among many people

widow *noun* a woman whose husband is dead

widower *noun* a man whose wife is dead

width *noun* **1** measurement across, from side to side **2** large extent

wield *verb* **1** to swing or handle (a cricket bat, sword, *etc*) **2** to use (power, authority, *etc*)

wife *noun* (*plural* **wives**) **1** a married woman **2** the woman to whom a man is married

wig *noun* an artificial covering of hair for the head

wiggle *verb* to move from side to side with jerky or twisting

movements ■ *noun* a jerky movement from side to side

wiggly *adjective* wriggly, wavy

wigwam *noun*, *history* a conical tent of skins made by some Native Americans

wild *adjective* **1** of an animal: not tamed **2** of a plant: not cultivated in a garden **3** uncivilized **4** unruly, uncontrolled **5** of weather: stormy **6** of a guess *etc*: rash, inaccurate ■ *noun* (usually **wilds**) an uncultivated or uncivilized region

wilderness *noun* a wild, uncultivated or desolate region

wild-goose chase a troublesome and useless errand

wildlife *noun* wild animals, birds, *etc* in their natural habitats

wile *noun* a crafty trick

wilful *adjective* **1** fond of having one's own way **2** intentional: *wilful damage*

will *noun* **1** the power to choose or decide **2** desire: *against my will* **3** determination: *the will to win* **4** feeling towards someone: *bear him no ill will* **5** a written statement about what is to be done with your property after your death ■ *verb* **1** to influence someone by exercising your will: *he willed her to win* **2** to hand down (property *etc*) by will **3** (*past form* **would**) also used to form future tenses of other verbs when the subject is *he, she, it, you* or *they*: *you will see me there* **4** *informal* often used for the same purpose when the subject is *I* or *we*: *I will tell you later* **5** used for emphasis, or to express a promise, when the subject is *I* or *we*: *I will do it if possible* (see also **shall**, **would**)

willing *adjective* ready to do what is asked; eager

will-o'-the-wisp *noun* a pale light sometimes seen at night over marshy places

willow *noun* **1** a tree with long slender branches **2** its wood, used in cricket bats

willy-nilly *adverb* **1** whether you wish or not **2** notwithstanding other people's feelings

wilt *verb* **1** of a flower or plant: to droop **2** to lose strength

wily *adjective* cunning

| **wily** ► wilier, wiliest

wimp *noun, informal* an ineffectual person

win *verb* **1** to gain by luck or in a contest **2** to gain (the love of someone *etc*) by effort **3** to come first in a contest **4** (often **win over**) to gain the support or friendship of ■ *noun* an act of winning; a victory

| **win** *verb* ► wins, winning, won

wince *verb* to shrink or start back in pain *etc*, flinch

winch *noun* (*plural* **winches**) **1** a handle or crank for turning a wheel **2** a machine for lifting things, worked by winding a rope round a revolving cylinder

■ **winch up** to lift up with a winch

wind[1] (*pronounced* wind) *noun* **1** a current of air **2** breath **3** air carrying a scent **4** air or gas in the stomach **5** the wind instruments in an orchestra ■ *verb* to put out of breath

wind[2] (*pronounced* waind) *verb* **1** to turn, twist or coil **2** (sometimes **wind up**) to screw up the spring of (a watch, clockwork toy, *etc*) **3** to wrap closely ■ **wind up 1** to bring or come to an end **2** *informal* to annoy, tease

| **wind** ► winds, winding, wound

winder *noun* a key *etc* for winding a clock

windfall *noun* **1** a fruit blown from a tree **2** an unexpected gain, *eg* a sum of money

winding *adjective* curving, twisting

wind instrument a musical instrument sounded by blowing into it

windmill *noun* a mill driven by sails which are moved by the wind, used for pumping water, grinding grain, *etc*

window *noun* an opening in a wall, protected by glass, which lets in light and air

Windows *noun singular, trademark* a type of computer operating system

windpipe *noun* the tube leading from the mouth to the lungs (*also called*: **trachea**)

windscreen noun a pane of glass in front of the driver of a car etc

windsurfer noun a board with a sail for riding the waves

windsurfing noun the sport of riding the waves on a board attached to a sail

windswept adjective exposed to strong winds and showing the effects of it

windward adjective & adverb in the direction from which the wind blows

windy adjective 1 of weather: with a strong wind blowing 2 of a place: exposed to strong winds

| **windy** ► windi**er**, windi**est**

wine noun 1 an alcoholic drink made from the fermented juice of grapes or other fruit 2 a rich dark red colour

wing noun 1 one of the arm-like limbs of a bird, bat or insect by means of which it flies 2 one of the two projections on the sides of an aeroplane 3 a part of a house built out to the side 4 the side of a stage, where actors wait to enter 5 football etc a player positioned at the edge of the field 6 a section of a political party: the left wing
■ verb 1 to wound (a bird) in the wing 2 to soar

winged adjective 1 having wings 2 swift

wink verb 1 to open and close an eye quickly 2 to give a hint by winking 3 of lights etc: to flicker, twinkle ■ noun 1 an act of winking 2 a hint given by winking

winkle noun a small edible shellfish ■ **winkle out** to force out gradually

winning adjective 1 victorious, successful 2 charming, attractive

winnings noun plural money etc that has been won

winsome adjective charming

winter noun the cold season of the year ■ adjective of or suitable for winter

winter sports sports on snow or ice, eg skiing, tobogganing, etc

wintry adjective 1 cold, frosty 2 cheerless, unfriendly

wipe verb 1 to clean or dry by rubbing 2 **wipe something away, out, off** or **up** to clear it away ■ noun the act of cleaning by rubbing ■ **wipe something out** to totally destroy it

wiper noun one of a pair of moving parts which wipe the windscreen of a car

wire noun 1 a thread-like length of metal 2 the metal thread used in communication by telephone etc ■ adjective made of wire ■ verb 1 informal to send a telegram 2 to supply (a building etc) with wires for carrying an electric current

wireless adjective of communication: by radio waves ■ noun, old a radio set

wiry adjective 1 made of wire 2 of a person: thin but strong

wisdom *noun* the quality of being wise

wisdom teeth four large back teeth which appear after childhood

wise *adjective* **1** very knowledgeable **2** judging rightly; sensible

-wise *suffix* **1** in the manner or way of: *crabwise* **2** with reference or regard to: *careerwise*

wish *verb* **1** to feel or express a desire: *I wish he'd leave* **2** (often **wish for**) to long for, desire **3** to hope for on behalf of (someone): *wish someone luck* ▪ *noun* (*plural* **wishes**) **1** desire, longing **2** a thing desired or wanted **3** an expression of desire: *make a wish* **4 wishes** expression of hope for another's happiness, good fortune, *etc*: *good wishes*

wishbone *noun* a forked bone in the breast of fowls

wishful *adjective* wishing, eager

wishful thinking basing your belief on (false) hopes rather than known facts

wishy-washy *adjective* **1** of liquid: thin and weak **2** feeble, not energetic or lively **3** lacking colour

wisp *noun* a small tuft or strand

wispy *adjective* wisp-like; light and fine in texture

wistful *adjective* thoughtful and rather sad ▪ **wistfully** *adverb*

wit *noun* **1** (often **wits**)

intelligence, common sense **2** the ability to express ideas neatly and funnily **3** someone who can do this

witch *noun* (*plural* **witches**) **1** a woman with magic power obtained through evil spirits **2** an ugly old woman

witchcraft *noun* magic performed by a witch

witch doctor someone believed to have magical powers to cure illnesses *etc*

with *preposition* **1** in the company of: *I was walking with my father* **2** by means of: *cut it with a knife* **3** in the same direction as: *drifting with the current* **4** against: *fighting with his brother* **5** on the same side as **6** having: *a man with a limp* **7** in the keeping of: *leave the keys with me*

withdraw *verb* **1** to go back or away **2** to take away, remove: *withdraw cash* **3** to take back (an insult *etc*) ▪ **withdrawal** *noun*

> **withdraw** ► withdraws, withdraw*ing*, withdrew, withdrawn

withdrawn *adjective* **1** of a place: lonely, isolated **2** of a person: unwilling to communicate with others, unsociable

wither *verb* to fade, dry up or decay

withering *adjective* **1** drying up, dying **2** of a remark *etc*: scornful, sarcastic

withhold verb to keep back, refuse to give

| **withhold** ► withhold**s**, withhold**ing**, with**held**

within preposition inside the limits of

without preposition **1** in the absence of: *we went without you* **2** not having: *without a penny*

withstand verb to oppose or resist successfully

witness noun (plural **witnesses**) **1** someone who sees or has direct knowledge of a thing **2** someone who gives evidence in a law court **3** proof, evidence ■ verb **1** to see, be present at **2** to sign your name to confirm the authenticity of (someone else's signature)

witticism noun a witty remark

witty adjective clever and amusing

| **witty** ► witt**ier**, witti**est**

wizard noun a man believed to have the power of magic

wizardry noun magic

wizened adjective dried up, shrivelled

woad noun **1** a blue dye **2** the plant from which it is obtained

wobble verb to rock unsteadily from side to side ■ noun an unsteady rocking

wobbly adjective unsteady, rocking

woe noun **1** grief, misery **2** a cause of sorrow, a trouble

woebegone adjective dismal, sad-looking

woeful adjective sorrowful; pitiful ■ **woefully** adverb

wok noun an Asian cooking-pan shaped like a large bowl

woke and **woken** see **wake**[1]

wolf noun (plural **wolves**) a wild animal like a dog that hunts in packs ■ verb to eat greedily

woman noun (plural **women**) **1** an adult human female **2** human females in general

womanhood noun the state of being a woman

womankind or **womenkind** noun women generally

womanly adjective like, or suitable for, a woman

womb noun the part of a female mammal's body in which the young develop and stay till birth

wombat noun a small, beaver-like Australian animal, with a pouch

women plural of **woman**

won past form of **win**

wonder noun **1** the feeling produced by something unexpected or extraordinary; surprise, awe **2** something strange, amazing or miraculous ■ verb **1** to be curious or in doubt: *I wonder what will happen* **2** to feel surprise or amazement (at, that)

wonderful adjective **1** arousing wonder; strange, marvellous **2** excellent

wondrous adjective, old wonderful

wont (*pronounced* wohnt) *noun* habit: *as is his wont*

won't *short for* will not

woo *verb* **1** to try to win the love of (someone) **2** to try to gain (*eg* success)

▌woo ► woos, wooing, wooed

wood *noun* **1** a group of growing trees **2** the hard part of a tree, especially when cut for use

wooded *adjective* covered with trees

wooden *adjective* **1** made of wood **2** dull, stiff, not lively

woodland *noun* land covered with trees

woodlouse *noun* (*plural* **woodlice**) a small beetle-like creature with a jointed shell, found under stones *etc*

woodpecker *noun* a bird that pecks holes in the bark of trees with its beak, in search of insects

woodwind *noun* wind instruments, made of wood or metal, *eg* the flute or clarinet

woodwork *noun* **1** the making of wooden articles **2** the wooden parts of a house, room, *etc*

woodworm *noun* the larva of a beetle that bores holes in wood and destroys it

woody *adjective* like wood

wool *noun* **1** the soft hair of sheep and other animals **2** yarn or cloth made of wool

woollen *adjective* made of wool ■ *noun* a knitted garment made of wool

woolly *adjective* **1** made of, or like, wool **2** vague, hazy: *a woolly argument* ■ *noun* (*plural* **woollies**) a knitted woollen garment

word *noun* **1** a written or spoken sign representing a thing or an idea **2** **words** talk, remarks **3** news: *word of his death* **4** a promise: *break your word* ■ *verb* to choose words for

wording *noun* choice or arrangement of words

word processor an electronic machine or computer program which can store, edit and print out text

wordy *adjective* using too many words

wore *past form of* **wear**

work *noun* **1** a physical or mental effort to achieve or make something **2** a job, employment **3** a task: *I've got work to do* **4** anything made or done **5** something produced by art, *eg* a book, musical composition, painting, *etc* **6** manner of working, workmanship: *poor work* **7 works** a factory **8 works** the mechanism (*eg* of a watch) ■ *verb* **1** to be engaged in physical or mental work **2** to be employed **3** to run or operate smoothly and efficiently **4** of a plan *etc*: to be successful **5** to get into a position slowly and gradually: *the screw worked loose* **6** to organize, manage, control ■ **work out 1** to solve **2** to discover as a result of deep thought **3** of a situation: to turn out all right in the end ▪ **work up** to arouse, excite: *working himself up into a fury*

workable *adjective* able to be done, practical

worker *noun* someone who works at a job

working *adjective* operating properly, not broken

working class the social class including manual workers

working day *or* **working hours** the hours each day that someone spends at work, on duty, *etc*

workman *noun* someone who works with their hands

workmanlike *adjective* done with skill

workmanship *noun* **1** the skill of a workman **2** manner of making something

workshop *noun* a room or building where manufacturing, handicraft, *etc* is done

world *noun* **1** the earth and all things on it **2** the people of the world **3** any planet or star **4** the universe **5** a state of existence: *the next world* **6** a particular area of life or activity: *the world of fashion* **7** a great deal: *a world of good*

worldly *adjective* concerned with material things such as money, possessions, *etc*, not the soul or spirit

worldwide *adjective* extending throughout the world ▪ *adverb* throughout the world

World Wide Web a vast collection of linked documents and stored information located on computers all around the world, which can be accessed via the Internet

worm *noun* **1** a small creeping animal without a backbone, often living in soil **2** *informal* a low, contemptible person **3** something spiral-shaped, *eg* the thread of a screw **4 worms** the condition of having threadworms *etc* in the intestines **5** *computing* a kind of virus ▪ *verb* **1** to move gradually and stealthily (in or into) **2 worm out** to draw out (information) bit by bit

worn *adjective* **1** damaged by use **2** tired, worn-out

worn-out *adjective* tired, exhausted

worried *adjective* in an unhappy and unrelaxed state, as a result of thinking about something bad which is happening, or which you fear may happen

worry *verb* **1** to annoy **2** to make troubled and anxious **3** to be troubled and anxious ▪ *noun* (*plural* **worries**) **1** uneasiness, anxiety **2** a cause of unease or anxiety

| **worry** *verb* ► worr*ies*, worry*ing*, worr*ied* |

worse *adjective* **1** bad or evil to a greater degree **2** more ill ▪ *adverb* badly to a greater degree, more severely

worsen *verb* to make or become worse

worship *noun* 1 a religious ceremony or service 2 deep reverence, adoration 3 a title used in addressing a mayor, magistrate, *etc* ■ *verb* 1 to pay honour to (a god) 2 to adore or admire deeply

| **worship** *verb* ► worship*s*, worship*ing*, worship*ped*

worst *adjective* bad or evil to the greatest degree ■ *adverb* badly to the greatest degree

worsted (*pronounced* woorstid) *noun* 1 a type of fine woollen yarn 2 a strong cloth made of this

worth *noun* 1 value; price 2 importance 3 excellence of character *etc* ■ *adjective* 1 equal in value to 2 deserving of: *worth considering*

worthless *adjective* of no merit or value

worthwhile *adjective* deserving time and effort

worthy *adjective* 1 (often **worthy of**) deserving, suitable 2 of good character

| **worthy** ► worth*ier*, worth*iest*

would *verb* 1 the form of the verb **will** used to express a condition: *he would go if he could* 2 used for emphasis: *I tell you I would do it if possible*

would-be *adjective* trying to be or pretending to be: *would-be actor*

wound[1] (*pronounced* woond) *noun* 1 a cut or injury caused by a weapon, in an accident, *etc* 2 a hurt to someone's feelings ■ *verb* 1 to make a cut or injury in 2 to hurt the feelings of

wound[2] (*pronounced* wownd) *past form of* **wind**[2]

wounded *adjective* having a wound, injured, hurt

wove *and* **woven** *see* weave

wraith (*pronounced* reith) *noun* an apparition of a living person, often as a warning of death

wrangle *verb* to quarrel noisily ■ *noun* a noisy quarrel

wrap *verb* 1 to fold or roll round 2 **wrap up** to cover by folding or winding something round ■ *noun* 1 a cloak or shawl 2 a snack made from a piece of tortilla rolled around a filling

| **wrap** *verb* ► wrap*s*, wrap*ping*, wrap*ped*

wrapper *noun* a loose paper cover, *eg* round a book or sweet

wrath (*pronounced* roth *or* rawth *or* rath) *noun* violent anger

wreak *verb* 1 to carry out: *wreak vengeance* 2 to cause: *wreak havoc*

wreath *noun* a ring of flowers or leaves

wreathe (*pronounced* reedh) *verb* to encircle

wreck *noun* 1 destruction, especially of a ship by the sea

2 the remains of anything destroyed, especially a ship **3** someone whose health or nerves are in bad condition ■ *verb* to destroy

wreckage *noun* the remains of something wrecked

wren *noun* a very small type of bird

wrench *verb* **1** to pull with a violent, often twisting, motion **2** to sprain (your ankle *etc*) ■ *noun* (*plural* **wrenches**) **1** a violent twist **2** a tool for gripping and turning nuts, bolts, *etc* **3** sadness caused by parting from someone or something

wrest (*pronounced* rest) *verb*, *formal* to twist or take by force

wrestle *verb* **1** to fight with someone, trying to bring them to the ground **2 wrestle with something** to think deeply about (a problem *etc*)

wrestler *noun* someone who wrestles as a sport

wrestling *noun* the sport in which two people fight to throw each other to the ground

wretch *noun* (*plural* **wretches**) **1** a miserable, pitiable person **2** a worthless or contemptible person

wretched (*pronounced* rech-id) *adjective* **1** very miserable **2** worthless, very bad

wriggle *verb* **1** to twist to and fro **2** to move by doing this, as a worm does **3** to escape (out of a difficulty *etc*)

wring *verb* **1** to twist or squeeze (especially water out of wet clothes) **2** to clasp and unclasp (your hands) in grief, anxiety, *etc*

| **wring** ► wrings, wring*ing*, wrung

wringer *noun* a machine for forcing water from wet clothes

wrinkle *noun* a small crease or fold on the skin or other surface ■ *verb* to make or become wrinkled

wrinkly *adjective* having wrinkles

wrist *noun* the joint by which the hand is joined to the arm

writ (*pronounced* rit) *noun* a formal document giving an order (especially to appear in a law court)

write *verb* **1** to form letters with a pen, pencil, *etc* **2** to put into writing **3** to compose (a letter, a book, *etc*) **4** to send a letter (to) **5** *computing* to copy (a data file)
■ **write down** to record in writing
■ **write off** to regard as lost for ever ■ **write up** to make a written record of

| **write** ► writes, writ*ing*, wrote, written

writer *noun* someone who writes, an author

writhe (*pronounced* raidh) *verb* to twist or roll about, *eg* in pain

writing *noun* a written text or texts

wrong *adjective* **1** not correct **2** not right or just **3** evil **4** not what is intended: *take the wrong turning* **5** unsuitable: *the wrong weather for camping* **6** mistaken ■ *noun* **1** whatever is not right or just **2** an injury done to another ■ *verb* to do wrong to, harm ■ **wrongly** *adverb*

wrongdoer *noun* someone who does wrong

wrongdoing *noun* immoral or illegal behaviour or actions

wrongful *adjective* not lawful or just

wrote *past form* of **write**

wrought iron iron hammered, rather than cast, into shape

wrung *past form* of **wring**

wry *adjective* **1** slightly mocking or bitter **2** twisted or turned to one side ■ **wryly** *adverb*

WWW *or* **www** *abbreviation* World Wide Web

X-chromosome *noun* the sex chromosome that is paired with another X-chromosome in female humans and with a Y-chromosome in males

xenophobia (*pronounced* zen-o-**foh**-bi-*a*) *noun* hatred of foreigners or strangers ∎ **xenophobic** *adjective*

Xmas *noun*, *informal* Christmas

X-ray *noun* **1** an electromagnetic ray that can pass through material impenetrable by light, and produce a photographic image of the object through which it has passed **2** a shadow picture produced by X-rays on photographic film ∎ *verb* to take a photographic image of with X-rays

xylophone *noun* a musical instrument consisting of a series of graded wooden bars which are struck with hammers

Y y

yacht *noun* a sailing or motor-driven boat for racing, cruising, *etc*

yachtsman, **yachtswoman** *noun* someone who sails a yacht

yak *noun* a Tibetan long-haired ox

yam *noun* a tropical root vegetable, similar to a potato

Yank *or* **Yankee** *noun*, *Brit informal* an American

yank *verb*, *informal* to tug or pull with a violent jerk ■ *noun* a violent tug

yap *verb* to bark sharply

| yap ▸ yaps, yapp*ing*, yapp*ed*

yard *noun* **1** a measure of length (0.9144 of a metre, or 3 feet) **2** a long beam on a mast for spreading sails **3** an enclosed space used for a particular purpose: *railway yard*

yardstick *noun* a standard for measurement

yarn *noun* **1** wool, cotton, *etc* spun into thread **2** a long, often improbable, story

yashmak *noun* a veil covering the lower half of the face, worn by Islamic women

yawn *verb* **1** to take a deep breath unintentionally with an open mouth, because of boredom or sleepiness **2** of a hole: to be wide open, gape ■ *noun* an open-mouthed deep breath

Y-chromosome *noun* the sex chromosome that is paired with a X-chromosome in males

ye *pronoun*, *old* you

year *noun* **1** the time taken by the earth to go once round the sun, about 365 days **2** the period 1 January to 31 December **3** a period of twelve months starting at any point **4** years age: *wise for her years*

yearling *noun* a year-old animal

yearly *adjective* happening every year, or once a year

yearn *verb* **1** to long (for, to do something, *etc*) **2** to feel pity or tenderness (for)

yearning *noun* an eager longing

yeast *noun* a substance which causes fermentation, used to make bread dough rise and in brewing

yell *verb* to give a loud, shrill cry; scream ■ *noun* a loud, shrill cry

yellow *noun* the colour of gold,

egg-yolks, *etc* ■ *adjective* of this colour ■ *verb* to become yellow, due to ageing

yelp *verb* to give a sharp bark or cry ■ *noun* a sharp bark or cry

yen[1] *noun* the standard unit of Japanese currency

yen[2] *noun, informal* a strong desire, longing: *a yen to return home*

yeoman *noun, history* a farmer with his own land

yes *exclamation* expressing agreement or consent ■ *noun* **1** an expression of agreement or consent **2** a vote in favour

yesterday *noun* **1** the day before today **2** the past ■ *adverb* on the day before today

yet *adverb* **1** by now, by this time: *have you seen that film yet?* **2** still, before the matter is finished: *we may win yet* ■ *conjunction* but, nevertheless: *I am defeated, yet I shall not surrender*

Yeti *another name for the* **Abominable Snowman**

yew *noun* **1** a tree with dark green leaves and red berries **2** its wood

yield *verb* **1** to give in, surrender **2** to give way to pressure or persuasion **3** to produce (a crop, results, *etc*) ■ *noun* an amount produced; a crop

yielding *adjective* giving way easily

yob *noun* a lout, a hooligan

yodel *verb* to sing in a style involving frequent changes

between an ordinary and a very high-pitched voice

yodel ▸ yodel*s*, yodell*ing*, yodell*ed*

yoga *noun* a Hindu system of philosophy and meditation, often involving special physical exercises

yogurt *or* **yoghurt** *noun* a semi-liquid food product made from fermented milk

yoke *noun* **1** a wooden frame joining oxen when pulling a plough or cart **2** something that joins together ■ *verb* to put a yoke on

yokel *noun, derogatory* an unsophisticated country person; a rustic

yolk *noun* the yellow part of an egg

Yom Kippur the Day of Atonement, a Jewish fast day

yonder *adverb, old* in that place (at a distance but within sight) ■ *adjective* that (object) over there: *by yonder tree*

you *pronoun* the person(s) spoken or written to, used as the *singular or plural* subject or object of a verb: *what did you say?/are you both free tomorrow?*

you'd *short for* **1** you would; you should **2** you had

you'll *short for* you will; you shall

young *adjective* **1** in early life **2** in the early part of mental or physical growth ■ *noun* **1** the offspring of animals **2** **the young** young people

youngster *noun* a young person

your *adjective* belonging to you: *it's your life*

you're short for you are

yours *pronoun* belonging to you: *is this pen yours?*

yourself *pronoun* (*plural* **yourselves**) **1** used reflexively: *don't trouble yourself* **2** used for emphasis: *you yourself can't go*

youth *noun* **1** the state of being young **2** the early part of life **3** a young person **4** young people in general

youthful *adjective* **1** young **2** fresh and vigorous

youth hostel a hostel where hikers *etc* may spend the night

you've short for you have

yo-yo *noun, trademark* a toy consisting of a reel which spins up and down on a string

Yule *noun, old* Christmas

Yuletide *noun, old* Christmas time

Zz

zany *adjective*, *informal* crazy, madcap

zap *verb* **1** to strike, shoot, *etc* suddenly **2** to move rapidly; zip

| **zap** ▶ zaps, zapping, zapped

zeal *noun* enthusiasm, keenness

zealous (*pronounced* zel-*us*) *adjective* full of zeal ■ **zealously** *adverb*

zebra *noun* a striped African animal of the horse family

zebra crossing a pedestrian street crossing, painted in black and white stripes

zenith *noun* **1** the point of the heavens exactly overhead **2** the highest point, the peak

zephyr (*pronounced* zef-*er*) *noun* a soft, gentle breeze

zero *noun* **1** nothing or the sign for it (0) **2** the point (marked 0) from which a scale (*eg* on a thermometer) begins

zest *noun* **1** relish, keen enjoyment **2** orange or lemon peel

zestful *adjective* keen; full of enjoyment

zigzag *adjective* having sharp bends or angles ■ *verb* move in a zigzag direction

| **zigzag** *verb* ▶ zigzags, zigzagging, zigzagged

zimmer *noun*, *trademark* a hand-held metal frame used to give support in walking

zinc *noun* a bluish-white metal

zip *noun* **1** a fastening device for clothes, bags, *etc*, consisting of two rows of metal or nylon teeth which interlock when a sliding tab is pulled between them **2** a whizzing sound, *eg* made by a fast-flying object ■ *verb* **1** to fasten with a zip **2** to whiz, fly past at speed **3** *computing* to compress the data in a computer file, so that it takes up less memory

| **zip** *verb* ▶ zips, zipping, zipped

zither *noun* a flat, stringed musical instrument, played with the fingers

zodiac *noun* an imaginary strip in space, divided into twelve equal parts ■ **signs of the zodiac** the divisions of the zodiac used in astrology, each named after a group of stars

zombie *noun* **1** a corpse

reanimated by witchcraft **2** a very slow or stupid person

zone *noun* **1** any of the five main bands into which the earth's surface is divided according to temperature: *temperate zone* **2** a section of a country, town, *etc* marked off for a particular purpose

zoo *noun* a place where wild animals are kept and shown to the public

zoological *adjective* **1** relating to animals **2** relating to zoos; containing a zoo: *zoological gardens*

zoologist *noun* someone who studies animal life

zoology *noun* the science of animal life

zoom *verb* **1** to move with a loud, low buzzing noise **2** to make such a noise

zoom lens a lens used in photography which makes a distant object appear gradually nearer without the camera being moved

Language workshop

Spelling

Below we have listed around 175 words that are frequently misspelled. Use your dictionary to make sure you know what they mean as well as how to spell them:

abbreviation	continuous	grammar
accelerator	correspondence	guarantee
accessible	definitely	guard
accommodation	desperate	guilty
achieve	diarrhoea	haemorrhage
address	disappoint	height
aerial	doubt	humorous
aeroplane	draughty	hygiene
almond	eccentric	illiterate
although	eczema	immediately
argument	embarrass	independent
asthma	environment	indispensable
autumn	exaggerate	innocent
bachelor	exceed	innocuous
battalion	excellent	inoculate
beautiful	exhaust	instalment
biscuit	experience	irresistible
broccoli	fascinate	jealous
business	February	jewellery
calendar	fierce	jodhpurs
ceiling	foreign	knowledge
cemetery	forty	laughter
changeable	friend	leisure
chaos	fulfil	leopard
character	gauge	liaise
column	ghastly	lieutenant
committee	ghost	liquorice
conscience	gorgeous	maintenance
consensus	government	manageable

728

manoeuvre	playwright	separate
marriage	pneumonia	sergeant
martyr	possession	shriek
mayonnaise	precede	siege
medicine	prejudice	silhouette
millennium	privilege	skilful
miniature	proceed	strength
miscellaneous	process	spaghetti
misspell	professor	subtle
mortgage	pronunciation	succeed
moustache	pyjamas	success
naive	questionnaire	supersede
necessary	queue	surprise
neighbour	receipt	technique
niece	receive	temperature
noticeable	recommend	truly
nuisance	refrigerator	vacuum
obscene	reign	valuable
occasion	reservoir	vehicle
occurred	restaurant	verruca
parallel	rhyme	villain
parliament	rhythm	Wednesday
people	righteous	weight
permanent	satellite	weird
perseverance	Saturday	wholly
Pharaoh	sausage	women
phenomenon	scissors	wrath
phlegm	secretary	yacht
physical	seize	zoological

Nouns

Nouns are words that name things. Nouns can be classified in many different ways.

Concrete and abstract nouns

Concrete nouns refer to physical things you can touch:

house, book, door, pig, tree

Abstract nouns refer to things you cannot touch, such as qualities or actions:

anger, sunshine, thought, kick, leap

Count and noncount/mass nouns

Count nouns name things that can be counted one by one, for example:

one *book*, two *bells*, three *flowers*, five hundred *apples*

Noncount nouns (also called **mass nouns**) name things that cannot be counted, for example:

help, excitement, luck, oxygen, milk, furniture

Some nouns can be count or noncount depending on what they mean:

Your *kindness* is much appreciated.
I appreciate all your little *kindnesses*.

 Is *dream* a count or noncount noun?
What about the word *life*?

Singular and plural nouns

Count nouns can be either singular or plural. A **singular noun** refers to one thing or person and takes a singular verb, for example:

The *boy runs*.
The *biceps is* an important muscle.

A **plural noun** refers to more than one thing or person and takes a plural verb, for example:

The *boys run*.
These *scissors are* sharp.

Some nouns can be treated as both singular and plural:

The family is on holiday.
The family are on holiday.

 Is *trousers* a singular or a plural noun?
What about the word *bacteria*?

Proper and common nouns

Proper nouns name particular people, groups, places, events and occasions, and they usually begin with a capital letter, for example:

Mr Green, Manchester United, The Louvre, Atlantic Ocean, Lake Geneva, Tuesday, April

Common nouns refer to any of a class of things, but do not specifically name them, for example:

my *teacher*, the *team*, a *museum*, an *ocean*, this *month*

 Is *brother* a proper or a common noun?

Collective nouns

Collective nouns refer to a group of similar people or things that make up a larger whole, for example:

a *flock* (of sheep), a *team* (of players), a *pile* (of coins, papers), a *bunch* (of flowers)

731

Verbs

A **verb** is often described as a 'doing' word, one that expresses an action or a happening, for example:

> *digs, ran, is shouting*

A verb can also be a 'being' word, one that expresses a process or a state, such as:

> *is, knew, becomes*

There is a verb in every sentence. A sentence cannot make sense without a verb.

Subjects and objects of verbs

Every verb has a **subject**. The subject is the person or thing doing the action:

> *The sun* shone.

In some sentences, the verb has an **object** as well as a subject. The object tells you whom or what the verb affects:

> The sun warmed *the earth*.

Agreement of verbs

Each verb has a number of different forms, and the form of the verb you use depends on the subject of the verb. The verb 'agrees' with the subject. It is important not to get this wrong when you are using Standard English:

> ✗ They was very clever.
> ✓ They *were* very clever.

Change the verb forms in these sentences
so they are correct:
1. You was wrong to say that.
2. These apples looks bad.
3. They is going to a party.

Auxiliary verbs

A verb is called an **auxiliary verb** when it is used with
another verb carrying the main meaning. The most common
auxiliary verbs are **be** and **have**, used in their different forms
to show tense:

> I *am* walking to school.
> The children *have* played all day.

Do is used for making questions and negatives:

> *Do* you like music?
> She *did not* want to go.

 Can you pick out the auxiliary verbs in
these sentences?
1. I was looking for Sally.
2. He has bought a new CD.
3. You don't know what I am talking about.

Tenses

All verbs have a **tense**. The tense indicates the time when an action happens – either in the present, the past or the future. A verb can be in one of a number of tenses.

The present tense

The **present tense** is used for actions or situations that are happening now:

> She *plays*.
> She *is playing*.

The past tense

The **past tense** describes actions that have already happened:

> She *played*.
> She *was playing*.

The future tense

There is no specific **future tense** in English. Actions that will happen in future time are expressed in several ways, using **auxiliary verbs**:

> She *will play* next week.
> She *will be playing* next week.
> She *is going to play* next week.
> She *is playing* next week.

Simple and continuous forms

The past and present tenses of verbs have **simple** and **continuous** forms. The continuous is made by using a form of the verb **be** with the **-ing** form of a verb:

| She *plays*. | (simple present) |
| She *is playing*. | (present continuous) |

| She *played*. | (simple past) |
| She *was playing*. | (past continuous) |

Simple and perfect forms

The past tense also has a **perfect** form. This uses a form of
the verb **have** with the **-ed** form of a verb:

| She *played*. | (simple past) |
| She *has played*. | (past perfect) |

Sometimes, the form of the verb you use in the simple past is
different from the one you use in the past perfect. In
Standard English, it is important to use the correct verb
forms for simple and perfect:

✗ She has went home.	✗ I have fell.
✓ She *has gone* home.	✓ I *have fallen*.
✓ She *went* home.	✓ I *fell*.

Using tense

The tense you use can have an effect on your writing. If you
use the present tense, for example, what you write will be
more vivid and immediate. However, it is important to be
consistent in the tense you use, and not change suddenly to
another unless you have a reason to do so.

> **?** There are various ways to change the
> tenses in this sentence so that it makes
> sense. What would you do?
> I will be shopping and I buy lots of
> new clothes, which I wore at Melissa's
> party.

Adjectives

Adjectives act as modifiers of nouns – that is, they tell us something about the noun they relate to. There are different types of adjective that give different types of information:

Descriptive adjectives give information about the qualities of people or things:

> The girl was *short* and wore a *blue* jacket.
> This woman is *British*.
> He is an *excellent* teacher.
> The *oval* table was covered with *hexagonal* tiles.
> We drank out of *plastic* cups.

Adjectives of quantity inform about the amount of something:

> She had a *few* cows, *several* pigs and *some* chickens.
> The *four* children drank *ten* bottles of lemonade and ate *half* an apple pie.

Emphasizing adjectives serve to emphasize the noun they relate to:

> The meeting was an *absolute* disaster.
> It rained for the *entire* weekend.

Possessive adjectives show who owns or has the noun:

> John washes *his* car every Sunday.
> Don't waste *your* time.

Distributive adjectives indicate how things are shared between people:

> She carried a box under *each* arm.
> She handed a letter to *every* pupil.

Demonstrative adjectives point to someone or something particular:

> Look at *this* letter.
> *These* children read *those* books.

Questioning or **interrogative adjectives** ask about something:

> *What* coat shall I wear?
> Show me *which* dress you like.

Identify the adjectives in these sentences:
1. You are getting on my nerves.
2. I saw a terrible play at that theatre.
3. The player had numerous chances to score easy goals.

Comparing adjectives

There are different degrees of comparison that can be expressed in the form of adjective you use.

A **positive adjective** does not convey any degree of comparison. It simply describes, and does not compare with anything else:

> Mount Everest is a *high* mountain.
> The weather is *bad*.
> History is *interesting*.

A **comparative adjective** shows a comparison between one thing and another. The word **than** follows it:

> Mount Everest is *higher* than Mont Blanc.
> The weather is *worse* than it was yesterday.
> I think history is *more interesting* than English.

A **superlative adjective** conveys the greatest degree of comparison. It tells you that something is the greatest of any in its class or category:

> Mount Everest is the *highest* mountain in the world.
> This is the *worst* weather for a week.
> I think history is the *most interesting* subject.

Forming comparatives and superlatives

Note that some comparatives and superlatives are formed by adding the endings **-er** and **-est**, and some are formed by putting the words **more** or **most** in front of the positive adjective.

In Standard English, it is important to use the right method:

- ✗ This is the beautifullest garden in the street.
- ✓ This is the *most beautiful* garden in the street.

It is important not to mix the two forms:

- ✗ This is the most happiest day of my life.
- ✓ This is the *happiest* day of my life.

Some comparatives and superlatives are not formed in either of these ways, and are known as **irregular** comparative and superlative forms.

It is important to use the correct form:

- ✗ Your calculator is gooder than mine.
- ✓ Your calculator is *better* than mine.

> **?** Are these positive, comparative or
> superlative adjectives?
>
> | pleasant | most |
> | more boring | bad |
> | better | least |

Adverbs

Adverbs act as modifiers of verbs – that is, they tell us something about the verb they relate to; for example, how, why, where, when or how often something happens:

> The explorers *cautiously* entered the cave.
> They went *inside* and *slowly* crept *upstairs*.
> The gang of children met at the cinema *yesterday*.

However, an adverb also can modify an adjective:

> The woods looked *very* different at night.

An adverb can also modify another adverb:

> They swam *remarkably* quickly.

> Identify the adverbs in these sentences:
> 1. She ran outside, looking rather frightened.
> 2. You acted very calmly in the circumstances.
> 3. We are quite excited because we are going to the cinema later.

Forming adverbs

Many adverbs are formed by adding **-ly** to an adjective. If an adjective ends in **-y**, the **y** changes into **i** before adding **-ly**:

> quiet - *quietly*
> weary - *wearily*

It is important that you do not use the adjective form when you should use the adverb form:

> ✗ Come quick, and look at this!
> ✓ Come *quickly*, and look at this!

740

Placing adverbs

Some adverbs can be placed at various points in a sentence without changing its meaning:

> The explorers *cautiously* entered the cave.
> The explorers entered the cave *cautiously*.
> *Cautiously*, the explorers entered the cave.

However, with other adverbs it is important to put them in the correct place in a sentence, otherwise the meaning of the sentence may be confused. Compare the different meanings of these two sentences:

> There was a report that the Prime Minister had lost his temper *on the evening news*.
> There was a report *on the evening news* that the Prime Minister had lost his temper.

The adverbs *almost*, *also*, *even*, *just*, *mainly* and *only* should always be placed immediately in front of the word they modify. Compare the change in meaning when the adverb *only* is put in front of different words in the following sentence:

> Jim gave Jane a kiss.
> *Only* Jim gave Jane a kiss.
> Jim *only* gave Jane a kiss.
> Jim gave *only* Jane a kiss.
> Jim gave Jane *only* a kiss.

Comparing adverbs

There are different degrees of comparison that can be expressed in the form of adverb you use.

A **positive adverb** does not convey any degree of comparison. It simply describes an action, and does not compare it with anything else:

> Chris ran *fast*.
> Serena played *well*.
> Rose behaved *courageously*.

A **comparative adverb** shows a comparison between one action and another:

> Chris ran *faster* when he realized he was late.
> Serena played *better* in the previous match.
> Rose behaved *more courageously* than Lisa.

A **superlative adverb** conveys the greatest degree of comparison:

> Chris ran *fastest* when he realized he would miss the bus.
> Serena played *best* in the final.
> Pauline behaved *most courageously* of all.

Forming comparatives and superlatives

Note that some comparatives and superlatives are formed by adding the endings **-er** and **-est**, and some are formed by putting the words **more** or **most** in front of the positive adverb.

It is important to use the right method:

- ✗ Brian ran quicklier.
- ✓ Brian ran *more quickly*.

It is important not to mix the two forms:

- ✗ Brian ran more faster.
- ✓ Brian ran *faster*.

Some comparatives and superlatives are not formed in either of these ways, and are known as **irregular** comparative and superlative forms.

It is important to use the correct form:

- ✗ You sang gooder than me.
- ✓ You sang *better* than me.

> **?** Are these positive, comparative or
> superlative adverbs?
>
> | | |
> |---|---|
> | pleasantly | well |
> | more happily | most warmly |
> | better | soonest |

Pronouns

Pronouns are essentially words that stand for nouns. There are many different types of pronoun.

Personal pronouns refer to specific people, places or things:

> We saw *him*.
> *They* went to see *it*.

Personal pronouns can have different forms depending on whether they are the subject or the object in a sentence. It is a common mistake to use the wrong one, so you should be careful with them when using Standard English:

> ✗ Him and me went to the shops.
> ✓ *He* and *I* went to the shops.

Some people wrongly use the subject form **I** when they should use the object form **me**, because they think it sounds better:

> ✗ Dad gave sweets to John and I.
> ✓ Dad gave sweets to John and *me*.

Reflexive pronouns are sometimes called **compound pronouns**. These are forms that end in **-self** or **-selves**:

> I hurt *myself*.
> I hope you enjoy *yourselves*.

Possessive pronouns indicate ownership:

> The cakes are *his*, the sweets are *mine*, and the biscuits are *theirs*.

Remember: possessive pronouns **never** have apostrophes.

Indefinite pronouns refer to non-specific people or things:

> *Nobody* knows *anything* about what happened.
> *Many* are called, *some* are chosen, but *few* succeed.

Interrogative pronouns begin questions:

> *Whose* is this?
> *Which* shirt should I wear?

Demonstrative pronouns 'point to' the nouns they replace:

> *These* (books) are good books.
> *That* (habit) is an annoying habit.

Relative pronouns are special pronouns that refer to someone or something already named and introduce additional information about them or it:

> Can we see a film *that* I like, for a change?
> The boy *who* was climbing the trees had an accident.

? What type of pronoun are the following?

I	someone
them	several
its	why
yours	those

Prepositions

A **preposition** is a word placed in front of a **noun** or **pronoun** to show how one person or thing relates to another:

> a class *of* students
> a cake *with* icing
> I walked *across* the road.
> John lives *in* Liverpool.
> Mum's birthday is *on* the 15th *of* June.
> The school holidays are *from* July *to* August.
> The building will be finished *within* a month.
> Grandad stayed *for* a month.
> I have been waiting *since* five o'clock.

 Can you pick out the prepositions in this sentence?
> After dinner I felt ill, so I climbed up the stairs and went to bed for two hours – from seven o'clock until nine o'clock.

Using prepositions

If a preposition is followed by a pronoun, the pronoun is always in its object form, that is, **me**, **him**, **her**, **them** or **whom**:

> He came *with* John and me.
> They walked *past* him.
> Chris is the friend *with whom* I went fishing.

In Standard English, it is important to use the correct preposition for what you mean:

> ✗ I went in the house.
> ✓ I went into the house.

746

Sometimes it is not necessary to use a preposition:

   ✗   Where are you going to?

   ✓   Where are you going?

> Can you rewrite these sentences correctly?
> 1. Which school do you attend at?
> 2. My pen fell off of the desk.
> 3. He wouldn't come inside of the classroom.

'Dangling' prepositions

A **dangling preposition** is what you get if you end a sentence in a preposition:

   This is the town I was born *in*.

Many people consider this to be wrong, and think that a **relative pronoun** should be used:

   This is the town *in which* I was born.

However, this can sometimes result in a clumsy sentence, so sometimes it is better to reword the sentence using a simpler structure:

   I was born in this town.

> How would you reword these sentences to avoid ending them with a preposition, and without making them sound clumsy?
> 1. She is someone I trust in.
> 2. Leeds is the city which I am moving to.

Phrases

Phrases are groups of linked words that make up a sentence:

(The poet) (was writing) (a poem).

You can add more information to the phrases:

(The clumsy poet) (was busily writing) (a dreadful poem).

There are different types of phrase.

Verb phrases

Verb phrases always contain a verb, and they can be expanded using adverbs:

Jane *was combing* her hair.
Jane *was hurriedly combing* her hair.

Noun phrases

Noun phrases always contain a noun, and they can be expanded using adjectives:

Jane was combing *her hair*.
Jane was hurriedly combing *her messy hair*.

Noun phrases can also be expanded using two special types of phrase:

Prepositional phrases, which begin with a preposition:

The girl *with messy hair* was combing it.

Genitive phrases, which show ownership and have 's added to them:

The girl's messy hair needed combing.

Adjective phrases

Adjective phrases always contain an adjective, and they can be expanded using adverbs. They are used with noun phrases:

> Jane's hair was *messy*.
> Jane's hair was *very messy*.

Adverb phrases

Adverb phrases always contain an adverb, and they can be expanded using more adverbs. They are used with verb phrases:

> Jane was *hurriedly* combing her hair.
> Jane was *very hurriedly* combing her hair.

Can you pick out the separate phrases making up these sentences?
1. I made a slow journey by train.
2. She agreed enthusiastically to walk Christopher's dog.
What kind of phrases are they?

Negatives

The process of turning a phrase or clause into a **negative** one (one that says something is *not*) is called **negation**.

This can be achieved by putting in the word **not**, or adding the ending **-n't** to a word:

> I am *not* going.
> Jane will *not* eat her lunch.
> They do*n't* know what is happening.

Using negatives

You should use the same verbs as you would for a positive structure:

> ✓   I *am* ready.
> ✓   I *am* not ready yet.
> ✗   I ain't ready yet.

It is important to put the word **not** in the correct place in a sentence, otherwise the meaning of the sentence may be confused. Compare the different meanings of these sentences:

> I do *not* think the instructions are clear and they need to be rewritten.
> I think the instructions are *not* clear and they need to be rewritten.

> All the villages do *not* have running water.
> *Not* all the villages have running water.

Double negatives

In Standard English only one word with negative meaning should be used in a sentence:

> I did *not* do anything.

A **double negative** is what you get if you have two words with negative meaning in one sentence:

> I did *not* do *nothing*.

This is not considered correct in Standard English, so it is best to avoid them in formal speech or writing.

How would you make these sentences negative?
1. Are you ready yet?
2. I am happy about this.
3. Listen to him!

Punctuation marks

Apostrophe (')

Apostrophes are used to show that one or more letters or figures have been missed out of a word or number, as in *can't* for *cannot*, *it's* for *it is*, and *the '30s* for *the 1930s*.

Apostrophes are also used with *s* to form possessive nouns:

the child's dog
James's dog

Brackets (( ))

Brackets are used to separate off comments from the rest of the sentence:

The leaflet (a copy of which is enclosed) has been sent to every house.

Capital letters

Capital letters are used to start the first word in a sentence.

Capital letters are also used to start proper nouns and words derived from proper nouns, for example:

Anne, South Africa, a South African dish

Capital letters are also used to start all the important words in the titles of books, plays, people, organizations, etc:

the Prince of Wales, the House of Commons

Colon (:)

Colons are used to create a break between an introductory statement and a statement or phrase that explains or expands on it:

> There are a great many things money can't buy: love is just one of them.

Colons are also used to mark the beginning of a list of items:

> Here are the things you will need: a hammer, some nails and a new pane of glass.

Colons are sometimes used instead of a comma to introduce direct speech:

> Peter's reply was immediate: 'I want to come too.'

Comma (,)

Commas are used in strings of adjectives and in lists, for example:

> a cold, wet, windy day

Commas are also used to mark a pause in a sentence:

> He seems unfriendly, but I think he's just shy.

Commas are also used to separate direct speech from the rest of the sentence:

> Peter at once said, 'I want to come too.'

Dash (–)

Dashes are used in a similar way to colons when introducing an explanation:

> More time, more money and more help – these are the three things we need.

Dashes are also used as a less formal alternative to brackets to mark off an aside:

> She told me she had inherited the money – over ten thousand pounds – from her aunt.

Dashes are also used to indicate ranges:

> the 1914–18 War
> pages 1–26

Exclamation mark (!)

Exclamation marks are used instead of a full stop to indicate emphasis or strong emotion such as anger or surprise, or to show that something has been shouted or exclaimed:

> What a lovely garden!
> Help!
> 'I can't stand working here any longer!' she screamed.

Full stop (.)

Full stops are used to mark the end of a sentence.

Hyphen (-)

Hyphens are used to link words:

> an up-to-date report
> his mother-in-law
> a bunch of forget-me-nots

Hyphens are also used to split a word where there is not enough room to fit it into a line of writing.

Inverted commas

See quotation marks

Question mark (?)

Question marks are used instead of a full stop to show that what comes before is a question:

How did he manage it?

Quotation marks (' ')

Quotation marks or inverted commas are used to enclose direct speech (the actual words spoken by someone):

'You must help her,' he said.

Semicolon (;)

Semicolons are used to mark a stronger and more definite break in a sentence than the break made by a comma, but less of a break than that between two separate sentences:

I will say no more about your behaviour; the subject is closed.

Semicolons are also used to separate groups of items in a list:

Among the area's chief industries are shipbuilding, automobile engineering and steel manufacturing; textiles and clothing; coalmining; and brewing.

Dictionary quiz

1 Without looking at your dictionary, name three other words which you would expect to find on the pages with these guide-words at the top: *archaic* to *argument*, *lancet* to *larch* and *vixen* to *volume*.

2 What are the adjectives from the nouns (a) *anomaly*, (b) *equinox*, and (c) *metropolis*?

3 What would (a) a *meteorologist*, (b) a *philatelist* and (c) an *apiarist* be interested in?

4 (a) Give each of the following words its part of speech: *pint, costly, me, for, although, enjoy, soon*.

   (b) How many parts of speech do you think the following words have: *master, ship, quick, glimmer, over, contact*?

5 What is the plural of the following nouns: *criterion, hanger-on, bacillus, corps, calypso*?

6 Choose the correct spelling of the word in brackets:

   I enclose two (complementary/complimentary) tickets for the show.
   Try to be (discreet/discrete) and don't ask awkward questions.
   It's impossible to get a (straight/strait) answer from him.
   He was (born/borne) in India.

7 Which of the words in the following sentences would you **not** use in a formal situation? What word might you use instead?

Do you suppose she's brainy enough to pass the exam?
The steak was served with broccoli, carrots and spuds.

8 What is another word for the *windpipe*?

9 What is the opposite of a *chronic* illness?

10 What two sorts of people could the word *clerical* refer to?

The answers are on page 758.

Answers

1 Check pages 31, 333 and 694 of your dictionary to see if your words are there.

2 **(a)** anomalous, **(b)** equinoctial, **(c)** metropolitan

3 **(a)** the weather, **(b)** stamps, **(c)** bees

4 Check in the dictionary to see if you were right.

5 criteria, hangers-on, bacilli, corps, calypsos

6 complimentary, discreet, straight, born

7 brainy (clever/intelligent), spuds (potatoes)

8 the trachea

9 an acute illness

10 office workers and members of the clergy